PUBLIC HEALTH
AND THE ENVIRONMENT

PUBLIC HEALTH AND THE ENVIRONMENT

The United States Experience

Edited by
MICHAEL R. GREENBERG, PH.D.
Rutgers—The State University of New Jersey
University of Medicine and Dentistry of New Jersey
Robert Wood Johnson Medical School

FOREWORD BY BERNARD D. GOLDSTEIN, M.D.

THE GUILFORD PRESS
NEW YORK   LONDON

To Sidney and Mildred Greenberg,
Sol Saletra, Miriam Barker,
and Kathleen Mason

© 1987 The Guilford Press
A Division of Guilford Publications, Inc.
200 Park Avenue South, New York, N.Y. 10003

Printed in the United States of America

Last digit is print number: 9 8 7 6 5 4 3 2 1

Library of Congress Cataloging in Publication Data

Public health and the environment

   Bibliography: p.
   Includes index.
   1. Environmental health—United States. 2. Chronic
diseases—United States—Etiology. 3. Chronic diseases—
United States—Prevention. 4. Environmental protection—
United States. 5. Environmental engineering—United
States. I. Greenberg, Michael R.
RA566.3.P83   1987   363.7′00973   86–18373
ISBN 0-89862-778-8

CONTRIBUTORS

RICHARD F. ANDERSON, Ph.D., Department of Urban Affairs and Planning, Boston University, Boston Massachusetts.

J. STANLEY BLACK, Ph.D., Office of Government and Community Affairs, Illinois Environmental Protection Agency, Springfield, Illinois.

BEVERLY M. CALKINS, D.H.Sc., Department of Epidemiology and Biostatistics, School of Medicine, Case Western Reserve University, Cleveland, Ohio.

AUDREY R. GOTSCH, Dr.P.H., Department of Environmental and Community Medicine, University of Medicine and Dentistry of New Jersey, Robert Wood Johnson Medical School, Piscataway, New Jersey.

MICHAEL R. GREENBERG, Ph.D., Department of Urban Studies, School of Urban and Regional Policy, Rutgers—The State University of New Jersey, New Brunswick, New Jersey; Department of Environmental and Community Medicine, University of Medicine and Dentistry of New Jersey, Robert Wood Johnson Medical School, Piscataway, New Jersey.

MARIAN MARBURY, Ph.D., Division of Chronic Disease and Environmental Epidemiology, Minnesota Department of Health, Minneapolis, Minnesota.

MICHAEL K. MILLER, Ph.D., Center for Health Policy Research and Department of Community Health and Family Medicine, University of Florida, Gainesville, Florida.

G. WILLIAM PAGE, III, Ph.D., Department of Urban Planning, School of Architecture and Urban Planning, and Center for Great Lakes Studies, Graduate School, University of Wisconsin—Milwaukee, Milwaukee, Wisconsin.

CLARENCE E. PEARSON, M.P.H., National Center for Health Education, New York, New York.

JOSEPH J. SENECA, Ph.D., Department of Economics, Rutgers—The State University of New Jersey, New Brunswick, New Jersey.

C. SHANNON STOKES, Ph.D., Department of Agricultural Economics and Rural Sociology, Pennsylvania State University, University Park, Pennsylvania.

DONALD B. STRAUS, M.B.A., American Arbitration Association, New York, New York.

ROBERT C. ZIEGENFUS, Ph.D., Department of Geography, Kutztown University, Kutztown, Pennsylvania.

RAE ZIMMERMAN, Ph.D., Urban Planning Program, Graduate School of Public Administration, New York University, New York, New York.

FOREWORD

Public Health and the Environment is a necessary and timely text. Environment is a vague term, having many different meanings depending upon context and mutual consent. At the present time environmental diseases have come to mean those whose causation is due to an external chemical or physical agent. This generally excludes conditions that are a direct consequence of our inheritance; are due to living organisms such as bacteria; are caused by nonoccupational violence, advertent or inadvertent; or are due to our encounters with physicians or other parts of the health care system.

Health, of course, is more than simply the absence of disease. It is a positive state of well-being allowing the maximum realization of human potential. Although the definition of environmental health has evolved over time, the goals of public health have remained constant: to maintain the health and well-being of every member of society, particularly through the prevention of disease and the prolongation of life. However, the tools of public health continue to change. In part this is due to an increased understanding of the basic biological processes involved in human health and disease. While fundamental biological truths are unalterable, and in essence await our discovery, changes in our society including its culture, mores, and political organization, all have a major impact on the practice of public health. Such changes alter the environment, thus affecting the health of the population, and in this sense of the environment I mean all of the diverse cultural, life-style, and other forces that interact with the basic biology of our inheritance. Our understanding of these societal forces also has a major impact on our ability to act preventively. The well-known story of the Broad Street water pump, in which, in 1854, Dr. John Snow recognized the causal role of contaminated water in a cholera epidemic, is often told in a way that implies that Dr. Snow personally removed the pump handle. In fact, it was the authorities who removed the pump handle. Effective action thus depended both on Dr. Snow's scientific understanding of the problem and his ability to identify and convince the appropriate authorities.

The organization of our society and the forces that shape responsiveness to public health needs have changed drastically since the time of Dr. Snow. In the United States among the most far-reaching of the rapid changes in the past decades have been those associated with what is loosely known as the environmental movement. Fueling concern about the role of chemical and physical factors in disease have been rapid advances in our understanding of the part played by nonmicrobial aspects of our food, water, and air, and our markedly enhanced ability to analyze and detect minute quantities of chemical contaminants. In the past, environmental health was nearly synonymous with control of infectious disease agents in food and water. Now that such problems are largely under control in this country, although not in all parts of the world, there has been a marked change in mortality and morbidity rates. Gone from the top of the mortality tables are the infectious diseases, which have been replaced by chronic disease processes such as cardiovascular disorders, cancer, pulmonary disease, and diabetes. Furthermore, chronic disease processes which previously seemed to be inevitable are more and more being recognized as having easily preventable environmental causes.

Let me emphasize that the evidence is clear that environmental factors play a major role in those diseases which are currently responsible for the overwhelming majority of deaths and of disabling diseases in the United States. Further, the evidence is that these diseases are preventable.

With the gradual recognition of the impact of nonmicrobial environmental factors on health has come a series of societal responses. As a simplification, they can be divided into two types of responses. For those problems due primarily to involuntary exposure, a series of regulatory approaches has developed, encompassing the establishment of such organizations as the Environmental Protection Agency and the Occupational Safety and Health Administration, both formed about 15 years ago. The second has been a public demand for the information necessary for us to be allowed to make our own choices concerning voluntary risk, including a healthy disrespect for experts providing paternalistic dicta.

As documented in the text, there have been many improvements in environmental parameters as a response to societal interest and demands in the past decade or two. The air pollutants associated with major disasters in areas such as London, England, and Donora, Pennsylvania, have been controlled to an extent that is beneficial to health and visible to the public. Known carcinogens have been removed from the food supply and there has been dramatic improvement in the purity of certain water supplies. However, at the same time we have learned more about the various risks posed by unwanted environmental chemicals. Furthermore, other chemicals of great value to our modern society have been shown to threaten health thereby posing difficult choices. Improvements in analytical chemistry have detected heretofore unrecognized problems. They have also led to the phenomenon of the vanishing zero, the ability to detect ever-decreasing amounts of compounds down to levels of negligible risk, but not zero risk. The concern about chemical and physical agents in the general environment has during this time period also led to a splitting away of environmental control functions from state health departments to newly formed state departments of environmental protection or related titles. Such programs have taken to themselves much of the public health function of the environment, particularly in relationship to prevention. The remaining environmental functions in departments of health have been less preventive and more oriented toward diagnosis or treatment once a problem is known to occur. Unfortunately, this has led to individuals without much training in public health being responsible for primary prevention in relationship to chemicals in the environment, while public health experts in state and federal organizations have tended to ignore noninfectious environmental aspects of disease.

In recent years there are signs that the core disciplines of public health and those involved in environmental protection are beginning to work together, a necessity for the solution of environmental problems. An important component that has been missing in this effort has been a text which thoroughly explores modern environmental problems from the point of view of public health. This is now provided by *Public Health and the Environment*. It contains excellent reviews of the various environmental health hazards present in modern America. The perspective is that of the objective health scientist and the result is an impressive marshalling of the factual basis for public health action to prevent environmentally related diseases. This approach is coupled with chapters which explore the basis for the necessary actions that will result in the desired changes within our society, changes based on individual actions following understandable communication of the risks, and changes based upon effective regulatory approaches. I know of no text which does a better job of combining environmental health science and environmental policy in such a comprehensive and readable format.

Bernard D. Goldstein, M.D.
University of Medicine and Dentistry of New Jersey
Robert Wood Johnson Medical School
January 30, 1987

PREFACE

Earth Day—April 1, 1970—symbolized a popular awakening of interest in protecting public health and the environment during the late 1960s and early 1970s. Unlike many other movements, which have had their day only to fade quickly, the movement to protect public health and the environment has more strength than this writer could have imagined two decades ago. Signs of this strength can be seen in the following:

1. Laws—More than 20 federal and many state laws have been passed to protect public health and the environment.

2. Public and Private Organizations—The laws are administered by official government agencies representing public health and the environment: U.S. EPA, OSHA, CPSC, and their state counterparts. Private organizations representing these interests, like the Environmental Defense Fund, the Natural Resources Defense Council, National Audubon Society, Sierra Club and others, have grown markedly in membership and influence.

3. Literature—A popular and technical literature informs the public about the state of public health and the environment. Special departments and institutes in universities have been created to study and find solutions to public health and environmental problems.

Yet, a decade after the celebration of the first Earth Day, I left Earth Day 1980 wondering whether I was celebrating a birthday or participating in a wake. The overwhelming majority of environmentalists I speak with are fearful that the environmental movement is at best treading water and at worst being whittled away.

Three issues are at the root of their fears. First, many people feel that public and private environmental organizations are becoming less able to defend the environment and even public health in the face of pressure for jobs, energy, and the movement to get government off people's backs. The second is that for every problem we find, understand, and begin to control, we find at least two other more difficult ones. The third issue is the threat of technology growing out of control, a theme that has been with us since the Industrial Revolution, but is now very strong in the mind of the public.

There is a literature on the history of the environmental movement and the growing fears about the future. *Man's Role in Changing the Face of the Earth* (1956), *Man's Impact on the Global Environment* (1970), *The Global 2000 Study* (1980), and the *State of the Environment* (1982) summarize the impact of people on the earth and follow trends into the future with generally depressing forecasts. The *EPA Journal*, *Environmental Awakening* (1980), *Environmental Science and Technology*, *Science*, and the newsletters of the Conservation Foundation and Resources for the Future along with other journals indirectly and sometimes quite directly address the growing anxiety about the next decade. Probably the best single piece was one of the 1980 issues of the *Conservation Foundation Newsletter*— "Environmentalists Savor Past, Look Anxiously Ahead."

There is no comprehensive volume that offers both an adequate benchmark treatment of the state of potential threats to public health in the United States and assessments of the means of coping with these threats. This book of two parts and 12 chapters seeks to fill that void. Its focus is on the causes and control of chronic diseases in the United States, and hence some important topics are not covered in detail or at all. Three are noteworthy. First, some issues of developing nations (e.g., infectious and parasitic diseases; widespread and extreme poverty; no sewage treatment or disposal; no or a totally inadequate potable water supply) are less important in the United States. These are noted, though in the American context. Second, there are many global and national resource issues that are indirectly related to public health and the environment and are incorporated into some of the chapters; but they will not be at the center of the representation. Included among these are water quantity and terrestrial and biological resources. Third, the impact of warfare and natural and technological disasters will not be included, although the consequences are potentially so catastrophic as to override all others.

The intended audience is public health professionals, environmental scientists, economists, geographers, planners, political scientists, sociologists, and other scientists, engineers and students concerned about public health and the environment. The authors of the individual chapters match the disciplinary and geographical diversity of the intended audience. They were trained in epidemiology, public health, environmental science, geography, economics, sociology, and political science. They have taught in university departments of environmental and community medicine, epidemiology, rural sociology, public administration, economics, geography, urban studies, sociology, and planning in the Northeast, Midwest, South, and Southwest. They have worked in public health and environmental agencies at the federal, state, and local government scales.

In addition to being interdisciplinary, the authors are diverse in experience. About half are young university faculty members with strong research records. The other half work for government public health and environmental agencies and private organizations, or they are senior university professors. Generally, the first group wrote Part I, which presents the state of protection of public health and the environment, and the second group wrote Part II, which considers alternative ways of better protecting public health.

PART I: STATE OF PUBLIC HEALTH AND THE ENVIRONMENT

Each of these six chapters focuses on the question of whether we are better off in the early 1980s than we were in 1970 and the early twentieth century and briefly indicates where we are heading.

In Chapter 1 health and disease are defined and their measurement explained. Trends in health are presented as is the changing association between urbanization and health in the United States. Following an overview of how risks to public health are assessed, the chapter briefly reviews options for controlling risks.

Many, if not most, of our health problems are primarily due to the way we live. The health effects of smoking tobacco and drinking alcohol, of nutritional habits, exercising, and psychological stresses are examined in Chapter 2. Cancer and heart disease are the major diseases that are considered because they are responsible for more than half of deaths in the United States. Prevention through personal and government intervention is weighed.

Injury is common in some jobs, and workers are usually the first group exposed to carcinogenic, mutagenic, and other harmful substances at high concentrations. They also have to adjust to changing schedules and to on-the-job pressures over which they may have little control. After a survey of the changing status of worker protection in the United States and the limitations of the epidemiological approach, Chapter 3 focuses on technical, medical, and political methods of reducing work-related morbidity and mortality and the advantages and disadvantages of each.

Much has been written about the threat to public health from contaminated drinking water. Following a review of waterborne infectious and parasitic diseases, a major cause of mortality among pre-twentieth-century Western nations and a major problem in today's developing nations, Chapter 4 deals with two major concerns of twentieth-century urban-industrial America: nonmalignant disease attributed to bacteria, viruses, protozoa, water hardness, fluoride, and nitrate; and malignant disease attributed to organic and inorganic microcontaminants and radioactivity.

Nearly all of us assume that air pollution is synonymous with contamination of the outdoor air with malodorous fumes, particles, and vapors. Chapter 5 begins by discussing the origin of this assumption and describes some early air pollution episodes of urban-industrial Western nations, which led the United States government to pass legislation aimed at improving outdoor air quality. Most of Chapter 5 focuses on indoor air pollution, which may be a far more serious threat to public health than outdoor pollution. A review of the new field of total exposure monitoring, which seeks to determine people's total exposure to air pollutants in the indoor and outdoor environments, concludes the chapter.

Chapter 6 analyzes the serious issue of the physical and mental health effects of improper solid waste management, especially that of hazardous waste. After reviewing the history of damage, which begins with a discussion of solid and hazardous wastes and their sources, the bulk of the chapter deals with the hotly debated evidence that hazardous waste facilities have directly affected public health.

PART II: CHOICES AND SOLUTIONS

Part 2 is about ways our society can cope with the public health and environmental issues described in Part 1. We consider approaches ranging from short-term technological fixes to long-term educational programs and from formal legal mechanisms to informal data mediation experiments. Some of the six chapters in this part of the book are standard issues, others are not often addressed in volumes concerned with public health and the environment.

Uncertainty and risk are facts of life in an urban-industrial society increasingly dependent on large-scale technologies for jobs and security. Chapter 7 focuses on the reasons for uncertainty and what, if anything, can be done to forecast more accurately the impacts of new technologies. The uncertainty of taking "hard" and "soft" technological paths is considered.

A web of more than 20 laws has been cast around public health and the environment during the last decade. But in the face of other priorities and pressure from business, there is great fear that this legislation will be changed or not enforced. Chapter 8 assesses the strength of the movement to protect public health and the environment at the seats of political power. Political, administrative, bureaucratic, and jurisdictional considerations influencing policy are critically analyzed.

Our adversary system was used to the advantage of the environmental movement during the 1970s, but opponents of the laws have begun to use it to undermine these programs. Litigation is costly and time consuming, and it often does not produce results that any parties to a dispute want. Chapter 9 describes alternatives to the adversary system.

Better education is essential—some say the most important factor—for better health. Chapter 10 reviews what school districts, industry, and organizations have been doing to educate Americans about specific threats to health and to adopt healthier life-styles. Case studies, many of which are new pilot projects, are used to illustrate the diversity of approaches.

Investments in health care have grown markedly in the last two decades. Yet many people contend that the accomplishments of the medical system have been minimal and that more money should be spent on prevention programs. Chapter 11 analyzes the contributions of the medical care system focusing on its historical development and the controversy over whether higher priority should be assigned to prevention (e.g., education, food stamps) and accordingly less to finding cures (e.g., high technology).

The environmental movement flourished during an upswing in the American economy. We have begun to learn how it functions during a declining period and will be learning about how it will function with a population that has a larger proportion of elderly and a smaller proportion of working-age people. These trends suggest that resources for protecting public health and the environment could rapidly decline. Chapter 12 examines the economic advantages and disadvantages of protecting public health and the environment.

Chapter 12 is followed by a glossary of medical, technical, and legal terms used in this book.

EDUCATION AS A COMMON THEME

There is a theme that is common to every chapter in this book—the need for applied research to narrow the range about issues in public health and the environment, and the need for education to convince the public that their environments can be more healthful. First, there are the conventional wisdoms about protecting public health and the environment, which upon close scrutiny are doubtful. Chapter 1, for example, questions the long-standing assumption that urban areas in the United States have much higher rates of many causes of death, such as cancer, than do rural areas. Chapter 2 questions the notion that smoking harms only smokers, Chapter 5 that outdoor air pollution should be our major concern, Chapter 9 that the adversarial approach is the approach to policy formation, and Chapter 11 examines the importance of the medical care system in contributing to better health.

Then there are things we know something about but not enough to be sure that we can make policy recommendations without trepidation. These include, for example, elements of nutrition, exercise, psychology, toxicology, epidemiology, sociology, and economics. Third, there are important things about which we know very little. Our lack of toxicological data about most of the chemicals in commerce is the best illustration. But gaps in bench sciences that are apparent in Chapters 1–6 are not the only major gaps. We do not, for example, know how well nonadversarial approaches work in public health and environmental disputes because they have rarely been tried here.

Finally, there are things we know a good deal about but are unable to communicate in a way that persuades people to make changes. Chapter 2, for example, summarizes convincing evidence against tobacco smoking and shows that rates of smoking have markedly decreased. But about one third of the American population smokes tobacco.

The book illustrates how much we have learned but also how little we know about protecting public health and the environment.

C O N T E N T S

STATE OF PUBLIC HEALTH
AND THE ENVIRONMENT

HEALTH AND RISK IN URBAN-INDUSTRIAL SOCIETY
An Introduction

Michael R. Greenberg
Rutgers—The State University of New Jersey
University of Medicine and Dentistry of New Jersey
Robert Wood Johnson Medical School

When we first open a book, there is a strong temptation to glance at the contents, preface, and first chapter and then to go directly to chapters we find most interesting. Before reading other chapters, please familiarize yourself with the contents of this chapter because it provides two essential perspectives that will make the remaining chapters easier to understand. One is the changing state of public health in the United States. The second is an overview of how urban-industrial America measures and copes with risks to public health and the environment. Readers with knowledge of epidemiology and risk assessment should glance through the chapter.

WHAT IS HEALTH AND HOW IS IT MEASURED?

Health is a state of physical and mental well-being. There is no widely agreed-upon way of measuring health, despite numerous attempts (Hennes, 1972; Lerner, 1973; Stewart, Ware, & Book, 1981). Therefore, health is almost always measured in terms of its opposite: disease. Poor health or disease may be defined as a morbid state brought about by the interaction of harmful environmental factors on a susceptible host.

Water, air, and food contamination are part of our human environment. But they are not synonymous with environment, as is sometimes erroneously reported. The environment also includes what we eat and drink; our recreation, sexual, and working behaviors; and other personal factors that influence the way we feel. Only illness or predisposition to illness due to genetic inheritance is not in some way an environmental factor. Each of us inherits biological characteristics that may increase or decrease our propensity to certain illnesses. Sickle cell anemia and hemophilia

3

are well-known inherited diseases. Heredity also contributes to our risk of infectious, chronic, and parasitic diseases to an unknown extent.

We use three measures of disease: incidence, prevalence, and mortality. *Incidence* (or *morbidity*) is a count of the number of people who contract a disease during a specific period of time, usually a year. *Prevalence* is the number of people who contracted the disease during the specific period of time plus the number of people who already had and still have the disease. *Mortality* is the number of deaths recorded on death certificates during a specific period of time, again usually a year.

Incidence and prevalence are preferred to mortality as indicators for many reasons. The most important is that mortality is not a good indicator of diseases such as measles or mumps that do not usually cause death. The U.S. Centers for Disease Control (CDC) maintain records of notifiable diseases such as measles, mumps, and anthrax. Recently acquired immunodeficiency syndrome (AIDS) was added to the notifiable disease list. Unfortunately, despite these CDC data sets, complete incidence and prevalence data are themselves not prevalent. Mortality data, however, are available for spans of many decades and for every county in the United States. Accordingly, this chapter uses mortality data as an indicator of health. All three measures are used in the book, although mortality is most often used.

Temporal Trends in Mortality Rates in the United States

The old testament allotted 70 years of life. But a male born in this country in 1880, about a century ago, could expect to live less than 42 years, a female less than 44 years (U.S. Bureau of the Census, 1960). Twenty years later, in 1900, an American male could expect to live 46 years, a female 48 years (U.S. Department of Health, Education and Welfare, 1973). Only during the next half century, between 1900 and 1950, did the average life span reach 70 years. Between 1950 and 1980, life expectancy once again began to level off. Since the genetic composition of our population has not substantially changed, these abrupt changes in mortality mark environmental changes.

1900–1950: Increase in Life Expectancy and Chronic Diseases

Three factors are thought to be responsible for the increase in life expectancy in the United States during the first half of the twentieth century. Medical research produced antibiotics and immunizations that dramatically lowered death rates from infectious and parasitic diseases like tuberculosis. Preventive public health measures such as water and sewage treatment eliminated the cholera and typhoid fever epidemics that had ravaged nineteenth-century cities. Increased agricultural productivity prevented the widespread famines that have decimated other nations.

The impact of better medicine, prevention, and nutrition is clear in the changed distribution of diseases in 1900, 1950, and 1981 (Table 1-1 and Figure 1-1). The

Table 1-1. Ten Leading Causes of Death in the United States, 1900 and 1950

Rank	Cause of death	Rate/100,000	% of deaths
	1900		
1	Pneumonia and influenza	202	11.8
2	Tuberculosis	194	11.3
3	Gastritis and related diseases	143	8.3
4	Heart diseases	137	8.0
5	Vascular lesions (central nervous system)	107	6.2
6	Chronic nephritis	81	4.7
7	Accidents	72	4.2
8	Cancer	64	3.7
9	Diseases of early infancy	63	3.6
10	Diphtheria	40	2.3
	All causes of death	1,719	—
	1950		
1	Heart diseases	366	38.7
2	Cancer	147	15.6
3	Vascular lesions (central nervous system)	107	11.3
4	Accidents	52	5.5
5	Diseases of early infancy	37	3.9
6	Pneumonia and influenza	36	3.5
7	Arteriosclerosis	20	2.1
8	Diabetes mellitus	17	1.8
9	Congenital malformations	12	1.3
10	Cirrhosis of the liver	11	1.2
	All causes of death	955	—

death rate from pneumonia and influenza, tuberculosis, and gastritis in 1900 was 539/100,000. In 1950, among the three, only pneumonia and influenza had a death rate exceeding 10/100,000. Infant mortality fell from more than 60/100,000 in 1900 to less than 40/100,000 in 1950 and to about 20/100,000 in 1960. And diphtheria was all but eliminated. The decline of deaths from these infectious and parasitic diseases had a marked impact on life span by dramatically lowering death rates among young people.

As infectious and parasitic diseases as a cause of death have declined, so has the total rate, and chronic diseases have become the leading cause of death in our urban-industrial society. In 1950 heart disease, cancer, cerebrovascular disease, diabetes, arteriosclerosis, and cirrhosis of the liver had a combined death rate of 668/100,000, or about 70% of all deaths (Table 1-1).

1950–1985: Slower Increase in Life Expectancy

The decline in the death rate began to level off in the 1950s and 1960s. The first reason is that unless one assumes that most people can live far beyond 70 years,

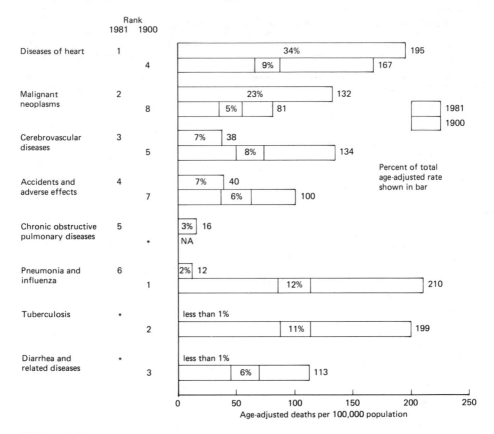

*Not a ranked cause

Figure 1-1. Age-adjusted death rates from leading causes of death in the United States per 100,000, 1981 and 1900. Source of basic data: National Center for Health Statistics, Division of Vital Statistics.

controlling many types of chronic disease will add only a few years to the average life span compared to the 20 or more years that were added when the major infectious and parasitic diseases were controlled. The second reason is that our attempts to prevent or cure chronic diseases have not been as successful as we hoped. Scientists observe changes in chronic disease rates, but are unsure why these changes occurred and how much, if any, is due to the medical care system. For example, quoting the Working Group on Heart Disease Epidemiology (1979, p. 1):

> One of the most important recent developments in regard to the major cardiovascular diseases (CVD) and their largest specific component—coronary heart disease (CHD)— is the accelerated decline in mortality rates recorded since the late 1960s. From 1968 to 1976, the mortality rate from premature CHD, for the age group 35–74, declined 24 percent. Over the same period, the death rate from cerebrovascular disease (stroke) fell 33 percent. As a consequence of these dramatic developments, the death rate from all major cardiovascular diseases dropped 25 percent, and the death rate from all

causes declined by 17 percent. This trend has been recorded for all four major sex-color groups in the United States: white men, white women, black men, and black women. The decline in death rate is all the more significant, since for the largest and most devastating form of premature cardiovascular disease, heart attack, the rates had been increasing—at least for men—during the preceding decades. Thus, a steep rise in heart attack death rates was recorded from 1940 into the 1950's, with a continuing less marked rise from the late 1950's into the 1960's. The steady decline over the last 8 to 9 years has brought the mortality rates for middle-aged men back down to approximately the 1940 levels. This fall is all the more impressive, and calls all the more for detailed attention, in view of the fact that mortality rates continue to rise in several other industrialized countries.

The authors of this report contend that these trends show that CHD disease is amenable to control. But to what controls? Research shows that people who eat diets high in fats and who smoke cigarettes, and those with high cholesterol levels and hypertension are at high risk of CHD disease. But we do not know which of these risk factors is the most important. Furthermore, all the important causes of CHD have not been identified. So it is hard to know if lower CHD rates are primarily due to high blood pressure control programs, bypass surgery, pacemakers, new drugs and coronary care units, or largely to public education about diet, exercise, smoking and tension (see Chapter 2.)

The failures to increase the life span markedly during the 1950s and 1960s and to explain changes that have subsequently occurred have led to much rancor and a good deal of political rhetoric. Of the many reasons why health trends have become a political issue two stand out. The federal contribution to medical research and care in the United States has markedly increased since 1950, but better results were expected than have been achieved. Second, there is a fundamental difference of opinion over how government health promotion funds should be spent. Some believe that government funding should concentrate on finding vaccines that will prevent and cure disease. Others argue that more money should be spent on preventing chronic diseases by protecting people against pollution and educating them about life-style and health. This book argues for the prevention approach.

The furor over a paper published by Pollack and Horm (1980) illustrates how changing disease rates are fertile grounds for fighting the battle of disease prevention. Their 13-page paper had a mild enough title: "Trends in Cancer Incidence and Mortality in the United States, 1969–1976." The paper contained numerous caveats about the quality of data. Pollack and Horm went so far as to say that their "analysis has focused more on the methodology of and problems in the analysis of trends over the period of time covered by the two nonrandom surveys of the U.S. populations than on the trends themselves" (p. 1100).

Their caveats were ignored. The 1969–1976 data suggested to some that incidence rates among white males for some types of cancer have begun to increase more rapidly than in the previous 25 years and that cancer rates among white females had reversed a long-standing trend and had begun to increase. Reversal of long-standing declines was suggested for cancer of the colon, rectum, and uterine corpus. When combined with continued increases of lung cancer, the seeming reversal of trends for these three types of cancer led to a net result of a 1.3% annual average increase in incidence for white males and 2.0% for white females. They also reported increasing annual average cancer mortality rates, 0.9% for white males and 0.2% for white females.

Actually, the 1969–1976 results are inconclusive because of data and methodological reasons that Pollack and Horm describe. The point of the controversy is political, not scientific. The political issue is whether chemical pollution in the workplace and outdoor environments has begun to cause large numbers of cancers (Smith, 1980). The chemical industry has, in fact, often cited relatively stable cancer rates as evidence that their products are not harming people. Environmental activists, on the other hand, see these cancer data as bearing witness to potential catastrophic health consequences of the unregulated production, sale, and disposal of chemicals. The debate over the Pollack and Horm paper did little to elucidate the causes of cancer, but it sharpened the level of rhetoric about them.

Other scientific studies (described in Chapters 2 through 6) have also provoked heated political as well as scientific debate. The second part of this chapter will show that the results of research on public health and the environment are so important that every research method is vigorously disputed.

Summarizing, life expectancy markedly increased between 1900 and 1950 as infectious and parasitic disease rates dropped sharply. Chronic disease rates increased as the population lived long enough to die from heart disease, stroke, and cancer. The life span has not increased as sharply during the last three decades as it did during the previous half century, leading to major scientific and political debates.

Temporal Trends in Cancer Mortality in Urban-Industrial America

Cancer is used here and elsewhere in this chapter to illustrate the major changes that have occurred in mortality in the United States. Four reasons prompted this choice. It is the second leading cause of death in the United States with about 475,000 deaths in 1986. Roughly half this number of people died of stroke, and about twice as many died of heart disease. Second, among these three leading causes of death, only cancer has not shown a long-term decline in death rates. Third, cancer is commonly thought to be directly linked to environmental pollution. Fourth, cancer is the most feared cause of death.

We use two death rates to study changing disease rates. One is the *crude death rate*, the number of deaths in a year per 100,000 people (sometimes 1,000 or 1 million people). The crude death rate for cancer rose from 101 deaths per 100,000 in 1930 to 172 in 1975 (1.6% per year).

The crude death rate is not very useful for studying the relationship between cancer and the environment. The American population has become older, and older people have higher rates of cancer than do younger people. So comparing the cancer rates of the American population in 1930 and 1975 is not very informative about environmental causes because the population was older in 1975 and should show higher cancer rates. The effect of aging of the population on cancer rates can be removed through a process called age adjustment. If we calculate the death rate as if the same proportion of Americans were 0–4, 5–9, 10–14, . . . 70–74, 75–84, 85 + in 1930 and 1975, the increase is from 117 in 1930 to 131 in 1975, a 0.3% annual increase. Most of the increase in the number of cancer deaths, then, is due to the aging of the American population.

An annual increase of 0.3% is less disturbing than one of 1.6%. But the total population age-adjusted rate hides important differences among specific subpopulations. We will use the period 1950–1977 to examine these marked differences by sex and race. Earlier data are not used because changes occurred in the classification of diseases, which make some specific types of cancer in the earlier data difficult to compare to the more recent data. The age distribution of the population in 1970 is used as the standard, which means that the cancer rates for 1950–1977 are higher than the 1930–1975 rates for the same years because the American population was older in 1970 (the standard used for the 1950–1977 calculations) than it had been for the standard used in the earlier calculations (the years 1930–1975). The four populations in the following presentation are white males, nonwhite males, white females, and nonwhite females. Nonwhite here includes blacks, Asians, and American Indians, but since blacks compose 88% of the nonwhite population, the nonwhite data primarily represent black Americans.

Remarkable changes occurred in cancer rates among the four subpopulations during the 1950–1977 period. In 1950, white males had the highest age-adjusted rate: 168/100,000 (Table 1-2). Nonwhite male, white female, and nonwhite female rates were 151, 148, and 146/100,000, about 10–15% less. A very different pattern was found in 1977. Nonwhite male rates increased 71% from 151 to 258 and were 24% higher than the white male rate, which rose from 168 to 208 (McKay, Hanson, & Miller, 1982). White female rates decreased, and nonwhite female rates were stable (Table 1-2).

Changes in white male and white female cancer mortality rates parallel those of most Western, urban-industrial nations (Greenberg, 1983). The alarming nonwhite male increase is probably explained by a combination of factors including underdiagnosis of cancer in earlier years, differences in medical care between nonwhites and whites, and increased nonwhite male exposure to carcinogens in the workplace and home that followed their migration from the rural South to the Urban North.

Space precludes a presentation of trends for all 200 different forms of cancer. Major groups and a few specific types will be used as illustrations.

During the period 1950–1977, age-adjusted death rates have sharply increased for the respiratory system among all four subpopulations. In 1950, trachea, bronchus, and lung cancer accounted for 13% of white male, 11% of nonwhite male, and 3% of white and nonwhite female cancer deaths. In 1977, the percentages increased to 33, 31, 13, and 12%. These increases are thought to be primarily due to cigarette smoking (see Chapter 2). But occupational and home environments are probably involved (see Chapters 3 and 5). Female lung cancer death rates are lower than male rates, but have been rising more rapidly. In 1950, cancer of the trachea, bronchus, and lung was the eleventh leading cancer-related cause of death among

Table 1-2. Selected Age-Adjusted Cancer Mortality Rates in the United States, 1950 and 1977

Type		White male			White female			Nonwhite male			Nonwhite female		
		1950	1977	% change	1950	1977	% change	1950	1977	% change	1950	1977	% change
All	Rate[a]	168.0	207.8	24	146.2	133.0	−9	150.9	258.2	71	147.7	148.1	<1
	Deaths[b]	98.8	184.3	87	94.9	157.1	66	8.2	25.2	207	8.8	18.3	108
Stomach[c]	Rate[a]	23.9	8.3	−66	13.1	3.8	−71	21.2	10.4	−51	16.1	7.5	−53
	Deaths[b]	13.6	7.2	−47	8.1	4.8	−41	1.6	1.5	−6	0.9	0.9	0
Lung[d]	Rate[a]	21.9	67.6	209	4.9	17.7	262	12.1	57.6	376	4.0	17.1	328
	Deaths[b]	14.0	60.7	334	3.2	20.0	525	0.9	8.0	789	0.2	2.1	950
Uterine[e]	Rate[a]				9.9	3.5	−65				17.9	8.0	−55
	Deaths[b]				6.9	4.0	−42				1.5	1.2	−20
Prostate[f]	Rate[a]	20.2	20.6	2				23.7	36.6	54			
	Deaths[b]	10.3	17.5	70				1.1	3.3	200			

[a]Age-adjusted rate per 100,000, 1970 standard population; [b]Number of deaths in 1,000s; [c]Cancer of the stomach; [d]Includes cancer of the trachea, bronchus, and lung; [e]Cancer of the uterine cervix; [f]Cancer of the prostate.

white females; in 1977 it was second. Only breast cancer caused more deaths. By the middle of the 1980s, lung cancer passed breast cancer.

This frightening increase closely parallels the female adoption of cigarette smoking. Men not only began smoking earlier than women, but in recent years, there has been a decrease in male smoking rates, especially in the urban-industrial Northeastern and North central states. This decrease will probably not be manifested in lower white male respiratory cancer death rates until the late 1980s or early 1990s because of the long incubation period of cancer. Much more will be said about smoking tobacco in Chapter 2.

The digestive system includes the esophagus, stomach, large and small intestines, pancreas, and liver. As a system, this group was the major cause of cancer-related deaths in the early 1950s. But since 1950, age-adjusted death rates for the digestive system have decreased by more than 25% among the white population and somewhat less among the nonwhite population. This decrease varies substantially by organ. Cancer rates of the stomach (Table 1-2), liver, and rectum have all decreased by about 50% or more. During the early 1950s, these three organs were responsible for two out of every ten cancer-related deaths. By the 1970s, only one of ten deaths were due to these three types.

Improved nutrition is considered to be the major factor in this change. However, the precise contribution of different factors is not known. For example, some scholars believe that food preservatives and refrigeration have been the major reasons for the international decrease in stomach cancer. Others are afraid that food additives cause cancer. Chapter 2 reviews the literature on nutrition and disease.

There are distinct differences by race and sex in genital cancer rates. Female rates of uterine cancer in 1977 were less than half of what they were in 1950. Some people attribute the decrease to improved screening methods and more frequent hysterectomies. But uterine cancer mortality rates were declining before the widespread adoption of these practices, so other factors must be involved (Cutler & Devesa, 1973).

Cancer of the prostate was the third leading cause of male cancer-related deaths in 1950. Nonwhite male rates were about 20% higher than white male rates. In 1977 it became the second leading cause among nonwhite males and the nonwhite male age-adjusted rate increased more than 50% (Table 1-2). White male rates stabilized. So in 1977 nonwhite male rates were 80% higher than male white rates. Along with cancer of the esophagus, cancer of the prostate has become the most race-differentiated type of cancer. No one knows why. One or more important environmental factors must be involved because U.S. nonwhite male rates have increased more than those of any nation, and they are higher than those of any nation, including black African nations, whereas U.S. white male rates were stable and were among the lowest in the world.

In conclusion, cancer has become the second leading cause of death in the United States, increasing at an annual rate of 1.6% per year since 1930. Most of the increase is due to the aging of the American population. The age-adjusted annual rate of increase is about 0.3%. This relatively small increase, however, hides marked differences by sex and race and type of cancer.

Geographical Trends in Mortality Rates in the United States

Elsewhere, I (Greenberg, 1983) proposed a two-part hypothesis to explain geographical differences in cancer and the subsequent narrowing of those differences. The first part of the hypothesis was that geographical differences in cancer resulted from cultural and economic conditions that led to the concentration of factors associated with increased risk of cancer in the cities of the Northeast and Northcentral United States. These risk factors include personal habits such as smoking tobacco, excess alcohol consumption, a diet closely identified with migrants from Europe that increased the risk of many digestive and urinary organ cancers, occupations that exposed workers to carcinogens, and an ambient environment that was more polluted than the remainder of the nation's. The second part of the hypothesis was that differences between cities, suburbs, towns, and villages in cancer have narrowed because of the diffusion of the urban-American culture and migration of American industry, American people, and the health care system from the Northeastern and Northcentral cities to the remainder of the United States.

This two-part hypothesis should be valid for chronic circulatory, respiratory, and endocrine diseases because many of the risk factors suggested for cancer are also suggested for these diseases (see Chapter 2). There should continue to be noticeable differences between suburbs and cities for infectious and parasitic diseases as a cause because they are so strongly differentiated by poverty (see Chapter 11). Despite the fact that suburbs have become the "outer city" (Muller, 1975), for almost every characteristic of American life, central city rates of poverty continue to be much higher than suburban rates (U.S. Bureau of the Census, 1982).

Changing City-Suburban Differences in Mortality

Let us look first for empirical evidence of differences between cities and suburbs. White male data will be used here and throughout this section to illustrate geographical trends in disease because there are not enough nonwhites living in suburbs to make city-suburban comparisons, and the white female data almost always show fewer differences than the white male data. So the white male data is the most interesting to use as an illustration.

Before discussing the trends, a few words must be said about the data. Mortality data are available for all counties in the United States. Cities and suburbs were approximated from county data using the standard metropolitan statistical areas (SMSA) as urban regions. The convention of calling the county or counties containing the central city the "central city" counties was adopted. Other counties in the SMSA were called the "suburbs." The data set is white male rates for the years 1959–1961 and 1973–1976 for 22 of the 25 most populous SMSA's in the United States in 1970 (Table 1-3). Three of the 25 most populous metropolitan areas were excluded from the study because the metropolitan area was a single county: Los Angeles, Miami, and San Diego. The 108 counties in 22 metropolises contained 30% of the American population in 1970 (62 million people). The 25 central city

Table 1-3. Metropolitan Areas Included in the Central City–Suburban Comparisons

1. Atlanta, Georgia
2. Baltimore, Maryland
3. Boston, Massachusetts
4. Buffalo, New York
5. Chicago, Illinois
6. Cincinnati, Ohio–Kentucky–Indiana
7. Cleveland, Ohio
8. Dallas, Texas
9. Detroit, Michigan
10. Houston, Texas
11. Kansas City, Kansas–Missouri
12. Milwaukee, Wisconsin
13. Minneapolis–St. Paul, Minnesota
14. Newark, New Jersey
15. New York City, New York
16. Paterson–Passaic–Clifton, New Jersey
17. Philadelphia, Pennsylvania–New Jersey
18. Pittsburgh, Pennsylvania
19. San Francisco, California
20. St. Louis, Missouri–Illinois
21. Seattle, Washington
22. Washington, DC–Virginia–Maryland

counties contained 36.9 million people (18% of the national population). In 1970, the 83 suburban counties had 25.1 million people (12% of the national population).

The results support the hypotheses. The most pronounced differences between cities and suburbs in 1959–1961 were for infectious and parasitic diseases: 63% for infectious and parasitic, 61% for kidney infections, and 41% for influenza and pneumonia (Table 1-4). These differences narrowed between 1959–1961 and 1973–1976 from 63, 61, and 41% to 54, 25, and 29%. But, as expected, they remained substantial.

Chronic diseases (chronic respiratory, diabetes, cancer, circulatory disease) show city-suburban differences ranging from 11 to 25% in 1959–1961. By 1973–1976, these differences were all less than 10% (Table 1-4). Clearly, convergence occurred.

Changing City-Rural Differences in Mortality: A Look at the Popular Image of "Healthy" and "Unhealthy" Places

The Grand Canyon and its northern neighbor Bryce Canyon are among the most beautiful places in the world. The clean air and breathtaking vistas engender feelings of awe and vigor. Surely, if there is a place in the United States where people live long and healthy lives, it must be these canyon areas. About 30,000 people live in the four counties that contain the two parks. In 1959–1961 the total male white death rate in the four counties was 942/100,000 (age-adjusted to the 1940 population of the United States). In comparison, the total male white death rate in New York

Table 1-4. A Comparison of Selected Causes of Death Among Male Whites in Central City and Surburban Counties of the United States, 1959–1961 and 1973–1976

| Type | Average rate[a] | | | | Comparisons | |
| | 1959–1961 | | 1973–1976 | | 1959–1961 | 1973–1976 |
	CC[b]	SU[c]	CC[b]	SU[c]	CC[b]/SU[c]	CC[b]/SU[c]
Circulatory[d]	519.6	468.4	427.4	394.8	1.11	1.08
Cancer	166.0	140.6	175.8	161.4	1.19	1.09
Influenza[e]	33.1	23.8	25.8	20.0	1.41	1.29
Respiratory[f]	18.1	14.7	29.6	27.2	1.25	1.09
Infectious[g]	14.3	9.4	8.0	5.3	1.63	1.54
Diabetes[h]	13.0	10.9	12.3	11.6	1.25	1.07
Kidney[i]	4.1	2.8	6.5	5.3	1.61	1.25

[a]Unweighted average of 22 areas; [b]CC, central city counties; [c]SU, suburban counties; [d]includes rheumatic heart disease and fever, hypertensive disease, ischemic heart diseases, myocardial degeneration, cerebrovascular diseases, arteriosclerosis, other disease of arteries and veins; [e]influenza and pneumonia; [f]chronic respiratory disease including asthma, bronchitis, and emphysema; [g]tuberculosis and other infectious and parasitic diseases; [h]diabetes mellitus; [i]kidney and other urinary infections.

City and Cook County, Illinois (which contains Chicago) was 988/100,000. The 5% difference between the canyon counties and big city counties is probably much less than most readers of this book would have expected, but is consistent with other studies (Miller, Voth, & Danforth, 1982).

Let us look at cancer in the canyon and two big city counties because among major chronic diseases cancer is thought to reflect most clearly the advantages of a rural life-style and rural occupations. In 1959–1961 the total male white cancer mortality rate in the four canyon counties was 107/100,000 or 62% of the rate in the two big city counties. The 62% figure is evidence of the conventional wisdom that rural people enjoy healthy environments, free of the carcinogenic burden surrounding city people.

The conventional wisdom no longer held by 1973–1976. The total male white mortality rate in the four canyon counties was 10% higher than the rate in the two big cities. Even more surprising was the marked decrease in the difference between the canyon and big city counties in cancer. The canyon counties' male white cancer mortality rate increased from 62% of the big city rate in 1959–1961 to 92% in 1973–1976.

Changing City-Suburban-Rural Differences in Cancer in the United States

A comparison of the rates of many types of cancer involving most of the population of the United States will serve as a final reference point, tying together temporal and geographical trends in disease and setting a foundation for a discussion of the role of environmental factors in disease in Chapters 2 through 6. The central cities and suburbs are defined as above (Table 1-3) The rural areas are all the counties in the continental United States that were more rural than urban in the year 1970.

Table 1-5. Age-Adjusted Cancer Mortality Rates[a] of the Male White Population, Central City, Suburban, and Rural Counties of the United States, 1950–1954 and 1970–1975

Type	1950–1954				1970–1975			
	CC[c]	CC[c]/USA[b]	CC[c]/RU[e]	CC[c]/SU[d]	CC[c]	CC[c]/USA[b]	CC[c]/RU[e]	CC[c]/SU[d]
Lung[f]	34.1	139	201	125	62.0	105	113	103
Stomach	26.0	126	138	124	11.1	126	144	117
Prostate	18.5	101	102	99	17.5	99	98	97
Large intestine	21.0	134	172	112	22.1	122	143	105
Rectum	13.2	153	224	127	7.3	128	152	109
Pancreas	9.9	121	143	115	11.1	108	112	105
Bladder[g]	9.3	137	190	115	7.8	115	134	101
Leukemia[h]	8.7	110	118	112	8.6	100	99	100
Esophagus	7.3	174	317	149	5.5	134	167	122
Liver	7.1	116	122	116	3.6	120	138	120
Tongue, mouth[i]	6.5	144	224	125	5.4	132	174	123
Lymphoma	4.6	118	139	112	6.2	109	117	105
Central nervous[j]	4.5	115	129	118	4.8	98	98	98
Kidney	4.2	124	150	114	4.6	105	110	100
Larynx	3.9	163	279	150	3.5	135	159	130
Hodgkin disease	2.5	109	119	109	2.0	111	111	105
All cancers	204.2	126	151	117	208.9	110	119	105

Note. From Urbanization and Cancer Mortality (p. 246) by M. Greenberg, 1983, New York: Oxford University Press. Reprinted by permission

[a]The 1960 population was used as the standard; all ratios have been multiplied by 100. [b]USA, United States; [c]CC, central city counties; [d]SU, suburban counties; [e]RU, rural counties; [f]also includes trachea and bronchus; [g]also includes other urinary, except kidney; [h]also includes aleukemia; [i]also includes oral mesopharynx and pharynx; [j]includes brain and all other central nervous system.

Twenty-four percent of the population of the United States lived in the approximately 2,000 rural counties. Overall, the city, suburban, and rural counties contained 54% of the American population in 1970.

Sixteen types of cancer with a rate exceeding 2/100,000 in 1950–1954 are used to compare city, suburban, rural, and total United States rates. The cancer rates are not directly comparable to the cancer rates in some other sections of this chapter because they were standardized to the 1960 United States population. What is comparable and most important are the ratios between the cities, suburbs, rural areas, and the United States (Table 1-5).

All 16 types of cancer show the expected higher rates in cities in 1950–1954. Five of 16 central city/rural ratios (central city rate divided by rural rate) exceed 2.0 in 1950–1954, 9 exceed 1.4. They are respiratory, digestive, and urinary cancers: esophagus; larynx; rectum; tongue and mouth; trachea, bronchus, and lung; bladder; large intestine; kidney; and pancreas. Lower ratios were observed for several digestive, lymphatic, and genital cancers. The central city/rural and central city/suburb ratios for all cancer sites are 1.51 and 1.17, respectively (Table 1-5).

Fourteen of the 16 ratios decreased between 1950–1954 and 1960–1964 with the total cancer sites central city/rural and central city/suburban ratios decreasing from 1.51 to 1.36 and 1.17 to 1.12. A more precipitous decrease took place during the next decade. By 1970–1975, the total cancer sites ratios decreased to 1.19 for cities/rural areas and to 1.05 for cities/suburbs. None of the 16 city/rural ratios exceeded 2.0. The most noteworthy convergence was for cancer of the trachea, bronchus, and lung, which dropped from a ratio of 2.01 in 1950–1954 to 1.13 in 1970–1975.

In conclusion, the dramatic convergence of different rates of disease among cities, suburbs and rural areas means that the geographical distribution of environmental risk in the United States has markedly changed. Methods used to figure out why these changes have occurred and cope with them are reviewed in the next section.

MEASURING AND COPING WITH RISK IN URBAN-INDUSTRIAL SOCIETY

This book is about how we cope with risks to public health. Chapters 2 through 6 describe how life-style, work, and pollution affect health, and chapters 7 through 12 describe ways of reducing risk through laws, education, scientific research, and medical care. The remainder of this chapter provides a foundation for the chapters that follow by an overview of how we measure risk and the major options we have for coping with it. The rest of the book assumes the knowledge presented here.

Measuring Risk

We measure risk in three ways: (1) by product performance, (2) by human experience, and (3) by animal and lower organism tests.

Product Performance

Tests have been developed by government agencies, insurance underwriters, engineering societies, and the American Society for Testing and Materials in order to determine the risk of products before they are marketed. The principle behind these tests is to determine product performance under normal and stressed conditions. Most products that can be stress tested are, and the tests are standardized, so that the product should be dependable, no matter who makes it.

The principle of stress testing is straightforward, but the practice is not. The biggest problem is defining normal and abnormal use. Products are usually designed with a specific audience in mind. But products are abused and used in unexpected ways. Should products be designed in ways that anticipate misuse? If your answer is yes, consider that such design may make the product more cumbersome and costly. Also consider that designing against an anticipated abuse of a product may mean that the product is made more dangerous in other ways. In short, product safety testing is an imperfect science.

Human Experience

Experience is a good teacher, hopefully. Our parents try to teach us to use common sense. This means constructing analogies that allow us to judge the implications of actions based on what we already know about similar actions. We learn this process at an early age, and most of us can judge the potential risk of our decisions. Common sense has its analogue in scientific risk assessment. Toxicologists infer that substances are potentially dangerous because they have physical, biological, and chemical properties similar to substances that are known to be dangerous. But Fiering and Wilson (1983) note that it is difficult to construct analogies where chemicals are concerned.

Field testing is widely used for cosmetics, toys, and other consumer products. The tests are conducted under codes of conduct that include revealing the methods of the test, obtaining consent, and supervising the test. However, codes were not always in place, and many people have tested toys, cosmetics, drugs, food additives, and pesticides under conditions that seem unethical in the context of the 1980s.

Ethical questions remain. Is it ethical to give toys to the children of employees? Is it morally acceptable to test cosmetics on a woman who needs the money and who hides information about preexisting health conditions?

Many workplaces are very dangerous. Documented risks to workers range from back injuries for those engaged in repeatedly lifting things to death for many exposed to asbestos (see Chapter 3). Signals of a problem include high injury, disease, and absentee rates. These signals lead to studies of those with occupational exposure and a control group that is similar in every respect (e.g., age, sex, race, smoking habits) except that the first group was exposed to the hazard in question and the control group was not. If the hypothesized hazard is very dangerous, then the exposed groups should manifest statistically significantly greater morbidity and/ or mortality rates than the control group.

Most studies of workers have been retrospective—that is, they were conducted on populations that were at risk long before the study was made. An alternative is the *prospective study*, which identifies a population that may be at high risk and then follows its future morbidity and mortality.

Epidemiological studies of workers have limitations. First, there are usually few cases to investigate because relatively few people develop obvious symptoms, and many who come into contact with the agent in question may die or move away by the time the effect becomes apparent. Second, the amount and duration of exposure are rarely known and have to be estimated. Third, some workers are at higher risk than others because of genetics and environmental exposures (e.g., smoking, living in an area with polluted air and water). In addition, most epidemiological analyses are expensive and time-consuming, which limits their use. The net result is that epidemiological studies of workers can identify only a small number of risks.

The general population can yield important clues about risk. Retrospective and, increasingly, prospective epidemiological studies of millions of deaths have convinced scientists that smoking, driving while intoxicated with alcohol or drugs and without seatbelts, being obese, and many other personal choices significantly increase the risk of morbidity and mortality. Another general population approach is to compare the morbidity and mortality rates of people in different countries, foreign and native-born people of the same country, and distinct subpopulations (e.g., Mormons). These studies have yielded clues about the relationship between disease and many life-style habits, especially nutrition.

Occupational and general population studies have taught us a good deal about risk, but we want to learn about the potential risk of a substance or action before people are exposed or shortly after they have received an initial and hopefully small dose. Researchers are searching for biological markers. Serum and urine specimens, hair, human milk, adipose tissue (in which fat is stored), neurotoxic damage, and chromosome effects have all been tested to a limited extent. Human monitoring through markers will become increasingly important.

Animal and Lower Organism Tests

Experiments with nonhumans produce estimates of risk faster and more cheaply than do human studies. One type uses rabbits, rats, mice, hamsters, and other animals. To test for toxicity, animals are given increasing doses until a predetermined percentage of the animals die. The best-known of the tests determines the median lethal dose (abbreviated LD50) that kills half of the animals. To test for cancer, birth defects, and mutations, sets of genetically identical test and control animals are kept in the same environment. The test animals are exposed to the agent being tested; the controls are not. The animals are followed for a period ranging from months to a few years. At the end of the test period, the animals are killed and examined for tumors and other effects.

Animal studies have disadvantages. The biggest is that animals and people differ in many ways, including metabolism and ability to repair damage to their organs. Often the animals that are selected have been bred to develop tumors and other effects. Second, animals are given much higher doses than humans would receive, and the doses administered to the animals are through routes that do not necessarily mirror human routes of exposure. In addition, the high doses are enhanced by the use of solvents. These steps are taken because a substance with a 1 to 3% chance of triggering a response might not produce statistically significant results in studies of 50 to 500 animals. These methods are conservative ways of trying to bring out the health effect. The third disadvantage of animal studies is that it is difficult to maintain the controlled environment of animals for the length of the experiment. Thus, despite the expenditure of between $200,000 and $750,000, every animal test is ripe for criticism by those who disagree with the results. Finally, animal tests raise ethical and legal questions about the use and abuse of animals.

Short-term tests conducted with bacteria (e.g., Ames test) and other simple organisms are the least expensive in time and money. A chemical can be tested for mutagenic properties in a matter of a few days for a few hundred dollars. A positive result is normally interpreted to mean that the chemical in question can cause mutations and perhaps cancer and other diseases in humans. Roughly 75% of the substances that have yielded positive results are known human carcinogens. Different short-term tests seem to work best for different classes of substances (de Serres, 1979; Hollstein, McCann, Angelosanto, & Nichols, 1979).

The major disadvantage of the short-term tests is that it is difficult to convince people that what happens to bacteria will happen to them. But these tests are finding a niche as a screening device to set priorities for animal and human studies.

Final Steps in Measurement

Extrapolating the results of the biomedical research produced by the above methods is the penultimate and most controversial step in measurement. No one seems to be satisfied with the state of the art. The focal point of the controversy is using the results of experimental studies of animals to estimate the impacts on humans. Recapitulating, animals are given much higher doses of substances than humans receive, and the probability of the animal manifesting an effect is enhanced by the use of solvents and by the choice of vulnerable species and routes for administering doses. The alternative is to use whatever epidemiological studies are available, or to assume that the substance in question will have the same effect as other substance(s) with similar chemical, biological, and physical properties.

There never seems to be enough data to satisfy researchers with extrapolations. Jacobs (1980) summarizes the arguments against extrapolation:

> "Everyone knows" that extrapolation is statistically unsound and that curves apply only to regions validated by data. In environmental issues extrapolation is routinely used, since no data exist in some important areas. The fallacy becomes obvious in looking at the case of trace elements in the human body. Copper and zinc, for example, are absolutely necessary to life. In larger doses they are dangerous poisons. No extrapolation could predict this reversal at low dosage. We need data, not bad guesses. (p. 1414)

A pragmatic position is represented by the United States Environmental Protection Agency (EPA), which uses several models, including the conservative linear, nonthreshold model to calculate the relationship between doses of substances and health responses. This model assumes that there is no safe dose. Each molecule of a substance has an equal chance of causing cell change. Anderson (1983) says that EPA uses this model to establish an upper limit of risk. One of the justifications for conservative models is that little is known about interactions among chemicals. Some chemicals become less harmful when they interact, but some become much more dangerous (a phenomenon called *synergism*). In recognition of the uncertainty about synergism that characterizes our knowledge about most chemicals, the use of a conservative model allows low doses of substances to cause some effect.

Industry and many scientists strongly oppose most uses of nonthreshold models (e.g., linear). Their most important argument is that nonthreshold models ignore the ability of the body to defend itself against low-dose assaults. Industry usually prefers multistage models, which require that multiple hits take place before an effect is produced.

Schneiderman (1981) summarizes the uncertainty about modeling dose-response relationships, saying, "The dose-response relationships that many of us considered 'conservative,' the linear, no threshold concepts are being challenged on both sides as both overstating and understating the risks" (p. 35).

The last step in the measurement of risk is estimating the population at risk. It is important to learn if the population at risk is confined to laboratories in which 100 people have to be protected, or is found in a limited number of factories, in which case a thousand workers may have to be protected, or is the general public, in which case millions of people are at risk, including people who may be at elevated risk because of genetics, existing health conditions, and bad habits.

In conclusion, there are ways to estimate potential risks to people from actions that range from canoeing, to spraying weeds, and to smoking tobacco. Our knowledge is very uneven. We have a pretty good idea about the dangers associated with many of the oldest physical activities such as childbirth and canoeing, and some of the newest such as riding a motorcycle and playing football.

Our knowledge about the potential risk of chemical, physical, and biological agents is clearly inadequate. People are exposed to more than 50,000 chemicals in commerce, foods, drugs, cosmetics, and pesticides. The National Research Council (*Nation's Health*, 1984) evaluated our knowledge of a random sample of 675 of more than 54,000 chemicals to which people are exposed. Based on that sample, the panel concluded that virtually none of the chemicals in commerce and only 5% of the food additives, about 10% of the pesticides and inert chemicals in pesticides, and 18% of drugs and substances in drugs have undergone sufficient testing to permit conclusions about their potential hazardousness. Furthermore, the panel added that we are falling farther behind, because 500 to 2,000 new chemicals are marketed every year.

For further reading about risk measurement see Lowrance (1976), Lave (1982), Hohenemser and Kasperson (1982), and National Research Council (1984).

Coping with Risk

Three mechanisms for coping with risk have been tried. Each will be briefly discussed here, and chapters 7 through 12 focus on specific methods. Chapters 2 through 6 also describe some coping mechanisms.

Market Mechanisms

Informed people can take direct action by boycotting products, refusing to live near unwanted facilities, and exerting pressure through lawsuits and the political system. But many risks are not so obvious, and not everyone is informed. So the public's evaluation of risk will lead to decisions that are at strong variance with scientific data.

In 1662 English scientists observed that people were extraordinarily fearful of lightning (Hacking, 1983). Nuclear power plants and hazardous waste facilities are today's lightning. The general public judges the risk of death from nuclear power and the automobile to be about the same, but actually the automobile is orders of magnitude more dangerous.

Many writers have tried to explain why people exaggerate some risks and understate others (Fischhoff, Slovic, & Lichtenstein, 1979; Lichtenstein, Slovic, Fischhoff, Layman, & Combs, 1978; Lowrance, 1976; Whyte & Burton, 1980). Exaggerated fears have the following characteristics:

1. The effect is latent, dreaded, irreversible, but not well measured.
2. The risk is involuntary.
3. The risk is associated with a nonessential activity and is likely to be misused.

These perceptual factors are not without logic. Lindell and Earle (1983) argue that people's judgments about how close they will live to a nuclear power plant, hazardous waste facility, and other unwanted land use is related to their perceptions of the consequences. Hacking (1983) argues that it is appropriate to be fearful of what he calls "interference effects," side effects of multiple new technologies that can act together to cause a disaster.

Whether our misperceptions of risk are justified or not, they mean that the marketplace cannot be trusted to protect public health and the environment. Some expert opinion is required in decision making.

Expert judgment can come in the form of consumer protection organizations, whose published evaluations directly benefit the public. Sometimes these organizations (e.g., Natural Resources Defense Council) directly confront industry and the government through the courts and the media. Indeed, these organizations often boast that much of the progress of the last decade is the result of lawsuits that forced industry and government to take action.

Voluntary Professional Standards

Industry has access to experts capable of designing tests and developing performance standards. In fact, there is a long history of industry self-policing in the United States. The American Society for Testing and Materials (ASTM) publishes standards for more than 4,000 consumer products or materials that go into consumer products. ASTM, the National Fire Protection Association, the American National Standards Institute, and many small trade associations concerned with a single product work in cooperation with government and increasingly with consumer groups. However, industry's credibility has suffered in the recent past, and it is unlikely that the public will trust it to be the sole risk assessor.

Government

Government is in the best position to evaluate risks objectively. The basis for a government role is what Maclean (1981) calls "hypothetical consent," which means that people consent to a set of principles and procedures for assessing risk. The process in the United States is described by Thompson (1983) as truculent, meaning that it is strongly adversarial.

Standards are the most publicized and controversial regulatory devices. Standards are prescribed goals that are to be met, not voluntary guidelines. They are in the form of ambient concentrations of substances, personal exposure limitations, product design requirements, work practices, packaging, and promotional claim requirements.

The U.S. Environmental Protection Agency is exemplary (see Chapter 8). It is responsible for water, air, solid and hazardous waste management, pesticide, and many other standards. Its standards aim at limiting the amount of effluent that can be discharged by a factory, constraining the type of equipment or raw materials that a factory may use, specifying licensing before someone can use a product, and restricting automobile emissions.

The automobile emission standards are among the most important government standards. Cars produced in the 1980s emit only 1 to 10% of the carbon monoxide emitted by cars built before 1970. Scientific studies of people, especially those with heart and lung diseases, form the basis for reductions in carbon monoxide, lead, and other automobile emissions.

Standards have been opposed on the grounds that they are not justified by the science (see discussion of limitations of risk measurement methods) and because of economic impact (see Chapter 12). Reductions of the magnitude required to meet the automobile standards, such as redesign of the engine, the addition of special pollution control devices, and changes in the fuel, have been expensive. These standards have been opposed by powerful interest groups like the automobile industry and producers of leaded gasoline. In addition, although the population as a whole has given its hypothetical consent to government regulations of automobile emissions, many Americans have tampered with emission controls and used leaded gasoline in engines designed for unleaded gasoline.

Direct costs are not the only economic argument against regulations. Standards, it is argued, hinder innovative approaches to pollution control, add to inflation, and hurt America's international competitive position.

These arguments have crystallized around the call for economic evaluation of all regulations. Three questions are at the heart of the debate about costs. They are:

1. What are the smallest effects to be included in the analysis (early death, acute illness, behavioral changes, property damage, damage to rivers, plants, and animals that do not directly effect people)?
2. How long are effects to be followed (immediately, a year, generations)?
3. How are effects to be measured in setting standards (natural background levels, multiples of background levels, risks compared to other risks commonly encountered)?

The greater the number of effects and the more subtle the effects, the greater the debate. Chapters 7, 8, and 12 assess the workings of our adversarial process. Chapter 9 presents a less adversarial approach to coping with decisions about risk.

There are two nonregulatory approaches. They are important, although they receive much less attention. One is health education. The objective is to teach people about risk, so that they will not smoke, will eat a balanced diet, use seat belts, be cognizant of workplace hazards, and so forth. Chapter 10 focuses on health education.

Medical care is the second nonregulatory approach. Rather than preventing the problem by education and regulation, vaccines and cures are sought. This approach is the focus of Chapter 11.

POINTS TO REMEMBER

This chapter has presented an introduction to health and disease in the United States and to methods for measuring and coping with risk. There are two main points to remember. One is that infectious and parasitic diseases have markedly declined as causes of death. Chronic diseases, principally heart disease, cancer, and cerebro-vascular disease, have become the leading causes of death. In addition, death rates in Northeastern cities and those near the Great Lakes were much higher than those of the rest of the United States. By the mid-1970s, these differences had shrunk in some areas and completely disappeared in others. The first point means that major environmental changes have occurred.

In light of this conclusion, it is important that we have methods to measure and cope with potential risk. We use tests of product performance, analyses of human experiences, and animal tests to assess the risk of consumer products, occupations, and many other potential hazards. The methods have limitations that lead to uncertain results. This uncertainty is magnified by our adversarial approach to decision making. Regulatory approaches to coping with risk are stressed in the media. Health education and medical care are alternatives.

References

Anderson, E., & The Carcinogen Assessment Group of the U.S. Environmental Protection Agency. (1983). Quantitative approaches in use of assess cancer risk. *Risk Analysis, 3,* 277–295.

Cutler, S., & Devesa, S. (1973). Trends in cancer incidence and mortality in the U.S.A. In R. Doll & I. Vodopija (Eds.), *Host environment interactions in the etiology of cancer in man.* Lyon, France: IARC Science Publication No. 7, IARC.

de Serres, F. (1979). Evaluation of tests for mutagencity as indicator of environmental mutagens and carcinogens. *Annals of the New York Academy of Science, 329,* 75–84.

Fiering, M., & Wilson, R. (1983). Attempting to establish a risk by analogy. *Risk Analysis, 3,* 207–216.

Fischhoff, B., Slovic, P., & Lichtenstein, S. (1979). Weighing the risks. *Environment, 21*, 17–20 and 32–38.

Greenberg, M. (1983). *Urbanization and cancer mortality*. New York: Oxford University Press.

Hacking, I. (1983). *Culpable ignorance of interference effects*. College Park, MD: Center for Philosophy and Public Policy, University of Maryland.

Hennes, J. (1972). The measurement of health. *Medical Care Review, 29*, 1268–1288.

Hohenemser, C., & Kasperson, J. (Eds.). (1982). *Risk in the technological society*. Boulder, CO: Westview Press.

Hollstein, M., McCann, J., Angelosanto, F., & Nichols, W. (1979). Short-term tests for carcinogens and mutagens. *Mutation Research, 65*, 133–226.

Jacobs, L. (1980). Environmental analysis. *Science, 207*, 1414.

Lave, L. (Ed.). (1982). *Quantitative risk assessment in regulation*. Washington, DC: The Brookings Institution.

Lerner, M. (1973). Conceptualization of health and social well-being. In R. Berg (Ed.), *Health status indexes, proceedings of a conference* (pp. 1–6). Chicago: Hospital Research and Educational Trust.

Lichtenstein, S., Slovic, P., Fischhoff, B., Layman, M., & Combs, B. (1978). Judged frequency of lethal events. *Journal of Experimental Psychology: Human Learning and Memory, 4*, 551–563.

Lindell, M., & Earle, T. (1983). How close is close enough: Public perceptions of the risks of industrial facilities. *Risk Analysis, 3*, 245–253.

Lowrance, W. (1976). *Of acceptable risk*. Los Altos, CA: William Kaufmann.

McKay, F., Hanson, M., & Miller, R. (1982). *Cancer mortality in the United States: 1950–1977*. Washington, DC: U.S. Government Printing Office.

Maclean, D. (1981). *Risk and consent: A survey of issues for centralized decision-making*. College Park, MD: Center for Philosophy and Public Policy, University of Maryland.

Miller, M., Voth, D., & Danforth, D. (1982). The medical care system and community malady: Rural, urban and suburban variations in impact. *Rural Sociology, 47*, 634–654.

Muller, P. (1975). *The outer city*. Washington, DC: Association of American Geographers.

National Research Council. (1984). *Toxicity testing: Strategies to determine needs and priorities*. Washington, DC: National Academy Press.

Nation's Health. (1984, April). NRC: Only a few chemicals tested for health effects, pp. 1, 3.

Pollack, E., & Horm, J. (1980). Trends in cancer incidence and mortality in the United States, 1969–1976. *Journal of the National Cancer Institute, 64*, 1091–1103.

Schneiderman, M. (1981). Extrapolation from incomplete data to total or lifetime risks at low doses. *Environmental Health Perspectives, 42*, 33–38.

Smith, S. (1980). Government says cancer rate is increasing. *Science, 209*, 998–1002.

Stewart, A., Ware J., Jr., & Book, R. (1981). Advances in the measurement of functional status: Construction of aggregate indexes. *Medical Care, 19*, 473–488.

Thompson, M. (1983). *To hell with the turkeys! A diatribe directed at the pernicious trepidity of the current intellectual debate on risk*. College Park, MD: Center for Philosophy and Public Policy, University of Maryland.

U.S. Bureau of the Census. (1960). *Historical statistics of the United States, colonial times to 1957*. Washington, DC: U.S. Government Printing Office.

U.S. Bureau of the Census. (1982). *Current population reports, series P-60, No. 133, Characteristics of the population below the poverty level: 1980*. Washington, DC: U.S. Government Printing Office.

U.S. Department of Health, Education and Welfare, National Center for Health Statistics. (1973). *Vital statistics of the United States, 1973, life tables*. Washington, DC: U.S. Government Printing Office.

Whyte, A., & Burton, I. (1980). *Environmental risk assessment*. New York: Wiley.

Working Group on Heart Disease Epidemiology, National Heart, Lung and Blood Institute. (1979). *Report* (NIH pub. no. 79-1667). Washington, DC: U.S. Department of Health, Education and Welfare.

C H A P T E R 2

LIFE-STYLE AND CHRONIC DISEASE IN WESTERN SOCIETY

Beverly M. Calkins

Case Western Reserve University

In Chapter 1 the magnitude of the contribution of the major causes of death in the United States was presented. The large contribution of chronic diseases to deaths is notable. In spite of recent encouraging declines, heart disease remains the number one cause of death for Americans today. Cancers are second. Note also that accidents are the fourth leading cause of death and of these about half are traffic accidents. Some known modifiable factors are associated with each of the ten leading causes of death. For example, 50% of traffic accidents are believed to involve alcohol. Assuming that this is true, the minimum preventable portion of all accidents is one out of four. In 1984, the surgeon general estimated that 80–90% of chronic lung diseases (the fifth leading cause of death) are due to smoking. If people stopped smoking, this cause of death would be almost entirely eliminated. Each of these leading causes of death could be explored in detail. For the sake of brevity, this chapter will focus mainly on cancer and heart diseases. Pulmonary diseases will be mentioned in connection with smoking; accidents and liver diseases will be discussed in connection with alcohol. Most of the references for each section have been chosen from summary publications, which will direct the reader to the original research.

Life-style factors will be the focus of this chapter. These are exposures over which each individual has control. Tobacco and alcohol use, wholly a matter of personal choice, have been shown to have profound effects on the user's health and on society through the impact of drunk driving, fires, and involuntary smoking. Diet (food items, preparation, combination, and amount) and exercise are factors that are also almost wholly a matter of personal choice. Psychological factors (i.e., stress and life events), social factors (i.e., occupation, marital status, and religion), and personality traits are more complex, but perhaps even here the role of individual choice is not lost. This chapter will emphasize four aspects of these life-style factors: (1) the extent to which, given current knowledge, they contribute to the disease process; (2) trends in population exposure to these factors; (3) intervention and

25

prevention strategies against diseases related to these factors; and (4) the role of government in developing public health policy as it pertains to these factors.

In the discussion about risk factors, strategies for approaching public health problems will be described primarily on two levels: prevention and intervention. The purpose of prevention is to stop a problem from developing; the purpose of intervention is to reverse a developing problem and prevent disease progression. Rehabilitation is an effort to restore health once a definitive problem has developed. Since this activity level is more often within the purview of clinical medicine or psychiatry than public health per se, little emphasis will be given here to rehabilitation. The summary of these perspectives on each factor is presented to enable the reader: (1) to become knowledgeable about personal and public health issues in the community at large as a voter and as a health professional and, even more important, (2) to make effective personal choices toward better health as a consumer of the retail market place and of health care services.

Evidence for a role of life-style factors in various chronic diseases accumulates as studies are completed and reported. If a large number of studies using different approaches to determine the association of a factor with a disease point in the same direction, then a strong case for causality can be made. Contradictory evidence may be found and should be "cross-examined" in an attempt to determine the reasons for contradictions. But it is not always necessary to wait until all the evidence is collected and all the contradictions are explained before public health policy and personal action are warranted. In particular, recommendations for action are warranted if they are of a prudent (conservative) nature and do not themselves incur any possibility of risk if they are followed.

A historical example of public health policy preceding concrete scientific evidence was the Broad Street pump cholera epidemic of 1854 in London. Dr. John Snow studied the association of water source with the occurrence of cholera in users and nonusers of the Broad Street water pump in London. Dr. Snow had no knowledge of the existence of the cholera bacteria, of the transmissibility of cholera through fecal contamination of water supplies, or of the pathological mechanism by which cholera caused disease. He simply observed that people who died of cholera had used this well as a water source more often than had persons who remained well and convinced authorities to remove the Broad Street pump handle to prevent Londoners from using it. The epidemic subsided, which was fortuitous because Snow had no evidence that the well was contaminated.

SMOKING AND CHRONIC DISEASE

Tobacco was unknown to Europeans until Christopher Columbus returned to Europe with samples of the plant instead of the gold and jewels of India he had hoped to find. Columbus noted that tobacco leaves were used by the natives of the islands for ceremonial purposes, a gesture of good intentions between tribesmen. The plant was smoked as leaves rolled together or in a pipe called tobac. Tobacco was believed to have medicinal properties and was promoted widely for such purposes. However, even in those early times dissenting opinions were heard. King James I of England, successor to Queen Elizabeth I, wrote that smoking was ''a custom loathsome to the eyes, harmful to the braine, dangerous to the lungs'' in his *Counterblast to Tobacco* and imposed a heavy tax on the plant (Fairholt, 1859). Several popes also denounced its use. Nevertheless, the practice spread.

The majority of the harmful constituents of tobacco smoke are formed when the tobacco leaf burns. The temperature in the cone may reach 950°C (1,742°F). Many of the toxic gaseous and particulate agents in cigarettes have been identified. More than 60 toxins, carcinogens, and cocarcinogens with known biological activity have been described, as well as a large number of compounds with unknown or suspected activity. Volumes have been written about these agents, but only two will be mentioned in some detail here.

Nicotine is believed to be the most important of these agents because of its immediate effect on human organ systems, apparent long-term addictive qualities, and potential as a cocarcinogen. It is known that nicotine is readily and rapidly absorbed by oral and intestinal lining, the lungs, and skin. The absorbed nicotine travels rapidly to the heart and then to the brain. The blood pressure and heart rate become elevated. A person who smokes just one pack of cigarettes per day will receive about 70,000 doses of nicotine in a year. Each dose has a half-life in the blood of approximately 30 minutes, which means that a pack-a-day smoker probably will maintain a constant level of nicotine by lighting up every 30–40 minutes. There is also evidence that a tolerance to nicotine can occur. The conditioning effect of repeated dosages, rapid brain feedback, and tolerance are indications that nicotine has addictive qualities. Whether the addictive process is due to simple Pavlovian conditioning, including the taste, feel, smell, and social setting of smoking, or due to a physical action (e.g., biological or chemical) or both is still under investigation. Smokers describe both an enhanced sense of alertness and energy and a calming effect of smoking, and report that they especially enjoy a cigarette with coffee and/or alcohol. The interaction of nicotine with the components of these two products is currently under study. Perhaps the most telling evidence of nicotine addiction is the withdrawal reactions that people experience when they stop smoking. Physiologically, the most immediate changes are decreased heart rate and blood pressure. Decreases in the levels of the hormones epinephrine (adrenalin) and norepinephrine have also been demonstrated. Weight gain, another documented physical change observed after smoking cessation, may result from increased appetite due to improvements in taste and smell or from metabolic changes. Whether weight gain can be attributed to nicotine withdrawal or to another constituent of tobacco is uncertain. Other symptoms that smokers may experience in the initial stages of nicotine withdrawal are nausea, headache, constipation, diarrhea, sleep disturbances, inability to concentrate, increased irritability, hostility, aggressive behavior, anxiety, and cravings for tobacco. Ninety percent of all smokers report some withdrawal symptoms. The symptoms and the craving for tobacco decrease in intensity with time and continued abstinence, but 20% of smokers report occasional cravings for 5 to 9 years after quitting. These facts illustrate why smokers find quitting so difficult (Krasnegor, 1979; Office on Smoking and Health [OSH], 1981, 1983b; Shiffman, 1979).

Carbon monoxide, a constituent of tobacco smoke formed by incomplete combustion of tobacco, has a great affinity for the oxygen-binding site on the hemoglobin (an iron-containing molecule) in the red blood cell, forming carboxyhemoglobin. It replaces oxygen and limits the ability of the blood to deliver oxygen to body tissues. Its role in disease development is under study, but its detrimental effects in persons with other conditions, such as heart disease, is known (OSH, 1981).

The mechanisms by which other constituents of tobacco smoke act in the body alone or interactively are less well understood. For instance, research is needed to clarify the steps involved in cellular changes that lead to tumor formation. The lack of an appropriate animal model is a practical limitation on research needed to discover these mechanisms. Rodents, often used in research, have respiratory tracts that differ in anatomy, physiology, and biochemistry from those of humans. Those animals similar to humans are expensive to procure and to maintain because of longer life spans. In addition, animals do not inhale as deeply or intensely as human smokers when exposed to cigarette smoke (OSH, 1982).

Epidemiological evidence about the effects of tobacco use on health began to be published in the 1950s. After a number of studies had been reported, the surgeon general of the United States announced in January 1964 that an association between smoking and lung cancer had been established. In the intervening two decades, a plethora of studies have linked smoking to cancers of the lung, mouth, pharynx, larynx, esophagus, bladder, and pancreas; cardiovascular disease and stroke; and asthma, bronchitis, and emphysema. In addition, hypertension, amblyopia (dimness of vision), allergies, and accidents have been associated with smoking (OSH, 1982, 1983a, 1983b).

Lung cancer is the leading cause of cancer death among American males. Among females, the rate has been rising so fast that in 1985 lung cancer became the leading cause of cancer death in women. The increase in death rates for lung cancer are alarming: 200% for males and 250% for females since 1950. Fifty retrospective studies have shown a higher risk of lung cancer among smokers than nonsmokers. The increased risk is consistently higher among smokers when different groups are studied: male and female, different occupational groups, international and regional studies, hospital and autopsy studies, and studies of different ethnic and racial groups. In addition, eight major cohort studies have also shown a consistently higher risk of lung cancer for smokers, ranging from 2 to 14 times that of nonsmokers. Higher death rates for lung cancer also were found among those who smoked a larger number of cigarettes daily, among those who started smoking early in life and continued to smoke, and among those who inhaled deeply. Increased risk of death due to lung cancer has also been shown to be directly related to the amount of tar and nicotine in the cigarettes smoked. But a much higher risk exists even for low tar and nicotine users when compared to nonsmokers. A lower but still increased risk of cancer has been shown for pipe and cigar smokers, possibly because these smokers do not inhale as often or as deeply. Finally, lung cancer death rates are lower among quitters. The reduction in risk is gradual but consistent in all studies reported; at about 15–20 years after smoking cessation the risk of lung cancer in an ex-smoker is approximately equal to that of the individual who never smoked. The mechanism by which smoking causes lung cancer has received considerable study. Premalignant changes in the lining of the bronchi and lungs have been noted. These changes involve the loss of typical cell structures and changes in the form of the cell. The specific components in tobacco smoke responsible for these changes are as yet not identified (OSH, 1982).

Smoking was recently declared by the surgeon general to be a definite causal factor in cardiovascular disease. Cardiovascular disease (CVD) should not be regarded as a single entity but as several: arteriosclerosis, coronary heart disease (CHD), cerebrovascular disease, peripheral vascular disease, and others. Arteriosclerosis is in itself not a single entity but several; the one most commonly associated with clinical disease is atherosclerosis, a fatty accumulation in the lining of arteries. Smoking has been well established as an important factor in all of these cardiovascular diseases. The role of smoking in atherosclerosis is believed to be as an aggravating and accelerating factor by altering the serum concentration of fats, such as cholesterol. Smokers have a 70% greater death rate than nonsmokers from coronary heart disease. And, as with cancer, higher death rates are related to the number of cigarettes used, the age smoking was started, the total number of years of smoking, and the degree of inhalation of smoke. But, in contrast to cancer, there is no consistent evidence of a reduction in risk from using low tar and nicotine cigarettes compared to regular cigarettes; cigar and pipe smokers do not appear to be at increased risk compared to nonsmokers. Smoking is in itself an important causal factor for coronary heart disease, but it also acts synergistically with other risk factors, hypertension and high serum cholesterol, to increase risk greatly. The surgeon general has estimated that 30% of all coronary heart disease deaths are due to smoking alone. This number translates into about one out of ten of all deaths in the United States every year. Stroke, CVD, and peripheral vascular disease have also been shown to be strongly associated with smoking. Smoking cessation appears to produce a rapid reduction in the risk of dying from CHD in just one year. One to ten years after cessation, CHD risk for ex-smokers is about equal to that of persons who never smoked (OSH, 1981, 1983a, 1983b).

Smoking is also recognized as the major cause of noncancerous respiratory diseases, collectively called chronic obstructive lung disease (COLD). Two in particular have been well studied: chronic bronchitis and emphysema. Eighty to 90% of COLD can be attributed to smoking, which is the only significant predictor of COLD development and its only established cause, with the exception of a rare genetic enzyme defect. Air pollution appears to be an exacerbating factor but does not seem to be causal. Occupational exposure to dust, heat, and gases may be important as causal factors but are far outweighed by the impact of smoking. As with cancer and cardiovascular diseases, the occurrence of COLD increases with numbers of cigarettes smoked. Pipe and cigar users have a lower risk than cigarette users but a higher risk than nonsmokers. The effects of the use of lower tar and nicotine cigarettes on risk are not definitively known but believed to be helpful. Important physiological changes in lung function have been demonstrated in smokers. Smokers produce more mucus and have narrower airways than nonsmokers. The ability of the lungs to expel air is decreased. This change begins soon after smoking is started and progresses with age at a faster rate than is observed in nonsmokers. When smoking is stopped, the ability of the lungs to expel air normalizes relatively quickly, within weeks or months. Important progress has been made in understanding the possible mechanisms by which smoking may cause COLD. Emphysema can be produced by the presence of excessive amounts of the enzyme elastase, which degrades the structural tissues of the lung. The amount of this enzyme is found to be higher in respiratory tissues of smokers (OSH, 1984).

A lower death rate from both lung cancer and CHD has been observed for women than men. Differences in hormone levels have been a traditional explanation of this difference, but differences in smoking prevalence and pattern may be responsible. Among women who have smoked as much and as long as men, the increased risk of developing lung cancer and CHD with increasing exposure (number of cigarettes smoked, number of years smoked, and so on) is similar to that of men (OSH, 1981).

The proportion of smokers in the United States population has declined. This decrease can be used as another way to examine the causal relationship of smoking to disease. To evaluate the potential role of a life-style change on the death rate, one must consider to what extent improvement in early detection and treatment for a disease may be responsible for changes in death rates. No improvements in the early detection or treatment of lung cancer to date have increased the survival of lung cancer patients. Lung cancer is approximately 90% fatal. No consistent evidence for improved survival for COLD has been shown either. Thus observed changes in death rates may be considered a direct response to change in smoking patterns. Since the latency periods for lung cancer and COLD are long and only 20 years have elapsed since the surgeon general's first report on the association of smoking and lung cancer, future decades should see the beginning of a downward trend in lung cancer, chronic bronchitis, and emphysema deaths (OSH, 1982, 1984).

Since the late 1960s there has been a substantial decline in deaths due to CHD and stroke. The latency period for CHD in relation to smoking may be shorter than cancer, and changes in death rates may respond more quickly than changes in smoking prevalence. Great improvements have been made in the treatment of CHD. Improvements in the training, distribution, and use of paramedic teams, coronary intensive care units, surgical treatments (bypass surgery of blocked arteries, heart transplants), drug therapy for hypertension and angina pectoris (chest pain), and diet and drug therapy for high serum cholesterol have greatly improved the chances that persons who develop heart problems will survive. These and other changes in life-style-related factors of CHD and stroke have been evaluated. Separation of the contribution of each to the lower heart disease death rate is difficult, but it can be concluded that the reduction in smoking has contributed to the change in death rates. Approximately 60–70% of all CHD deaths are "sudden" deaths, deaths that occur within 24 hours of the onset of symptoms and without a medical history of problems. Most of these are persons found dead or unconscious at the scene and are not revived by paramedic or emergency room assistance. Improvements in medical care are not helpful to such individuals. For this large group, prevention may be the only approach to effectively reduce risk of sudden death, since treatment does not appear to be a possible option (National Institutes of Health [NIH], 1979).

Adverse effects of smoking have been found to occur to smoking pregnant women, the placenta, and the unborn child. Pregnant women who smoke are at greater risk of spontaneous abortions, but this fetal loss is not due to any abnormality in the fetus. Women who smoke during pregnancy are also more likely to experience placenta previa, abruptio placentae, vaginal bleeding during pregnancy, amnionitis, and premature rupture of amniotic membrane surrounding the fetus in utero, all of which increase in turn the likelihood of hemorrhage in the mother. The potential threat to the unborn child from these problems cannot be overstated. The fetus of a smoking mother is exposed to the effects of tobacco smoke through changes in the ability of maternal blood and the placenta to deliver oxygen. The blood of smokers is known to carry a higher amount of carboxyhemoglobin, a combination of hemoglobin and carbon monoxide. Carbon monoxide replaces oxygen in the red blood cells, which prevents blood from delivering oxygen to the body. Fetal blood can have 10% higher levels of carboxyhemoglobin than maternal blood, and thus the fetus is placed at risk from oxygen deprivation in utero. Nicotine rapidly crosses the placental barrier and produces increased blood pressure, acidosis, rapid heart rate, and hypoxia in the fetus. The effects on the fetus of other constituents of tobacco such as cyanide, cadmium, and polycyclic aromatic hydrocarbons have yet to be adequately studied. Nicotine is also present in breast fluids in the same concentration as in plasma. The effect of nicotine in breast milk of nursing infants needs further study. Infants born to women who smoke are underweight, are at greater risk of sudden infant death syndrome (crib death), and have been shown to have small but measurably slower physical, intellectual, and emotional development after birth, even into adolescence. Behavioral problems, such as hyperkinesis (purposeless, excessive, involuntary movements), are more common as well (OSH, 1981, 1983b).

Smoking is also known to interfere with drug therapy and nutrition. Drugs such as clorpromazine, diazepam, and chlorodiazepoxide (all tranquilizers) have been shown to be less effective in smokers than nonsmokers, which may tend to result in increased doses being used by smokers, increasing the likelihood of side effects and overdosing. Smoking has been shown to have a profound interaction with oral contraceptives. Both stroke and heart attack risk are increased among women who smoke *and* use oral contraceptives. Smokers have also been shown to need additional vitamin C in the diet. Further studies of the effects of smoking on nutrition are needed (OSH, 1983b).

Occupational exposures to various substances can act synergistically or additively to increase the risk for exposed workers who also smoke. Asbestos, uranium, silica talc, carbon black, cotton and coal dust, aromatic amines, and cadmium exposure all increase the risk of cancer in workers who smoke. Synergistic or cocarcinogenic activity with tobacco smoke is suspected also for exposure to nickel, chromium, ansenicals, vinyl chloride, and halogenated ethers (OSH, 1981, 1982, 1983a, 1983b).

Table 2-1. Comparison of Mainstream and Sidestream Cigarette Smoke[a]

Compound	Mainstream	Sidestream
General characteristics		
Duration of smoke production	20 sec.	550 sec.
Tobacco burnt	347	411
Particulates, no. per cigarette	1.05×10^{12}	3.5×10^{12}
Particulate phase (mg/cig.)[b]		
Tar (chloroform extract)	20.8	44.1 (Nonfilter)
	10.2	34.5 (Filter)
Nicotine	.92	1.69 (Nonfilter)
	.46	1.27 (Filter)
Benzo(a)pyrene	3.5×10^{-5}	13.5×10^{-5}
Pyrene	13×10^{-5}	39×10^{-5}
Total phenols	0.228	0.603
Cadmium	12.5×10^{-5}	45×10^{-5}
Gases and vapors (mg/cig.)[b]		
Water	7.5	298
Ammonia	.16	7.4
Carbon monoxide	31.4	148
Carbon dioxide	63.5	79.5
Oxides of nitrogen	.014	.051

Note. Adapted from Centers for Disease Control (1976).
[a]For 35 ml puff volume, 2 sec puff duration, one puff per min and 23 or 30 mm butt length and 10% tobacco moisture.
[b]Milligrams per cigarette.

　　The determination of the risk of disease in those who "smoke" secondarily or "involuntarily" due to the presence of sidestream smoke in the ambient air has also been evaluated, but the results are controversial. *Sidestream* smoke is that which drifts into the ambient air from the tip of a smoldering cigarette; mainstream smoke is that which the smoker inhales. Sidestream smoke has higher concentrations of carbon monoxide, nicotine, and other constituents of tobacco smoke than mainstream smoke (see Table 2-1). Eighty-four percent of smoking air pollution is sidestream smoke. Thus smokers as well as nonsmokers are exposed to sidestream smoke. Most nonsmokers report some ill effects as a result of being in a smoky atmosphere (OSH, 1984).

　　If not properly ventilated, confined areas can achieve carbon monoxide, nicotine, and other substances levels from cigarette smoking that exceed standards set for work areas by Occupational Safety and Health Administration. Recent studies also indicate that nonsmokers in a smoky atmosphere do absorb significant amounts of nicotine (OSH, 1984). The most common complaints from smokers as a result of exposure to tobacco smoke are eye irritation (69%), headache (32%), nasal symptoms (29%), and cough (25%) (Speer, 1968). These are usually temporary symptoms, but evidence is accumulating that permanent pulmonary changes may be experienced by otherwise healthy nonsmokers who are chronically exposed to smoky atmospheres at work or at home.

Studies on the risk of developing cancer, heart disease, or respiratory disease in nonsmokers exposed to smoky ambient air have been attempted. These studies are not easily designed because of methodological difficulties, the most prominent of which are quantifying the amount of exposure and the long latency period between exposure and disease onset. It is also difficult to separate the effects of smoky atmospheres from what may be occupational or other environmental exposures. The accumulating evidence suggests that nonsmokers chronically exposed to cigarette smoke are at increased risk of lung cancer and heart disease (Garfinkel, 1981). Heart, asthmatic, and allergy patients have definitely been shown to be adversely affected by breathing smoky air (OSH, 1981, 1984). More studies are needed with attention to other groups who also may be seriously affected, such as the elderly and persons confined to a bed or wheelchair. Children of smokers seem to be at increased risk of developing respiratory infections, such as pneumonia and bronchitis (OSH, 1984). One of the limitations of respiratory disease studies in children and parents is the ability of any study design to separate a possible inherited tendency toward respiratory problems from strictly environmental factors. The relationship of parental smoking to illness in children would also be explained if parental smoking caused a higher level of respiratory infections in the parents, which are then transmitted to the children. Thus, parental smoking would be only indirectly responsible for infections in their children. These considerations should illustrate why not all experts agree on this issue. After 10 years of evaluation and debate, it can be concluded that children of smoking parents are adversely affected and that the problems experienced by children are more severe if both parents smoke as opposed to one parent. Whether the ill effects result in increased incidence or severity of disease in adulthood is not yet known (OSH, 1982, 1984).

Trends in Cigarette Usage

In the United States cigarette consumption has soared from less than 10 per capita of the adult population in 1880 to 4,300 per capita of the adult population in 1980. Since the surgeon general's announcement in 1964, the per capita consumption declined slightly between 1964 and 1970, peaked again in 1976, and declined slightly again to about 3,950 per capita in 1978 (OSH, 1981). Since 1964 the proportion of adult smokers in the population has declined, but number of cigarettes consumed by the remaining smokers has not. In fact, those men and women who continue to smoke appear to be smoking more cigarettes than ever before. Cigarette consumption has declined about equally for white and black males and females in the United States. The proportion of black males who smoke is higher at every age level than that for white males. The proportion of black females who smoke is about equal to the proportion of white females at each age level. Currently, about 45% and 31% of black males and females, respectively, are smokers as compared to 37% and 30% for white males and females. Blacks of both sexes use cigarettes with higher tar and nicotine content than do whites (Moss, 1979; National Center of Health Statistics [NCHS], 1984). The higher proportion of cigarette smokers among black males and the heavier use of high tar cigarettes are major contributing factors to the higher death rates among black males. From surveys conducted between 1968 and 1979, the percentage of male teenage smokers has declined in recent years after remaining at a fairly constant proportion from 1968 to 1974. Currently, 3% of 12- to 14-year-olds; 13% of 15- and 16-year-olds and about 19% of 17- and 18-year-old males smoke. Among teenage females a steady and alarming increase in the percentage of smokers at all of these ages was observed between 1968 and 1974; the proportion in younger teenagers declined between 1974 and 1979, but the proportion of smokers among older teenage females has remained disturbingly high. Currently, smoking proportions for female teenagers are about 4.5%, 12%, and 16% for these respective age categories (OSH, 1983b).

The tar and nicotine components of the cigarette have received considerable attention for their carcinogenic and addictive qualities respectively. Manufacturers of cigarettes have marketed low tar and nicotine products with considerable success. The tar content of the average cigarette sold has declined from about 37 mg in 1954 to about 18 mg in 1978. The nicotine content of cigarettes has also declined parallel with tar content (OSH, 1981). It appears that while smokers as a proportion of the total population have declined, the remaining minority of the population who are smokers are, on the average, smoking lower tar and nicotine filter cigarettes but more cigarettes. Warnings by the surgeon general have stated that if in addition to smoking more, smokers are inhaling more deeply, any benefit derived from the lower tar/nicotine and filter cigarettes may be nullified (OSH, 1979).

Prevention and Intervention Programs against Smoking

Persuading young people not to smoke and smoking cessation programs are two very important keys to the success of improving public health. Of these, one has not been shown to be more easily accomplished than the other, but both are vital if the future health of the American population is to be improved. Prevention programs started with antismoking ads as public service announcements in the mid-1960s. Recently, these ads have more directly focused on a younger audience. School-based smoking prevention programs have been developed and tested. Those that show consistent success (50% or more reduction of smoking initiation) share several common features. All are based on (1) social-psychological theory and research, (2) social learning theory, and (3) attribution theory. These programs emphasize the immediate social and health advantages of not smoking rather than the long-term consequences of smoking. The smoking prevention model has been important in developing an approach to combating alcohol and drug abuse problems in the young as well (McAlister, Perry, Killen, Slinkard, & Maccoby, 1980).

Public and private agencies have developed intervention programs with a wide variety of strategies to assist smokers to stop. These programs might be grouped into these categories:

1. *Self-Help*. Most reports indicate that a self-devised and implemented program is the preferred method for the majority of those who stop smoking. Both the American Cancer Society and the National Clearinghouse for Smoking and Health have self-help kits available. Unfortunately, evaluation of the effectiveness of these kits is difficult, but estimates suggest that 96% of ex-smokers quit without the aid of an organized program.

2. *Educational Programs*. A host of educational materials are available through the National Clearinghouse for Smoking and Health, but the most prominent educational program is the *Five-Day Plan* to stop smoking, which was developed and is offered through the Seventh-day Adventist Church and has served approximately 11 million smokers worldwide. Educational programs feature films, lectures, discussions, and counseling by physicians, clergy, and psychologists and often a "buddy" system, which pairs a smoker with a nonsmoker or two smokers to provide encouragement. The 6–12 months success rate for educational programs ranges from 20–26%.

3. *Medication*. Smoking deterrents have been developed. Astringent mouthwashes are available which are mainly prepared from silver nitrate, copper sulfate, or potassium permanganate and have an irritating effect on oral and nasal mucosa. Other products such as local anesthetics and bitters of quinine and/or taste substitutes are intended to reduce the sensory drive. Substitutes for smoking, such as nicotine-containing gum, recently have become available. About 25% of subjects using nicotine-containing gum are able to stop smoking. Other pharmaceuticals are also available, which are intended to reduce withdrawal symptoms. Overall, medications have been shown to be effective for about 20% of smokers trying this approach.

4. and 5. *Individual and Group Counseling*. Of these two approaches, individual or one-to-one sessions show the best results with 32–35% success after 6–12 months of smoking cessation. Group counseling shows a 27–30% success rate after 6–12 months. Counselors use a wide variety of formats and counseling styles and the length of time necessary for counseling also varies. Some evidence does exist that the practice of physicians counseling their patients to stop is a good motivation for some smokers.

6. *Hypnosis*. Hypnosis has been adapted for smoking cessation. Claims of very high quit rates (up 68%) have been made, but the evidence for the effectiveness of hypnosis is contradictory. Overall, a success rate of 35–47% for 6–12 months may be more likely.

7. *Behavior Modification*. This approach may be summarized as adverse conditioning. The use of mild electric shock, rapid smoking, and sensory deprivation as well as other aversion techniques are used. This approach generally yields poor results, although claims of great success are made by some users of these methods (National Cancer Institute [NCI], 1977).

Some rather more exotic methods such as transcendental meditation, telephone messages, and Caribbean cruises also have been tried. Community intervention programs conducted through the media, principally television, have also been tried. These also have been evaluated but show less than a 20% quit rate. It should be clear that further study and development of smoking cessation strategies are necessary. None of the approaches suggested is even 50% effective. Evaluation of these programs is very difficult because many "graduates" cannot be located for follow-up evaluation. Validation of smoking cessation is also a problem. New and more effective approaches are needed to assist smokers to quit.

The workplace is becoming a more common site for smoking cessation programs. Smokers have an absentee rate 33–45% higher than nonsmokers or about 2 extra days per year. If an average worker earned about $40 per day (1980 dollars), the additional cost to the employer would be about $80 per employee per year. In addition, the average productivity loss to business is estimated to be between $50 and $166 per smoking employee per year. A successful smoking cessation program can return these costs plus additional savings from lower insurance costs including fire, accident, life, disability, and workers' compensation. These savings have been estimated at $274 per smoker per year. In addition, higher insurance costs and other benefits paid to nonsmokers affected by workplace exposure are about $104 per smoker per year. The total cost estimate ranges from $625 to $4,611 per smoker per year (1980 dollars). The total savings after a smoking cessation program is conservatively estimated to be between $12,634–40,829 for male and $3,003–13,594 for female employees 35–39 years of age, depending on the quantity of cigarettes smoked.[1] Despite these staggering numbers, only 8–14% of businesses report having any kind of cessation program for their employees. The total economic cost, both direct medical costs and indirect costs of lost wages and premature mortality, of smoking to Americans is $47.5 billion annually (1980 estimates). About 49% of this amount is heart disease-related. Another 32%, 16%, and 3% respectively, are respiratory, cancer, and fire-related costs. These costs break down to about $811 per adult smoker or about $1.56 per pack of cigarettes sold (Oster, Colditz, & Kelly, 1984).

Smoking and Public Policy

Public legislation restricting smoking is not unique to recent times. Between 1895 and 1921, 14 states had banned smoking altogether as a response to public outrage and concern over its health effects. But by 1927 as state legislatures began to view the taxation of the tobacco industry as a source of revenue, all antismoking laws had been repealed. Almost immediately after the surgeon general's announcement in 1964 the Federal Trade Commission (FTC) ruled that health warnings must appear on all cigarette packs. After a successful lobbying campaign by tobacco interests, in 1965 Congress passed the Cigarette Labeling and Advertising Act which, although requiring a warning on cigarette packages, prohibited the FTC or any other federal agency from further regulating cigarette advertising and set aside

---

1. The differential in the cost estimates between the sexes is due to a difference in the risk between the sexes for developing serious smoking-related diseases.

any state or local advertising regulations. Tobacco interests were not able to stop passage of FTC rulings in 1967 allowing free air time for antismoking public service announcements. Cigarette ads were finally banned from radio and television in 1970, but no new antismoking legislation has been enacted since that time. However, Congress did strengthen the wording of warnings on cigarette packaging in the spring of 1984. Federal agencies do have the authority to restrict smoking in the transportation industry. The Interstate Commerce Commission (ICC) ruling has restricted smoking to the rear 30% of seats on buses and to designated cars on trains. The Civil Aeronautics Board (CAB) has designated nonsmoking areas on aircraft and established rules to protect the right of nonsmokers to a nonsmoking seat (NCI, 1977).

For decades, the federal government has engaged in a very delicate political balancing act on tobacco-related issues. As a health advocate, the federal government has poured millions of tax dollars into health and tobacco-related disease research and has developed antismoking literature, public service announcements, and prevention and cessation programs. However, the federal government also provides support for tobacco agriculture with tax dollars (Iglehart, 1984). Price supports and low-cost loans to tobacco growers began in 1938 with congressional passage of the Agricultural Adjustment Act. These subsidies have been continued through very careful lobbying and regional politicking by the tobacco industry. Politicians from tobacco-growing states trade support of tobacco subsidies for support of subsidies of other agricultural products such as cotton, milk, and wheat with representatives from regions where these products are important (Iglehart, 1984). The local impact of withdrawing the tobacco subsidies has been evaluated. Land values and tobacco prices would most likely decline. The loss of jobs, tax revenue, and personal expenditures in tobacco-growing areas are effects for which politicians generally do not wish to take responsibility. And resistance to change after generations of tobacco growing in these areas has made the introduction of new agriculture or industry difficult. Price supports for tobacco continue as do well-financed campaigns by the tobacco industry to oppose federal, state, and local legislation that would further limit tobacco interests.

Since 1964, consideration of state legislation for the regulation or limitation of various smoking-related activities has steadily increased. Proposed legislation can be categorized as: (1) "clean air" regulation or limitations on indoor smoking, (2) intra- and interstate commercial regulation of tobacco transactions, (3) smoking and health education in schools, (4) cigarette advertising, (5) the sale of products to minors, and (6) reduced insurance premiums for nonsmokers. In 1975 only nine states had enacted comprehensive clean-air legislation.[2] Just 5 years later 36 states had passed laws limiting indoor smoking. Such legislation requires careful drafting,

---

2. Smoking is regulated in public areas in a broad range of facilities including public buildings, elevators, theaters, sports arenas, schools, drug and department stores, supermarkets, hospitals and health care facilities, public transportation facilities, restaurants, and certain government buildings.

since poorly written laws are confusing and unenforceable. Four states have enacted legislation restricting smoking in public and private schools and/or supporting the inclusion of antismoking health education in school curricula. Five states have enacted legislation restricting the sale to and use of cigarettes by minors. Seven states (Colorado, Minnesota, Montana, Nebraska, Oregon, Utah, and Connecticut) and four cities in California (San Francisco, San Diego, Sacramento, and Palo Alto) have enacted legislation limiting smoking in the workplace. This legislation has been controversial and has received considerable media attention. Some of the early limitations on smoking in the workplace resulted from suits brought to court by individual employees. Certainly one of the more prominent of these was a landmark decision against the New Jersey Bell Telephone Company. This company, which manufactures communications equipment sensitive to smoke, had a policy of smoking restriction in work areas near this equipment. The receptionist, who developed an allergy to smoke, asked for smoking to be further restricted to the lunchrooms and lounges. In finding for the employee, the court reasoned:

> Human beings are also very sensitive and can be damaged by cigarette smoke. Unlike a piece of machinery, the damage to a human is all too often irreparable. . . . A company which has demonstrated such concern for its mechanical components should have at least as much concern for its human beings. Plaintiff asks nothing more than to be able to breathe the air in its clear and natural state. (*Shimp* v. *New Jersey Bell Telephone*, 1976)

The court further defined the rights of smokers and nonsmokers by asserting:

> The evidence is clear and overwhelming. Cigarette smoke contaminates and pollutes the air, creating a health hazard not merely to the smoker but to all those around . . . who must rely on the same air supply. The right of an individual to risk his or her own health does not include the right to jeopardize the health of those who must remain around him or her in order to properly perform the duty of their jobs. (*Shimp* v. *New Jersey Bell Telephone*, 1976)

Other court actions have awarded disability to employees who developed illnesses as a result of both personal or secondary smoking on the job (*Los Angeles Times*, 1977). However, countersuits by smokers also have been filed and are in litigation at the time of this writing.

Nonsmoker rights have received considerable media attention and some media support. The National Association of Broadcasters television code has suggested that programming should de-emphasize cigarette smoking. The movie industry has not followed suit. Two organizations have been founded with the protection of nonsmokers' rights as the specific objective: Action on Smoking and Health (ASH) and Group Against Smoking Pollution (GASP). The effectiveness of GASP is illustrated by its efforts to pass antismoking legislation in California and Miami, Florida. In 1979 in California, tobacco interests spent 10 times the $500,000 GASP budget to defeat a statewide smoking restriction referendum which lost by only a narrow margin. In 1979 in Miami, GASP spent only $5,000 in a campaign to restrict smoking in certain offices and public places. Tobacco interests spent nearly $1 million to vote down the initiative, which lost only by .5% of the votes cast. Tobacco interests have capitalized on a growing resistance to governmental regulation in order to defeat these measures.

Summary

The association between smoking and a wide variety of illnesses and adverse events is strong, well studied, and documented. Despite gaps in knowledge of how smoking causes problems, experts now agree that a causal association exists between smoking and a variety of cancers, heart diseases, and respiratory diseases. Smoking is the single most preventable cause of death. Mortality from all causes of death is 70% higher for smokers than nonsmokers. Thirty percent of all cancers and cardiovascular diseases are smoking-related. This represents an enormous number of persons dying prematurely and unnecessarily each year. The life expectancy for a 30-year-old, two-pack-a-day smoker is 8 years less than a nonsmoker of the same age. The total yearly cost of smoking has been estimated to be over $45 billion (1980 estimates). It is clear, however, that information alone will not stop some individuals from taking up the habit or motivate some smokers to stop. New motivational strategies need to be found to address the pressing need for more effective prevention and cessation programs.

ALCOHOL AND CHRONIC DISEASE

Human use of alcohol is recorded in the earliest literature. Alcohol abuse is equally old. Alcohol is used by almost all cultural groups, Islamic societies excepted. In both primitive and developed societies, alcohol is an important part of religious ceremonies, celebrations, and social gatherings. Alcohol is also important, though less so, as a source of calories, as a drink in cultures where water sources are not dependably potable, and as a medicine. But in Westernized societies, its most important function is social, as a means of creating a pleasurable sense of social unity and temporary mood modification. It also is used as an escape from unpleasant social situations or personal crises. In the history of the United States, it has unquestionably made its impact. Early colonial trade was based on the trading of rum and molasses for African slaves. The first civil crisis faced by the infant U.S. federal government was the Whiskey Rebellion of 1794. The temperance movement, which began as an attempt to foster moderation in alcohol use, culminated in the passage of the Eighteenth (Prohibition) Amendment to the Constitution, later repealed by the Twenty-first Amendment and the only amendment to be repealed. Even customs and language have been affected by alcohol: ships are launched with champagne, an evening gown is sometimes called a cocktail dress, and even the evening hours used for drinking are called ''the happy hour'' (a reference to the mood-altering aspects of alcohol). It is clear that the influence of alcohol is large, pervasive, and most likely permanent. Thus, it should not be surprising that the problems produced by alcohol overconsumption and abuse are equally large and pervasive. The permanence of alcohol-produced problems depends on whether individuals and society as a whole continue to tolerate alcohol abuse.

Alcohol is the most widely available, used, and abused drug in America. When consumed, a portion is rapidly absorbed into the bloodstream by the stomach lining. For the average adult, one shot of hard liquor (1.5 oz. of 80–100 proof [40–50%] ethanol), one glass of wine (5 oz. of 12% ethanol), or one pint of beer (16 oz. of 5% ethanol) will raise the blood alcohol level to about 0.02% (the amount of alcohol in 100 ml of blood). At this level, mild alterations and intensification of mood are the primary effects. After two to six drinks (depending on body weight), the blood level of most persons is 0.05–0.09%. At this level, ability and judgment are impaired, reaction time is prolonged, visual and hearing ability are reduced, but the individual may feel only warm, relaxed, and elated (or depressed). After four to seven drinks, a blood alcohol level of 0.10% is reached. This level is legal intoxication in most states (Smith & Hanham, 1982).

Of the many chronic effects of alcohol on various organ systems only a few will be mentioned here. Alcohol-caused chronic brain damage is second only to Alzheimer's disease as a cause of mental deterioration in adults. Physical effects can be detected by a CT scan (computerized tomography) even before overt abnormalities are noticed. Brain injury occurs even with adequate nutrition and in the absence of other medical problems. Interest in the mechanism for dependency development has recently been stimulated by the discovery of naturally produced opiate-like compounds in the brain as a result of alcohol consumption. Alcohol acts as an irritant to the lining of the digestive tract, particularly the esophagus and stomach. It impairs vitamin (thiamin and folic acid) and zinc absorption and alters cholesterol metabolism. Alcohol consumption has profound effects on the function of the pancreas, gallbladder, and liver. Alcohol is metabolized by the liver to acetaldehyde, which is itself toxic, and finally to acetate. Both alcohol and acetaldehyde have independent toxic effects on liver function. Cirrhosis, hepatitis, and fatty liver are the three most common conditions due to long-term alcohol damage. Chronic and excessive alcohol consumption results in cardiomyopathy, a condition characterized by failure of the heart muscle to function properly. Myopathy of skeletal and smooth muscles also occur as results of alcohol abuse. Alcohol decreases the production of sex hormones. The thyroid and adrenal hormone production are also chronically and acutely affected by alcohol ingestion (National Institute on Alcohol Abuse and Alcoholism [NIAAA], 1984).

Mortality rates among alcohol abusers are 2.5 times greater than among non-alcohol abusers. For the three causes of death most universally recognized as alcohol-related, cirrhosis of the liver, alcoholism, and alcohol psychosis, the rates of death have remained relatively constant except for cirrhosis, which has declined somewhat from an apparent peak in 1973. Cirrhosis of the liver is also caused by factors other than alcohol. A decline in non-alcohol-related cirrhosis is most likely responsible for the downward trend in cirrhosis deaths, since alcohol-related cirrhosis death rates are not declining. The death rates are higher for males than

Table 2-2. The Proportion of Deaths Attributable to Alcohol for Selected Causes

	Proportion related to alcohol
Alcohol as a direct cause	
Alcoholism	100%
Alcohol psychosis	100%
Cirrhosis	41–95%
Alcohol as an indirect cause	
Accidents	
Motor vehicle	30–50%
Young drivers	40–60%
Falls	44%
Fires	26%
Drownings	50–68%
Others	11%
Violence	
Homicide	49–70%
Suicides	25–37%

Note. Adapted from National Clearinghouse for Alcohol Information (1981).

females, and that for blacks is higher than that for whites. Rates of death due to cirrhosis are particularly disproportionately high, nearly ten times higher among black young males than among white young males (NIAAA, 1981, 1984).

As with smoking, the relationship of alcohol use and chronic disease may be viewed as strictly personal effects, and those effects extend beyond the individual user into the larger society. Even more thoroughly than smoking, the societal effects of alcohol abuse can be documented and are more serious. Table 2-2 summarizes the estimated proportion of alcohol-related causes of death. In addition other estimates have been made with regard to the consequences of alcohol use. Up to 33% of child abuse and 50% of spousal abuse cases, and 40% of divorces involve alcohol. Job absenteeism and industrial accidents are two to four times more frequent among alcohol abusers (NIAAA, 1981).

The effect of alcohol on the developing fetus has been vigorously debated in a see-saw fashion. As recently as 1964, claims of absolute safety for the fetus were made (Montagu, 1964), regardless of the amount of alcohol consumed by the mother. But even in the nineteenth century, children of alcoholic women were noted as "starved, shriveled and imperfect" (Jones & Smith, 1973). The identification of fetal alcohol syndrome (FAS) as an entity in 1970 renewed interest in the effects of alcohol during pregnancy. Like the effects of smoking, FAS is characterized by underweight children at birth and slower-than-normal growth and development. Birth defects, brain dysfunction, and abnormal behavior in the child are also the result of alcohol abuse during pregnancy (NIAAA, 1978). These are serious problems and occur with heavy consumption of alcohol. Many other factors associated with alcohol use, such as maternal smoking, drug use, or poor nutrition, affect the fetus. Thus, the effects of alcohol use are difficult to study separately. The existing studies on humans, however, together with the historical recognition of FAS-like symptoms and its occurrence in controlled animal studies are compelling evidence against the use of alcohol during pregnancy. The timing of alcohol use during the developmental process may be critical in determining the type and extent of the effects on the fetus. Particularly important may be the first trimester (first three months), a time when very rapid fetal development (differentiation) is occurring, before many women know for certain that they are pregnant (NIAAA, 1981). Two drinks or more per day or the consumption of five drinks or more at a single occasion are considered likely to result in some impairment of the fetus. Lesser amounts of alcohol may also produce negative effects. FAS is estimated to occur in 26–29 of every 1,000 births. Estimates of adverse alcohol-related effects, however, vary widely from 73 to 690 of every 1,000 births (NIAAA, 1984). About 5% of all congenital abnormalities may be attributable to fetal alcohol exposure (65–70% of developmental defects are of unknown origin) (Sokol, 1981). Alcohol is believed to be "the most frequent known teratogenic cause of mental retardation in the Western World" (Clarren & Smith, 1978). Thus, acting on the side of caution, the National Institute on Alcohol Abuse and Alcoholism recommends that pregnant women discontinue alcohol use altogether during pregnancy.

The problems presented so far are the result of alcohol abuse and excessive use. The moderate or light use of alcohol has also been examined. In terms of the chronic disease conditions with which this chapter has been concerned, heart disease appears to occur less frequently in moderate users (not over two drinks per day) than in heavy users or even abstainers (Fraser, 1986). This finding and a possible mechanism by which alcohol may function are still being studied. Paradoxically, the same "moderate" use of alcohol has already been noted to be detrimental to the fetus and has been shown to be associated with hypertension, a prominent risk factor for heart disease, with cancer of the colon, rectum, and lung, and with changes in the liver associated with early stages of cirrhosis (Klatsky, Friedman & Siegelaub, 1981; Kono et al., 1983; NIAAA, 1981; Pollack, Nomura, Keilbrun, Stemmermann, & Green, 1984).

Trends in Alcohol Use

Alcohol consumption declined in the United States to a low in 1920 (the first year of prohibition) and has since increased substantially to a current per capita consumption of 2.7 gallons of ethanol per year.[3] This figure is somewhat deceiving, since one third of the adult U.S. population do not drink. The average consumption of persons who do drink is 1.5 ounces of pure ethanol or about three drinks per day. The beverage of choice in the United States by per capita consumption is beer, followed by distilled spirits and wines (Distilled Spirits Councils of the United States [DISCUS], 1978a, 1978b). Among drinkers, 11% consume about half of the alcohol beverages sold. In 1980, Alcoholics Anonymous (AA) had a membership

---

3. This amount is pure ethanol and represents nearly 33 gallons of alcoholic beverages.

of 476,000 persons in the United States and Canada, a 280% increase from 1968 membership estimates; the proportion of women and young persons (under 30 years of age) also has increased. In 1980, 1,058,000 persons were admitted to state or federally funded alcohol treatment programs, but the combined estimates from AA and government treatment facilities probably represent only 15% of the total number of persons needing treatment. About 10 million persons in the United States are alcoholics by conservative estimates. For every one of these persons, another four to five persons, family members, friends, and coworkers are "para-alcoholics," persons negatively affected by alcoholic drinking. It is estimated that one out of every ten Americans is a problem drinker and that nearly one out of every five adolescents (14–17 years of age) may be problem drinkers (National Council on Alcoholism [NCA], 1984). The percentage of males who are drinkers is larger than the percentage of females in every age group. Native Americans are at very great risk of becoming alcohol abusers, as are persons of Irish descent. Other ethnic groups (Jewish, Chinese, Italians) do not show this strong tendency toward alcoholism in spite of routine use of alcohol in these populations. Data on other ethnic groups are somewhat limited, but some studies indicate that alcohol-related problems may be greater among Hispanics than among the general population. Data on black drinking behavior need further development, as they are conflicting. Although a higher rate of alcohol-related deaths occur among blacks, a larger proportion of blacks classify themselves as abstainers than do Hispanics or whites (Milt, 1974; NIAAA, 1981).

The extent of the alcohol problem among the elderly may be substantial but is not well known because the consequences of their drinking are not usually socially disruptive. Particularly at risk among the elderly may be recently widowed or retired men. The 1970s saw increased attention to the problem of drinking among women. Historically, it has been less acceptable for women to use or abuse alcohol. Thus, it should not be surprising that alcohol abuse and dependence among women is often concealed. The consequences to the health of women who drink are the same as would occur to men who drink, however. Women who drink appear to develop problems at an earlier age, after a shorter period of alcohol use than men, and after a smaller quantity of alcohol is ingested (NIAAA, 1981).

Alcohol abuse among adolescents recently has received more thorough attention. Adolescents who drink often cite peer pressure as a factor in their drinking behavior but most often list home as their usual drinking place. Heavy alcohol use and abuse are associated with those adolescents who are introduced to alcohol and consume it outside their homes. Parental attitude and drinking behavior correlate strongly with adolescent alcohol abuse as does religious affiliation. Heavy alcohol use apparently precedes the development of problem behaviors, including precocious sexual behavior, poor school performance, interpersonal problems in school and the family, and dropping out of school (NIAAA, 1981).

A history of parental alcohol abuse is reported in a large number of alcoholics. This finding has led to many studies designed to separate the possible genetic and environmental determinants of alcoholism. Studies of the occurrence of alcoholism in families do not necessarily indicate a genetic causality for alcoholism, since families share both common genes and a common environment. Well-designed studies of children adopted from alcoholic and nonalcoholic biological parents, identical and fraternal twins, and ethnic groups with different tolerance levels for alcohol have indicated that a genetic predisposition to alcoholism may account for 35–40% of alcoholism and alcohol abuse. Selective breeding of animals has clearly shown a genetic influence in alcohol tolerance and the extent of dependence (NIAAA, 1984). Subtypes of alcoholism have also been identified that suggest that the interaction of genetic and environment may be variable. Nevertheless, the sociocultural influences are regarded as being critical in the developmental process of genetically predisposed individuals.

Prevention and Intervention against Alcohol Abuse

Since alcoholism may be a function of multiple patterns of dysfunctional alcohol use and results in a variety of disabilities, the diagnostic definition of alcoholism has not always been clear and distinct. The general definition of alcoholism suggested by the World Health Organization (WHO) is:

> a dependence on alcohol, characterized by an overwhelming need to ingest large amounts of alcohol . . . marked by loss or impairment of control over drinking. There is a drive to obtain the gratification of intoxication . . . by means of self-alcoholization. (Milt, 1974, p. 7)

Diagnostic criteria for alcohol abuse have been suggested recently by the American Psychiatric Association (1980) and are as follows:

1. Pattern of pathological alcohol use: need for daily use of alcohol for adequate functioning, inability to cut down or stop drinking, repeated efforts to control or reduce excess drinking by "going on the wagon" (periods of temporary abstinence) or restricting drinking to certain times of the day, binges (remaining intoxicated throughout the day for a least 2 days), occasional consumption of a fifth of spirits (or its equivalent in wine or beer), amnesic periods for events occurring while intoxicated (blackouts), continuation of drinking despite a serious physical disorder that the individual knows is exacerbated by alcohol use, drinking of non-beverage alcohol.
2. Impairment in social or occupational functioning due to alcohol use: violence while intoxicated, absence from work, loss of job, legal difficulties (e.g., arrest for intoxicated behavior, traffic accidents while intoxicated), arguments or difficulties with family or friends because of excessive alcohol use.

Alcohol dependence is further differentiated from alcohol abuse by the presence of either evidence for increased tolerance (larger amounts needed for desired effect) or development of withdrawal symptoms (i.e., morning "shakes" and malaise after drinking). The operational criteria of problem drinking suggested by the National Institute on Alcohol Abuse and Alcoholism (1982) are:

- changes in personality or behavior after drinking,
- is drunk often,
- is arrested as a result of drinking,
- has family or job problems because of drinking,
- takes alcohol before going to work,
- drives a car while drunk,
- is injured while intoxicated,
- is advised to stop or reduce drinking by a physician,
- has financial problems because of drinking.

Alcoholism prevention is a growing concern but a consensus on a model for an approach to the problem is yet to be achieved. Several models have been proposed. One, the "public health" model, views the alcohol problem in a manner similar to one which has been used quite effectively in communicable disease problems. It involves three concepts: the host, the agent, and the environment. The host is the individual involved in the drinking problem, the agent is alcohol, and the environment, social or psychological, is the context in which the problem occurs. This model is not universally accepted, since alcoholism is regarded by some as having a more social than medical basis.

Another model sees the control of distribution of consumption as an effective prevention approach. The consumption of alcohol is an integral element in the development of both problem drinking and alcoholism. If alcohol consumption is limited or eliminated, alcoholism and problem drinking cannot occur. There is good evidence that a direct relationship exists between per capita consumption and the prevalence of heavy alcohol use. Thus, it would seem to follow that limitation of consumption would limit the number of heavy users and therefore the problems, either personal or societal, produced by heavy use. Prohibition in the 1920s was an experiment with this approach. While such a broad action is not likely to occur again in American society, restrictions on a smaller scale are being considered. In particular, the drinking age is being raised from 18 to 21 in many states that had lowered it in the early 1970s. Other restrictions have been tried in other countries with varying degrees of success. For instance, changing the closing hours for retail outlets of alcohol merely changes the peak time during which accidents and other problems occur. An experiment tried in Finland, where all outlets were closed one day a week, did result in fewer drunken arrests and other alcohol-related problems, without an increase in illicit alcohol use (Saila, 1978). Raising prices through taxation has also been studied, and this approach does appear to reduce both overall consumption and consumption among heavy drinkers (Smart, 1982). This strategy is being widely used in European countries.

The sociocultural model approaches alcoholism prevention in the context of the relationship between alcohol problems and normal use of alcohol in society. This may be important, since the way alcohol is viewed by a society may influence its use and the potential for abuse. For example, although 90% of Jewish persons use alcohol, very low levels of alcoholism have been noted in this ethnic group. In the Jewish culture, alcohol is used in religious and cultural ceremonies. Alcohol is also used in high proportions by Catholics and in the Catholic worship service, but the proportion of alcohol problems among Catholics and some typically Catholic ethnic groups (i.e., Irish Catholics)) is very high. The differences in the cultural view of alcohol between these groups would be an interesting and important link in the understanding of the alcoholism problem (NIAAA, 1981, 1982).

Putting all theoretical models aside, health professionals and concerned citizens must act to find pragmatic solutions to the problem of alcohol abuse in lieu of a definitive model. Prevention is of primary importance. Research on a broad range of approaches is needed. Whatever approaches are developed, of primary concern must be high-risk groups: pregnant women, children of alcoholics, native Americans, young blacks, Hispanics, and the elderly.

Considering the large number of persons in the United States who are alcoholics or problem drinkers, intervention must be a high priority. Current research is being directed toward a biochemical marker or dependable psychosocial indicators that can be used in the screening and early detection of alcohol-related problems. A drawback to early detection and intervention is a tendency on the part of drinkers to deny and conceal the problem, even from themselves, and a tendency for family, friends, and coworkers to protect the drinker from the truth. In addition, physicians who treat drinkers for gastrointestinal problems, hypertension, and other medical conditions related to alcohol abuse may not recognize the connection to drinking in their patients or may not be comfortable prescribing therapy for alcohol abuse. Intervention programs that have been tested have clearly demonstrated their effectiveness through reductions in job absenteeism, hospitalizations, and mortality (Kristenson, 1982). And the feasibility of such programs in large populations has also been demonstrated (Babor, Treffardier, Weill, Fegueur, & Ferrant, 1983). One of the most important opportunities for intervention is the workplace. Compassionate supervisors can be helpful motivaters to assist an employee slipping into alcoholism. An estimated 10% of the industrial work force are alcoholics. Alcoholic workers have two to four times the accident and absenteeism rate, and receive three times more sickness, accident, and disability payments than other employees. The cost per employee to industry is 25% of the gross salary. Overall, this represents an annual loss of $25 billion (1977 estimates). Where intervention programs have been established, companies not only have recovered valuable employees but have saved money as well. In 1980 about 4,400 such occupational programs existed, a small number compared to the number of businesses in America. But the phenomenal growth of these programs is encouraging (NCA, 1984; NIAAA, 1981, 1984).

Alcohol and Public Policy

The role of the federal government and its agencies in the alcohol industry were changed by the Twenty-first Amendment repealing prohibition. Broader powers to regulate alcohol production, distribution, marketing, and taxation were given to the states. But the federal government through the U.S. Bureau of Alcohol, Tobacco, and Firearms still has substantial influence. Many agencies of the federal government have increased their collaboration on alcohol prevention, intervention, and research activities. The Department of Defense has initiated a comprehensive health promotion effort, which includes alcoholism prevention and intervention within the military. A Presidential Commission on Drunk Driving was established in 1982 to examine appropriate strategies to address this problem. Included in their recommendations were raising the drinking age and establishing a uniform legal intoxication level in all states. The National Institute on Alcohol Abuse and Alcoholism (1984) has developed objectives for the United States for 1990 for reduction of alcohol-related problems. Summarized, they are:

- a reduction in alcohol-related fatalities from cirrhosis and automobile and other accidents,
- reduction in FAS occurrence,
- maintenance of per capita alcohol consumption at current levels,
- reduction of adolescent alcohol abusers to less than 17% and expansion of adolescent abstainers to 46%,
- reduction of adult alcohol abusers to 8%,
- expansion of industrial prevention and referral programs in major industries to 70%.

Educational objectives include increasing adult awareness of additional alcohol-related disease risk to 75% and increasing adolescent (specifically high school seniors') awareness of greater risk associated with alcohol intoxication to 80%.

Any prevention activity is essentially political in the sense that it cannot succeed without grass-roots support. The potential impact of prevention is substantial through the state alcohol beverage control boards and the state legislatures. The movement called MADD (Mothers Against Drunk Driving) is an example of a current grass-roots effort attempting to effect changes in alcohol-related legislation. Many states have become quite aggressive in their efforts to develop solutions to the drinking/driving problem. The drinking age has been raised to 21 in some states, and tougher penalties for convicted offenders have been enacted. Public education campaigns via all forms of media have been aimed at high-risk audiences (i.e., women and adolescents). It remains for an intelligent citizenry to become personally involved and respond to proposed changes to create the desired environment in which preventive measures can be effective.

Summary

Alcohol is involved as a direct causal agent in many deaths and as an aggravating factor in others. Controversial associations with heart disease and recent associations with cancer are still being studied. Like smoking, alcohol-related deaths are totally preventable. Like smoking, the costs, direct and indirect, are enormous, about $50 billion per year (1977 estimates). Recent research developments and mounting public support have created a need for more research and new strategies in education (prevention), legislation, intervention, and treatment.

DIET AND CHRONIC DISEASE

That diet can cause disease, even cancer, in animals has been a known and accepted scientific phenomenon for some time. That diet may be related to disease in humans is an idea relatively recently researched and only beginning to be accepted in scientific circles. Although it is true that "man does not live by bread alone," it is also certain that, unlike tobacco and alcohol, one cannot live without food. So research questions about diet are generally complex ones of how much, what kind, and in what proportion various nutrients or foods should be represented in the diet.

The investigation of diet-related chronic disease began in earnest after World War II with studies of the relationship of diet, serum lipid levels, and CHD. CHD is characterized by lesions, or atheromas, in the lining of the coronary arteries of the heart and in the aorta. These lesions, described as early as 1727, are "mushy" in appearance and have a high content of cholesterol, hence the Greek word *athere* meaning "gruel." Since World War II, evidence based on international comparisons of food consumption patterns and death rates, has accumulated consistently, showing an association of increased amounts of cholesterol, total calories, total fat, animal fat, saturated fat, total protein, animal protein, and sugar and decreased amounts of vegetable protein, vegetable fat, and total carbohydrate in the diet with CHD mortality rates. Evidence has also been gathered from studies of the change in mortality experienced by immigrants to the United States. Several studies have reported increased dietary fat, serum cholesterol, and CHD in ethnic groups moving from less affluent areas of the globe to the United States. The emigrants were also shown to be more obese and less physically active than nonemigrants in the country of origin. A decline in CHD mortality has been noted when diets are restricted as they were in Europe during World War II. Studies of selected populations who restrict diet by choice, such as vegetarians, have shown lower dietary cholesterol and fat, lower serum lipid levels, and lower CHD mortality rates (Stamler, 1979).

Research on heart disease does not pinpoint a single entity as the sole cause. Factors other than serum cholesterol and diet have been suggested as important contributing factors to the disease process. Cigarette smoking plays a major role as an aggravating factor during the developmental process of atherosclerosis. It also elevates blood pressure and aggravates angina pectoris by lowering the oxygen-carrying ability of the blood. Hypertension, or high blood pressure, is another factor that independently contributes to risk. Excessive salt consumption, smoking, and obesity are the major contributing factors to hypertension. Obesity elevates risk of CHD, but since obesity is closely related to both hypertension and high cholesterol blood levels, it is not clear that it is an independent risk factor. Sedentary life-styles are shown to elevate risk of CHD mortality. An active life-style may reduce risk via the moderating effect of exercise on both hypertension and obesity. The effect of "moderate" consumption of alcohol has been mentioned. The role of coffee in CHD risk has been studied but appears to be small. Other factors that have been studied are psychosocial factors, diabetes, family history of heart disease, and use of oral contraceptives. Adult diabetes is obesity-related and therefore also diet-related. A family history of heart disease is associated with heart disease. Since families share both genes and life-style, efforts to separate the role of each in heart disease have been made. Migrant studies indicate that a change in diet rather than genetics is the more likely origin for family disease patterns (Kritchevsky, 1979). Psychological research is presented elsewhere in this chapter. The role of oral contraceptives has already been discussed in connection with smoking.

Because of its presence in the atheroma (fatty plaque in arterial lining) and its relationship to heart disease, cholesterol has received considerable research attention and deserves separate attention. Cholesterol is synthesized in all cells for use in hormones, cell membranes, and other essential functions. Cholesterol, when synthesized in the liver, is formed into bile, enters the digestive system in the duodenum, and is readily reabsorbed. Because of this synthesis and reabsorption, shortage of cholesterol due to its absence in the diet is not likely. Cholesterol is consumed in the diet from products of animal origin (red meats, seafood, eggs, and milk products). The average consumption in the diet is between 400 and 700 mg per day (Grundy, 1979).

Cholesterol, a lipid, is not soluble in the aqueous plasma of the blood. For cholesterol to be solubilized, it must be joined to lipoproteins, which attach to cholesterol and other lipids for transport through the bloodstream. Three major lipoproteins groups have been identified: VLDL (very low density lipoproteins), LDL (low density lipoproteins), and HDL (high density lipoproteins). Of these, the HDL fraction, if high in proportion to the others, is believed to be protective against heart disease (Grundy, 1979). Exercise and moderate amounts of alcohol have been shown to raise HDL levels. High VLDL, but principally LDL, levels have been associated with high serum cholesterol, atherosclerosis, and CHD mortality. Removing or decreasing cholesterol in the diet and replacing saturated fat (animal fat) with unsaturated fat (vegetable fat) have also been shown to lower serum cholesterol. Animal protein and sugars (particularly the refined table type) can also raise serum lipids. Diets relatively high in starches and fiber are believed to reduce serum cholesterol, but whether these dietary constituents act independently or whether their presence in the diet simply reflects an absence of foods high in fat and cholesterol is uncertain. Water hardness has been suggested to be protective. Sodium, consumed principally in salt, has been associated with high blood pressure and high serum cholesterol. Some investigators have suggested mechanisms by which some minerals, such as fluoride and selenium, may be protective, but conclusions are not possible with existing data. Of the vitamins only niacin in very large doses has demonstrated efficacy in reducing serum cholesterol. Vitamin C and E and lecithin have also been suggested as beneficial in lowering blood lipids, but little evidence for this exists (Grundy, 1979; Kritchevsky, 1979; Merz, 1979; Zilversmit, 1979).

Diet has been accepted as a causal factor of cancer in animal studies. Both excess calories and fat have been demonstrated to produce cancer in mice (National Research Council [NRC], 1982). That diet may be an etiological factor in human cancers has only recently received scientific investigation. The two organ systems which currently are suggested as being diet-sensitive are the gastrointestinal tract (esophagus, stomach, colon, rectum, liver, pancreas tumors), and the sex-hormone-responsive organs (breast, prostate, endometrium, ovary tumors). Diet may also be involved in the development of respiratory and bladder cancers. These cancers represent a large proportion of cancers in humans. Stomach, colon, breast, and bladder account for about 43% of cancers in women. Adding prostate to this list accounts for about 39% of cancers in men. International comparisons of rates of death and incidence have shown that these cancers occur more prominently in affluent populations.

More specifically, comparisons of per capita consumption patterns for various nutrients have suggested that high dietary fat (specifically of animal origin) and diets low in fiber and vitamin A are related to the occurrence of cancer. Studies of migrant populations from low-cancer-incidence countries who come to the United States have shown that an increase in cancer follows. Studies of populations with very different dietary habits such as Seventh-day Adventists and Mormons have also shown lower cancer rates than the general U.S. population. Seventh-day Adventists abstain from alcohol, tobacco, and caffeine-containing beverages. About 50% of Seventh-day Adventists also follow a lacto-ovo-vegetarian life-style. Deaths due to heart disease, colo-rectal, and smoking-related cancers are lower than expected for the general U.S. population. Mormons also do not use alcohol, tobacco, coffee, or tea. Vegetarianism is not practiced by this group, but recommendations for a well-balanced diet including grains, fruits, vegetables, and a moderate use of meat are given to church members. The usual smoking-related sites, colon, breast, and ovarian cancers are lower among Mormon females than among non-Mormon females. Smoking-related cancers and stomach cancer (but not colon cancer) are lower among Mormon males than among non-Mormon males. The lower incidence of these cancers in Utah (a largely Mormon population) are also found in Idaho and Wyoming, adjacent non-Mormon states (NRC, 1982).

The possible dietary factors related to development of specific cancer sites have been summarized in Table 2-3. Each of the dietary relationships in Table 2-3 might be explored in some detail. Because of their prominence in society, only breast and colo-rectal cancer will be mentioned here. Breast cancer is the second most common cause of death due to cancer among American women (exceeded by lung cancer in 1985). Studies comparing the consumption patterns in different cultures with incidence in those cultures point to diet as a major difference between them (NRC, 1982). Studies of migrants have shown an increase in incidence of breast cancer with changes to Westernized dietary patterns (Dunn, 1977). Retrospective studies have shown a fairly consistent association with total fat and fatty foods, but a weaker one with saturated fat. Animal studies have also shown dietary fat-related association with breast cancer (NRC, 1982). Polyunsaturated fats, with a low total fat intake, were shown in one study to promote tumors in animals (Carroll & Khor, 1971). Polyunsaturated fats (vegetable fats) are the principal source of fats in vegetarian diets. However, vegetable fats are not found to be associated with human breast cancer when studies of vegetarian and nonvegetarian populations are made. A different mechanism of action may be operable for the carcinogenic action of polyunsaturated fats in animal populations, since the findings in animals do not agree with the finding of lower levels of dietary fat (but a high proportion of polyunsaturated fat) and lower rates of cancer in human vegetarians (Calkins, Whittaker, Nair, Rider, & Turjman, 1984). Obesity and an early age for menarche are both diet-related and closely associated with breast cancer (NRC, 1982).

Studies of the cultural dietary patterns of migrants to the United States from areas of low colo-rectal cancer incidence have shown associations of colo-rectal cancer with diet. Colo-rectal cancer is associated with higher socioeconomic status and with changes in the diet as shown in Japan since World War II. Total fat, saturated fat, and cholesterol have been correlated in various studies. A diet lacking in fiber or low in particular foods (especially vegetables called crucifers—broccoli, kale, brussels sprouts, and the like) have also been suggested as playing a role in colo-rectal cancer. Not all investigators have found this association, however. Some studies have found an association between colo-rectal cancer and alcohol consumption, principally beer, but again not all studies have found this association. Some investigators regard the findings on fat and fiber as supportive of each other, since foods high in fat are generally low in fiber and *vice versa* (NRC, 1982).

In the cancer patients a sudden drop in serum cholesterol has been found to coincide with exacerbation of cancer. Studies have been conducted which have examined the possibility that very low serum cholesterol levels may be a risk factor for cancer (or possibly a symptom of subclinical disease). In 1981 a workshop composed of a large number of scientists from many countries reviewed the available data. Some studies did show a possible association of very low serum cholesterol with colon cancer. But the studies were inconsistent, and the association was very weak. The finding is not supported by studies of vegetarians, who have been found to have low cholesterol levels and both low heart disease and colon cancer rates. Thus, the finding of an association of low serum cholesterol with increased risk of cancer was not regarded as sufficiently important to alter any public health recommendations with respect to serum cholesterol (Feinleib, 1982).

Foods in the diet convey not only nutrients but other substances as well, which may be important in cancer development. For simplicity, these substances will be divided into four groups: naturally occurring carcinogens, mutagens, additives and contaminants, and inhibitors of carcinogens. The majority of naturally occurring carcinogens are mycotoxins, the by-products of the metabolism of molds in foods. Of these, aflatoxins are associated with liver cancer and may be an important exposure in cancer development in Africa and Asia. No evidence suggests that mycotoxins are a significant exposure in the United States. Mutagens can occur in meat and fish when they are cooked at high temperatures, smoked, or charcoal broiled. The importance of mutagens in human cancer is not clear. Additives and contaminants include such compounds as nonnutritive sweeteners, preservatives, hormones used in animal production, pesticide residues, and other environmental toxins. Of the nonnutritive sweeteners, saccharin and cyclomates are associated

Table 2-3. The Relationship of Diet to Specific Cancer Sites

Site	Dietary factor(s)	
Esophagus	Risk factors:	Alcohol
		Pickles
		Moldy foods
		Trace minerals
		Very hot beverages
	Protective:	Fresh fruits and vegetables
Stomach	Risk factors:	Smoked foods
		Salt-canned foods
		Nitrate or nitrite preserved foods
	Protective:	Milk
		Green and yellow vegetables
		Vitamin C containing foods
Colon and rectum	Risk factors:	Total fat
		Saturated fat (?)[a]
		Alcohol (?)
	Protective:	Fiber
		Cruciferous vegetables
Liver	Risk factors:	Aflatoxins in foods
		Chronic hepatitis B infectives
		Alcohol (?)
Pancreas	Risk factors:	Alcohol (?)
		Coffee (?)
		Meat (?)
Gallbladder	Risk factors:	Diets leading to obesity
		High fat (?)
		Excess calories (?)
Lungs	Risk factors:	Diets low in Vitamin A foods
		Alcohol
Bladder	Risk factors:	Coffee
		Low Vitamin A diet
		Saccharin (?)
Kidney	Risk factor:	Total cadmium exposure
		(diet, smoking, occupation)
Breast	Risk factor:	High-fat diet
Endometrium	Risk factor:	No direct relationship—association due mainly to close association with breast cancer
Ovary	Risk factor:	High-fat diet (indirect)
Prostate	Risk factors:	High-fat diet
		High-protein foods
	Protective:	Vitamin A diet

Note. Adapted from National Research Council (1982).

[a]A question indicates that the association is based on a limited number of studies, is not consistently found, or is not strong.

with cancer in animals but not in humans. Aspartame, another recently FDA-approved nonnutritive sweetener, does not show an association with cancer in animals, and no human studies of its cancer associations exist. Vinyl chloride (used as polyvinyl chloride in food packaging) is important as an occupation-association carcinogen. Butylated hydroxytoluene (BHT) shows conflicting evidence as both a tumor promoter and inhibitor. Butylated hydroxyanisole (BHA) shows no carcinogencity. Diethylstilbestrol (DES) was used as a growth promoter in animals until 1979. There is sufficient evidence to associate DES with vaginal and cervical cancer in female offspring of women using this drug therapeutically. Its epidemiological importance in the food chain is not clear. Of the pesticides, the organochlorides, but not organophosphates or -carbonates, show carcinogencity in animals. The importance of the organochlorides is that they are slowly metabolized and have a tendency to accumulate in body tissues. Polychlorinated biphenyls (PCBs), polybrominated biphenyls (PBBs), and polycyclic aromatic hydrocarbons (PAHs) are all established carcinogens, but epidemiological evidence for exposures in humans are lacking. Inhibitors of carcinogenesis also occur in foods, such as indoles and aromatic isothiocyanates (found primarily in cruciferous vegetables), flavones (found in both fruits and vegetables), protease inhibitors (found in seeds, soybeans, and lima beans), and beta-sitosterol (found in vegetables and vegetable oils) (NRC, 1982). The influence these substances may have as inhibitors of carcinogenic mechanisms is not yet clearly understood.

Several possible hypotheses by which diet may act in the development of cancer have been suggested (Doll & Peto, 1981). First, carcinogens might be ingested with foods. The origins of the carcinogens might be naturally occurring, produced during cooking, or produced by microorganisms during storage. Second, carcinogens might be formed in the body by substrates in the food, by altering the flora of the gut, or by altering the cholesterol and bile acid metabolism of the body. Third, different diets might expose the gut to fecal contents for different amounts of time, change the transport of carcinogens to target organs, stimulate or inhibit relevant enzymes which would be effective on target organs, or inhibit the development of intermediate "species" essential in the conversion of a normal cell to a cancer cell. Fourth, cancer development might represent a chronic dietary deficiency such as vitamin A. Finally, cancer may be the result of overnutrition. Research exists supporting each of these hypotheses, and one or more may be functional as a mechanism for one cancer or another.

With respect to colon and breast cancer, diet could function as a causal agent (initiator) in cancer development or as a promoter or inhibitor in the presence of other causal agents. The latter, seems theoretically more likely than the former in view of the diversity of dietary constituents. As a promoter, diet could function by creating a condition of susceptibility for an initiator as well as maintaining favorable growth conditions for a tumor. As an inhibitor, diet could function by preventing the contact of an initiator with body cells, by fostering natural body defense mechanisms against an initiator, and by blocking enzymatic or biochemical pathways necessary for normal cells to become transformed into tumor cells. In the case of colon cancer, fiber may act as an inhibitor by diluting the contents of the bowel and decreasing the amount of time the contents spend in transit within the bowel, thereby limiting contact of potential carcinogens with the cells in the wall of the bowel. Fat may promote the production of secondary bile acids (known to be carcinogenic and in greater concentration in the stool of nonvegetarians than vegetarians) by microorganisms in the gut (Nair, 1984).

Trends in Diet

Along with changing transportation and communication methods, in this century the American population has experienced great changes in the food supply. The livestock, poultry, seafood, dairy and grain products, and produce are produced in plentiful supplies. However, the consumer is farther removed from the source. Food no longer comes primarily from the garden behind the house, from a small roadside stand, or even from the corner market. The main sources are large retail chains, which have nearly eclipsed the corner market. Rapid interstate transportation and more effective food preservation and processing techniques have created a constant, relatively inexpensive, and varied food supply. The frozen, canned, boxed, or otherwise prepared and processed food products are increasingly staple items of the American larder. In fact 10,000 different processed items are currently available where only 1,000 such items were available at the end of World War II (Molitor, 1980).

Rigorous surveys of the individual American diet as are currently conducted are not available for earlier periods, making nutrient intake comparison impossible. Per capita consumption of nutrients based on total available food for consumption has been examined and appears to have remained fairly stable. When the consumption of food items is compared (Table 2-4), it is clear that there has been a shift away from grain products (which have generally declined to half of the level of earlier decades) and toward more calorie-concentrated or calorie-dense source (meat products, sugar, fats, and oils) (Friend, Page, & Marston, 1979). Although Table 2-4 indicates that the consumption of fruits and vegetables has recently increased slightly, the consumption of fresh fruits and vegetables has actually declined.[4] The change in the consumption of fresh potatoes is particularly striking. A decline in the consumption of cruciferous vegetables (broccoli, cabbage, kale, etc.) has also been noted (not shown). In 1961 the American Heart Association published its recommendations with respect to dietary fat and cholesterol and their relation to heart disease and stroke. Even before this, however, declines in the per capita consumption of eggs, lard, butter, whole milk, and cream had been noted; the consumption of cheese and ice cream is up, however. The use of vegetable fats

---

4. The definition of fresh is generally taken to mean at most washed and chilled, uncanned, unfrozen, and additives and preservatives lacking.

Table 2-4. Trends in Per Capita Consumption of Foods in Pounds per Year

Food group	Year			% Change 1912 to 1975–76
	1912	1948	1975–76	
Fats and oils	41	46	59	up 44%
Butter	18	11	4	down 78%
Sugar and sweets	89	110	119	up 34%
Red meat	141	141	165	up 17%
Poultry	18	22	53	up 194%
Fish and shellfish	13	13	15	up 15%
Dairy products	177	236	222	up 25%
Eggs	37	47	35	down 5%
				(down 26% from 1948)
Dry beans, peas, nuts, and legumes	16	17	18	up 13%
Flour and cereal products	291	171	140	down 52%
Fruits	176	208	188	up 7%
Vegetables	203	232	213	up 5%
Potatoes	205	123	80	down 61%

Note. Adapted from Friend, Page, and Martson (1979).

in spreads and oils has gone up about threefold. Beef consumption increased over the same period (Friend et al., 1979).

Between 1940 and 1977 the consumption of food color additives increased tenfold (per capita). Soft drink consumption also increased 50% between 1960 and 1976 (Brewster & Jacobson, 1978). Many food products now available were unknown in earlier decades (such as imitation whipping cream, ice creams, cheeses and milks, most based on soy protein and fats). The production techniques used for processed foods may also be a source of mutagenic substances, particularly with foods that are cooked at high temperatures or cooked in superheated fats. The consumption of supplemental vitamins and minerals (usually in tablet or capsule form) has skyrocketed. In addition, the population has had increased exposure to pesticide residues and drugs used in the production of plant and animal foods.

Dietary Prevention and Intervention

Within the confines of income, the diet of Americans is an almost entirely self-selected exposure. Changes in diet can be effected only through the education of the public on nutrition issues. Using the guidelines set forward by the American Heart Association, prevention and intervention studies have been designed to reduce serum cholesterol through voluntary compliance with recommendations on dietary intake. Serum cholesterol levels have been reduced 7–16% by dietary intervention regimens. Several drugs also have been effective in reducing serum cholesterol levels 5–10% (Ahrens, 1976). But these studies have not measured any changes in mortality that might have resulted from the lower cholesterol levels.

A large-scale long-term prevention/intervention study of serum cholesterol (and other risk factors) with risk reduction has recently been completed. The Multiple

Risk Factor Intervention Trial (MRFIT) was initiated in 1972 by the National Heart, Lung, and Blood Institute. The objectives of the study were to reduce serum cholesterol, blood pressure, and smoking using special intervention techniques in a selected group of individuals deemed at high risk for CHD. The occurrence of heart disease was measured in this group and a similar high risk group of "controls," who were not given any special intervention. The results of the intervention group showed that serum cholesterol declined in response to the dietary changes, and the magnitude of change was greater for those who also lost weight and did not smoke or have high blood pressure. Lowering blood pressure and cessation of smoking were also successful in a large proportion of subjects. However, the nonintervention group also showed changes in serum cholesterol, smoking, and blood pressure (perhaps in response to public education on these issues). The decline in morbidity and mortality for both the intervention and nonintervention group was similar. As a result, the change in disease occurrence cannot be definitively credited to changes in risk factors. One of the criticisms of this study is that the target reduction levels for the intervention group were too modest. However, another carefully designed and implemented intervention study, also recently completed, did show clearly that lowering serum cholesterol resulted in a reduction of heart disease occurrence (Benfari & Sherwin, 1981; Lipids Research Clinics Program [LRCP], 1984a, 1984b).

The average serum cholesterol level of Americans has declined for both sexes at every age level since the early 1960s. The proportion of the population with high serum cholesterol has declined 12–22% (Abraham, Johnson, & Carroll, 1977). These changes combined with changes in smoking and exercise habits, and improved treatment for high blood pressure may account, to some extent, for the decline in heart disease, which began in the late 1960s. The amount of the decline attributable to these changes or a separation of the effect of each factor changed is not available with current statistics.

These results are encouraging because they indicate that changes in risk factors in adults can be made and are effective in reducing risk. And these results are also an indication that dietary regimes for infants and children should be reevaluated, such as those recommended by pediatricians and those used in school lunch programs. Dietary patterns established in infancy and childhood could potentially reduce or eliminate the development of a risk factor such as high serum cholesterol. Establishing early in life a preventive pattern of food consumption for heart disease should be a priority concern of parents, educators, and public health professionals.

The results of intervention studies on heart disease risk factors also indicate that since dietary changes are possible in large populations, similar prevention/intervention studies of dietary risk factor reduction for cancer are warranted. Much study, however, of dietary behavioral patterns is also necessary, since an improved knowledge of the determinants of dietary behavior is essential in the development of strategies for dietary changes. Undoubtedly, one of the key elements in the determinants of dietary behavior is social pressure: ethnic custom, family customs, and advertising. Studies of the development of ethnic or regional food patterns may also be useful in the educational process.

Diet and Public Policy

Sixteen expert committees have reviewed the research and issues involved in the question of diet and CHD death. The following recommendations have been suggested (Blackburn, 1979):

- Decrease consumption of fatty red meats.
- Increase consumption of lean meats.
- Increase consumption of fish and poultry.
- Decrease consumption of commercially baked foods high in saturated fats.
- Partially replace decreased fat intake with foods high in polyunsaturated fats, including vegetable oils.
- Use only low-fat or nonfat milk and milk products, except for infants.
- Decrease butter consumption.
- Decrease egg yolk consumption to three per week.

These were suggested in response to the dietary goals set forward to reduce CHD mortality as follows:

- Reduce fat consumption to 30% of total calories.
- Reduce saturated fat consumption to 10% of total calories.
- Balance mono- and polyunsaturated fat intake to 10% of total calories each.
- Reduce cholesterol intake to about 300 mg daily.
- Increase complex carbohydrate consumption to 48% of total calories.
- Reduce sugar consumption to 10% of total calories.
- Reduce salt consumption to about 5 g daily.

After a similar review process of the research on cancer and diet, the National Research Council of the National Academy of Sciences issued its recommendations for a diet protective against cancer in 1982. The guidelines used as the basis for these recommendations are summarized as follows:

- Reduce fat intake to 30% or less of total calories in the diet.
- Increase the consumption of fresh fruits and vegetables (especially citrus fruits and carotene-containing and cruciferous vegetables), and whole-grain cereal products in the daily diet.
- Minimize the consumption of salt-cured, pickled, and smoked foods.
- Minimize contamination of foods with carcinogens whether occurring naturally or introduced inadvertently during production, processing, and storage.
- Identify mutagens in foods and remove or reduce their concentration without jeopardizing the nutritive value of foods or introducing other hazardous substances into the diet.
- Reduce consumption of alcoholic beverages to a moderate level.

The similarity of the two sets of guidelines is noteworthy. Some investigators believe that recommendations for a cancer prevention diet are premature (Graham, 1983a,

1983b; Willett & MacMahon, 1984a, 1984b). As with the tobacco issue, counter-interests, livestock ranchers, and egg and dairy farmers are involved, and the U.S. government again must carefully balance its price support policies with public health issues. Increasing pressure is being brought to bear on the food industry to indicate the nutrient contents as well as the ingredients of food items. Such labeling would allow interested and aware consumers to monitor their intake of key nutrients such as sodium, cholesterol, and fat. Efforts are also being made to breed and feed animals for lower saturated fat content. The food industry is being encouraged to produce and promote lower calorie and fat items as well as the use of fats lower in saturated fat and cholesterol in the production of foods (McNutt, 1979; NRC, 1982).

Summary

Diet appears to be important in the development of both heart disease and cancer. High serum cholesterol is believed to cause many forms of heart disease. Reducing dietary consumption of saturated fat and cholesterol has been shown to be effective in reducing serum lipid levels. Reduction of serum lipids, smoking cessation, and blood pressure control are all regarded as keys to risk reduction of heart disease. Dietary factors associated with breast, colo-rectal, and prostatic cancers are high fat, low fiber, and low Vitamin A diets. Alcohol is associated with liver, pancreas, and esophageal cancers and possibly lung cancer. Foods pickled, smoked, or pre-served with nitrate have been associated with stomach cancer. Contaminants in food (mutagens, toxins, and the like) have been suggested as associated with esoph-ageal and liver cancers.

The economic cost of heart disease and cancers are enormous: $175 billion annually (1981 estimates). Heart diseases and related conditions (hypertension) are the most prevalent chronic conditions and the most common reasons for limitations of activity in the United States (National Heart, Lung, and Blood Institute [NHLBI], 1983). The impact of heart disease and cancer morbidity and mortality on the American population is extensive economically and disruptive socially. Heart disease (plus stroke and atherosclerosis deaths) and cancer account for 70% of all deaths in the United States. About half of all these deaths remain when the proportion of smoking-related deaths is taken into account. Some investigators estimate that 35–40% of all cancers can be attributed to diet (Doll & Peto, 1981). The role of diet in specific cancer sites may be more variable (90% for stomach and colo-rectal; 50% for endometrial, gallbladder, pancreatic, and breast; 20% for lung, larynx, bladder, cervical, oral, pharynx, and esophageal) (Doll & Peto, 1981). Due to the complex interaction of known risk factors, estimates of this kind are not available for diet alone with respect to heart disease. Despite this, the role of diet in heart disease is undoubtedly considerable.

In spite of the recent decline in heart diseases deaths and improved treatment for heart diseases and cancer, their impact continues to be enormous. Prevention and intervention are essential in both public health policy and in personal practice.

Dietary guidelines for the prevention of both heart diseases and cancer have been proposed. The efficacy of these guidelines with respect to risk reduction for heart disease appear to have some support. Similar guidelines for dietary prevention of cancer have also been suggested and are consistent with the guidelines for heart disease prevention. However, the efficacy of these guidelines still remains to be tested. Nevertheless, they can be recommended, since they are prudent and promote good general nutrition.

EXERCISE AND CHRONIC DISEASE

In less developed societies, exercise is mandatory for survival; hunting, fishing, and food gathering are still a necessary part of day-to-day life for much of the world. But in the United States and Westernized societies sedentary work has become the rule even in occupations that have traditionally involved hard labor. Carpenters now have power nail-guns, power saws, and power drills. Ditch digging now involves the use of powerful machinery that can do in minutes what would take arms and backs hours to do. As a consequence for the first time in history a very large proportion of society, both blue- and white-collar, can make a living without the kind of back-breaking labor once characteristic of many occupations. Recreational exercise in less developed societies is limited to activities such as contests between two tribes at festive occasions. This was also true for preindustrial America. As television became the central form of entertainment in the American home, modern Americans, who no longer vigorously exercised on the job, have become accustomed to spectator participation in sports.

Exercise may be defined as either static or dynamic in nature. Static exercise, also called isometric, involves activities in which muscles do not change length and joints do not move. No work is performed during this exercise: only tension is created in the muscles involved in the exercise. Dynamic exercise, also called isotonic, involves the muscle contraction and joint movement. External work is performed during dynamic exercise. Muscles are attached by tendons between two bones. Because of this, muscles can only pull, contract, or shorten in length. Exercise involves the expenditure of energy (calories derived from carbohydrate, fat, and protein). Even at complete bed rest, a certain level of energy is burned to continue the basic functions of the body. During exercise the rate of energy use climbs sharply and drops back again after exercise. Table 2-5 shows the relative amount of energy required for various activities as compared to the resting energy needs. Dynamic exercise increases the breathing and heart rate because oxygen is required to burn energy efficiently. The climatic temperature and altitude also affect exercise (WHO, 1978).

At least five parameters of muscle activity are improved by exercise: (1) strength, (2) endurance, (3) efficiency, (4) muscle size, and (5) blood supply. The heart itself is a muscle and is exercised when it beats rapidly. The heart fills with blood between beats and is itself nourished at that time. A high heart rate at rest is inefficient,

Table 2-5. Average Values of Energy Expenditure for Selected Activities

Activity	Energy expenditure kcal/min[a]	
	Males	Females
Rest		
Lying	1.1	.9
Sitting	1.4	1.1
Standing	1.7	1.4
Work		
Office work	1.8	1.6
Light industry	2.3–4.1	1.9–3.4
Farming	5.0	4.8
Heavy industry	6.5–11.6	2.4–4.0
Recreation		
Cards	2.5	2.0
Walking	2.6–4.0	2.2–3.4
Golf	5.2	4.4
Bicycling	5.9	5.0
Dancing	4.3–11.3	3.6–9.6
Swimming	9.1	7.7
Tennis	9.1–11.1	7.7–9.4
Running	10.4	8.8
Skiing	12.0	11.0
Basketball	14.3	12.1
Handball	13.7	11.6

Note. From World Health Organization (1978).

[a]The values refer to energy (kilocalories) spent per minute for a 145-lb man and a 120-lb woman, and represent energy expenditure during the actual performance of the specified activities.

since the heart fills less efficiently and has less time to be perfused with its own blood. The "training" effect of exercise is to reduce the resting heart rate, so that the heart beats more slowly. Two additional effects of exercise on the heart are to increase the efficiency of the heart output (amount of blood expelled during each beat) and the vascularization of the heart (the number of small blood vessels in the heart muscle). The function of the blood vessels and lungs are also shown to be positively improved through exercise (Cooper, 1968).

Exercise at some level is necessary to maintain the most basic function of muscles and joints. Wasting of muscles and stiffness of joints occurs when a limb of the body must be immobilized for a period of time such as when a bone is broken. A level of proficiency for a particular activity such as dancing, may be "lost" through lack of practice. Thus, exercise is essential to maintain freedom of motion in the joints, a certain level of strength of muscles, and a correct responsiveness for a desired movement. Exercise is well accepted as a means of controlling weight. Since the importance of some level of exercise to health needs no further defense or explanation, this discussion will concentrate on the role of exercise in the prevention of chronic disease to the extent of present knowledge.

Most of the studies of exercise associations with chronic disease have measured exercise in terms of the amount involved in occupations. Studies of active and nonactive occupational groups have shown that exercise may be important in the prevention of death due to heart disease, but the studies are not all consistent in this conclusion (Leon & Blackburn, 1977). Studies of exercise are limited by the ability to estimate correctly the amount of exercise levels required in various occupations. Most studies estimate exercise based on last known occupation as it is listed on the death certificate or as self-reported activity. Either could be wrong. Studies have indicated that active persons have lower resting heart rates, lower blood pressure and a lower prevalence of hypertension. Obesity and high blood levels of cholesterol are also reduced by regular exercise. Exercise has been shown to raise HDL cholesterol, believed to be beneficial rather than harmful in preventing heart disease (Fraser, 1986). In addition, exercise has been shown to reduce muscle tension which may contribute to psychological health by assisting an individual to cope with stress, sleep and feel better, creating a "safety valve" for tension, anxiety, and frustration, and improving self-image. Thus, exercise, while perhaps not a direct factor in the prevention of heart disease, is helpful in modifying other important risk factors.

Four excellent studies have recently been published showing an association between various cancers and low levels of exercise. Three cancer sites appear to be responsive to exercise: colon, breast and reproductive organs (Frisch *et al.*, 1985; Vena *et al.*, 1985; Gerhardson, Norell, Kiviranta, Pedersen, & Ahlbom, 1986). The association between low exercise and colon cancer has been shown to be present in all races, at all income levels, and for each subsection of the colon studied (Garabrant, Peters, Mack, & Bernstein, 1984). The colon cancer studies are especially intriguing, since the findings are consistent with what is known about colon physiology and colon cancer pathogenesis. Much more study is necessary, however, before the suggested association between exercise and these cancers can be determined to be independently causal of other factors.

Trends in Exercise

A growing awareness of a need for more physical activity and fitness began with a report by Hans Krans in 1955, which showed American children to be less fit than children of Western Europe. The report triggered the formation of the President's Conference on the Fitness of American Youth in 1956 under President Dwight D. Eisenhower. During the presidency of John F. Kennedy, the name of the council was changed to the President's Council on Physical Fitness, so that its efforts could be more broadly directed to fitness at every age level. An ambitious series of public service announcements, a series of teaching clinics for physical educators and recreational leaders, and a series of pilot programs were established in local school systems for the testing and training of school children. But not until the 1970s did Americans begin to take an active part in personal exercise programs.

The increased use of fitness facilities, parks, and roadways by joggers as well as the growth in the sales of sport and physical fitness paraphernalia is remarkable. Also notable is the plethora of books, cassettes, records, and video instructions for home use by the fitness-conscious consumer. This change is not due totally to improved health consciousness. Fashion has made being slender important and brought exercise back as a necessary part of the daily routine. The relative importance of job-related exercise is illustrated by a 1979 survey by the National Center for Health Statistics. One out of four males, but only one out of ten females, reported vigorous exercise on the job. One out of four males and one out of five females reported at least some exercise on the job. Survey results are not consistent with respect to the proportion of the population who participate in recreational exercise, but most agree that more Americans are exercising today. A 1979 survey indicated that between one third and one half of Americans, both men and women, regularly exercised by walking, gardening, or dancing. Between 10 and 15% indicated that they jogged regularly. A 1983 Gallup poll indicated that 77% of Americans exercised, about half on a daily basis. A Harris survey (1978) indicated that participation in exercise was directly proportional with income. Among the elderly, about one third indicated in a 1975 survey that they take regular walks. Only one third of children and adolescents participated in regular physical education programs at school, and more disturbing, the proportion is declining. Many high school programs focus on competitive sports, which involve a relatively small number of students. Fitness programs are available in only 2.5% of all businesses. The trend toward awareness and participation is encouraging, but the need for greater involvement is also apparent (Public Health Service [PHS], 1980).

The proportion of the decline in heart disease possibly attributable to increased activity cannot yet be determined by current statistics. While lack of exercise may not be definitively determined to be causal in chronic disease, much evidence exists, as has been suggested, to recommend exercise as a means to reduce other risk factors and generally to improve health.

Exercise Programs for Prevention and Intervention

An abundance of books, tapes, videocassettes, exercise paraphernalia, health clubs, and exercise experts are available in the retail market place for the choosing. The extent to which an exercise program is carried depends entirely on an individual's choice. It need not be of such an extent as would be necessary to develop Olympic or professional athletes. A physical fitness program should at a minimum result in the ability of the participant to maintain a desirable weight, reduce the resting heart rate to 60 or below, allow the individual to participate in exercise without chronic residual discomfort, and increase the strength and agility of the body and cardiovascular fitness of the heart. Thirty minutes of sustained activity three days per week of an activity which uses large muscle groups and raises the heart rate is considered a minimum for cardiovascular fitness. "Crash" programs are not recommended. Common sense caution should be used in choosing a program or selecting equipment.

In the development of public health programs for the promotion of health special attention should be given to groups that have shown disproportionately low use of fitness programs: girls and women, the elderly, physically and mentally handicapped, institutionalized persons, the poor, and inner-city and rural residents.

Exercise and Public Policy

The Federal government has developed specific objectives for 1990 with respect to exercise. These objectives are:

- increase to 90% the participation of children and adolescents in cardiovascular fitness programs,
- increase to 60% the participation of children in school physical fitness programs,
- increase to 60% the participation of adults in vigorous exercise, and
- increase to 50% the participation of the elderly in daily appropriately scaled exercise activities.

Education objectives include increasing to 70% the proportion of adults who can accurately identify the kind and duration of exercise believed to promote cardiovascular fitness and increasing to 50% the proportion of physicians who include an evaluation of exercise history as a part of their initial examination of patients. It is also hoped to increase to 25% the proportion of businesses offering fitness activities to their employees. Surveillance and evaluation mechanisms have been planned both in terms of use of fitness services and health status of the population. Plans to meet these objectives include: promotion of fitness education through media, educational institutions, health care facilities, and service organizations; promotion of worksite fitness programs through education, tax incentives, and reduced health and life insurance premiums; and promotion of fitness facility development through public, private, and corporate entities (PHS, 1980).

Summary

Exercise of some kind is clearly important to health. Current statistics at this time do not allow a determination of the amount of risk associated with lack of exercise. However, exercise can be recommended as a means of reducing risk of disease by modifying other risk factors. Participation in exercise at some level should be encouraged for everyone.

PSYCHOSOCIAL FACTORS IN CHRONIC DISEASE

The influence of the emotions on health has been known for centuries. In 1676 Wiseman in England attributed cancer to "black bile" and "melancholy" (Selye,

1950). In 1701 Deshaires Gendron suggested an association between emotions and cancer from his observations that cancer development followed fright or grief. In 1747 Gaub of Leyden wrote "the reason why a sound body becomes ill, or an ailing body recovers, very often lies in the mind" (Menninger, 1954).

Much research has been devoted to the psychological and social factors associated with disease in recent decades. Heart disease since the late 1950s has received much attention after the pioneer efforts of Drs. Rosenman and Friedman. More recently, the relationship of cancer occurrence with psychological factors has been studied. Psychological and social factors related to overall mortality have also been studied. It should be mentioned that the psychological and social factors to be reviewed here are conceptually quite distinct from factors indicative of mental illness. However, mental illness, a very large and complex area of study, may or may not have similar risk factors and may contribute independently to risk of chronic disease, but a review of this possibility is beyond the scope of this discussion.

Psychological and social factors related to heart disease occurrence have been separated into a variety of categories: sociological indexes, social mobility and status incongruity, anxiety and neurosis, other reactive characteristics, life dissatisfactions and interpersonal problems, stress and life changes, and coronary-prone behavior pattern. Sociological indexes may be described by such environmental and personal characteristics as industrialization, urbanization, occupation, education, income, religion, and marital status. Heart diseases are more common in highly industrialized and urbanized societies, and in upper education, occupation, and income levels. Heart diseases occur more commonly in unmarried persons: separated, divorced, widowed, and never married. The higher risk of unmarried persons cannot be explained by higher levels of other risk factors such as high blood pressure, serum cholesterol, and weight. The relationship of heart diseases to marital status is not consistent, however. Conversely, persons who attend religious services regularly have consistently been shown to have lower risk of heart diseases, but a particular religious affiliation has not been found to be associated positively or negatively (Jenkins, 1976).

The category of social mobility and status incongruity refers to movement and to discrepancies within or between generations with respect to education, occupation, and income. The hypothesis suggest that such movement and discrepancies between or within generations may contribute to tension and conflict (particularly if social status is lost). But contradictory evidence has been found for this hypothesis, and the association with heart disease is not certain (Jenkins, 1976).

Anxiety and neuroticism characterized by depression, psychosomatic complaints, nervousness, fatigue, emotional drain, and sleep disturbances have been hypothesized as associated with heart disease. A large number of studies seem to indicate that an association with coronary disease is likely, but some findings also suggest that these symptoms may be more likely prodromes of disease, a manifestation of subclinical disease, than true risk factors. Other reactive characteristics such as exaggerated denial, obsessive/compulsive defenses, and repression are less well studied. Of all the reactive characteristics, only the cold-pressor test (submerging a subject's forearm into ice water) is consistently shown to be related to elevated blood pressure, a heart disease risk factor (Keys *et al.*, 1971).

Another hypothesis is that life dissatisfactions, changes, and problems may be precursors to chronic disease development, specifically heart disease. Work and financial problems have been suggested by several studies as precursors to heart disease development, but contradictory findings have also been reported (Jenkins, 1976). Some researchers have suggested that the intensity, uncertainty, or ambiguity of the problem and not the specific problem per se may be the critical issue.

Both supportive and contradictory evidence have also been reported for the hypothesized association of heart disease with stress (such as excessive overtime) and life changes (events such as loss of a job, buying a house, or a death, divorce, marriage, and so on). Some studies have shown a crescendo in life events preceding the occurrence of a myocardial infarction (Rahe & Paasikivi, 1971). Contradictory studies that have used powerful methodological designs are negative (Jenkins, 1976).

Of these categories of psychological and social factors, the most promising with respect to cardiovascular risk is the Type A–Type B behavior pattern. Type A behavior is characterized by some or all of the following: intense striving for achievement, competitiveness, easily provoked impatience, time urgency, abruptness of gesture and speech, overcommitment to work, excessive drive, and hostility. It should be noted that this is a behavior pattern, believed to be deeply ingrained, and not a response to "stress" or a distressful situation. The Type B behavior pattern is characterized by the converse: relaxed and easygoing. The reported studies of the Type A behavior pattern consistently show an association with heart disease. Such a behavior pattern might raise risk by the mechanism of promoting the development of atherosclerotic lesions. Two models for the mechanism of interaction between Type A behavior and heart disease have been proposed. The first model suggests Type A as a causal factor mediated by stress-related autonomic neuroendocrine mechanisms. The second suggests that both Type A and heart disease are independent and parallel expressions of a central aggression constitutional trait, which expresses itself behaviorally as Type A and somatically as heart disease (Review Panel, 1981).

Studies of the occurrence of precursor psychological or social changes with respect to cancer development are even less clear. Cancers of different organs have different associated risk factors. The length of time believed to be required for most cancers to develop further confuses the issue. In children, for instance, shortness of the time interval would tend to suggest that life events or psychological factors are perhaps not involved. In adults, however, the longer time interval during which psychological factors can develop or have an effect as well as allowing life events to accumulate may allow for real *or* spurious associations to be made. The very fact that a serious disease has been diagnosed may influence the emotional health of patients such that spurious associations again might be made, particularly if the retrospective study design is used. Prospective studies are difficult to conduct because they require large amounts of time and money. Despite these problems, studies of the psychosocial aspects of cancer development have been attempted. Feelings of alienation from family, hopelessness, helplessness, and despair have been found to occur more frequently among cancer patients than controls (LeShan, 1966). Relationships between life event and depression (Brown, Seggie, & Ettigi,

1979), between depression and decreased immunocompetence (Schlesser, Winokur, & Sherman, 1980), and decreased immunocompetence and subsequent cancer development have been shown (McQueen & Siegrist, 1982). Conclusions with regard to these associations would be premature, given the state of the art of psychological assessment and the methodological problems confronting this area of research.

The association of sexual behavior with chronic disease must be mentioned for completeness. The risks to health as a result of the diverse communicable venereal diseases will not be detailed here. The occurrence of cervical cancer has been determined to be more frequent among women who marry or give birth at an early age. Cervical cancer rarely occurs among unmarried persons, such as nuns (Fraumeni, Lloyd, Smith, & Wagoner, 1969). Parallels in the pattern of the occurrence of cervical, penile, and testicular cancer have also been noticed. A larger proportion of cervical cancer occurs among women whose husbands had penile cancer (Graham et al., 1979). Cervical cancer cases admit to a larger number of sexual partners than controls (Terris, Wilson, Smith, Sprung, & Nelson, 1967), which has led to the suggestion that increased exposure to the Herpes simplex II virus may be involved in the cancer development (Berg & Lampe, 1981). This hypothesis needs further study, since it does not concur with the declining incidence of cervical cancer, with a larger prevalence of Herpes simplex II, or with more relaxed social mores with respect to sexual behavior. Nor does this hypothesis of increased risk due to exposure to Herpes simplex II account for a larger number of cases, since both death and incidence rates for cervical cancer have fallen sharply. A downward trend in incidence of cervical cancer cannot be explained by the use of the Papanicolaou (Pap) test for early detection either, since the decline began before widespread use of screening.

Another dimension of psychosocial factors that has been studied are those factors in the social milieu that protect health and well-being. Foremost of these is the social network, the social ties maintained with individuals or groups in the community at large. Four types of social ties (networks) have been studied: (1) marriage, (2) extended family and close friends, (3) church membership, and (4) other formal and informal group affiliations. Married persons have been consistently shown to have lower death rates than unmarried persons in a number of studies. The much higher death rates among the unmarried cannot be explained by any single cause of death but are shown for all causes except leukemia. The higher death rates for unmarried persons persist after other risk factors are taken into account, such as smoking or socioeconomic levels, and for many years after the termination of a marriage (as in widowhood). Death rates following loss of a spouse have been shown to be higher among men. One mechanism by which confiding relationships (spouse, extended family, and friends) may function to protect health is that they have been shown to be important in the avoidance of depression, in compliance with a prescribed medical regime, and in coping with illness, recovery, and rehabilitation. Lower risk for chronic disease for regular church-goers has already been mentioned. Persons who report having many contacts outside the home also report "being happy" more often and are not as likely to score "impaired" on psychiatric evaluation as are persons with few contacts. The number and strength of social bonds are both inversely related to the occurrence of neurotic symptoms. Inferences from these findings must be carefully drawn, since the presence of illness often changes social bonds, mobility, and opportunity to develop and maintain contacts (Berkman & Breslow, 1983).

Many studies have indicated that race, social class, urbanization, geographical and occupational mobility, and use of preventive health status are important in health risk and promotion. The interaction of these variables with psychological and social network variables has been evaluated together with other risk factors. Lower social class is associated with both a higher occurrence of most diseases and with such risk factors as smoking, drinking, and obesity. Whites show more inclination toward non–church membership and marriage. Blacks are more frequently unmarried but show a stronger tendency toward church attendance and extended family ties. Both geographical (number of addresses) and occupational (number of different jobs) mobility are negatively associated with maintenance of social ties. However, urbanization shows an independent increase of mortality risk when social network factors are taken into account. Predictably, the use of preventive health care is inversely associated with mortality. The interaction of psychological factors with social network surprisingly does not show that isolation/depression indices are significantly associated social network integration. But the combination of social network and psychological factors (specifically life satisfaction) is a powerful predictor of mortality (Berkman & Breslow, 1983).

Trends in Psychological and Social Factors

As mentioned previously, heart disease death rates have been declining markedly since the late 1960s. The contribution of psychological factors to the decline have not been evaluated. If it is assumed, for instance, that Type A behavior is a cause in heart disease development, would the decline represent a declining prevalence of Type A behavior? If stress is a causal factor, has stress become less prevalent in society or has society learned to cope with it? These questions cannot be answered from existing research.

Since 1970 the number of community mental health facilities have increased by 2.5 times and now account for 25% of the use of mental health care services. The trend since 1975 has been for a larger use of mental health care by younger persons, age 18–44. The rates of diagnosis of neurosis, psychosis, personality disorders, and depression have all declined since 1975, as estimated by inpatient discharge records. A trend toward the de-institutionalization of mentally ill persons since World War II might account for increasing use of community mental health facilities and for the declining rate of certain diagnoses based on inpatient records. Alcohol- and drug-related diagnosis, however, have increased (National Institute of Mental Health [NIMH], 1983). Thus, these trends are not necessarily helpful indications of whether the psychological or social factors associated with chronic disease are declining in prevalence in the population. There have also been changes in the average income, educational distribution, urban-rural residence pattern, and the proportion of males and females. The extent and effect of such trends need further research. Further research on the contribution of social ties to specific causes of death is also needed.

Psychosocial Factors and Prevention and Intervention

Strategies for prevention of the development of negatively associated psychological factors and fostering of positively associated psychological and social variables have not been proposed. In the 1978 Report of the President's Commission on Mental Health (PCMH, 1978), recommendations and strategies for meeting the needs of only the mentally ill and the underserved populations of handicapped, alcoholics, and others were suggested. However, recommendations of the commission's report might be useful in preventive strategies for psychosocial factors as well. Particularly appropriate among the recommendations was suggestion for the development of community support with existing mental health care services.

Useful approaches in the prevention of or intervention against specific psychological factors requires further research. It is not clear how, for example, Type A behavior might be prevented, since its developmental process and origin are not yet known. Predictors of Type A-Type B behavior might be studied in children to develop such a profile. Further, it is not clear how or to what extent intervention with respect to these factors may be useful in modifying risk. The intervention with respect to Type A behavior has been attempted, but a lack of quantitative data about behavior phenomena has restricted the reproducibility and precision of assessment. The design of an intervention study also could depend on the choice of a model for the mechanism of effect of Type A behavior.

Psychosocial Factors and Public Policy

In 1978 the President's Commission on Mental Health issued a comprehensive report on the status of the mental health of Americans and the research, personnel, and facility requirements for the nation. The goal stated in the report was to extend the availability of mental health care particularly to the underserved, alcoholics, abusive families, physically handicapped, learning disabled, and drug abusers. The recommendations were also primarily directed toward meeting the needs of the chronically mentally ill (PCMH, 1978). Thus, attention to the distribution and development of services or recommendations for persons with the type of psychological and social factors discussed here was not addressed by this report.

Given the state of knowledge of the associations of psychological factors with chronic disease, the development of public policy or definitive recommendations would be premature. Counseling for psychological and social problems should be encouraged. Type A personalities are sometimes encouraged to relax more often. Research findings, however, are too limited to suggest that even such basic mental health activities are effective in reducing disease risk. Support for further research is certainly warranted.

Summary

With the exception of demographic social factors and Type A behavior, psychological factors are only tentatively associated with chronic disease. No recommendations can be made with regard to risk reduction, but appropriate psychological health care can be suggested as a means for achieving a more pleasant life regardless of its role in chronic disease.

POINTS TO REMEMBER

A review of the large body of research with respect to tobacco and alcohol use, diet, exercise, and psychosocial factors in chronic disease has indicated that these life-style factors contribute significantly to the risk of developing disease. To be complete, other important factors must be mentioned. For instance, a tendency within a family toward high serum cholesterol and heart disease is important. As has already been suggested, such a tendency may be due as much to genetics as to common life-styles in families. A genetic tendency is not a factor over which control can be exercised. Exposure to dietary cholesterol and fats, smoking, and other factors are controllable, however. Other factors must be considered also with respect to cancer development. Table 2-6 summarizes the proportion of cancers attributed to various environmental exposures, including some already mentioned (diet, tobacco, and so on) and some exposures not already mentioned (occupation, radiation, etc.). The relatively small amount of risk attributed to exposures such as occupation, pollution, and radiation is notable in comparison to that attributed to tobacco and diet. This information should not be construed to mean that protection of the environment, testing or consumer products, or limiting occupational exposures are not important activities. They most definitely are, but they are currently estimated to be causal only in a relatively small number of cancers, perhaps because many of these factors are relatively recent as an exposure problem or because a relatively small proportion of the population receives large or chronic exposure. With sufficient passage of time, if environmental problems intensify and/or occupational exposures broaden, these factors may account for a larger proportion of the cancer problem in the future. Currently, however, Table 2-6 indicates that a substantial proportion (65–80%) of cancers are attributable to tobacco and diet alone. These exposures are of immediate, not future, concern. The enormous economic burden, both public and private, and the large proportion of the population affected require that attention be focused on modification of life-style factors as the highest priority. Unless prompt attention is given to health education and modification of life-style, the future health care of Americans may become a crisis situ-

Table 2-6. Summary of the Proportion of Cancers Attributed to Various Factors

Factor	Estimated percentage of all cancer deaths attributed to factor
Tobacco	30%
Alcohol	3–13%
Diet	35–50%
Food additives[a]	<1%
Occupation	4%
Asbestos	3%
Radiation[b]	8%
Drugs and medical procedures[c]	4%
Pollution	2%
Sexual behavior[d]	7%
Infection	5–10%
Consumer products	<1%

Note. Adapted from Doll and Peto (1981) and U.S. Congress Office of Technology Assessment (1982).

[a]Allowing that some preservatives may be protective.

[b]Includes natural and X-ray. This estimate does not include nonfatal skin cancers; the inclusion of these (largely attributable to excessive exposure to sunshine) would increase the contribution of this factor to about 30%.

[c]Primarily exogenous hormones (estrogen), which are believed to cause uterine cancer.

[d]Includes reproductive practices also.

ation. By the year 2000, it is expected that the post World War II baby boom generation will begin to arrive at the age of retirement and of high risk for chronic diseases. The demand for health services and financial resources will become even more critical than it is presently. A projected proportionally smaller group of persons of employment age will be available to contribute to the public health-care dollar. This will require that priorities for the distribution of services be established. Undoubtedly such a process will require that uncomfortable questions be addressed challenging the values and humanitarian soul of America as well as stretching or redefining its laws. A crisis of some proportion seems inevitable. Only prevention activities *now* can limit the impact of this developing crisis in health care. And prevention involving modification of life-style, can *only* be accomplished through the exercise of choice by each individual.

Acknowledgments

The author wishes to thank Drs. Albert I. Mendeloff, M. G. Hardinge, David D. Celantano, and Ernst Wynder for reading this manuscript; a special thank you is in order for Fanchon Finucane for assisting in the location of resource materials and preparation of the final manuscript.

References

Abraham, S., Johnson, C. L., & Carroll, M. D. (1977). A comparison of levels of serum cholesterol of adults 18–74 years of age in the United States in 1960–62 and 1971–74. *Advancedata: Vital and Health Statistics*, (No. 5).

Ahrens, E. H. (1976). The management of hyperlipidemias: Whether, rather than how. *Annals of Internal Medicine, 85*, 87–93.

American Psychiatric Association. (1980). *Diagnostic and statistical manual of mental disorders*, (3rd ed.). Washington, DC: American Psychiatric Association.

Babor, T. F., Treffardier, M., Weill, J., Fegueur, L., & Ferrant, J-P. (1983). Early detection and the secondary prevention of alcoholism in France: A quoi bon? *Journal of Studies on Alcohol, 44*, 600–616.

Benfari, R. C., & Sherwin, R. (1981). The Multiple Risk Factor Intervention Trial after 4 years: A summing up. *Preventive Medicine, 10*, 544–546.

Berg, J. W., & Lampe, J. (1981). High-risk factors in gynecologic cancer. *Cancer, 48*, 429–441.

Berkman, L. F., & Breslow, L. (1983). *Health and ways of living: The Alameda County Study*. New York: Oxford University Press.

Blackburn, H. (1979). Diet and mass hyperlipidemia: Public health considerations: A point of view. In R. I. Levy, B. M. Rifkind, B. H. Dennis, & N. D. Ernst (Eds.), *Nutrition, lipids, and coronary heart disease: Nutrition in health and disease*, (Vol. 1). New York: Raven Press.

Brewster, L. M., & Jacobson, M. (1978). *The changing American diet*. Washington, DC: Center for Science in the Public Interest.

Brown, G. M., Seggie, J., & Ettigi, P. (1979). Stress, hormone responses and cancer. In J. Tache, H. Selye, & S. B. Day (Eds.), *Cancer, stress and death*. New York: Plenum Press.

Calkins, B. M., Whittaker, D. J., Nair, P. P., Rider, A. A., & Turjman, N. (1984). Diet, nutrient intake and metabolism in populations at high and low risk for colon cancer. 3. Nutrient intake. *American Journal of Clinical Nutrition, 40*, 896–905.

Carroll, K. K., & Khor, H. T. (1971). Effects of level and type of dietary fat on incidence of mammary tumors induced in female Sprague-Dawley rats by 7,12 dimethylbenz(a)anthracene. *Lipids, 6*, 415–420.

Center for Disease Control (1976). *The health consequences of smoking: A reference edition: Selected chapters from 1971 through 1975 reports with cumulative index for all reports, 1964–1975* (DHEW pub. no. (CDC) 78-8357). Washington, DC: U.S. Department of Health, Education, and Welfare; Public Health Service.

Clarren, S. K., & Smith, D. W. (1978). The fetal alcohol syndrome: A review of the world literature. *New England Journal of Medicine, 298*, 1063–1067.

Cooper, K. H. (1968). *Aerobics*. New York: Bantam Books.

Distilled Spirits Councils of the U.S., Inc. (1978a). *Distilled spirit industry statistical report, apparent consumption of distilled spirits by months and states, 1977*. Washington, DC: DISCUS.

Distilled Spirits Council of the United States, Inc. (1978b). *Distilled spirits industry statistical report, apparent consumption of distilled spirits by states in wine gallons* (Report G-78-12). Washington, DC: DISCUS.

Doll, R., & Peto, R. (1981). The causes of cancer: Quantitative estimates of avoidable risks of cancer in the United States today. *Journal of National Cancer Institute, 66*, 1191–1308.

Dunn, J. E. (1977). Breast cancer among American Japanese in the San Francisco Bay area. *National Cancer Institute Monographs, 47*, 157–160.

Fairholt, F. W. (1859). *Tobacco: Its history and associations*. London: Chapman and Hall.

Feinleib, M. (1982). Summary of a workshop on cholesterol and noncardiovascular disease mortality. *Preventive Medicine, 11*, 360–367.

Fraser, G. E. (1986). *Preventive cardiology*. New York: Oxford University Press.

Fraumeni, J. F., Lloyd, J. W., Smith, E. M., & Wagoner, J. K. (1969). Cancer mortality among nuns: Role of marital status in etiology of neoplastic disease in women. *Journal of the National Cancer Institute, 42*, 455–468.

Friend, B., Page, L., & Marston, R. (1979). Food consumption patterns, U.S.A.: 1909–13 to 1976. In R. I. Levy, B. M. Rifkind, B. H. Dennis & N. D. Ernst (Eds.), *Nutrition, lipids, and coronary heart disease: Nutrition in health and disease* (Vol. 1). New York: Raven Press.

Frisch, R. E., Wyshak, G., Albright, N. L., Albright, T. E., Schiff, I., Jones, K. P., Witschi, J., Shiang, E., Koff, E., & Marguglio, M. (1985). Lower prevalence of breast cancer and cancers of the reproductive system among former college athletes compared to non-athletes. *British Journal of Cancer, 52*, 885–891.

Garabrant, D. H., Peters, J. M., Mack, T. M., & Bernstein, L. (1984). Job activity and colon cancer risk. *American Journal of Epidemiology, 119*, 1005–1014.

Garfinkel, L. (1981). Time trends in lung cancer mortality among non-smokers and a note on passive smoking. *Journal of the National Cancer Institute, 66*, 1061–1066.

Gerhardsson, M., Norell, S. E., Kivirant, H., Pedersen, N. L., & Ahlbom, A. (1986). Sedentary jobs and colon cancer. *American Journal of Epidemiology, 123*, 775–780.

Graham, S. (1983a). Diet and cancer: Epidemiologic aspects. *Epidemiologic Reviews, 2*, 1–45.

Graham, S. (1983b). Toward a dietary prevention of cancer. *Epidemiologic Reviews, 5*, 38–50.

Graham, S., Priore, R., Graham, M., Browne, R., Burnett, W., & West, D. (1979). Genital cancer in wives of penile cancer patients. *Cancer, 44*, 1870–1874.

Grundy, S. M. (1979). Dietary fats and sterols. In R. I. Levy, B. M. Rifkind, B. H. Dennis, & N. D. Ernst (Eds.), *Nutrition, lipids, and coronary heart disease: Nutrition in health and disease* (Vol. 1). New York: Raven Press.

Iglehart, J. K. (1984). Health policy report: Smoking and public policy. *New England Journal of Medicine, 310*, 539–544.

Jenkins, C. D. (1976). Recent evidence supporting psychologic and social risk factors for coronary disease (first of two parts). *New England Journal of Medicine, 294*, 987–994.

Jones, K. L., & Smith, D. W. (1973). Recognition of the fetal alcohol syndrome in early infancy. *Lancet, 2*, 999–1001.

Keys, A., Taylor, H. L., Blackburn, H., Brozek, J., Anderson, J. T., & Simonson, E. (1971). Mortality and coronary heart disease among men studied for 23 years. *Archives of Internal Medicine, 128*, 201–214.

Klatsky, A. L., Friedman, G. D., & Siegelaub, A. B. (1981). Alcohol use and cardiovascular disease: The Kaiser-Permanente experience. *Circulation, 64*, (Suppl. III), 32–41.

Kono, S., Ikeda, M., Ogata, M., Tokudome, S., Nishizumi, M., & Kuratsune, M. (1983). The relationship between alcohol and mortality among Japanese physicians. *International Journal of Epidemiology, 12*, 437–441.

Krasnegor, N. A. (Ed.). (1979). *Cigarette smoking as a dependence process* (NIDA research monograph 23). Washington, DC: Department of Health, Education and Welfare; Public Health Service; Alcohol, Drug Abuse, and Mental Health Administration.

Kristenson, H. (1982). Studies on alcohol related disabilities in a medical intervention programme in middle-aged males. Doctoral dissertation, Lund University, Sweden.

Kritchevsky, D. (1979). Dietary interactions. In R. I. Levy, B. M. Rifkind, B. H. Dennis, & N. D. Ernst (Eds.), *Nutrition, lipids, and coronary heart disease. Nutrition in health and disease* (Vol. 1). New York: Raven Press.

Leon, A. S., & Blackburn, H. (1977). The relationship of physical activity to coronary heart disease and life expectancy. *Annals of the New York Academy of Sciences, 301*, 561–578.

LeShan, L. (1966). An emotional life history pattern associated with neoplastic disease. *Annals of the New York Academy of Sciences, 125*, 780–793.

Lipids Research Clinics Program. (1984a). The Lipid Research Clinics Coronary Primary Prevention Trial results. I. Reduction of incidence of coronary heart disease. *Journal of the American Medical Association, 251*, 351–364.

Lipids Research Clinics Program. (1984b). The Lipid Research Clinics Coronary Primary Prevention Trial results. II. The relationship of reduction in incidence of coronary heart disease to cholesterol lowering. *Journal of the American Medical Association, 251*, 365–374.

Los Angeles Times. (1977, April 8). Stewardess grounded by smokers wins $3,657 suit.

McAlister, A., Perry, C., Killen, J., Slinkard, L. A., & Maccoby, N. (1980). Pilot study of smoking, alcohol and drug abuse prevention. *American Journal of Public Health, 70*, 719–721.

McNutt, K. W. (1979). Nutrition labeling: A tool for diet planning. In R. I. Levy, B. M. Rifkind, B. H. Dennis, & N. D. Ernst (Eds.), *Nutrition, lipids, and coronary heart disease: Nutrition in health and disease* (Vol. 1). New York: Raven Press.

McQueen, D. V., & Siegrist, J. (1982). Social factors in the etiology of chronic disease: An overview. *Social Science and Medicine, 16*, 353–367.

Menninger, K. (1954). Psychological aspects of the organism under stress; Part 2: Regulatory devices of the ego under major stress. *International Journal of Psycho-analysis, 35*, 412–420.

Merz, W. (1979). Effect of dietary components on lipids and lipoproteins: mineral elements. In R. I. Levy, B. M. Rifkind, B. H. Dennis, & N. D. Ernst (Eds.), *Nutrition, lipids, and coronary heart disease: Nutrition in health and disease* (Vol. 1). New York: Raven Press.

Milt, H. (1974). *Basic handbook on alcoholism*. Maplewood, NJ: Scientific Aids Publications.

Molitor, G. T. T. (1980). The food system in the 1980s. *Journal of Nutrition Education, 12* (Suppl. 1), 103–111.

Montagu, A. (1964). *Life before birth*. New York: New American Library.

Moss, A. J. (1979). Changes in cigarette smoking and current smoking practices among adults: United States, 1978. *Advancedata: Vital and Health Statistics, No. 52*, 1–16.

Nair, P. P. (1984). Diet, nutrient intake and metabolism in populations at high and low risk for colon cancer. 1. Introduction: correlates of diet, nutrient intake, and metabolism in relation to colon cancer. *American Journal of Clinical Nutrition, 40*, 880–886.

National Cancer Institute (1977). *The smoking digest: Progress report on a nation kicking the habit*. Washington, DC: U.S. Department of Health, Education, and Welfare; Public Health Service, National Institutes of Health.

National Center for Health Statistics. Annual summary of births, deaths, marriages, and divorces, Untied States, 1980. *Monthly Vital Statistics Report*, 1981, *29* (13), 1–31.

National Center for Health Statistics. (1984). *Health, United States, 1983, and prevention profile*. (DHHS pub. no. (PHS) 84-1232). Washington, DC: U.S. Department of Health and Human Services; Public Health Service.

National Clearinghouse for Alcohol Information (1981). *Fact sheet: Selected statistics on alcohol and alcoholism*. Rockville, MD: National Clearinghouse for Alcohol Information.

National Council on Alcoholism, New York City Affiliate, Inc. (1984). *Some facts on alcoholism in industry*. New York: National Council on Alcoholism.

National Heart, Lung, and Blood Institute. (1983). *Fiscal year 1983 fact book*. Washington, DC: U.S. Department of Health and Human Services; Public Health Service; National Institutes of Health.

National Institute of Mental Health. (1983). *Mental health, United States, 1983* (DHHS pub. no. (ADM) 83-1275). Washington, DC: U.S. Department of Health and Human Services; Public Service; Alcohol, Drug Abuse, and Mental Health Administration.

National Institutes of Health. (1979). *Proceedings of the Conference on the Decline in Coronary Heart Disease and Mortality* (NIH pub. no. 79-1610). Washington, DC: U.S. Department of Health, Education, and Welfare; Public Health Service.

National Institute on Alcohol Abuse and Alcoholism. (1978). Fetal alcohol syndrome: New perspectives. *Alcohol Health and Research World, 2* (3), 1–12. Washington, DC: U.S. Department of Health, Education, and Welfare; Public Health Service; Alcohol, Drug Abuse, and Mental Health Administration.

National Institute on Alcohol Abuse and Alcoholism. (1981). *Fourth special report to the U.S. Congress on alcohol and health from the Secretary of Health and Human Services, January 1981* (DHHS pub. no. (ADM) 82-1080). Washington, DC: U.S. Department of Health and Human Services; Public Health Service; Alcohol, Drug Abuse, and Mental Health Administration.

National Institute on Alcohol Abuse and Alcoholism. (1982). *Treating alcoholism: The illness, the symptoms, the treatment* (DHHS pub. no. (ADM) 82-128). Washington, DC: U.S. Department of Health and Human Services; Public Health Service; Alcohol, Drug Abuse, and Mental Health Administration.

National Institute on Alcohol Abuse and Alcoholism. (1984). *Fifth special report to the U.S. Congress on alcohol and health from the Secretary of Health and Human Services, December 1983* (DHHS pub. no. (ADM) 84-1291). Washington, DC: U.S. Department of Health and Human Services; Public Health Service; Alcohol, Drug Abuse, and Mental Health Administration.

National Research Council of the National Academy of Sciences. (1982). *Diet, nutrition, and cancer.* Washington, DC: National Academy Press.

Office on Smoking and Health. (1979). *The health consequences of smoking 1977–1978* (DHEW pub. no. (PHS) 79-50065). Washington, DC: U.S. Department of Health and Human Services; Public Health Service.

Office on Smoking and Health. (1981). *The health consequences of smoking: The changing cigarette: A report of the Surgeon General* (DHHS pub. no. (PHS) 81-51056). Washington, DC: U.S. Department of Health and Human Services; Public Health Service.

Office on Smoking and Health. (1982). *The health consequences of smoking: Cancer: A report of the Surgeon General.* Washington, DC: U.S. Department of Health and Human Services; Public Health Service.

Office on Smoking and Health. (1983a). *The health consequences of smoking: Cardiovascular disease: A report of the Surgeon General.* Washington, DC: U.S. Department of Health and Human Services; Public Health Service.

Office on Smoking and Health. (1983b). *The health consequences of smoking for women: A report of the Surgeon General.* Washington, DC: U.S. Department of Health and Human Services; Public Health Service.

Office on Smoking and Health. (1984). *The health consequences of smoking: Chronic obstructive lung disease: A report of the Surgeon General.* Washington, DC: U.S. Department of Health and Human Services; Public Health Service.

Oster, G., Colditz, G. A., & Kelly, N. L. (1984). The economic costs of smoking and benefits of quitting for individual smokers. *Preventive Medicine, 13*, 377–398.

Pollack, E. S., Nomura, A. M., Keilbrun, L. K., Stemmermann, G. N., & Green, S. B. (1984). Prospective study of alcohol consumption and cancer. *The New England Journal of Medicine, 310*, 617–621.

President's Commission on Mental Health. (1978). *Report to the President from the President's Commission on Mental Health* (Vol. 1). Washington, DC: U.S. Government Printing Office.

Public Health Service. (1980). *Promoting health/preventing disease: Objectives for the nation.* Washington, DC: U.S. Department of Health and Human Services.

Rahe, R. H., & Paasikivi, J. (1971). Psychosocial factors and myocardial infarction. II. An outpatient study in Sweden. *Journal of Psychosomatic Research, 15*, 33–39.

Review Panel on Coronary-Prone Behavior and Coronary Heart Disease. (1981). Coronary-prone behavior and coronary heart disease: A critical review. *Circulation, 63*, 1199–1215.

Saila, S. L. (1978). A trial closure of Alko retail outlets on Saturdays and its effect on alcohol consumption and disturbances caused by intoxication. Paper presented at the 24th International Institute on the Prevention and Treatment of Alcoholism, Zurich.

Schlesser, M. A., Winokur, G., & Sherman, B. M. (1980). Hypothamic-pituitary-adrenal axis activity in depressive illness. *Archives of General Psychiatry, 37*, 737–743.

Selye, H. (1950). *The physiology and pathology of exposure to stress.* Montreal: Acta.

Shiffman, S. M. (1979). The tobacco withdrawal syndrome. In N. A. Krasnegor (Ed.), *NIDA research monograph 23: Cigarette smoking as a dependence process.* Washington, DC: Department of Health Education, and Welfare; Public Health Service; Alcohol, Drug Abuse, and Mental Health Administration.

Shimp v. *New Jersey Bell Telephone.* 1976, *NJ Supre 145* 516, 368 A.2d 408.

Smart, R. G. (1982). The impact of prevention measures: An examination of research findings. *Legislative approaches to prevention of alcohol-related problems: An inter-American workshop* (pub. no. (IOM) 82-003). Washington, DC: National Academy Press.

Smith, C. J., and Hanham, R. Q. (1982). *Alcohol abuse: Geographical perspectives.* Washington, DC: Association of American Geographers.

Sokol, R. J. (1981). Alcohol and abnormal outcomes of pregnancy. *Canadian Medical Association Journal, 125*, 143–148.

Speer, F. (1968). Tobacco and the non-smoker: A study of subjective symptoms. *Archives of Environmental Health, 16*, 443–446.

Stamler, J. (1979). Population studies. In R. I. Levy, B. M. Rifkind, B. H. Dennis, & N. D. Ernst (Eds.), *Nutrition, lipids, and coronary heart disease: Nutrition in health and disease* (Vol. 1). New York: Raven Press.

Terris, M., Wilson, F., Smith, H., Sprung, E., & Nelson, J. H., Jr. (1967). The relationship of coitus to carcinoma of the cervix. *American Journal of Public Health, 57*, 840–847.

Vena, J. E., Graham, S., Zielezny, M., Swanson, M. K., Barnes, R. E., & Nolan, J. (1985). Lifetime occupational exercise and colon cancer. *American Journal of Epidemiology, 122*, 357–365.

U.S. Congress Office of Technology Assessment. (1982). *Cancer risk: Assessing and reducing the dangers in our society.* Boulder, CO: Westview Press.

Willett, W. C., & MacMahon, B. (1984a). Diet and cancer—an overview (first of two parts). *New England Journal of Medicine, 310*, 633–638.

Willett, W. C., & MacMahon, B. (1984b). Diet and cancer—an overview (second of two parts). *New England Journal of Medicine, 310*, 697–703.

World Health Organization, Regional Office for Europe. (1978). *European series no. 6: Habitual physical activity and health.* Copenhagen: World Health Organization.

Zilversmit, D. B. (1979). Dietary fiber. In R. I. Levy, B. M. Rifkind, B. H. Dennis, & N. D. Ernst (Eds.), *Nutrition, lipids, and coronary heart disease: Nutrition in health and disease* (Vol. 1). New York: Raven Press.

WORKER HEALTH

Marian Marbury
Minnesota Department of Health, Minneapolis

A clerical worker leaves the office every day with a headache, feeling tired and washed out. A nurse working in an operating room has a miscarriage and remembers that several of her coworkers have had similar problems. A dry cleaner often leaves work light-headed and dizzy from smelling the solvents in the shop, and one day has a car accident on the way home. An unusually large number of young employees at a chemical plant develop lung cancer. Production workers involved in the manufacture of DBCP, a pesticide, are found to be sterile.

Hearing about workplace disasters in which hundreds are killed or hurt is not uncommon. But these kinds of occurrences, important as they are and newsworthy as they are made to be, are only the tip of the occupational disease and injury iceberg. Concentrating solely on disasters obscures the fact that health can be affected by workplace conditions or exposures in many more subtle ways. Occupational health is not just the concern of the blue-collar or industrial worker; it is an issue for everyone.

Formally, occupational health and safety is that field of public health concerned with the recognition and prevention of work-related disease and injury. In principle, all work-related health problems are preventable. In reality, an estimated 20 million injuries and 390,000 new cases of disease each year are recognized as primarily work related (Levy & Wegman, 1982). These figures do not begin to reflect all the health problems that are never reported or connected to the workplace. Why so much preventable ill health occurs and what can be done about it are the questions that form the focus of this chapter. Throughout, an attempt is made to balance factual information necessary for understanding the field with discussion of the most important controversies within it. Some of the most difficult issues are noted as questions. We recommend that you try to answer them before and after you read this and other chapters in this book.

AN OVERVIEW OF THE ISSUES

Since occupational health is concerned with the recognition and prevention of disease, an important initial consideration is the definition of disease. Most people would agree that conditions with clear underlying pathology (changes in structure and/or function of the affected organ) are diseases. But how should symptoms such as headaches or fatigue or physiological changes with no apparent serious pathological significance be regarded? Are these best viewed as inevitable problems of everyday life or as problems that can and should be prevented?

Three methods are available for assessing health effects in populations of physical or chemical exposures: *in vitro* (test-tube) methods, animal tests, and studies of human populations. Each method has strengths and limitations. What kinds of evidence of adverse health effects should be required before steps are taken to limit human exposure? Should the evidence have to meet rigorous standards of scientific ''proof''? Should a substance be considered safe until proven harmful, or harmful until proven safe?

Another issue is the diagnosis of disease in individuals. Many large companies employ full-time occupational physicians or nurses, while smaller companies may have no program at all. An increasing number of independent clinics, not affiliated with any particular company, are springing up to fill in the gap for small companies or to provide workers with alternative care that is perceived as being less subject to corporate influence. What can be done to ensure that work-related disease is properly diagnosed and treated in everyone?

Prevention of disease can be achieved by both technical/medical approaches and political approaches. Technical/medical approaches involve removing a hazard or protecting the worker from it in some other ways, such as by the use of respirators and other protective equipment or by installing engineering controls. Political approaches define the authority and responsibility of individuals and institutions (employers, workers, labor unions, governmental agencies, etc.) to employ technical/medical approaches. Such definition is commonly achieved through legislative and regulatory actions by the state or federal government but may also occur through labor-management negotiation.

In terms of technical/medical approaches, how should illness and injury be prevented? Should the source of the problem be identified and modified? Alternatively, should workers less likely to be bothered by the hazard be selected to perform that work? In other words, should the goal be to fit the worker to the job or the job to the worker? What is the role of worker education in illness/injury prevention?

The major political initiative in occupational disease and injury prevention in the past 15 years has been the Occupational Safety and Health Act (OSHA) of 1970. How effective has this act been in meeting its goals? What roles have state governments and organized labor played? Does or should the current worker's compensation system play a role in prevention, or should compensation be divorced from prevention?

Finally, the likely future directions of the field will be examined. Our economy is currently undergoing a structural transformation, with more jobs in the service sector and fewer in manufacturing. What impact will this have on the types of occupational health problems that workers experience? What types of research and services will professionals in the field need to provide?

THE NATURE OF WORKPLACE HAZARDS

Before examining specific issues, some basic concepts and terminology must be introduced. The term *health hazard* is commonly used to indicate workplace conditions or exposures that result in disease, usually over a long period of time. *Safety hazards* involve exposures or conditions that can cause acute traumatic injury. This distinction is not absolute: A substance can be both a health and a safety hazard. For example, at high levels solvents can cause explosions; at low levels they can cause central nervous system damage. Sometimes it is difficult to determine the appropriate classification. A worker may perform the same bending and lifting motion every day. One day that motion results in an acute back strain, keeping her out of work for 6 weeks. Was that an accident, a sudden traumatic injury, or the gradual accumulation of repeated minor injuries to the back that finally became apparent?

Despite such ambiguous cases, however, this distinction between health and safety hazards has generally proved useful. Traditionally, safety hazards have received more attention than health hazards for several reasons. Usually the cause of an accident is more readily apparent than the cause of an illness because the time between cause and effect is so much shorter. Illnesses may not show up until 20 to 40 years after the exposure, and at that time the cause is hard to determine. Work-related illnesses may also be indistinguishable from chronic illnesses with other causes, such as emphysema, or even be confused with common results of the normal aging process such as loss of memory and mental ability. For these reasons, the cost of injuries is also more readily apparent: Injured workers lose work, accidents may damage property, and the company may have to pay the worker compensation.

Another useful way to classify hazards is by their nature rather than their effect on workers. The most widely used classification scheme divides hazards into physical, biological, chemical, and ergonomic categories. Physical hazards include agents that are without substance but are capable of affecting biological mechanisms, such as ionizing and nonionizing radiation, noise, vibration, electromagnetic fields, and atmospheric variations, including extremes of heat and cold. Noise is one of the most widespread occupational health problems, occurring in workplaces as diverse as manufacturing plants and offices. Ionizing radiation is also a common hazard in many settings, although the fact that its health effects have been studied since it was first used has led to the development and implementation of effective programs for reducing worker exposures.

Biological hazards are living agents capable of causing toxic or allergic reactions. Exposure to biological hazards is a common problem for health care personnel who come into direct contact with infected patients or with body material such as urine and blood. Exposure to such hazards can also occur in other ways: through work involving contact with animals or animal products (e.g., meat packers and poultry workers) or with plants (farmers and foresters). Travelers to foreign countries may also be exposed to biological agents. And it is common knowledge among school teachers that new teachers frequently get an excessive number of colds and other infections during their first few years of teaching.

Chemical hazards include not only liquid and solid chemicals, but also dusts, vapors, gases, and fumes. Many people automatically think of toxic chemicals when they think about workplace hazards, since this category has probably received more attention and study than any other because of their obvious potential to cause harm. The concepts of hazard and toxicity in regard to chemicals are important to distinguish. A substance's toxicity refers to its inherent ability to cause damage. The toxicity of two chemicals can be compared by determining the relative amounts necessary to cause biologic damage. For example, it clearly requires more ethanol to poison a person than it does cyanide. Cyanide is much more toxic. A substance's hazard depends both on its toxicity and on the circumstances of intended or actual use. Alcohol is a greater hazard than cyanide in today's society, since its use is much more widespread and not uncommonly results in accidents and disease (see Chapter 2). A chemical can thus be quite toxic without being greatly hazardous, providing it is used with proper precautions.

Little attention has been paid to ergonomic hazards until recently. Ergonomics, also called human factors engineering, is a science concerned with the design of facilities, equipment, tools, and tasks that are compatible with the physiological, perceptual, biomechanical, and behavioral characteristics of human beings. Ergonomic hazards occur wherever there is a lack of fit between an aspect of the job and a characteristic of the worker. Many accidents blamed on worker carelessness are actually the result of poor job design. For example, a worker may slip on a wet floor because his shoes or the floor are not slip-resistant. Depending on the exact nature of the hazard, the result may range from something as dramatic as an accidental death to something as subtle as headaches or muscle fatigue. Many office workers are unnecessarily tired at the end of the day because they have been sitting in chairs that do not provide adequate support for their backs, are not adjustable for their height, and provide insufficient padding on the seat. Taking human characteristics into account when designing tools and tasks not only improves workers' safety and health, but often increases efficiency as well.

A HISTORICAL OVERVIEW OF OCCUPATIONAL SAFETY AND HEALTH

Although European writings on occupational safety and health date back to the sixteenth century, concern with these issues in the United States really began with the Industrial Revolution of the 1800s. Rapid industrialization brought with it increasingly adverse workplace conditions, with workers forced to toil long hours in dirty and often dangerous conditions. A growing number of labor protests and progressive social reformers brought these conditions to the public attention, and in the last half of the nineteenth century states began to pass legislation to address some of these issues. Massachusetts created the first Department of Factory Inspection in 1867 and the first legislation to mandate certain safety precautions, such as machine guards, in 1877. Other states followed suit, and subsequently legislation restricting child labor and shortening the workweek was also passed.

While initial attention was focused on workplace safety, the early twentieth century saw some interest in workplace health. Dr. Alice Hamilton, widely regarded as one of the pioneers of American occupational medicine, began her studies of lead-induced disease in 1908. By 1912 the U.S. Public Health Service (which had started in 1798 to provide medical care for American seamen and been gradually transformed into the primary federal health agency) began the first of its many industrial studies. These efforts, however, were still limited, and the importance of occupational disease gained little recognition (Felton, 1976).

Pressure to develop a system for compensating injured workers also began to build at this time (see section on workers' compensation for a full discussion). Simultaneously the "voluntary" safety movement commenced with the formation of the National Safety Council (NSC) in 1913. The movement had the support of most of the major corporations, took place without government compulsion, and virtually excluded unions and workers from all decision-making processes. While the NSC had some success in decreasing the industrial accident rate with its "Safety Pays" campaigns, not all of its effects were beneficial. It advanced the concept of the accident-prone individual and stressed worker carelessness as the major factor in accidents, rather than considering underlying causes such as long working hours and speedups. It also served to keep the focus almost entirely on safety, obscuring the importance of health hazards in the workplace (Berman, 1978).

With the development of workers' compensation systems and corporate safety programs, most people felt that the problems of unsafe working conditions had been dealt with satisfactorily. Surprisingly little public concern was expressed for the next 50 years. The one exception was the period around World War II. In 1936 the federal government passed the Walsh-Healey Public Contracts Act, which required compliance with health and safety standards by any company that received over $10,000 in federal contracts. Although this act marked the first effort by the federal government to regulate unsafe working conditions, it was never adequately enforced and thus never very effective. As World War II approached and the necessity to conserve human resources became paramount, the federal government started to provide funds to state industrial health programs, and the Bureau of Mines, in existence since 1910, was authorized to inspect mines and enforce regulations.

In the late 1960s, a number of factors coalesced to bring workplace health and safety to national attention once again. The environmental movement increased awareness of industrial pollution not only of the environment but also of the workplace. The industrial accident rate increased 29% from 1961 to 1970, a fact that attracted the attention of the public and organized labor. In this context, the final straw was the Farmington mine disaster in 1968. All through the 1960s miners had actively struggled for safer working conditions and better disability benefits. They finally gained national sympathy and support when millions of people watched on television the aftermath of the mine explosion that killed 78 people. In 1969 the Coal Mine Health and Safety Act was passed, followed a year later by the Occupational Safety and Health Act. The latter has proven to be a major landmark in the history of workplace health in the United States. While the legislation has not proven to be as effective as was once hoped, it has served to put the issue on the permanent agenda of worker, businesses, and public health professionals, as well as increased public awareness about the nature of the problems. There is still a long way to go, but the period of silence and inactivity is over.

RECOGNIZING DISEASE IN POPULATIONS

What Is Disease?

Although everyone has a general idea of what disease is, agreeing on a functional definition is difficult. On the one hand the World Health Organization (WHO, 1948) says, "Health is a state of complete physical, mental, and social well-being and not merely the absence of disease or infirmity." On the other hand, there is the definition of disease as obvious impairment, deformity, or death. Somewhere in between is an ambiguous area, in which the WHO criteria are not met and yet no observable pathological changes have taken place. Should we consider healthy the worker who goes home every day feeling fatigued and irritable, with little interest in or energy for family or social activities? Is this condition simply part of living in the modern world that must be accepted and adapted to? Or is it indicative of a problem in the workplace that should be investigated and corrected? If our society is interested in preventing workplace disease, a consensus about what we are trying to prevent is necessary to guide our actions.

A good example of the difficulty in defining occupational ill health is the controversy over the appropriate regulation of lead. In 1978 the federal government proposed a standard regulating the allowable amount of lead measurable in the blood serum (the blood lead level). While humans do not normally have any lead in their blood, it is not uncommon to find levels of 10–20 micrograms (μg) per deciliter (dl) in the blood of urban dwellers from lead in paints, in motor vehicle fuel, and from industrial pollution. At slightly higher levels, on the order of 20–25 μg/dl, lead inhibits an enzyme necessary in the synthesis of the hemeprotein (which is then incorporated into hemoglobin, the oxygen-carrying molecule in red blood cells). However, the body is still able to manufacture sufficient hemoglobin, and no adverse effects are noticed by the affected individual. Lead levels of 40–

50 μg/dl have been shown to slow nerve conduction velocity, that is, the time it takes for a nerve impulse to travel from one part of the body to another (Seppalainen & Hernberg, 1980). Again the individual is not aware of any symptoms; this effect can only be detected by special diagnostic tests, called electromyograms. In addition, since lead crosses the placental barrier, the fetus of a pregnant woman who has blood lead levels this high might be adversely affected. While fetal effects have never been demonstrated directly, there is evidence that children with levels of 30–35 μg/dl suffer damage to their nervous system, resulting in impaired intellectual functioning (Rom, 1980).

Blood lead levels of 60 μg/dl have been reported to produce symptoms such as fatigue, irritability, and difficulty in concentrating. Psychological tests show a decrease in memory and perceptual speed (Haenninen, Hernberg, Mantere, Vesanto, & Jalkanen, 1978). Often the symptoms are vague and may go unheeded by the worker and others. At blood lead levels of 80 μg/dl, more classic symptoms of lead poisoning begin to appear: loss of appetite, anemia, depression, stomach pain, constipation, muscle weakness, delayed reaction time, and so forth. At very high levels coma, convulsions, and death can occur.

What has been outlined above is not universally accepted by all scientists who have studied the health effects of lead. Furthermore, it should be noted these are the average blood lead levels at which specific symptoms begin to appear. Some workers will develop them at lower levels and some at higher levels. The higher the population average, the more common these symptoms will be in a population.

When the federal government proposed to set a maximum allowable level for blood lead, controversy arose over several related issues. Most people agreed that the allowable level should certainly not be above 80 μg/dl and that levels at which enzyme inhibition could be prevented were not feasible to achieve. But there was disagreement over the exact blood lead levels that cause specific psychological and physical effects, and whether effects such as enzyme inhibition constitute adverse health effects. Debate particularly focused on the significance of decreased nerve conduction velocity. On the one hand, some argued that it did not impair the worker and had not been shown to have any long-term consequences. On the other hand, some scientists felt that it clearly indicated a toxic effect on the nervous system, one of the most essential and sensitive body systems, and therefore should not be ignored.

In summary, while no one argued about the importance of preventing obvious lead poisoning, there was sharp disagreement over the necessity of preventing effects whose long-term health significance was unclear. The final standard was set at 40 μg/dl, to be achieved over several years of declining levels. The future of the standard is still unclear.

Methods for Assessing the Health Effects of Exposures

Toxicology and epidemiology are the two disciplines involved in determining the health effects of exposures. *Toxicology*, often called the science of poisons, is the study of the harmful effects of chemicals on biological (usually nonhuman) systems. *Epidemiology* is the study of the distribution of disease, its causes, and its risk factors in human populations. (See Chapter 1 for an overview of related methodology.) Some examples of recent studies will serve to illustrate the epidemiological approach, as well as its strengths and limitations.

In the 1960s, epidemiologists from the University of Pittsburgh studied the causes of death among 59,000 members of the United Steelworkers of America (Lloyd, Lundin, & Redmond, 1970). They used a study design called a retrospective cohort mortality study: "retrospective" because they were examining deaths that had already occurred and "cohort" because the study group was composed of a fixed population of exposed people. The cohort in this case consisted of everyone who was a member of the steelworkers' union in 1953. The work histories of each person were determined from work records. Death certificates were then collected for everyone who had died between 1953 and 1961, and the specific cause of death was recorded. Mortality rates for each cause were then computed and compared to the United States national mortality rates during the same period, taking into account differences in the age structures of the two populations. The United States rates served as a comparison group, to provide an estimate of what the mortality rate should have been in the steelworkers if they were not being exposed to any health hazard.

The first analysis showed that, as a group, the steelworkers were actually healthier than the general population and their overall mortality rate was lower. There was, however, a twofold increase in the lung cancer rate among men who worked in the coke plant, as compared to all other steelworkers, and this increase occurred largely among the black workers, whose lung cancer rate was three times higher than that of their white colleagues (Lloyd *et al.*, 1970). Further analysis of job histories then showed that the increase was almost all among members who worked around the coke ovens. In particular there was a fivefold increase among those who worked on the top of the ovens. The final picture that emerged was that workers who worked on top of the ovens for more than 5 years had a tenfold increase in lung cancer and that almost everyone who did this work was black (not coincidentally, it was widely regarded as one of the dirtiest jobs). Analysis of the fumes to which the workers were exposed showed that coal tar pitch volatiles contain benzoapyrene, a known carcinogen, along with a number of other known or suspected carcinogens (Lloyd, 1971).

One objection to the study that was raised was that researchers had not collected information on smoking, and it was suggested that perhaps workers on the coke ovens had higher lung cancer rates because they smoked more than other steelworkers. While it was later demonstrated that smoking alone could not account for a lung cancer rate that was increased tenfold, this objection exemplifies an issue of crucial concern in all epidemiologic studies. When an exposed population is compared to a nonexposed population and the former is found to have more disease than the latter, the assumption is usually made that the exposure is causing the increase. There is always the possibility, however, that there is another factor or exposure that can also cause the disease and that is more common among the exposed group than the comparison group. This problem is called *confounding*, and the extraneous exposure is called a *confounding factor*. A simple example is a comparison of overall mortality rates between Florida and Maryland. If nothing else were known about either state, the conclusion would be reached that Florida is an unhealthier place to live because its mortality rate is higher. The real cause, of course, is the fact that more elderly and retired people move to Florida and die there. Age is the confounding factor. If the presence of a confounding factor is known, it can be controlled, that is, its misleading effects can be adjusted statistically. This is the reason that mortality rates are age adjusted (controlled for age): to permit comparison between two populations whose age structures are different. In short, in every epidemiological study there is a possibility that an unknown confounding factor (or factors) is causing the differences between the two groups in the study.

Another cohort study, conducted among rubberworkers in the 1970s, found an excess of cases of leukemia, although they were not confined to people with one particular type of job (McMichael, Spirtas, & Kupper, 1975). The researchers then switched to a *case control* study design, in which they compared past workplace exposures of rubberworkers who had developed leukemia with a control group of rubberworkers who were selected from the rest of the cohort. The advantage of this study design was that the researchers could thoroughly investigate the past exposures of everyone in the smaller study, a task that would have been impossible to complete for the entire cohort. This study showed that workers with leukemia were more apt to have been exposed to solvents such as benzene than those without leukemia, leading to the strong suspicion that leukemia and benzene are causally related.

The health outcomes that epidemiologists investigate do not have to be cancer or other fatal diseases, and the exposures that are studied can be in any category of hazards. For example, a study of women who work as stitchers in a garment shop is currently underway. The researchers are investigating whether stitchers have a higher prevalence of musculoskeletal complaints than other workers of the same age and sex, and, if so, whether they are related to the repetitive motions (an ergonomic hazard) that the stitchers must perform in their work (Punnett, personal communication, 1984). Another ongoing study examines the question of whether workers exposed to solvents such as paint thinners are more apt to have neuropsychiatric problems than other workers (Baker, 1984).

Epidemiological studies are necessary to detect patterns of illness that are not obvious. In 1974 a physician in Kentucky noted that one of his patients had angiosarcoma of the liver, an extremely rare type of cancer (Creech & Johnson, 1974). This was the third such patient with this rare cancer that he had seen in the last 6 years, all of whom had worked at a plant where vinyl chloride was used. From this he surmised that vinyl chloride might have caused the cancer. This clinical deduction was possible because the cancer was so rare that just three cases constituted an epidemic, and because he observed that all shared a common and unusual exposure. Further epidemiological studies showed that lung and brain cancer were also associated with the manufacture of vinyl chloride in this and other plants. The physician had not detected this association because these two types of cancer, particularly lung cancer, are much more common and are also known to be caused by other common exposures.

But if epidemiological study is negative, that is, if it fails to demonstrate a disease-exposure relationship, does it prove that the exposure is not harmful to health? Unfortunately, it does not. Such studies may be negative because the exposure is not harmful or because the sample studied was not large enough, the study design was poor, the exposure and/or the health effect was not measured accurately, or the health effect has a long latency period, that is, a long period of time between exposure and appearance of the effect. Consequently, negative studies, unless they are large and very well done, can be given little weight. Positive studies, because of the possibility of confounding and other sources of error, should also not be considered definitive proof that an exposure causes an effect, but they should raise serious concern. This is especially true when several different studies show similar results.

Epidemiological studies are an important way to properly evaluate certain hazards, particularly ergonomic ones, and certain health effects, especially effects involving nonfatal illness or symptoms and declines in physiological function. They are not the best way, however, to evaluate exposures that cause serious illness or death, since they can only be done after a sufficient number of people have developed the disease. Asbestos was not found to be a carcinogen until 40 years after widespread use had exposed millions of people. It is estimated that a minimum of 1% of all cancers in the next decade will be due to this exposure (Doll & Peto, 1981).

Since there is almost always some scientific uncertainty about whether a specific exposure causes a specific health effect, people with different interests and perspectives often disagree on the credibility or the strength of the evidence, and the issue becomes political. From a public health perspective, the major priority must be the prevention of disease. If there is uncertainty about the effect of an exposure, it is better to err on the side of conservatism and limit exposure to several substances that might be harmless than to permit widespread exposure to one that causes serious disease. If in vitro and animal tests indicate that an agent is carcinogenic, then exposure to it should be minimized without awaiting the results of epidemiological studies. From a short-run economic perspective, this approach appears unnecessarily costly. While limiting proven causes of significant disease is important, decreasing or eliminating exposure is expensive, deprives society of the usefulness of the substance, and thus should be delayed until the evidence is conclusive. These competing perspectives on the meaning and implementation of research findings have often resulted in intense debates that will undoubtedly continue in a variety of public arenas.

Another issue affected by political as well as scientific considerations is the acceptance of disease as being occupational in origin. The history of coal workers' pneumoconiosis, commonly called black lung, provides a good example. For many years scientists and physicians have recognized that chest X rays of coal miners show certain characteristic changes due to dust accumulation after a number of years of work. It is also clear that some miners develop a very disabling lung disease called progressive massive fibrosis, resulting in clear loss of lung function and specific changes on the chest X ray. Considerable disagreement has centered on people in the first category, with characteristic chest X rays but without massive fibrosis, who are said to have simple pneumoconiosis. Some studies have shown that people with the simple form also have some loss of lung function, but other researchers have argued that this is due to cigarette smoking and that the simple changes on the chest X rays by themselves do not indicate disease. Until the 1970s, U.S. coal miners had great trouble getting workers' compensation for simple pneumoconiosis, regardless of how long they had worked in the mines or how symptomatic they were. Finally in 1977 a group of retired disabled miners formed the Black Lung Association and conducted an intensive and successful lobbying effort for passage of a federal act mandating benefits for any coal miner who met certain employment history and medical criteria. In contrast, the United Kingdom had been recognizing and compensating black lung since the 1950s. It is probably no coincidence that the miners there were represented by an extremely strong and politically active union. The major point here, however, is that the recognition of black lung as a real (and compensable) disease occurred for political as much as for scientific reasons.

In summary, the most crucial issue, which is at the basis of much political controversy in this and other public health fields, is whether measures should be taken in the face of scientific uncertainty. Should action be delayed until the uncertainty is resolved? Or is it more appropriate to act conservatively and ensure that the public's health is protected?

RECOGNIZING DISEASE IN INDIVIDUALS

The field of occupational health, while it primarily has a public health orientation, also has a clinical medicine component. Occupational health nurses and physicians, although concerned with recognition and prevention of disease in populations, usually spend a large proportion of their time diagnosing disease in individuals. Obviously the line between the two is ambiguous: Recognizing that an individual is sick may lead to a more careful investigation of the workplace that results in measures being taken to prevent illness in other workers. The focus though is on the individual, and the activities undertaken in this pursuit are thus substantially different from those discussed previously.

Occupational Health Programs in the Workplace

Occupational health programs vary in size and complexity, from units staffed by a single nurse to large departments that involve physicians, nurses, industrial hygienists, safety inspectors, toxicologists, and epidemiologists. The size and scope of a program are determined by a multitude of factors, including the size of the workplace, the nature of the workplace hazards, relevant regulatory requirements, and employer and employee attitudes. The major auto manufacturers all have fairly extensive programs, a reflection of the number and diversity of hazards encountered in their many workplaces, the number of government regulations affecting them (the size of their programs has increased substantially since the federal government started issuing regulations in the 1970s) and, arguably, a large active union. The vast majority of small workplaces, where the hazards are often as great or greater, have no formal program and often rely on a neighborhood general practitioner or surgeon to handle their emergencies.

While the more advanced programs are involved in recognition and prevention of disease in populations (this will be discussed in detail later and in Chapter 10), the most basic function of them all is the diagnosis and treatment of the individual worker. The effectiveness and scope of a program in this endeavor can vary greatly depending on the training and motivation of the health professionals, their proximity to and knowledge of the workplace, and the discretion given them by management. Correct diagnosis often depends not only on clinical skills, but in being knowledgeable about workplace exposures and conditions, so that correlations between exposures and diseases can be drawn. A physician with no training in occupational medicine who comes to the workplace twice a week to see patients is unlikely to understand the conditions of a particular patient's job. A nurse who is supposed to stay at his clinic in case of emergency will see only the workers who choose to come and be largely unaware of the general health of the work force.

Ethical questions have been raised about possible conflicts of interest when a health professional treating an employee is also employed by the same company as her patient. The major question is whether a division of loyalty occurs, since the interests of the patient and the company may be quite different. For example, back pain is very common in the workplace. In the majority of cases there is no objectively measurable evidence of damage, only the patient's report of pain. On the one hand, management's interest is in having the person return to work whenever possible and avoid a compensation claim. On the other hand, it is usually in the patient's interest to be sent home. No matter what the professional does, someone is bound to be dissatisfied.

Unfortunately this is a relatively minor example of the conflicts that can occur. Physicians have been known not to report test results or chest X ray changes to patients, to reassure their patients that they are in good health when in fact evidence to the contrary exists, or to change their professional opinions when it was advantageous to the company to do so. While such flagrantly unethical conduct is not common today, in many workplaces there is a bitter legacy of mistrust between workers and "company doctors" or their equivalents.

Occupational Health Clinics

A number of occupational health clinics have sprung up in the past few years. These clinics may be attached to a hospital or neighborhood health center or be completely independent. They are usually staffed by at least one physician with training in occupational medicine, and may also have industrial hygienists and/or lawyers as staff members or consultants.

Clinics may come from one of two origins, which determines the functions they perform. Some have been established expressly to meet the needs of small businesses that lack their own programs. Functions of these larger clinics may include offering health and safety evaluation of the workplace and medical screening mandated by the government, as well as providing preemployment physicals and routine and emergency care. In some areas several smaller workplaces have joined together in setting up such clinics.

Other clinics act primarily as referral centers. Commonly, their patients are most often referred by general practitioners who suspect that their patient's problem is work-related, lawyers who want their clients evaluated for disability or compensation, or by labor unions or patients themselves who want an independent medical opinion on the work-relatedness of their disease. Sometimes these clinics will also employ lawyers who counsel patients about their legal options, or industrial hygienists who may contact the management of a plant (with the patient's permission) and attempt to determine if there is a correctable problem that caused the illness. There are also clinics that serve both functions, as consultants or providers of health care for management and as independent practitioners for workers.

General Practitioners

In the past, medical schools have taught little or nothing about occupational health, and many physicians still know little or nothing about their patient's occupation. Occupation has been regarded more as an indicator of socioeconomic status than a piece of information that might have direct bearing on their patients' health status. Consequently, occupational diseases are frequently overlooked or misdiagnosed, or their work-relatedness is not ascertained. Although this has begun to change with increasing awareness of the relation between work and health, a great need still exists for more public and professional education.

TECHNICAL AND MEDICAL APPROACHES TO DISEASE AND INJURY PREVENTION

Industrial Hygiene

Industrial hygiene is concerned with the identification, evaluation, and control of physical, chemical, and biological hazards in the workplace. Traditionally industrial hygienists have been employed by large industries, where they have often been placed in organizational units, such as engineering, that are separate from the medical department. More recently there has been a trend toward integrated occupational health programs, as described previously.

Identification of potential hazards depends on a thorough familiarity with the industrial processes being evaluated. Some hazards, such as excessive noise or heat or improper ventilation of fumes, can be identified through simple inspection. Others require a knowledge of what materials are being used and what byproducts are generated as a result of the process. An industrial hygienist must know the particular substance she is sampling. She can evaluate the levels of exposures she knows or suspects are present, but she cannot walk into a workplace and determine what exposures are present without prior knowledge of the materials or processes.

Evaluation of the potential hazard is then required to determine if, in fact, an actual hazard is present. Knowing that a particular chemical is being used in a workplace is not sufficient: It may be used in a completely enclosed process or in some other way such that workers are never exposed to it. The particular method used for evaluation depends on the type of hazard. Air sampling is used to evaluate the concentration of dusts, gases, and vapors. Noise dosimeters are used to measure noise levels. Radiation badges measure the amount of radiation an individual is exposed to.

Once the concentrations of each potential hazard have been determined, the industrial hygienist compares these to legal or recommended standards or recommendations from the scientific literature. The American Conference of Governmental Industrial Hygienists (ACGIH) has developed and periodically updates recommended safe exposure levels, called Threshold Limit Values (TLVs), for 400 chemicals. The federal government adopted these in 1971 as mandatory legal standards. Since the government standards have not been updated since then, some of the TLVs now recommended by the ACGIH are more stringent than the mandatory ones. But the TLVs can only be considered to be guidelines as to what levels are safe: They have largely been based on evidence of acute effects rather than more recent evidence of mutagenicity or carcinogenicity. In some cases they are based only on animal tests of acute effects. Additionally, some workers have adverse reactions to exposures at lower levels than others. Therefore, if health effects are present, a hazard may exist even if all exposures are below recommended or legal limits.

After the nature and extent of the hazard has been evaluated, the decision must be made regarding methods to control it. Control efforts may be directed toward controlling the hazard at its source, in the path from the source to the worker, or toward the worker who is exposed to the hazard. Generally, controlling the hazard at its source is the most effective approach. This can take several forms depending on the particular hazard. Substitution of a less hazardous material or process may be made. For example, asbestos was a fiber widely used in insulation until recently. When it was discovered to cause various kinds of cancer as well as lung disease, it was replaced by fiberglass. Spray painting of objects has been largely replaced by dipping them into paint to reduce the amount released into the air. Occasionally a toxic substance has been replaced by another substance that later also proved to be toxic, pointing out the need for adequate testing before use.

Another method for controlling a problem at the source is either to enclose or to isolate the process. A noisy process can be placed in an isolated part of the plant, only performed at a time when few workers are present, or enclosed with noise-insulating material. Sometimes automating or mechanizing the process is helpful, such as using mechanical lifting devices for heavy loads. Finally, most equipment and machinery run more efficiently and cleanly when regularly serviced and repaired.

The major method for controlling a hazard in its path is ventilation. General room ventilation prevents the buildup of emissions in the workplace, and may be adequate if the emissions are of low toxicity. If they are toxic, however, this approach may simply dilute and disseminate the exposures throughout the workplace, exposing more people. In this case a local exhaust ventilation system that captures emissions right at their source, before they escape into the atmosphere, is necessary.

Finally, control efforts may be directed toward the worker. These may take the form of administrative directives, such as controlling the number of hours worked in a hazardous location, or personal protective equipment, such as protective clothing, safety glasses, hearing protection, and respirators. This latter approach, particularly in regards to hearing protection and respirators, has been a major source of controversy. Most public health professionals agree that relying on personal protection to protect health is insufficient. Workers often do not wear the equipment provided because it is uncomfortable, may increase hearing or breathing difficulties, and interferes with communication. In addition, to provide adequate protection, it must fit properly and be maintained regularly; even then the degree of protection provided is quite variable. The cost of an adequate respirator program may be substantially underestimated if the costs of adequate maintenance are not taken into account. And, finally, they do not get rid of the problem and thus, at best, are only an interim solution. Others have countered that such equipment can provide adequate protection, is often the only technologically feasible method of control, or is much cheaper than providing engineering controls (e.g., substitution, enclosure, ventilation). When federal standards regulating hazards have been issued, one of the recurring debates has been whether the federal government should mandate engineering controls or allow companies to employ any method they choose in meeting the standard, including the use of personal protection. This debate will continue.

Administrative controls usually involve scheduling work so that an individual's exposure to a hazard is limited. For example, since continuous work on a video display terminal often results in stress and fatigue, one reasonable solution is to limit the number of hours an individual works on a terminal. This is not a useful approach in a situation involving exposure to a mutagen or a carcinogen, which theoretically has no safe exposure levels, since it will simply result in a larger number of people being exposed.

Control of hazards is more difficult when the hazards are already present in the workplace. Many opportunities for prevention are missed due to lack of proper consultation between industrial hygienists and the engineers who design the equipment and processes. Engineers usually have had no training in health and safety and thus may pick a solvent based on its manufacturing specifications rather than its health effects. Designing equipment with health and safety in mind is always cheaper and more effective than having to retrofit it or modify the process after the problems become apparent.

As the name implies, industrial hygiene has largely been practiced in industry. However, the methods of evaluation and principles of control are equally applicable in nonindustrial workplaces. For example, offices are often relatively noisy environments. This exposure to noise can be greatly alleviated by the installation of noise absorbing partitions and acoustical tile, proper maintenance of office machinery, and use of quiet typewriters.

Ergonomics and Safety

Normally, workplace safety personnel have had little or no formal training in safety. Furthermore, in most workplaces the major safety activities have been accident investigations and other after-the-fact inspections to uncover major, obvious hazards. In general, there has been little scientific basis to these activities and little attempt to go beyond dealing with the symptoms of underlying problems.

These deficiencies have decreased in the last few years as more safety professionals have been educated. Concommitantly there has been a growing understanding and awareness of ergonomic principles and practices. Safety and ergonomics, although not synonymous, are closely related. While accidents are often blamed on worker carelessness or performance of an unsafe act, frequently the underlying cause is poor ergonomic design. For example, a machine guard may be installed to prevent a worker from accidentally getting her hands or fingers caught in the machine. If the guard has been installed in such a way as to slow down production, or make the task harder for the worker, she may well devise a method for circumventing the guard, such as removing it! If an accident then occurs, the worker will be blamed for committing the unsafe act of removing the guard. The underlying problem, however, was poor design of the guard, and if not corrected, additional accidents may occur.

Poor ergonomic design may also result in cumulative trauma. In contrast to accidents, cumulative trauma is not caused by a specific event but rather is the result of repeated minor insults to the body. Back problems, tendonitis, carpal tunnel syndrome (median nerve entrapment caused by swelling of the carpal tunnel, a structure in the wrist), and degenerative joint disease are all the results of cumulative trauma. For example, certain repetitive motions involving forceful hand exertion, especially with a bent wrist, can result in carpal tunnel syndrome. Often redesigning a hand tool so that the worker can use it without bending the wrist will alleviate the problem.

Paying attention to ergonomic principles can often result not only in making jobs safer and healthier, but also in improved efficiency and production. When video display terminals were first introduced, people who worked on them complained of visual disturbances, neck and back pain, and headaches. Experimentation and application of knowledge about illumination and biomechanical requirements resulted in redesigning the screen to reduce glare, limiting background light and adding adjustable spot lighting, creating an adjustable work station so that desk and chair heights can be altered, and making the keyboard detachable. In short, increasing the ability of the individual to adjust the workspace to his own physical capabilities can greatly alleviate the symptoms and thus increase efficiency.

The increasing number of women in blue-collar jobs has served to focus attention on tool and equipment design. Since the average woman is smaller than the average man, equipment is often too large for women. But in fact, equipment that does not fit is not just a woman's problem; equipment designed for the average man will not fit many workers of both sexes. This realization, prompted by the more obvious discrepancy with women, has led to the design of equipment to fit a wider variety of body sizes and shapes.

Occupational Health Programs in the Workplace

As mentioned previously, the most common activity of a workplace occupational health program is the diagnosis and treatment of disease or injury in the individual worker. Larger, more comprehensive programs aim to prevent or to detect early disease (often called secondary prevention) in individuals and the entire workforce. This may take several forms.

Most programs perform some type of preplacement medical evaluation. Its sophistication may vary considerably. The basic purpose of this evaluation is to determine if the worker can perform a specific job without undue risk of injury to herself or others. To evaluate this adequately the medical department should have a clearly written job description, detailing the physical requirements. Even then, of course, judging fitness is a somewhat subjective task. If a worker can perform a job safely but not with maximum efficiency, is he still fit for the job? At times there may be a tension between the wish to employ people in adequate jobs and the desire to maximize production.

A related issue is that of exclusionary policies. Some companies have instituted policies stating that women of childbearing age cannot work in certain areas where they might be exposed to an agent capable of causing damage to a fetus. Often the jobs women have been barred or removed from are among those with higher pay. Many businesses with this type of policy argue that it is the only sure preventive approach. At the same time they are concerned that they could be sued if a child were born with birth defects. Others, including labor unions, women's groups, and many health professionals, state that such policies are discriminatory, deny women equal employment opportunity, ignore the fact that the reproductive ability of men can also be harmed, and divert attention from the necessity to clean up the workplace so that it is safe for everyone. This undoubtedly will be an issue of continuing importance.

Surveillance, defined as the systematic collection, analysis, and dissemination of disease data on populations, is another important preventive function of workplace programs. Medical data may come from preplacement or annual physical exams, collection of information on injury and illness, screening programs aimed at detecting particular diseases in the population, and death benefit data. These data should then be integrated with industrial hygiene and safety data. Analysis of these data may indicate whether or not existing control efforts are adequate or may result in the recognition of previously undetected problems. For example, federal standards mandate that blood lead levels must be periodically determined for anyone exposed to lead. Simply looking at a listing of surveillance results will only be useful in identifying the individuals with high lead levels for their medical removal. In order to find the source of the high lead exposure, analysis of the results in relation to industrial hygiene data and other relevant variables, such as length of employment and work station of people who have high levels compared to others, may reveal patterns that would provide information for further control efforts.

Education and Training

The concept that people should be trained about the safety aspects of their job has been generally accepted for a long time, at least for industrial workers. Surprisingly, the notion that other people such as hospital or office workers also need this information and that everyone, industrial and nonindustrial workers alike, needs education about both health and safety as well as training, is fairly new. The difference between training and education is the difference between telling people what to do and giving them enough basic information to understand why they need to do it.

How much and what people should know is sometimes a controversial question. Some health and safety professionals believe that workers should not be told a certain agent is carcinogenic in animals because it would upset them "unnecessarily," or that workers do not have the education to understand the intricacies of a particular situation. On the other hand there is increasing recognition that people are more apt to act safely, (e.g., wear respirators or follow safe handling precautions) if they know the risks to them should they not follow instructions. Optimally, education increases workers' awareness and enhances their ability to detect dangerous situations that might otherwise go unnoticed and to make suggestions about hazard reduction.

This controversy can be seen in the current pressure for "right to know" laws. These laws may be federal, state, or municipal and vary in detail, but their essential thrust is that workers have a right to know the names and health effects of the chemicals they work with, and that such materials should be clearly labeled. Some laws also require that the communities in which workplaces are located have access to the same information. Business opposition to these laws has usually centered around two issues: expense and revelation of trade secrets. They argue that the requirements of such a law will result in unnecessary expense, when the same end results could be more economically achieved. They also claim that the law will result in their having to reveal trade secrets that will destroy their competitive edge.

Most laws that have been passed to date have attempted to achieve some kind of compromise, setting up a mechanism for releasing trade secret information in a more limited way. Coalitions of labor, community, and environmental groups have formed to lobby for such legislation, since communities are often concerned with the transportation of chemicals and illegal dumping of toxic wastes.

Education of workers is also increasingly occurring outside the workplace. Courses in occupational health offered by community colleges or labor education centers aimed specifically at workers have become more commonplace. Some labor unions have sponsored conferences on health and safety issues for their memberships, or offered special training courses for safety stewards. Education is also an important function of Coalitions for Occupational Safety and Health (COSH groups) that have sprung up in a number of areas in the country. These groups are usually comprised of labor unions, individual workers, health and safety professionals, and lawyers. In addition to general education, COSH groups offer technical assistance with specific hazards and help workers establish and strengthen health and safety committees.

Employee education and training about certain substances is specifically mandated by federal regulations. Regulations specify the kinds of information that must be presented, such as sources of exposure, adverse effects, engineering controls and work practices, appropriate first aid treatment, and procedures used to monitor controls and the health status of employees. In some larger companies these regulations have stimulated the provision of general safety and health educational programs.

In the long run this increased emphasis on education should be beneficial, resulting in a more informed work force that is capable of playing an active role in health and safety surveillance. In order for this to become a reality, however, more attention needs to be paid to the manner in which these efforts take place. Simply giving people information is not sufficient if the purpose is to enable them to use that information. This is particularly true when the goal also involves some sort of behavioral change. In order to determine the effectiveness of different educational approaches, evaluation must be built in as part of any educational program. Only through a process of trial and evaluation will the optimal ways to inform people become apparent. (See Chapter 10 for other approaches to and case studies of health education.)

POLITICAL APPROACHES TO DISEASE AND INJURY PREVENTION

As was mentioned earlier, the participation of the federal government in occupational safety and health regulation increased dramatically with the passage of the Occupational Safety and Health Act of 1970. The purpose of the act was "to assure so far as possible every working man and woman in the nation safe and healthful working conditions." This act put health and safety on the national agenda in an unprecedented way. It set up two new agencies, defined how legal standards should be set, and gave workers new rights. Its subsequent history has not always lived up to its promise, but it remains a major piece of legislation that has had a marked effect on health and safety in this country.

Occupational Safety and Health Administration

The major new agency mandated by the act was the Occupational Safety and Health Administration, commonly called OSHA, in the Department of Labor. Its most important functions are setting and enforcing safety and health standards. For the first two years following passage of the act, OSHA was empowered to adopt any nationally recognized consensus standards (i.e., standards that had been developed by professional organizations and thus represented general agreement among experts). The threshold limit values developed by the American Conference of Governmental Industrial Hygienists were adopted under this provision.

Since 1972 OSHA has had to go through a formal rule-making procedure to promulgate new standards. Usually, after being petitioned by an outside party or deciding through an internal decision-making process to propose a standard for a new substance or safety practice, OSHA convenes an advisory panel of experts representing management, labor, academia, and the government to provide input. A proposed standard is published in the *Federal Register*, and comments from interested parties are invited. Public hearings, which have often become quite combative, are then held. After taking all testimony into account, OSHA is supposed to issue a final standard within 90 days. It often takes considerably longer. Almost every standard has then been challenged in court by labor or industry, resulting in further delay in implementation. Initial hearings for a standard on noise took place in 1976; the final complete standard had still not been issued in 1984. This process, while designed to invite participation by all affected parties, has proven to be cumbersome and slow in practice. Only 14 new standards were issued in the first 10 years of OSHA's existence.

OSHA also has the authority to set an emergency temporary standard without any hearing if it determines that workers are in imminent danger from exposure to serious hazards. In theory this imposition is to be followed within 6 months by a proposal for a new permanent standard that must go through the formal rule-making procedure. Some emergency standards have later been adopted as permanent standards, while others have been allowed to lapse after 6 months with no further action.

A standard promulgated in this way specifies more than a permissible exposure level (PEL, the equivalent of a TLV). It also details requirements for industrial hygiene monitoring, medical screening of exposed workers, engineering controls, personal protective equipment, and worker education and training. The TLVs initially adopted by OSHA have none of these provisions, and thus it is important to distinguish between standards adopted in the first 2 years and those that have gone through the formal rule-making procedure.

OSHA is also charged with the enforcement of all standards, primarily through inspection of workplaces. Such inspections are supposed by law to be unannounced, although employers can insist that OSHA obtain a court order before entry. Since there are about 5 million workplaces and about 1,700 inspectors, OSHA has developed various policies to target the largest industries and the most hazardous industries for frequent inspections. It is also supposed to respond to any employee complaints that it receives about conditions. OSHA can impose fines of up to $1,000 for each violation and up to $10,000 if the violation is willful or repeated. In practice, actual fines are usually much less.

OSHA does not have authority over all workplaces. Since 1979 it has been prevented from inspecting workplaces with fewer than ten employees. It also does not cover public employees or workplaces covered by other federal agencies (such as coal mines). The act encourages states to set up their own programs. If a state program is approved, it can take over enforcement activities, although it continues to be monitored by the federal OSHA. State OSHAs must also set and enforce standards that are at least as stringent as the federal requirements. Currently about one half of the states have their own programs. Most states, whether or not they have state OSHAs, may also offer on-site consultations to employers. This is a particular benefit to small companies that lack health and safety expertise, since it permits evaluation and correction of hazardous conditions without fear of penalties and fines.

A major limitation of OSHA is that, in both its standard-setting and enforcement activities, it has chosen to concentrate almost solely on the industrial sector. This is in line with the traditional orientation of occupational safety and health activities toward heavy industry, where hazards are more obvious. For example, people who work in hospitals usually do not think of calling in an OSHA inspector when confronted with a safety or health problem, and OSHA does not routinely inspect hospitals. Even if it did, most of the hazards that exist in that type of environment are not covered by the existing standards. Yet hospitals contain more physical (e.g., heat), biologic (infectious patients), chemical (drugs and laboratory chemicals), and ergonomic (heavy lifting) hazards than many other workplaces. It is to be hoped that as the perspective of occupational health professionals broadens to include all types of work and workplaces, a concomitant change will occur in OSHA.

Another major limitation of OSHA is that it is greatly affected by a changing political climate. The assistant secretary of labor for OSHA is appointed by the secretary of labor, himself a political appointee. OSHA's first director, who had no public health background, focused most of his attention on staffing and organizing administrative units but gave little sense of direction or purpose to the agency. The next two directors, both public health scientists, increased the level of scientific expertise within the agency and took a more aggressive attitude toward disease prevention, both through standard setting and enforcement activities. The fourth director, appointed in 1981, has changed the emphasis of the agency to that of encouraging voluntary compliance (the number of inspectors was cut significantly). He has also stressed supposedly cost-effective ways of controlling hazards, which in practice has meant increased reliance on personal protective equipment and less on engineering controls. Many health professionals have been concerned about the impact these changes will have on workplace health and safety.

National Institute of Occupational Safety and Health

The second agency created by the Occupational Safety and Health Act is the National Institute of Occupational Safety and Health, or NIOSH, located in the Department of Health and Human Services. NIOSH's major function is to perform research of several types. One type of project is a health hazard evaluation, conducted at the request of labor and/or management. Its purpose is to investigate the underlying causes of health problems experienced by people in a particular workplace to see if they might be work-related and to make recommendations for control. For example, in the last 5 years there have been an increasing number of reports of large numbers of office workers, particularly those who work in new hermetically sealed office buildings, complaining of nausea, dizziness, and eye irritation. While the specific causes have not been elucidated, the underlying problem seems to be inadequate fresh air ventilation. This has led NIOSH to make recommendations for air circulation in all such office buildings. NIOSH also undertakes industry-wide studies of workers with chronic exposure to materials, processes, and stressors. Additionally, NIOSH conducts testing and certification of personal protective equipment and develops sampling and measurement methods for hazard evaluation.

Another major function of NIOSH is to develop recommended standards for OSHA based on the best scientific data available. These are issued in the format of Criteria Documents, which contain exhaustive, although uncritical, reviews of the literature. The standards recommended by NIOSH are often more stringent than the ones enacted by OSHA, since OSHA is mandated to take questions of economic and technologic feasibility into account.

Finally, NIOSH is also directly and indirectly involved in the training of occupational safety and health professionals, including physicians, nurses, industrial hygienists, epidemiologists, safety specialists, and others. Directly, the agency sponsors relevant training courses (such as certification courses in pulmonary function testing) and educational seminars and symposia. Indirectly, it funds regional Educational Resource Centers (ERC) which provide graduate and community education in health and safety. ERCs have trained a large number of new professionals in the past 8 years.

State Governments

Most states have some sort of agency, located in the state labor or health department, that provides evaluation of health and safety conditions in workplaces. Most offer consultative services, where the evaluation takes place at the request of management to determine if they are in compliance with the law. The agency may also evaluate specific health complaints or problems experienced by workers. As with NIOSH, most of these agencies have no enforcement powers; they can, however, inform OSHA if a violation is found that the management refuses to correct. As mentioned previously, some states have their own OSHA programs that can enforce both state and federal regulations.

As the federal government has turned away from regulation in recent years, there is some evidence that more legislative action will take place at a state level. It is important to realize, however, that it is against an individual state's short-term economic interest to impose strict environmental or occupational health regulation, since this may serve as a disincentive for companies (and the jobs they bring) to locate there. Consequently, action is most likely to occur in areas that are also of concern to community groups concerned with environmental or related issues. The passage of "right to know" laws has been most successful in areas where a coalition of labor and community groups has formed. (The movement toward local right to know laws received added impetus after a proposed federal regulation was withdrawn by the new OSHA administrator in 1981.) Concern over hazardous waste may well generate new legislation that has an impact on workplace health and safety.

Labor Unions

With the exception of the United Mine Workers and occasional local protests, labor unions have been actively involved in occupational safety and health issues only since 1970. Traditionally unions have focused on "bread and butter" issues, such as wages, benefits and hours of work. This reflects the major concerns of union memberships, and the understanding that only a limited number of issues can be fought for at any one time through collective bargaining.

A number of forces coalesced in the late 1960s that helped change this orientation: a relative labor shortage due to the Vietnam war, which produced higher wages and greater employment security; growing environmental consciousness and social unrest; a rising industrial injury rate; and the influence of a handful of progressive people both inside and outside the labor movement. Not surprisingly, with the recession and high unemployment of the early 1980s, unions have again shifted their focus toward dealing with plant closings, job security, and minimizing givebacks (cuts in wages and benefits). The concern with health and safety has not disappeared, however. Unions continue to play an important role at both the international and local union level.

While 15 years ago the idea of a health professional working for an international union was almost unheard of, today most of the large unions have at least one, and often several such professionals on staff. These include physicians, industrial hygienists, health and safety specialists, and even a few epidemiologists. Their roles vary depending on the union, but may include giving technical assistance to locals with problems, providing education and training of union membership, helping formulate appropriate health and safety demands for collective bargaining, and helping define the union's public posture and activities, including lobbying for health and safety legislation and OSHA standards. Unions have played a very active role in setting standards. In addition to testifying at OSHA hearings, labor unions have initiated many of the current regulations by petitions for emergency temporary standards.

Activity at the local level also varies considerably, depending on the interests and expertise of union members, their perception of the degree of hazard involved in their work, and the economic condition of the plant. At times, unions have been fearful of pressing health and safety demands for fear that the workplace would be closed. An increasingly common vehicle for labor involvement at the local level has been the creation of health and safety committees, which may be independent or joint with management. The functions of such committees may include walk-through inspections, monitoring injury and illness reports, investigating workers' complaints, and devising strategies for control of hazards. Some locals have negotiated for a safety steward, a union member with interest and training in health and safety who is given the time and freedom to investigate problems.

Unionized workplaces are generally believed to have safer conditions than comparable nonunion ones. This is due partly to having a formal bargaining mechanism, through which labor and management are forced to negotiate, and partly to the fact that workers in unionized plants are less likely to be arbitrarily fired. Cases have been documented of workers being fired for raising health and safety issues with their fellow workers or with management. This is much harder with a union with a formal grievance procedure. For these reasons, health and safety concerns have sometimes spurred unionization drives.

WORKERS' COMPENSATION

Workers' compensation is the system under state law that compensates workers financially for work-related illness and injury. The specific provisions of these laws vary from state to state but in general they provide for income benefits and medical and rehabilitation payments.

Workers' compensation laws were enacted in Europe as early as the 1880s, but comparable legislation was not passed in the U.S. until 1911, when New York became the first state to do so. Prior to such legislation, a worker's only recourse when injured was to sue his employer. Such suits were difficult to win, since the worker had to prove that the employer had been negligent, that the worker had sustained a work-related injury, and that the injury had been caused by the negligence of the employer. Even when these points were proved, the suit would still be lost if the employer could prove that the injury was at least in part due to the negligence of the worker or a fellow employee or that the worker had been or should have been aware of the hazard and "assumed the risk" when taking the job. Many suits were not even brought, since the chance of winning was low (fewer than a third of such suits were successful) and the chance of losing a job as a result of the suit was high.

In the early 1900s there was pressure from several sides to enact legislation similar to that in Europe. In addition to labor leaders and progressive social reformers, many of the major corporations joined in this effort. Their reasons for doing so are not clear, but have been attributed to several factors: the fact that workers were starting to win more suits as a result of changes in state laws that weakened employers' defenses; fear of rising radical political action among workers; and simple humanitarian concern for workers who were disabled and left without support. For whatever reasons, the pressure was largely successful, and by 1920 all but eight states had passed some form of workers' compensation. Mississippi, in 1948, was the last to do so.

Workers' compensation is a "no fault" system. Regardless of who is at fault, the worker will be compensated for injury or illness if she can prove that it is work-related. Most companies pay annual premiums to insurance companies, which then process claims and distribute payments. Some companies choose to insure themselves, and in some states the state acts as the insuring agent. For companies, the advantage to this system is that they know in advance each year the amount of their premiums and can thus budget accordingly. This assures them protection from a sudden unplanned monetary loss. In turn, the worker gives up the right to sue the employer and in exchange, at least theoretically, is guaranteed certain compensation without having to go through litigation. Uncertainty for both parties is thus reduced.

Workers' compensation provides for payment of all medical and rehabilitation costs, and partial replacement of lost income. This last component varies considerably from state to state. Generally the worker receives two thirds of his usual wage or a maximum weekly total, whichever is lowest. In 1981, maximum payment ranged from a high of $895.00 a week in Alaska to a low of $98.00 a week in Mississippi. Particularly when a worker is permanently disabled, this system can result in a large loss of potential income over a working life. In many states there is no cost-of-living increase, so that a worker is frozen at two thirds of the wage he was receiving when injured. He also will not be compensated for the increases in salary that he would have received had he stayed in the work force. There is also no payment for pain and suffering.

Generally workers' compensation systems have been most successful, that is workers have been most promptly and adequately compensated, in cases where workers suffer temporary disability from an acute traumatic injury. While it is usually straightforward to prove that such an injury has arisen "out of and in the course of employment," this is much more difficult to prove in cases of cumulative trauma injuries or occupational diseases. Many workers as well as their physicians are unaware that their problem is work-related and thus do not file for workers' compensation. This may be due to the long latency period between exposure and disease, so that the physician is not even aware of what the worker was exposed to 30 years ago; the fact that many diseases caused by occupational exposures are indistinguishable on clinical grounds from nonoccupational diseases; and many physicians' lack of training in occupational health.

Various states have regulations that compound the difficulty of providing adequate compensation for occupational disease. Some will only compensate a narrow list of "prescribed diseases." Others will only compensate diseases that are characteristic of a particular occupation or are not "ordinary diseases of life," which excludes common conditions that are often work related, such as hearing loss and chronic lung disease. All states have a statute of limitations (a specified period of time between some event and the filing of a claim). The statute presents no problems if the event is the diagnosis of the disease. If, however, the event is the end of exposure or the beginning of symptoms, many workers will be unjustly excluded. Another difficulty is that the occupational exposure may be only one of several exposures the worker sustained that could result in the disease. There is nothing to differentiate a lung cancer caused by vinyl chloride from a lung cancer caused by smoking. If the worker has exposure to both, a physician cannot definitely determine which is responsible for the disease. A worker who lifts heavy loads every day and then suffers from an acute back injury while lifting something at home will not be able to prove that his injury is actually the result of cumulative trauma to his back sustained at work. Thus many claims for occupational disease are contested by insurance companies, and on the average it takes over a year before the worker receives any payment. Clearly then, the goal of prompt compensation without litigation is not being met where occupational disease is concerned.

Another general criticism of the workers' compensation system is that it may result in the full cost of illness and injury not being born by the company responsible for it, and thus is in conflict with the goal of disease prevention. Only about 25% of companies are merit rated; that is, their insurance premiums depend on their injury and illness rate. Other companies are assessed premiums based on the average experience of companies of the same size and type. Thus, unless their illness and injury rates are much worse than others (in which case they are assigned to a special high-risk class), they have no economic incentive to go beyond a limited point in making their workplaces safer. Their costs do not reflect the true costs of the injuries and illnesses for which they are responsible, which allows premiums to be set too low. It is not in a company's economic interest to invest money in cleaning up a workplace, since a lower accident rate will not result in money being saved. Additionally, the present compensation system can lead to the institutionalization of disease. In other words, a certain amount of disease and disability becomes expected and is considered part of the standard operating procedure. For this reason, a recent resolution by the American Public Health Association states that all compensation systems should be explicitly tied to prevention efforts through the use of penalties and economic incentives, and the liability for the costs of occupational disease should be internalized within the industry that is producing it.

Another reflection of the inadequacy of the workers' compensation system has been the growing use by workers of third-party suits. Workers cannot sue their employers, but they can under certain circumstances sue other manufacturers who have provided tools, equipment, or materials which result in injury to the worker. To win such a suit, the injured worker must prove that the third party was negligent in either the design or the manufacture of the machine causing the accident or failed to warn of the hazards of the machine or material or to prove that the third party had warranted it was safe when it was not. This type of suit has been brought against Johns Manville, the major manufacturer of asbestos products, in the past few years. Since workers suffering from asbestos-related cancer and lung disease cannot sue their employers, they have sued the supplier of the material, charging that the company knew that asbestos caused disease and failed to warn the companies to whom they sold the product. The increasing frequency of such suits may serve to provide a stronger incentive for companies to assess health and safety aspects of their products thoroughly before releasing them on to the market.

FUTURE DIRECTIONS

Clearly, responses to occupational health problems in the United States are strongly affected by the political, economic, and social forces at work at any one point in time. In the 1970s, the amount of government regulation pertaining to workplace health and safety, as well as to broader issues of environmental protection, increased. Along with this, new money was available for research and training of professionals and workers, and awareness of these issues greatly increased. The early 1980s have seen a change in the federal government's attitude toward regulation and less money available to support health and safety activities at all levels. Although awareness is unlikely to decline to pre-1970 levels, the amount of activity that will be sustained in various sectors is not yet clear.

Several major trends in the field are apparent. In general, workplaces are much cleaner than they were 20 years ago. While lead poisoning of the kind Alice Hamilton saw still occurs, it is very unusual. A disaster of the magnitude that asbestos has caused is still possible, but it is less likely today than before. Consequently the aims of scientific research are changing. Scientists are trying to find more sensitive indicators of adverse toxic exposure, so that workers do not have to die or become severely impaired before the effects are noticed. For example, if lead levels are identified that will prevent slowing of nerve conduction velocity in 90% of exposed workers, then we can be confident that the same levels will prevent lead poisoning in 100%.

Another major trend in the field is related to the broader changes in the economy. The percentage of the work force employed in heavy manufacturing is declining, while employment in the service industry is increasing. This has resulted in new scientific research and increased public interest in occupations and workplaces that have largely been ignored until the present. There is new awareness that jobs can impact on people's health in a number of ways. For example, new research has shown that people who have jobs that are demanding but offer little control over how the demands are met are more likely to develop heart disease than others. These high-demand, low-control jobs are likely to increase in number as more workplaces, such as the office, acquire new technology.

In summary, the breadth of the field in increasing. Researchers and workers now recognize that all workplaces, including hospitals and offices, have at least the potential for health and safety problems. Researchers are moving past the "count the bodies" approach and looking for earlier indicators of toxic effects. The concept of exposure has been extended to include the social as well as the physical environment of the workplace.

As always, the accumulation of scientific knowledge is not sufficient by itself to protect public health. The dissemination of that knowledge to the people who need it and the creation of ways in which people can use that knowledge effectively are the biggest challenges and the ultimate determinants of the level of workplace disease and injury that is allowed to exist.

POINTS TO REMEMBER

Occupational health is the field that deals with the relationship between work and health. Since essentially everyone works, whether inside or outside the home, in volunteer work or for money, everyone potentially has occupational health problems. Although the field of occupational health was largely developed to address the problems of industrial environments, much of the knowledge and many of the techniques used to prevent disease and injury there can be applied in other workplaces. Headaches caused by improper illumination in an office are no more an inevitable part of work than lead poisoning.

The fundamental objective of all occupational health is the prevention of work-related disease and injury. Early detection of disease is also essential, as prevention cannot always be achieved. The most important method for achieving prevention is the elimination of unsafe and unhealthy working conditions. This is done most easily by initially designing workplaces and processes with health and safety in mind. Uses of methods that do not eliminate the actual hazard should always be the last choice.

Most public health decisions have to be made in the face of some degree of scientific uncertainty. To wait until there is a scientifically acceptable level of proof that something is harmful will result in more workers being unnecessarily harmed. The level of evidence that is necessary to take conservative public health action is of necessity lower than the level needed to establish something as a scientific fact.

While strong legislation to protect workers' health is necessary, it is not in itself sufficient to prevent disease and injury. Widespread worker education and awareness, coupled with the power to affect working conditions, is essential. Management and physician education is also important.

References

Baker, E. L., Feldman, R. G., White, R. A., Harley, J. P., Niles, C. A., Dinse, G. E., & Berkey, C. S. (1984). Occupational lead neurotoxicity: A behavioral and electrophysiological evaluation. Study design and year one results. *British Journal of Industrial Medicine, 41*, 352.

Berman, D. (1978). *Death on the job*. New York: Monthly Review Press.

Creech, J. W. & Johnson, M. N. (1974). Angiosarcoma of the liver in the manufacture of vinyl chloride. *Journal of Occupational Medicine, 16*, 150.

Doll, R., & Peto, R. (1981). The Causes of cancer: Quantitative estimates of avoidable risk of cancer in the United States today. *Journal of the National Cancer Institute, 66*, 1191.

Felton, J. S. (1976). 200 years of occupational medicine in the United States. *Journal of Occupational Medicine, 28*, 809–815.

Haenninen, H., Hernberg, S., Mantere, P., Vesanto, R., & Jalkanen, M. (1978). Psychological performance of subjects with low exposure to lead. *Journal of Occupational Medicine, 20*, 683–689.

Levy, B., & Wegman, D. H. (Eds.). (1982). *Occupational health.* Boston: Little, Brown.

Lloyd, J. W. (1971). Long term mortality study of steelworkers. V: Respiratory cancer in coke plant workers. *Journal of Occupational Medicine, 13*, 153–167.

Lloyd, J. W., Lundin, F. E., & Redmond, C. K. (1970). Long term mortality study of steelworkers. IV: Mortality by work area. *Journal of Occupational Medicine, 12*, 151–157.

McMichael, A. J., Spirtas, R., & Kupper, L. (1975). Solvent exposure and leukemia among rubber workers: An epidemiologic study. *Journal of Occupational Medicine, 17*, 234–239.

Rom, W. (1981). Effects of lead on reproduction. In P. F. Infante & M. S. Legator (Eds.), *Proceedings of a workshop on methodology for assessing reproductive hazards in the workplace.* Cincinnati, OH: National Institute of Occupational Safety and Health.

Seppalainen, A. M., & Hernberg, S. (1980). Subclinical lead neuropathy. *American Journal of Industrial Medicine, 1*, 413–420.

WATER AND HEALTH

G. William Page, III
University of Wisconsin–Milwaukee

Water is essential to life. We consume it to replenish the approximately 90% of our bodies that is water. It is also directly related to disease and death. The World Health Organization has estimated that as much as 80% of all disease is water-related (Guest, 1979). Less direct impacts of water on human health come from: (1) supplying food—the bountiful supplies of fish, shellfish, water fowl, and aquatic plants we consume, the water used for agricultural and animal production; (2) protecting humans—the water we use for fire protection; (3) producing goods and services—the use of rivers, canals, lakes, and the oceans for transport; water bodies for the disposal of sewage effluent and industrial wastes; water for the production of hydroelectric power and the cooling of electric power generating plants; and the use of water for recreational opportunities, which are extremely important to the mental and physical health of large segments of human populations.

The relationship of water to human health is the focus of this chapter. The topic is large. This chapter will concentrate on the direct impacts on human health in industrially developed countries. The indirect health impacts and the special problems of the less developed countries will be briefly described in order to understand the context of water-related health problems.

The chapter has four major sections. The first provides a historical perspective on the impact of water on health since prehistoric times: the role of water in the development of civilization, the great pandemics, yellow fever and typhoid fever in the United States, chlorination and other technological advances in water treatment, current problems, and the environmental movement and legislation in the United States. The second section discusses nonmalignant (noncancerous) water-related diseases, including those caused by bacteria, viruses, and protozoa. It also discusses improving human health through the control of water hardness and fluoridation. The relationship of microcontaminants in drinking water to malignant disease is the next topic. This is an area of water and health research that is currently most active and the subject of considerable scientific and policy debate. The focus here is on the relationship of water to cancer, radioactivity in water, solid particles including asbestos in water, and inorganic and organic microcontaminants. Conclusions and a brief review conclude the chapter.

HISTORICAL AND CURRENT PERSPECTIVES

The health of humans and their civilizations has been closely interwoven with water resources throughout the history of human habitation on the earth. A historical perspective helps us understand current and future problems of human health as related to water. Understanding how practices, policies, and technologies developed is important in evaluating our present potable water treatment and distribution systems. Furthermore, it is possible that the ways water-related health problems were resolved in the past may help in developing models for contending with current and future problems.

Prehistory and Ancient Times

Anthropologist Mary D. Leaky has found evidence that people created small, elementary networks for water 500,000 years ago (Nature/Science Annual, 1973). By 4000 B.C., communities had developed in flat, fertile lands adjacent to rivers. Agricultural societies developed in the fertile crescent of Mesopotamia, and along the Nile, the Indus, and the Hwang Ho rivers. There are fascinating and well-developed theories that argue that the organization necessary for society to control water for irrigation contributed to the development of distinctive sociopolitical forms, which shaped civilizations and history (Bennett, 1974; Wittfogel, 1957). The control over water resources for large areas under a central administrative system provided the prerequisites for political and military power. Extensive irrigation led to the concentration of population and agricultural surpluses that permitted the emergence of urban civilizations. These developed first in river valleys in warm semiarid parts of the world where the control of water for agriculture was essential for human populations.

Many achievements of ancient civilizations in controlling water in order to protect their collective health were impressive. The system of terraces, check dams, and directed runoff developed in Bronze and Iron Age times in the Negev and the Sinai Peninsula have been used as models for managing water in present-day Israel. In some successful modern projects designed to turn desert land into productive agricultural land, these ancient systems have simply been restored (Evenari, 1961). In the fourth and fifth centuries B.C., the Greeks constructed substantial public water supply systems. Athens developed a system of wells and tunnels from 18 different sources, and on the island of Samos a water supply tunnel 5½ feet square and 3,300 feet long built in 450 B.C. is still in existence (Vallentine, 1967). There is evidence of complete sewerage systems constructed 3,750 years ago in Nippur, India (Babbit, 1953).

The Roman Empire appreciated high-quality drinking water and its relationship to good health. At the beginning of the Christian era, Rome had an estimated population of about 1 million and was supplied with water at the rate of approximately 100 million gallons per day (Vallentine, 1967). The per capita average consumption of water is thus estimated to be 100 gallons per day, which is a reasonable estimate of residential water consumption in a modern city, although the patterns of water use were very different. Few houses had running water. Most water in ancient Rome was used in public fountains and public baths. Sources were selected far from the city to ensure good-quality water. There were over 30 miles of raised aqueducts in the 250 miles of channels and tunnels that carried water to Rome (Vallentine, 1967). One theory on the reasons for the empire's decline and fall blames lead poisoning from the ingestion of lead from water pipes and water and wine vessels (Nriagu, 1983). Another argues that the demise of empires and civilizations in history may have been due more to infectious diseases, many of them waterborne, than to political or economic factors (McNeill, 1976). As commerce and warfare brought remote civilizations into contact with each other, populations without inherited or acquired resistance or cultural adaptations were exposed to new diseases. There is historical evidence of repeated outbreaks of diseases, often carried back to Rome from Asia by soldiers, which decimated the population of the empire. As many as a quarter to a third of the entire population died in some of these plagues (McNeill, 1976).

The Great Pandemics

As population concentrated in urban centers in Europe during the Middle Ages and as trade and travel between distant areas developed, severe outbreaks of disease became regular events. Many of these epidemic or pandemic outbreaks such as the bubonic plague (the Black Death) are not directly water related, since the bacilli are transmitted from rodents via flea bites.

Water as the breeding place for mosquitoes is directly related to two of the most important epidemic diseases: malaria and yellow fever. Malaria, which is carried by the anopheles mosquito, is a collective term for four types of protozoan infections caused by the parasitic species *Plasmodium* (Savage, 1980). Yellow fever, carried by the *Aedes aegypti* mosquito, is a viral infection that was almost always fatal in adults until a vaccine was developed in 1937 (McNeill, 1976).

Water serves as the medium for the transmission of some of the most important epidemic diseases. These waterborne illnesses include cholera, typhoid and paratyphoid fevers, bacillary dysentery, amoebic dysentery, and infectious hepatitis. Infected persons carry the microorganisms that cause these diseases in their digestive tracts. Feces from infected persons can carry these organisms to surface and groundwater supplies, and people drinking this water would be unknowingly exposed. In densely populated areas without sophisticated sewage disposal and drinking water treatment facilities, it is easy to imagine how these diseases could and did reach epidemic proportions. Public supply systems distributing water to large populations carried something that was essential to life, but was often the cause of widespread death. Indeed, dense concentrations of population such as are found in large cities or are brought together by warfare are usually necessary for waterborne diseases to attain epidemic proportions.

Cholera was one of the most often-recurring and deadliest of epidemics in Europe and many other parts of the world until the late nineteenth century. The water supply system in London played a major role in the discovery that the transmitter of cholera was water. London's water came from a variety of sources. By 1822, there were eight private water supply companies providing the city with over 28 million gallons of water per day (Blake, 1956). Of this total, about half was drawn from the River Lea and other sources more than 38 miles north of London and transported to London by the New River Canal, which had been constructed in 1609. The other half of London's water supply was pumped from the River Thames close to the city. In 1854 Dr. John Snow studied the spread of cholera throughout London in areas supplied water by two of the private water supply companies. One of these companies used the Thames in central London as its source of water. In the vicinity of London in the mid-nineteenth century, the Thames was a very polluted river. The other company used water from a distant and undoubtedly much less polluted source. In one particular area the pipes of these two companies were both under the streets and the 300,000 residents of the area had their houses connected to the water pipes of one or the other of the two water companies. The climate, soil conditions, educational attainments, wealth, and many other potential factors that might explain who did and who did not contract cholera were nearly identical in this study area for the customers of both water supply companies. Dr. Snow's study is considered a classic in the field of epidemiology. He found that those houses served by the Lambeth Company, using a water source far from London, had a lower incidence of cholera than the average for the city of London. Those houses served by the Southwark and Vauxhall Company, using water taken from the Thames within London, had a very high incidence of cholera. From this data, Dr. Snow concluded that the water supply was responsible for transmitting cholera. (National Research Council, 1977; Snow, 1936).

Not until the 1880s were scientists able to understand how cholera and other diseases were transmitted by water. Advances in scientific technology, especially microscopes, played a large role by enabling scientists to see objects as small as bacteria. Around 1880, the germ theory of disease was established when Louis Pasteur identified the bacilli of anthrax and Robert Koch the bacilli of tuberculosis (McNeill, 1976). In 1883 Koch announced that he had identified the bacilli of cholera (Howard-Jones, 1972).

Yellow Fever and Typhoid in the United States

The experiences with water-related diseases of cities in the United States are somewhat different from those in Europe but have also contributed to the evolution of measures to protect the public's health. Unlike Europe where cholera was the most important water-related epidemic disease, yellow fever and typhoid were the major epidemics in the United States. In the early years of the nation, the summer months brought repeated epidemics of yellow fever. In 1793 it caused more than 4,000 deaths in Philadelphia, approximately 10% of the population, and about half the population fled the city, which was then the capital of the nation (Powell, 1949). Epidemics of yellow fever were a summer occurrence in most of the major U.S. cities for many years. Gradual improvements in sanitation helped reduce the severity of the epidemics until eventually in 1937 an inexpensive and effective vaccine was developed and became widely available (McNeill, 1976).

By the nineteenth century typhoid fever had become the most important epidemic disease in the United States. It remained so even after its causal agent, the bacilli *Salmonella typhi*, was identified in the early 1880s, and it was recognized that one of the major sources of exposure was through water supplies (National Research Council, 1977).

Most cities in the United States suffered epidemics of typhoid fever in the nineteenth century. In 1880, the mortality rate (per 100,000 population) from typhoid fever was 31.9 in New York City, 57.6 in Philadelphia, 42.4 in Boston, and 59.0 in Baltimore (Whipple, 1908). Typhoid fever provided the motivation to find ways to provide higher-quality water. One way was for the cities themselves to purchase and carefully control land uses in distant, upland watersheds developed as sources of less polluted water and as sites for reservoirs. In 1890 Newark, New Jersey, which took its water from the polluted Passaic River, had a typhoid mortality rate of over 100. In 1892 Newark developed its water supply source in the headwaters of the Pequannock River more than 30 miles from the city, and its annual typhoid mortality rate dropped to about 20 deaths (Whipple, 1908). New York City, Jersey City, and Boston also developed distant, unpolluted water supply sources about this time with similar reductions in their typhoid fever mortality rates. Chicago used a unique water supply planning option to reduce its typhoid mortality rate that was over 173 in 1891. At that time Chicago and other cities took their drinking water and disposed of their sewage in Lake Michigan. Chicago built the Chicago Drainage Canal, which reversed the flow of the Chicago River so that its sewage would flow away from Lake Michigan down the Des Plaines and Illinois rivers into the Mississippi. After the canal was opened in 1900, Chicago's typhoid rate fell to about 20 (Blake, 1956).

Advances in Water Treatment

About the turn of the century in the industrialized nations of Europe and North America, three very significant measures to control waterborne diseases were introduced: (1) slow sand filtration, (2) methods for bacteriological examination of water and indicator bacteria, and (3) chlorination. There have been no innovations of comparable importance since. While the turn of the century is a reasonable date for widespread use of filtration, Paisley, Scotland used it in 1804. Copenhagen and Odense, Denmark, and Hamburg-Altona, Germany, also filtered their water before the first use in the United States in Poughkeepsie, New York, in 1872 (Blake, 1956; Bonde, 1981). Sand filters were constructed in 1893 in Lawrence, Massachusetts, in connection with an earlier experimental station. For 7 years the typhoid fever mortality rate had never fallen below 80 and had reached 134. After the filters were built, the mortality rate for typhoid in Lawrence fell to between 20 and 30 (Blake, 1956).

Bacteriological test procedures, the second major innovation, cannot always be expected to isolate and identify all waterborne pathogenic bacteria. The presence of the indicator organism is a signal that there may be a problem. Tests for fecal coliform bacteria have successfully served as indicators of pathogens in water supplies since about the turn of the century.

The third innovation, chlorination of water supplies, has proven to be the most important of the water treatment innovations in terms of protecting public health. In 1908 Jersey City, New Jersey, was the first city in the world to introduce chlorination. Not only did chlorine destroy pathogens on contact, but the concentration of chlorine in water could be regulated so that a small residual concentration would remain to provide protection as it passed through miles of water pipes. It proved to be so effective, simple, and inexpensive that by 1914 most U.S. cities were chlorinating their water (Hazen, 1914; National Research Council, 1977).

These innovations in water treatment had a major impact on protecting the health of the public. During the decade 1880–1890, the average typhoid mortality rate per 100,000 population for 47 American cities was 58. By 1910 the rate for an expanded list of 78 cities had fallen to 20.5. In 1938 the rate had fallen to 0.67 deaths from typhoid fever per 100,000 population (Blake, 1956). On the one hand, we must acknowledge that these innovations of water treatment were not the only public health improvements that contributed to the decline in typhoid fever, but on the other hand their importance extends far beyond typhoid fever. The Mills-Reincke theorem states that for every death from waterborne typhoid, there were several deaths from other water-transmitted diseases (National Research Council, 1977).

Current Problems in Water and Health

Despite great progress in controlling water-related disease in most industrially advanced countries, it remains a devastating problem in much of the world. The problem is getting worse instead of better because the world's population is increasing most rapidly in those areas with the worst water-related health problems. By 1990 the world population is estimated to be about 5 billion, with 2 billion estimated to be without adequate water supply and even worse sanitation (Van Damme, 1981). At present in less developed countries, 86% of the rural population are estimated to lack an adequate water supply, and 92% lack adequate facilities for excreta disposal (Feachem, McGarry, & Mara, 1977). While urban areas in less developed countries are better off than rural areas, even in urban areas between 22 and 42% of the population lack adequate access to water (Linn, 1979). The quality of water supply affects between 20 and 30 diseases in tropical areas (Bradley, 1977). Many infections that are spread by an insect, snail, or other cold-blooded organism, or that spend part of their life cycle in the soil, require a warm climate to survive the stages of their life cycle spent outside of humans. These diseases are not problems in most temperate climates, but are major problems in many of the less developed countries that have tropical or semitropical climates.

The industrialized nations have a different set of water-related health problems. Most are located in temperate climates where the number of diseases is smaller than in tropical climates, and most have water distribution systems with sophisticated water treatment and disinfection. The water-related health problems of developed nations result from high population concentrations, dependence on a water treatment apparatus that must continually function at a high level of performance, and potentially dangerous levels of pollutants in water supply sources.

Concentrated populations, fallible water treatment systems, and other problems have caused outbreaks of waterborne diseases, illness, and death in the United States and in other developed nations. Infants are the most likely to become severely ill and die. In the United States there was a consistent and dramatic decrease in the number of waterborne-disease outbreaks from the period 1938–1940 to 1951–1955 when the number dropped from an average of 45 per year to 10 (Craun & McCabe, 1973). Since the 1951–1955 period, there has been an increase in the number of waterborne-disease outbreaks, and since 1971 this increase has been steep (Figure 4-1). An outbreak is defined as two or more cases linked to the same causal event. The data on outbreaks and illness probably represent only a small portion of the true number, as the number and kinds of reported outbreaks and of some of the suspected or known causes of the illness may depend upon the interests or capabilities of particular health agencies or individuals. For example in the 15-year period 1946–1960, 36% of the 228 reported outbreaks of disease or poisoning attributed to drinking water were reported by New York State, while in an earlier period New York State had reported 50% of the nation's outbreaks (Weibel, Dixon, Weidner, & McCabe, 1964). An example from Richmond Heights, Florida, in 1974 illustrates some of the problems of underreporting. Originally ten cases of waterborne shigellosis were reported, but an epidemiological investigation determined that 1,200 cases actually occurred (Craun, McCabe, & Hughes, 1976). It is commonly estimated that the reported outbreaks of waterborne disease represent about 10% of the true number; the remainder are unreported (U.S. General Accounting Office, 1982b). Improved reporting may explain the increasing number of waterborne-disease outbreaks in the U.S. as shown in Figure 4-1, but other explanations are possible. Our increasingly complex water treatment plants may be experiencing operating problems because of either equipment failures or operator errors, or the water supply sources we are drawing upon may be becoming increasingly polluted.

Waterborne-disease outbreaks occur in all types of systems, but there are some patterns to the outbreaks. Publicly owned and privately owned water utilities have been found to experience similar patterns (Craun & McCabe, 1973). Municipal water systems experience fewer outbreaks than nonmunicipal systems, which include institutions, industries, camps, parks, hotels, and service stations that have

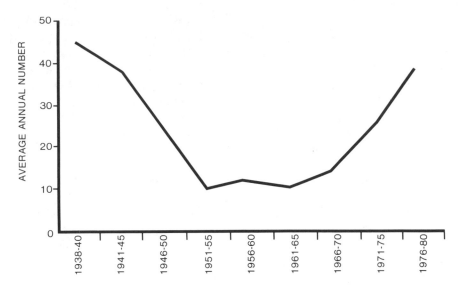

Figure 4-1. Average number of waterborne disease outbreaks, 1938–1980. From *Water-Related Disease Outbreaks, Annual Summary 1975, 1976, 1977, 1978, 1979, 1980.* (Centers for Disease Control, 1976, 1977, 1979, 1980, 1981, 1982).

their own water supply for public use. Such private supplies accounted for 70% of the outbreaks in the United States in the period 1971–1977. The major causes of outbreaks in nonmunicipal water systems were untreated groundwater, which caused 44% of the outbreaks and the illness, and treatment deficiencies such as inadequate chlorination, which caused 34% of the outbreaks and 50% of the illness (Craun, 1979). While municipal water systems account for fewer outbreaks, they are responsible for a much larger number of the illnesses, 67% in the 1971–1977 period, because they serve large numbers of people. Contamination of the distribution system caused 68% of the outbreaks, and treatment deficiencies caused 75% of the illness in the municipal systems (Craun, 1979). Individual systems, mostly private wells in rural areas, have reported about 14% of the outbreaks and 1% of the illness, but they are thought to be greatly underreported (Bonde, 1981). For all water supply systems combined, 49% of the outbreaks and 42% of the illness were caused by the use of untreated or inadequately treated groundwater (Craun, 1979).

The relationship of water to health in the industrialized nations in the past few years has focused on the possibility of increased cancer and mortality from ingestion of microcontaminants in drinking water consumed over long periods. Since the 1940s, industry has directly and indirectly released large quantities of toxic substances into the environment and specifically into our water supplies. Many of these toxic substances are organic chemicals. In the late nineteenth century, advances in microscopes led to the identification of germs in water and produced a revolution in water treatment technology. In the 1970s, advances in computer-aided mass spectrometers, gas chromatographs, and other devices led to the detection of many toxic substances in our drinking water at concentrations so small that we had previously been unable to detect them. Some of these microcontaminants are known and suspected human carcinogens. Most have never been tested thoroughly for carcinogenicity, mutagenicity, or teratogenicity. Problems of synergisms and bioaccumulation make the issue more complicated. This topic will be explored in more detail later in this chapter.

The Environmental Movement and Water-Related Legislation in the United States

The environmental movement in the United States burst upon the political system of the nation with remarkable force in the late 1960s and early 1970s. The broad-based popular support of its objectives combined with the suddenness of its manifestation produced substantial changes in environmental legislation and a heightened consciousness of environmental degradation and its relationship to health. Significant improvement was achieved in controlling air pollution, noise pollution, and solid and hazardous waste management as well as in improving the control of water pollution.

Water quality was not a major concern in the United States in the years between the widespread adoption of the water treatment innovations around the turn of the century and the environmental movement that became a powerful force with the first Earth Day in 1970. The combination of filtration, biological indicators, and chlorination had reduced water-related health problems to unprecedented low levels. As population increased and industrial expansion took place, rivers, lakes, estuaries, and the oceans became widely used for the disposal of industrial wastes and municipal sewage. The natural assimilative capacity of these water bodies was often exceeded by the quantities disposed and by the characteristics of the wastes they were receiving. Many rivers and lakes, especially in urban areas, became septic and could no longer support fish populations and were unpleasant and unsafe for human recreation. Water pollution control legislation passed in 1948, 1956, and 1965 was cumbersome and ineffective (Page & Weinstein, 1982). This legislation tried to take into account the nature and the uses of individual water bodies by evaluating variations in the physical, chemical, and biological properties of each stream segment or lake. This requirement for detailed site-specific analysis was combined with a three-step enforcement process. The result approached bureaucratic gridlock, and much less was accomplished then was needed to control the steady increase in water pollution.

The 1972 amendments to the Clean Water Act (P.L. 92-500) made an important change by providing for a comprehensive national approach to combating water pollution by setting uniform standards and guidelines on the basis of an administrative process geared to handling complex technical and scientific information. It also provided a more effective enforcement mechanism of those standards and regulations. Progress was made.

But again, the results have been less than had been expected. The widely held view was that we could identify all the pipes that were emptying pollution into our water bodies and cleanse them by forcing all dischargers to have permits and by applying uniform standards and technology. In 1980, 63% of large municipal sewage treatment plants were not yet in compliance with national standards (Council of Environmental Quality, 1980). In a study of major municipal and industrial dischargers for the period October 1980 to March 1982, 82% had exceeded their permit limits at least once, and 31% of the dischargers that exceeded the permit limits for one or more pollutants did so by 50% or more for at least four consecutive months (U.S. General Accounting Office, 1983). Overall, the billions of dollars spent on treating wastes following out of pipes (point sources) had achieved a substantial reduction in pollution even though the program has fallen short of its ambitious goals.

One of the reasons that the control of point sources has not resulted in pollution-free water bodies is that in the early 1970s the problem of controlling nonpoint source pollution was not recognized. Nonpoint source pollution does not come from a pipe or other single point source but from a broad area such as runoff from parking lots, animal feed lots, crop lands, and other areas. It is now thought that about half of the pollution in our water has been caused by nonpoint sources and that we have done very little to control this important cause (U.S. General Accounting Office, 1982a).

In addition to the amendments to the Clean Water Act, the environmental movement prompted other legislation important in protecting health from water-related disease. This body of legislation includes the National Environmental Policy Act of 1969 (P.L. 91-190), the Resource Conservation and Recovery Act of 1976 (P.L. 94-580), the Toxic Substances Control Act (P.L. 94-469), the Federal Insecticide, Fungicide and Rodenticide Act, as amended (P.L. 92-516, P.L. 94-140, P.L. 95-396), the Safe Drinking Water Act (P.L. 93-523), and the Comprehensive Environmental Response, Compensation and Liability Act (P.L. 96-510). While all are important and will be discussed elsewhere in this volume, space limitations will allow only a brief discussion of the Safe Drinking Water Act of 1974. It was enacted to insure that the nation's public water supply systems meet minimum national standards for the protection of public health. Previously, federal authority to regulate drinking water was limited to that provided on interstate carriers. The act required the Environmental Protection Agency (EPA) to establish national health standards for drinking water and gave the states responsibility for enforcing these standards in the approximately 215,000 water supply systems with at least 15 service connections or regularly serve a minimum of 25 people at least 60 days a year. The EPA issued the national interim primary drinking water regulations in December 1975 and has since added to them.

Compliance with the requirements of the Safe Drinking Water Act has not been good. Analysis of EPA data reveals that in 1980 there were 146,000 violations reported against 28,000 of the 65,000 (43%) community (year-round) water systems in the nation for either failing to test or for not meeting the drinking water quality standards (U.S. General Accounting Office, 1982b). These data also indicate that 13,600 public water systems cannot meet one or more of the water quality standards without improving their facilities. Explanations for this very poor compliance record include the lack of full-time and properly trained operators, operator apathy toward the federal requirements, and insufficient financial resources and personnel to meet the federal requirements (U.S. General Accounting Office, 1982b).

CAUSES OF NONMALIGNANT WATER-RELATED DISEASES

Bacteria

In developed countries bacterial diseases transmitted by water can be, and in most cases are, effectively controlled by water treatment. The classic, epidemic-causing waterborne bacterial diseases such as cholera, typhoid fever, and dysentery have been largely controlled in the developed countries. But there continue to be some outbreaks of disease and even deaths. In urban industrialized nations, large concentrations of people depend upon the proper functioning of sophisticated water treatment facilities and water distribution systems. Occasional malfunctions of these systems can result in serious bacterial or other types of waterborne illness. In the United States the most frequently occurring waterborne disease is acute gastroenteritis, for which the specific etiologic agent is usually not identified. Some gastroenteritis may be caused by bacterial infections. Bacillary dysentery, shigellosis, has been in recent years the most commonly identified bacterial disease and has most often been found in nonmunicipal water systems (National Research Council, 1977). Some of the data for outbreaks of waterborne disease in the United States were shown in Figure 4-1 and analyzed in the section titled "Current Problems." While the relative importance of the respective causes fluctuates, in 1975, 25% of the cases of waterborne disease were caused by water treatment deficiencies, and 64% were caused by deficiencies in the water distribution systems (Centers for Disease Control, 1976). The most frequently identified cause of deficiencies in the water distribution systems have been indirect cross-connections, which allow wastewater or toxic chemicals into the water distribution system by back-siphonage through hoses or through defects in water pipes during periods of low water pressure (National Research Council, 1982). Water treatment facilities and distribution systems are relatively fragile. In addition to occasional human error and mechanical breakdown, they are subject to disruption by environmental or human-caused disasters. As long as 10 years after damage to waterworks infrastructure during World War II, 20.4% of deaths in Japan were attributable to waterborne infectious disease (Bonde, 1981).

There is a substantial body of literature on waterborne bacterial disease. The

National Centers for Disease Control, a unit of the federal government's Department of Health and Human Services located in Atlanta, Georgia, publishes an annual summary of water-related disease outbreaks. Each state has a department that publishes vital statistics including incidence and mortality by disease. The most thorough analysis of this subject is the series *Drinking Water and Health* by the National Research Council of the National Academy of Science. There are presently five volumes with a wealth of information and specific references to the original research.

The process of humans contracting bacterial diseases through water starts with human and animal feces. Modern sewage treatment plants can greatly reduce the introduction of human wastes directly into our water resources. But bacteria from human and animal wastes do find their way into the sources of our drinking water. We are almost always exposed to some bacteria in our water supplies. There are four factors that determine whether we will become ill: (1) The species of bacteria present, as only a small number of species cause human illness; (2) the number or quantity of pathogenic bacteria in the treated water to which we are exposed; (3) the minimum dose of infection; some species of pathogenic bacteria are much more virulent than others and exposure to a relatively small number of these bacteria may result in illness. Bacteria of the genus *shigella*, which cause bacillary dysentery, are known to be highly virulent, with very small numbers often causing infection (National Research Council, 1977); (4) the age and general health of individuals. The aged and children are thought to be especially susceptible (MacKenzie & Livingstone, 1968; National Research Council, 1977).

To protect the health of the public from waterborne bacterial disease, it is necessary to understand the factors that determine the species and the numbers of pathogenic bacteria that may be present in local water supplies. The health characteristics of the population are the starting point, especially the presence of individuals who are "carriers" of some of the diseases more likely to cause epidemics. For instance, 2 to 5% of typhoid fever patients become permanent carriers of the disease (Bonde, 1981). Tourism, commercial travel, and the import of live animals and food are also possible sources of pathogenic bacteria. Our large urban centers with many possible sources are very likely to have a wide array of pathogenic bacteria present. The survival in nature of bacteria varies greatly depending on the species and environmental factors such as temperature, sunlight, and the natural microbial flora. Bacteria may live in the environment from a matter of seconds to several months. The last and most important factor that determines which pathogenic bacteria may be present in our water supplies is the extent of effective treatment.

Intervention to protect the public from pathogenic bacteria can be used effectively against any of these factors. In developed countries the treatment of raw water supplies prior to distribution to consumers is the most effective means of protecting the public's health. Proper treatment of water including disinfection with chlorine, ozone, or other means can effectively reduce the risk of waterborne bacterial illness to minuscule levels. The important issue is proper treatment. Since every pathogenic bacteria cannot be routinely isolated and tested individually, indicator bacteria are used to determine if the proper degree of treatment has been achieved. This approach has been found to be very reliable. Using this approach, the present U.S. standard of a monthly mean of less than one coliform per 100 ml of water achieves a high level, but not necessarily perfect treatment, at a reasonable cost. This approach does not entirely exclude the possibility of waterborne bacterial illness especially from low levels of virulent pathogens (Wolf, 1972). International and European standards are slightly different, but comparable (National Research Council, 1977).

In conclusion the problem of waterborne bacterial health problems is well controlled in developed countries with modern water treatment and distribution facilities that function properly. Rural areas of developed countries may have problems if groundwater sources are not treated prior to use. In the United States, 58.8% of water supply systems serving fewer than 100 people do not use disinfection (U.S. Environmental Protection Agency, 1982). The consequences of water treatment and distribution facilities failing to function properly in a large urban system can cause serious bacterial illness. The potential seriousness of this problem increases as our water supply sources become more polluted, thus requiring greater and more consistent treatment, and as the risk of mechanical or human error becomes greater with the increased technical sophistication of the processes.

Viruses

Viruses differ in several important ways from other microorganisms that can occur in water supplies. These differences raise some important issues and questions concerning our ability to protect the health of the public from illness they cause. We know that viruses are present in water supplies and that viruses in water can retain the ability to cause human infections. Unfortunately, there are no quick and effective methods to detect viruses in water. Detection of viruses takes a minimum of two days for even the most severe contamination and usually takes one to two weeks (National Research Council, 1977). The procedures are also expensive and require highly skilled laboratory personnel. Considerable human illness can occur while waiting for laboratory results that can be the basis of action. The important questions concerning virus in water supplies are: (1) What is the safe dosage or number of viral particles in water below which human infection will not occur? and (2) Can water treatment methods, using bacteriological indicators to establish the level of treatment, protect humans from viral infection?

The viruses most often identified in water are the enteroviruses, which are adapted to the gastrointestinal track of humans. This group of viruses include the poliovirus, coxsackie, echo, infectious hepatitis A, reoviruses, adenovirus, rotavirus, and Norwalk agent (Kott, 1981). The extent of illness caused by waterborne viral infection is unknown and is likely to remain unknown for the foreseeable future. But is is not considered to be great. One estimate is that in a city of 1 million inhabitants each drinking 1 litre of water per day, 3,650 people per year would contract a viral illness from the water (World Health Organization, 1979).

Before the 1940s infection from waterborne viruses was not an established fact. In the late 1940s and 1950s, the spread of poliomyelitis and hepatitis through water supplies was accepted (Berg, 1965; Little, 1954). Transmission by water was blamed for eight outbreaks of poliomyelitis in the United States and in Europe (Mosley, 1967). The Salk and Sabin polio vaccines virtually eliminated the threat of polio in developed countries in the late 1950s. Hepatitis A is now the most important viral disease that is sometimes transmitted by water. It can also be transmitted by person-to-person contact and by food. More than 30,000 cases of hepatitis A were counted in 1956 in Delhi, India, after sewage contaminated the drinking water supplies (Melnick, 1957). In the United States, the reported cases of waterborne infectious hepatitis have increased sharply since 1946. In the 25-year period from 1946 to 1970 in the United States, there were 53 reported outbreaks of waterborne hepatitis involving 1,833 cases (Craun & McCabe, 1973), but the number of outbreaks and cases is probably grossly underreported. The majority of outbreaks from public water supply systems were the result of contamination of the distribution system, primarily through cross-connections or back-siphonage. In private systems, outbreaks were the result of contamination of groundwater (Craun & McCabe, 1973). There has been no evidence of hepatitis A virus being transmitted through properly functioning modern water treatment plants in the United States (Craun et al., 1976).

The most common waterborne disease in the United States and other developed countries, gastroenteritis, may be the result of a viral infection. But no virus or other cause is usually identified. Symptoms include nausea, vomiting, and diarrhea. Enteric viruses were recovered from unchlorinated well water in a Michigan restaurant after patrons became ill and from a Florida migrant labor camp that experienced repeated illness (Mack, Yue-Shoung, & Coohon, 1972; Wellings, Lewis, & Mountain, 1976). The contribution of waterborne viruses to gastroenteritis outbreaks remains speculative.

There is an extensive body of literature and reviews on the topic of waterborne viral diseases. A good overview is provided by Berg (1965) and by Kott (1981). The questions of safe levels of viruses and the disinfection of viruses are treated in detail in volumes I and II respectively of the series by the National Research Council (1977, 1980a).

The process by which humans become infected by waterborne viruses starts with human wastes. Large numbers of enteric viruses are contained in human feces. Sewage treatment plants cannot destroy all of these submicroscopic, inert particles or virions, which have the potential to produce disease in humans ingesting them in water. Wastewaters have been found to contain more than 100 different enteric viruses (Davis, Dulbecco, Eisen, Ginsburg, & Wood, 1967). Virions lose their ability to cause infections as time passes, but in many cases this does not happen quickly.

Methods to protect public health from illness caused by waterborne viruses are based on standard water treatment technology using bacterial indicators. Since these indicator bacteria reveal the presence of microorganisms originating in the intestines of mammals, they are the best available indicators of possible enteric virus contamination of water for routine use in water treatment facilities.

About one fifth of U.S. plants begin water treatment with coagulation and settling prior to disinfection (Temple, Barker, & Sloane, Inc., 1982). Coagulation involves adding substances such as aluminum sulfate, ferric chloride, polyelectrolytes, acids, alkalis, or clays to the water to cause suspended substances in the water and any organic or inorganic contaminants attached to them to coagulate and settle to the bottom, where they can be easily removed. Several studies indicate that coagulation and settling under ideal circumstances can be very effective in removing from 90 to 98% of the virus present in raw water (National Research Council, 1977). There is also evidence that the duration of contact time during disinfection and the pH (acidity) of the water being treated are very important to the successful destruction of viruses (Kott, 1981). As stated above, there have been no reported cases of waterborne viral outbreaks from properly functioning water treatment and distribution facilities. Viruses have been found to survive longer during water treatment than bacterial pathogens and indicator bacteria, thus raising the possibility of outbreaks of viral illness if water sources were sufficiently contaminated (Colwell & Hetrick, 1976; National Research Council, 1977).

In conclusion the problem of waterborne viral disease is usually well controlled in developed countries with modern, properly functioning water treatment and distribution facilities. Viruses in water supplies do, however, represent a potential threat to public health because many fewer organisms are needed to cause a viral infection in humans than are needed to cause bacterial infections, and because viruses can survive longer in natural waters and in water undergoing disinfection in a water treatment plant. Even in developed countries, problems can exist in rural areas where groundwater sources are not treated prior to use. The consequences of water treatment and distribution facilities failing to function properly in a large urban system could cause serious viral illness.

Protozoa

Protozoa are parasites, and a number of them can be transmitted to humans through water. Waterborne protozoa are a major public health problem in many less developed countries, especially in tropical regions. In the developed countries, some health problems caused by protozoa have been a minor nuisance for many years, while others are becoming increasingly important.

In the less developed countries, some of the most intractable public health problems are caused by waterborne protozoa. Of the many protozoa-caused problems only a few of the worst can be briefly mentioned here. Schistosomiasis is a generic name for a series of illnesses caused by liver flukes that are human parasites. The eggs of the liver flukes are excreted, and some find their way into water where they hatch and enter water snails for a stage in their life cycle. In their final larval stage, they swim freely in water bodies, where they can burrow into the exposed skin of humans who come in contact with infected water. They then cause schistosomiasis, which is debilitating and difficult to treat (Weir, 1969).

Onchocerciasis, or river blindness, is caused by the filarial worm, which is spread by black flies (Hunter, 1966). Sleeping sickness, trypanosomiasis, is transmitted by the tsetse fly (Bradley, 1977). Both the black fly and the tsetse fly breed in water and usually bite victims who approach water bodies.

Guinea-worm infection, or dracunculiasis, is transmitted to humans who consume water that contains a minute crustacean, cyclops, which is itself infected with guinea-worm larva. In some affected African villages more than 70% of the population are afflicted with guinea-worm (Bradley, 1977).

In developed countries, the health problems caused by protozoa are not as severe as in the less developed countries, but they do exist, and they may be increasing. The public health questions are: (1) Are waterborne protozoa becoming an important public health problem? and (2) What water treatment processes can be effectively used to protect the health of the public?

The principal pathogenic protozoa with the potential to cause public health problems in the developed countries are *Entamoeba histolytica* and *Giardia lamblia*. Their wide distribution in water supplies and resistance of the ova and larvae to current chlorination procedures make these organisms a potential problem (National Research Council, 1980a). In the past decade, *Giardia lamblia* in water supplies has become a major cause of illness throughout developed nations, even in wilderness areas. In remote wilderness areas of the United States it is recognized as the most important cause of waterborne disease (Knotts, 1983). The *Giardia lamblia* protozoa causes giardiasis, which may involve diarrhea, loss of appetite, dehydration, cramps, and in some cases vomiting. Since 1970 in the United States, giardiasis has caused more cases of waterborne illness (18% in the period 1971–1977) than anything else except acute gastrointestinal illness (Craun, 1979; National Research Council, 1977).

Protozoa waterborne disease begins in human and animal intestines. The cysts of protozoa are excreted and can enter water supplies through feces. It is estimated that between 3 and 20% of the U.S. population and about 30 species of animals, including beavers, dogs, cattle, coyotes, deer, muskrats, cats, marmots, and ground squirrels are carriers of *Giardia* (Knotts, 1983). Some species of *Giardia* that infect animals do not infect humans, but some do. Excreta deposited in water that runs off into water bodies or is treated and released from sewage treatment plants can carry protozoa into water supplies.

Water treatment plants can remove protozoa from drinking water. Most rely on disinfection of water with chlorine, ozone, or some other product, and a residual concentration of disinfectant in the distribution system. But the cysts of *Giardia* and other protozoa are not destroyed by these processes. In the United States all outbreaks of giardiasis involving municipal water supply systems, with one exception in a system using groundwater, have been associated with surface water supply sources where disinfection was the only treatment (National Research Council, 1977). The cysts of *Giardia lamblia, Entamoeba histolytica*, and other protozoa can be removed by sedimentation and filtration through sand. The use of coagulation, sedimentation, and filtration in water treatment plants in the United States varies with the number of customers of the water supply system. In the smallest systems serving fewer than 100 people, 4.3% use coagulation, sedimentation, and filtration, while in the largest systems serving more than 1 million customers, 78.5% use coagulation, settling, and filtration (U.S. Environmental Protection Agency, 1982). The filters must be of adequate depth, and proper maintenance is essential to be effective in removing protozoa from water.

Waterborne disease outbreaks caused by protozoa are likely to remain a public health problem, and possibly increasingly so. Even when municipal water treatment facilities install sufficient coagulation and filtration to remove the cysts, water supplies taken from contaminated groundwater and from improperly functioning water treatment plants will continue to expose large numbers of people.

Two related topics will be briefly mentioned, but at this time they can only be considered potential public health problems. Helminths, a class of protozoa, are intestinal worms. Several of them can be transmitted in drinking water (National Research Council, 1977). Coagulation and filtration are effective in removing these protozoa, but disinfection practices are not effective. Certain algae, including the common blue-green algae, can produce a diarrhea-causing toxin (Aziz, 1974). These bloom-forming species of algae release their toxins in the water, and these toxins are responsible for large outbreaks of diarrhea in parts of India (Gupta & Dashora, 1977). This process also is possible in many developed countries and may be responsible for some of the gastroenteritis for which no known eitological agent could be identified (Kappers, Leeuwangh, Dekker, & Koerselman, 1981).

Water Hardness

In the past two decades there has been a great deal of interest in the possible relationship between hardness of drinking water and human health, especially between water hardness and cardiovascular disease. While there have been many studies, the results are still not conclusive. This is an issue on which research is very active. The three major questions about water hardness are: (1) What is water hardness? (2) Is water hardness associated with any human diseases? and (3) What steps should be taken to protect human health?

Hardness is one of the oldest and most widely used parameters used to characterize water for both public consumption and for industrial uses. In technical terms, hardness is the sum of the polyvalent cations present in water (National Research Council, 1977). In lay terms, hardness is mostly determined by how much calcium and magnesium are present in the water plus some traces of strontium, barium, iron, manganese, and other metals. Unfortunately from a health perspective, hardness is a very imprecise term. When a statistical association is found between water hardness and human health, we cannot determine which, if any, of these elements that comprise hardness is causing the disease.

Many studies have found that people consuming hard water have lower mortality from cardiovascular disease than do people who drink soft water. The earliest studies were completed in Japan and the United States (Kobayashi, 1957; Schroeder, 1960). Since then, more than 50 studies in nine countries have found that cardiovascular mortality is lower in areas where water is hard (National Research Council, 1977). There are many other studies that did not find such a relationship, for example Zielhuis (1981) and Sonneborn and Mandelkow (1981). There are also studies that report that areas with hard water have a significantly lower incidence or mortality from other diseases such as bronchitis, neural tube defect, cleft lip and palate, and sudden death syndrome ("How trace elements," 1978; Roberts, 1976).

Since total hardness is primarily determined by the presence of calcium and magnesium and the proportion in water of these two substances varies widely, it is logical to consider health effects of calcium and magnesium hardness. These two elements have different physiological effects on humans despite being chemically similar (De Fulvio & Olori, 1976). Some research indicates that calcium hardness is much more important to cardiovascular disease than magnesium (Crawford, Gardner, & Morris, 1968, 1971). Other research shows that greater quantities of calcium ingested in drinking water are more highly associated with reduced risk of cardiovascular disease than calcium in the diet, rainfall, temperature, socioeconomic status, and other potentially confounding factors (Clayton, 1976).

There are some excellent guides to the literature of this large body of research. The proceedings of the European Scientific Colloquium held in Luxembourg in 1975 focuses on this issue (Amavis, Hunter, & Smeets, 1976). Volumes 1 and 3 of the series *Drinking Water and Health* by the National Research Council are very good. The National Academy of Sciences report of the Panel on Geochemistry of Water in Relation to Cardiovascular Disease is excellent (National Academy of Sciences, 1979).

The influence of water hardness on cardiovascular and other diseases is not proven, and the process by which such a relationship might function is not well understood. If one assumes that water hardness does cause disease, then control of the hardness of water could reduce the annual deaths from cardiovascular disease in the United States by as many as 150,000 persons (8% of mortality) (Tate, 1978).

In many places in developed countries the opposite is, in fact, done. Hard water is often softened to reduce scale buildup in industrial boilers and wear and tear on household appliances such as dishwashers and washing machines. Soft water is more likely to cause corrosion in the water supply distribution system and in turn, public health problems from high levels of trace metals. Some methods of water softening may also produce other human health problems. Ion-exchange resins soften water by replacing calcium or magnesium with sodium. High concentrations of sodium in drinking water have been implicated in hypertension (elevated blood pressure) and increased risks of heart and kidney ailments (Calabrese & Tuthill, 1981).

At this time, officials in most developed countries believe that further research is necessary before taking any action to protect the public health by changing the hardness of water (National Academy of Sciences, 1979). Studies have not made clear which, if any, additions to soft water would best protect public health.

Fluoride

Fluoride, which both occurs naturally and is added to water supplies in many places throughout the world, has both positive and negative human health impacts. Fluoride is the 17th most abundant element in the earth's crust, and it is found in almost all foods as well as in water. From a public health perspective the questions concerning fluoride are: (1) Does fluoride help prevent dental caries? (2) Does fluoride cause human illness? and (3) Is there a safe level of fluoride in drinking water?

The concentration of fluoride varies in rocks, soils, and water supplies. This natural variation in human exposure to fluoride led to the observation in Great Britain that areas with high concentrations in drinking water had a high prevalence of mottling of teeth and lower than expected rates of dental caries (McKay, 1928). Mottling is a brownish discoloration of tooth enamel, which is caused by exposure to high concentrations of naturally occurring fluoride in drinking water supplies. Dental caries or tooth cavities vary in humans for many reasons, but fewer were found in areas with high concentrations of fluoride in the drinking water. In 1945 two U.S. cities and one in Canada began to add fluoride to water and found that dental caries among young people decreased to less than half their former level (Gorchev, 1981). Today 200 million people in more than 40 countries drink water that is artificially fluoridated (Van Burkalow, 1982).

There are several good sources of information on the human health effects of fluoride in drinking water. Shaw (1954) covers the basic issues. The World Health Organization (1970), the Royal College of Physicians in Great Britain (1975), and the National Research Council in the United States (1977) have also published information.

There is nearly universal agreement that the addition of fluoride to drinking water helps reduce dental caries. The fluoride alters the crystalline structure of tooth enamel making teeth harder and more resistant. Too much fluoride in drinking water, the diet, or in other sources does cause mottling. Some recent research contends that considerable dental mottling (fluorosis) is due to factors other than fluoride, and that optimal concentrations of fluoride may decrease the amount of dental mottling (Al-Alousi, Jackson, Compton, & Jenkins, 1975).

The most important question concerning fluoride in water supplies is the possibility that it might cause illness. Acute toxicity from fluoride is rare but can happen if enough is ingested. The real fear is that long-term ingestion of small amounts of fluoride may cause illness. Some evidence of illness has been reported from clinical observations. Among the adverse health effects that scientists think might be associated with fluoride are skeletal fluorosis, renal problems, Down's syndrome, cancer, and birth defects (National Research Council, 1977). These suggested associations have not been supported by systematic research. There is no generally accepted evidence that anyone has been harmed by fluoride concentrations that are considered optimal for the prevention of tooth decay (National Research Council, 1977). The usual fluoride dosage of 1 mg/litre is widely accepted, depending on temperature and local conditions.

Over all, adding fluoride to drinking water supplies has been beneficial in protecting the health of the public. There has been a significant reduction in dental caries, especially among the young. While further research is necessary on the possibility of adverse human health effects, at this time the possibility is not supported by the available evidence.

Nitrate

Nitrate in drinking water supplies is known to cause some diseases and is suspected of causing others. The public health issues are: (1) What is the maximum allowable concentration of nitrate in drinking water that will protect the health of infants? (2) Does nitrate in drinking water cause stomach cancer? (3) What intervention mechanisms are available to protect the public health?

The literature on human health effects of nitrate in drinking water dates only from the post–World War II era. Infant methemoglobinemia, sometimes referred to as blue-baby disease, was first associated in 1945 with ingestion of water with high nitrate concentrations (Comly, 1945). Many studies have since confirmed this association. Good reviews of this literature are found in Volume I of the *Drinking Water and Health* series (National Research Council, 1977) and in Fraser and Chilvers (1981). Although nitrate in drinking water supplies has been implicated in some other human illness, to date, these associations have not been supported by sufficient evidence to be widely accepted. The strongest case has been made for an association with stomach cancer. Besides the two sources cited above some of the best sources for this association include Hill, Hawksworth, & Tattersall (1973) and Cuello *et al.* (1976).

The process by which nitrate causes human illness starts in the many sources from which nitrogen enters our water supplies. Some nitrate reaches our water supplies as a result of natural processes. Bacteria, which consume natural organic material, release nitrogen that becomes nitrate, since that is the stable form of combined nitrogen in oxygenated aqueous systems. High nitrate concentrations are more likely to result from human activities. The disposal of human waste after treatment in sewage treatment plants or in septic tank systems, fertilization of croplands, and the confinement of large numbers of farm animals in small spaces are all potential causes of nitrate contamination. Problem-causing concentrations of nitrate are possible in water from either surface or groundwater sources, but most nitrate-related health problems in the United States have involved shallow wells located near barnyards, septic tanks, fertilized, or irrigated fields (Delfino, 1977).

The process by which nitrates in drinking water cause methemoglobinaemia in infants involves the conversion of nitrate (NO_3) to nitrite (NO_2). Nitrate-reducing bacteria are present in humans, but in adults their numbers and presence in the lower intestinal tract do not cause these problems. In infants, whose principal food is milk, the low gastric acidity of the upper digestive tract enables these bacteria to flourish. Infants also have a higher fluid intake in relation to their body weight than adults. High concentrations of nitrate in drinking water in bottle-fed infants can be converted by bacteria to high levels of nitrite. On absorption to the blood, nitrite combines with hemoglobin to form methemoglobin. Methemoglobin does not have the capacity to transport oxygen. When between 5 and 10% of total hemoglobin is methemoglobin, symptoms of cellular anoxia, manifest as clinical cyanosis, show up (Knotek & Schmidt, 1964). Severe cases can lead to death by suffocation.

We do not know how nitrates in drinking water cause cancer in humans. The suspected process involves nitrites, which readily react with secondary amines and similar nitrogenous compounds that are likely to be present in the human digestive tract. The combination forms N-nitroso compounds, many of which are potent carcinogens.

Intervention to protect the health of the public from risks caused by nitrates in drinking water relies on standards for acceptable concentrations. In the United States the recommended drinking water standard is 45 mg/l of nitrate, which is equivalent to approximately 10 mg/l of nitrate as nitrogen (Public Health Service, 1962). The World Health Organization (WHO) has established a European standard of 50 mg/l and an international standard of 45 mg/l of nitrate (WHO, 1970, 1971). These standards are thought to be adequate to protect the public from methemo-globinemia, but it is recognized they provide little margin of safety (National Research Council, 1977).

Public water supply systems that meet the standard for nitrate concentration in drinking water probably protect the public from these health risks. The problem is that many countries do not routinely test their water supplies for nitrate levels. The majority of people in the developed and developing countries consume water from private wells, and they are the population at highest risk, especially in areas where agricultural sources of nitrate contamination may be plentiful.

CAUSES OF MALIGNANT WATER-RELATED DISEASES

Possible relationships between water contamination and cancers receive prominent media coverage because of the public's great fear of cancer.

Organic Microcontaminants

Improvements in chemical instrumentation permit us to detect a wide variety of organic chemicals in water supplies. In most cases these substance are found at concentrations near the lower limit of analytic chemists' ability to detect compounds in water. Because the concentrations are so low, these substances are often referred to as microcontaminants. The issues concerning organic microcontaminants are: (1) What organic microcontaminants are found in water? (2) What are the health implications of ingesting organic microcontaminants in drinking water? and (3) How can we protect the health of the public from the risks of exposure to organic chemicals in drinking water?

There has been a chemical revolution in the past four decades. Insights into the structure of organic molecules led to the synthesis of vast numbers of organic chemicals that do not occur naturally. More than 2 million new compounds were registered in the United States from 1965 to 1972. Less than 1 billion pounds of synthetic organic compounds were produced in the United States in 1941, but by 1978 production of just 50 of the most common synthetic organic chemicals amounted to 172 billion pounds (Council on Environmental Quality, 1980). Shackelford and Keith (1977) reported that 1,259 different organic compounds have been identified in water samples. Chemists can identify only about 10% of the organic compounds in water and have had very little success in identifying nonvolatile compounds (Kool, Van Kreijl, Van Kranen, & De Greef, 1981; Rohlich, 1978). As an example of the dimensions of the identification problem, the 89 toxic organic compounds identified in New Orleans drinking water represent approximately 2% by weight of the total organic chemicals in that water (Guinan, Shaver, & Adams, 1978).

The health implications of exposure to organic microcontaminants in drinking water are the subject of considerable controversy. There is no doubt that exposure to large doses of many of these chemicals causes acute illness; however, concentrations large enough to cause these health effects are very rarely found in water supplies. The real question is what are the health effects of drinking water with low concentrations of organic microcontaminants over the course of a lifetime. In earlier centuries, human populations often suffered serious epidemics caused by bacteria, viruses, or parasites that originated in distant lands and to which they had not developed biological resistance or cultural adaptation. Most of the organic microcontaminants of concern in water supplies are man-made chemicals. Humans have evolved without prior exposure to these substances and lack defense mechanisms, acclimation capabilities, or excretion pathways to contend with these chemicals once they have entered the body. Many of these microcontaminants are stored in fat cells where they can accumulate from contaminants in the water and food faster than they are degraded or eliminated. The long-term health implications are presently unknown. There is widespread agreement that they are adding to the disease burden in a significant, although as yet not precisely defined way (U.S. Department of Health and Human Services, 1980).

The greatest concern from the long-term exposure to organic microcontaminants in drinking water is cancer. As early as the 1960s, warnings were sounded that microcontaminants in our drinking water supplies were animal carcinogens and that the threat of cancer from these pollutants was a rapidly increasing danger to humans (Hueper, 1960; Hueper & Payne, 1963). Most of the organic microcontaminants that have been identified in samples of drinking water have not yet been tested for carcinogenicity. We have virtually no information on potential synergisms among the large numbers of microcontaminants that may be present in water supplies.

There has been considerable epidemiologic research on a link between water supplies containing microcontaminants and increased cancer mortality. This epidemiologic research has included both ecological studies and case control studies. The ecological studies compare cancer rates to aggregate measures of exposure, usually with the county as the unit of analysis. There have been many ecological studies since T. Page, Harris, and Epstein (1976) first reported elevated cancer mortality in New Orleans, presumably caused by microcontaminants in water supplies. Almost all epidemiologic studies have found significant statistical associations with several body site cancers. The strongest and most consistent associations have been with rectal, bladder, and colon cancer (Alavanga, Goldstein, & Susser, 1978; Brenniman, Lagos, Amsel, Namekata, & Wolff, 1980; Struba, 1979).

In addition to being suspected of causing cancer, many of the organic microcontaminants found in water supplies are also suspected human teratogens and mutagens. The organic microcontaminants that are teratogens can produce birth defects or congenital abnormalities. Those which are mutagens can be increasing the genetic load of recessive mutant alleles, which can lead to an increasing incidence of genetic diseases in future generations (Page, 1987a).

The literature on organic microcontaminants and health is large and growing, but there are some excellent reviews. The best single source is the five-volume series *Drinking Water and Health* (National Research Council, 1977, 1980a, 1980b, 1982, 1984). These volumes are the result of a study mandated by the U.S. Congress in order to get a dispassionate, objective review of the evidence available to make a specific judgment concerning contaminant levels that may have an adverse health effect on people drinking water. The best review of the epidemiologic literature on this subject is Crump and Guess (1980). Good reviews of the policy implications of these issues can be found in Greenberg and Page (1981) and Page (1984).

There are a variety of processes by which our drinking water may become contaminated with toxic chemicals. Microcontaminants can pollute our water supply sources, they can be created in the water treatment process, and they can originate in the drinking water distribution system. The most serious problems are with our sources of drinking water. Some microcontaminants such as pesticides and herbicides are intentionally released in the environment. Others result from transportation accidents and chemical spills. Microcontaminants escape landfills, effluent lagoons, and petroleum storage and distribution facilities. To take one example, there are an estimated 1.5 to 2 million buried gasoline storage tanks in the United States. About 35% of the underground motor fuel storage tanks and nearly half of such tanks located below the water table may be leaking (Environment Reporter, 1986).

Contamination of groundwater with toxic chemicals is an especially serious problem. Traditionally groundwater has been assumed to be pure. Even in developed countries, groundwater often is not treated. Nevertheless, groundwater has been found to be at least as contaminated with organic and other microcontaminants as surface water, and that contamination is likely to be in higher concentrations in groundwater than in surface water (Page, 1981). Contaminants move through an aquifer as a discrete plume that is not subject to rapid dilution because of its slow movement and nonturbulent flow. Once below the water table, microcontaminants are not in contact with the atmosphere, which means that even volatile organic chemicals cannot escape solution, and that aerobic degradation processes are highly restricted. A plume of contaminants in groundwater may move slowly in unpredictable directions for years before being pumped from the ground in a private or public water supply (Page, 1987b).

The process of treatment and distribution has been found to introduce organic microcontaminants into drinking water. Chlorination, which is used to disinfect water, combines with naturally occurring humic and fluvic acids to create a class of organic microcontaminants known as trihalomethanes, the most widely identified toxic organic chemicals in U.S. water supplies. The U.S. Environmental Protection Agency water supply survey of finished drinking water from both ground and surface sources indicated that 95–100% of the systems surveyed contained chloroform, one of the trihalomethanes (Office of Toxic Substances, 1975). Chloroform and others of the trihalomethanes are suspected human carcinogens (National Research Council, 1977). Other research has identified organic microcontaminants that originate in the water pipes of the distribution system possibly from microbial action on the walls of the pipes or from the coal tar used to line some pipes (Schwartz, Saxena, Kopfler, 1979).

There are several distinct approaches that could be used to protect public health from risks posed by organic microcontaminants in drinking water. Keeping these pollutants out of water supply sources is by far the best approach. Unfortunately so many toxic chemicals have been released to the environment that there are precious few water supply sources that do not already contain organic microcontaminants. Most are present in extremely low concentrations, and the most effective intervention is to keep additional toxic chemicals out of water supply sources, especially groundwater sources (Page, 1987b). The available legislation to protect water sources in the United States was discussed earlier. But there are so many water supply sources and so many sources of toxic chemicals that this approach is unlikely to be completely successful.

Another approach is to establish standards for the maximum allowable concentration of each microcontaminant in drinking water. In the United States, the Environmental Protection Agency has established maximum contaminant levels for a very small number of organic and inorganic microcontaminants. The National Interim Primary Drinking Water Regulations include maximum contaminant levels for six specific organic microcontaminants plus a group of chemically related compounds known as total trihalomethanes (40 Code of Federal Regulations part 141). The process of establishing these standards is extremely contentious and time-consuming because the long-term human health effects are unknown (Page, 1987a; Page & Greenberg, 1982).

The last intervention approach to be discussed is technological. Alternative water treatment processes to disinfect water are being tested in an attempt to avoid the creation of trihalomethanes (National Research Council, 1980b). While there are alternatives to the use of chlorine as a disinfectant, none are widely considered to be better than chlorine because each alternative has known or potential problems. Other technological approaches are being evaluated as a means of removing organic microcontaminants from water. The present water treatment techniques such as filtration, coagulation and settling, and disinfection are not effective in removing organic microcontaminants. Activated carbon has been extensively studied and does remove many, but not all, microcontaminants from water (National Research Council, 1980b). This technology is not widely used because of the high operating expenses required to regenerate the activated carbon at frequent intervals.

The consequences of failing to keep our drinking water supplies free of organic microcontaminants are unknown. Because there is usually an interval of 20 to 30 years between exposure to a carcinogen and the incidence of the disease in humans, it is possible that the widespread exposure to organic microcontaminants in water supplies now taking place may produce substantial increases in cancer in the future. The best available information indicates that this will not happen. Risk assessments of consuming water with the low concentrations of carcinogens and other microcontaminants estimate that this exposure will produce some cancers that would not otherwise have occurred, but that the number may not be very great compared to other causes of mortality (Crouch, Wilson, & Zeise, 1983; Greenberg & Page, 1981; National Research Council, 1980b). Present risk assessment methods are designed to be conservative, but they cannot include the presently unknown risks caused by synergistic effects of the mixtures of many different microcontaminants that may simultaneously be present in drinking water.

Inorganic Microcontaminants

There are many inorganic microcontaminants in water supplies that are a threat to the health of the public. This section will describe some of these substances and examine the health risk that they pose. These substances include trace metals, other inorganic elements like arsenic and selenium, and inorganic particles such as asbestos. All these inorganic substances are found in very low concentrations. We will consider how these substances get into our water supplies, what the health effects of ingesting these substances with our drinking water might be, and what interventions are currently possible to protect the public from the potential health risks.

The literature on health effects of inorganic microcontaminants in water supplies is substantial. As was the case for the organic microcontaminants, the series *Drinking Water and Health* is the best summary source of information and the best review of the literature on inorganic microcontaminants and health (National Research Council, 1977, 1980a, 1980b, 1982, 1984). In Volume 1, each inorganic element is briefly described along with a review of its occurrence, chemical characteristics, health effects, methods of analyzing for its presence in water, and conclusions and recommendations concerning the risk to public health.

All inorganic microcontaminants can enter our water supplies through natural processes or as a result of human activity, since they are all present in rocks and soil. As a result, chemical weathering and soil leaching wash trace concentrations into virtually all natural waters. Many are used extensively by industrial societies, and mineral extraction and manufacturing produce products and wastes that often contain large quantities of these substances.

The health effects of some of these inorganic microcontaminants are very complex because some of the metals are essential to human health at trace concentrations but are toxic at slightly higher concentrations (Mertz, 1981). The metals chromium, cobalt, copper, magnesium, manganese, molybdenum, tin, and zinc are known to be essential to human health, and nickel and vanadium may be (National Research Council, 1977). Other metals such as lead, mercury, and cadmium are not known to have any beneficial effect. To protect the public health in the Untied States, the National Interim Primary Drinking Water Regulations have established maximum contaminant levels expressed in milligrams per litre of water for several of the inorganic microcontaminants: arsenic 0.05, barium 1.0, cadmium 0.01, chromium 0.05, lead 0.05, mercury 0.002, selenium 0.01, and silver 0.05 (Federal Register, 1982). Acute health problems caused by exposure to high concentrations of inorganic microcontaminants in water supplies are rare. The concern is more with the unknown effects of long-term exposure to the low concentrations that are most often found in water supplies. Some of the inorganic microcontaminants are suspected carcinogens. Some of the heavy metals are probably not carcinogens, but may act as cocarcinogens by depressing the function of enzymes involved in the metabolism of organic carcinogens (Berg & Burbank, 1972).

Of the inorganic microcontaminants routinely found in water supplies lead is probably the best known and has been identified as causing the most serious health threat. Its maximum permissible contaminant level also may not provide adequate protection for certain populations (Rohlich, 1978). Lead in drinking water may originate in natural sources, pollution, or the solvent action of water on any lead in domestic plumbing or the pipes that connect households to water mains. Areas with soft, acidic water usually have greater concentrations of lead in their water. The long-term effects from exposure to lead in drinking water in amounts too small to cause classical lead poisoning, are not completely known. One of the major problems is to determine the importance of the contribution that lead in drinking water makes to the total human exposure to lead. Humans are exposed to lead from many sources, especially in the diet and in the air we breathe. There is considerable evidence that children are exposed to more lead, absorb more lead, and are more susceptible to its toxic effects than adults (Matthew, 1981). Children with high lead levels in their bodies have been found to score significantly lower on standard intelligence tests including verbal subtests and on three other measures of auditory or speech processing. Their attention spans were found to be shorter and their classroom behavior was judged to be less adaptive than students with lower body burdens of lead (Needleman et al., 1979).

Intervention to protect the health of the public from inorganic microcontaminants in water supplies depends upon maximum contaminant levels. Based on the best scientific knowledge available, concentrations of inorganic microcontaminants in water supplies below the established maximum contaminant level are considered to be safe. Standard water treatment methods are not generally effective in removing inorganic microcontaminants from water. Alternative water treatment techniques that might be effective are being studied (National Research Council, 1980a).

The long-term health consequences of exposure to low concentrations of inorganic microcontaminants in drinking water are unknown. The best scientific estimates are that they will be very small as long as the maximum contaminant levels are enforced. The importance of their roles as carcinogens, cocarcinogens, promoters of cancer, and the synergisms among themselves and with organic microcontaminants are all potential problems that are presently unknown.

Radioactivity

All drinking water supplies contain some traces of radioactivity that represent a potential threat to the health of the public. Exposure to the radioactivity in drinking water generally represents a very small percentage of our total exposure to radiation. The quantity of radioactivity found in water supplies varies greatly, determined largely by the composition of the rocks and soil through which the water has passed. This section considers what kind of radioactivity is found in water and where it comes from, what the potential health effects of exposure to radioactivity in drinking water are, and what can be done to protect the health of the public.

The literature on the health effects of exposure to radiation consists of small portions of the large body of literature on the biological effects of ionizing radiation. Volume 1 of the series *Drinking Water and Health* presents a good review of the literature and an excellent overview of the topic (National Research Council, 1977). The U.S. Environmental Protection Agency has some technical publications that are very useful (1978, 1983). Another good source of information is the National Institutes of Health (1980).

Radiation on the earth includes cosmic rays, products of the decay of radioactive elements in the earth and its atmosphere, and man-made radiation. Humans are exposed to radiation from all of these external sources as well as from the radioactive material in the air we breathe and in the food and water we consume. There are two types of radiation in drinking water that are of potential health significance: low linear energy transfer (LET) and high-LET.

Low-LET radiation in sufficient dosage can cause cancer of the soft tissues. Some of the common, naturally occurring contaminants emitting low-LET radiation in water are potassium-40, tritium, carbon-14, and rubidium. Of these radioactive substances, potassium-40 is usually the largest source of radioactivity in water supplies because it occurs as a constant percentage (0.0118%) of total potassium (National Research Council, 1977). The quantity of potassium-40 consumed in drinking water is usually not a serious threat to health because it is a minute amount (less than 0.004%) of the total quantity from the diet and other sources (National Research Council, 1977).

High-LET radiation in drinking water is attracted to the bones where it may cause cancer. Some common sources in drinking water of high-LET radiation include radium-226, the daughters (decay products) of radium-228, uranium, thorium, radon-220, and radon-222 from natural sources and strontium-90, cesium-137, iodine-131, and others from human activities such as the testing of nuclear weapons, the discharge of radiopharmaceuticals, and the use and processing of nuclear fuel by electric generating plants. Of these, radium-226 and its daughters and the daughters of radium-228 probably have the greatest potential for producing adverse health effect in humans (National Research Council, 1977). These daughters of radium are often more important than the isotopic mixture measured in freshly drawn drinking water because they contribute significantly to the long-term alpha dose that can be accumulated in the body. These forms of radium vary in their distribution. In the United States they are found at high levels in drinking water in parts of the Midwest where they are thought to be caused by leaching of radium-bearing rock strata into the deep sandstone aquifers, and in Florida where they are thought to result from leaching from phosphate rock deposits into the Floridian aquifer (U.S. Environmental Protection Agency, 1983). A typical water supply in the United States accounts for less than 10% of the annual background dose from high-LET radiation (Rohlich, 1978). In some locations, radium in drinking water is found at high levels and can be a more substantial source of exposure and cause for concern. In the United States, approximately 1.1 million people consume water that contains more than 3 picocuries per litre (National Research Council, 1977).

Intervention to protect the health of the public from radioactivity in drinking water in the United States is based on maximum contaminant levels for radionuclides in water supplies. The National Interim Primary Drinking Water Regulations specify maximum contaminant levels of 5 picocuries per litre (pci/l) for combined radium 226 and 228, 15 pci/l for gross alpha particle activity, 20,000 pci/l for tritium in the total body, 8 pci/l strontium-90 in the bone marrow, and an annual average concentration of beta particle and photon radioactivity from man-made radionuclides in drinking water that does not produce a total body or internal organ dose equivalent greater than 4 millirem per year (Federal Register, 1976). For those water supply systems not meeting these standards, there are a variety of options available to enable the system to provide water that does meet these maximum contaminant levels (U.S. Environmental Protection Agency, 1978, 1983).

The consequences of being exposed to radionuclides in drinking water do not appear to be a major threat to human health though radiation in drinking water has the potential of causing teratogenic effects, genetic effects, and carcinogenic effects. Teratogenic effects are particularly important because the unborn and children are much more sensitive to radioactivity than adults are (National Research Council, 1972). Despite the sensitivity of the developing fetus, the teratogenic and genetic risks caused by consuming radionuclides in drinking water are extremely low (National Research Council, 1977). The risk of cancer because of skeletal-seeking high-LET radiation from sources that vary greatly in drinking water is more important, but still small. Only in those locations with very high concentrations of radium in drinking water would there be any possibility of a measurable health effect.

POINTS TO REMEMBER

The less developed nations experience the most severe water-related health problems. An estimated 2 billion people in these countries presently lack an adequate water supply. This is predominently a rural problem with 86% of these estimated 2 billion people living in rural areas of the less developed nations. The concentration of this problem in the less developed nations is likely to persist or even intensify because the countries with the worst water-related health problems are among those with the fastest growing populations.

The United States and other industrialized nations have fewer and different water-related health problems. Unlike the less developed nations, the industrialized nations have an operating water supply infrastructure that provides people with relatively high-quality drinking water. Documented waterborne-disease outbreaks in the developed nations are generally the result of inadequacies or breakdowns in the water supply treatment and delivery infrastructure, usually in water supply systems that use untreated groundwater. These systems are usually small nonmunicipal systems. Breakdowns occur in the water supply infrastructure because of both machinery and operator failure. As water treatment technology becomes more complex, both causes of system failure are likely to increase. In urban areas, a breakdown of the water treatment system can expose very large numbers of people to the threat of water-related diseases.

Both the less developed and the developed nations will continue to experience some water-related health problems in response to the ongoing processes of urbanization and industrialization. As populations grow and become increasingly concentrated, it often becomes very difficult to find new, high-quality water supply sources to provide water to the growing population. Residential, commercial and industrial growth all contribute to an increase in the pollutant load to surface water and groundwater. This produces a situation of reduced supply and increased demand for high-quality water. In the developed nations, reuse of wastewater effluents is now an integral part of water-resource management. In the United States there are no federal treatment requirements or water quality criteria for wastewater reuse. The increasing use of wastewater effluents as raw water sources for water supply systems may cause increased waterborne diseases caused by viruses and protozoa, which are not always destroyed by water treatment either in sewage or in water treatment.

The increasing use of products composed of or containing toxic substances also contributes to the threat of water-related disease. We know that virtually all municipal water supplies contain low concentrations of toxic substances. Some of these substances are suspected human carcinogens. We do not know the health impacts of exposure to the low concentrations of these substances in drinking water over a lifetime. Most risk assessments estimate a relatively small number of additional cancers will be caused by the ingestion of these substances in drinking water. Other risk assessments estimate a much more substantial problem. Because of the lag time between exposure to a carcinogen and incidence of the cancer, we will not be certain of the true risk for many years. As we learn more about which substances are present in our water supplies, their toxicity, and their synergisms and antagonisms with other microcontaminants found in water supplies, we will be better able to assess the human health impacts of these substances in our water supplies.

References

Al-Alousi, W., Jackson, D., Compton, G., & Jenkins, O. C. (1975). Enamel mottling in a fluoride and in a non-fluoride community: A study. *British Dental Journal, 138*, 9–15.

Alavanja, M., Goldstein, I., & Susser, M. (1978). Case control study of gastrointestinal and urinary cancer mortality and drinking water chlorination. In R. J. Jolley, H. Gorchen, & D. Hamilton (Eds.), *Water chlorination, environmental impact and health effects* (Vol. 2). Ann Arbor, MI: Ann Arbor Science.

Amavis, R., Hunter, W. J., & Smeets, J. G. (Eds.). (1976). *Hardness of drinking water and public health*. Oxford: Pergamon Press.

Aziz, K. M. (1974). Diarrhea toxin obtained from a waterbloom-producing species, Microcystis aeruginosa Kutzing. *Science, 183*, 1206–1207.

Babbit, H. E. (1953). *Sewerage and sewage treatment*. New York: Wiley.

Bennett, J. W. (1974). Anthropological contributions to the cultural ecology and management of water resources. In L. D. James (Ed.), *Man and water*. Lexington, KY: University of Kentucky Press.

Berg, G. (1965). *Transmission of viruses by the water route*. New York: Wiley.

Berg, J. W., & Burbank, F. (1972). Correlations between carcinogenic trace metals in water supplies and cancer mortality. *Annals of the New York Academy of Science, 199*, 249–262.

Blake, N. M. (1956). *Water for the cities*. Syracuse, NY: Syracuse University Press

Bonde, G. J. (1981). Salmonella and other bacteria. In H. van Lelyveld & B. C. J. Zoeteman (Eds.), *Water supply and health*. Amsterdam: Elsevier Scientific.

Bradley, D A. (1977). Health aspects of water supplies in tropical countries. In R. Feachem, M. McGarry, & D. Mara (Eds.), *Water, wastes and health in hot climates*. New York: Wiley.

Brenninman, G., Lagos, J., Amsel, J., Namekata, T., & Wolff, A. (1980). Case-control study of cancer death in Illinois communities served by chlorinated or nonchlorinated water. In R. J. Jolley, W. A. Brungs, & R. B. Cummin (Eds.), *Water chlorination, environmental impact and health effects* (Vol. 3). Ann Arbor, MI: Ann Arbor Science.

Calabrese, E. J., & Tuthill, R. W. (1981). The influence of elevated sodium in drinking water on elementary and high school students in Massachusetts. In H. van Lelyveld & B. C. Zoeteman, (Eds.), *Water supply and health*. Amsterdam: Elsevier Scientific.

Centers for Disease Control. (1976, 1977, 1979, 1980, 1981, 1982). *Water-related disease outbreaks, annual summary, 1975, 1976, 1977, 1978, 1979, 1980*. Atlanta, GA: U.S. Department of Health, Education and Welfare.

Clayton, D. G. (1976). Water hardness and cardiovascular mortality in England and Wales. In R. Amavis, W. J. Hunter, & J. G. Smeets (Eds.), *Hardness of drinking water and public health*. Oxford: Pergamon Press.

Colwell, R. R., & Hetrick, F. M. (1976). Annual report, Office of Naval Research. In A. L. Gameson, (Ed.), *Discharge of sewage from sea outfalls* (Proceedings of symposium, August 27–September 2, 1974). Elmsford, NY: Pergamon Press.

Comly, H. R. (1945). Cyanosis in infants caused by nitrates in well water. *Journal of the American Medical Association, 129*, 112–116.

Council on Environmental Quality. (1980). *Environmental quality 1980*. Washington, DC: U.S. Government Printing Office.

Craun, G. F. (1979). Waterborne disease—A status report emphasizing outbreaks in ground-water systems. *Ground Water, 17*, 183–191.

Craun, G., & McCabe, L. (1973). Review of the causes of waterborne-disease outbreaks. *Journal of the American Water Works Association*, 74–84.

Craun, G. F., McCabe, L. J., & Hughes, J. M. (1976). Waterborne disease outbreaks in the U.S. 1971–1974. *Journal of the American Water Works Association*, 420–424.

Crawford, M. D., Gardner, M. J., & Morris, J. N. (1968). Mortality and hardness of local water supplies. *Lancet, 1*, 827–831.

Crawford, M. D., Gardner, M. J., & Morris, J. N. (1971). Cardiovascular disease and the mineral content of drinking water. *British Medical Bulletin, 27*, 21–24.

Crouch, E., Wilson, R., & Zeise, L. (1983). The risks of drinking water. *Water Resources Research, 19*(6), 1359–1375.

Crump, K S., & Guess, H. A. (1980). *Drinking water and cancer: Review of recent findings and assessment of risks*. Washington, DC: Council on Environmental Quality.

Cuello, C., Correa, P., Haenszel, W., Gordillo, G., Brown, C., Archer, M., & Tannenbaum, S. (1976). Gastric cancer in Columbia. 1. Cancer risk and suspect environmental agents. *Journal of the National Cancer Institute, 57*, 1015–1020.

Davis, B. D., Dulbecco, R., Eisen, H. N., Ginsburg, H. S., Wood, W. B. (1967). *Microbiology*. New York: Harper & Row.

De Fulvio, S., & Olori, L. (1976). Definitions and classifications of naturally soft and naturally hard waters. In R. Amavis, W. J. Hunter, & J. G. Smeets (Eds.), *Hardness of drinking water and public health*. Oxford: Pergamon Press.

Delfino, J. (1977). Contamination of potable ground water supplies in rural areas. In R. B. Pojasek (Ed.), *Drinking water quality enhancement through source protection*. Ann Arbor, MI: Ann Arbor Science.

Environmental Reporter, 1986. EPA Survey of Storage Tanks, 17(9), 253–254.

Evenari, M. (1961). Ancient agriculture in the Negev. *Science, 133*, 979–996.

Feachem, M., McGarry, M., & Mara, D. (1977). Water, wastes and health in hot climates. New York: Wiley.

Federal Register. Drinking Water Regulations, 41, 28404-28409, 1976.

Federal Register. National Primary Drinking Water Regulations, Amendments, Correction, 47, 10998, March 12, 1982.

Fraser, P., & Chilvers, C. (1981). Health aspects of nitrate in drinking water. In H. van Lelyveld & B. C. Zoeteman (Eds.), *Water supply and health*. Amsterdam: Elsevier Scientific.

Gorchev, H. G. (1981, June). Fluoride saves teeth. *World Health*, pp. 15–17.

Greenberg, M. R., & Page, G. W. (1981). Planning with great uncertainty: A review and case study of the safe drinking water controversy. *Socio-Economic Planning Sciences, 15*, 65–74.

Guest, I. (1979, January). The water decade 1981–1990. *World Health*, pp. 2–5.

Guinan, D. K., Shaver, R. G., & Adams, E. F. (1978). Identification of organic compounds in effluents from industrial sources. In R. B. Pojasek (Ed.), *Drinking water quality through source protection*. Ann Arbor, MI: Ann Arbor Science.

Gupta, R., & Dashora, M. (1977). Algal pollutants and potable water. In R. Pojasek (Ed.), *Drinking water quality enhancement through source protection*. Ann Arbor, MI: Ann Arbor Science.

Hazen, A. (1914). *Clean water and how to get it* (2d ed.). New York: Wiley.

Hill, M. J., Hawksworth, G., & Tattersall, G. (1973). Bacteria, nitrosamines and cancer of the stomach. *British Journal of Cancer, 28*, 562–567.

How trace elements in water contribute to health. (1978). *World Health Organization Chronicle, 32*, 382–385.

Howard-Jones, N. (1972). Choleranomalies: The unhistory of medicine as exemplified by cholera. *Perspectives in Biology and Medicine, 15*, 422–433.

Hueper, W. C. (1960). Cancer hazards from natural and artificial water pollutants. In *Proceedings, Conference on Physiological Aspects of Water Quality*. Washington, DC: U.S. Public Health Service.

Hueper, W. C., & Payne, W. W. (1963). Carcinogenic effects of adsorbates of raw and finished water supplies. *American Journal of Clinical Pathology, 39*, 475–481.

Hunter, J. M. (1966). River blindness in Naggoldi, Northern Ghana. *Geographical Review, 56*, 391–416.

Kappers, F. I., Leeuwangh, P., Dekker, M., & Koerselman, W. (1981). Investigation of the presence of toxins produced by cyanobacteria (blue-green algae) in the Netherlands. In H. van Lelyveld & B. C. J. Zoeteman (Eds.), *Water supply and health*. Amsterdam: Elsevier Scientific.

Knotek, Z., & Schmidt, P. (1964). Pathogenesis, incidence, and possibilities of preventing alimentary nitrate methemoglobinemia in infants. *Pediatrics, 34*, 78–83.

Knotts, D. M. (1983). Purifying water in the wild. *Sierra, 68*(3), 57–59.

Kobayashi, K. (1957). Geographical relationship between the chemical nature of river water and the death rate from apoplexy. *Berichtedes Institution fuer Landwirtschaftliche Biologie, 11*, 12.

Kool, H. J., Van Kreijl, C. F., Van Kranen, H. J., & De Greef, E., (1981). Toxicity assessment of organic compounds in drinking water in the Netherlands. In H. van Lelyveld & B. C. Zoeteman (Eds.), *Water supply and health*. Amsterdam: Elsevier Scientific.

Kott, Y. (1981). Viruses and bacteriophages. In H. van Lelyveld & B. C. Zoeteman (Eds.), *Water supply and health*. Amsterdam: Elsevier Scientific.

Linn, J. F. (1979). *Policies for efficient and equitable growth of cities in developing countries* (Staff Working Paper No. 342). Washington, DC: World Bank.

Little, G. M. (1954). Poliomyelitis and water supply. *Canadian Journal of Public Health, 45*, 100–102.

Mack, W. N., Yue-Shoung, L., & Coohon, D. B. (1972). Isolation of poliomyelitis virus from a contaminated well. *Health Service Report, 87*, 271–274.

MacKenzie, C. R., & Livingstone, D. J. (1968). Salmonellae in fish and food. *South African Medical Journal, 42*, 999–1003.

Matthew, G. K. (1981). Lead in drinking water and health. In H. van Lelyveld & B. C. Zoeteman (Eds.), *Water supply and health*. Amsterdam: Elsevier Scientific.

McKay, F. S. (1928). The relation of mottled enamel to caries. *Journal of the American Dental Association, 15*, 1429–1437.

McNeill, W. H. (1976). *Plagues and peoples*. Garden City, NY: Anchor Press.

Melnick, J. L. (1957). A waterborne urban epidemic of hepatitis. In F. W. Hartman (Ed.), *Hepatitis frontiers*. Boston: Little, Brown.

Mertz, W. (1981). The essential trace elements. *Science, 213*, 1332–1338.

Mosley, J. W. (1967). Transmission of viral disease by drinking water. In G. Berg (Ed.), *Transmission of viruses by the water route*. New York: Wiley Interscience.

National Academy of Sciences. (1979). *Geochemistry of water in relation to cardiovascular disease*. Washington, DC: National Academy Press.

National Institutes of Health. (1980). Known effects of low-level radiation exposure (NIH pub. no. 80-2087). Washington, DC: U.S. Department of Health, Education and Welfare, Public Health Service.

National Research Council. (1972). *The effects on populations of exposure to low levels of ionizing radiation*. Advisory Committee on the Biological Effects of Ionizing Radiation. Washington, DC: National Academy Press.

National Research Council. (1977). *Drinking water and health* (Vol. 1). Washington, DC: National Academy Press.

National Research Council. (1980a). *Drinking water and health* (Vol. 2). Washington, DC: National Academy Press.

National Research Council. (1980b). *Drinking water and health* (Vol. 3). Washington, DC: National Academy Press.

National Research Council. (1982). *Drinking water and health* (Vol. 4). Washington, DC: National Academy Press.

National Research Council. (1984). *Drinking water and health* (Vol. 5). Washington, DC: National Academy Press.

Nature/Science Annual. (1973). Summing up the year. New York: Time-Life Books.

Needleman, H. L., Gunnoe, C., Leviton, A., Reed, R., Peresie, H., Maher, C., & Barrett, P. (1979). Deficits in psychologic and classroom performance of children with elevated dentine lead levels. *New England Journal of Medicine, 300*, 689–732.

Nriagu, J. O. (1983). *Lead and lead poisoning in antiquity.* New York: Wiley.

Office of Toxic Substances, U.S. Environmental Protection Agency. (1975). *Preliminary assessment of suspected carcinogens in drinking water* (Report to Congress). Springfield, VA: National Technical Information Service.

Page, G. W. (1981). Comparison of groundwater and surface water for patterns and levels of contamination by toxic substances. *Environmental Science and Technology, 15*, 1475–1481.

Page, G. W. (1984). Toxic contaminants in water supplies and the implications for policy. *The Environmentalist, 4*, 131–138.

Page, G. W. (1987a). Drinking water and health. In G. W. Page (Ed.). *Planning for groundwater protection.* New York: Academic Press.

Page, G. W. (Ed.). (1987b). *Planning for groundwater protection.* New York: Academic Press.

Page, G. W., & Greenberg, M. R. (1982). Maximum contaminant levels for toxic substances in water: A statistical approach. *Water Resources Bulletin, 18*(6), 955–963.

Page, G. W., & Weinstein, A. (1982). The costs of conflicting environmental policy: A case study in Milwaukee. *Water Resources Bulletin, 18*(4), 671–677.

Page, T., Harris, R., & Epstein, S. (1976). Drinking water and cancer mortality in Louisiana. *Science, 193*, 55–57.

Powell, J. H. (1949). *Bring out your dead: The great plague of yellow fever in Philadelphia in 1793.* Philadelphia: University of Pennsylvania Press.

Public Health Service. (1962). *Public Health Service drinking water standards.* Washington, DC: Department of Health, Education and Welfare.

Roberts, C. J. (1976). Diseases other than cardiovascular disease and their association with the physicochemical quality of drinking water. In R. Amavis, W. J. Hunter, & J. G. Smeets (Eds.), *Hardness of drinking water and public health.* Oxford: Pergamon Press.

Rohlich, G. A. (1978). Drinking water and health. In C. S. Russell (Ed.), *Safe drinking water: Current and future problems.* Washington, DC: Resources for the Future.

Royal College of Physicians. (1975). *Fluoride, teeth and health.* Bath, England: Pitman Medical.

Savage, E. P., (1980). Disease vectors. In P. W. Purdom (Ed.), *Environmental health.* New York: Academic Press.

Schroeder, H. A. (1960). Relation between mortality from cardiovascular disease and treated water supplies: Variations in states and 163 largest municipalities in the United States. *Journal of the American Medical Association, 172*, 1902.

Schwartz, D. J., Saxena, J., & Kopfler, F. C. (1979). Water distribution system, a new source of mutagens in drinking waters, *Environmental Science and Technology, 13*, 1138–1141.

Shackelford, W. M., & Keith, L. H. (1977). *Frequency of organic compounds identified in water* (NTIS PB-265 470). Athens, GA: Environmental Research Laboratory.

Shaw, J. H. (Ed.). (1954). *Fluoridation as a public health measure.* Washington, DC: American Association for the Advancement of Science.

Snow, J. (1936). *A reprint of two papers by John Snow, M.D.* New York: Commonwealth Fund.

Sonneborn, M., & Mandelkow, J. (1981). German studies on health effects of inorganic drinking water constituents. In H. van Lelyveld & B. C. Zoeteman (Eds.), *Water supply and health.* Amsterdam: Elsevier Scientific.

Struba, R. J. (1979). Cancer and drinking water quality. Ph.D. dissertation, Department of Epidemiology, University of North Carolina, Chapel Hill.

Tate, C. (1978). Discussion of drinking water and health. In C. Russell (Ed.), *Safe drinking water: Current and future problems* (pp. 76–103). Washington, DC: Resources for the Future.

Temple, Barker, & Sloane, Inc. (1982). Survey of operating and financial characteristics of community water systems, prepared for the Office of Drinking Water, EPA (570/9-82-006, NTIS PB 83-180539). Arlington, VA: National Technical Information Service.

U.S. Department of Health and Human Services. (1980). *Health effects of toxic pollutants* (Report prepared for the U.S. Senate by the surgeon general, serial no. 96-15). Washington, DC: U.S. Government Printing Office.

U.S. Environmental Protection Agency. (1978). *Costs of radium removal from potable water supplies* (EPA-600/2-77-073). Washington, DC: U.S. Government Printing Office.

U.S. Environmental Protection Agency. (1982). *Descriptive summary: Survey of operating and financial characteristics of community water systems.* Washington, DC: U.S. Government Printing Office.

U.S. Environmental Protection Agency. (1983). *Radionuclide removal for small public water systems* (EPA-570/0-83-010). Washington, DC: U.S. Government Printing Office.

U.S. General Accounting Office. (1982a). *Cleaning up the environment: Progress achieved but major unresolved issues remain* (GAO/CED-82-72). Washington, DC: U.S. Government Printing Office.

U.S. General Accounting Office. (1982b). *State's compliance lacking in meeting safe drinking water regulations* (CED-82-43). Washington, DC: U.S. Government Printing Office.

U.S. General Accounting Office (1983). *Wastewater dischargers are not complying with EPA pollution control permits* (GAO/RCED-84-53). Washington, DC: U.S. Government Printing Office.

Vallentine, H. R. (1967). *Water in the service of man.* Baltimore: Penguin Books.

Van Burkalow, A. (1982). Water resources and human health: The viewpoint of medical geography. *Water Resources Bulletin, 18,* 869–874.

Van Damme, J. M. G. (1981). Strategies for water supplies systems in developing countries. In H. van Lelyveld & B. C. Zoeteman (Eds.), *Water supply and health.* Amsterdam: Elsevier Scientific.

Weibel, S. R., Dixon, F. R., Weidner, R. B., & McCabe, L. J. (1964). Waterborne-disease outbreaks, 1946–60, *Journal of the American Water Works Association,* 947–957.

Wellings, F. M., Lewis, A. L., & Mountain, C. W. (1976). Demonstration of solids-associated virus in wastewater and sludge. *Applied Environmental Microbiology, 31,* 354–358.

Weir, J. M. (1969). The unconquered plague. *Rockefeller Foundation Quarterly, 2,* 4–23.

Whipple, G. C. (1908). *Typhoid fever: Its causation, transmission, and prevention.* New York: Wiley.

Wittfogel, K. A. (1957). *Oriental despotism.* New Haven, CT: Yale University Press.

Wolf, H. W. (1972). The coliform count as a measure of water quality. In R. Mitchell (Ed.), *Water pollution microbiology.* New York: Wiley Interscience.

World Heath Organization. (1970). *European standards for drinking water* (2nd ed.). Geneva: World Health Organization.

World Health Organization, (1971). *International standards for drinking water* (3rd ed.). Geneva: World Health Organization.

World Health Organization. (1979). Report of WHO scientific group (Technical Report Series 639). Geneva: World Health Organization.

Young, T., Kanarek, M., & Tsiatis, A. (1981). Epidemiologic study of drinking water chlorination and Wisconsin female cancer mortality. *Journal of the National Cancer Institute, 67,* 1191–1198.

Zielhuis, R. L. (1981). Water hardness and mortality in the Netherlands. In H. van Lelyveld & B. C. Zoeteman (Eds.), *Water supply and health.* Amsterdam: Elsevier Scientific.

C H A P T E R   5

AIR QUALITY AND HEALTH

Robert C. Ziegenfus
Kutztown University

We do not at this time have an agreed-upon definition of adverse health effects as it pertains to air pollution

SHERWIN, 1983

AIR QUALITY CONCERNS IN THE 1950s AND EARLIER: A CASE OF NEGLECT

Despite numerous studies that have attempted to discern the relationship between air pollution and human health there is much that we still don't know. Public health tragedies brought on by high concentrations of air pollutants before 1960 are among the worst effects of air pollution ever recorded. From an overview of these disasters we move on in this chapter to discuss attempts at regulating air pollution in the 1960s and 1970s. The third section examines perhaps the single most important emerging air quality issue of the 1980s, indoor air pollution, and the most promising method to help formulate the elusive definition mentioned in the opening quote, total exposure monitoring. A deliberate decision was made to emphasize these two topics because of their demonstrated direct link to public health. Both will probably be under intensive scrutiny in this decade in order to understand the public health effects of air quality. Consequently, we are devoting less attention to the regulated outdoor pollutants. (For discussion of these and other subjects see Stern, 1977; Lynn, 1976; and Perkins, 1974.) Finally, no space is devoted to acid rain despite the raging controversy over its ecosystem impact. Acid rain is an important environmental issue, but it is not discussed here because it is much less important than indoor air as a public health issue.

Air Pollution Tragedies

Among the television humorists of the 1970s a common line about the air in New York or Los Angeles was that residents of either city were uncomfortable in a clean environment because they "didn't like to breath air they couldn't see." Unfortunately, air that was so dirty that it could be seen was no joke for the population of several places where sickness, even death, was the reward for breathing ambient air. Many writers refer to these instances of acute responses to air pollution as *episodes*, but this word seems more indicative of the pollutant concentrations recorded over a short time (days) than the true cost in health-effect terms. The term *tragedy* is preferred to describe the effects, since it reflects the human experience.

Some of the earliest recorded observations of pollution and their attendant effects are from London. Holland *et al.* (1979) constructed a table that identifies 5 years from 1873 to 1892 when 600 or more excess deaths took place. Not much official reaction resulted. Possibly, the sole permanent consequence of note is the coining of the word *smog* by some anonymous resident of London before World War II (Lynn, 1976).

In the twentieth century, events conspired to strike the Meuse Valley of Belgium in December 1930, thereby rendering false the notion that only London need be concerned. The narrow river valley experienced a temperature inversion from December 1–5, and the effluent from the coke ovens, steel mills, zinc smelters, glass factories, and sulfuric acid plants accumulated under this meteorological lid. Several hundred people became ill with an assortment of respiratory ailments. Another 63 people died, mostly elderly and those with lung or heart disease. Subsequent analysis (there was no monitoring during the event) suggested that the cause of the illness was a combination of sulfur dioxide (SO_2) and sulfuric acid mist that entered the lungs.

Donora, Pennsylvania, became the first place in the United States where air pollutants were directly linked to sickness and death. The conditions in Donora on October 26–31, 1948, were remarkably similar to what had happened in the Meuse Valley—a temperature inversion over a valley trapped the pollutants from a sulfuric acid plant, zinc plant, and steel mill. Again, no instruments were in place to record what are assumed to have been high levels of sulfur dioxide and particulates. Health effects were, however, quite measurable. Slightly more than 40% of the total population became ill within two days, and 10% had severe reactions including coughing, vomiting, headaches, nausea, and irritation of the eyes, nose, and throat (Schrenk, 1949). A total of 20 people died, most on the third day, which is 18 more than would have been normal for Donora. All those who died were 52 to 84 years of age, suggesting the hazards of high pollution levels to the elderly and the infirm.

London possesses the dubious distinction of having experienced the worst single air pollution tragedy ever recorded. From December 5–9, 1952, a temperature inversion controlled the weather pattern. In addition, lower-than-average temperatures led to greater than normal coal burning in power plants and fireplaces, all in addition to the contributions from industry. What began as white fog ended as black from the accumulation of particles and sulfur dioxide. More accurate information is available for this case because of some monitoring of pollutants and weather conditions. Holland *et al.* (1979) cite the maximum 24-hour pollution readings as 4,460 $\mu g/m^3$ for smoke and 3,830 $\mu g/m^3$ for sulfur dioxide. With the caveat that British smoke readings do not correspond precisely with particulates, one can compare the London levels with the levels established by law in the United States: 260 $\mu g/m^3$ (maximum daily average) for particulates and 365 $\mu g/m^3$ (maximum daily average) for sulfur dioxide. As will be discussed below, these United States standards are established at levels to protect human health. A comparison of the numbers reveals, perhaps, why 4,000 people died in London in those 5 days. As in other cases the elderly and those with respiratory problems succumbed first. Specific diseases that were recorded in excess numbers include bronchitis by a factor of 10, influenza by 7, respiratory diseases by 6, pneumonia by 5, heart disease by 3, and lung cancer by 2 (Bach, 1972). Also, applications for emergency bed service more than doubled that week and did not return to normal until 2 to 3 weeks after the air cleared up. Regrettably, similar conditions plagued London again in 1956, 1957, and 1959 with the estimated excess deaths at 1,000, 750, and 250 respectively (Holland *et al.*, 1979).

New York City had its first recorded incident in 1953. From November 18–22, particulate and sulfur dioxide levels rose as a stagnant air mass dominated the weather pattern of the eastern United States (Goldsmith & Friberg, 1977). Approximately 250 excess deaths were attributed to the effect of the air pollutants (Bach, 1972).

Three main lessons came from these and other tragedies in the 1950s and earlier. First, certain meteorological and topographical conditions in winter could produce an environment in which pollutants could accumulate to extraordinary levels. Second, interactions between particulates and sulfur dioxide seemed to be the dominant hazard to human health, perhaps in association with other substances as well such as fog droplets. Third, morbidity and mortality occurred among those in the most susceptible groups; namely, the aged and those with preexisting conditions, particularly of the respiratory system.

Unfortunately, substantive action following these disasters was limited in proportion to the damage inflicted on humans. In England the primary goal of the Clean Air Act, passed in 1956, was to reduce the smoke content of the ambient air in the whole country (Holland *et al.*, 1979). Meanwhile, across the Atlantic, the United States response to deteriorating air quality had actually started before the Donora tragedy. In 1881 Chicago passed the first smoke-control law, and most other major cities had followed suit by 1912. Two world wars moved attention away from the environment, but in 1945 Pittsburgh implemented an effective smoke-control program, and Los Angeles established an air pollution control district that led to smoke and SO_2 regulations within 2 years (Lynn, 1976).

The Donora incident did, however, serve to galvanize action and thought about air quality. It showed that small towns were not immune from danger. In addition, the Public Health Service Service completed a study of the residual health effects among Donora residents. One result was the establishment of the first formal federal air pollution program as a result of passage of the Air Pollution Control Act of 1955. The Public Health Service had primary responsibility for its administration with the specific charge to do research on air pollution effects, train air pollution personnel, and provide technical assistance to the states (Bach, 1972). But the locus of control of air pollution sources remained where it had always been—in the hands of state and local governments.

The tragedies described above were the outgrowth of a long series of singular events related to the Industrial Revolution that, when combined, had a most sinister effect. The steam engine's fuel demands caused an almost immediate spatial concentration of early industry near coal resources with a consequent impact on population distribution. In general, public health implications of the numerous economic interactions through the nineteenth and first half of the twentieth century were rarely, if ever, questioned. Smoke, odors, and other pollutants were symbols of economic growth. Effluents were discharged in any convenient manner: they were released into the lowest-lying layers of air over industrialized regions. To a limited degree, the atmosphere has the ability to disperse, dilute, and remove material in the air, and the observations of these processes likely sanctioned the idea that the solution to pollution is dilution. What the tragedies began to bring into focus was that human activities had exceeded the atmosphere's capacity. The penalty was substantial.

THE 1960s AND 1970s: THE MOVEMENT TOWARD REGULATION

The decade of the 1960s had hardly begun when tragedy struck once more. Again, London, in the winter of 1962, felt the brunt of the same type of conditions it had experienced for years. Credit is usually given to the enforcement of the Clean Air Act of 1956 for having reduced smoke levels to the extent that the total accumulations never reached the truly massive levels of a decade earlier. Holland *et al.* (1979) argue that these lower smoke readings are the reason why the mortality reached only 700 excess deaths rather than the 4,000 in 1952 when the pollution came at the same time of the year, lasted just as long and produced almost exactly the same SO_2 levels. Two alternatives and/or additional reasons for the smaller number of deaths may be a greater effort on the part of the susceptible population to protect themselves or that by 1962 there fewer people with preexisting conditions alive after the toll taken by the tragedies in the 1950s. Absence of any further tragedies in London since the mid-1960s seems to favor the smoke-reduction theory, but SO_2 levels have also fallen at the same time (Holland *et al.*, 1979).

Data from other world regions suggests that the conditions in London were only a part of the worldwide trend of elevated pollutant levels. Monitoring stations across the eastern United States recorded increasing particulate and SO_2 values between November 27 and December 5, 1962 (Bach, 1972). New York City experienced a rise in the death rate compared to the normal seasonal levels as well as a rise in the number of upper respiratory complaints among the elderly (Goldsmith

& Friberg, 1977). Less is known about the health effects in other cities where high readings were recorded such as Cincinnati, Philadelphia, and Washington, D.C.— where the event coincided with the start of a national conference on air pollution (Lynn, 1976)! On the European continent Rotterdam had SO_2 levels about five times the norm with an increase in mortality and hospital admissions. Hamburg recorded similar levels of SO_2 and double its dust levels without sizable health impacts. Neither acute nor chronic effects have been documented for the increased pollutant burdens in Paris, Frankfurt, or Prague. The last city to be affected by the incident was Osaka, Japan, from December 7–10 with a consequent 60 excess deaths (Goldsmith & Friberg, 1977).

In New York City at least twice again in the 1960s there were excess deaths from air pollution. A few months after the worldwide episode, January 29–February 13, 1963, similar conditions prevailed again (McCarroll & Bradley, 1966). It is difficult to assess the role of meteorological and pollutant conditions in this rise in mortality, because there was an influenza outbreak at the same time. The best estimate is 405 excess deaths from pollutant levels. More accurate information has been obtained on the tragedy in New York City during the Thanksgiving Day weekend of November 23–25, 1966. Once again, the stagnant high pressure system fostered elevated readings for SO_2 and particulates. An analysis of the data revealed that "daily deaths due to all causes immediately rose to higher than expected levels for seven consecutive days" (Glasser, Greenberg, & Field, 1967, p. 694). Excess deaths totaled 168 and affected all age groups, but increased with advancing age.

The most deadly tragedies were events of the 1960s or earlier, but there is no cause for complacency. A reminder of the ability of humans to overload natural atmospheric conditions occurred in the Pittsburgh metropolitan area from November 16–20, 1975. Stationary high pressure, a temperature inversion, and light winds combined to elevate SO_2 and particulate levels. By 1975, however, regulations were in effect that triggered a series of responses to avoid worsening the situation. An official air alert was declared in several portions of the city, and abatement procedures were instituted. Further, U.S. Environmental Protection Agency (EPA) personnel flew to Pittsburgh in case they were needed to invoke more stringent controls on the major pollutant sources. In spite of a quick response by officials and voluntary changes by the polluters, the total impact was approximately 14–23 excess deaths. No details are available about morbidity (U.S. EPA, 1976).

Pollutant problems on the west coast of the United States were different. No "body count" was apparent. Instead, coughing and watering eyes were the primary symptoms of the malaise. Los Angeles responded with attempts to reduce smoke and SO_2 concentrations as other cities had done, but success in this control effort yielded little improvement. Slowly, research efforts began to outline a type of pollution that focused on the interactions in the atmosphere between sunlight, hydrocarbons (HC), and nitrogen oxides (NO_x). A series of additional control measures on the suspected sources of these pollutants, in particular petroleum refineries, again produced only minimal progress. Having eliminated or controlled virtually all the obvious sources led to a realization that automobile exhaust had to be the chief cause of the problems. The label coined in London was quickly adopted, and soon smog and Los Angeles became synonymous. To be precise and to avoid confusion, there really are two types of pollution: London smog had a fog-smoke-SO_2 base whereas the Los Angeles smog is the result of secondary reactions in the atmosphere of NO_x and HC—given the technical label *photochemical smog* (Lynn, 1976).

The Awakening of Concern

The air pollution control problems that became ever more apparent in the late 1950s and early 1960s motivated the United States Congress to act. In 1963 the Clean Air Act was passed, amending the 1955 legislation. Very little, if any, substantive improvement resulted. More research, training, and money for state and local programs did not make any important difference. The only possible impact that the act could have had was the clause about "federal authority to abate interstate air pollution" (Perkins, 1974, p. 362). Nothing came of this potential because of the nonbinding nature of the recommendations made to states. Two years later the act was amended again; this time the administrator (the secretary of health, education and welfare) was given authority to enforce automobile emission standards. This amendment marked the first time that enforcement powers were given to the federal air pollution agency. Several of the provisions of the 1967 Air Quality Act were ambitious. One called for the establishment of air quality standards by the states, based on criteria relating pollutants to health effects. Another mandated the creation of air quality control regions for the whole country. Still, there was no provision for federal national standards other than those for autos.

The environmental fervor of the late 1960s had a major effect on public policy about air pollution in the form of the 1970 amendment to the Clean Air Act. Three "firsts" were written into law by Congress: the first national ambient air quality standards (NAAQS) to be established by a federal agency; the first national performance standards for stationary sources; and the first national emissions standards for hazardous pollutants. Federal emission standards for cars were retained as another key provision of the 1970 amendments. By far the majority of issues generated by the act were related to the NAAQS and, therefore, this subject will be the major focus of the discussion.

Stationary sources are those large plants that usually produce huge quantities of particles and/or gases (e.g., power plants, cement plants, acid plants). These sources were to be governed by an interesting dual provision. On the one hand, new or modified sources would be under federal purview, but existing sources would be responsible for meeting the requirements established by the state in which the plant was located. In essence, both the federal and state governments were to set standards that would specify the maximum permissible emission level for a pollutant at a source. Health effects of these emissions come from the various gases and especially the vast quantities of particles small enough to settle and remain in the lungs (commonly called *respirable particulates*).

Probably all reasonable people would agree that hazardous pollutants require control; what becomes controversial is the degree. Congress rejected the "zero emissions" concept even though it was recognized that the pollutants in this class are substances that can accumulate in the body (Massey, 1972). Instead, the EPA was authorized to establish an emission standard that provided an ample margin of safety to protect public health. Initial substances listed as hazardous were asbestos, beryllium, and mercury. The carcinogenic and other morbidity-causing properties of asbestos are well known. Beryllium poisoning is an established risk in industrial applications. Slow excretion rates from the body and chronic effects on the nervous system are among the more important reasons for concern about mercury.

Without a doubt, the regulatory focus of the 1970 amendments to the Clean Air Act was the provision that a federal agency promulgate air quality standards for the ambient air. According to the report of the National Commission on Air Quality (1981):

> Congress based the Clean Air Act on the principle that to protect public health, government must act to control potentially harmful pollutants despite scientific uncertainty about the precise harm they cause and the levels of exposure that cause that harm. (p. 117)

The result was the creation of primary standards to protect public health with "an adequate margin of safety" and secondary standards for the protection of public welfare. Congress defined neither the standards nor the criteria to establish the standards within the act itself. Rather, the law set forth a procedure for the development of what are called "criteria documents." A criteria document is a compendium of the latest scientific information that identifies the kind and extent of the effects of the pollutant in question on the public health and welfare. Six pollutants were mandated for action by the 1970 amendments. The standards have been modified several times since then and those currently in effect are listed in Table 5-1. This section will review briefly the health-effects basis for regulation of each.

Particulate matter includes a wide variety of particles found in the ambient air. Variety in this instance refers to size, shape, and chemical composition. From the perspective of human health, size may be the most significant of the three because the smaller the particle, the greater the chance for penetration into the lungs. Particle size is measured in microns (or micrometer for one millionth of a meter or 1/25,000 of an inch). On this basis, particles larger than about 10 microns are large enough to fall to a nearby surface after being emitted from a source, hence the term *settleable particulate matter*. Anything smaller can remain in the air for long periods, and they constitute what is called *suspended particulate matter*. The EPA standard shown in Table 5-1 is for measurements of total suspended particulates (TSP). There seem to be at least three ways that urban particulate matter is harmful: (1) some of the particles themselves may be toxic and/or have toxic elements adsorbed onto the particle; (2) too many particles within a short time can tax or overwhelm the normal lung-clearing functions; and (3) the particles may interact with gaseous pollutants in synergistic ways (Lynn, 1976). The annual geometric mean primary standard 75 $\mu g/m^3$ seems to be related to the findings in the criteria document that revealed adverse health effects when the annual mean reached 80

Table 5-1. National Ambient Air Quality Standards (NAAQS)

Pollutant	Primary (Health Related)		Secondary (Welfare Related)	
	Averaging time	Concentration	Averaging time	Concentration
Total suspended particulate	Annual geometric mean	75 $\mu g/m^3$	Annual geometric mean	60 $\mu g/m^3$[a]
	24-hour	260 $\mu g/m^3$	24-hour	150 $\mu g/m^3$
Sulfur dioxide	Annual arithmetic mean	(0.03 ppm) 80 $\mu g/m^3$	3-hour	1300 $\mu g/m^3$ (0.50 ppm)
	24-hour	(0.14 ppm) 365 $\mu g/m^3$		
Carbon monoxide	8-hour	9 ppm (10 $\mu g/m^3$)	No secondary standard[b]	
	1-hour	(35 ppm) 40 $\mu g/m^3$	No secondary standard	
Nitrogen dioxide	Annual arithmetic mean	0.053 ppm (100 $\mu g/m^3$)	Same as primary	
Ozone	Maximum daily 1-hour average	0.12 ppm (235 $\mu g/m^3$)	Same as primary	
Lead	Maximum quarterly average	1.5 $\mu g/m^3$	Same as primary	

Note. From U.S. Environmental Protection Agency (1986).

[a]This annual geometric mean is a guide to be used in assessing implementation plans to achieve the 24-hour standard of 150 $\mu g/m^3$.

[b]Because no standards appear to be requisite to protect the public welfare from any known or anticipated adverse effects from ambient CO exposures, EPA rescinded the existing secondary standards.

μg/m^3 (Massey, 1972). One does wonder, however, if 5 μg/m^3 is an "adequate margin of safety." A very critical review of these standards and a retort are well worth reading. The *American Journal of Epidemiology* devoted an entire issue ("Particulate Air Pollution," 1979) and then a reply (Shy, 1979) to this subject.

Sulfur oxides are the gaseous pollutants sulfur dioxide (SO$_2$) and sulfur trioxide (SO$_3$). In effect, the EPA standard is really for SO$_2$ because it is more prevalent in ambient air. The main effect of SO$_2$ seems to be as an irritant to the human respiratory system causing increased airway resistance as the bronchi begin to constrict. The solubility of SO$_2$ in the nasal passages often restricts its impact to the upper respiratory tract, but when adsorbed onto small particles, it can inflict damage deep within the lung. (Recall that it was the combination of particulate matter and SO$_2$ many blame for the mortality in the early air pollution tragedies.) The appropriateness of the standard is supported in the criteria document's report that increased mortality could be determined when SO$_2$ levels were 115 μg/m^3 (annual genetic mean), and other adverse health effects could be measured when 300 μg/m^3 existed for a period of a few days (Massey, 1972).

Carbon monoxide (CO) is unique among the six pollutants for which NAAQS were promulgated in 1971. First, it is a gaseous compound that is colorless, odorless, and tasteless. Consequently, its presence may remain undetected and its effects misunderstood, especially since it seems to affect brain functions such as mental alertness, response time, and judgment (Lynn, 1976). Second, it is the only one of the six to have its standards based on direct health effects measured in laboratory settings. By contrast, the other pollutants have standards derived from air quality readings at fixed monitoring stations. The ability to obtain relatively precise data on CO stems from the bonding that occurs between it and hemoglobin in the blood. Hemoglobin combines much more readily with CO than with oxygen, thereby interfering with the latter's transport of oxygen from the lungs to the cells. Measuring carboxyhemoglobin, then, becomes a sensitive indicator of exposure to CO. A third unique aspect of CO is that it rapidly causes death, the final stage in a series of effects beginning with headaches, then nausea, vomiting, breathing difficulty, and unconsciousness. The standards for CO were based on the findings, as stated in the criteria document, that 30 parts per million (ppm) will inactivate about 5% of the blood's hemoglobin after only a few hours of exposure, with a consequent loss of certain brain functions. Higher exposures seem to place an undue burden on those with preexisting heart conditions (Massey, 1972).

Two other pollutants are primary pollutants; they are emitted into the atmosphere directly, not formed in the atmosphere through a series of reactions. Hydrocarbons (HC) and nitrogen oxides (NO$_x$) were both part of the original NAAQS based on their role as contributors to the production of the secondary pollutant photochemical oxidants (i.e., the Los Angeles smog). The term *hydrocarbon* refers to a group of organic chemicals containing carbon and hydrogen. There are a great many different hydrocarbons, which vary widely in their reactivity to create oxidants. Measuring each substance would be impossible and not very practical, so that the typical approach is to measure all hydrocarbons and subtract the methane portion, which is measurable by itself though it is not a precursor to smog. As a result, one can categorize the nonmethane hydrocarbons, and the NAAQS are based on this group. No health effects have been observed for HC at the levels found in the ambient air. It was a regulated pollutant solely because of its role in smog formation. Hydrocarbons were later dropped by the federal government as a NAAQS.

Oxides of nitrogen, for the purpose of the NAAQS, consist of nitrogen oxide and nitrogen dioxide. The latter forms when the former oxidizes; therefore, the standard treats them as one. Like HC, their regulation is a function of their chemical involvement in the formation of photochemical oxidants. In fact, the brown color of Los Angeles smog comes from NO_2. Nitrogen dioxide, unlike HC, has been implicated in human health effects. Elevated levels of chronic bronchitis were found in children (Massey, 1972), and lowered lung function and respiratory illness occurred in neighborhoods near a chemical plant (Lynn, 1976). Prior to these findings, it had been the conventional wisdom to assume that NO_2 had few, if any, impacts at levels typically found in an urban atmosphere.

As mentioned above, photochemical oxidants form as a result of reactions in ambient air; thus they are called *secondary pollutants*. These reactions lead to a plethora of substances among which it is difficult to detect and measure any one individually other than ozone. The health effects associated with ozone seem to be confined to pulmonary stress of one type or another. Yet, the dominant complaint from smog exposure in Los Angeles (and other cities with photochemical smog) is irritation of the eyes, but ozone has no known association with this type of symptom. Consequently, researchers believe that the true chemical culprit in photochemical oxidation remains unknown. Nevertheless, standards of oxidant control were promulgated mostly on the basis of the ozone effect, especially the impairment of performance of student athletes when subjected to 60–590 $\mu g/m^3$ of hourly levels and the increased frequency of asthma attacks at 100–120 $\mu g/m^3$ (Massey, 1972).

A seventh substance has been added to the NAAQS since the initial six were set forth in the 1970 amendments of the Clean Air Act. The only experience with the procedures for including a new pollutant on the official NAAQS list came about as a result of the controversy surrounding lead (Hattis, Goble, & Ashford, 1982). The EPA was reluctant to act until forced to when the National Resources Defense Council sued in 1975; the lead standard was promulgated in 1978. A host of data show the health effects of lead on adults and children of all ages. EPA focused attention on what is considered to be the most susceptible population—children under 5 years of age who lived in inner-city areas. The final product of all the work was a lead standard of 1.5 μg of lead per cubic meter of air as a maximum average for the readings in one quarter of a year (based on summer exposure of children). Basically, the action on lead is a reflection of its relatively ubiquitous presence in urban environments that offer numerous avenues of exposure in air, water, food, and even nonfood items. Some of the more common health effects are anemia, kidney malfunction, and brain damage (Lynn, 1976). The latter, once initiated, can produce retardation as well as death. It is not clear from the available research what the chronic effects are of long-term low-level exposure. What is clear is that the U.S. EPA is moving to limit automobile lead emissions even further. The maximum allowable lead content of gasoline after January 1, 1986, was planned to be 90%

lower than the maximum of just 1 year earlier. A complete ban could occur by 1988 (EPA, 1985).

Reaffirmation of the Federal Role in 1977

Clearly the 1970 amendments to the Clean Air Act represented a significant departure from the previous approaches. Most of the subsequent action (legal, political, scientific) has revolved around the ambient air quality standards. As one might assume, significant controversies arose regarding the new federal authority and the mechanisms of implementation of the various procedures. Evidence that the political process had produced a reasonable law in 1970 came in 1977 when new amendments to the Clean Air Act reaffirmed its basic goals and strategies. While the EPA was given somewhat greater latitude in enforcing various provisions of the act, the nucleus of the legislation remained the NAAQS. In that regard, the 1977 amendment required the EPA to review all existing standards and revise them where necessary by December 31, 1980 (National Commission on Air Quality, 1981). Response to this mandate was less than complete: a revised ozone standard appeared in 1979; a proposal to change the CO standard surfaced in 1980 (but was never approved); a combined particulate matter and SO_2 criteria document appeared in 1981 that recommended elimination of the primary standard for SO_2, the retention of the 24-hour standard, and the consideration of a new 1-hour standard; a NO_x criteria document was published in September 1982, though no official procedures for changing the standard have been initiated. In early 1984 the EPA administrator took the first step toward revising the standards for particulate matter (EPA, 1984). The proposal is to replace the current standard for total suspended particulates with a new standard for only those particles of 10 microns or smaller. As indicated above, it is the size range of less than 10 microns that can penetrate deeply into the lungs and inflict most of the damage thought to be done by particulates. A most unusual aspect of the EPA action concerns the administrator's decision to propose a range of values (150–250 $\mu g/m^3$) for the primary standard and a range (70–90 $\mu g/m^3$) for the secondary standard. Public comment has been invited on what number should be chosen, though the administrator suggested that he would be inclined toward a lower number in order to provide a greater margin of safety to public health. It will be interesting, indeed, to see the final result of this approach to standard setting.

Given the importance of the ambient air quality standards, you might legitimately wonder why the health effects of each pollutant were not discussed in detail rather than in summary fashion. Three reasons can be given for this action. First, there are numerous articles, books, and monographs on each of the criteria pollutants. It would have been difficult to do justice to these six, let alone the hazardous pollutants. Second, health effects research and the process of developing and evaluating criteria documents have all changed greatly since the initial work more than a decade ago. For example, Sherwin (1983b) contends that the ambient standards should consider health effects at the subclinical level, which would require a much finer distinction than ever before, while Jordon, Richmond, and McCurdy (1983) document the current procedure for review and promulgation of the NAAQS including a new risk analysis framework. The third and most important reason for not considering the detailed health effects of the NAAQS is that the pollutant burden an individual bears is less a function of what can be measured at a fixed monitoring station miles away from the person and more a function of where and how a person spends his/her time during a 24-hour period. New concepts of exposure have appeared recently, and the next section of this chapter turns attention to these matters.

AIR QUALITY IN THE 1980s: OLD AND NEW THREATS TO HEALTH OUTSIDE AND INSIDE HOMES

Indoor Air Pollution

An informed citizen with perspective on air quality issues over the years might well wonder why the cause for alarm about the indoor environment. Frankly, it was an article of faith that polluted air outdoors caused human health problems, but that we were all safe in our homes. Now, little more than a decade after the smog alerts in California and the air pollution episodes in other cities with their appeals for people at greatest risk to remain inside, a flurry of reports in the popular and scientific literature call attention to a greater variety of potentially harmful pollutants indoors than had ever been of concern outdoors. For example, a 1979 World Health Organization (WHO) report concluded, "contaminants are being introduced into the indoor atmosphere from new building materials, contents and furnishings, and from a growing range of consumer products which release chemicals" (p. 20). In January 1981, the *New York Times* was less reticent about calling attention to specific items of concern:

> nitrogen dioxide, carbon monoxide, hydrocarbons, formaldehyde, radon, . . . sulphur dioxide, asbestos, not to mention the chemicals in hairsprays, deodorants, oven cleaners, paints, pesticides, laundry aids, floor and furniture polishes, glue and, ironically, air fresheners. (*New York Times*, January 28, 1981)

"Indoor air pollution poses a potentially serious health hazard," says the U.S. General Accounting Office (GAO) (1980) in its conclusion to a report to the Congress entitled, *Indoor Air Pollution: An Emerging Health Problem*. While the specific health effects of each indoor pollutant are not yet known, the cause for concern reflected in the GAO publication has a substantive basis. This necessarily selective review will examine the human health effects related to two well-established considerations. First, several studies have documented that the indoor levels of certain criteria pollutants exceed ambient levels and, at times, the NAAQS. Second, several known and/or suspected carcinogens have been detected in a variety of indoor environments.

People spend much more time indoors than outdoors. According to the National

Academy of Sciences (NAS) (1981b), the typical American worker is inside 90% of the time while young children, their mothers, the elderly, and the infirm may spend about 95% of their time at home. Therefore, low concentrations over extended periods of time can contribute substantially to a person's total exposure to pollutants. This section reviews the indoor air quality problem as measured by the criteria pollutants.

Criteria Pollutants

A long-term prospective epidemiologic project undertaken by Harvard University, commonly known as the Six City Study (see Embers, 1977, for an overview), has generated some of the most convincing evidence for the existence of high levels of NO_2 inside homes. In a 1979 paper, Spengler, Ferris, and Dockery found that cooking with unvented gas stoves led to NO_2 exposures in excess of the ambient levels while cooking with vented gas or electric stoves kept NO_2 levels lower than ambient levels. But the data Spengler speaks of were obtained at monitors located primarily in the living room, not the kitchen. He went on to speculate about possible kitchen readings:

> Kitchen annual mean values in our study may exceed 100 $\mu g/m^3$ if we extrapolate from other studies. Further, the short-term hourly kitchen NO_2 levels during cooking may be 5 to 10 times higher than measured values. (p. 1280)

A follow-up paper by Sexton, Letz, and Spengler (1983), using additional data from the Harvard Study, presented a simple deterministic model to estimate human exposure to NO_2 in homes with gas versus electric cooking. The results confirm the speculative comments in the earlier paper:

> residents of gas-cooking homes are commonly exposed to elevated NO_2 levels during cooking episodes. In homes with low air-exchange rates and high gas consumption, occupants may experience NO_2 concentrations substantially above existing long-term standards. Associated peak values are likely to be much higher and probably exceed promulgated and recommended short-term standards on a regular basis. (p. 163)

The Harvard research seems to confirm other earlier findings. In one study, Wade, Cote, and Yocom (1975) found that gas stove operations in four different homes produced NO_2 concentrations in kitchens above the NAAQS during a 2-week sampling period. In another study, Palmes, Tomczyk, and March (1979) summarized the evidence from studies conducted in New York, London, and Gainesville, Florida, by stating that in all three places kitchens with gas stoves had average NO_2 readings virtually equal to or above the NAAQS.

If one considers the current NO_2 ambient standard of 100 $\mu g/m^3$ to be reasonable, given the health-effects research, then the evidence to date is a powerful argument for additional research that will allow for more thorough characterization of the potential harm to residents of homes that use gas stoves. Two major studies continue: (1) the Southern California Gas Company is measuring 600 homes in Los

Angeles over three different seasons; and (2) the Gas Research Institute is sponsoring a study of 600 homes in Boston over all four seasons.

All these studies tested the use of gas stoves for cooking. Sterling and Kolayaski (1981), however, have assembled evidence that seems to reveal conclusively that the urban poor in New York City use gas stoves for supplemental heating. If this practice in other cold-climate cities approximates that of New York City, then the number of people, among them large numbers of children and the elderly, exposed to chronic and perhaps acute levels of NO_2 could number in the hundreds of thousands.

Another criteria pollutant for which indoor levels have occasionally been found to exceed the ambient is CO. Carbon monoxide is a well-studied pollutant because of its ability to interfere with oxygen diffusion to the blood. Therefore, any elevated measurements indoors should be evaluated carefully. One of the earliest concerns about CO stemmed from the identification of high levels in homes with defective gas stoves. Yates (1967) recorded readings as high as 2,500 ppm. Sterling and Sterling (1979) completed a study devoted exclusively to CO in homes with gas stoves. Their findings disputed the notion that CO would be minimal in properly adjusted stoves in the presence of ventilation and a hood-fan combination over the stove. What they found was that: (1) CO production increases in a linear fashion with cooking time and number of burners active; (2) CO production increases rapidly when cooking utensils are placed over the flame; (3) CO diffusion throughout a home occurs rapidly and as a function of house volume; and (4) CO dissipation varies directly with the amount of ventilation. The NAAQS for a maximum hourly average is 35 ppm, and only two of the nine kitchens in the study remained below this level after only 20 minutes of cooking. In fact, one kitchen attained a value of 120 ppm. Kitchen levels above the 8-hour ambient standard have been confirmed by other studies as well (Yocom, 1982). Some doubt has recently been cast on the representativeness of these high readings. An EPA study of CO in 712 homes in Washington, D.C., and in 459 homes in Denver found average levels while cooking with gas stoves to be 2.59 ppm. Additional insight may become available when EPA publishes the result of this study.

In addition to studies of residential dwellings, there are increasing concerns about the pollutant levels inside other structures. A new term, sick building, has even appeared to describe a place whose occupants complain of various maladies. Both the Consumer Product Safety Commission and the National Institute for Occupational Safety and Health (NIOSH) have received thousands of complaints regarding alleged health problems caused by building materials, furnishings, operations, and ventilation rates. Wallace (1983) discovered one such condition in a large office building with basement offices next to an underground garage. Carbon monoxide levels often double the NAAQS 8-hour standard were commonplace, and by the end of the workweek nonsmokers had carboxyhemoglobin (COHb) levels similar to that of smokers. In this instance, remedial action was rather straightforward: The building operator closed the fire doors to the parking garage as required by law and started to operate the ventilation system in the garage as the building design specified. The applicability of this study to other settings is clear when one considers the vast number of office buildings with underground garages in large and medium-sized cities throughout the United States.

Spengler, Stone, and Lilley (1978) reported on the carbon monoxide threat in a typical recreational building in New England and the upper Midwest—enclosed ice-skating rinks. Of the 26 hours of monitoring, 21 had hourly CO levels above the 1-hour NAAQS of 35 ppm; one-third of the values exceeded 60 ppm, and peak values reached 192 ppm. The measurement of COHb levels in hockey players showed levels that could produce chronic and perhaps even acute health problems. Once again, the solution is known. Rink managers could replace the gas-powered ice-making equipment and/or ventilate the arenas.

Very few of the hundreds of "sick buildings" studied by NIOSH and state agencies have had such an easy diagnosis as these two. What these two examples do signify is the insidious nature of the carbon monoxide problem because in neither case was the building operator aware of any problem. More important, without the benefit of the studies, the health risks would have remained unknown as well.

A third criteria pollutant of concern indoors is particulate matter. An inherent problem in measuring particulate pollution is deciding whether one will collect all particles, called total particulate matter (TPM), or create a create a dichotomous split of the sizes that can penetrate the lungs—mass respirable particulates (MRP)—versus those that cannot (larger than 10 microns in diameter). One of the early studies cited by Yocom (1982) reported residential structures with TPM in excess of the NAAQS for TSP. More to the point, however, since EPA is on the verge of promulgating what it calls an inhalable particulate (IP) standard to replace the TSP, is the large data base of MRP values generated by the Harvard Six City Study. Spengler, Dockery, Turner, Wolfson, and Ferris (1981) have shown conclusively that mean indoor readings exceeded those outdoors. Therefore, MRP matter is being generated indoors, though all sources and their exact contribution to the total could not be estimated given the data aggregation. One source of indoor MRP was identified. Cigarette smoke increases the mean concentration dramatically from 24.4 μg/m^3 in a home with no smokers to 36.5 μg/m^3 with one smoker to 51.8 μg/m^3 with two or more smokers for "a mean MRP impact per smoker in the home of 20 μg/m^3" (Spengler et al., 1981, p. 26). In a related study, Dockery and Spengler (1981a) found that airconditioning increases the mean contribution from smoking to nearly 42 μg/m^3 while other sources add another 15 μg/m^3 to the MRP.

One of the more comprehensive attempts to understand the contribution of smoking to the levels of respirable suspended particulates (RSP) indoors was the work of Repace and Lowrey (1980). In brief, they found that the smoking-induced RSP levels inside buildings of various types were higher than those measured in the ambient air, in vehicles inhabited by nonsmokers on commuter highways during rush hours, and in smoke-free rooms. Mean levels of RSP in each nonsmoking environment are: (1) smoke-free, 40 μg/m^3; (2) automobiles in rush hour, 38 μg/m^3; (3) ambient outside smoking locations, 46 μg/m^3. By contrast, the range of values (average of 2-minute samples) in 20 indoor smoking locations was 86–697 μg/m^3. Seven of the readings exceeded the 24-hours ambient standard of 260 μg/m^3 for TSP! Such a finding would suggest that the people in these rooms are at risk because Repace and Lowrey measured only the respirable fraction. Furthermore, they make a convincing case for a ban on smoking in public-access buildings. Their readings were made in the presence of ventilation and occupancy rates within the acceptable range of such practices. They note that increasing ventilation rates or filtration of the air yields exponentially diminishing returns. Also, since tobacco smoke levels are directly proportional to smoker density, any reduction in the number of smokers will yield immediate results.

The move to pare energy costs in the Unites States has taken many forms. Perhaps the one of most concern from the standpoint of particulate matter is the burning wood for home heating. A recent estimate (U.S. EPA, 1981) placed the number of American homes heated solely with wood at 1% but estimated that 10 million homes would be using some wood as fuel by 1985. These numbers suggest that research will be needed to assess the impact of residential wood combustion on indoor particulate levels. Only recently has the first set of results become available from the Harvard Wood-Burning Study conducted in Waterbury, Vermont, from January to March 1982 (Sexton, Treitman, Spengler, & Turner, 1984). Similar to the findings reported above, they found that the indoor concentrations were higher than outdoors, but they found no statistical difference between the wood-burning versus the non-wood-burning homes even though all the residents in the study were nonsmokers. Particulate levels varied greatly among the homes. While wood-burning had an impact on the levels, it was not judged to be the most important source of respirable particulates.

Even though hydrocarbons (HC) are no longer regulated by the NAAQS, they seem to occur at elevated levels indoors. Yocom (1982) cites a study of New York high-rise apartments where the average HC levels were higher inside than outside for buildings situated in street canyons and air rights. Another study in the same article cited indoor values that ranged from 0 to 8 ppm while the outdoor levels ranged from 0 to 3.5 ppm (NAAQS were 0.24 ppm for nonmethane hydrocarbons). These levels would lead one to conclude that the former outdoor standard can be exceeded indoors. A later study by the same contractor duplicated the earlier findings. Moreover, they suggested that the amount of HC is a function of the use of paint and cleaning materials indoors.

Less is known about the indoor air quality as measured by the other criteria pollutants (SO_2, ozone, lead). Traditionally, it was assumed that when any of these were found inside, their presence was a function of the ambient levels although in lesser amounts because of losses sustained while penetrating a structure. Consequently, any effort to weatherize a home would provide additional protection. A faulty flue was thought to be the only potential source of SO_2 inside a building. Recently, however, kerosene heaters, now used as a source of supplemental heat in millions of homes, have been found capable of producing SO_2 concentrations in excess of the ambient air quality standard (Leaderer, 1982). Lead can enter the indoor air as a pollutant from outside and as part of the material carried into a house on shoes or boots which then becomes airborne. It must also be noted that lead paint in the home is a major concern in terms of the public health of children.

A major concern relates to the measurement of several known or suspected carcinogens inside at levels that have raised grave questions about human impacts. Formaldehyde, radon, and organics have received most of the attention in the literature and will be reviewed here.

As you may recall from high school biology class, formaldehyde is a liquid in which animals are preserved for study. Recently, however, it has become quite clear that contact with formaldehyde in some forms is harmful. The most important function of formaldehyde is as a component in resins. Ureaformaldehyde is the principal resin in building materials such as foam insulation, particleboard, and plywood. Human exposure to the formaldehyde derives from the excess amounts in the wood product as well as the incomplete mixing of the resin, especially in the foam insulation. Hence, formaldehyde emissions from these products are at their maximum immediately after manufacture and tend to decrease over time. Moisture and heat can contribute to the continuation of the outgoing effect (Yocom, 1982). Other sources of formaldehyde in the home are combustion appliances, tobacco smoke, and a variety of consumer products.

Potential and actual formaldehyde exposure became an issue during the late 1970s. The Consumer Product Safety Commission (CPSC) had received several hundred complaints from residents of mobile and conventional homes insulated with ureaformaldehyde foam during this time. Subsequent research by CPSC led to the issuing of a consumer advisory on August 1, 1979, because of what it called "possible" health problems. At the same time, the Department of Housing and Urban Development noticed that its number of complaints about formaldehyde had increased (NAS, 1981a). This heightened consciousness on the part of the public did not go unnoticed at the EPA. That agency requested the National Research Council to prepare a report to help assess the need for some regulation. The resulting report entitled *Formaldehyde and Other Aldehydes* (NAS, 1981a) is probably the single best source of information on the subject.

The cause for alarm on the part of the thousands who have complained seems justified. Monitoring studies summarized in the NAS document reveal that levels of all aldehydes (of which formaldehyde is the dominant constituent) in a clean environment are in the range of .0005–.002 ppm; in ambient air at .004–.05 ppm (hourly average); and indoors 24-hour formaldehyde averages of .05–.2 ppm are typical (NAS, 1981a). Other formaldehyde readings reported in the literature include: (1) a study of 23 new Danish homes with chipboard as a component revealed concentrations of .06–1.83 ppm with a mean of .51 ppm; (2) a Swedish study of 319 homes of persons who filed complaints found an average level of .58 ppm, but 38 homes had readings of more than 1 ppm; (3) a Washington state study contained a range of 0–3.4 ppm; and (4) a Connecticut survey of 68 homes had a range of .41–8.2 ppm (Dally, Hanrahan, Woodbury, & Kanarck, 1981). Dally *et al.* conducted their own study on 100 structures after receiving complaints from occupants and reported a range in formaldehyde from below detection (.1 ppm) to 4.18 ppm with an overall mean of .35 ppm. Mobile homes had a mean of .47 while conventional homes had a mean of .10.

Most of the monitoring studies of formaldehyde completed to date have been the direct result of consumer complaints. The medical symptoms catalogued from these people include eye irritations, respiratory tract discomfort, nausea, headache, tiredness, and thirst. A number of studies have shown that formaldehyde can aggravate already existing conditions, particularly asthma. According to the distillation of data in the NAS report (1981), levels of formaldehyde need not be high to induce the symptoms that bothered these people. Specifically, the NAS (1981a) estimates that between 10 and 20% of the general population may be susceptible to irritant effects at concentrations between .5 and 1 ppm. Moreover, laboratory tests have revealed effects at levels as low as .01 ppm, though in this case formaldehyde was mixed with other air pollutants. More serious is the evidence for carcinogenicity in rats, though no similar documented information has been discovered for humans. But the accepted scientific practice is to assume that a substance is a likely carcinogen in humans when it is found to be a carcinogen in animal tests (Perera & Petito, 1982).

Occupational standards exist for formaldehyde, but there is no nonoccupational standard in the United States. The American Society of Heating, Refrigerating, and Air-Conditioning Engineers has recommended a 24-hour residential maximum of .20 ppm. By contrast, a few European countries have even more stringent standards: Germany (.10), Denmark (.12), and the Netherlands (.10). Whether the American government will ever establish a standard is an open question. For a while in 1981 and 1982, it appeared that the Formaldehyde Institute and the EPA leadership were attempting to scuttle any attempt to list formaldehyde as a priority candidate for regulation under the Toxic Substances Control Act (Perera & Petito, 1982). The return of William Ruckelshaus as EPA administrator seems to have changed EPA's interest in indoor air, if the testimony at the August 1983 hearings of two subcommittees of the House Committee on Science and Technology is an accurate indicator (Hileman, 1983).

The substantial attention given to radon as an indoor air pollutant is not for radon per se because it is a gas capable of being inhaled and exhaled as well. Rather, the concern arises because radon is a radioactive decay product from radium and further decays to a group of what are called *daughter* (or *progeny*) elements. These progeny are solids that can attach themselves to particulates in the air. When the particulates enter the lungs, the radon daughters irradiate the tissue.

According to Hileman (1983), Spengler of Harvard has testified that radon's health effects are the best known and understood of all indoor pollutants. Much of this knowledge has come from studies of miners. There may be some question as to whether the miners' exposure, at two to three orders of magnitude higher than normal indoor readings, is relevant, but "there is no doubt that radon and its progeny in sufficient doses can produce lung cancer in man" (NAS, 1981b, p. 317). A more recent publication indicates that certain types of nasal cancers may also be related to radon exposure (Hileman, 1983).

In-home exposure to radon and its progeny can come from three main sources: building materials, groundwater, and soil. The first two were originally considered the principal avenues of exposure, but a number of studies in several geographic locations in the United States has caused the NAS (1981b) to consider soil as perhaps the major source of exposure. Apparently the radon diffuses out of the soil and into buildings, from which it cannot easily escape.

Radon levels indoors are commonly an order of magnitude higher than outdoors. When measured in picocuries per liter (pci/l), Spengler and Sexton (1983) reported a range of .01–4 pci/l from their survey of the literature. They did, however, find an instance of where energy-efficient houses had readings in excess of 20 pci/l. Conventional homes, too, have been found to have high levels, especially in granitic, phosphate, and other mining regions (Hileman, 1983). One corporation that pioneered the development of a radon monitor (Terradex) has taken thousands of measurements in widely scattered locations throughout the United States and discovered exceedingly high levels, up to 133 pci/l, in Maine.

One way to assess the importance of these readings is to compare them to the standard that the EPA established in January 1983 for houses built on contaminated sites near inactive mill tailings sites. This standard mandates levels of less than 3 pci/l for indoor air. By this yardstick, many of the homes surveyed by Terradex are above the standard. More than 40% of the homes in Pennsylvania measure above 3 pci/l and 15% above 20 pci/l. Consider the following contrast as a way of placing radon exposures into a context. A person living in a house with 3 pci/l of radon receives approximately 3,000 millirems of radiation each year while the average annual exposure from a nuclear power plant is 0.3 millirems (Hileman, 1983). Virtually everyone is aware of nuclear power plants. It would seem appropriate that more individuals begin to investigate the levels of radon they may be exposed to every day.

Organic chemicals are a third class of substances for which known or suspected carcinogens have been detected indoors. Unfortunately, it is the least understood group of compounds compared to formaldehyde, radon, and most other indoor pollutants, at least partly because the number of potential chemicals involved could be enormous. Americans use and store at home a bewildering array of substances for cleaning, deodorizing, disinfecting, exterminating, painting, polishing, and personal grooming. The NAS (1981b), in its report *Indoor Pollutants* cites a study that estimates the number of aerosol sprays in the average residence to be 45. It will be difficult to assess the health effects of these exposures accurately because of their irregular and sporadic nature, and because of the myriad number of substances in the product. Add to this mix the potential plethora of chemicals from the bioeffluents emitted by humans, gases from building materials, and the constituents of tobacco smoke (NAS, 1981b), and one can appreciate the difficulty of establishing controls for research on organics in homes.

Nevertheless, the EPA has conducted two studies on exposure to volatile organic compounds (VOCs) in family homes. One was a relatively small study of 150 households in three cities by the Office of Toxic Substances; the other was a much larger undertaking by the Office of Research and Development (ORD) of 650 households in six cities (Wallace, 1984). The ORD study obtained 12-hour integrated exposures of 20–25 VOCs, so that one sample represented the daytime (6:00 AM–6:00 PM) and the other the nighttime (6:00 PM–6:00 AM). Identical equipment was placed in the backyard of a subgroup of households in order to compare outdoor to indoor values. Not all the results of this study have been analyzed, but for the 11 most prevalent chemicals among the households in Bayonne and Elizabeth, New Jersey, the indoor concentrations were all higher than outdoor readings, by a factor of 2 to 4 at median levels to more than 10 at higher levels. Wallace (1984) has found that these 11 chemicals are of three types. The aromatics contain benzene (a known human carcinogen), styrene, ethylbenzene, and the xylenes, the total indicating exposure to gasoline, paint, and plastics. The chlorinated solvents suggest contact with household cleaning products, dry-cleaning fluids, and metal degreasers. A miscellaneous group revealed no clear pattern of singular exposure. Considered together, the implications of the findings about these 11 chemicals strongly suggest that exposure is a function of one's personal activities. This, in turn, means that one may be able to minimize health effects if given the required information.

As a separate entity, apart from the two studies that had objectives beyond just indoor air concerns, the EPA launched an indoor air monitoring program in 1982 to examine structures other than family residences. The program has monitored two homes for the elderly, one school, and one office building (Wallace et al., 1984). A five-story home for the elderly was the first structure to be studied and is the one for which some preliminary data are now available. Each efficiency apartment has its own electric stove, but the building's heating fuel is gas. Six monitoring locations were established: one on the rooftop to indicate the outdoor levels, a nonsmoking lounge, a smoking lounge, a nonsmoker's apartment, a smoker's apartment, and a dining area without smoking restrictions. Keeping in mind that this is a home for about 200 individuals of a population that is more susceptible to pollutant burdens, the monitoring discovered approximately 350 VOCs in the building with a distinct gradient of higher readings from the outdoor monitor to the lounges to the apartments. Fifty-three chemicals were detected at all the indoor sites (see Table 5-2), and of these 14 are carcinogens, cocarcinogens, or mutagens. These results suggest that as in homes, there are a large number of sources of indoor pollutants. In fact, over 800 separate organic compounds were identified in the four buildings (Wallace, personal communication, October, 1984).

Office buildings have been evaluated, often because of complaints from workers. Lawrence Berkeley Laboratories (LBL) of the University of California has conducted studies on a number of these structures. Hollowell and Miksch (1981) reported that three types of organic compounds dominated the indoor environment: (1) hydrocarbons derived from petroleum-type solvents, (2) aromatic hydrocarbons, and (3) chlorinated hydrocarbons. Not one of the organics was detected at levels near the Occupational Safety and Health Administration (OSHA) standards. But this does not indicate an absence of potential health effects because long-term, low-level exposure in a diverse population may lead to additive or synergistic effects. The LBL (Hollowell & Miksch, 1981) research identified building materials, wet-process photocopiers, tobacco smoke, and building maintenance products as the major sources of organics in closed office spaces. While removal of some of these sources is possible (tobacco smoke, photocopiers), others would be impossible (building materials). Therefore, more information is needed to identify how exposure can be minimized, given the economic realities of building construction and maintenance.

Table 5-2. Chemicals Present in All Indoor Monitoring Sites at Home for the Elderly in Washington, D.C., March 1983

Acetone	Methyl decalin	Propylbenzene
*Benzene	4-Methyldecane	i-Propylbenzene
*Carbon tetrachloride	5-Methyldecane	Propylcyclohexane
*Chloroform	*Methylene chloride	*Styrene
Cyclohexane	2-Methylheptane	*Tetrachloroethylene
Decalin	2-Methylhexane	Toluene
Decanal	3-Methylhexane	*1,1,1-Trichloroethane
*Decane	1-Methylnaphthalene	*Trichloroethylene
*m,p-Dichlorobenzene	2-Methylnaphthalene	Trichlorofluoromethane
1,4-Diethylbenzene	2-Methylnonane	1,3,5-Trimethylbenzene
*1,4-Dioxane	2-Methyloctane	1,2,4-Trimethylcyclohexane
*Dodecane	2-Methylundecane	1,3,5-Trimethylcyclohexane
Ethyl acetate	Naphthalene	2,2,4-Trimethylhexane
Ethylbenzene	Nonanal	2,4,4-Trimethyl-i-pentene
Heptane	Nonane	*Undecane
Hexane	*Octane	m,p-Xylene
Hexanol	Pentane	o-Xylene
Methylcyclohexane		

Note. From Wallace (1984).
*An asterisk indicates a chemical with mutagenic, carcinogenic, or cocarcinogenic properties.

Exposure Determinants

From this discussion of elevated levels of several criteria pollutants and the detection of carcinogenic substances indoors, one might assume that there are literally hundreds of sources of specific substances of potential concern and that protecting oneself from this onslaught would be impossible. Such is not the case. At the risk of overgeneralization, it appears as though three primary factors can largely govern one's exposure to indoor pollutants: air-exchange rate, smoking, and household activities.

Rising energy costs in the 1970s, spurred by inflation and oil embargos, caused the American public to be much more conscious about the retention of warm air in winter and cool air in summer. Adding more insulation, replacing old windows with double-paned glass, caulking all cracks, placing plastic over windows, and installing storm doors and windows were some of the responses. This wholesale adoption of energy conservation strategies produced savings on utility bills and federal tax bills as well because of tax credits for certain energy-saving measures. The net effect of these collective actions was successful; the amount of air escaping from inside and being replaced by outside air declined. It is difficult to be precise about the degree of change because ventilation rates for the United States housing stock have not been well established (NAS, 1981b). Repace (1981), however, reports that typical closed-window rates in the past averaged approximately one complete air change per hour (ach). Builders know that energy conservation "sells," so new homes have a range of .5 to .7 ach with the most energy-efficient homes as low as .3 ach. Even retrofitted residences can achieve levels in the .5 to .8 ach range (NAS, 1981b).

The consequence of reduced air-exchange rates has been greater exposure to indoor pollutants. A myriad of substances can be present indoors as the EPA Indoor Monitoring Program has confirmed. The health effects of some of these substances are already well known while others are virtually unknown. While research continues, so will exposure. Hence, it appears the public is forced to choose between higher immediate utility bills from greater ventilation or perhaps higher medical bills in the future from greater exposure. The alternatives to these undesirable choices are to ventilate without energy loss using heat-exchange technology, clean the air, or remove the sources of pollution. The installation of a heat exchanger is a viable option at the present time, but the drawback is the cost. Filtering the air inside a structure, especially a detached home, is not yet economically, and, for some pollutants technically, feasible. As a result, source removal may be the most effective strategy where applicable. Clearly, one cannot economically remove the insulation from a home that is the source of formaldehyde exposure. Many other cost-effective approaches are within reach of every household, and a number of these will be noted below.

People have the power to control tobacco smoke in the indoor environment. That they should do so is rather apparent, as "over 2,000 compounds have been identified in cigarette smoke; many are established carcinogens" (NAS, 1981b, p. 150). The concern here is not only for the smoker who is voluntarily exposing himself or herself to these substances, but for those involuntarily exposed (commonly called passive smokers). A significant proportion of the American population must be exposed, as 33% of all adults are smokers (NAS, 1981b). It is estimated that 60% of children live in homes with at least one smoker. Of course, some of the contact between smokers and nonsmokers is probably incidental, but many nonsmokers indicate they suffer a variety of chronic effects in the presence of tobacco smoke.

If passive smoking produced an occasional cough, it might be appropriate to question the need for further research on the specific health impacts on nonsmokers. Evidence is beginning to accumulate, however, that the influence of tobacco smoke transcends mere anecdotal responses. Repace (1981) has summarized the evidence of recent epidemiologic and clinical studies, and he classified the health effects into four categories. Symptomatic effects ranged from eye irritation to aggravation of preexisting conditions in a study of 10,000 nonsmoking office workers. A number of studies on respiratory effects found dose-response relationships between exposure to tobacco smoke and pulmonary function of paramount concern especially because one of these studies was restricted to children. Another survey of children found more chronic problems in those from homes with smokers than those from smoke-free homes. While the evidence for cardiovascular effects is extremely limited because of small sample sizes, measured effects include higher blood pressure, heart rate, and COHb. Repace's fourth category was cancer. He cites two studies that compared housewives to the husband's smoking habits, and both reported statistically significant dose-response relationships.

All of us have seen smoke disperse from a cigarette. We might, therefore, be tempted to assume that ventilation is the solution to removing tobacco smoke from indoor environments. Research by Repace and Lowrey (1980) discovered tobacco smoke concentration to be inversely proportional to the ventilation rate. One can assume that respirable particulate pollution from tobacco smoke is increasing because of the reduced air-exchange rates instituted in many buildings and private homes. In addition, Repace and Lowrey found tobacco smoke levels to be directly proportional to the number of smokers.

The third of the three major exposure determinants to be discussed is the household activity pattern of Americans. As noted above, people use and store a wide variety of substances to accomplish various tasks around the home. One might question the need for several of the products that contain chemicals implicated in health effects research. Conversely, the presence of ants or silverfish usually prompts a desire for something that will stop the critters dead in their tracks. What seems to be required is an effective campaign to promote more intelligent use of consumer products. How many of us have used the philosophy that if one ounce or tablespoon or cupful of a chemical will do the job, then a little more will do even better? A disregard for the proper use of these substances exposes not only the user but those in the household as well. Inadequate labeling laws and hazard warnings may account for a certain portion of the misuse; the remainder is simply abuse. Storage is yet another issue. A typical home often has a laundry room on the same floor as the most used activity area for the sake of convenience. Such places are commonly the repository of detergents, bleaches, and presoaks. Cleansers, polishes, and associated items may also be located there or even within the kitchen or bathroom. An attached garage or basement will usually have gasoline for the lawnmower, paints, varnishes, oils, "industrial-strength" cleaners, and other supplies for hobbies like woodworking or modelbuilding. Virtually nothing is known about the specific health effects of these activities except that "a number of chemicals with serious toxic potential continue to be used" (NAS, 1981b, p. 107). Public education to the possible dangers and prudent use and storage appear to be the twin approaches most likely to reduce exposure.

Recommendations

After all of the seemingly negative pronouncements in this section, you may think that the only way to avoid the dangers of indoor pollution is to move outdoors. One could, though, begin to construct a tentative list of ways to minimize human health effects from indoor pollutants. All of the evidence from numerous reports suggests that tobacco smoke may be one of the most harmful exposures over which the populace has immediate and decisive control. Efforts to remove it ought to be intensified. Sexton, Webber, Hayward, Sextro, and Offerman (1984) recently presented the preliminary results of a chamber study wherein they found cigarette smoke "high in particle phase organic carbon, and [it] tests positive for mutagenicity on the . . . modified Ames test" (p. 6). Another change, if possible, would be from gas to electric cooking because of the elevated CO and NO_2 emissions that seem to influence chronic respiratory symptoms in children. Any gas stove should be well ventilated. A third way to reduce exposure would be to avoid using wood-burning stoves and kerosene space heaters for heating. Particles and gases from the combustion have not yet been carefully researched, but stock samples from wood-heated residences were found to be mutagenic and cytotoxic in an EPA study (U.S. EPA, 1981). Avoiding the use of formaldehyde-bearing substances is a fourth suggestion. Fifth, assess one's radon exposure by using one of the commercially available monitors. Sixth, use and store all necessary consumer products in a safe manner, and reduce the frequency of use whereever possible. Finally, maintain ventilation rates at practical levels given the constraints of house type, ambient environment, and climate. Consider the installation of a heat exchanger if circumstances warrant.

One of the major caveats in these data is that almost all were averages over various time periods. A key question could be whether or not these average concentrations are the critical ones for determining human health. Perhaps the peak value and its duration is of greater singular importance. Few studies to date have considered this issue, but there is general agreement that episodic levels are the ones that may trigger acute responses, especially in those with preexisting chronic conditions.

Potential additive or synergistic relationships are another relatively unknown quantity in the indoor air quality formula. We have noted several times that there is a tremendous variety of substances indoors. In this instance, there will be little equivalent ambient air research to draw upon for ideas. Even where available, the outdoor levels would probably be quite low in contrast to the levels achieved by entrapment inside a structure.

As noted at the outset of this section, people generally spend approximately 90% or more of their time indoors. The aged, infirm, and mothers with young children may even approach 95% of the time inside. Given what we already know about the human health effects of indoor air quality, there seems to be no sensible recourse other than to begin to move public policy toward the development of an effective and fair response to the numerous issues raised in this chapter. It is time for the designation of a lead agency. It is time for the establishment of an agenda for indoor air quality research. Perhaps these efforts at the federal level could profit from an examination of California's pioneering legislation mandating a permanent research program on the subject (Wesolowski, Sexton, Liu, & Twiss, 1984). Conferences, workshops, international symposia, and the recent spate of articles in the popular and scientific press have all addressed what might be recognized as the first phase of coming to grips with the problem of indoor air quality. Phase two will require a concerted effort to determine the spatial and temporal variation within homes and buildings in the United States, establish the dose-response relationships for the human health effects, and move toward the implementation of public policy that minimizes exposure. (For related discussion, see also *Proceedings of the 3rd International Conference on Indoor Air Quality and Climate*, Volumes 1–5.) The impetus for a reasonable public policy on indoor air will likely emanate from the states. For example, within the last few years there has been a great deal of activity at the state level because radon by-products have been found at elevated levels in numerous homes in politically active states like New Jersey and Pennsylvania. The federal government may be forced to respond to the upwelling of state pressure due to the threats of indoor air pollution.

Total Exposure Monitoring

As noted earlier, the principal motivation for the promulgation of standards for ambient air is the desire to protect human health. The determination of whether or not these standards are being achieved stems from measurements derived from a network of monitoring stations located at specific places that, more or less, attempt to approximate the population distribution of the United States. Implicit in this approach is the assumption that these fixed stations are an accurate indicator of the population's exposure to the criteria pollutants. Such an assumption has proved to be erroneous. Ott (1982), Cortese and Spengler (1976), and Petersen and Allen (1982) all cite evidence from their own research that calls into serious question the use of fixed site stations to characterize CO exposure. Moreover, Ott (1982) reviews several additional studies that arrive at similar conclusions for CO. Spengler and Tosteson (1981) and Dockery and Spengler (1981) investigated the levels of respirable particulates both indoors and outdoors and found the outdoor readings to be unreliable as a basis for predicting indoor concentrations. Wallace (1982) claims that the same relationship holds true for nitrogen dioxide and volatile organic gases.

All this is not meant to suggest that the ambient readings are worthless. Various publications based on the Harvard Six City Study have concluded that outdoor levels have an influence on exposure under certain circumstances. Indoor measurements are usually, however, of greater significance as we have seen. One additional exposure that has been found to be of paramount importance in CO studies depends on a person's mode of transportation. Wallace (1979) used a portable monitor to measure CO levels in several different types of cars and buses during his commute to downtown Washington, D.C., from Reston, Virginia, and return. He concluded, "This study, like many others, indicates that commuter exposures to carbon monoxide are considerably higher than could be estimated from ambient readings" (Wallace, 1979, p. 7). Repace, Ott, and Wallace (1980) cite evidence of episodic CO exposure at levels of 20–50 ppm during commuting between Virginia and Washington, D.C., the latter reading associated with an interior parking garage. An EPA study of more than 1,000 vehicles (buses, taxis, police cars) in two major metropolitan areas found that more than 50% of the 132 vehicle trips measured by a personal sampler had average CO concentrations above the CO NAAQS of 9 ppm for 8 hours while the fixed monitoring site had comparatively low values (U.S. EPA, 1982). Pedestrians, too, can be exposed to CO concentrations well above those recorded at official monitoring stations (Ott, 1982).

Knowledge about indoor and in-transit pollutant levels has certainly augmented the air quality community's awareness of the potential matrix of exposures a person can experience. In the last few years the quest for comprehensiveness has led to the concept of total exposure. *Exposure* means the amount of a substance present at the point of contact with a surface (lung, skin, gut) through which the pollutant can penetrate, and a *dose* is the quantity that actually passes through the surface. *Total exposure* can be defined as the amount of pollutant(s) that exist(s) in all three pathways of exposure (air, food, water) and then comparing the exposure to a dose as calculated by measuring the same pollutant(s) in the breath, blood, and urine (Wallace, 1982/1983). The objective, then, is to determine the relative contribution of each pathway for a particular substance.

A careful reading of this definition should make it quite apparent that such a study cannot rely on fixed-station measurements. Each day an individual is in all sorts of settings, each with different pollutant levels. A typical day might include sleeping, driving to work, walking to the office, working inside a building, walking outside at lunch time, eating inside, walking back to the office, working the rest of the day, driving home with a stop to fill the gas tank or pick up the dry cleaning, eating dinner, working in the garage, and watching TV. To assess the exposures occurring in these different places (often called microenvironments) accurately requires that an individual have a portable monitor on or near his/her person at all times. These personal monitors would have to be small, lightweight, and compact to minimize their interference in a person's daily activities.

There has been more research on total exposure to CO than any other single pollutant. The main reason has been the existence of instruments originally designed for occupational use that have been sufficiently sensitive and portable to be used for environmental applications. Another reason is "technology forcing" of the well-established health effects of CO. The desire for federal agencies such as the EPA, NIOSH, and the Department of Energy (DOE) to understand CO exposure has prompted the development of appropriate instruments. The EPA has funded several CO personal exposure studies; the most recent one involved data collection in Washington, D.C., and Denver during the winter of 1982–1983. Participants monitored their CO exposure, had their breath CO levels (the dose) measured by technicians, and kept a diary of their daily activities. A diary is an essential document in total exposure work, as it serves as the only mechanism by which CO readings can be directly linked to a specific microenvironment. Analysis of this large data base continues, but a special effort has been made to use the data in a computer program that simulates exposure to CO. The model, Simulation of Human Air Pollution Exposure (SHAPE), was developed by Dr. Wayne Ott of the EPA. SHAPE input includes ambient and microenvironment CO readings and the activity pattern of individuals while the output consists of several types of CO averages and blood COHb levels. This study is an excellent example of how total exposure field studies can be related to computer modeling efforts for the mutual enhancement of both.

More comprehensive in scope is another EPA effort entitled the Total Exposure Assessment Methodology (TEAM) study. This 5-year effort represents the largest study yet conducted on volatile organic compounds (VOC). It would have been impossible to screen all organic chemicals because of the large potential number eligible for review. Therefore, financial considerations forced attention to those toxic, mutagenic, or carcinogenic volatile organics known or thought to be prevalent. The term *methodology* in the title of the study is central to a consideration of the overall goal; the TEAM study was specifically designed to test different pieces of equipment and other methods to perform total exposure assessments. To achieve this objective, the planners of the TEAM study incorporated several distinct steps into the overall plan.

The initial effort involved 17 university students in a petrochemical manufacturing area in Texas and a nonindustrial area in North Carolina (Wallace *et al.*, 1982). The methodological objectives were to field test the following: a personal monitor for air within a person's breathing zone; a spirometer to sample exhaled breath; and analytical protocols for measuring VOCs in air, tap water, breath, blood, and urine. The exposure objective was to compare the VOC levels in the breathing-zone air and drinking water (i.e., the exposure) with the dose as measured by the VOC levels present in the exhaled breath, blood, and urine. The breathing-zone air seemed to be correlated with the exhaled breath. Such a result is exactly what the total exposure concept implies—the ability to detect an exposure and its resultant dose. An unanticipated discovery of breathing-zone air values that varied by two to three orders of magnitude among similarly situated participants on the same day within the small area of a college campus calls into question the validity of assuming relatively uniform exposure among such individuals as is the case in much of epidemiologic research (Wallace, 1982/1983).

A second effort on 12 New Jersey and North Carolina subjects tested equipment and methods for four groups of substances: VOCs; metals; pesticides and PCBs; and polyaromatic hydrocarbons (PAHs). A total of more than 3,000 samples were collected. Exposure to VOCs in food and beverages was added to the testing for the same substances in breathing-zone air and drinking water. Breath and blood measurements for VOCs were retained, but pesticides in blood and urine and metals in blood, urine, and hair represented new efforts. An entirely different approach was taken in the attempt to select and gather data from the participants; five different questionnaires were employed for these purposes, instead of the one in the first step. Nine people from two communities in northeastern New Jersey were chosen as the participants, while three people in North Carolina served as controls. The reasons for choosing New Jersey as the field location are: (1) the state has a number of industries that either manufacture or use substances with VOCs; (2) the state has the highest population density of all the 50 states; (3) the state environmental and health agencies have performed more research on toxic substances than most other states; and (4) the communities identified for sampling have provided support for the study. Each participant was monitored for a total of 9 days over three different seasons.

As in the first step, the majority of methodological objectives of the second step were found to be appropriate for the purposes of the study. Methods for determining the VOC levels in breathing-zone air, drinking water, food, and exhaled breath were quite successful. Indeed, confidence in the validity of the low concentrations in food may lend support to the argument that food is a relatively unimportant pathway of exposure to VOCs. A few of the methods, however, will have to be reevaluated. For example, the procedures for VOCs in blood and urine were deemed unsatisfactory.

A diversity of statistical procedures were employed to discern the value of the data to an understanding of exposure-dose relationships. First, looking simply at presence or absence, several VOCs and metals were found in a high percentage of the samples in more than one media. Lead, cadmium, chloroform, and benzene were virtually ubiquitous. Second, the surprising degree of individual variability discovered during step one surfaced again. This variability was often a function of the season of the year, occupational exposure, type of day (weekday versus weekend), or some combination. Third, a few significant correlations were found between exposure levels in air and water and dose levels in breath, another confirmation of the ability to assess total exposure (Pellizzari et al., 1983). Fourth, the procedure for selecting control subjects becomes even more of an enigma because the differences between the New Jersey participants and the North Carolina volunteers were so small.

Step three of the TEAM study had a goal of estimating the exposures to VOCs of an entire urban population. The result of the first two steps indicated that only a few of the volatile organic compounds had methodologies deemed acceptable for a full-scale study. Moreover, exposure pathways could be limited to air and water, as food and beverages were thought to be relatively minor sources. Knowledge about doses was to be obtained by breath samples. The participants were selected using a stratified design sampling method that began with a survey of more than 5,000 households and ended with the selection of 362 individuals to represent the 128,000 people in the study area. New Jersey was the site for this phase for the same reasons as before.

To provide some appreciation for what was involved in being a participant, here are the tasks each subject performed: (1) completed a 51-question survey form on socioeconomic and personal matters; (2) carried or wore a personal monitor for the two 12-hour sampling times; (3) collected a drinking water sample during each 12-hour period; (4) maintained a diary of activities for the 24-hour monitoring period; (5) provided a breath sample at the end of the 24-hour monitoring period; and (6) completed a 12-question recall survey about exposure variables. Also, a small subset of the participants agreed to have an air monitor identical to the one worn or carried to be installed outside their home to obtain the equivalent of fixed-station monitors for comparison to the breathing-zone air and exhaled breath measurements.

Results are available for only the first season of monitoring (Wallace, Pellizzari, Hartwell, Sparacino, & Zelon, 1983) as of this writing. Generally, the findings are consistent with the results of the first two steps. In particular, personal exposures in breathing-zone air were 70–80% of the time in excess of the outdoor concentrations, sometimes by orders of magnitude. Median personal air values for all 11 prevalent chemicals were 2 to 5 times median outdoor levels. This confirms both the extreme variability and frequency of detection issues discovered in the earlier studies. One of the generalizations to be gleaned from the first-season data is the poor correlation between breathing-zone air and the outdoor sample measurements. This revelation seems especially important because both samples are of the exact same type and "outdoors" in this study means in one's backyard, not some station that may be miles away from the person sampled. Since the fixed air values are considerably less than the personal exposures and correlate poorly, one can see that:

> it is scientifically invalid to estimate exposures to these compounds from outdoor measurements. Personal air, indoor air, or breath measurements are far superior to outdoor measurements in estimating exposures. (Wallace *et al.*, 1983, p. 10)

Finally, it is important to remember that the participants were chosen on a probability basis to represent the population of the two cities. Given this fact, the first-season data showed that virtually every participant was exposed to at least 6–10 hazardous chemicals. While the exposure levels were lower than occupational standards, we still don't know whether these chronic exposures represent an important public health problem.

The TEAM data base for the first season of the main study will soon be bolstered by the values for the second and third seasons. Additional information will come from an effort to derive background levels for the same VOCs in what is assumed to be a clean environment in North Dakota. Even more data will eventually flow from a study in another manufacturing, but non-chemical-based city in the South and from two cities on the West Coast with different economic bases. Clearly, the TEAM studies will generate a wealth of data to be sifted by reseachers at the EPA and elsewhere. That other total exposure work will emerge is, in all likelihood, a safe assumption. One need only read Wallace's 1978 paper on the state of personal air quality monitors and compare it to the Wallace and Ott paper in 1982 to comprehend the dramatic progress that has been made in a short time.

In closing, it seems safe to pose three conclusions based on the analysis of TEAM data to this point. First, the TEAM studies have been the vehicle for developing and testing methodologies that now allow for accurate determination of personal exposures to a significant group of toxic substances—the volatile organics. Second, outdoor concentrations are of minimal value in understanding total exposures, but indoor readings in the breathing zone must be considered essential. Third, exhaled breath is an extremely sensitive and reliable indicator of recent exposure. The concept of total exposure assumes the ability to detect dosages received, and the exhaled-breath methodologies appear to be the best noninvasive means to achieve this goal. The comprehensive objective of the TEAM study to assess statistical and chemical methods to estimate total human exposure to certain toxic substances has to be considered well along the path to achievement.

POINTS TO REMEMBER

This chapter has attempted to portray the air quality–health effects nexus as having three principal stages. In stage one, before 1960, a series of air pollution disasters caused substantial loss of life. London's experiences were the worst in terms of the number of excess deaths, but this fact was little solace to the residents who suffered similar events in Belgium, Pennsylvania, and New York.

Response to these incidents was smoke control legislation in England and the first federal law on air pollution in the United States, although the latter provided money for only research and training.

The 1960s and 1970s can be identified as a second stage in the development of the interrelationship between air quality and health. During the 1960s, London and New York City again were subjected to virtually the same meteorological conditions and pollutants that had taken such a toll in previous years. At the same time, the residents of Los Angeles came to recognize that their own somewhat unique brand of smog was photochemical in nature rather than the smoke and SO_2 variety typical of London. Concern began to mount about air pollution. Congress responded with amendments to the 1955 act in 1963, 1965, and 1967. Only the 1965 effort was noteworthy, because it provided for the first federal enforcement of automobile emission standards. Not until the 1970 amendments did the nation have national ambient air quality standards, along with performance standards for stationary sources and emission standards for hazardous pollutants. Initially, six ambient air quality standards were set forth: particulate matter, sulfur oxides, carbon monoxide, photochemical oxidants, hydrocarbons, and nitrogen oxides. Lead was added to the list in 1978 as a result of a lawsuit requesting the administrator of EPA to promulgate a standard. The standards must under the 1970 amendments be set at levels that will protect public health with "an adequate margin of safety." An exact level was to be established by review of the pertinent health effects literature in criteria documents. In 1977 Congress amended the Clean Air Act once more, but kept intact the procedures for establishing air quality standards. One new facet related to the standards, perhaps in recognition of the changing nature of research on health effects, was the requirement that the standards then in effect be reviewed by 1980 and then every 5 years thereafter. The EPA has been attempting to respond to the mandate, though the schedule has not been adhered to.

An interest in more realistic measures of pollutant burden in the 1980s is a recognizable third stage in the quest for the true connection between air quality and health. One direction in this search has been toward an understanding of the contribution of indoor air pollution to a person's overall air exposures. Since most people spend most of their time indoors, it seems reasonable to assume that even low levels of exposure could be potentially troublesome. A disquieting finding of many studies has been that the exposures have *not* been low; levels above ambient are commonplace and levels above the national standards are documented. Moreover, known and/or suspected carcinogens have been found indoors. For the criteria pollutants, serious questions have emerged about indoor levels of NO_2 and particulates. Carbon monoxide may have to be reevaluated in light of a recent, large-scale study. Sulfur dioxide, ozone, and lead are of lesser concern at this time. The carcinogenic potential of formaldehyde, volatile organics, and radon pose perhaps the most disturbing issues, partially, in the case the first two, because of their ubiquitous nature in many types of building materials, furnishings, and household consumer products. It appears feasible, however, to reduce one's exposure in the home by considering the implications of air exchange rates, household activities, and smoking habits. Exposure to radon, which may be the most serious threat in some places, can best be assessed by the use of relatively inexpensive monitors.

The other direction in the search for better estimates of air quality–health effects, and one complementary to the indoor air approach, is termed total exposure monitoring. A number of investigations in the late 1970s and early 1980s demonstrated the futility of trying to predict a person's air quality exposure from measurements recorded only at a fixed monitoring station. Consequently, emphasis has begun to shift toward a recognition of the need to know all the different types of exposure one experiences and then compare these readings with those obtained by an evaluation of the actual dose received. Toward this end, the EPA has sponsored a research effort called the Total Exposure Assessment Methodology (TEAM). This project has focused on a group of toxic air pollutants known as volatile organics. Through the several steps of the TEAM study, the EPA has improved the ability to measure an individual's exposure with personal monitors and confirm the exposures with readings based primarily on exhaled breath but also to a lesser extent, on blood, urine, and hair. Total exposure monitoring has been given a tremendous impetus by the TEAM study. It may soon be feasible to state that a person's total air pollutant burden can be measured and assessed. Then it may be possible to develop an agreed upon definition of adverse health effects due to air pollution.

References

Bach, W. (1972). *Atmospheric pollution*. New York: McGraw-Hill.

Cortese, A. D., & Spengler, J. D. (1976). Ability of fixed monitoring stations to represent personal carbon monoxide exposure. *Journal of the Air Pollution Control Association, 26*, 1144–1150.

Dally, K. A., Hanrahan, L. P., Woodbury, M. A., & Kanarek, M. S. (1981). Formaldehyde exposure in nonoccupational environments. *Archives of Environmental Health, 36*, 277–284.

"Dangers of Indoor Air Pollution." (1981). *New York Times*, January 28.

Dockery, D. W., & Spengler, J. D. (1981a). Indoor-outdoor relationships of respirable sulfates and particules. *Atmospheric Environment, 15*, 335–343.

Dockery, D. W., & Spengler, J. D. (1981b). Personal exposure to respirable particulates and sulfates. *Journal of the Air Pollution Control Association, 31*, 153–159.

Embers, L. P. (1977). Air pollutants and health: An epidemiologic approach. *Environmental Science, 11*, 648–650.

Glasser, M., Greenberg, L., & Field, F. (1967). Mortality and morbidity during a period of high levels of air pollution. *Archives of Environmental Health, 15*, 684–694.

Goldsmith, J. R., & Friberg, L. T. (1977). Effects of air pollution on human health. In A. C. Stern (Ed.), *Air pollution* (3rd ed.), *Vol. 3: The effects of air pollution*. New York: Academic Press.

Hattis, D. R., Goble, R., & Ashford, N. (1982). Airborn lead: A clearcut case of differential protection. *Environment, 24*, 14–20, 33–42.

Hileman, B. (1983). Indoor air pollution. *Environmental Science and Technology, 17*, 469a–472a.

Holland, W. W., Bennett, A. E., Cameron, I. R., Florey, C. du V., Leeder, S. R., Schilling, R. S. F., Swan, A. V., & Waller, R. E. (1979). Health effects of particulate pollution: Reappraising the evidence. *American Journal of Epidemiology*, Special Issue on Particulate Air Pollution, *110*.

Hollowell, C. D., & Miksch, R. R. (1981). Sources and concentrations of organic compounds in indoor environments. *Bulletin of the New York Academy of Medicine, 57*, 962–977.

Jordan, B. C., Richmond, H. M., & McCurdy, T. (1983). The use of scientific information in setting ambient air standards. *Environmental Health Perspectives, 52*, 233–240.

Leaderer, B. P. (1982). Air pollution emissions from kerosene space heaters. *Science, 218*, 1113–1115.

Lynn, D. A. (1976). *Air pollution: Threat and response*. Reading, MA: Addison-Wesley.

McCarroll, J., & Bradley, W. (1966). Excess mortality as an indicator of health effects of air pollution. *American Journal of Public Health, 56*, 1933–1942.

Massey, M. A. (1972). *A citizen's guide to clean air*. Washington, DC: Conservation Foundation.

National Academy of Sciences. (1981a). *Formaldehyde and other aldehyes*. Washington, DC: National Academy Press.

National Academy of Sciences. (1981b). *Indoor pollutants*. Washington, DC: National Academy Press.

National Commission on Air Quality. (1981). *To breathe clean air: Report of the National Commission on Air Quality*. Washington, DC: U.S. Government Printing Office.

Ott, W. R. (1982). Concepts of human exposure to air pollution. *Environment International, 7*, 179–196.

Palmes, E. D., Tomczyk, C., & March, A. W. (1979). Relationship of indoor NO_2 concentrations to use of unvented gas appliances. *Journal of the Air Pollution Control Association, 29*, 392–393.

Particulate Air Pollution. (1979). *American Journal of Epidemiology, 110* [Special Issue], 525–659.

Pellizzari, E. D., Hartwell, T., Zelon, H., Leninger, C., Erickson, M., & Sparacino, C. (1983). *Total Exposure Assessment Methodology (TEAM): Prepilot study-northern New Jersey*. Washington, DC: Environmental Protection Agency.

Perera, F., & Petito, C. (1982). Formaldehyde: A question of cancer policy? *Science, 216*, 1285–1291.

Perkins, H. C. (1974). *Air pollution*. New York: McGraw-Hill.

Petersen, W. B., & Allen, R., (1982). Carbon monoxide exposure to Los Angeles Area Commuters. *Journal of the Air Pollution Control Association, 32*, 826–833.

Proceedings of the 3rd International Conference on Indoor Air Quality and Climate (Vols. 1–5). (1984, August). Stockholm: Swedish Council for Building Research.

Repace, J. L. (1981). The problem of passive smoking. *Bulletin of the New York Academy of Medicine, 57*, 936–946.

Repace, J. L., & Lowrey, A. H. (1980). Indoor air pollution, tobacco smoke, and public health. *Science, 208*, 464–472.

Repace, J. L., Ott, W. R., & Wallace, L. A. (1980, June). Total human exposure to air pollution. Paper presented at 73rd Annual Meeting of the Air Pollution Control Association, Montreal, Quebec.

Schrenk, H. H. (1949). Air pollution in Donora, Pa.: Epidemiology of the unusual smog episode of October, 1948. *Public Health Bulletin, 306*.

Sexton, K., Letz, R., & Spengler, J. D. (1983). Estimating human exposure to nitrogen dioxide: An indoor/outdoor modeling approach. *Environmental Research, 32*, 151–166.

Sexton, K., Treitman, R. D., Spengler, J. D., & Turner, W. A. (1984, August). The effects of residential wood combustion on indoor and outdoor air quality: A case study in Waterbury, Vermont. *Proceedings of the 3rd International Conference on Indoor Air Quality and Climate.*

Sexton, K., Webber, L. M., Hayward, S. B., Sextro, R. G., & Offerman, F. J. (1984, August). Characterization of particulate and organic emissions from major indoor sources. *Proceedings of the 3rd International Conference on Indoor Air Quality and Climate.*

Sherwin, R. P. (1983a). Preface. *Environmental health perspectives, 52*, 151.

Sherwin, R. P. (1983b). What Is an Adverse Health Effect? *Environmental Health Perspectives, 52*, 177–182.

Shy, C. (1979). Epidemiologic evidence and the Unites States air quality standards. *American Journal of Epidemiology, 110*, 661–671.

Spengler, J. D., Dockery, D. W., Turner, W. A., Wolfson, J. M., & Ferris, B. G., Jr. (1981). Long-term measurements of respirable sulfates and particles inside and outside homes. *Atmospheric Environment, 15*, 23–30.

Spengler, J. D., Ferris, B. G., Jr., & Dockery, D. W. (1979). Sulfur dioxide and nitrogen dioxide levels inside and outside homes and the implications on health effects research. *Environmental Science and Technology, 13*, 1276–1280.

Spengler, J. D., & Sexton, K. (1983). Indoor air pollution: A public health perspective. *Science, 221*, 9–17.

Spengler, J. D., Stone, K. R., & Lilley, F. W. (1978). High carbon monoxide levels measured in enclosed skating rinks. *Journal of the Air Pollution Control Association, 28*, 776–779.

Spengler, J., & Tosteson, T. (1981). Personal exposures to respirable particles. In *Environmetrics 81 Summaries of Conference Presentations*. Philadelphia: Society for Industrial and Applied Mathematics.

Sterling, T. D., & Kobayaski, D. (1981). Use of gas ranges for cooking and heating in urban dwellings. *Journal of the Air Pollution Control Association, 31*, 162–165.

Sterling, T. D., & Sterling, E. (1979). Carbon monoxide levels in kitchens and homes with gas cookers. *Journal of the Air Pollution Control Association, 29*, 238–241.

Stern, A. C. (Ed.). (1977). *Air pollution* (3rd ed.). New York: Academic Press.

U.S. Environmental Protection Agency. (1976, April). *The Allegheny County air pollution episode*. Air Programs Branch, EPA Region III. Philadelphia: Environmental Protection Agency.

U.S. Environmental Protection Agency. (1981). CCEA continues study of residential wood combustion. *Conventional Combustion Environmental Assessment Program Report, 3*, 1–2.

U.S. Environmental Protection Agency. (1982). *Carbon monoxide intrusion in sustained-use vehicles*. Research Triangle Park, NC: Environmental Protection Agency.

U.S. Environmental Protection Agency. (1984). New air rules proposed for particulate matter. *EPA Journal, 10*, 19–21.

U.S. Environmental Protection Agency. (1985). EPA's lead phasedown action. *EPA Journal, 11*, 2–5.

U.S. Environmental Protection Agency. (1986). National air quality and emissions trends report, 1984 (EPA-450/4-86-001). Washington, DC: Environmental Protection Agency.

U.S. General Accounting Office. (1980). *Indoor air pollution: An emerging health problem* (CED-80-111). Washington, DC: General Accounting Office.

Wallace, L. A. (1978). Personal air quality monitors: Past uses and present prospects. In *Proceedings, 4th Joint Conference on Sensing of Environment Pollutants*. Washington, DC: American Chemical Society.

Wallace, L. A. (1979, June). *Use of personal monitor to measure commuter exposure to carbon monoxide in vehicle passenger compartments*. Paper presented at the 72nd Annual Meeting of the Air Pollution Association, Cincinnati, Ohio.

Wallace, L. A. (1982). Direct measurement of individual human exposure and body burden: Research needs. *Journal of Environmental Science and Health*, Part A, A17, 532–539.

Wallace, L. A. (1982/1983). Measuring direct individual exposure to toxic substances. *Toxic Substances Journal, 4*, 174–183.

Wallace, L. A. (1983). Carbon monoxide in air and breath of employees in an underground office. *Journal of the Air Pollution Control Association, 33*, 678–682.

Wallace, L. A. (1984, May). *Organic chemicals in indoor air: A review of recent findings*. Paper presented at Annual Meeting of American Association of the Advancement of Science, New York.

Wallace, L. A., Bromberg, S., Pellizzari, E., Hartwell, T., Zelon, H., & Sheldon, L. (1984, August). Plan and preliminary results of the U.S. Environmental Protection Agency's indoor air monitoring program: 1982. *Proceedings of the 3rd International Conference on Indoor Air Quality and Climate*.

Wallace, L. A., & Ott, W. R. (1982). Personal monitors: A state-of-the-art survey. *Journal of the Air Pollution Control Association, 32*, 601–610.

Wallace, L. A., Pellizzari, E. D., Hartwell, T. D., Sparacino, C., & Zelon, H. (1983, June). *Personal exposure to volatile organics and other compounds indoors and outdoors—the TEAM study*. Paper presented at the 76th Annual Meeting of the Air Pollution Control Association, Atlanta, GA.

Wallace, L. A., Zweidinger, R., Erickson, M., Cooper, S., Whitaker, D., & Pellizzari, E. (1982). Monitoring individual exposure. Measurements of volatile organic compounds in breathing-zone air, drinking water, and exhaled breath. *Environment International, 8*, 269–282.

Weslowski, J. J., Sexton, K., Liu, K., & Twiss, S. (1984, August). The California indoor air quality program: An integrated approach. *Proceedings of the 3rd International Conference on Indoor Air Quality and Climate.*

World Health Organization. (1979). *Health aspects related to indoor air quality. Report on a WHO working Group.* Copenhagen: World Health Organization.

Yates, M. W. (1967). A preliminary study of carbon monoxide gas in the home. *Journal of Environmental Health, 29,* 413–420.

Yocom, J. E. (1982). Indoor-outdoor air quality relationships: A critical review. *Journal of the Air Pollution Control Association, 32,* 500–520.

SOLID WASTE AND PUBLIC HEALTH

Richard F. Anderson
Boston University

That the waste products of urban industrial societies like the United States threaten public health should come as no surprise. Technological progress and rises in living standards have led to widespread distribution of all kinds of consumer products made from a host of new chemical substances, and consequently more—and more diverse—solid waste. This chapter examines the public health implications of the way we deal with that solid waste.

We begin by presenting the legal definitions of solid waste, and specifically hazardous waste, and a brief overview of who produces how much of what types of it. In the second section we review the various ways by which those who create and handle waste try to control the spread of dangerous substances. Such a review must also include the most common types of damage and threats to public health, and the routes by which contaminants move from place to place in the environment. The third section presents the special case of hazardous waste and how scientists study the public health effects of these wastes and waste- disposal sites. Studies of three well-publicized cases illustrate research methods for investigating the association between public health problems and waste sites. A comparison of such studies highlights some of the difficulties in examining public health–solid waste connections. Finally, the problems and promises of monitoring the physical and mental health in the neighborhoods around waste-disposal sites are discussed.

The key issue in this chapter is the great difficulty of scientifically determining public health effects of solid waste disposal. The bulk of this chapter is devoted to this issue, and consequently important issues such as conservation, recycling, regulation, and many others can only be touched upon.

WHAT IS SOLID WASTE?

One of the biggest problems in managing solid wastes is that the term includes so much, and different kinds of solid waste vary substantially in potential risk to the public. The very word "waste" evokes no less than three functional forms of speech in the English language (adjective, noun, and verb). And then for each form there are a host of different definitions. Today we usually think of waste as a noun and define it as any useless byproduct, refuse, garbage, or trash.

For our purposes in this book the legal definition of waste is the most important because of its implication for management. The Resource Conservation and Recovery Act (RCRA), enacted in 1976 (Public Law 94-580), was designed to upgrade waste management technology and practices. RCRA specifically defines waste under separate categories. Solid waste includes

> any garbage, refuse, sludge from a waste treatment plant, water supply treatment plant, or air pollution control facility and other discarded material, including solid, liquid, semisolid, or contained gaseous material resulting from industrial, commercial, mining, and agricultural operations, and from community activities, but does not include solid or dissolved material in domestic sewage, or solid or dissolved materials in irrigation return flows or industrial discharges which are point sources subject to permits under section 402 of the Federal Water Pollution Control Act. (P.L. 94-580, Sec. 1004 [27]: 42 USC 6902)

As you see, "solid waste" under regulation by this law includes material that is actually liquids and gases as well as solids. Note also that domestic sewage, irrigation flows, and industrial discharges, including nuclear wastes, are regulated under other laws, and are thus excluded from attention under RCRA. Household wastes, which may contain extremely toxic substances that would be regulated if generated by an industry, are also excluded.

Hazardous wastes are a specific group of solid wastes. They have received a great deal of publicity because improper handling greatly increases the risk to the health of nearby residents. RCRA defines hazardous waste as:

> a solid waste, or combination of solid wastes, which because of its quantity, concentration, or physical, chemical, or infectious characteristics may—(A) cause, or significantly contribute to an increase in serious irreversible, or incapacitating reversible, illness; or (B) pose a substantial present or potential hazard to human health or the environment when improperly treated, stored, transported, or disposed of, or otherwise managed. (P.L. 94-580, Sec. 1004 [5]: 42 USC 6902).

The hazardous portion of solid waste is the primary reason why people so adamantly oppose new waste facilities near their homes. This fear has spread to new sanitary landfills because virtually every place where waste is dumped has, or has had, contact with something that is at least potentially toxic to human health.

What Does Waste Consist of?

A major difficulty in trying to manage solid waste is the monumental task of really knowing what's in it. Aside from the fact mentioned above that much of it is not solid, even the best attempts to sort it by what it contains and how much leave a good deal to be desired. (Greenberg & Anderson, 1984). Estimates of the quantity

Table 6-1. Estimated Quantities of Solid Waste Generated, 1977

Waste source	Metric tons (millions)	% of total
Municipal		
Residential/Commerical/Institutional	132	2.4
Sewage sludge	4.5	.1
Junked Auto and Construction/		
Demolition[a]	41	.5
Industrial		
Nonhazardous	292–310	5.5
Hazardous	34–52	.8
Radioactive[a]	.04	<.1
Mining/milling[a]	2,086	39.0
(including uranium tailings)		
Agricultural[b]	2,265–3,014	50.3
Utility[c]	70	1.2

Note. From Lacomber (1979).
[a]In dry weight (all other source tonnages are in wet weights).
[b]Includes residues from crop growing, harvesting, and processing: meat, poultry, and dairy products, and logging and wood manufacture.
[c]Includes fly and bottom ash and scrubber sludge, excludes radioactive waste.

of solid waste generated in 1977 indicate that the vast majority comes from agriculture and mining (Table 6-1). The more toxic categories (sewage sludge, hazardous industrial wastes, and radioactive substances) account for less than 2% of the estimated volume. The bulk of municipal wastes, that ends up in the city landfill (residential, commercial, institutional, and construction trash) represents roughly 3% of the estimated total (or about 175 million metric tons).

Generation of residential, institutional, and commercial solid waste (which we will call municipal solid waste in this discussion) has been steadily increasing in recent years. JRB Associates, Inc. (1981) cites unpublished U.S. Environmental Protection Agency (EPA) data that show an increase in volume from 95 million tons in 1960 to 150 million tons in 1978. In other words, each of us increased our output of trash from about 2.9 pounds per day to 3.7 pounds. It's impossible to say exactly because measurements of volume are influenced by methods of reporting and estimating, inconsistent record keeping, and confusion about exactly what should be included. But the point that Americans continue to generate more trash all the time still holds.

Not all trash is, of course, harmful to human health. The major nontoxic constituents are listed in Table 6-2. But that's not all, because commercial and institutional wastes have routinely been dumped with household waste in the same municipal incinerator, landfill, or sewer system. Because their volume is so small, these wastes have been exempt from strict regulation. However, many commercial and institutional enterprises generate the same types of wastes that *are* regulated when produced by industry. Even very common small businesses such as dry cleaners, photography labs, pesticide formulators, construction, car repair shops, and others use—and throw out—a variety of substances that could cause serious public health problems. The Environmental Protection Agency (EPA) is currently conducting a national survey to find out what and how much such establishments produce of these wastes and how they handle them.

The Special Problem of Hazardous Waste

Spewing industrial wastes into the air or through pipes into streams has been regulated for some time. Ironically, controlling these sources of pollution has had the inadvertent effect of increasing the volume of wastes that has had to be disposed of in landfills. Thus in more recent years the EPA has focused attention on this special problem of hazardous waste (U.S. Environmental Protection Agency, 1974, 1977). Even though hazardous waste constitutes only 2% of all waste, there is still a lot of it. One estimate suggests that industries annually generate about 42 million metric tons of hazardous waste (Booz-Allen & Hamilton, & Putnam, Hayes, & Bartlett, Inc. 1980). Westat Inc. (1984) conducted a 2-year sample survey of generators regulated under RCRA and estimated that they produce about 250 million metric tons per year (or 71 billion gallons). This study also suggested that there were at least 14,100 active firms that produce large quantities of hazardous waste in the United States. They were primarily chemical, equipment and metals manufacturing, motor transport, and utility companies (Table 6-3).

Like the figures for waste in general, these estimates of hazardous waste are necessarily imperfect. Many sources are never included in the calculations. RCRA exempts from regulation any generator that accumulates less than 1,000 kg/month of a hazardous waste and 1 kg/month of what are considered acutely hazardous wastes.[1] Some states have more stringent requirements and have lowered the exemption to 100 kg/month, or even lower. As the exemption level decreases, the number of sources of waste increases, bringing on other headaches for the regulators. Since many of these smaller operations are widely dispersed and engage in very different activities, it becomes practically impossible to inventory who they are, let alone enforce the regulations.

MUNICIPAL WASTE AND ITS PROBLEMS

We have seen that the United States—its industry, its commercial and institutional establishments, and its individuals in their households—generate huge quantities

---

1. The legal definition for a large quantity generator is any one which produces 1,000 or more kg/month of hazardous waste or any one which generates more than 1 kg/month of acutely hazardous waste.

Table 6-2. Net Quantity and Composition of Solid Waste by Detailed Product Category, 1978

Product category	Net waste disposed of	
	Quantity (thousands of tons)	% of total waste
Durable goods	16,525	12
Major appliances	2,330	2
Furniture, furnishings	5,410	4
Rubber Tires	1,650	1
Miscellaneous durables	7,135	5
Nondurable goods, excluding food	28,110	20
Newspapers	7,570	5
Books, magazines	6,400	5
Office paper	4,305	3
Tissue paper, including towels	2,190	2
Paper plates, cups	370	<0.5
Other nonpackaging paper	2,475	2
Clothing, footwear	2,765	2
Other misc. nondurables	1,935	1
Containers and packaging	42,125	30
Glass containers	13,680	10
Beer, soft drink	6,690	5
Wine, Liquor	2,165	2
Food and other	4,625	3
Steel cans	4,235	3
Beer, soft drink	995	1
Food	2,165	1
Other nonfood	1,075	1
Aluminum	935	<0.5
Beer, soft drink	610	<0.5
Other cans	35	<0.5
Aluminum foil	290	
Paper, paperboard	17,890	13
Corrugated	10,315	7
Other paperboard	3,915	3
Paper packaging	3,660	3
Plastics	3,640	2
Plastic containers	1,735	1
Other plastic packaging	1,905	1
Wood packaging	1,570	1
Other misc. packaging	175	
Total nonfood product waste	86,760	62
Add: Food waste	23,400	17
Yard waste	26,600	19
Misc. inorganic wastes	2,100	2
Total	138,360	100

Note. From Franklin Associates, Ltd., Unpublished data based on National Flow Estimation Procedures developed by the Office of Solid Waste, U.S. EPA (1981).

Table 6-3. Numbers of Generators and Quantities Generated by Industry

| Industry | | Quantity generated | |
(Standard Industrial Code)	Number of generators	Billion gallons	%
Chemicals (28)	2,440	28.4	71%
Machinery (35)	700	2.3	6
Transportation equipment (37)	680	2.3	6
Motor freight transport (42)	80	1.7	4
Petroleum refining (29)	370	1.3	3
Primary metals (33)	850	1.0	3
Fabricated metals (34)	2,640	0.8	2
Electrical machinery (36)	1,510	0.7	1
Electric, gas, and sanitary services (49)	250	0.5	1
Other	4,580	1.0	3
All industries	14,100	40.0	100%

Note. From U.S. Environmental Protection Agency (1983).

of waste each year. Now we look at what all this means to public health and why we should all be concerned with how this waste is handled and disposed of. In this section we review the problems municipal solid waste and hazardous waste sites can create. At this point we won't make a clear distinction between them, because hazardous waste has often been dumped in the same landfills as municipal waste.

Public health problems traced to waste dumps pepper the daily news; new ones come to light frequently. They vary slightly depending on the type of waste site (whether land disposal, incineration, storage, or treatment) and the physical and demographic characteristics of surrounding areas.

In the past, the standard procedure for municipal solid waste was to dump it in an open pit and burn it. As recently as 10 years ago, there were 18,539 known "sanitary" landfills for nonhazardous industrial waste in the nation. Only 5,600 of these were duly licensed and therefore legal (Petersen, 1983). By 1983 the number had dropped to less than 13,000 as states cracked down on unlicensed and poorly run dumps. The number will continue to shrink for the same reasons.

Municipal Waste Disposal and Disease

Potential environmental health problems associated with landfills and incinerators are listed in Table 6-4. First, the organic material (garbage) is a fertile breeding ground for bacteria and viruses that cause disease in humans as well as for flies, mosquitoes, and rodents, which transmit the germs to people (Rajagapolan & Schiffman, 1974). Keswick and Gerba (1980) suggest that contamination of groundwater by such disease-causing organisms from water seeping through dumps is likely to include the viruses of hepatitis A, poliomyelitis, and gastroenteritis. Thus, not only do people get sick where wastes contaminate local groundwater supplies, but some of the illnesses have long-term—even lifelong—aftereffects.

Table 6-4. Solid Waste Health Effects and Mechanisms

Vectors causing digestive tract diseases:
- flies
- mosquitos
- rodents
- birds
- bacteria
- viruses

Explosions

Fires

Groundwater pollution

Surface water pollution via runoff

Odors from garbage

Noise from traffic and bulldozing operations

Traffic safety

Air pollution from incineration

Declining property values

Overall decline in the quality of life in the neighborhood

Poor choice of site, poor design, and careless operation are major factors leading to environmental health problems. Solid waste composed of organic matter that is normally decomposed by microorganisms—what we commonly call garbage—in municipal landfills attracts flies and rodents (Versar, Inc., 1981). A daily cover of compacted soil about 6 in. thick will keep out rodents and probably flies (SCS Engineers, 1981). Mosquitoes can be controlled by minimizing puddles on the surface of the landfill.

Birds that eat organic waste, such as gulls, are also attracted to dumps. They have been known to threaten public safety by interfering with air traffic when airports or flight paths are located near sanitary landfills. They can also cause other problems. For example, sea gulls are often implicated in potential public health problems. Bird droppings from gulls feeding in great numbers at nearby municipal sanitary landfills contaminate reservoirs to the point that even though the water is chemically treated, it has to be boiled before use. Simply covering the landfill with soil could keep the gulls out of the garbage and avoid the problem.

Keeping insects, birds, and vermin out of garbage, then, is a relatively simple problem technologically. But contaminants can also reach humans through drinking water, and that can pose a greater challenge. As rain water percolates through the material in a waste disposal site, it dissolves and carries with it water-soluble matter. It also picks up bacteria and viruses. Eventually, the water and whatever it has picked up on the way become part of the groundwater, the moisture deep in the soil that many communities and individuals depend on for their water supply through wells.

Several engineering techniques are available to slow down the movement of water through a waste disposal site into groundwater. The most important is the use of a natural or synthetic liner (U.S. Environmental Protection Agency, 1978). A system to collect and treat this water may be installed. Permit conditions may specify that an owner or operator must install one or more groundwater monitoring wells, from which water samples will be drawn to test for certain *criterion pollutants*, which are substances known to present potential danger to public health. Presence of these criterion pollutants would indicate that hazardous substances had made their way into the groundwater.

The extent of the contamination, the degree to which the local population depend on the groundwater source for drinking water, and the type of contaminants involved greatly influence the seriousness of the health problem that the site presents. The Safe Drinking Water Act (SDWA) of 1974 specifies standards for evaluating groundwater contamination by municipal solid waste landfills, surface impoundments (large dug out area filled with solid waste) and farms. Any site that contaminates a groundwater supply with 10,000 mg/l of total dissolved solvents (e.g., tricholorethylene, a substance widely used in degreasing agents, thought by some to be a carcinogen) or exceeds the maximum contamination level for criterion inorganic or organic substances as specified in the law requires action. If the source of contamination is located over what the law calls a *designated sole source aquifer*, that is, a water-bearing rock layer that provides most or all the drinking water for a community, it automatically becomes a high-priority site requiring some form of enforcement. If, on the other hand, the site contaminates groundwater that is not a source of drinking water, state authorities may or may not have a statutory basis for taking action.

Other Dangers of Municipal Waste

Fires and explosions are an ever-present danger at solid waste landfills. Most are caused by accumulations of methane, the main gas produced by decomposing organic wastes. Traces of nitrogen, carbon dioxide, ammonia, hydrogen sulfide, hydrogen, and volatile organic substances are also usually present at landfills (SCS Engineers, 1981). Versar (1981) suggests that the landfill sites with the highest degree of danger are those that have concentrations of methane at 5 to 15% in the surrounding air. Methane is also toxic to vegetation, so the presence of unhealthy or dead vegetation is a good clue that methane is highly concentrated in the air. Even a 5% concentration of methane approaches the lower explosion level and is considered a hazard.

Methane will move quite freely through clean gravels and sands in the ground; less freely in silty gravels, loam, or sand; and is most confined by heavy clay soils. Municipal solid waste generates methane at a rate of 5 to 8 cubic feet per pound of decomposed waste, and the gas can move through the soil in any direction. Nearby structures where the gas may accumulate, explode, or flare are thus in considerable danger.

Proper venting by several methods greatly reduces the chance that the gas will concentrate enough to explode or catch fire (Moore & Rai, 1977). The permeable method entails installation of a gravel-filled trench. As gases migrate and reach the gravel pit, they move up through it and are vented into the open atmosphere. The impermeable method relies on construction of a natural or synthetic barrier, so that the gas cannot migrate at all. Then vacuum extraction wells are placed at peripheral areas of the solid waste landfill to vent the gas. The methane may then be collected through a piping distribution network and used as a fuel.

In some communities waste is burned, or *incinerated*, rather than being dumped directly into a landfill. About 4% of the residential/commercial/institutional waste in the United States is incinerated (JRB Associates, 1981). But incineration is expensive and can only compete with landfills in crowded urban and industrial centers where the cost of land is greater than the cost of equipment, labor, operation, and maintenance for incinerators.

Incinerators have also been blamed for causing particulate air pollution and odors. Particulates can be controlled to a large degree by devices installed in the smokestack. Odors may be impossible to eliminate from the trucks delivering and unloading the waste, especially if it contains garbage; such stench definitely decreases the overall quality of life for the incinerator's neighbors.

Another health risk of incineration of municipal solid waste is incomplete combustion of hazardous substances. Most organic material burns completely at temperatures of 750 to 1,000°C (Rajagopalan & Schiffman, 1974). Lower temperatures result in incomplete combustion and leave residues that enhance breeding of flies and rats. Temperature control of incinerators is difficult because of air turbulence, the creation of carbon dioxide, and the dwell time of the waste mass being burned. We know that some hazardous wastes enter municipal and privately owned facilities and are treated at suboptimal temperatures. Many organic chemicals require extremely high temperatures and special super-oxygenated burning to complete the combustion process. Hazardous metallic wastes may also escape combustion. Lack of these extensive controls results in products of incomplete combustion and the potential for multiple hazardous emissions. They may then pose a threat to public health.

Noise and traffic safety and the mental and physical stress they create are other problems of most municipal solid waste sites. Access roads must accommodate large numbers of heavy trucks, sometimes through residential neighborhoods. Local ordinances have tried to reduce the noise and improve traffic safety by diverting traffic, restricting traffic schedules, requiring use of special noise-control devices, speed limits, requiring driving with flashing lights, personnel training in handling emergency spills, and other measures. Noise from solid waste sites can be controlled. Separating waste sites from other land use by standard zoning ordinances is often an effective mechanism. Barriers, natural vegetation buffers, and earth berms can also be effective.

We know now how to control these common risks of disposal of nonhazardous wastes, and many of these measures have been enacted as laws. Municipal solid waste landfill owners or operators are now required to apply for a license and permit to begin or to continue operations. Permits are issued to owners/operators who have demonstrated ability and willingness to comply with regulations for operating practices. Indeed, the EPA contracted with Versar, Inc. (1981) to develop a guidance manual to be used by local and state waste managers to evaluate the possible health problems caused by waste sites. Any state that received solid waste funding from the EPA for waste management programs under RCRA was required to conduct an inventory of all waste sites and use the manual to identify dumps that required either upgrading or closing. The manual provides a set of evaluation criteria that are sensitive to the possible problems listed in Table 6-4 and ways contamination might spread. The criteria are also intended to provided "minimum national standards for the protection of health and the environment from adverse effects resulting from solid waste disposal."

This introduction to problems generated by municipal solid waste dumps does not pretend to be exhaustive. The spread of infectious diseases is routinely controlled at most landfills in this country. Since the 1970s attention has focused on the link between chronic disease and waste sites; now the chronic diseases that seem to be associated with hazardous waste sites command our attention. We now turn to a consideration of this concern.

HAZARDOUS WASTE

No one knows exactly how many hazardous waste sites there are in this country. The often-quoted Fred C. Hart Associates (1979) study suggested that the number was somewhere between 35,000 and 50,000, which seems high. An estimate of 17,000–22,000 is probably more accurate (Greenberg & Anderson, 1984). While most researchers agree that the vast majority of sites have been identified, there are probably a few remaining unidentified ones that could cause serious damage to environmental resources and public health.

Actually only a small percentage of all the waste we generate is hazardous. However, the EPA (1974) estimated that 90% of all hazardous wastes were improperly disposed of in open pits, surface impoundments, vacant land, farmlands, and water bodies. Media stories about the resulting damage have become a daily routine in many metropolitan areas.

Hazardous substances spread from waste sites through air, soil, and water. A review of 421 specific incidents (Table 6-5) shows that the environment and public health were harmed by groundwater contamination, surface water contamination via runoff, air pollution from burning in open pits, fires and explosions, direct poisoning of humans, and indirect poisoning via the food chain (U.S. Environmental Protection Agency, 1977).

In all cases the problems were directly related to the design, operation, and siting of waste-disposal sites. Unfortunately most decisions about where to dump hazardous waste are made with almost total ignorance of whether or not the land is suitable for dumping. A suitable area for hazardous waste facilities would be an area that impedes contamination migration and contact with community residents.

Table 6-5. Mechanisms Involved in Incidents of Damage by Disposal Method[a]

Disposal method	Surface impoundments	Landfills, dumps	Other land disposal[c]	Storage of wastes	Smeltings, slag, mine tailings
Number of Cases	89	99	203	15	15
Damage mechanism[b]					
Groundwater (259)	57	64	117	10	11
Surface water (170)	42	49	71	—	8
Air (17)	3	5	9	—	—
Fires, explosions (14)	—	11	3	—	—
Direct contact					
poisoning (52)	1	6	40	5	—
Wells affected (140)	32	28	74	4	2

Note. From U.S. Environmental Protection Agency (1977). The data presented in this table have been derived solely from the case studies associated with land disposal of industrial wastes.

[a]The tabulation is based on 421 cases studied thus far. The numbers in the matrix add up to more than 421, because several damage incidents involved more than one damage mechanism.

[b]Numbers in parentheses indicate total number of cases.

[c]Haphazard disposal on vacant properties, on farmland, spray irrigation, etc.

For example, if you site a land disposal facility, it is preferable to locate it where the soil strata is thick with a highly impermeable clay, overlying an area where groundwater is not used or essential to public consumption. A suitable site for a hazardous waste incinerator would be a site where the resulting air emissions would not diminish the air quality for the residents of a city or town. However as indicated above, many sites are not well located; in point, a review of 46 landfills in the lower Raritan River drainage basin of central New Jersey revealed that only four sites were situated in somewhat suitable areas, and these four sites were probably chosen by good luck (Anderson & Greenberg, 1984).

From the point of view of protecting public health, until the late 1970s solid waste, including hazardous waste, was grossly mismanaged. The fundamental management principle was out of sight, out of mind.

Then Love Canal burst into national attention and became a household word. Local public pressure came to bear on state health authorities and public health professionals to find out just what the actual and potential health problems were. Was the old waste dump really causing the illnesses? A number of investigative studies were conducted in a rather short period of time, and peer review has cast doubt on the reliability of some of them. General problems with these studies included lack of control populations, inadequate knowledge about when and in what order contamination and environmental exposure took place, scientific uncertainty about the impact of low-dose exposure, and the often inconclusive nature of findings. (See Chapter 1 for a discussion of these generic problems.)

The scientific community, especially environment and health officials, criticized the methods of the studies and expressed general dissatisfaction with their rigor. One result was an effort to develop broadly accepted guidelines for conducting meaningful investigations.

This section discusses the methodological guidelines health researchers have suggested. Then we will look at three waste sites that have won notoriety and see how the studies of them stand up to the rigors of the guidelines. We cannot review all the available studies. We will look at a few in detail, rather than many in brief.

Methods of Study

Studies of hazardous waste's effects on health are usually triggered by a geographic cluster of cases of disease, or by residents who live near existing waste sites and are assumed to be exposed to hazardous substances from it. In some instances, researchers investigating established data bases such as birth and death certificates, hospital records, or physician records come upon such a cluster. Other studies are sparked by impassioned pleas from local residents and officials when an uncontrolled waste site is discovered. Bloom (1981) cautions that symptom reporting by neighboring residents is likely to be biased if they know of a nearby waste site. While there is a potential for a cause-effect relationship between waste site contaminants and disease, the more likely case is that the anxiety and stress present a greater psychological burden (Lumb, 1984; Lowrance, 1981).

There are no guarantees that a health study will discover minor changes in disease patterns. Lowrance (1981) states that other than direct contact poisoning, health effects are more likely to be subtle, chronic, and to have long latency periods, going undetected for years by either the patient or physician. Nevertheless, many specific effects on health have been enumerated in Table 6-6.

Attention has focused on both chronic, long-term effects such as cancer and genetic mutation (changes in genes that pass on inherited information to offspring), and on acute effects such as miscarriages, stillbirths, changes in cell structure, and damage to nerves. There are probably other problems, too, such as liver and kidney damage (Lowrance, 1981). However, research on all of these effects, as well as others not mentioned, is still in its infancy.

Designing the Health Study

A variety of guidelines have been developed to aid researchers in choosing and implementing research techniques. The U.S. Centers for Disease Control (1984) outlines a 14-step process to decide if a waste site health study is warranted in the first place and how to conduct it if it is. Ing (1983) outlined approaches appropriate for waste site health investigations using data on individuals. Stephens (1981) discussed some early experiences with investigations, their accomplishments and their failures. Bloom (1981) proposed guidelines for a three-stage process. Briefly, it begins with the screening of readily available data on effects. Next, if warranted, is the study of individuals, which considers a wider range of effects. Finally, where appropriate, a long-term follow-up investigation of an entire exposed population may be implemented. Tokuhata (1984) emphasizes

Table 6-6. Acute and Chronic Public Health Indices Related to Waste Sites

Adult health indices	
Chest pains	Persistent colds
Loss of weight without dieting	Bruising and bleeding easily
Numbness of fingers and toes	Respiratory problems
Nausea	Neurological problems
Dizziness	Kidney problems
Skin and eye irritation	Liver disease
Cough	Digestive disease
Fatigue	Cancer
Nervousness	Other blood problems
Anemia	Chromosomal aberrations

Confounding factors[a]	
Age	Education
Sex	Smoking history
Race/ethnicity	Alcohol use
Marital status	Occupational/avocational
Income	Exposure history
Housing	

Reproductive dysfunction indices	
Sexual dysfunction	Early fetal loss (to 28 weeks)
Decreased libido	Perinatal death
Impotence	Late fetal loss (after 28 weeks)
Sperm abnormalities	Stillbirth
Decreased number	Intrapartum death
Decreased motility	Low birth weight (under 2,500 g)
Abnormal morphology	Altered sex ratio
Subfecundity	Multiple births
Abnormal gonads, ducts, external genitalia	Birth defects
Abnormal pubertal development	Major
Infertility (male/female)	Minor
Amenorrhea	Chromosome anomalies
Anovulatory cycles	Infant mortality
Delay in conception	Childhood morbidity
Illness during pregnancy	Childhood malignancies
Toxemia	
Hemorrhage	

Note. Adapted from Ozonoff *et al.* (1983) and Warburton (1981).
[a]Confounding factors are background information useful for isolating the effects of waste site exposure from characteristics of the personal environment.

the task of assessing health risks associated with toxic agents is extremely complex because of the multiplicity of ways in which they can interact with biologic systems.

Thus there are many problems besetting health effects studies, and there is no general framework that all interested parties agree upon. Part of the problem is that each case is somewhat unique, and a meaningful investigation must be site-specific.

A team effort using local physicians, environmental health specialists, residents, and state and local officials is required. Lumb (1984) cautions against relying too heavily on local physicians:

> When confronted with a variety of possible etiologic agents, physicians are not accustomed to assess the capacity for disease production in the absence of prior knowledge of established associations with illness.

Diseases are caused by many factors working together, especially in the case of hazardous waste sites, and a highly controlled investigation is consequently necessary. Unquestionably, a rigorous health study requires a major effort on the part of a multidisciplinary research team, which makes the health study costly and time-consuming.

A symposium held at the Rockefeller University, New York, in 1981 attempted to reach some consensus about proper methods for assessing health effects of waste sites. Stephens (1981) points out that the state of the art in chemical analyses far surpasses our scientific ability to put such data into a meaningful context for risk assessment. There is no great problem in detecting chemicals at the parts per billion or smaller concentrations in air, soil, water, and body fluid and tissue mediums. But then how do we apply that information? A number of participants at the symposium warned of the extremely limited scientific knowledge about how hazardous substances spread out from waste sites and the uncertainty about the environmental pathways they follow. Miller (1981) discussed the inherent difficulties in tracking contaminants moving in groundwater. Contaminants from waste sites often travel extremely slowly as what is called a "slug." The mobility of chemicals traveling underground is a function of such factors as the slope of the rock layers, chemical solubility and density, soil adsorption, fluctuation in seasonal water table, the permeability of the rocks, rate at which water is pumped for use, and other factors. There is no firm guide for determining the sampling locations, chemicals to sample for, and the problems of intermediate and complex chemical compounds resulting from interaction with soil and water mediums.

Another problem besetting researchers is the fact that the contents of many waste sites are often an undefined, even unknown, potpourri of exotic organic and inorganic chemicals. This is further complicated when the waste site has no documented history of contents and operational practices. Chemical analyses performed at different laboratories have a tendency to report vastly different concentrations because procedures for analysis are not standardized. While partial records of disposal, aerial photographs, and historical maps of the site are helpful for estimating exposures, they are no substitute for accurate data to determine the extent of the health risk. Even where many of the chemicals at a waste site can be identified and measured, there are unfortunately no "adequate methods for assessing human risks for most toxicological effects" (Voytek, 1981, p. 150).

Many researchers stress the necessity of finely calibrated exposure data for risk assessment. Heath (1984a, p. 378) argues that

> risk assessment is a matter of measuring clinical illness in an exposed population and relating those measurements to levels of exposure.

Heath warns of two common misconceptions concerning cause-and-effect relationships between exposure and the incidence of disease. The first is the tendency for people to blame all illness on an exposure. The second involves dose–response relationships, which are discussed in a later section.

Choosing a Research Technique

Most investigations fall under two methodological approaches: studies of individuals, and analyses of data for groups of people living in states, counties, census tracts, and health districts. The choice of whether to study individuals or groups is often influenced by the availability and possibility of collecting data. Secondary (that is, existing or published) data are often readily available in the form of, for example, birth and death certificates. These data are of varying quality, depending on the specific variable in question. Birth weight, for example, is consistently and accurately reported on birth certificates. Congenital (birth) defects, on the other hand, may be less accurately recorded. Some birth defects don't even become apparent until some time after birth.

Death certificates also vary in accuracy. For example, lung cancer is usually accurately reported (over 90%). On the other hand, reports of cancers of the brain, large intestine, and rectum are less than 60% accurate. This difficulty may sometimes be overcome by examination of physician or hospital records. If the state has a tumor registry—and many do not—it can provide valuable information on cancer incidence. Another problem with using death certificate data is that technical and clinical advances in diagnoses or changes in disease classifications may cause an abrupt change in the number of reported cases.

Despite these limitations, a major advantage of screening secondary data sources is the relative ease of using such information with automated data processing. In addition to the disadvantages already mentioned, researchers have only partial information on sources of exposure. There is no nationwide collection of data about alcohol and tobacco consumption or dietary intake, all of which are confounding factors. Essentially, secondary data sources may be helpful in identifying problem areas, which then require the collection, processing, and analysis of primary data.

Primary data are gathered directly by the researcher. They fall into two general types: biological and environmental. Both are normally very expensive and time-consuming to obtain. Biological data (data from the subjects' bodies) may be obtained by chemical diagnoses of blood cells; tissue, hair, and nail samples; nerve conductivity measurement; or saliva and urine analysis. Some tests, such as blood and urine analysis may reveal recent exposures. Tissue samples (e.g., fat cells) may suggest past exposures that have accumulated in the body. Other biological data may be obtained using survey techniques. These data include self-reporting of headaches, infections, nausea, respiratory discomfort, and vertigo (dizziness). These symptoms are prone to self-reporting bias.

Environmental data reveal information about the physical environment of the area being studied and are obviously essential. Air, water, and soil analyses are required to detect the presence of chemicals, and the consequent potential for human exposure. There are considerable problems with obtaining accurate measurements of chemicals believed to be present at waste sites. The reader should consult specialized sources (Maugh, 1982; Miller, 1981; Voytek, 1981; Greenberg & Anderson, 1984) for a detailed discussion of the complexities of sampling procedures and methods for obtaining reliable laboratory measurements.

Finally, after all the data are assembled, there are issues related to the use of statistics. Much of the controversy over reports of findings in the early Love Canal health investigations centered on choice of study design and statistical reliability. The problems of these studies and society's growing need to understand the health consequences of waste sites, especially when proposals are made for new facilities, has prompted many scientists and decision makers to suggest guidelines to insure the statistical integrity of health studies (Stein, Hatch, Kline, Shrout, & Warburton, 1981; Bloom, 1981). The study of statistics is beyond the scope of this volume; you should consult specialized references on ways to plan a study so that it will be statistically valid.

Establishing Cause-Effect Relationships

The health study begins by focusing on either a geographical cluster or potential exposure. In either case, the researchers must clearly state the observed or expected adverse effects (Table 6-6). The nature of the cluster or potential exposure may greatly influence study design and effects to study. The study area is defined by delimiting the assumed area of effective exposure and incidence of disease. Careful definition of the study region right at the start is essential.

Once a study area is defined and data gathered, the character of the assumed hazardous exposure determines what effects will be studied. A broad literature should be established describing the effects of chemicals on human health. Such a literature is glaringly absent. A few resources on the effects of specific chemicals are available to aid researchers (Bloom, 1981; Hu, Weaver, & Kaltreider, 1984; Longo, 1980), but many experts point out that cause-effect relationships between chemicals and human disease are still largely uncertain. Much is unknown about the health effects of specific chemical exposures. Moreover, individuals vary considerably in their physiological responses to exposure because they differ in metabolism and in general ability to resist disease.

Tokuhata (1984) points out the need for three types of exposure information: (1) duration of exposure, (2) mode of exposure, and (3) cumulative dose. Tokuhata suggests that contaminants traveling in different ways through the environment may lead to multiple exposures at different parts of the body. For example, a contaminant in the air would affect the respiratory system, water would affect the urinary tract, and soil and crops the gastrointestinal tract.

Another uncertainty related to establishing plausible cause and effect involves the interaction among chemicals and changes in contaminants as they travel through the environment in various ways. Interaction of chemicals presents two types of problems. Stephens (1981) notes that searching for many chemicals is costly. Multiple chemicals in one waste site may undergo complex chemical reactions, producing a unique chemical compound with no established literature on its health effects. This is further complicated by the incomplete and sketchy history of waste sites and their chemical constituents.

Another difficulty is exposure to many chemicals at the same time. Animal studies on exposure and effects have focused on one suspected agent at a time. In reality people are exposed to all sorts of harmful substances in their personal environment (for example, smoking, alcohol consumption, diet, occupation, and outdoor activities). These exposures complicate studies of the impact of the chemicals found in waste sites on public health, for isolating just which substance is causing the problem becomes that much more difficult.

In addition to scientific uncertainty about what is in waste sites and how much is escaping, the dose–response issue has been a constant source of professional disagreement. Division of opinion centers on judgment regarding two models of response to various doses: the linear model and the threshold model. The linear dose–response model suggests that human health is affected at very low levels of exposure, and the effects increase proportionately with increases in exposure level. The threshold model holds that at very low doses chemicals have no observable effects on human health. This theory has important implications for waste sites that expose people to very small amounts of potentially dangerous chemicals. Conclusive scientific evidence to substantiate either theory is lacking (see Chapter 1).

The length of time that most chronic disease takes to develop (the latency period) is yet another difficulty. Exposed people may have died from a disease not easily linked to the waste at a site by the time the waste is found. The problem of keeping track of people who may have been exposed increases because people move around so much. For example, mutagenic cell effects vary based on the extent and nature of exposure and the susceptibility of the individual. There are two types of damage: chromosomal aberrations and sister chromatid exchanges. Chromosomal aberrations, which occur in the cells that make up the individual body, are more likely to affect the health of the exposed individual. Wolff (1981) suggests that serious changes are easily detected, but usually lead to cell death. Thus, they are probably not passed on to future generations. Individuals also have widely varying capabilities to repair cell damage and thus confound the researcher's investigation by making a cluster of incidents less pronounced.

Sister chromatid exchanges, occur in the germ cells, which transfer the genetic code from adults to offspring. These changes tend to occur as chromosomes duplicate themselves in preparation for cell division (Bloom, 1981). Thus mutations (changes) can show up in future generations. The rate of such change may serve as an indicator of chemical exposure, but there are no firm scientific guidelines for concluding that health damage is inevitable. Contact with other substances that cause mutations may complicate our understanding of the timing and sequence of exposure-effect. At best, cell damage can be used as an early warning of present or past exposure.

The same is probably true of chemical exposure that damages the nerves that provide the electrical impulses for maintaining biological mechanisms. Schaumberg, Arezzo, Markowitz, and Spencer (1981) suggest that such effects are widespread in the body and include the neurons, myelin sheaths, and axons (nerve junctions). Nerve-damaging chemicals tend to act quickly with brief latency periods. Effects differ dramatically depending on dose, and one chemical can trigger the toxic effects of another. Nerve conductivity measurements are useful in detecting the extent of nerve dysfunction. However, it is extremely difficult to detect potential psychological manifestations from nerve dysfunction. Therefore, neurotoxic damage serves best as a "flag" indicating recent or chronic exposure.

Effects on pregnancy and childbirth, such as miscarriage and stillbirths have a relatively short latency period. Tokuhata (1984) suggests that a systematic study of such cases would be a profitable area of investigation. Furthermore, since they have such a short latency period, they may also serve as an early warning of incidence of adult chronic disease. However, Warburton (1981) argues that

> major differences in susceptibility among test species, and even among different strains of the same species, and differences in drug metabolism among species, make the tests' predictive value for human reproduction very questionable. (p. 106)

Again, the question of confounding factors such as alcohol consumption, diet, drug use, prenatal care, and smoking makes it difficult to isolate the role of waste site chemicals.

We have reviewed some key considerations for conducting waste site health investigations. This discussion has included choosing the appropriate research technique, the availability and proper use of primary and secondary data, and establishing plausible cause–effect hypotheses. The complexities of all these stages make it extremely difficult to declare defensible positive findings. The following section reviews three waste site health studies and some of the problems that each encounters.

Three Case Studies

Love Canal

The Love Canal chemical dump in Niagara Falls, New York, has brought to focus the intense controversy surrounding efforts to investigate public health effects of toxic waste. Numerous studies have been conducted and much debate has raged concerning the short- and long-term safety of neighboring residents. Love Canal, more than any other single site, has been reported in great detail (Brown, 1980; Epstein, Brown, & Pope, 1982; New York Department of Public Health, 1978; Gibbs, 1983; Segel, Kamlet, Clark, & Veraska, 1979; U.S. Environmental Protection Agency, 1980). The goal here is to review briefly the types of health studies carried out, their findings, and their strengths and weaknesses. This discussion also serves to illustrate the difficulty inherent in investigations of releases of hazardous substances that travel through the environment by air, soil, and water.

Environmental monitoring of the Love Canal area revealed that people were indeed potentially exposed repeatedly to various chemical contaminants that were traveling through the environment from the place where they had been dumped. Residents had been saying for a long time that they had seen this happening (Leonard, Wetham, & Ziegler, 1977; Kim et al., 1980; U.S. Environmental Protection Agency, 1982). Now they demanded government action to protect them from the health effects. An early state survey revealed that the rate of miscarriages among women between the ages of 30 and 34 who lived in the southern section of the canal was four times what would normally be expected (Epstein et al., 1982). This survey also found an increased risk of birth defects and chronic disease. The residents of Love Canal were told of the state survey, but were not asked to participate, since the state focused on off-the-shelf secondary data (birth and death certificates).

In 1978 local residents did join Beverly Paigen, a researcher from Roswell Park Memorial Institute in Buffalo, in conducting a telephone survey of over 1,100 residents to obtain initial information on their health status. The survey was intended to be a preliminary investigation. Comparisons were made between self-reported symptoms of residents living in the ''wet'' areas (e.g., old streambeds, marshes, high water table) assumed to contain chemical contaminants moving in the water, and ''dry'' areas, which presumably had less chemical contamination. Paigen reported that indeed ''wet'' area residents experienced higher rates of miscarriages, birth defects, asthma, urinary-tract disease, severe nervous disorders, and nervous breakdowns than residents in ''dry'' areas.

Judged by considerations of formal scientific method, the Paigen study has many weaknesses. They include the lack of controls, potential bias in self-reported symptoms, absence of medical records and clinical diagnoses to confirm symptoms, and great uncertainty over the type, dose, and frequency of exposure. Yet, in terms of triggering more scientifically controlled studies, the Paigen study was very successful.

In 1979 the EPA contracted for a pilot study of changes in cell structure among volunteer residents to aid their enforcement actions against Hooker Chemical Company (assumed to be responsible for the dump in the first place). Picciano (1980a) studied 36 high-risk Love Canal residents, ''high-risk'' in this case meaning that these residents had experienced symptoms or disease, and had suffered pregnancy complications such as miscarriage or stillbirth. The research goal was to ascertain whether changes in the cells' chromosomes could be detected. Picciano (1980b) reported that 11 of the 36 subjects studied exhibited a rare chromosomal change called unique long acentric fragmentation. These conclusions were supported by at least one other researcher (Shaw, 1980). Picciano cautioned that the study group was not complemented with a control group because of funding limitations. Thus the study samples were compared to historical controls (that is, populations in past time), an admittedly undesirable design flaw. He also cautiously concluded that the chemical exposures at Love Canal may be responsible for increased cell aberrations and that residents could be at increased risk of cancer, birth defects, and spontaneous abortion. Later Picciano (1980c) suggested that the study results, though controversial, were grossly overshadowed by the fact that 16 of the last 18 pregnant women had lost their babies.

The weaknesses of the study were many. The most important were the lack of population controls, participant screening, interpretation, and the overall lack of understanding of what the chromosomal changes mean in terms of disease in the individual in which they occur and in future generations. Kolata (1980) reported that the expert panel of reviewers concluded that this was a classic case of how *not* to do such a study! Yet another panel found weaknesses in the method that was used but did not consider the identification of the chromosomal changes to be controversial.

The Paigen and Picciano studies caused alarm in the scientific community, but more importantly they caused increased anxiety among Love Canal residents. Both the state of New York and the U.S. EPA began a series of more rigorously designed investigations. Vianna (1980) reported preliminary results of an analysis of individuals who had suffered pregnancy complications, based on certificate and other data. He observed that some kinds of complications occurred more frequently than normal in the Love Canal area, but the increased frequency was not statistically significant. Therefore, the major preliminary conclusion was that the dump had no effect on public health. However, Vianna has continued to research the Love Canal residents' health effects, and his most recent report (Vianna & Polan, 1984) shows higher percentages of low-birth-weight babies during the active dumping period than during the period of no chemical dumping.

Janerich *et al.* (1981) examined age-adjusted cancer incidence data at the census-tract level for areas surrounding the canal. These rates were compared for a limited number of cancer organ sites or systems (e.g., lung, leukemia, brain, liver) to county and state rates. A statistically higher-than-normal incidence of brain tumors was the only observable excess cancer incidence. His study used county and state data instead of a control group and failed to consider the appropriate latency period for cancer. He also failed to match his cases of cancer with data on exposure to chemicals. On the other hand, the study illustrates very well the advantages and limitations of using off-the-shelf data to examine hypotheses relating waste sites to public health effects. This study, as well as those reported by Paigen, Picciano, and Vianna, all concluded that some health problems appeared to be higher than normal, but nearly all excess illness and death could be explained by random chance.

Heath (1984b) did not find a strong positive correlation and statistically significant excess of public health effects. In response to the Picciano study Heath (1983) investigated the potential for cell damage among Love Canal residents. Heath reported that both chromosomal changes and sister chromatid exchanges did not differ significantly between 46 subjects who lived or had lived in the ring of homes around the canal and control subjects who did not. While the results were negative, the study is very instructive in its design and use of data. Study participants were screened by questionnaire, and blood samples were taken. Geographic controls were used to identify varying levels of exposure of organic chemical levels as measured in basement air samples. Controls were selected from another section of Niagara Falls. Screening for confounding factors such as smoking and contact recreation with the waste site (touching contaminated grounds) were obtained by questionnaire. The study appears to have met the major criteria for a controlled, scientific study; it has satisfied the immediate peer review; and it awaits broad acceptance in the research community. The only positive finding was a statistically higher frequency of sister chromatid exchanges among those who smoked than those who did not, regardless of whether the person lived near Love Canal or was in the control group.

To summarize, some studies have found health problems among people who lived around Love Canal before the area was evacuated. However, these effects are seldom found to be of sufficient magnitude to be statistically significant. While the debate over the extent and importance of public health effects and the uncertainties involved assessing risk continue, there is pressure to rehabitate part of the residential neighborhood, allowing people to live there again. It remains to be seen what government and health officials will do in this situation.

Silresim Corporation, Lowell, Massachusetts

The Silresim Corporation operated a 5-acre chemical reclamation and recycling facility in the city of Lowell from 1971 to 1977. Silresim collected a wide variety of waste chemicals that were thought to have a commercial value for resale. The wastes were stored on the site in surface containers. Around 1974 neighboring residents complained to local health officials and the Massachusetts Department of Environmental Quality Engineering (DEQE) about odors from the haphazardly stored material and contaminated soil on the site. Meanwhile, Silresim ran into financial trouble, and it ceased operations by late 1977. The DEQE secured the site, since it posed an environmental threat, and it was eventually included in the National Priority (Superfund) List under the Comprehensive Environmental Response Compensation and Liability Act (CERCLA). Meanwhile more residents complained more about pregnancy complications than complained about merely annoying odors. By 1981 all the surface containers had been cleared away, but contaminated soil remained, and residents voiced concern about past and future health threats related to the site. The Silresim case and the studies of it illustrate the difficulty of assessing the risk to human health from a waste site where air exposure is the primary source of contamination.

Ozonoff et al. (1983) conducted a symptom-prevalence study of 1,015 households (513 residents of the area and 502 controls), resulting in data collection on 1,997 adults (1,049 residents and 948 control) and 1,106 children (594 residents and 512 control). The research hypothesis was:

> Exposure to airborne chemicals from the Silresim site is associated with increased prevalence of self-reported adverse health outcomes and/or altered patterns in cause of death for deceased residents.

The research strategy was to compare health data between the resident and control groups, and then measure the levels of airborne pollutants to correlate with reported symptoms and deaths.

Identifying and measuring the levels of airborne chemicals proved very difficult. A first air-sampling study obtained samples at the site, at three locations in the immediate neighborhood of the site, and one location some distance away that served as a control to establish background levels. This first study concluded that levels of benzene, toluene, trichloroethylene, and tetrachlorethylene detected were not significantly different from background levels.

A second air study conducted by a private contractor, using a different air-monitoring instrument, found positive results. Aliphatic amines were detected in the hundreds of parts per billion (ppb). Phtalic anhydride and total phtalate compounds were detected at up to 100 ppb. These findings suggested that the first air study was not sufficiently sensitive to actual and transient pollutants.

A third air study was conducted to try to resolve the different results from the first two. Four different sampling techniques and analytical methods were employed, and the results confirmed the first air study, concluding that levels of organic emissions were not significantly different from background levels. This study also uncovered volatile emissions originating from two industrial facilities situated to the northeast of the Silresim site. These emissions included significant quantities of dimethyl formamide, toluene, and xylene. It is speculated that the emissions detected in the second air study were really confirmed by identifying the new sources in the third air study.

Ozonoff *et al.* (1983) used proximity to site as the index of exposure, and the study group was composed of people who lived within one-quarter mile of the Silresim site. The control group consisted of Lowell residents who lived between one-half and three-quarters of a mile from the Silresim site. The control area was chosen on the assumption that effects of exposure would decrease with distance. The effects that were being studied included cancer deaths, information from certificates regarding miscarriages and stillbirths, and finally a laundry list of self-reported symptoms by the study participants. The researchers also controlled for confounding variables such as age, education, smoking, workplace exposures, sex, marital status, and type of residence. The study team concluded:

> based on currently available evidence there is no increase in the reproductive hazard, cancer risk, or mortality in the target area. (p. 5)

Statistically significant increases were found in self-reported symptoms of wheezing and tightness in chest, coughing, chest discomfort, shortness of breath, and persistent colds. Residents of the study area also reported more fatigue, bowel discomfort, headaches, easy bruising, and bleeding problems. The authors expressed serious questions concerning bias in self-reporting, but they were reluctant to ignore these reports:

> insofar as some kind of bias is not at work to produce an artifactual difference, there is no question that perception of symptoms, whether or not there is a documented physiological basis for it, has an impact on the quality of life, the efficiency and the productivity of a community. (Ozonoff *et al.*, 1983, p. 8)

The study authors site the uncertainties imposed by the exposure data, the bias in self-reporting, the latency period for cancer, the time sequence of exposure and the appearance of the numbers of problems, and the small sample size as complicating factors. Concern was also expressed about the possible presence of additional volatile substances, which may have introduced "noise" (extraneous variables) into the analysis. On the other hand, the study followed guidelines for scientific investigation with great rigor.

Industriplex Industrial Park, Woburn, Massachusetts

In 1979 workmen were digging foundations for the 800-acre Industriplex industrial park in Woburn, Massachusetts. As they worked, they repeatedly unearthed chemical wastes, which it turns out, had been accumulating for over 130 years. The site had been a routine dumping ground for area industry, and with no engineering controls was little more than a series of open dumps and abandoned surface impoundments. Samples taken in 1979 revealed a potpourri of chemical constituents. Furthermore, chlorinated organic compounds were found to contaminate two of the wells (wells G and H) from which the town obtained its water supply. Public concern about the incidence of chronic disease, especially leukemia, prompted health officials to investigate the relationship between the waste site and the health of residents. This case illustrates a health study involving groundwater contamination as the primary way that humans were exposed. The Woburn study has been hailed as a landmark investigation showing conclusive positive results. But critics claim that the study was faulty and not definitive.

The first two studies of health in Woburn produced mixed results. Parker and Rosen (1981), working for the Massachusetts Department of Public Health, found abnormally high rates of cancer deaths (e.g., liver, female organs other than cervix, and kidney) after screening death certificates from 1969 to 1978. Significant rises in rates of childhood leukemia were also reported. These researchers recognized the effect but were unable to identify an environmental cause.

Rowe (1981) examined cancer deaths in the Woburn area for the years 1949 to 1968 by census tracts. Since no evidence of anything that would cause leukemia was found, Rowe concluded that the high rates of leukemia were attributable to random fluctuation over time and space.

In early 1979 the DEQE shut down the two wells when samples revealed presence of 48 organic priority pollutants and significant levels of trichloroethylene, 1-1-1-trichloroethane, tetrachloroethylene, chloroform, and dibromochloromethane (Ecology and Environment, Inc. 1982a, 1982b). Thus, it became reasonable to assume that people whose water came from wells G and H had been exposed long before 1979 when DEQE shut down the wells.

Two other reports were instrumental in relating levels of exposure to public health problems. Waldorf and Cleary (1983) reported on the Woburn water distribution system between the years 1964 to 1979. From this report it was possible to determine which houses were being served by water pumped from wells G and H. This study used a water distribution simulation model developed earlier by Camp, Dresser and McKee, Inc. (1976) to estimate the levels of water consumption from well G and H by residential users. The researchers were able to identify different gradients, or zones, based on estimated percentage of their water that came from the contaminated wells. This form of geographic knowledge allowed the researchers to examine the hypothesis that a higher percentage of water consumed from the contaminated wells would lead to more problems in pregnancy and more childhood disease.

The target group for the study was all households with listed telephone numbers where at least one resident was born in Woburn after 1920, a total of 3,257 (slightly over 50% of the known residents). Information on childbearing for the years 1960 to 1982 was obtained, along with controls for mother's age, smoking habits, number of children born previously, and a number of socioeconomic factors (e.g., income, education, home values). Information was also obtained concerning early childhood leukemia incidence. The results showed that households receiving their water from wells G and H did experience more problems.

Lagakos, Wessen, and Zelen (1984) also reported that increased use of water from contaminated wells G and H was associated with newborn deaths, eye and ear birth defects, other environmentally linked birth defects, and childhood leukemia, lung/respiratory disorders, and kidney and urinary-tract disorders. The authors concluded that these statistical associations do not confirm a cause–effect relationship, but are still important.

As mentioned above, the study results have become controversial. Some residents, researchers, and health officials have said that they feel vindicated. However, a prominent epidemiologist at the Harvard School of Public Health, Brian McMahon, has disputed the study, its method, and its results (Knox, 1984). McMahon argues that the study suffers from the unexplained exclusion of almost 47% of the target group, the use of small numbers of disease cases, and the ''naiveté'' of grouping nerve and chromosomal damage as environmentally related.

In any case, a group of neighbors of the Industriplex Industrial Park have brought a personal injury suit against two corporations alleged to have improperly disposed of hazardous waste on the site. The plaintiffs (neighborhood residents) have set forth two legal arguments. First, the defendants (Beatrice Foods, Inc., and W. R. Grace, Inc.) poisoned the groundwater supplying the residents' water source with hazardous contaminants. The second argument deals with medical causation, and the plaintiffs argue that the excessive health problems they have experienced are a result of the groundwater poisoning.

Trial of the case began in the federal district court in Boston in early 1986. The defendants have disclaimed responsibility for the groundwater contamination and the health problems of the plaintiffs. Present and former employees at the site, subpoenaed by the plaintiffs, have testified that dumping hazardous waste disposal on the land and in the ground was routine.

The outcome of this personal injury suit might have been expected to have broad implications for the future conduct of waste site health studies. In part, some of the issues became moot, because the plaintiffs made a multimillion dollar cash settlement with the defendants in the summer of 1986. However, it is still particularly important to evaluate whether the Woburn study, a scientific study based on hypotheses testing using techniques of statistical inference and revealing evidence of contamination and impaired health, is accepted as valid legal evidence. Witness testimony has established as fact routine improper hazardous waste disposal. Whether or not the improper disposal is linked to the contamination and health problems will have to be determined. Researchers investigating other waste sites with ground-water contamination will rely on the Woburn study as a precedent.

To summarize, these three examples illustrate the difficulty of investigating waste site health effects when air and soil, air, and groundwater are the paths by which contamination travels. Other than an inferential association between repro-ductive and childhood disorders and groundwater contamination with organic chem-icals, there is little scientific evidence to conclude that waste sites have exacted a gross price in danger to public health. The later Love Canal studies and the two Massachusetts waste site studies adhered to many of the guidelines for conducting scientific investigations; yet, each could be faulted on some grounds. The major research problems included the lack of knowledge about the extent of human ex-posure to hazardous substances, weak statistical power of explanation, bias in self-reporting of symptoms, the difficulty of obtaining appropriate control groups, and the limitations of working with relatively small numbers of cases. Although many researchers and especially neighbors of waste sites have intuitive feelings that the waste dumps are the cause of their problems, state-of-the-art methodological ap-proaches have not verified such notion with 100% certainty. Either the public health effects are extremely subtle so far, or the methods are not sensitive enough to reveal them. In light of this serious degree of uncertainty it is not surprising that local residents are fearful of and strongly opposed to allowing new facilities to be es-tablished in their communities.

Mental Health Problems of Waste Sites

The most obvious health effects that waste sites have caused are psychological. Known or possible exposure, especially involuntary exposure, strikes fear into people's hearts and has often led to prolonged controversy. The Reverend Ted Creen (1983) discussed psychological impact on residents of the town of Whit-church-Stouffville, Ontario, of the proposal to extend the York Sanitation Landfill. Public controversy and prolonged confrontation over the proposed expansion height-ened community stress, deepened personal depression, and even developed into some cases of paranoia and psychosis. The Reverend Creen (1983, p. 58) wrote that the Whitchurch-Stouffville incident

> will have lasting effects upon the wider community, effects unfortunately of a negative nature such as division, animosity, distrust, cynicism, and despair.

While we have seen that science has not definitively related physical health problems to waste sites, the mental health effects abound. However, they remain unquantified and unsubstantiated by other than anecdotal description.

Dramatic accounts of the psychological trauma among residents of Love Canal can be found in transcripts of hearings held before the Subcommittee on Oversight and Investigations of the U.S. House of Representatives Committee on Interstate and Foreign Commerce (1979). Gibbs (1983) describes in detail the psychological trauma that her family endured as a result of chemical exposure from Love Canal and the confrontation with private and industrial officials who denied responsibility. Perhaps the most devastating account of this confrontation is documented in a film called *PCBs: A Plague on our Children*, produced by the Public Broadcasting Service and broadcast as part of the NOVA television series. In this film the neighbors of Love Canal were nearly hysterical as they attempted to convince state and federal officials that residents should be evacuated. Expressing fears that they were being victimized, residents not only challenged the credibility of government officials at all levels, but they planned civil disobedience. Greenberg and Anderson (1984) summarized a number of other incidents across the country where acts of violence, sabotage, and general civil disobedience were the reaction to new or existing waste sites. The participants in these acts and demonstrations were not only environmental activists. They constituted a heterogeneous cross section of American society. Despite the potential importance of civil disobedience as a possible trend, there is relatively little formal research to help understand these psychological impacts.

Research on the psychological effects of *natural* disasters such as floods, hurricanes, and earthquakes, has appeared in the literature for some time (White, 1974; Jackson & Mukerjee, 1974; Burton, Kates, & White, 1978; Shippee, Burroughs, & Wakefield, 1980). Only recently has there appeared literature on *technological* hazards. Much of it was derived from the natural hazards literature.

Baum, Fleming, and Singer (1983) identify seven characteristics that may be used to compare natural and technological hazards (Table 6-7). The key difference is that while the natural hazard is accepted as uncontrollable, the technological hazard is seen as evidence of the human failure in design or control. Thus, it evokes feelings of helplessness and anger at managers and government regulators considered responsible for the technology. Not all the disasters that have been studied deal with hazardous waste specifically, but their findings are still instructive.

Researchers who have studied the behavior of residents in neighborhoods experiencing natural or technological disasters have reported unsettling findings. For example, when danger threatens, removing people from the hazard becomes important. Smith and Fisher (1981) reveal the difficulties of developing an evacuation plan for over 200,000 residents, including those in short-term and long-term care medical facilities, living within a 20-mile radius of the Three Mile Island Nuclear Generating Station (TMI), near Harrisburg, Pennsylvania.

Nor do people necessarily move away from a dangerous area voluntarily. Goldhaber, Houts, and DiSabella (1983) reported that residential mobility within 5 miles of the plant remained unchanged from the year before the TMI accident to the year after. Only 15% of those who did move claimed that the accident was the primary reason. They also report that those who moved because of the accident had financial and social characteristics that made them more likely to move any way. Preston, Taylor, and Hodge (1983) reported that residents had adjusted their activities in line with natural and technological hazards, but they still perceived their situation to be extremely risky. A low rate of mobility, these authors concluded,

Table 6-7. Characterstics of Natural versus Technological Hazards

Characteristic	Natural	Technological[a]
Causes	Known	Usually known
Damage	Visible, measurable, usually reparable	Sometimes invisible and immeasurable, often irreparable
Predictability	Estimation and forecasts based on previous experience	Low or nonexistent; safeguards are intended to make risks negligible
Low point	Identifiable, after which recovery begins	Often unknown without clear turning point
Control	Uncontrollable	Occurrence results from loss of normal control mechanism
Extent of effects	Usually limited to immediate victims and vicinity	Initially limited to immediate victims and vicinity; engenders widespread loss of confidence among populations in comparable situations
Persistence of effects	Relatively short-lived	Relatively long-lived

Note. Adapted from Baum, Fleming, and Singer (1983) and White (1983).
[a]With emphasis on chemical waste hazards.

is due chiefly to the need for low-cost housing and a tightly knit social structure in the affected communities. In other words, most people couldn't afford to move and were unable and unwilling to tear up roots and start over elsewhere.

It seems likely that the mental health effects from existing or proposed waste sites will likewise be heightened among populations that are economically or socially bound to an area of potential exposure. This may be an important reason why vociferous opposition to new facilities may be a normal reaction.

Scientists are working on developing attitudinal surveys to inventory and measure symptoms and stress. There are a number of test batteries with different scaling systems that could be beneficially employed. White (1983) suggests two possible psychological tests that could be used to establish baseline conditions (before any problem develops), to identify sensitive populations, and to monitor changes over time. One 20-question battery is designed to detect stress indicators such as alcohol abuse, headaches, lethargy, loss of appetite, and nervousness.

The second test is known as the SCL-90-R. It is a 10- to 20-minute self-test designed to distinguish among nine different types of psychological stress: anxiety, depression, hostility, interpersonal sensitivity, obsessive-compulsive behavior, paranoid ideation (disordered ways of thinking such as suspicion, feelings of grandiosity, fear of loss of autonomy), phobic anxiety (persistent and disproportionate fear of a specific person, place, object, or situation), psychoticism (withdrawn, isolated, or schizoid life-style), and somatization (distress arising from perceptions of bodily dysfunction such as pains, breathing difficulties, lump in throat, hot or cold spells) (Derogatis, 1977). Derogatis was instrumental in developing the SCL-90-R and suggests the use of composite scores based on average responses in order to identify stress. In addition, there are two indices that combine the composite scores to measure the presence of distress (Positive Symptom Distress Index) and the level of general severity of impacts (General Severity Index). Results of such a survey could be compared with a control group. Comparison could also be made to a variety of historical control groups including "normal" populations as well as homogeneous populations.

The results from psychological tests could guide decision makers about what should be done to prevent or reduce stress. Opening the lines of communication and involving community residents in such a survey could lead to wider understanding of the problem. Sensitive populations could be targeted for special counseling. Most importantly, conducting such surveys could send a clear signal to the residents that the decision makers care and are competent enough to take early precautions. This step is one of many that will be necessary to reestablish the credibility of government officials who work with the hazardous waste problem as protectors of public health.

Similar tests can be designed and administered to populations surrounding existing sites. Indeed, CERCLA requires the Centers for Disease Control to maintain a registry of persons exposed to toxic substances and to conduct health effects investigations, including psychological impacts, periodically. The most severe limitation with investigations of populations near existing waste sites include obtaining a proper control group, bias in self-reporting on questionnaires, and distinguishing between stages of mental health effects with regard to duration of effects and behavior adjustment. It would be profitable to develop and conduct a number of testing procedures on populations of people living near some of the worst sites in the United States (National Priority List under CERCLA).

POINTS TO REMEMBER

The purpose of this chapter has been to introduce the public health effects of solid waste and its management in the United States. Solid wastes are everywhere in our society. Yet we have only an imperfect knowledge of the types, volumes, and characteristics of these wastes. Regulations to protect health have focused on technological design and operation standards at waste sites, from the municipal sanitary landfill to the large hazardous waste management facility.

The numerous investigations of the public health problems resulting from hazardous waste sites usually are faulted for methodological reasons. Rarely is a plausible linkage confirmed, and even then there is a strong possibility that the results may be confused or spurious. There is also a singular lack of scientific investigation of the mental health effects related to living near waste sites.

Industry and government officials face growing opposition to plans for expanding or creating waste disposal facilities because of the great uncertainty over what might happen to—indeed may already slowly be happening to—public health. The many unanswered questions and the risk of irreversible chronic disease and pregnancy and childbirth problems signal that those responsible for managing hazardous waste, land use, and protection of public health and the environment should proceed cautiously. Rather than rushing into the development of a supposedly superior and safe new hazardous waste technology at new sites, decision makers should seriously consider what effects existing sites have had. Priority should be given to developing processes that do not create waste and that recycle the waste on-site. Rather than find new sites, it should be possible to identify the least dangerous existing sites and refurbish them with new and upgraded technology. It is clear that each new or upgraded waste facility will undergo extreme public scrutiny. Unless decision makers can show caution and prove that control programs work, then the unfortunate neighbors of waste facilities will continue to be victimized, will continue to suffer, and probably will escalate their opposition to new facilities.

References

Anderson, R. F., & Greenberg, M. R. (1984). Siting hazardous waste management facilities: Theory versus reality. In S. Majumdar & W. Miller (Eds.), *Hazardous and toxic wastes: technology, management, and health effects.* Philadelphia: Pennsylvania Academy of Sciences.

Baum, A., Fleming, R., & Singer, J. E. (1983). Stress at Three Mile Island: Applying psychological impact analysis. In L. Bickman (Ed.), Applied social psychology annual. Beverly Hills, CA: Sage.

Bloom, A. D. (1981). *Guidelines for studies of human populations exposed to mutagenic and reproductive hazards.* White Plains, NY: March of Dimes Birth Defects Foundation.

Booz-Allen & Hamilton, Inc., & Putman, Hayes, and Bartlett, Inc. (198). *Hazardous waste generation and commercial hazardous waste capacity* (SW-894). Washington, DC: U.S. Environmental Protection Agency.

Brown, M. (1980). *Laying waste: The poisoning of America by toxic chemicals.* New York: Pantheon.

Burton, I., Kates, R. W., & White, G. W. (1978). *The environment as hazard.* New York: Oxford University Press.

Camp, Dresser, and McKee, Inc. (1976). *Metropolitan water transmission and distribution system simulation model.* Boston: Metropolitan District Commission.

Creen, T. (1983). The social and psychological impact of NIMBY disputes. In A. Armour (Ed.), *Hazardous Waste Management: The Not-In-My-Backyard Syndrome, Symposium Proceedings.* Toronto: York University.

Derogatis, L. R. (1977). *SCL-90-R Manual—I.* Baltimore: Johns Hopkins University School of Medicine.

Ecology and Environment, Inc. (1982a). *Chlorinated solvent contamination of the groundwater: East Central Woburn, Massachusetts* (Final Report). Boston: U.S. EPA Region 1.

Ecology and Environment, Inc. (1982b). *Evaluation of the Hydrogeology and Groundwater quality of East and North Woburn, Massachusetts: Volume I: Final Report.* Boston: U.S. EPA Region 1.

Epstein, S. S., Brown, L. O., & Pope, C. (1982). *Hazardous waste in America.* San Francisco: Sierra Club Books.

Gibbs, L. (1983). Community response to an emergency situation: Psychological destruction and the Love Canal in Niagara Falls, N.Y. *American Journal of Community Psychology, 11*(2), 115–125.

Goldhaber, M. K., Houts, P. S., & DiSabella, R. (1983). Moving after the crises: A prospective study of Three Mile Island area population mobility. *Environment and Behavior, 15*(1), 93–120.

Greenberg, M. R., & Anderson, R. F. (1984). *Hazardous waste sites: The credibility gap.* Piscataway, NJ: Center for Urban Policy Research.

Fred C. Hart Associates, Inc. (1979). *Preliminary assessment of clean-up costs for national hazardous waste problems.* (prepared for U.S. Environmental Protection Agency, Office of Solid Waste, EPA Contract #68015063).

Heath, C. W. (1983). Field epidemiologic studies of populations exposed to waste dumps. *Environmental Health Perspectives, 48*, 3–7.

Heath, C. W. (1984a). The effects of hazardous waste on public health. In S. Majumdar & W. Miller (Eds.), *Hazardous and toxic wastes: Technology, management, and health effects.* Philadelphia: Pennsylvania Academy of Sciences.

Heath, C. W. (1984b). Cytogenic findings in persons living near the Love Canal. *Science, 251*, 1437–1439.

Hu, T., Weaver, J. A., & Kaltreider, D. L. (1984). Empirical estimation of hazardous waste disposal damage costs. In S. Majumdar & W. Miller (Eds.), *Hazardous and Toxic wastes: Technology, management, and health effects.* Philadelphia: Pennsylvania Academy of Science.

Ing, R. (1983). *Uniform methods to collect information on mortality, serious diseases, and human exposure to toxic substances: Recommendations from an epidemiologic perspective.* Atlanta, GA: Centers for Disease Control.

Jackson, E. L., & Mukerjee, T. (1974). Human adjustment to the earthquake hazard of San Francisco, California. In G. F. White (Ed.), *Natural Hazards.* New York: Oxford University Press.

Janerich, D. T., Burnett, W. S., Feck, G., Hoff, M., Nasca, P., Polednak, A. P., Greenwald, P., & Vianna, N. (1981). Cancer incidence in the Love Canal Area. *Science, 212*, 1404–1407.

JRB Associates, Inc. (1981). *Solid waste data: A compilation of statistics on solid waste management within the United States.* Springfield, VA: NTIS, PB82-107301.

Keswick, B. H., & Gerba, C. P. (1980). Viruses in groundwater. *Environmental Science and Technology, 14*(11), 1290–1297.

Kim, C. S., *et al.* (1980). Love Canal: Chemical contamination and migration. In *Proceedings of the*

National Conference on Management of Uncontrolled Hazardous Waste Sites. Washington, DC: U.S. Environmental Protection Agency.

Knox, R. A. (1984). Professor criticizes Woburn health study. *Boston Globe*, June 8.

Kolata, G. B. (1980). Love Canal: False alarm caused by botched study. *Science, 209*, 1239–1243.

Lacomber, D. M. (1979). *An overview of solid waste generation in the United States*. Los Alamos, NM: Los Alamos Scientific Laboratory.

Lagakos, S. W., Wessen, B. J., & Zelen, M. (1984). *The Woburn health study: An analysis of reproductive and childhood disorders and their relation to environmental contamination*. Boston: Department of Biostatistics, Harvard School of Public Health.

Leonard, R. P., Wetham, P. H., Ziegler, R. C. (1977). *Characterization and abatement of groundwater pollution from Love Canal chemical landfill, Niagara Falls, New York*. Buffalo, NY: CALSPAN Corporation.

Longo, L. D. (1980). Environmental pollution and pregnancy: Risks and uncertainties for the fetus and infant. *Journal of Obstetrics and Gynecology, 137*(2), 162–173.

Lowrance, W. W. (Ed.). (1981). *Assessment of health effects at chemical disposal sites*. New York: Rockefeller University.

Lumb, G. (1984). Health effects of hazardous wastes. In S. Majumdar & W. Miller (Eds.), *Hazardous and toxic wastes: Technology, management, and health effects*. Philadelphia: Pennsylvania Academy of Science.

Maugh, T. H. (1982). Just how hazardous are dumps? *Science, 215*(4,532), 490–493.

Miller, D. W. (1981). Geohydrological surveys at chemical disposal sites. In W. W. Lowrance (Ed.), *Assessment of health effects at chemical disposal sites*. New York: Rockefeller University.

Moore, C. A., & Rai, I. S. (1977). Design criteria for gas migration control devices. In *Management of Gas and Leachate in Landfills* (EPA-600/9-77-026). Washington, DC: U.S. Environmental Protection Agency.

New York Department of Public Health. (1978). *Love Canal: Public health time bomb, Special report to the governor and legislature*. Albany: New York State Department of Health.

Ozonoff, D., Colten, M. E., Cupples, A., Heeren, T., Schatzkin, A., Mangione, T., Dresner, M., & Colter, T. (1983). *Silresim area health study—Report of findings*. Boston: Boston University School of Public Health.

Parker, G. S., & Rosen, S. L. (1981). *Woburn: Cancer incidence and environmental hazards 1969–1978*. Boston: Massachusetts Department of Public Health.

Petersen, N. M. (1983, March). 1983 Survey of Landfills. *Waste Age*, 37–40.

Picciano, D. (1980a). *Pilot cytogenic study of Love Canal, New York*. Washington, DC: U.S. Environmental Protection Agency, prepared by the Biogenics Corporation.

Picciano, D. (1980b). Pilot cytogenic study of the residents living near Love Canal: Hazardous waste site. *Mammalian Chromosome Newsletter, 21*, 86–93.

Picciano, D. (1980c). Letter to the editor. *Science, 209*, 755–756.

Preston, V., Taylor, S. M., & Hodge, D. C. (1983). Adjustment to natural and technological hazards: A study of an urban residential community. *Environment and Behavior, 15*(2), 143–164.

Rajagopalan, S., & Schiffman, M. A. (1974). *Guide to simple sanitary measures for the control of enteric diseases*. Geneva: World Health Organization.

Rowe, R. (1981). *A retrospective study of Woburn mortality 1949–1968*. Boston: Massachusetts Department of Public Health.

Schaumberg, N. H., Arezzo, J. C., Markowitz, L., Spencer, P. S. (1981). Neurotoxicity Assessment. In W. W. Lowrance (Ed.), *Assessment of health effects at chemical disposal sites*. New York: Rockefeller University.

SCS Engineers. (1981). *Solid waste landfill design and operation practices—draft*. Washington, DC: U.S. Environmental Protection Agency.

Segel, E., Kamlet, K. S., Clark, B., & Veraska, W. (1979). *The toxic substances dilemma—A plan for citizen action*. Washington, DC: National Wildlife Federation.

Shaw, M. W. (1980). Love Canal chromosome study. *Science, 209*, 751–752.

Shippee, G., Burroughs, J., & Wakefield, S. (1980). Dissonance theory revisited: Perception of environmental hazards in residential areas. *Environment and Behavior, 12*(1), 33–51.

Smith, J. S., & Fisher, J. H. (1981). Three Mile Island: The silent disaster. *Journal of the American Medical Association, 245*(16), 1656–1659.

Stein, Z., Hatch, M., Kline, J., Shrout, P., & Warburton, D. (1981). Epidemiologic consideration. In W. W. Lowrance (Ed.), *Assessing health effects at chemical disposal sites*. New York: Rockefeller University.

Stephens, R. D. (1981). Experimental design for wastesite investigations. In W. W. Lowrance (Ed.), *Assessment of health effects at chemical disposal sites*. New York: Rockefeller University.

Tokuhata, G. K. (1984). Epidemiologic methods for investigating potential health effects of toxic waste sites: A case of asbestos. In S. Majumdar & W. Miller (Eds.), *Hazardous and toxic wastes: Technology, Management and health effects*. Philadelphia: Pennsylvania Academy of Science.

U.S. Centers for Disease Control. (1984). *A system for prevention, assessment, and control of exposures and health effects from hazardous sites*. Atlanta, GA: U.S. Department of Health and Human Services, Public Health Service.

U.S. Environmental Protection Agency. (1974). *Report to Congress: Hazardous Waste* (SW-115). Washington, DC: U.S. Environmental Protection Agency.

U.S. Environmental Protection Agency. (1977). *State decision makers' guide for hazardous waste management* (SW-612). Washington, DC: U.S. Environmental Protection Agency.

U.S. Environmental Protection Agency. (1978). Surface impoundments and their effects on groundwater quality in the United States—A preliminary survey (570/9-78-004). Washington, DC: U.S. Environmental Protection Agency.

U.S. Environmental Protection Agency. (1980). Damages and threats caused by hazardous material sites (EPA/430/9-80/004). Washington, DC: U.S. Environmental Protection Agency.

U.S. Environmental Protection Agency. (1982). Environmental monitoring at Love Canal (EPA-600/4-82-030a). Washington, DC: U.S. Government Printing Office.

U.S. Environmental Protection Agency. (1983). *National survey of hazardous waste generators and treatment, storage and disposal facilities regulated under RCRA in 1981: Preliminary highlights of findings*. Washington, DC: U.S. Environmental Protection Agency.

U.S. House of Representatives Subcommittee on Oversight and Investigations of the House Committee on Interstate and Foreign Commerce. (1979). Hearings on Hazardous Waste Disposal, 96th Congress, 1st Session, Ser. No. 96-48.

Versar, Inc. (1981). *Guidance manual for the classification of solid waste disposal facilities—Final*. Washington, DC: U.S. Environmental Protection Agency.

Vianna, N. (1980). Adverse pregnancy outcome: Potential endpoints of human toxicity in the Love Canal: Preliminary results. In I. H. Porter & E. B. Hook (Eds.), *Human embryonic and fetal death*. New York: Academic Press.

Vianna, N., & Polan, A. (1984). Incidence of low birth weight among Love Canal residents. *Science, 226*, 1217–1219.

Voytek, P. E. (1981). Aspects of risk assessment strategy. In W. W. Lowrance (Ed.), *Assessment of health effects at chemical disposal sites*. New York: Rockefeller University.

Waldorf, H., & Cleary, R. (1983). *Water distribution system, Woburn, Massachusetts, 1964–1979, Draft report*. Boston: Massachusetts Department of Environmental Quality Engineering.

Warburton, D. (1981). Selection of human reproductive effects for study. In W. W. Lowrance (Ed.), *Assessment of health effects at chemical disposal sites*. New York: Rockefeller University.

Westat, Inc. (1984). *National survey of hazardous waste generators and treatment, storage and disposal facilities regulated under RCRA in 1981*. Washington, DC: U.S. Environmental Protection Agency.

White, A. (1983). *Potential psychological and sociological effects of the IT facility on Warren and abutting communities, Memorandum to Warren, Massachusetts, Local Assessment Committee*. Boston: Boston Planning Group.

White, G. F. (1974). Natural hazards research: Concepts, methods, and policy implications. In G. F. White (Ed.), *Natural Hazards*. New York: Oxford University Press.

Wolff, S. (1981). Cytogenic analysis: Problems and prospects. In W. W. Lowrance (Ed.), *Assessment of health effects at chemical disposal sites*. New York: Rockefeller University.

II

CHOICES AND SOLUTIONS

THE TECHNOLOGICAL SOLUTION

Hard and Soft Paths, Scientific Uncertainty, and the Control of Technology

J. Stanley Black
Illinois Environmental Protection Agency

This chapter explores the role of technology, and of proposed technological "solutions," in protecting public health and the environment. As the title suggests, I will address the "hard path–soft path" controversy, but with an emphasis on the role of uncertainty in limiting our control over technology. Thus a portion of the discussion will draw upon research on the factors influencing perception of technological risk, the acceptability of such risk to various affected "publics," and some of the difficulties of arriving at mutually acceptable risk-management decisions regarding technologies.

This effort has been profoundly influenced by two very different developments. The first was the publication in mid-1984 of Charles Perrow's book, *Normal Accidents*, in which he sets forth a thesis that we cannot ignore. The second event was the catastrophic release in December 1984 of tons of highly toxic methyl isocyanate gas from a chemical facility in Bhopal, India, resulting in the deaths of over 2,500 people and severe toxic exposure of tens of thousands more.

"HARD" AND "SOFT" TECHNOLOGICAL PATHS: NO SURE PATH TO PUBLIC SAFETY

There have been perhaps as many different definitions of what constitute "hard" and "soft" technologies as there have been the many writers who have addressed the issue since Amory Lovins first introduced the distinction in his 1976 *Foreign Affairs* article. I do not propose to continue this proliferation here but will rely on Lovins's own words, from *Soft Energy Paths* (1977). To Lovins, the hard technology path "relies on rapid expansion of centralized high technologies to increase supplies of energy, especially in the form of electricity," whereas the soft path "combines a prompt and serious commitment to efficient use of energy, rapid development of renewable energy sources matched in scale and in energy quality to end use needs, and special transitional fossil fuel technologies" (Lovins, 1977, p. 25).

Lovins's argument (see also Lovins, 1975; Lovins & Price, 1975; Lovins, 1978) was quickly taken up by others and expanded to include not only energy technologies, but other "unforgiving" technologies as well. Despite differences in terminology and definitions among those who expounded and expanded Lovins's critique of the "hard path," there has been reasonably good agreement as to which technologies belong on which path. Nuclear fission and fast breeder reactors, and prolonged dependence on centralized coal plants fed by strip mines formed the core of the hard path. Continued and increasing dependence on synthetic organic chemicals as insecticides and herbicides in agriculture and an increasing tendency to replace natural materials with chemically manufactured synthetic materials represented a second branch of the hard path. In contrast, the soft path would rely on energy conservation through increasing efficiency of end-use, solar, and other renewable energy sources, decentralization of energy production and consumption to reduce demand further, reduced use of synthetic materials, and increased use of biological controls and "integrated pest management" in agriculture.

A major component of the controversy over the relative merits of "the paths" has been the conflicting claims of the proponents of each about the public health impacts of the other. On the one hand, soft path advocates emphasize the potential path for catastrophe and for a slow poisoning of the populace by high-tech nuclear and chemical technology. They warn ominously of a future humanity sickened by toxic chemicals and afflicted with widespread cancer and genetic mutations. Soft path detractors counter that high technology has brought a high standard of living, an improved quality of life, and increased longevity. They warn equally ominously that the soft path leads, not to a utopian idyll, but to the Hobbesian nightmare of a life "poor, nasty, brutish, and short."

The large problem thus facing the United States today is how to evaluate and compare the varying risks—to the public and to the environment—posed by either existing or proposed technologies, or combinations of technologies.

The Attractions of Hard and Soft Paths: The Roles of Values, Special Interests, and Social Agendas

It is inevitable that a controversy as basic and far-reaching as the hard path–soft path debates would reflect many of the fundamental underlying conflicts—of assumptions, of values, of interests, and of agendas—present in our society. It is perhaps equally certain that these conflicts would more often be reflected implicitly than explicitly during much of the debate. The discourse often appears to hinge upon differing views of the *facts*—of what the health and environmental consequences of a given technology "actually" are, or will be—when the primary differences between the parties relate to values, special interests, and social agendas. A number of authors have addressed this issue more or less directly, so it will not be discussed in great detail here (e.g., Fischhoff, Lichtenstein, Slovik, Derby, & Keeney, 1981; Humphrey & Buttel, 1982; Lowrance, 1976; Mazur, 1981).

It is noteworthy that Lovins himself made the social agenda and value premises of his soft path advocacy quite explicit in his works (Lovins, 1975, 1976, 1977, 1978; Lovins & Price, 1975). He argues that the soft path is conducive to democratic institutions, a more equitable distribution of both wealth and power, full employment, increased local control over both working conditions and the quality of life, and a variety of other societal changes he would favor (see also Humphrey & Buttel, 1982, pp. 187–193). I am not suggesting here that questions of value or the societal implications of technologies do not belong in the debate—on the contrary, I would argue, with these authors, that such questions should be addressed *explicitly* in the debate over technological safety, rather than be relegated to second-class status. Societal decisions regarding the regulation of potentially hazardous technologies can literally mean the difference between billions of dollars of profit and equally huge losses. It would be naive to imagine that groups and organizations with an economic interest in such decisions approach their own analysis in a totally dispassionate manner; yet, the dialogue on technological risk assessment and evaluation most often lacks any explicit recognition of this fundamental reality.

Unseen Pitfalls on the Paths: Normal Accidents

Part of the argument against hard path technologies has been not merely that they are unsafe now but that they cannot be made safe. This claim especially has been vehemently denied by hard path advocates, even those willing to admit that these technologies are not presently safe enough. A great deal of the dialogue concerning the hard path technologies has in fact assumed that they can be made safe, or at least "safe enough." In mid-1984 Charles Perrow added a new analysis to the discourse; his conclusion was that indeed some technological systems, by their very nature, cannot feasibly be made accident-free. Perrow went on to argue that if the "normal accidents" to which such systems are prone have significant catastrophic potential for communities or society as a whole, the systems may be unacceptable. Because I believe that Perrow may have identified a crucial factor in the debate over the safety of technologies, I will outline at some length his line of argument. I am aware that the brief description I can present here cannot do justice to the wealth of detail in Perrow's book, *Normal Accidents*, and I urge the interested and/ or unconvinced reader to go to the original source.

Complex Interactions

Perrow begins by identifying the major generic components essential to the operation of a technical system: Design, equipment, procedures, operators, supplies and equipment, and the environment (DEPOSE, as a mnemonic). He then differentiates the types of interactions among these components into "linear" and "complex" interactions. Linear interactions occur between one component of the DEPOSE system and "one or more components that precede or follow it immediately in the sequence of production." Complex interactions, in contrast, "are those in which one component can interact with one or more other components outside of the normal production sequence, either by design or not by design" (Perrow, 1984, p. 77). He goes on to suggest that linear interactions tend to occur in normal sequence and to be visible and understandable even when unintended, whereas complex interactions tend to be found in "unfamiliar sequences, or unplanned and unexpected sequences, and either not visible or not immediately comprehensible" (Perrow, 1984, p. 78). *Complex systems*, then, in Perrow's words, are characterized by:

- Proximity of parts or units that are not in production sequence;
- Many common mode connections between components (parts, units, or subsystems) not in a production sequence;
- Unfamiliar or unintended feedback loops;
- Many control parameters with potential interactions;
- Indirect or inferential information sources; and
- Limited understanding of some processes. (Perrow, 1984, p. 85)

Tight Coupling

The second factor crucial to system accidents, in Perrow's view, is "tight coupling," characterized by the absence of "slack" in a system, the presence of time-dependent processes, invariant sequences, and generally limited flexibility in the system's operations. Because of their limited flexibility, the design of tightly coupled systems must include buffers and redundant subsystems to assure that component failures will not necessitate system shutdown or catastrophic failure.

System Accidents

The essence of Perrow's argument is that a system will be prone to accidents if it is both very complex interactively and very tightly coupled. He supports this claim by both the analysis of system characteristics in the abstract and the analysis of a wide variety of real-world technological systems and their accident records. His abstract analysis points out that highly complex systems contain numerous subsystems and components, each one designed, built, operated, maintained and repaired by fallible human beings operating within imperfect organizational structures. Given this basic fact, he predicts that in complex systems there will inevitably be component and subsystem malfunctions that can interact, *often in unforeseen ways*, with other components and subsystems, due to the common-mode connections, interconnections, and close proximity characteristic of such systems. When these systems are also characterized by tight coupling, Perrow notes, the lack of slack in the system is likely to allow unforeseen subsystem interactions to propagate or "feed back" through the system rapidly enough and with sufficient effect to result in a major accident.

In Perrow's view, such an event will often be attributed to component failure, or even more often to "human error," but the true culprit is the combination of the system's complexity and tight coupling. In fact, he points out that the human operators of tightly coupled systems are often acting on the basis of rigidly prescribed operating instructions, which never foresaw the unique accident sequence unfolding. In this case, the centralized control and invariant sequences of tightly coupled systems serve to block the independent and creative action by on-scene operators to halt an unexpected and unwanted series of interactions within the system. Further, he points out that designed-in buffers and safety systems cannot in themselves *guarantee* against a system accident, simply because the designers cannot realistically be expected to have designed against absolutely every possible interaction of subsystem component failures and malfunctions. In fact, he points out numerous instances in which safety subsystems have themselves contributed to system accidents.

If Perrow's analysis is correct, then technological systems that are designed for both great complexity and tight coupling can be *expected* to suffer system accidents—in his words, "normal accidents"—with some regularity. Perhaps in a more perfect world, with better design and higher levels of quality control, such accidents could be minimized; but Perrow, as an organizational researcher, makes this observation after his study of a wide variety of existing technological organizations:

> Time and again warnings are ignored, unnecessary risks taken, sloppy work done, deception and outright lying practiced. As an organizational theorist, I am reasonably unshaken by this; it occurs in all organizations, and it is a part of the human condition. But when it comes to systems with radioactive, toxic, or explosive materials, or those operating in an unforgiving, hostile environment in the air, at sea, or under the ground, these routine sins of organizations have very nonroutine consequences. Our ability to organize does not match the inherent hazards of some of our organized activities. (Perrow, 1984, p. 10)

This quote brings us to the final concern presented by Perrow: the hazard potential of the technological system under consideration.

Catastrophic Potential

Even if two technological systems have the same capacity for a "normal accident," they may differ greatly in their capacities to produce health, social, and economic damage as a result of these accidents. As Perrow suggests, some technological systems have a high potential to produce catastrophic accidents with dire and lasting consequences. Perrow classifies the victims of a technological accident as "first-party victims," for example, operators or workers in a plant; "second-party victims," passengers or others who have no direct influence over the operation of the system, but who have voluntarily associated themselves with the system; "third-party victims," so-called innocent bystanders who are injured by an accident due to location or chance; and "fourth-party victims," fetuses and members of future generations who would suffcr from the long-lasting effects of chemical or radiological accidents. In considering the catastrophic potential of a system, Perrow ignores first-party victims altogether, emphasizing the potential threat to "passengers" or users of a technological system or to bystanders or future generations who might be harmed by an accident. He then attempts to rank technologies on their catastrophic potential, based on past performance and inherent potential for catastrophic accident.

High-Risk Systems

The result of this analysis is Perrow's ranking of technological systems by their complexity and close coupling—hence, their system accident potential—and by their catastrophic potential. Technological systems that are high on both dimensions include nuclear power, recombinant DNA technology ("genetic engineering"), nuclear weapons systems, and to a somewhat lesser degree (in Perrow's view) chemical plants. (It should perhaps be noted that a major source of Perrow's concern with DNA has to do less with the inherent danger it presents than with a recent effort, in the face of competitive economic and academic pressures, to relax the regulatory safeguards established after the historic Asilomar Conference in 1975.) On the basis of his analysis, Perrow states that "the case for abandoning nuclear power strikes me as very strong" (Perrow, 1984, p. 348), in the absence of a reactor design less prone to system accidents. He recognizes the economic and generating-capacity implications of such a move, however, and he seems resigned to the continued operation of the present generation of nuclear power reactors. However, he points out that the public's concern over economic and power grid disruption could pale before the results of a nuclear power catastrophe, and he leaves us with a dire prophecy:

> I would expect a worse accident than TMI in ten years—one that will kill and contaminate. . . . There will be more system accidents; according to my analysis, there have to be. One or more will include a release of radioactive substances to the environment in quantities sufficient to kill many people, irradiate others, and poison some acres of land. There is no organizational structure that we would or should tolerate that could prevent it. None of our existing reactors has a design capable of preventing system accidents. (Perrow, 1984, p. 348)

Perrow is less harsh in his conclusions regarding chemical technology, but he might have been more concerned if he had included a "cradle-to-grave" analysis of both the chemicals being manufactured and used and their hazardous waste byproducts. Certainly our recent history is rife with examples of chemicals and their toxic wastes being mishandled and carelessly discarded in ways that threatened public health and the environment (see Chapter 6). Perhaps these examples seem less catastrophic because their effects are often delayed and initially invisible. Certainly the ultimate public health impacts remain to be weighed.

However we evaluate the impacts of chronic chemical exposure, the disastrous release of methyl isocyanate from a chemical facility in Bhopal, India, on December 3, 1984, has unequivocally shown the catastrophic potential of chemical accidents. Bhopal, now being called "the Three Mile Island for chemicals," caused over 2,500 deaths and serious respiratory and eye injuries to literally tens of thousands of other third-party victims. The harm to fourth-party victims is so far unclear, though news accounts mention numerous stillbirths in the weeks following the tragedy. This may not have been a "system accident," in Perrow's terms, but if we view the chemical plant "system" in broad terms, it may yet prove to have been such an accident. In any case, a close reading of a series of *New York Times* summary articles (January 28, 30, 31, and February 3—the most complete account and analysis of the case I have seen as of early 1985) suggests that a multitude of design, operational, training, and safety system decisions left almost no hope of averting the release of the chemical. The fact that each of three backup safety systems was disabled at the time of the release made some exposure of the public inevitable. The apparent lack of effective emergency planning or prior efforts to educate the residents of the surrounding (densely populated) area to the hazard posed by potential chemical releases, and the ultimate failure to alert and evacuate the populace in the face of the release of tons of lethal gas seem to have combined to turn a serious accident into a historic calamity.

Perrow's Challenge

Having raised this example, I will move on from the discussion of Perrow's thesis, but not before I state that I believe it poses the greatest challenge to the hard path advocates yet offered in the name of public health and safety and environmental protection. His analysis leads to the conclusion that there can be no "technological fix" that will assure safety for systems that are both highly complex and tightly coupled. The only "fix" available would be to reduce interactive complexity or to eliminate the tight coupling, or both. Because the hard path technologies tend to fall in this category, and because they also tend to pose the risk of catastrophic damage, it remains to refute Perrow's arguments or to consider whether hard path technologies could be altered to make them less complex and/or less coupled. One recent proposition seemingly aimed at this goal is the suggestion that a gas-cooled nuclear reactor design be adopted in place of current water-cooled designs, on the basis that the new system is inherently more stable and has a much lower catastrophic potential. In any case, the challenge awaits.

Evaluating Risk: The Crucial Role of Uncertainty

In answer to growing public and governmental concern over the increasing hazard potential of complex technologies a new field of research has appeared—risk assessment. The assessment of risk assessment itself has been mixed, however. Perrow puts it this way: "the new risks have produced a new breed of shamans, called risk assessors. As with the shamans and the physicians of old, it might be more dangerous to go to them for advice than to suffer unattended (Perrow, 1984, p. 12).

Although this statement may seem overly harsh to some, there are few who would deny that the practice of risk assessment for complex technological systems is not long out of infancy. Consequently, there are many sources of concern over the growing power of risk assessors in the technology policy arena. However, my focus at the moment is the very *fact* of present uncertainty regarding many technological risks and the implications of various kinds of uncertainties for the endeavor of assessing and managing technological risks. In introducing these issues here, I draw on a wide variety of sources without attempting either to be exhaustive or to resolve the considerable conflicts contained within these sources (Douglas & Wildavsky, 1982a, 1982b; Fischhoff *et al.*, 1981; Kates, 1978; Rowe, 1977; Royal Society Study Group, 1983; Schneiderman, 1980; Sorenson, 1984; Veseley & Rasmuson, 1984; Wynne, 1980). I will merely introduce some of these major areas of uncertainty here without discussing them in great detail:

- *Uncertainties in problem definition.* Precisely *what* hazards must be accounted for; what is the *scope* of the analysis in terms of "system boundaries" and consequences considered; what alternatives are considered; and how is the analysis "operationalized"?
- *Uncertainties about facts.* Crucial research data and parameters may be missing or ambiguous; probabilities of system or component failure may have to be estimated; causal factors may not be well understood and theoretical "models" of crucial processes may be unverified; and the full health or environmental consequences of an effect may not be clear.
- *Uncertainties about values.* The *evaluation* of the policy or management implications once an objective level of risk has been established can be difficult because values can be unclear or conflicting or can be manipulated; because of problems inferring or eliciting values; and because societal values are continually evolving.
- *Uncertainties due to human fallibility.* Both "average citizens" and "experts" are prone to errors in risk perception and estimation and tend to be overly confident of the accuracy of their assessments.
- *Uncertainties about decision quality.* In risk assessment for complex and hazardous technology the "track record" of assessment approaches is often unclear or even untestable (with outcomes revealed only by sudden catastrophic or belated revelation of delayed damage); sensitivity analyses are often inadequate; the impacts of errors in assessment or the meaning of "unusual" events may be misjudged; and the threat of "groupthink" (in which experts take false comfort from the "convergent validation" derived from only *superficially* different approaches) is ever present.

PUBLIC HEALTH THREATS FROM HARD PATH AND SOFT PATH TECHNOLOGIES

Rhetoric and self-interest aside, there are some very real public health and environmental threats present in many of the hard path technologies. What has not always been acknowledged, and what many hard path advocates have been at pains to emphasize over the past 10 years, is that the soft path technologies themselves have a dark side in public health and environmental terms.

Some Hard Path Threats: Nuclear and Fusion Power and Chemicals

The concern for the safety of hard path technologies is far from universal. It is often argued that opposition to these technologies is based primarily on ignorance, misinformation, and essentially superstitious fears. Although it is certain that some of the opposition to these technologies rests on this base, I am equally sure that a sizable portion of the popular support for these same technologies has an equally shaky basis. In fact, I suspect that some of the residual support and quite visceral opposition enjoyed by the hard path is due to the fact that these technologies were "oversold" in an earlier era.

In the 1950s the public was told that nuclear power would soon make electricity "too cheap to meter." The reality has proved to be "rate-shockingly" the opposite. Similarly, the public was being told only recently that "Without chemicals, life would be impossible." In the late 1970s the public was awakened suddenly to the reality of literally thousands of hazardous waste sites spread all over the nation. Fusion power is still being touted by many as the option that will *really* be both environmentally safe and "too cheap to meter" at last, the technological panacea. The following discussion of these technologies makes no attempt to paint them as irredeemably hazardous. It merely seeks to establish that there is considerable *uncertainty* about the overall safety of each technology as it now exists or is envisioned (in the case of fusion power).

Nuclear Power

A great deal has been written on the subject of nuclear power and its safety, in addition to the Lovins work already cited. An entire literature has grown up assessing, attacking, and defending the economics and general safety of nuclear power (e.g., Bupp, 1979; Glasstone & Jordan, 1980; Hileman, 1982; Kaku & Trainer, 1982; Komanoff & Van Loon, 1982; Marshall, 1982; Pasqualetti & Pijawka, 1982). Still another library has emerged to analyze the environmental, economic, sociopolitical, health, and many other consequences and implications of the Three Mile Island (TMI) accident (e.g., Ford, 1981; Moss & Sills, 1981; Sills, Wolf, & Shelanski, 1982; Union of Concerned Scientists, 1979). The economic, political, environmental, and human health concerns associated with the long-term storage of nuclear wastes, once shrugged off by the nuclear industry as a minor technical problem, are now being recognized as significant (Murdock, Leistritz, & Hamm, 1983). Finally, the erosion of previously unquestioned public support for nuclear power has led to studies of the sources of both societal support and opposition to "nukes" (e.g., Freudenberg & Rosa, 1984).

Economics and politics aside, the literature on nuclear power reveals a substantial number of still-unanswered safety questions. These include the radiation-induced "embrittlement" of the steel reactor vessel and the consequent threat of failure due to the "thermal shock" of cold emergency core coolant water on hot reactor vessel walls (Hileman, 1982; Marshall, 1982). Another concern is the degradation of steam generator integrity through "stress-corrosion cracking," "wastage," "flow-induced vibration cracking," "erosion-cavitation," and "denting," all leading to leaking of radioactive primary-loop water into the secondary loop, increasing both the likelihood of contamination of workers and the levels of radiation chronically released into the surrounding environment (Hileman, 1982, p. 376A). Still another hazard was highly radioactive spent fuel that has been "doubled up" in the storage racks of cooling water pools, reducing the safety factor of their original design (Hileman, 1982). There are many, many more examples of unanswered technical concerns.

Perhaps the most telling critique of both the safety of nuclear power and the adequacy of its assessments to date was that the TMI accident resulted from a sequence that had not been considered by its designers, its operators, or the authors of the so-called Rasmussen Report (U.S. Nuclear Regulatory Commission, 1975). Furthermore, as Glasstone and Jordan note, the *Reactor Safety Study* estimated the probability of a core meltdown as less than 1 in 10,000 "reactor-years" of operation. In contrast, the *partial melting* of radioactive fuel rods now known to have occurred in the core of TMI reactor on March 28, 1979, took place after less than 800 reactor years of operation (Glasstone & Jordan, 1980, p. 107.)

It is a measure of the state of the nuclear debate that no few defenders of nuclear power were reported to see the TMI accident as *support* for the ultimate safety of nuclear power, on the grounds that no one was harmed by the accident. It seemed initially that we might fall into the trap that so damaged the Rasmussen Report's credibility if we assumed that TMI had shown us the worst accident that could befall a nuclear power plant.

Subsequently the April 1986 nuclear power disaster at Chernobyl, in the Soviet Union, with hundreds hospitalized and dozens dying from immediate radiation effects and millions of Europeans exposed to increased risks from radiation exposure, dwarfed all previous mishaps involving nuclear power. Chernobyl was clearly a watershed event, in a real sense a "loss of innocence" for nuclear power. This was the first nuclear power accident to have significant health, economic, and political impacts far from the accident site itself, the first to have international effects.

The long-term implications that will be drawn from the Chernobyl disaster are clouded by both technological and societal differences between the Soviet and various Western nuclear power systems. Certainly the advocates of nuclear power in the West wasted no time in emphasizing—sometimes incorrectly—those differences. Although no U.S. commercial reactors use the graphite-moderated reactor design that contributed so much to the severity of the Chernobyl accident, a large number of U.S. reactors do employ pressure-suppression systems similar to those which failed to prevent containment failure at Chernobyl. (On the other hand, and perhaps most important, the widespread criticism in the West of the delay in evacuating affected area residents and the eventual need to evacuate more than 100,000 people from the region can be expected to spur already existing efforts to require more realistic and effective evacuation plans for U.S. nuclear plants.)

Perhaps the greatest irony of the Chernobyl tragedy has been the resulting demand for greater international openness and accountability for the safety of nuclear power systems. This emphasis is now primarily aimed at the Soviet Union because of Chernobyl's dramatic example of the potential for a hard path disaster to have impacts far beyond national borders. It remains to be seen whether these concerns, and the calls for more openness and accountability, will be applied as well to the nuclear industries of the United States and other Western nations.

In summary, I believe that a fair reading of the literature on the present state of nuclear power reveals a number of areas of uncertainty about the safety of nuclear power. The reactor core and spent fuel rods contain enormous loads of highly radioactive and long-lived radionuclides, with a real but indefinite probability of release to the environment, with effects that could range from serious to devastating. Add to this the uncertainties about the health and environmental effects of "routine" releases of radioactivity from daily operation and the long-term consequences of decommissioning highly radioactive reactors and disposing of spent fuel, and the burden of uncertainty borne by nuclear power is considerable.

This discussion intentionally ignores perhaps the most inherently dangerous fission reactor technology yet considered, the "fast breeder" reactor. In its most common design, this reactor employs extremely hazardous liquid sodium to cool the radioactive core and "breeds" weapons-grade plutonium to be used (and transported) as fuel for future reactors. At present, the breeder reactor's primary *raison d'être*, the need for more fuel to supply a rapidly increasing number of nuclear power plants, has disappeared as projections of nuclear power plant numbers have dwindled all around the globe. Present sources of uranium promise to be ample to supply all planned reactors into the next century.

The Chemical Industry

We have certainly come a long way in the United States since the era when the benefits of new chemical products were casually assumed to outweigh their possible risks—when risks were considered at all. That era saw the widespread adoption of pesticides, from DDT through aldrin and dieldrin to a host of other, more sophisticated but often still very hazardous compounds. It also saw the substitution of relatively cheap synthetics for natural materials in a wide variety of products, with fabrics being perhaps the most ubiquitous example. And, of course, it saw the introduction of a fantastic variety of inexpensive new products that either could not or probably would not have been fashioned from natural materials. Perhaps some readers would not equate these developments with the "hard path"—in fact, they appeared to be a deceptively *easy* path to travel. I would argue, however, that the heavy reliance on the synthetic chemical industry has been an important aspect of the hard path, due to its heavy reliance on high-quality energy sources, its profligate use of hydrocarbon energy resources, and its widespread negative effects on natural systems—particularly so in the case of pesticides. And, of course, the incident in Bhopal has clearly demonstrated the catastrophic potential of chemical industry as such.

Without making any systematic effort here to cite the voluminous literature on the health and environmental effects of chemicals, health and environmental risk analysis is now routinely being performed in regard to the production and use of chemicals (e.g., Conway, 1982), the disposal of hazardous chemicals (e.g., Hileman, 1984a; Long & Schweitzer, 1982), and the threat of groundwater contamination by toxic chemicals (e.g., Hileman, 1984b; U.S. Office of Technology Assessment, 1984).

Human exposure to toxic chemicals in food has occurred accidentally, as in the tragic PBB (polybrominated biphenyl) poisoning of Michigan residents in the mid-1970s (Chen, 1979; Egginton, 1980) or the contamination of a large proportion of the dairy products in Hawaii by the pesticide heptachlor, lasting for about a year in 1981 and 1982.

More often, the adulteration of food by chemicals is intentional, as in the past use of ethylene dibromide to protect citrus fruit and grain from pests (Sun, 1984) or the decaffeination of coffee by a process which leaves minute amounts of a solvent, methylene chloride, in the coffee (see also Weir & Schapiro, 1981). The health implications of each of these cases remain uncertain, but the proliferation of such uncertainties is a cause for concern.

The use of synthesized chemicals in manufactured goods and industrial processes leads to both occupational and consumption-mediated exposures to chemicals with effects that may not be known for decades, if ever. Recently, health effects studies have begun on some of the plasticizers widely used in consumer products. Such studies inevitably take years, and a chemical is nearly always held to "innocent until proven guilty," sometimes guilty by a number of such studies. PCBs (polychlorinated biphenyls) are another example of a widely used industrial material whose use has been sharply curtailed because of concerns about health effects (Haley, 1984). It is notable that some researchers have asserted that the health effects attributed to PCBs are in fact due to the low levels of the (*much* more toxic) dioxins and dibenzofurans with which commercial quantities of PCBs were universally contaminated (Miller, 1983). Even if true, this point would seem to have little, if any, policy relevance to the question of the acceptability of human exposure to "real world" PCBs.

Besides the health impacts of chemical exposures from foods and products, we are faced with occupational exposures suffered in chemical plants and the exposures of off-site populations due to "routine" or accidental releases. Probably the three most prominent workplace substances to be banned as proven human carcinogens are vinyl chloride, benzene, and asbestos. In each case, industry groups lobbied, argued, and litigated for years before succumbing to regulation (Environmental Defense Fund & Boyle, 1979; Epstein, 1979). Concern for the possible health effects off-site of air and water releases of toxic and hazardous chemicals is a relatively recent phenomenon. In the wake of the Bhopal accident, for example, it was noted that a health study had recently begun in the West Virginia valley that held the parent company's "twin" MIC (methyl isocyanate) plant. Apparently, patterns of disease in the area had been sufficiently disturbing to warrant a large-scale study effort.

The "final" chapter in the story of the threat posed by chemical technology is that of hazardous waste disposal. Decades of inattention to this issue have resulted in a truly staggering burden of unwanted toxic chemicals, stored in leaking or soon-to-be-leaking landfills, industrial holding ponds and lagoons, euphemistically named "recycling centers" that are actually dump sites, and the widely scattered results of "midnight dumping." In this area, two principal "schools" of literature seem to complement each other. The first, which might be thought of as the "cautionary tale" school, uses a more or less reportorial style to convey the human and policy consequences of hazardous waste disposal problems and disasters to the lay reader (e.g., Brown, 1979; Environmental Defense Fund & Boyle, 1979; Epstein, 1979). The purpose of these works is both to inform and to arouse citizens, with the goal of changing policy, and they may be a necessary precursor to create the societal support and the policy context within which the second "school" can thrive.

This second approach, focusing more narrowly on technical analysis and using established research techniques, can nevertheless produce very disturbing results in this area (e.g., Hileman, 1984a, 1984b; Levine, 1982; U.S. Office of Technology Assessment, 1984). As an example, this second type of literature has identified major problems with the present system of permitted secure landfills for hazardous disposal, as well as a serious threat of groundwater contamination by toxic substances in many areas of the country (Hileman, 1984a, 1984b; U.S. Office of Technology Assessment, 1984). Based on the track record of hazardous chemical waste production, storage, and disposal so far, it is not surprising that the "not in my backyard" (NIMBY) syndrome has typified the response of communities to proposed hazardous waste disposal facilities. Works about siting such facilities rightly emphasize the role of uncertain health effects (e.g., Elliott, 1984a, 1984b; Hirschhorn, 1984; Paigen, 1984; Willard & Swenson, 1984).

All this acknowledged uncertainty about the potential effects of any given chemical exposure gains its emotional and policy impact from the fact that we know quite a bit about what chemicals *can* do. In fact, we have demonstrated, or discovered by tragic experience, that chemicals can be both acutely and chronically toxic, that they can have neurological or behavioral effects, can be teratogenic, mutagenic, or carcinogenic, and (more recently) that they can have subtle—or disastrous—immunological consequences. The fact that many of these effects can be delayed by years or even generations can make them even more dreaded.

Fusion Power

After such a recitation, fusion power, with its shining reputation as a potentially inexhaustible, cheap, environmentally benign source of power, might scarcely seem to be in the "hard tech" league. Indeed, assuming that fusion technology proves feasible, it seems probable that it *will* be "cleaner" and safer than either present fission reactors or proposed breeder technologies. However, at least two major sources of concern have been identified regarding the magnetic containment approach to fusion reactors. First, in these systems the steel "first wall" that maintains the necessary vacuum will be exposed to intense neutron bombardment during reactor operation. Research shows that the steel will suffer internal structural damage and become brittle as a result. Because intense magnetic fields are necessary to confine the plasma "fuel" within the first wall, the weakening of the wall's material over time would eventually necessitate completely removing and replacing the wall, perhaps every ten years. Unfortunately, the same neutron bombardment that would cause this problem would also induce intense radioactivity in the steel, making the process of removal extremely costly, difficult, and hazardous. The "first wall" materials would then have to be disposed of as highly radioactive wastes (Kenward, 1976, pp. 122–127; Priest, 1979, p. 334f).

A second and potentially even more serious problem with fusion is its reliance, at least in the designs now contemplated, on tritium for fuel. Tritium is a highly radioactive isotope of hydrogen and like hydrogen is extremely hard to confine. There would inevitably be routine releases of tritium from a fusion reactor, and the inventory of tritium in the reactor would be sufficient (perhaps 10 kilograms) to qualify its release in an accident as a catastrophe. Any releases of tritium would be made more serious by the fact that its chemical behavior is just like that of hydrogen. Thus, it would take the place of hydrogen atoms in water, biochemical processes, and elsewhere and would pose a potential threat to ecosystems and the human food chain.

Thus, while fusion energy may yet prove feasible, it may not be either as inexpensive or as benign in health and environmental terms as its supporters would wish it to be. It would seem to belong in the "hard path" category.

Some Soft Path Threats: Energy Conservation, Biofuels, Solar Photovoltaics

The "paths" debate can be disconcerting and frustrating because it is so often couched in the most absolute terms. On the one hand, the advocates of the soft path approach often appear to believe that there are no health and environmental problems associated with "soft" technologies. In contrast, to hear such hard path advocates as Herman Kahn and Julian Simon tell it, the greatest environmental and public health threat posed by a total commitment to the soft path would be the resulting widespread poverty, pestilence, and starvation. Leaving the broader social welfare consequence of soft path approaches for others to contest (and they will certainly continue to do so), I will focus on a few examples of very real threats from "soft" technologies that have already been identified. If this discussion includes less detail than in the hard path case, at least part of the reason is that many of these techniques, while not new, have only recently been placed under close scrutiny and research attention.

Energy Conservation

One of the most basic elements of the soft energy path approach has been the more efficient use of energy in buildings, industry, and power generation, to reduce energy demand. One aspect of this approach involves "tightening up" the building envelope, so that less heat is lost (Black, Stern, & Elworth, 1985; Stern, Black & Elworth, 1981, 1983). One potential health threat posed by the "tightening" of housing units was the potential for increasing indoor air pollution by trapping inside the structure increased amounts of a number of pollutants (Hurwitz, 1983; Kirsch, 1983; Spengler & Sexton, 1983; see also Chapter 5, this volume, for a discussion of indoor air pollution). These health threats include radon and its decay products from structural stone, soil, or water supplies. Combustion products such as carbon monoxide, nitrogen oxides and particulates, from gas stoves, kerosene heaters, wood stoves, fireplaces, and other sources are also a greater problem in well-insulated structures. Formaldehyde builds up, especially in homes containing large amounts of particle board, fiberboard, or plywood. However, there are numerous other products commonly found in homes and offices that emit formaldehyde—carpets and carpet pads, a wide variety of textiles, paper products—the list goes on. Household chemicals are a further source of indoor air pollution, with aerosol sprays contributing both their active ingredients and their propellant to the mix. Cleaning products, deodorizers, plastics, and a variety of other products are also sources.

It can be argued—persuasively, I think—that most of the indoor air pollutants in this list are more representative of the hard path than the soft path. One can thus view their presence as a result of *inadequate* adherence to the soft path. In addition, research has shown that, without sacrificing efficiency, tightly weatherized structures can be brought back to normal levels of indoor air quality or better by bringing in fresh outside air and exhausting stale indoor air through an inexpensive air-to-air heat exchanger. However, the essential point still stands: that much about the effects of even the most apparently innocuous soft path technologies is unknown. The uncertainties may not be insurmountable, but they are present.

Biofuels

The substitution of fuels derived from "recent" biological activity (recent compared with the activity that produced coal, oil, and natural gas, that is) is another centerpiece of soft path technology. Recently, however, considerable attention has been drawn to the contribution of wood-burning stoves to both indoor and outdoor air pollution. Some valley communities are even beginning to develop regulations on wood burning, which in some cases may require the use of small electrostatic precipitators to remove particulate matter from the chimney smoke. There has also been a suggestion that widespread use of relatively volatile methanol ("wood alcohol") fuels could contribute to some air pollution mechanisms. Again, even age-old "technologies" can present hazards that are not clearly understood (Rom & Lee, 1983).

Solar Photovoltaics

Yet another central aspect of the soft path is the use of solar energy technologies. While "passive solar" approaches are generally viewed most favorably for applications requiring "low-quality" heat sources, the generation of electricity directly from sunlight, via photovoltaics, is an important component of the soft path society. Until recently, most analysts would probably have agreed that the principal health threat from photovoltaics would come from falls from ladders while installing them on roofs. In the early 1980s, however Silicon Valley, California, the home of the solid state technology upon which photovoltaics are based, was shocked by the revelation of numerous leaks of toxic solvents from tanks at many semiconductor firms in the area, some of which had already polluted drinking water sources. In fact semiconductor technology is highly chemical-intensive, and its workers are now exposed to solvents and toxic gases such as arsine and phosphine, and etching acids. The levels of exposure and the health consequences for workers have only recently begun to be explored (Sanger, 1984). And of course, the solvents and acids must be disposed of as hazardous waste (see also Rom & Lee, 1983).

Having noted all of the above regarding both hard and soft path technologies, Perrow's earlier argument remains, and it can hardly be argued that *any* of the soft path technologies suffers from the same interactive complexity and close coupling that is characteristic of the centralized nuclear power plant. Moreover, part of the difficulty with the "paths" debate is the frequent feeling that not all of the participants are "playing fair" with the data. One notable example is the heated controversy that surrounded the publication in 1979 in the highly respected journal, *Science*, of an article by Herbert Inhaber, assessing the relative risks of coal, nuclear, and renewable energy resources. Several months later a letter to the editor from three researchers charged, "Inhaber's report is a morass of mistakes, including double counting, highly selective use (and misuse) of data, untenable assumptions, inconsistencies in the treatment of different technologies, and conceptual confusions" (Holdren, Smith, & Morris, 1979, p. 564). The letter went on to rebut Inhaber's work at length and in great detail.

THE NEED TO TRANSCEND LABELS TO ASSURE PUBLIC HEALTH PROTECTION

The common elements in all these cases have been the lack of relevant information regarding the risks of technologies and the resultant uncertainty. I have long felt that the policy debate has been better served when it has transcended the labels and looked more carefully at the details of the technologies in question.

An example from Perrow's analysis is particularly enlightening in this regard: Recombinant DNA, or "genetic engineering." Which "path" is this technology traveling? On the one hand, it can be carried out by relatively small-scale laboratories with modest resources of funds and equipment. It also involves living organisms, so shouldn't it be classified as soft path? On the other hand, some analysts fear that biotechnology carries the potential of enormous public health hazards and environmental disruption (e.g., Alexander, 1985; McGarity, 1985; Rifkin, 1984), because of the possibility of unseen, unexpected, and uncontrollable consequences. In this, it would seem to have much in common with some of the hard path technologies.

Perrow emphasizes that his knowledge is insufficient to judge whether or not recombinant DNA technology represents a serious threat, but he worries that this is a wholly new area of human endeavor, with all too much room for surprises of all sorts. Most important is that while it may be difficult to categorize biotechnology by "path," such labeling is also irrelevant to making useful policy decisions. What *is* relevant, as Perrow suggests (1984, pp. 293–303 and 348–350), is that we have inadequate experience with this technology to judge its risks fully while the economic and academic pressures for its increased application are enormous. What, then, must we do to overcome the uncertainties and make more reliable judgments about technological risks and their control?

The Crucial Role of Information

It seems absurdly obvious to state that the solution to the uncertainties regarding technological risk is to obtain more information. However, there are often serious obstacles in the way of discovering and disseminating the relevant information regarding competing technological alternatives. In addition to institutional and political obstacles, Slovic and his colleagues have identified psychological barriers, which were discussed briefly earlier in this chapter: Values affect "facts," and perceived "facts" influence values. And even "experts" in risk assessment are subject to some extremely tenacious fallacies and perceptual biases, compounded by overconfidence in their judgments (Fischhoff *et al.*, 1981).

The Role of Research and the Source of Research Funding

Without high-quality research into the environmental and public health consequences of the technological options facing our society, it will be impossible to reduce the uncertainties in our assessments of risk, much less come to a consensus decision regarding the acceptability of such risks. Yet the proportion of our nation's resources allotted to research into the *consequences* of technology is minuscule, compared with the proportion committed to the development, implementation, and expansion of new and established technologies. In addition, the research resources are for the most part heavily overbalanced on the side of established economic and political interests. In our free society, the powerful interest groups may not actively *suppress* information, but they are often in a position either to withhold support for research that might damage their interests, or to provide support to researchers who will attempt to refute their critics. This situation leads to two corollary conditions.

"Regulatory Lag": Outspent and Outclassed

The term "regulatory lag" commonly refers to the reputed lack of responsiveness of regulatory agencies, presumably due to bureaucratic inefficiency. I am here referring to a quite different sort of lag, the seemingly inevitable lag between the time a new technology, such as a new chemical, is developed and introduced and the time academic researchers and regulatory agencies are able to determine what, if any, unintended negative consequences are associated with it. I say "seemingly inevitable" because at least a part of this lag would exist even in the "best of all possible" regulatory worlds simply because no one could devise and perform enough tests in advance of its implementation to be sure of predicting all possible consequences in the real world.

However, given that initial handicap, academic and regulatory bodies in every part of the world also operate at an extreme disadvantage in terms of resources, relative to those who wield and profit by the technologies. For example, salaries for academic and regulatory agency researchers are typically much lower than for their industry counterparts, and "defections" of technically trained members are common. Academic and regulatory researchers also tend to get by with less adequate, often older and less sophisticated, equipment than their industry counterparts. It seems that these facts are consistent with a strain of American pragmatism, a respect for the "do-er" and an underlying disdain for the "know-er." This disdain for "knowing" may serve our society ill in the area of technological risk evaluation, if these priorities remain.

Depending on Industry for Data: Faking It

One consequence of the unequal matchup between regulators and industry is regulators' dependence for data and analyses on the very industries they regulate. One recent example of the potentially disastrous consequences of this situation is the case of Industrial Bio-Test Laboratories (IBT) (Schneider, 1983a, 1983b). In the 1970s IBT was a thriving contract lab firm based in Illinois. In fact, it was getting so many contracts from industry to test chemicals for health and environmental effects that it expanded its activities far beyond its capacity to perform valid research. Industries hired IBT to test over 200 agricultural chemicals and drugs over the years, and the firm submitted more than 2,000 reports to federal agencies on these products, many of which were approved for market on the basis of these reports.

In the wake of a scandal, the U.S. Environmental Protection Agency (EPA) spent 7 years auditing the firm's records and interviewing IBT personnel, finally concluding that less than 10% of the reported results were valid (Schneider, 1983a). In many cases, data were blatantly fabricated. For years, these data were taken as "facts" by industry, regulators, and consumers alike. Only recently one of the herbicides "tested" by IBT and approved for market was found to be a probable carcinogen upon retesting, 7 years later, after having become the nation's number one selling herbicide. The fact that three former IBT executives were convicted of fraud in the case late in 1983 should not allay the concern this case has aroused. What the IBT case has shown is that industry was unable or unwilling to assure the quality of the studies it was paying for, even though retrospective reports suggest that many of the problems should have been evident. The case has also shown the regulatory body—EPA in this case—to have been at the mercy of the industries it is attempting to regulate and of the laboratories they hire to perform studies of the products they are eager to market.

Constraints on Information—Proprietary Data

In the name of preserving the secrecy of proprietary information to avoid giving away a competitive edge to a rival firm, industries often resist providing information or plant access to regulatory bodies. This same reasoning was applied in resisting worker right-to-know legislation, requiring that employees be informed of the characteristics and hazards of chemicals to which they were exposed. The same argument is now being applied to counter growing demands for community right-to-know legislation along the same lines.

There may indeed be some validity to the industry claims for a possible loss of a competitive margin through information exchange. However, this issue surely demands the sort of balancing of the costs and benefits of which industry is so fond. Certainly in some cases the evident benefits of shared knowledge far outweigh the hypothetical costs; indeed in some cases, industry may benefit by gaining credibility with the public.

The Need for Research and Regulatory Institutions

Market forces are not enough to guarantee public health and environmental protection in the face of technological uncertainties. While the discipline of the marketplace serves a vital function in our society in many areas, in the area of collective goods, it does not operate so well. (A common, collective, or public good is defined as a good that is available for *all* members of a group to use and enjoy or is available to none.) Mancur Olson's *Logic of Collective Action* demonstrated that where collective goods are concerned, some external or collective norm or coercive force may be necessary to assure that the good is provided (Olson, 1968). National defense, for example, has long been recognized as such a collective good.

The protection of public health and the preservation of the quality of the natural resources and ecosystem that support society are the most fundamental and necessary collective goods for any society. Research institutions thus serve a vital purpose when they independently seek to discover the unintended effects of technologies. At the same time, regulatory institutions are essential in attempting to define and enforce normative standards of "good behavior" needed to assure that the society as a whole can enjoy the collective goods of public health and environmental quality. Our society and its people are not well served by any deregulation that sacrifices these two essential elements.

The Role of Norms

As long as crimes against public health and the environment, such as the fabrication of experimental results for chemicals, willful or negligent dumping of hazardous wastes, or intentional exposure of workers or consumers to hazardous chemicals, are treated by the public and by the legal system as minor infractions, we will be far from technological safety. A feeling of individual and corporate responsibility for the consequences of our technological actions seems to be essential.

A societal norm for technological safety would involve a shared feeling, backed up by legal and social sanctions, of the obligation of individuals and corporate entities to consider public health and environmental quality consequences, along with more narrowly defined self-interest, in making technological decisions. Those who followed this normative standard would be admired and respected, even treated as heroes if they did so at great personal cost or risk. Those who acted counter to this norm would be criticized or—in extreme cases—treated as criminals. No such norm is generally present in our society, though there are many *individuals* who follow it, rigorously.

The Role of Whistle-Blowers

In a society filled with complex and potentially hazardous technology, those who act to reveal a technological hazard before it harms public health or the environment are truly heroes. In our society, these "whistle blowers" are more often treated as scapegoats or traitors. In that social context, how many technological hazards go unreported that would otherwise be corrected? This issue was virtually ignored in the literature until recent times (Nader, Petkas, & Blackwell, 1972; Westin, 1981), and much remains to be discovered about the social and psychological conditions which would be conducive to whistle blowing. A society that fosters such conditions would be a safer, healthier society.

POINTS TO REMEMBER

1. The debate about the relative merits of the hard and soft path technologies often has more to do with differences in the *values* served by the two approaches than with the *facts* regarding their relative safety.

2. There may be no "technological fix" to provide adequate safety for some technologies, many of which are in the hard path category. Perrow has argued persuasively that technologies that are both interactively complex and tightly coupled are subject to "normal accidents." When the results of such accidents are also potentially catastrophic, as with many hard path technologies, society may need to re-evaluate the acceptability of such technologies or at least take steps to put the population "out of harm's way."

3. Public concerns about the safety of a technology are often characterized as "irrational," especially by proponents of the technology in question. In fact, uncertainties in the actual levels of risk and/or differences in values often make public concern both rational and valid. Especially for relatively new technologies, the actual level of risk may be quite uncertain; and even when there is agreement on the *level* of risk involved, there will often be disagreement over the *acceptability* of this risk, based on conflicting values. Acceptability of risks is inherently a value question, belonging to the sphere of public policy and politics, rather than to science and technology.

4. The reduction of uncertainty regarding a technology, whether it represents the hard or soft path, is a key factor in reducing technological threats to public health and the environment. We need strong and independent research institutions, in order to obtain better and more timely information on the unintended consequences of technologies. We need strong regulatory institutions to make decisions on new and existing technologies with less uncertainty and delay. Finally, we need strong *norms* in society in support of actions which reveal existing or threatened technological hazards and against actions which tend to conceal them.

References

Alexander, M. (1985). Ecological consequences: Reducing the uncertainties. *Issues in Science and Technology, 1*(3), 57–68.

Black, J. S., Stern, P. C., & Elworth, J. T. (1985). Personal and contextual influences on household energy adaptations. *Journal of Applied Psychology, 70*(1), 3–21.

Brown, M. H. (1980). *Laying waste: The poisoning of America by toxic chemicals.* New York: Pantheon Books.

Bupp, I. C. (1979). The nuclear stalemate. In R. Stobaugh & D. Yergin (Eds.), *Energy future.* New York: Random House.

Chen, E. (1979). *PBB: An American tragedy.* Englewood Cliffs, NJ: Prentice-Hall.

Conway, R. A. (Ed.) (1982). *Environmental risk analysis for chemicals.* New York: Van Nostrand Reinhold.

Douglas, M., & Wildavsky, A. (1982a). How can we know the risks we face? Why risk selection is a social process. *Risk Analysis, 2*(2), 49–51.

Douglas, M., & Wildavsky, A. (1982b). *Risk and culture.* Berkeley: University of California Press.

Egginton, J. (1980). *The poisoning of Michigan.* New York: Norton.

Elliott, M. L. P. (1984a). *Coping with conflicting perceptions of risk in hazardous waste facility siting disputes.* Unpublished doctoral dissertation, Massachusetts Institute of Technology.

Elliott, M. L. P. (1984b). Improving community acceptance of hazardous waste facilities through alternative systems for mitigating and managing risk. *Hazardous Waste, 1*(3), 397–410.

Environmental Defense Fund & Boyle, R. H. (1979). *Malignant neglect.* New York: Knopf.

Epstein, S. S. (1979). *The politics of cancer.* Garden City, NY: Anchor Books.

Fischhoff, B., Lichtenstein, S., Slovic, P., Derby, S. L., & Keeney, R. L. (1981). *Acceptable risk.* New York: Cambridge University Press.

Ford, D. F. (1982). *Three Mile Island: Thirty minutes to meltdown.* New York: Penguin Books.

Freudenburg, W. R., & Rosa, E. A. (Eds.). (1984). *Public reaction to nuclear power: Are there critical masses?* Boulder, CO: Westview Press.

Glasstone, S., & Jordan, W. H. (1980). *Nuclear power and its environmental effects.* LaGrange Park, IL: American Nuclear Society.

Haley, T. J. (1984, Nov./ Dec.). Pentachlorobiphenyls. *Dangerous Properties of Industrial Materials Report, 2*–17.

Hileman, B. (1982). Trends in nuclear power. *Environmental Science and Technology, 16*(7), 373A–378A.

Hileman, B. (1984a). RCRA groundwater protection standards. *Environmental Science & Technology, 18*(9), 282A–284A.

Hileman, B. (1984b). Water quality uncertainties. *Environmental Science and Technology, 18*(4), 124A–126A.

Hirschhorn, J. S. (1984). Siting hazardous waste facilities. *Hazardous Waste, 1*(1), 423–429.

Holdren, J. P., Smith, K. R., & Morris, G. (1979). Energy: Calculating the risks (II). *Science, 204,* 564–567.

Humphrey, C. R., & Buttel, F. R. (1982). *Environment, energy, and society.* Belmont, CA: Wadsworth.

Hurwitz, H., Jr. (1983). The indoor radiological problem in perspective. *Risk Analysis, 3*(1), 63–77.

Inhaber, H. (1979). Risk with energy from conventional and non-conventional sources. *Science, 203,* 718–723.

Kaku, M., & Trainer, J. (Eds.). (1982). *Nuclear power: Both sides.* New York: Norton.

Kates, R. W. (1978). *Risk assessment of environmental hazard.* New York: Wiley.

Kenward, M. (1976). *Potential energy: An analysis of world energy technology.* New York: Cambridge University Press.

Kirsh, L. S. (1983). Behind closed doors: The problem of indoor pollutants. *Environment, 25*(2), 16–20, 37–42.

Komanoff, C., & Van Loon, E. (1982). "Too cheap to meter" or "too costly to build"? *Nucleus, 4*(1), 3–7.

Levine, A. G. (1982). *Love Canal: Science, politics, and people.* Lexington, MA: Lexington Books.

Long, F. A., & Schweitzer, G. E. (Eds.). (1982). *Risk assessment at hazardous waste sites.* Washington, DC: American Chemical Society.

Lovins, A. B. (1975). *World energy strategies: Facts, issues and options.* New York: Harper & Row.

Lovins, A. B. (1976). Energy strategy: The road not taken? *Foreign Affairs, 55*(1), 65–96.

Lovins, A. B. (1977). *Soft energy paths: Toward a durable peace.* New York: Harper & Row.

Lovins, A. B. (1978). Soft energy technologies. *Annual Review of Energy, 3,* 477–517.

Lovins, A. B., & Price, J. H. (1975). *Non-nuclear futures: The case for an ethical energy strategy.* New York: Harper & Row.

Lowrance, W. W. (1976). *Of acceptable risk.* Los Altos, CA: William Kaufmann.

Marshall, E. (1982). NRC reviews brittle reactor hazard. *Science, 215,* 1596–1597.

Mazur, A. (1981). *The dynamics of technical controversy.* Washington, DC: Communications Press.

McGarity, T. O. (1985). Regulating biotechnology. *Issues in Science and Technology, 1*(3), 40–56.

Miller, S. (1983). The PCB imbroglio. *Environmental Science and Technology, 17*(1), 11A–14A.

Moss, T. H., & Sills, D. L. (Eds.). (1981). *The Three Mile Island nuclear accident: Lessons and implications.* New York: The New York Academy of Sciences.

Murdock, S. H., Leistritz, F. L., & Hamm, R. R. (Eds.). (1983). *Nuclear waste: Socioeconomic dimensions of long-term storage.* Boulder, CO: Westview Press.

Nader, R., Petkas, P. J., & Blackwell, K. (Eds.). (1972). *Whistle blowing: The report of the Conference on Professional Responsibility.* New York: Grossman.

Olson, M. (1968). *The logic of collective action.* New York: Schocken Books.

Paigen, B. J. (1984). Methods for assessing health. In M. Harthill (Ed.), *Hazardous waste management*. Boulder, CO: Westview Press.

Pasqualetti, M. J., & Pijawka, K. D. (Eds.). (1984). *Nuclear power: Assessing and managing hazardous technology*. Boulder, CO: Westview Press.

Perrow, C. (1984). *Normal accidents: Living with high-risk technologies*. New York: Basic Books.

Priest, J. (1979). *Energy for a technological society: Principles, problems, alternatives*. Reading, MA: Addison-Wesley.

Rifkin, J. (1984). *Algeny: A new word—A new world*. New York: Penguin.

Rom, W. N., & Lee, J. (1983). Energy alternatives: What are their possible health effects? *Environmental Science and Technology, 17*(3), 132A–144A.

Rowe, W. D. (1977). *An anatomy of risk*. New York: Wiley.

Royal Society Study Group. (1983). *Risk assessment*. London: The Royal Society.

Sanger, D. E. (1984). Worries over toxins grow in Silicon Valley. *New York Times*, November 10.

Schneider, K. (1983a). Faking it: The case against Industrial Bio-Test Laboratories. *The Amicus Journal, 4*(4), 14–26.

Schneider, K. (1983b). IBT—Guilty: How many studies are no good? *The Amicus Journal, 5*(2), 4–7.

Schneiderman, M. A. (1980). The uncertain risks we run: Hazardous materials. In R. C. Schwing & W. A. Albers, Jr. (Eds.), *Societal risk assessment: How safe is safe enough?* New York: Plenum Press.

Sills, D. L., Wolf, C. R., & Shelanski, V. B. (Eds.). (1982). *Accident at Three Mile Island: The human dimensions*. Boulder, CO: Westview Press.

Sorenson, J. B. (1984). The assurance of reasonable toxic risk? The problem: Inadequate methods to assure reasonable risk. *Natural Resources Journal, 24*, 549–569.

Spengler, J. D., & Sexton, K. (1983). Indoor air pollution: A public health perspective. *Science, 221*(4605), 9–17.

Stern, P. C., Black, J. S., & Elworth, J. T. (1981). *Home energy conservation: Programs and strategies for the 1980's*. Mount Vernon, NY: Consumers Union Foundation.

Stern, P. C., Black, J. S., & Elworth, J. T. (1983). Responses to changing energy conditions among Massachusetts households. *Energy, 8*(7), 515–523.

Sun, M. (1984). EDB contamination kindles federal action. *Science, 223*, 464–466.

Union of Concerned Scientists. (1979). To the brink of the abyss: The first hours of Three Mile Island. *Nucleus, 1*(4), 1–10.

U.S. Nuclear Regulatory Commission. (1975). *Reactor safety study: An assessment of accident risks in U.S. commercial nuclear power plants*. Washington, DC: U.S. Nuclear Regulatory Commission.

U.S. Office of Technology Assessment. (1984). *Protecting the nation's groundwater from contamination*. Washington, DC: U.S. Office of Technology Assessment.

Vesely, W. E., & Rasmuson, D. M. (1984). Uncertainties in nuclear probabilistic risk analyses. *Risk Analysis, 4*(4), 313–322.

Weir, D., & Schapiro, M. (1981). *Circle of poison: Pesticides and people in a hungry world*. San Francisco: Institute for Food and Development Policy.

Westin, A. F. (Ed.). (1981). *Whistle blowing: Loyalty and dissent in the corporation*. New York: McGraw Hill.

Willard, D. E., & Swenson, M. M. (1984). Why not in your backyard? Scientific data and nonrational decisions about risk. *Environmental Management, 8*(2), 93–99.

Wynne, B. (1980). Technology, risk and participation: On the social treatment of uncertainty. In J. Conrad (Ed.), *Society, technology and risk assessment*. New York: Academic Press.

C H A P T E R   8

POLICY, LEGAL, AND ADMINISTRATIVE CONSIDERATIONS FOR THE CONTROL OF THE OUTDOOR ENVIRONMENT

Rae Zimmerman
New York University

Public and private institutions are responsible for the trade-offs society makes between personal lifestyle decisions and the maintenance of environmental quality and human health. These institutions consist of legal, administrative, and political systems that develop and implement environmental policy. This chapter examines the role of governmental institutions in the historical context of the environmental movement. It emphasizes the form in which institutional strategies and programs have emerged in response to changing societal goals and technology, and finally takes a brief look at the performance of these institutions in terms of their objectives.

This chapter focuses on the outdoor environment as distinct from personal (Chapter 2) and occupational environments (Chapter 3). It does not attempt to provide complete coverage of the dozens of laws and agencies that regulate the outdoor environment. Instead, it focuses on how numerous laws and programs have been administered by a complex bureaucracy. It provides a framework for understanding the tools used by government as it undertakes its responsibilities and the means of measuring the success of these efforts.

Trends in environmental quality, which are a major indicator of the performance of environmental programs, are first reviewed over the past decade or so. One finds that no matter how environmental quality is measured—by means of physical, chemical or biological parameters, or by public perceptions of quality—the trend is mixed. This is shown to be associated with changes in two factors—societal goals for environmental quality and the technology for implementing programs— during the period that environmental programs have been operating. It is also shown that changes in the design and performance of environmental institutions have accompanied changes in goals and technology. This institutional response is cast in terms of developments in laws, administrative organization, and the role of the public. These institutions have employed various technical strategies and implementation programs to carry out their responsibilities. Finally, the overall performance of these institutions is evaluated, in terms of measures of institutional process. The objective of the performance evaluation is to see whether they have kept pace with changing goals and technology or if technology and goals have had any effect at all on performance.

MIXED REVIEWS OF PROGRESS

The bottom line in evaluating the performance of governmental institutions that manage the quality of health and the environment is whether environmental quality has improved in response to a century of public and private intervention. Chapters 4 through 6 described the condition of the outdoor environment in considerable depth. While the precision and design of indicators of environmental quality are not perfect, certain general conclusions have been drawn from the trends by the Council on Environmental Quality ([CEQ], 12th Ann. Report–1981, 14th Ann. Report–1984).

On the one hand, some improvements have been made in reducing contaminant inputs into the environment. This is reflected in some modest improvements in the quality of the environment in certain geographic areas and for certain kinds of contaminants. On the other hand, there are still areas that are not in compliance with outdoor environmental standards. In addition, residues of complex organic chemicals and heavy metals are being detected in certain species of lower organisms and in human tissue, and levels of carbon dioxide (which can affect global temperatures) continue to rise in the atmosphere. Reports issued by the U.S. General Accounting Office (GAO) in the early 1980s also highlighted the mixed trends in environmental quality. They note the improvements in air quality, drinking water, and wastewater treatment, but point to solid waste disposal, groundwater contamination, pesticide contamination, radiation releases, and acid rain as areas of growing concern (U.S. General Accounting Office, 1982a, 1982b).

Public perceptions and attitudes of the quality of the environment also reflect this mixed pattern: public opinion polls show that in recent years the quality of the ambient environment has generally been perceived as improving, though concerns are escalating in the area of health risks from toxic and hazardous substances (Marsh & McLennan Co., 1980). A recent Harris survey shows the heightened concern over hazardous wastes between 1981 and 1985: the proportion of its survey sample that regarded the disposal of hazardous wastes as "very serious" rose from 60% to 74% over the 4-year period (Harris, 1985).

One explanation for the ambiguities in environmental trends is that the elements of progress may have been overshadowed by (1) changing societal values with regard to the quality of the environment, and (2) technological advances in detecting environmental contaminants and their health effects. Changing societal values are reflected in the increasing stringency of standards for environmental quality and environmental health: the number of regulated pollutants has increased and the acceptable concentrations to which they are controlled have been lowered. Technological advances (as defined in this chapter) are multidimensional. They pertain to the increase in the number and type of sources of contaminants that can be detected, the introduction of new information about the environmental pathways and fate of contaminants, and improvements in medical techniques for evaluating the effect of environmental contaminants on human health. The institutions that manage the environment have continually had to adapt over time to these changing values, attitudes, and goals toward the risks and costs posed by environmental contaminants and to the technologies that shape the boundaries of knowledge about the quantities and effects of these contaminants.

SHAPING POLICIES TOWARD ENVIRONMENTAL PROTECTION AND HEALTH

Changes in societal goals and technology shape institutional design and performance. Before exploring the operation and performance of governmental institutions, it is important to see how goals and technology have actually changed.

Changes in Environmental Goals

Since societal goals provide a framework for the functions of government institutions, such goals are important end points against which to evaluate the design and performance of these institutions.

The goals of environmental policy have substantially shifted over the course of the last century. These changes have influenced how environmental quality is measured and the kinds of controls that are considered acceptable. The changes have in part been driven by popular movements that have focused on environmental issues. The emergence of these movements has been characterized as cyclical (Downs, 1972). Pepper (1984) identified four periods with strong environmental movements, the 1890s, the 1920s, the 1950s, and the early 1970s, and links them to periods of economic prosperity and disillusionment with materialism. What is particularly striking about the early environmental movement is its heterogeneity, with interests ranging from wildlife and resource protection to human survival (Cotgrove & Duff, 1980; O'Riordan & Turner, 1983).

In the first half of the century, resource conservation was the major objective of environmental laws. The environmental problem that was being addressed was the expansive growth and associated resource exploitation characteristic of the utilitarian thinking of the late nineteenth century and the depletion of plant and animal species, water, and mineral resources that resulted. As Kenneth Boulding so aptly put it, there was a gradual shift from the "cowboy" economy of expansionism of the late nineteenth century to the "spaceship" economy of conservation (Boulding, 1971). A common approach to the resolution of the conflicts among various ways of using resources was to redistribute the benefits of resource use more broadly among both users and nonusers or to distribute the adverse impacts brought about by their exploitation among the beneficiaries.

A distinction has often been made between the conservation movement of the early twentieth century and a second movement occuring about the same time. The conservationists were oriented toward the use of resources for economic development goals. A second group, the preservationists or transcendentalists, identified with such people as John Muir, was oriented toward the aesthetic and health aspects of natural resources (CEQ, 12th Ann. Report–1981; O'Riordan & Turner, 1983). Environmental laws reflected the differences in these two ideologies. For example, early water resource laws were conservation oriented: they emphasized the use of water for navigation and the sufficiency of water supplies for economic activities. Laws and court cases dealing with forest management and wilderness preservation were examples of the aesthetic orientation.

The growing public health concerns of the early part of this century were also a major objective of environmental policy. An important example was the regulation of contaminants in water and air, which were seen as agents of human disease or as public nuisances. Later, health and environmental concerns separated for more than a half a century, to recombine in the mid-1970s in a different form. In the 1970s, the emphasis was on exposure to chemical toxicity over long periods of time rather than on biological vectors or the immediate effects of poisons, whose impacts showed up after a short exposure period. A new set of pathologies, often taking many years to appear, was associated with these chemical toxins: carcinogenesis, teratogenesis, and mutagenesis. The concerns over and, consequently, the measures of environmental contamination focused on toxicity. The agents and indicators of disease shifted from the biological to the chemical arena.

Environmental policies shifted toward a stronger policy of protectionism in the late 1960s and 1970s. While some policy analysts have emphasized the integrating effect of ecology on environmental policy at this point (Vig & Kraft, 1984), the problem identified for environmental policy actually first appeared in a variety of forms. First, was the old issue of resource scarcity. Others saw the environmental problem as a function of population growth alone (Ehrlich, 1970) or combined with the resource scarcity issue (Cole, Freeman, Jahoda, & Pavitt, 1973). Still others saw it in terms of the conflict between environmental values and the goals of new technological innovations for the production of goods and services for society and technologies specifically designed to improve the quality of life, such as waste disposal and treatment systems (Commoner, 1971; Pepper, 1984, p. 20). The environmental goals and the strategies advanced to meet these goals depended on the way problems were perceived. The legislation of the 1970s reflects a mix of philosophies and strategies, since the nature of the problem was conceived of so differently by different groups.

When the environmental problem was viewed in terms of population growth and resource scarcity, strategies appeared in the form of growth control. A number of laws required that human activity should not promote excessive growth or population concentration. Another strategy for the population question was the complete reversal in societal behavior, such as a reduction in the scale of human activity (Schumacher, 1973). Where the environmental problem was conceived in terms of technology, the strategies put forth were mixed. The technological fix (through pollution control) was still seen as a way of expanding limited resources. In contrast, technological innovations (in the form of industrial activity) were seen as the source of the strain on those resources and had to be controlled.

The environmental movement has largely continued through the 1980s because of the relaxation in certain environmental standards, nuclear crises such as Three Mile Island (Pepper, 1984, p. 19) and Chernobyl, the abandonment of certain standards because of the energy crisis, chemical emergencies such as Bhopal, and the public attention drawn to Anne Gorsuch's controversial leadership of the U.S. Environmental Protection Agency (EPA) and James Watt's leadership of the U.S. Department of the Interior in the early 1980s.

As pointed out earlier, an important difference between the goals and orientation of the environmental movement of the 1960s through the 1980s and earlier movements prior to the 1960s was the later movement's recognition that environmental problems (and their underpinnings in terms of population growth and resource use) were composed of interrelated phenomena. These processes were understood to a greater extent by the 1970s, because of scientific advances in environmental science (Caldwell, 1982). Pollution problems and strategies for their resolution were put in that context. By contrast, at the turn of the century, pollution problems were considered as isolated events, that is, as nuisances or isolated health incidents, unrelated to the larger context of urban crowding and poor living conditions (Melosi, 1980, p. 21).

The recognition of interrelationships among biological, chemical, and geological processes and human activity in recent times grew out of principles of ecology and geophysics, many of which had appeared in the scientific literature much earlier. In ecology, principles emphasizing the limits of the natural environment to absorb change, such as "carrying capacity," were put forth. While the first references to this concept have been traced back to the eighteenth century with mathematical formulations following in the 1920s (Bishop, Fullerton, Crawford, Chambers, & McKee, 1974, p. 14–15), not until the late 1960s and early 1970s did the concept come to be systematically applied to the relationship between human populations and environmental resources. In recent times, the carrying capacity concept was applied to the assessment of the environmental impact of human activity and the calculation of thresholds of activity that the environment could withstand (Baldwin, 1985). In the area of geophysics, a considerable amount of work was done on the cycling of individual elements through the air, water, and land environments. In the 1960s, human origins of each element were introduced into the formulation of such biogeochemical cycles, and the models were used to compute the relative burden that man-made sources were contributing to the natural occurrence of each element. Thus, it is this understanding of process and the interrelationships among natural and human phenomena that distinguishes recent environmental goals from earlier ones, and influences the strategies that are pursued.

Changes in Technology

Technology has influenced environmental management in a number of different and even opposite ways. First, changes in scientific and industrial engineering technology have enabled society to introduce substances into common use in unprecedented proportions. Second, changes in instrumentation and pollution control technology strongly influenced (and in turn, were influenced by) the direction of environmental management by increasing the level of detection of substances in the environment and the ability to track and control their movement in the environment. To a large extent advances in instrumentation were market induced, that is, initiated partly by the need to resolve uncertainties in the environmental arena that were becoming the focal point of extreme controversy. This second area of technological change is discussed below.

In the middle part of the century, the technology for measuring contaminants and the understanding of the medical basis for diseases whose onset from the time of infection had a long duration were still relatively primitive. The parameters chosen to measure the environment and the numerical limits assigned to such parameters reflected this level of knowledge. In air quality, for example, particulates were an initial indicator of quality. The Ringlemann chart, which measured smoke-shade very qualitatively against a series of shadings, was one of the first devices for measuring the degree of particulate concentration. Similarly, in the area of water quality, such gross measures as total solids, floating or suspended solids, or total organic carbon were the initial measures of quality rather than specific chemical compounds. While many of these earlier measures have been superseded by more refined measures, they are still valuable as initial screening procedures that direct and prioritize more detailed study.

The gradual refinement in instrumentation technology (see, for instance, Lisk, 1974) was accompanied by several dramatic shifts in environmental policy. First, there was an increase in the number of parameters regulated. Second, limits on each parameter were made more stringent, and these limits were often set at the limits of detectability. Third, compliance procedures or methods to establish proof of meeting prescribed limits became more complex. Fourth, because of the large number of parameters involved in characterizing the environment, indexes were designed to combine parameters, and models were developed to simulate cause and effect relationships.

Technological advances allowed environmental analysts to pursue stringent goals such as ''zero discharge'' of pollutants into navigable waterways in the Clean Water Act (CWA) and ''zero tolerance'' for any food contaminants in the Delaney clause of the Food and Drug Act.

Thus, the combination of changes in both environmental goals and technological innovation produced a number of shifts in environmental policy and law, whose ramifications are discussed in more detail below. First, an emphasis upon the most visible, nuisance-causing pollutants and water- and airborne contaminants that were vectors of disease of local importance shifted to the more persistant and toxic contaminants whose effects were of regional, national, and even global significance. Second, the emphasis upon resource conservation shifted to an emphasis upon the use of technology either to expand resource capacity (within the limits of environmental carrying capacity) or to constrain human activity to fall within resource constraints.

INSTITUTIONAL PATTERNS AND RESPONSES

Institutional responses to changes in environmental goals and technology have occurred along a number of dimensions: law, administration, and the role of the public as a major force in shaping governmental policy and procedures.

Legislative Change

In the 1970s there was a relatively large increase in the number of laws and programs for environmental protection and environmental health. Between 1970 and 1983 alone, over three dozen major environmental (non-energy-related) laws appeared, compared with only a dozen or so in the first two thirds of the century. If one considers modifications to existing laws rather than the emergence of new ones, the difference between the decade of the 1970s and the first half of the century is even more striking.

In reviewing environmental laws in historical perspective, it should be kept in mind that the passage of a number of them were responses to catastrophes or crises. Some examples of this are (1) the Santa Barbara oil spill that coincided with the passage of the National Environmental Policy Act (NEPA), though the actual act had been debated in Congress as early as 1959 (Andrews, 1976, p. 7), (2) Love Canal and the passage of the Comprehensive Environmental Response Compensation and Liability Act (or Superfund), (3) various air pollution episodes and the Clean Air Act (CAA) Amendments, and (4) polychlorinated biphenyls (PCB) contamination problems and the Toxic Substances Control Act (TSCA). Other environmental programs appeared in the form of gradual, episodic program modifications. The Clean Water Act (CWA), amended at least seven times since 1948, is an example of legislation that changed more incrementally.

Table 8-1 summarizes the changes in federal environmental legislation over time. Regardless of the area of emphasis (water, air, solid waste), legislative developments show that over time the number and complexity of standards increased, the kinds of proof required to demonstrate compliance with standards and the requirements for obtaining federal money increased in number and complexity, and

Table 8-1. Summary of Federal Legislative Histories

Air Quality[a]	
1955	Federal role emphasizes research and data collection and technical assistance to states.
1963	Grants awarded to states for air quality programs; Federal-state conferences used for enforcement.
1965	Emission standards for new motor vehicles introduced.
1967	Mandates federal air quality criteria, and provisions for the states to set ambient air quality standards; designation of air quality control regions for planning purposes.
1970:CAA	National Ambient Air Quality Standards (NAAQS); emission standards for new motor vehicles and facilities; emission standards for new sources (NSPS) and for hazardous substances (NESHAPs) for existing facilities; provisions for the development of state implementation plans (SIPs).
1977:CAA Amendments	More stringent controls on air quality degradation: prevention of significant deterioration provision added, construction of new sources contingent on state approved air quality plan.
1978	Lead added as a national ambient air quality standard.
1980s	Health effects studies developed for noncriteria air pollutants under NESHAPs; extensive delegation of permit programs for new sources of air pollution and the development of hazardous air pollution standards to state agencies with continued federal oversight responsibilities; development of regulations for an emissions trading policy; increased stringency of standards for lead content of gasoline.

Water Quality[b]	
Late 1800s–early 1900s	1899 Rivers and Harbors Act used for pollution control through the late 1960's; 1924 Oil Pollution Control Act used similarly; both Acts administered by the U.S. Army Corps of Engineers.
1948	Grants for state programs and facility plans; orientation of federal effort is toward interstate waterways.
1956	Authorized federal wastewater treatment facility construction grants (up to 30% of the costs) and grants for state programs; continuation of emphasis on data collection, research and technical assistance to states; enforcement procedures use a federal-state conference, and require that endangerment of health or welfare has occurred.
1961	Expansion of federal jurisdiction from interstate waters to coastal waters; incentives for interjurisdictional projects for wastewater treatment; increases in funding to most areas.
1965:WQA	State to set and enforce water quality standards for interstate, navigable waterways; enforcement plans developed, conformance of projects with local area plans encouraged.
1966	Increased authorizations for construction grants up to 50% of costs; formulas for increases based on federal-state shares and other incentives; allotment formula becomes more complex.
1970	State certification of compliance with water quality standards as a condition for issuing wastewater discharge permits; strengthening of marine vessel and oil pollution controls.

Table 8-1. *Continued*

1972:FWPCAA	Extensive controls for industrial, municipal and other sources of pollution; standards for ambient quality, effluent discharges; NPDES permit program for wastewater discharges; provision for areawide planning; coverage of grants for wastewater facility construction increased up to 75% of costs.
1972:CZMA	Planning for the development of coastal areas, incorporating environmental and economic criteria.
1972:MPRSA	Permits for ocean disposal of wastes; provisions for establishing criteria for the quality of material for disposal.
1974:SDWA	Standards for public water supply systems; designation of sole source drinking water aquifers; development of an underground injection control program.
1977:MPRSAA	Prohibition of ocean disposal of sewage sludge after 1981 (however, this provision was the subject of a number of court cases and subsequent revisions of the deadline); five classes of ocean disposal permits established.
1977:CWAA	Extensive delegation of programs to the States; extension of construction grant funding and applicability to operation and maintenance; provision for 85% federal share for innovative projects; delegation of Sec. 404 provisions for dredging and filling in wetlands assigned to the Corps of Engineers; expansion in the number of toxic substances covered under water quality standards and expansion in the use of pretreatment standards for wastes entering municipal wastewater treatment systems; compliance deadlines extended.
1981	Reduction in the applicability and scope of construction grant awards for wastewater treatment plants and reduction in the federal share of such grants to 55% after 1985; extensive delegation of programs to state agencies, including construction grants program, NPDES program, underground injection control program and coastal management programs; prohibitions on ocean disposal of hazardous waste.
1986:SDWAA	Standards-setting is considerably expanded: the number of standards to be set for drinking water supplies is increased to 83 chemicals over three years; a list of chemicals is to be developed from which chemicals are drawn for standards-setting. Monitoring and treatment requirements are expanded to meet the new standards. Filtration or equivalent treatment method is required for surface water supplies. Underground injection program requirements and ground water protection provisions have been added.

Pesticides[c]	
1910	General standards for insecticides and fungicides; specific standards for a couple of pesticides; basic purpose is protection from consumer fraud.
1938	Food, Drug and Cosmetic Act—certain sections regulate pesticide residues in food.
1947:FIFRA	Registration and labeling system established.
1964	Safety considerations included in registration process; explicit references to registration, cancellation/suspension.
1972:FEPCA	Regulation orientation supplants registration orientation of earlier statutes; cost-benefit analysis included.

Table 8-1. *Continued*

1975	Cost impacts of suspension and cancellation of registration required; formal RPAR process is adopted for premarket registration of pesticides; Science Advisory Panel created to review regulations and product bans; Amendments weaken overall cost/benefit analysis and strengthen agricultural interests—agricultural economic impact statements required.
1978:FPA	Development of generic standards based on active ingredients rather than on each individual pesticide preparation.
1980s	Streamlining of the registration process; review of existing pesticide process through registration standards program; expansion in the number of registration standards; expansion in the delegation of pesticide applicator and training programs to the states.

Manufacture of Toxic Substances and Hazardous Waste Disposal[d,e]

1976:TSCA	Registration system for toxic substances prior to manufacture (PMN system); ban on the manufacture of PCBs.
1976:RCRA	Permit program with a preventive orientation for hazardous waste generators, transporters, and treatment, storage, and disposal facilities under a "cradle to grave" manifest system; development of performance standards for these regulations; mandatory solid waste plan development by the states; grants and technical assistance to states; federal government authorized to perform emergency cleanup of sites by responsible parties.
1980	RCRA regulations provide criteria for the designation of hazardous wastes and delisting provisions; technical standards for incinerators and land disposal facilities adopted, such as percent removal efficiencies, liners for landfills, and groundwater monitoring.
1980:CERCLA	Mandatory cleanup of illegal hazardous waste disposal sites by private parties or the federal government (with reimbursement provisions by responsible parties); authorizes both emergency removal actions and more long-term removal actions; financing of federal cleanup activities by a chemical feedstock tax; National Contingency Plan describing criteria and methods of cleanup; National Priorities List for the prioritization of hazardous waste sites for cleanup; listing of hazardous wastes and reportable quantities above which cleanup is required.
1982:TSCAA	Expansion in the reporting requirements for chemicals; rule-making on asbestos in schools and for manufacturers and handlers.
1984:HSWA	More stringent requirements for land disposal facilities: double liners and leachate control systems for land disposal facilities, restrictions on the land disposal of solvents, underground storage tank restrictions; requirements for resource recovery facilities, such as dioxin emission limits; increase in the number of wastes regulated; improvements in the test procedures for hazardous wastes; lowering of the limit of applicability of the permit program to facilities generating 100 kg/mo. or more of hazardous wastes; restrictions on the burning of fuel containing hazardous wastes.
1986:SARA	$9 billion is authorized for hazardous waste site and underground storage tank cleanup. Schedules are required for cleanup of sites on the National Priorities List and for the preparation of cleanup plans. A cost-effectiveness test is required

Table 8-1. *Continued*

for evaluating cleanup options and rules are developed to evaluate cleanup levels. Health assessment studies are authorized for chemicals found at hazardous waste sites and at specific hazardous waste sites. Liability protection is provided for hazardous waste contractors. Emergency management through state emergency response commissions and emergency planning districts is provided. The provision of information by industry to communities (right-to-know provision) is required through inventory mechanisms for generators and treatment facilities. The method of providing funds under Superfund (the Hazardous Substances Superfund) is revised to include governmental appropriations as well as various taxes on industry. The chemical feedstock tax is supplemented by a corporate income tax. Limits are placed on the use of Superfund monies for damage claims. Authorizations are made from the fund for special cleanups. A connection is provided between regulation of chemicals under Superfund and under the Hazardous Materials Transportation Act. A special provision is made for radon gas research.

Note. Explanation of abbreviations: CAA, Clean Air Act; NAAQSS, National Ambient Air Quality Standards; NSPS, New Source Performance Standard; NESHAP, National Emission Standards for Hazardous Air Pollutants; SIP, State Implementation Plan; WQA, Water Quality Act; FWPCAA, Federal Water Pollution Control Act Amendments; NPDES, National Pollutant Discharge Elimination System; CZMA, Coastal Zone Management Act; MPRSA, Marine Protection, Research and Sanctuaries Act; SDWA, Safe Drinking Water Act; MPRSAA, Marine Protection, Research and Sanctuaries Act Amendments; CWAA, Clean Water Act Amendments; SDWAA, Safe Drinking Water Act Amendments; FIFRA, Federal Insecticide Rodenticide and Fungicide Act; FEPCA, Federal Pesticide Control Act; RPAR, Rebuttable Presumption Against Registration Program; FPA, Federal Pesticides Act; TSCA, Toxic Substances Control Act; PMN, Premanufacture Notice; RCRA, Resource Conservation and Recovery Act; CERCLA, Comprehensive Environmental Response Compensation and Liability Act; TSCAA, Toxic Substances Control Act Amendments; HSWA, Hazardous and Solid Waste Amendments; SARA, Superfund Amendments and Reauthorization Act.
[a]Adapted from Council on Environmental Quality (12th Ann. Report–1981, 13th Ann. Report—1982).
[b]Adapted from Council on Environmental Quality (12th Ann. Report–1981, 13th Ann. Report–1982) and Lamb (1980).
[c]Adapted from National Research Council (1980) and Council on Environmental Quality (13th Ann. Report–1982).
[d]Adapted from Council on Environmental Quality (13th Ann. Report–1982, 15th Ann. Report–1984).
[e]This section excludes the review of various statutes pertaining to hazardous substances that fall within the jurisdiction of the Food and Drug Administration, the Consumer Product Safety Commission, the Nuclear Regulatory Commission, and the Department of Transportation.

the opportunities for state government in planning and accepting the delegation of federal programs increased.

In addition, the amount of cross-referencing of technical requirements from one statute to another increased with each successive environmental law in the 1970s. For example, the requirements for environmental impact statements were originally incorporated under the National Environmental Policy Act and its regulations. Environmental legislation that followed NEPA in the 1970s, directly included special provisions for the conduct of environmental impact assessment to conform with NEPA. Other examples of cross-referencing are that grant awards for constructing wastewater treatment plants under the Clean Water Act are contingent on the elimination of air quality violations under the Clean Air Act, and solid waste facilities cannot be approved under the Resource Conservation and Recovery Act where they violate water quality standards. These cross-references were a way of dealing with the new goal of confronting ecological relationships and the complexities of unforeseen impacts of various activities across environmental mediums.

The direction of these changes partly reflects the emphasis upon the interrelationships between natural phenomena and human activity and the recognition that technology both solves environmental problems and has adverse environmental impacts if uncontrolled. The legislative pattern also reflects the changing nature of the regulatory reform movement and its impact on environmental legislation. Bardach and Kagan (1982) have pointed out that the regulatory reform movement had different meanings at different periods of time. In the 1960s and 1970s it meant developing more stringent environmental standards. In the areas shown in Table 8-1, the requirements for standards increased in stringency through the mid-1970s. By the late 1970s and early 1980s, it meant the opposite: reducing paperwork and the adverse economic impacts seen as resulting from the implementation of environmental laws. Programs in Table 8-1 show an emphasis upon consolidation and delegation of programs to state government in line with this policy of shrinkage.

To summarize, the legal framework for environmental policy appears to have shown considerable sensitivity to changes in technology and goals. Legal requirements for both environmental monitoring and source controls have reflected advances in technology. The stringency of requirements for environmental discharges, especially toward the late 1970s, reflected the shift of societal goals toward regulating more complex health risks.

Administrative Change

The organization of government to a large extent paralleled the changes in the environmental laws. From the early 1900s to the 1970s, one sees a gradual but only minimal attempts at integration and centralization of environmental management at the federal level relative to the need to coordinate and control the growing number of programs. A decentralization of programs to other federal agencies and state and local governments followed in the late 1970s and early 1980s as programs moved from a policy and technical development phase to implementation.

The Period of Centralization: The Federal Role

At the federal level, the Public Health Service administered some environmental programs at the turn of the century. Their work reflected the close alliance of health and environmental concerns. Other environmental programs were divided among agencies whose responsibilities were in the area of economic development. The evolution of water pollution control programs illustrates the direction of change in federal environmental administration. At one point water pollution control functions were transferred to the Department of Health, Education and Welfare (HEW). The relatively low priority of these functions was reflected in the fact that they were still administratively located several levels down from the top departmental official. In 1966 water-quality functions were transferred to the Department of Interior and given the status of an administration within the department. The new agency was called the Federal Water Pollution Control Administration. Some water-related functions in the areas of flood control and navigation were retained by the Corps of Engineers in the Department of the Army. In 1970 water pollution control functions merged with other environmental programs within the Environmental Protection Agency and were given a higher administrative status as an office. The formation of the EPA marked the first time that environmental functions were located within a cabinet-level agency. The centralization phenomenon is illustrated by the formation of EPA from 15 governmental units in the Departments of Agriculture, Health, Education and Welfare, and the Interior. Six thousand employees were transferred from these other agencies to EPA (Marcus, 1980, p. 275).

Some environmental functions, however, were still divided among other federal agencies. The Council on Environmental Quality, also established in 1970, was responsible for coordinating the environmental impact assessment process under the National Environmental Policy Act. The National Oceanic and Atmospheric Administration (NOAA) in the Department of Commerce was responsible for long-term marine and atmospheric research and the administration of the coastal zone management program. The Corps of Engineers retained its regulatory authority over flood control and navigable waters.

The Beginnings of Decentralization: The Role of Other Federal Agencies

During the 1970s, as toxic and hazardous substances began to emerge as a major environmental concern, the EPA still emerged as the dominant agency for regulating hazardous materials under nine major statutes covering air, water, pesticides, and solid and hazardous waste disposal, and the manufacture of toxic substances. But other agencies played major roles as well and have continued these roles through the 1980s. The relative importance of each of the agencies is illustrated by the size of budgets and personnel assigned to them for conducting environmental protection and health functions (see table following on page 243).

The formation of the EPA had been the answer to the consolidation of programs in the early 1960s, but it could not keep up with the rate at which programs were emerging. This was especially true in light of the severe budget cuts it experienced during the early 1980s. Between 1981 and 1983, EPA experienced a 22.6% cut in employment, the third largest percentage (excluding Superfund) of any federal agency (Conservation Foundation, 1982, p. 388). There are numerous examples of other agencies assuming environmental functions. For example, the U.S. Department of Agriculture continued to play a major role in decisions about pesticide use.

Agency	Employees[a] (1984)	Budgetary Appropriations[b] (in millions of 1984 dollars)
Environmental Protection Agency	12,650	$4,064
Food and Drug Administration	7,437	408
Nuclear Regulatory Commission	3,578	466
Occupational Safety and Health Administration	2,277	213
Consumer Product Safety Administration	567	69

[a]U.S. Senate Committee on Government Affairs. Personnel figures as of January 1, 1985.

[b]Executive Office of the President, Office of Management and Budget (1985, February). *Budget of the United States Government*. Fiscal Year 1986. Washington, DC: Office of Management and Budget.

The Food and Drug Administration regulated chemicals in products commercially available for human consumption. The Occupational Safety and Health Administration regulated chemicals in the workplace. The Department of Transportation exercised authority over the transport of over 2,000 hazardous materials under the Hazardous Materials Transportation Act. The Consumer Product Safety Commission developed standards as the basis for bans on certain chemical hazards associated with consumer products. Thus, in spite of the attempts in the early 1970s at administrative consolidation, growing environmental concerns emerging in the mid-1970s resulted in a continued division of authority among a number of different federal agencies by type of victim or circumstances of exposure.

Continued Decentralization: Delegation to State and Local Government

As major federal environmental laws were passed in the early 1970s, states began to gear up their programs to parallel federal requirements. This was partially made possible by provisions for federal assistance to state agencies for program development and planning. Cuts in the federal budget and employment in the late 1970s and early 1980s were accompanied by substantial delegation provisions to state and local governments. Some of the major programs that have been delegated include the construction grants program for sewage treatment plants and the permit program for wastewater discharges (National Pollutant Discharge Elimination System [NPDES]) under the Clean Water Act, the permitting of facility air emissions under the Clean Air Act, and the permitting of solid and hazardous waste treatment and disposal facilities under the Resource Conservation and Recovery Act. The extent of delegation of these programs across the country depends upon whether the states have met federal delegation requirements.

Trends in the organization of state government functions over the 1970s roughly paralleled federal trends. Environmental functions were initially divided among health departments, conservation departments, and economic development departments. Major consolidations occurred at the state level following the formation of the U.S. EPA in 1970. Unlike the EPA, state administration of environmental protection functions took two forms. States formed either line agencies[1] or full- or part-time commissions or boards to oversee pollution control. The commission and board form came under attack because interests or organizations being regulated were often represented on them. By the late 1970s state administration had shifted away from these boards and commissions to the line agency form. The shift to the agency form helped to integrate environmental functions by substituting many separate independent boards for departments responsible to a single administrator. Similarly, the "superagency" concept, which integrated environmental functions that had been scattered among many other agencies into one, also improved co-ordination. Nevertheless, a separation of authority often remained between health and environmental protection departments, especially in the area of water quality. Also, environmental functions were often divided between labor or commerce departments and environmental agencies. This became a particular problem for the administration of toxic and hazardous waste issues.

State government, in the area of environmental facility development, also resorted to a functional decentralization of its responsibilities to special agencies. By the 1970s, environmental control facilities became a popular strategy induced by many technological advances in pollution control technology. Management schemes for these environmental control facilities were accomplished by authorities or corporations set up under state legislation. These organizations performed a variety of functions including management, financing, construction, and operation of disposal and treatment facilities. Early examples included the Maryland Environmental Service and the New York State Environmental Facilities Corporation.

Local government responses to environmental management were similar to those of federal and state government as they received delegation of or assumed environmental functions. Environmental departments assumed environmental protection functions from health agencies or public works departments, where the size of the locality and magnitude of environmental concerns could support a new agency. One administrative development was unique to local government: the integration of land use and comprehensive planning with environmental control. This drew environmental programs to the local level that relied on land use controls for implementation. While some advocated that land use and environmental control should be integrated at the state level (Haskell & Price, 1973), it typically occurred at the local level. Local control over land use and zoning was the basis for local dominance.

The form that local administration of environmental programs assumed was primarily a function of the size of the locality and the importance assigned to environmental functions. A survey in the early 1970s (Carter, Frost, Rubin & Sumek, 1974) showed the following distribution of forms for the environmental function among cities and counties:

---

1. A line agency is directly responsible for an output or end product of an organization, whereas a staff agency is responsible for support services or for providing the means to produce the output.

Nature of the environmental function	Cities	Counties
Environmental department or agency	23%	55%
Staff committee	20	42
Individual staff member	40	48

In the 1980s, the environmental department or agency became more popular.

Emergence of Coordination Strategies

A number of management strategies for the coordination of federal and state environmental functions appeared in reaction to the growing complexity of environmental laws and administrative fragmentation accompanying decentralization. Interagency arrangements have grown in popularity in both federal and state government. In the area of toxic substances, the federal Interagency Regulatory Liaison Group (IRLG) brought a number of federal agencies together over the issue of toxic substances. A variety of advisory groups were formed within EPA, such as the Science Advisory Board (SAB), whose membership is drawn from other agencies such as the Occupational Safety and Health Administration (OSHA).

Interagency coordination among states was attempted by the formation of multistate regional agencies. Where such agencies existed prior to the major changes in environmental laws, new responsibilities were added to their existing functions. One of the models for such a regional agency was the interstate water resource commission; another was the interstate compact agreement (see Advisory Commission on Intergovernmental Relations [ACIR], 1972; Derthick, 1974). Substate regional agencies were also popular.

To summarize, the response of administrative agencies to changing goals and technologies has been to decentralize and specialize. To avoid this occurring at the expense of coordination, special entities have been set up to integrate responsibilities on a program-by-program or, in some cases, project-by-project basis.

The Role of the Public

The public as an institution in environmental decision making is another important component of environmental management. The public's role has undergone considerable change during the past decade as goals and technology have changed. One major change has been the gradual institutionalization of public participation processes directly into environmental legislation. Much of the modern-day environmental legislation was initiated by extensive public intervention symbolized by the Earth Day movement. Yet, it took many years before public participation was formally incorporated into legislation. Many of the earlier federal laws incorporated the minimum requirements for notifying the public of new regulations and administrative actions ("notice and comment procedures") dictated by the Administrative Procedures Act. Public hearings were held as a means to obtain public input. In spite of these requirements, there was little obligation on the part of the hearing officer to incorporate comments into agency decisions, nor any mechanism to weigh and evaluate each claim systematically. In the mid-1970s the role of public participation gradually grew, especially in the context of environmental planning processes. The common administrative mechanism that state and local government used for citizen involvement was the environmental commission or council (Carter et al., 1974; Kundell, 1977). While these organizations proliferated in the early to mid-1970s, many were eventually disbanded or absorbed into local governmental environmental agencies. Thus, the institutionalization of public participation has had mixed success.

Another change has been the increased technical demands on the public in order to participate. With the growth in complexity of environmental decision making due to the greater emphasis upon individual chemicals and the complex technology needed to manage them under the Toxic Substances Control Act (TSCA) and cleanup actions under the Comprehensive Environmental Response Compensation and Liability Act (CERCLA), public participation became much more specialized and technically informed. It was placed in the hands of a few national organizations that could afford the expertise required to address these new technical issues. A major exception is environmental impact statements (EISs), where the input of the general public has remained strong and is still largely locally based. Public views can be directly incorporated into EISs in the form of plans for the preservation of neighborhood or community character.

A third change has been the growing political influence of the public. The major environmental interest groups have been responsible for introducing and influencing major environmental programs. Some of the major law suits that have considerably changed the programs were brought by these organizations. For example, the case of *Natural Resources Defense Council (NRDC)* v. *Train* in the mid-1970s resulted in the expansion of substances covered under federal and state water quality criteria. The Federal Water Pollution Control Act Amendments (FWPCAA) of 1972 required that toxic substances be included in water quality criteria, but EPA set only a few such criteria. The NRDC case expanded the list to 129, which was ultimately reduced to 65. Another indication of the strength of the role of both environmental and citizen groups is the fact that they consistently bring the majority of cases under NEPA (CEQ, 13th Ann. Report–1982; 14th Ann. Report–1983; 15th Ann. Report–1984). Their record over the past three years has been as follows:

	Number of Cases Filed		
	1981	1982	1983
Total cases brought	114	157	146
Environmental organizations	40	58	55
Individuals or citizen groups	32	62	57

To summarize, the public has adapted to changing goals and technology by

becoming increasingly institutionalized, technically oriented, and influential politically especially in the area of litigation.

MANAGEMENT STRATEGIES TO COPE WITH COMPLEXITY AND FRAGMENTATION

The trends toward integration, consolidation, and coordination of laws and administrative organizations to deal with the explosion of environmental programs were
paralleled by a similar development in the technical approaches and implementation
strategies for environmental protection.

In the early 1970s, the environmental issues were organized separately by
environmental medium or type of pollutant—air, land, water; pesticides, solid
wastes, radiation. This became even worse by the early 1980s when management
strategies took a chemical-by-chemical approach. As in the case of administrative
structure and laws, strategies and technical methods emerged to introduce integrated
problem solving across environmental mediums. Individual chemicals presented an
even greater challenge to environmental administration. the new strategies and
techniques included multipurpose resource use, land use management, environmental planning, dispute resolution, environmental impact assessment, and risk
assessment.

Multipurpose Resource Use

Multipurpose resource use was a more common technique in the 1960s than in the
1970s to integrate and coordinate competing uses for a given resource. One example
of this strategy was the promotion of multiuse concepts for resources under the
Multiple Use–Sustained Yield Act of 1960. The act was under the jurisdiction of
the U.S. Bureau of Land Management and the Forest Service. Encouraged by the
Water Resources Development Act of 1965, similar strategies were explored for
water resource management combining the multiple uses of water resources (e.g.,
recreation, power, water supply, flood protection) and the accomplishment of such
uses by multiple means (e.g., waterworks construction, land use controls) (White,
1969). The major shortcoming of these efforts is their inability "for resolving
conflicts between competing, mutually exclusive uses" (CEQ, 12th Ann. Report–
1981, p. 9). More specifically, these efforts never directly addressed the political
mechanisms for resolving these conflicts. Also, the technical basis for usage patterns
was not as sophisticated as those in later programs.

Land Use Management

A considerable effort was made during the 1960s and 1970s to relate the uses of
land to the quality of air, land, and water resources. Even before this, it was known

that poor land management practices could degrade environmental quality through severe soil erosion, desert formation, landslides, and flooding. As a result of recent studies, the control over land use became an important strategy to simultaneously control discharges to water, air, and land resources (for a discussion see, for example, Bishop, 1974; Bosselman & Callies, 1971; Bosselman, Callies, & Banta, 1973; Kaiser *et al.*, 1973; Keyes, 1976; McAllister, 1973).

The interest in land use controls as a strategy for controlling environmental quality paralleled the delegation of federal environmental programs to state and local government. New regulatory mechanisms emerged at the local level to meet the needs of both land use and environmental controls, such as the creation of special environmental zoning districts, environmental control ordinances to protect sensitive lands from degradation, and special tax or other financial incentives to develop land in environmentally sound ways. However, the technical capabilities and resources of local government to implement land use and environmental controls were often limited.

Environmental Planning

Environmental planning was a technique for evaluating the effect of alternative land development scenarios on a number of different environmental attributes or conditions simultaneously. It was also used to identify environmentally sensitive areas where development should be avoided or constrained. The pioneering work in environmental planning is Ian McHarg's *Design with Nature* (1969). A parallel effort was the work in water resources begun by Leopold and associates (1971). Leopold developed a two-dimensional matrix to tabulate the impacts of components of a development project on attributes of the affected environment.

These early efforts soon blossomed into more advanced techniques involving decision trees and simulation models, often taking on a global perspective (Dee, Drobny, Baker, Duke, & Fahringer, 1973; Forrester, 1969; Leontief, 1970; Sorensen, 1971; Williams & House, 1974). In response to the data demands of these techniques, many states began to develop environmental data bases such as the LUNR system in New York, the FLORIS system in Florida, the LOIS system in New Jersey, and the MNRIS system in Minnesota. Some states developed their own tools for environmental planning, such as the CRIP system in Wisconsin.

Dispute Resolution

Another process that has become a popular means of integrating a variety of environmental concerns simultaneously as well as resolving conflicts is dispute resolution. This actually consists of a number of different approaches, such as negotiation, mediation, and arbitration. These techniques have been implemented in particular cases by organizations such as the American Arbitration Association and various mediation centers established throughout the United States (see Chapter 9). Dispute resolution is built upon the premise that negotiation is more effective and less costly than litigation, that the parties involved are willing to bargain, that there has to be an initial agreement on the nature of the problem, and that the findings or recommendations for action are binding (Susskind, Bacow, & Wheeler, 1983). It acts as a vehicle for integrating environmental concerns by providing a common framework applicable to many environmental problems (often simultaneously). It can deal with many different aspects of a problem at once.

Environmental Impact Assessment

Another process that was used more frequently than (but was related to) environmental planning was the environmental impact assessment process established under National Environmental Policy Act (NEPA). The purpose of environmental impact assessment was to provide a comprehensive coverage of environmental issues in the review of projects that the categorical legislation could not provide. The "full-disclosure" and "action-forcing" provisions of NEPA have had perhaps the most pervasive influence on environmental decision making of any statute (Anderson, 1973; Andrews, 1976; Caldwell, 1982). Between 1977 and 1984, close to 7,000 impact statements were filed at the federal level. The number generally declined annually from about 1,500 statements in 1977 to about 600 by 1984 (CEQ, 15th Ann. Report–1984, p. 719). This decline came during a period when many states and localities were passing their own versions of NEPA, and delegations of the environmental impact statement process to these other levels of government were common. This delegation may account for some of the decline in federal activity.

The process has somewhat limited effectiveness in integrating environmental concerns. For example, it has been argued that the orientation of environmental impact statements toward individual projects is the antithesis of comprehensive planning. It allows projects to develop incrementally in the absence of an overall plan. Environmental issues are often skewed toward those of immediate concern to the public, leaving open the possibility of new problems being discovered in the future (see Zimmerman, 1985a). Second, the process is fraught with uncertainties. The complexity of the NEPA process is reflected in the number of court cases that have been brought under the act: over 100 cases are typically filed each year (CEQ, 13th Ann. Report–1982, p. 234). For example, in 1982, 157 cases were brought (CEQ, 14th Ann. Report–1983, p. 265) and in 1983 another 146 (CEQ, 15th Ann. Report–1984, p. 522). About 10 to 15% of the cases lead to injunctions.

Risk Assessment

Another recent analytical process that integrates a number of technical concerns simultaneously is risk assessment. Risk assessment integrates the analysis of the transport and fate of environmental contaminants with the exposure of humans to toxic substances. Risk assessment or estimation is one component of the decision-making process for environmental risks. It consists of identifying the source of risk, establishing its magnitude and severity and its consequences, and computing the probability of its occurrence. Risk evaluation weighs the benefits against both the costs and risks. A second component is the determination of risk acceptability, which introduces values, attitudes, and perceptions about risk into the decision to accept or reject it. Finally, risk management combines these steps within decision-making and institutional systems to arrive at and implement an outcome (Zimmerman, 1983; see also Chapters 1 and 7, this volume).

There are many indications that risk assessment has become an important strategy for environmental administration at least at the federal and state levels of government. At the federal level:

- A previous EPA administrator, William Ruckelshaus, advocated risk assessment as a means of implementing environmental policy for the agency (U.S. EPA, 1984);
- A tradition of risk assessment has been established in and coordinated by the Science Advisory Board within EPA to develop water and air quality standards;
- A major research program was developed within the National Science Foundation to study risks in the environmental area;
- A recent study of risk assessment at the federal level analyzed where risk assessments should be placed organizationally (National Research Council, 1983);
- A number of bills have been introduced into Congress mandating risk assessment by government agencies;
- Risk assessment is slowly appearing in federal regulations to implement toxic and hazardous waste laws.

At the state level risk assessments have been conducted in connection with the evaluation of health risks for setting drinking water and air quality standards, the disposition of hazardous wastes, and in some cases for environmental impact assessments. The state of New Jersey, for example, requires an Environmental Health Impact Statement for hazardous waste facilities, which includes a risk analysis. In New York state, risk assessment is being used for the development of "acceptable ambient levels" (AALs) for air pollutants not covered by national ambient air quality standards under the Clean Air Act.

THE INCORPORATION OF MANAGEMENT STRATEGIES INTO SPECIFIC ENVIRONMENTAL PROGRAMS

The previous section showed that management techniques and strategies developed and implemented by society's institutions were largely guided by environmental goals and changes in the technologies for detecting and removing environmental contaminants. The strategies were based on a mix of conservationist and public health concerns. They often incorporated stringent technological controls reflecting the refinements in the detection of pollutants in the environment and in human organisms. Most notably, environmental management was placed in the context of the complex interrelationships between human activity and natural phenomena, and attempts were made to integrate widely disparate phenomena.

The management strategies that institutions use to maintain the quality of health and the environment can be defined in terms of a cause-effect framework that relates some initial condition of the environment to changes in this condition as a result of human activity. This framework reflects the growing concern with ecological relationships and consists of the following components:

- the condition of the ambient environment
- the potential sources and pathways of contamination of the ambient environment, and source reductions through technological or behavioral change
- the effects of contamination as portrayed by the health and welfare of human receptors and the health of lower-order organisms.

Tables 8-2 through 8-6 categorize most of the major environmental programs that exist today in terms of the three components of that framework: programs that refer to ambient environmental conditions, programs pertaining to sources of contamination and source reduction, and programs pertaining to the condition of receptors. (These programs have been categorized in a similar way for stages in an emergency management process [Zimmerman, 1985b]). The tables show that by far the largest number of programs applies to sources of environmental contaminants rather than being directed toward the ambient environment or to receptors. This reflects the major orientation of environmental policy toward source controls or technological controls.

While the legislative references in these tables are to federal statutes, in many cases states and even local jurisdictions now have primary responsibility for the programs. Two major programmatic themes run through all these programs: (1) the development of environmental standards, and (2) the development of implementation mechanisms, which include planning, nonregulatory management alternatives, and regulation. These two programs are central to the development and application of environmental policy. A third theme is setting priorities. Prioritization systems are applicable to both standards-setting and implementation, and are discussed as well in the context of the environmental programs.

Standards provide a measurement system against which the environmental ramifications of all activities can be gauged. The development and application of scientific standards theoretically allows information and values to be integrated outside the context of any particular decision. Implementation demonstrates the feasibility of environmental policy against resource, political, and other constraints.

The Standards-Setting Process

The development of standards should precede decisions about environmental quality and then can be the basis for these decisions. Standards reflect human-environmental

Table 8-2. Federal Environmental Programs Applicable to Ambient Environmental Conditions

Domain	Activity	Reference
	Setting of Standards	
	(Including development of criteria and designation of geographic areas to which standards are applicable.)	
Air	National Ambient Air Quality Standards (NAAQS) Primary Standards Secondary Standards	CAA, Sec. 106
	Designation and Classification of Air Quality Control Regions	CAA
Water	Water Quality Criteria	CWA, Sec. 304(a)
	Water Quality Standards	CWA, Sec. 303
	National Interim Primary Drinking Water Standards; Maximum Contaminant Levels	SDWA, Sec. 1412
	Sole Source Aquifer Designations	SDWA, Sec. 1424(e)
	Marine Sanctuary Designations	MPRSA, Sec. 302
	Restrictions for Wild and Scenic Rivers	WSRA, Sec. 7(a)
	Coastal Zone Management Area and Boundary Designations	CZMA
	Implementation	
	(Only plans and related monitoring and surveillance programs are the relevant implementation mechanisms for ambient environmental condition.)	
Air	Plans	
	State Implementation Plans	CAA, Sec. 110
	Monitoring and Surveillance	CAA, Secs. 113, 114
	State and Local Air Quality Monitoring System (SLAMS)	
	National Air Quality Monitoring System (NAMS)	
Water	Plans	
	Areawide Waste Treatment Management Plans	CWA, Sec. 208
	Basin Plans	CWA, Sec. 209
	State Plans	CWA, Sec. 303(e)
	Monitoring and Surveillance	
	State water quality reports	CWA, Sec. 305(b)
	National Stream Quality Accounting Network (NASQAN)- (USGS)	
	National Eutrophication Program	
	Federal-State Cooperative Program for groundwater monitoring (USGS)	
	Northeast Monitoring Program (NEMP)-(NOAA)	
	National Organics Monitoring Survey	SDWA
	National Screening Program	SDWA
	Community Water Supply Survey	SDWA
	State drinking water supply surveys	SDWA
	Groundwater monitoring at hazardous waste sites	RCRA

Note. Explanation of abbreviations: CAA, Clean Air Act; CWA, Clean Water Act; SDWA, Safe Drinking Water Act; MPRSA, Marine Protection, Research and Sanctuaries Act; WSRA, Wild and Scenic Rivers Act; CZMA, Coastal Zone Management Act; SLAMS, State and Local Air Quality Monitoring System; NAMS, National Air Quality Monitoring System; NASQAN, National Stream Quality Accounting Network; USGS, United States Geological Survey; NEMP, Northeast Monitoring Program; NOAA, National Oceanic and Atmospheric Administration, RCRA, Resource Conservation and Recovery Act.

Table 8-3. Federal Environmental Programs in Air, Pesticides, and Toxic Substances Applicable to Sources and Source Reduction

	Federal law		
Activity	CAA	FIFRA/FEPCA	TSCA

	Setting of Standards		
Standards	New Source Performance Standards—Sec. 109 National Emission Standards for Hazardous Air Pollutants—Sec. 112 Motor Vehicle Emission Standards Lead content in gasoline		PCB disposal, standards

	Implementation		
Planning	State Implementation Plans—Sec. 110 Transportation Control Plans—Sec. 105		
Monitoring and surveillance	National Emissions Inventory	Pesticide reporting system	Inventory of Chemicals in Commerce
Nonregulatory alternatives	Emissions Trading Policy (offsets, banks, bubbles)	Not applicable	Not applicable
Regulation			
Notifications, Registrations, Certifications, and Permits	Mobile Source Certification (testing of prototype vehicles)	Rebuttable Presumption Against Registration (RPAR)—Sec. 3 Certification of Pesticide Applicators—Sec. 4	Premanufacture Notification (PMN)
Enforcement	Motor Vehicle Recall—Sec. 207(c)(1) Motor Vehicle Warranty—Sec. 207(a) and (b) Antitampering Provision for Emission Control Equipment—Sec. 203 Inspection & Maintenance	Suspension of Registration—Sec. 6 Seizure Orders—Sec. 7	Control/limitation of manufacture—Sec. 6 Penalties—Sec. 16

Note. Explanation of abbreviations: CAA, Clean Air Act; FIFRA, Federal Insecticide, Fungicide, and Rodenticide Act; FEPCA, Federal Pesticide Control Act; TSCA, Toxic Substances Control Act.

Table 8-4. Federal Environmental Programs in Water Quality Applicable to Sources and Source Reductions

Activity	Federal Law		
	CWA	SDWA	R&HA, MPRSA
Setting of Standards			
Standards	Effluent Limitations— Secs. 301(b)(2), 304(b)(2), 307 Water Quality-based Effluent Limits—Sec. 302 New Source Performance Standards—Sec. 306 Toxic & Pretreatment Standards—Sec. 307 Ocean Discharge Criteria—Sec. 403	National Primary Drinking Water Regulations; Maximum Contaminant Levels Goal Sec. 1412	Special environmental policies for evaluating permits
Implementation			
Planning	Waste Treatment Management Plans— Sec. 201 Areawide Water Quality Management Plans— Sec. 208 Basin Plans—Sec. 209 State Plans—Sec. 303	State Groundwater Management Plans— Sec. 1443	
Monitoring and surveillance	Effluent violations—Sec. 308 Discharge Monitoring Quality Assurance	Public water systems— Sec. 1445(a)	
Regulation			
Notifications, Registrations, Certifications, and Permits	Water Quality Certification—Sec. 401 NPDES permit—Sec. 402 Disposal of dredge and fill material—Sec. 404	Connection to Public Water Supplies	Ocean Disposal Permit (6 types) (MPRSA)— Sec. 103 Permit to Construct in Navigable Waters (R&H)—Sec. 9, 10, 11
Grant requirements	Construction grant conditions for publicly owned wastewater treatment facilities		
Enforcement	Orders—Sec. 309 Spills—Sec. 311	Well Closings Underground Injection Control—Sec. 1423	

Note. Explanation of abbreviations: CWA, Clean Water Act; SDWA and Amendments of 1985, Safe Drinking Water Act; R&HA, Rivers and Harbors Act; MPRSA, Marine Protection Research and Sanctuaries Act; NPDES, National Pollutant Discharge Elimination System.

Table 8-5. Environmental Programs in Solid and Hazardous Wastes Applicable to Sources and Source Reductions

Activity	RCRA	CERCLA, SARA
	Setting of Standards	
Standards	Hazardous Waste Generator Standards— Sec. 3002 Hazardous Waste Transporter Standards— Sec. 3003 Hazardous Waste Facility Standards—Sec. 3004: —Interim Status Standards —General Status Standards —Interim Standards for New Facilities —Standards for design, construction, and installation of underground storage tanks —Standards for burning hazardous waste-fuel mixtures	Reference standards for environmental quality drawn from other federal environmental laws. Remedial action cleanup standards—Sec. 121 (SARA)
	Implementation	
Planning	Solid Waste Management Plans—Sec. 4001 Hazardous Waste Facility Plans, e.g., closure and postclosure—Sec. 3004	National Contingency Plan— immediate removal, planned removal, remedial action— Sec. 105 Remedial investigation/ feasibility studies—Sec. 104
Regulation		
Notifications, Registrations, Certifications, and Permits	Construct/operate Hazardous Waste Management Facility—Sec. 3005 Uniform Hazardous Manifest for Transport New underground petroleum and chemical storage facilities Burning hazardous waste-fuel mixtures	Record of Decision, consent decrees for remedial actions
Enforcement	Permit Revokation—Sec. 3005(d) Compliance Orders—Sec. 3008	Abatement Orders, penalties, and cost recovery provisions—Sec. 106

Note. Explanaton of abbreviations: RCRA, Resource Conservation and Recovery Act; CERCLA, Comprehensive Environmental Response Compensation and Liability Act; SARA, Superfund Amendments and Reauthorization Act.

interrelationships and emphasize health-oriented and technological solutions to environmental problems. Tolerance limits are set for living organisms based on known health effects associated with different levels of a pollutant; these are then used as the basis for ambient environmental standards for water, air, and land (the vehicles of exposure) that reflect these tolerances; finally, facility and activity standards or technological standards are developed that allow the ambient standards to be met.

Table 8-6. Federal Environmental Programs Applicable to Receptors

Environmental Program	Type of receptor	
	Humans	Lower organisms
Setting of Standards		
Not applicable (Except for radiation standards under the Atomic Energy Acts)		
Implementation		
Plans and monitoring and surveillance programs		
Pesticides, Toxics	National Human Monitoring Program	National Residue Program (USDA)
	National Adipose Tissue Survey Health and Nutrition Examination Survey	Various trace element and toxics surveys (National Marine Fisheries Service)
Water		Aquatic Life Survey (EPA, FWS)
		Mussel Watch Program
Regulation		
After-the-fact emergency measures		

Note. Explanaton of abbreviations: USDA, U.S. Department of Agriculture; EPA, Environmental Protection Agency; FWS, Fish and Wildlife Service.

The programs shown in Tables 8-2 through 8-6 give many examples of each kind of standard. Some types are more common than others. An example of a tolerance limit is an allowable average daily intake of a water supply contaminant. Examples of ambient standards are allowable concentrations of dissolved oxygen, suspended solids, or toxic substances in surface and groundwaters and sulfur and nitrogen oxides in the air. Examples of technology-based standards are the limits placed on the pollutants in wastewater discharges, air emissions from a stack, or design parameters such as treatment capacity for a pollution control device.

While conceptually a logical relationship exists among the three types of standards, it is often difficult to apply the logic in any particular situation. Setting ambient standards to reflect the tolerances of living organisms is initially constrained by the tremendous variability in the sensitivity of organisms and their susceptability to environmental contaminants by stage in the life-style, type of species, and condition (e.g., age, health) of the individual organism. Thus, tolerance standards may not exist before ambient or technology-based source standards have to be developed. Even if ambient standards exist, the relationship between technology-based standards for sources of contamination and ambient environmental standards has always been difficult to establish. the major difficulty has been in developing facility standards that at the same time reflect current technologies and are stringent enough to be consistent with ambient environmental standards when pollutants are released. Complex environmental models are often employed to set standards for sources of pollutants that will meet ambient standards.

Implementation Devices

Implementation programs to achieve environmental goals consist of plans, various nonregulatory alternatives, and regulations.

Plans

In the spirit of the environmental goals of the 1970s and 1980s, some plans lay the foundation for broad, long-term coverage of these goals. These plans more than any other type of program are based on ecological principles, such as carrying capacity and biogeochemical cycles. Examples of these plans are areawide environmental plans, such as Areawide Water Quality Management Plans prepared under Section 208 of the Clean Water Act, the State Air Quality Implementation Plans under the Clean Air Act, and solid waste management plans under the Resource Conservation and Recovery Act and its predecessors. These planning programs are shown in Tables 8-2 through 8-6. Plans emphasize an integrated framework by proceeding from sources of pollution to their reduction. They typically require the identification of sources of pollution, a description of the state of and trends in ambient environmental quality relative to environmental standards, and mitigation measures to avoid the transport of pollutants from one medium to another. The effectiveness of these plans depends on how complete their coverage of sources and environmental conditions is, how much funding is available to implement and continue modifying them, whether they are endorsed by political officials, and whether a management commitment exists at high, politically influential levels of government.

Water quality planning under Section 208 was one of the largest programs of this type. These plans ultimately extended over every geographic area in the country. While extensive data bases were developed under the plans, evaluations of the program reveal jurisdictional and financial problems that were obstacles to their implementation (see, for instance, Lamb, 1980). Air quality plans have actually played a relatively larger role in land development decisions.

Other kinds of plans have a more technological orientation. These provide the specifics of facility design to meet environmental standards rather than being broad-based. The wastewater facility plans under Section 201 of the Clean Water Act and the Remedial Action Master Plans under the Comprehensive Environmental Response Compensation and Liability Act (CERCLA) fall into this category.

Nonregulatory Alternatives

Nonregulatory alternatives pertain to a wide variety of economic incentives or legal rights doctrines, such as common law, to achieve environmental goals. Many of these mechanisms were explored early in the environmental movement in the form of taxes on wastewater effluents and air emissions as a means of encouraging the reduction of such discharges. Other kinds of incentive systems were developed as well (Kneese & Schultze, 1975). Innovative land use controls, such as transfer of development rights (TDRs), were borrowed from growth management. TDRs enabled a landowner to sell his allotment of pollutant emissions to another developer in return for a fee. The "emission offset" policies in the Clean Air Act are examples of this concept also. Various financial and legal tools to implement nonregulatory concepts have been developed (see Baram, 1982; Breyer, 1982).

Regulation

Regulatory programs are still the most popular form of implementation. These include various legal sanctions related to enforcement, permits, licenses, registrations, and certifications. Most are designed for individual cases and are based on an extensive array of technology-based standards. The most common instrument is a permit or license applicable to an individual source of pollution.

Permits are a common device for identifying, characterizing, and placing conditions upon pollutant discharges into the environment. Across the country permit holders in many of the environmental programs now number many thousands. A given facility can hold many permits, one for each pollutant discharge location. In order to reduce the regulatory burden imposed by the sheer numbers of permits involved, streamlining mechanisms were designed in the late 1970s. These were partly motivated by a regulatory reform movement started in the Carter administration, prompted by the findings of the Federal Paperwork Commission and mandated by the Regulatory Reform Act of 1979 and Regulatory Impact Analyses (RIAs). Five federal permits were collapsed into a single permit (40 Code of Federal Regulations [CFR] 122 through 125). This ultimately proved to be too cumbersome, and a deconsolidation of the permits followed.

The permit proliferation problem has been addressed in a number of places (Bosselman, Feurer, & Siemon, 1976; Noble, Banta, and Rosenberg, 1977; Zimmerman, 1980a). Some of the techniques (Zimmerman, 1980a) for streamlining permitting that have emerged, primarily at the state and local levels, are:

- Joint application submission (same application for several permits)
- Listing of all required permits on a single application
- Joint submission of environmental assessments or impact statements
- Joint hearings
- Joint issuance of permits (joint permit forms)
- Requiring that conditions of one permit be met to issue another kind of permit
- Sequencing or scheduling the issuance of multiple permits

These joint procedures are often carried out at different levels of government as well as within one level of government.

Particular examples of the mechanisms developed to reduce both the numbers of applicants for any given type of permit as well as the number of different types of permits a given applicant had to apply for are:

- Permits issued for classes or categories of sources rather than individual sources (National Pollutant Discharge Elimination System (NPDES) permits for stormwater discharges under the Clean Water Act)

- General permits (nationwide or regional permits issued for a class of activities that are similar in nature or have cumulative environmental impacts issued by the U.S. Army Corps of Engineers under the Rivers and Harbors Act and the Clean Water Act, 33 CFR Part 330)
- Single permits for multiple discharges from a single source (e.g., Clean Air Act "bubble policy")

A similar kind of streamlining occurred for environmental impact statements. Page limits were placed on environmental impact statements. "Generic" EISs were developed to cover similar kinds of actions (e.g., activities that were similar in type or location or were part of the same project). "Programmatic" EISs were used for activities that fell under the requirements of the same program and for which similar guidelines were applicable. Programmatic EISs were a substitute for EISs for each source issued a permit under a given regulatory program. The case of *Kalur* v. *Resor* (335 F. Supp. 1 [D.D.C. 1971]) initially challenged the federal government's issuance of wastewater discharge permits without EISs for each discharge. The decision exempted individual discharge permits from EISs, but required the impacts to be considered in the EIS accompanying the 208 Plan encompassing the geographic area within which a particular discharge was located.

Setting Priorities for Environmental Management

Beginning with the last decade, legislators and administrative agencies were faced with the enormity of the management process involving a large number of potential contaminants, categories of effects, and receptors. Attempts at consolidation were not entirely successful, and in fact, deconsolidation of major federal permits followed their consolidation. Integration of environmental regulations through comprehensive planning was hampered by limited funds for continuing the processes. Prioritization schemes, therefore, were used in almost every program. Their use represents a major response of environmental institutions to the growing regulatory complexities created by the introduction of ecological concerns. Such schemes now precede standards-setting and implementation functions. Practically all laws or regulations now contain some provision for prioritization of the agents of pollution, sources, transport mechanisms, target organisms, and their locations.

Screening was designed in a number of different ways. Some programs screened categories of pollutant sources (emitters or substances emitted) geographically, some by degree of toxicity, and some by amount of the contaminant discharged. Some examples of priority systems that are based upon the biological, physical, and chemical characteristics of pollutant sources are:

1. The Rebuttable Presumption Against Registration (RPAR) program under the Federal Insecticide Fungicide and Rodenticide Act (FIFRA) was limited to the review of active ingredients in pesticides rather than to each pesticide

preparation. This relieved the bottleneck of reviews under the RPAR process by reducing the number of reviews that had to be conducted. The justification for restricting detailed analyses to this subset only is that "the same basic ingredients appear repeatedly, singly, or in combination in the 35,000 pesticide formulations for which reregistration is being sought" (National Research Council (NRC), 1980, p. 30). Generic standards would then be developed for each active ingredient. Apparently, the program to establish generic standards for active ingredients "began late in 1978, with 47 scheduled for completion and another 50 scheduled for initiation in 1980" (NRC, 1980, p. 30).

2. The development of the National Priorities List under the Comprehensive Environmental Response Compensation and Liability Act (CERCLA) was a means of prioritizing hazardous waste sites for cleanup actions. As of June 1986 close to 900 sites have been listed by the U.S. EPA.

3. The hazardous substances ranking systems under CERCLA (Sec. 105(8)(A) gives the ranking criteria) and Toxic Substances Control Act (TSCA) (Office of Technology Assessment, 1983, pp. 237, 383, 386) prioritize chemicals for regulation in hazardous waste sites or during a premanufacturing review process respectively.

4. The Consumer Product Safety Commission's chemical screening program screens new chemicals found in consumer products based on toxicity and economic value of the product.

Examples of prioritization schemes based on the magnitude of the pollution problem are:

1. Financial responsibility must be demonstrated for vessels exceeding a size limit of 300 gross tons under CERCLA Section 108 (a)(1).

2. The Resource Conservation and Recovery Act (RCRA) and its amendments of 1984 exclude small generators of hazardous wastes (discharging 100 kg or less per month) from hazardous waste disposal requirements.

3. Under the National Pollutant Discharge Elimination System (NPDES) program of the Clean Water Act (CWA), wastewater dischargers are classified into major and minor dischargers for the purpose of processing permit applications.

4. The applicability of the Safe Drinking Water Act is restricted to systems that are public water supplies or have 25 connections or more.

State environmental programs employ still other priorities and thresholds. The problem with priorities is that they change over time, are different for different groups, and may be poorly designed or difficult to justify.

The choice of prioritization criteria has not gone unchallenged. For example, irrigation return flow waters from areas of less than 3,000 acres were originally exempted from the requirements of the NPDES permit under the CWA. The Natural Resources Defense Council challenged this in *NRDC* v. *Train* (396 F. Supp. 1393, 1395 [D.D.C. 1975]) and won (Gould, 1980, p. 95). The size threshold for applicability of hazardous waste laws to small hazardous waste generators was recently lowered in amendments to RCRA after it received considerable criticism by the U.S. General Accounting Office and others as being a loophole in the law and allowing the incremental buildup of hazardous wastes.

OVERVIEW OF PROGRAM PERFORMANCE

Program performance can be measured in a number of ways. Vig and Kraft (1984) have suggested three measures of agency performance relevant to environmental agencies—means-ends measures (measuring performance as improvements in environmental quality), cost-benefit analysis (measuring performance as benefits exceeding costs), and process-oriented measures (measuring performance in terms of the functions the agency performs). The process-oriented measures are the ones that are explored here. The dilemmas associated with accurate means-ends measures were discussed earlier. Cost-benefit analysis presents only a very partial picture of performance and its utility has been much debated.

Some process-oriented measures relate to the response of agencies to explicit legislative mandates—the timely scheduling and comprehensiveness of rules and regulations that have to be promulgated, the development of plans and program standards that are required by law, and enforcement of agency programs through the development and implementation of compliance schedules. Other dimensions of performance relate to how the programs deal with uncertainties—constantly changing technologies, information about environmental conditions and their health effects— and how well uncertainties are translated into program modifications.

Some of the aspects of performance that appear to have drawn more attention than others are the timeliness of program implementation relative to mandated legislative schedules and deadlines, the use of sophisticated techniques (such as models) in the development and implementation of standards, the design and strength of enforcement efforts, the extent to which agencies have used programs and powers delegated to them, particularly in the area of standards setting, and the overall efficiency and effectiveness of the implementation and management of technological controls.

Compliance with Statutory Deadlines and Schedules

The environmental laws of the 1970s were unprecedented in their use of precise deadlines for many regulatory activities as well as in prescribing the kinds of solutions agencies could use to achieve environmental quality goals. Deadlines were applied to the development of standards, issuance of guidelines, development of implementation plans, and other regulatory activities.

The use of statutory deadlines is one means that Congress uses to limit the discretionary authority of agencies. While a comprehensive analysis of the existence of these schedules and the extent to which agencies have complied with them is beyond the scope of this chapter, a few examples illustrate that a number of environmental agencies have had trouble meeting the requirements. This is not necessarily indicative of agency performance only—it may also demonstrate that the deadlines set by Congress were unrealistic in the first place. Some of these examples are given below.

- TSCA required that the manufacture of polychlorinated biphenyls cease by 1978, and that existing PCBs be properly labeled and disposed of. The GAO found that EPA issued regulations on labeling and disposal 7 months after the statutory deadline. Regulations for the ban were issued as much as 18 months late (U.S. GAO, 1981).
- The Department of Energy has been given the authority to develop siting criteria for nuclear waste repositories under the Nuclear Waste Policy Act of 1982. Its guidelines were issued 17 months after the statutory deadline (U.S. GAO, 1985b).

Use of State-of-the-Art Analytical Techniques Such as Models

The complexity of decision making has prompted decision makers to use models throughout the management process to integrate multidimensional characteristics of the environment and the activities that impinge on it. These environmental models followed the wave of urban development and ecological models of the 1960s (e.g., Forrester, 1969), which, in turn, came out of the postwar tradition in operations research and systems theory.

Models are used to characterize the entire causal linkage pathway from sources through ambient environmental condition to receptor. They are used to establish standards as well as extent of compliance for individual sources. In the air quality area alone, EPA lists close to a dozen models for recommended use for environmental impact assessment and estimates of compliance with air quality standards. EPA lists another two dozen or so as a guide for compliance with the technical aspects of regulations.

Models have been criticized over the years for their complexity on the one hand and tendency to oversimplify on the other hand (Lee, 1973; Ackerman, Ackerman, Sawyer, & Henderson, 1974). Nevertheless, reliance upon them has been increasing, especially in the environmental impact assessment process (for a discussion of the application of models in the EIS process, see Zimmerman, 1985a).

The interest in risk assessment discussed earlier has added a new family of models to the environmental ones of the early 1970s. From concentrations of substances in the environment one can calculate the probable occurrence of a given health effect. Alternatively, given a desired or acceptable probability of getting a disease, one can back calculate to the environmental concentration that will yield that probability, using risk assessment models. These models are fraught with the same uncertainties as environmental models; nevertheless, they have become a popular technique for evaluating alternatives. Under the Clean Air Act, EPA recently used risk assessments to control benzene emissions under the hazardous air pollution program. The agency was criticized for not having formal procedures for quantitative risk assessment (though guidelines had been proposed in November 1985) and for not including recent health effects studies in the assessment (U.S. GAO, 1986). To summarize, the use of risk assessment techniques in environmental decision making is limited by the lack of a consensus on many of the methodologies and assumptions that underly such assessments and the unavailability of much of the data required to run the models.

Enforcement

Performance in enforcement functions has many different dimensions. A few of these are the extent to which agencies carry out surveillance functions such as inspections and monitoring; the extent of reliance upon voluntary negotiation as an enforcement strategy and the success of such an effort; and the completeness of agency case reviews, including the sufficiency of information for those reviews. While a comprehensive review of all of these areas is beyond the scope of this chapter, some examples of insufficient information for effective enforcement are:

- As part of the Premanufacture Notice (PMN) provision issued for new chemicals under Section 5 of TSCA, manufacturers are required to provide certain information, including toxicity testing. Few PMN applications are submitted with test data adequate for EPA to make a decision, and as of 1982 half of the applications did not contain any toxicological data (CEQ, 13th Annual Report–1982, p. 194). Part of the problem may be that regulations for the PMN program are issued under Section 5 of the act, while regulations for the testing programs are issued under Section 4 (White, 1981, p. 138). Another explanation may be that testing requirements are negotiated (U.S. GAO, 1982d).

- Air quality decisions depend on data from air quality monitoring networks. Many models that are run for air quality permits and environmental impact statements depend on data inputs from the monitoring. While 70% of the air quality monitors were operational by June 1982, EPA's quality assurance program was such that the data coming from the monitors were not considered reliable (U.S. GAO, 1982c).

- The hazardous waste management program under both CERCLA and RCRA is beset by a number of information problems that have been identified by the General Accounting Office. First, the tracking system for the enforcement of the Superfund program is decentralized into regional offices. No national management information system exists (U.S. GAO, 1984). This limits the extent to which information on procedures and standards can be shared. Second, the data on illegal waste disposers are also very limited, since inventory information on many illegal generators and types of waste they generate is not complete, even though required by law. The problem is especially acute for small generators of hazardous wastes (U.S. GAO, 1985a). Third, inventories of hazardous waste sites also lack accuracy. Fourth, knowledge of groundwater conditions beneath hazardous waste sites is not complete. A recent study found that three quarters of the facilities in only two states did not have adequate groundwater monitoring capability (U.S. GAO, 1983b).

Extent of Program Use

The wide range of programs developed under environmental legislation was described in Tables 8-1 through 8-6. A critical question in program performance is how extensively programs are used.

The RPAR Process under FIFRA

Some registration and permit programs should be applicable to a wide range of activities, but some have not been used very much since their creation. The major process administered by the U.S. EPA for evaluating the toxicity of pesticides and subsequently deciding on the registration of a pesticide is the Rebuttable Presumption Against Registration (RPAR) process instituted in 1975 under the Federal Insecticide, Fungicide, and Rodenticide Act (FIFRA) as amended by the Federal Pesticide Control Act (FEPCA). In 1980, the National Research Council commented on the program's slow start: "the full process is only in the incipient stage, in that it has been initiated less than thirty times and completed only seven" (NRC, 1980, p. 29). The scope of the RPAR process is to review about 35,000 pesticides or their common ingredients.

The Development of NESHAPs under the CAA

The extent to which standards are set that are called for in legislation is another indication of program performance. The setting of the National Emission Standards for Hazardous Air Pollutants (NESHAPs) under Section 112 of the Clean Air Act (CAA) by EPA is an example of a program that has been slow to evolve. The EPA has been criticized for having listed only seven hazardous air pollutants and setting emission limits for only four of them by mid-1983, in spite of the fact that 37 candidate pollutants had been identified for the program (U.S. GAO, 1983a).

Standards and Product Bans Under CPSC

The Consumer Product Safety Commission (CPSC) has among its program responsibilities the regulation of acute and chronic chemical and environmental hazards (these accounted for 28% of the CPSC budget in 1978) and the development of safety standards within these areas (Bick & Kasperson, 1978). Prior to the development of a standard, the economic and environmental impacts must be assessed. The CPSC has been criticized for developing standards too slowly: the first standard appeared only 3½ years after the CPSC was established, but as of 1978 only 11 standards and bans were in force. A number of standards were not even upheld by the courts, including vinyl chloride in aerosols, because of failures to follow procedures (Bick & Kasperson, 1978, pp. 33, 35). On the other hand, the CPSC was the only agency that issued a ban on urea-formaldehyde foam insulation, while the EPA and OSHA failed to do so (Ashford, Ryan, & Caldart, 1983b, p. 894).

Efficiency of Program Operators

There are numerous examples of contamination partly attributable to inadequate performance of operating personnel. For example, in the pesticides control area, pesticide applicators are registered by state agencies. Since the programs are not directly oriented toward efficiency, practices occur that can be environmentally detrimental. For example, a CEQ report noted, "Two-thirds of the insecticides used in agriculture are applied by aircraft, but only 25% to 50% of it reaches the crop. A large portion remains airborne and drifts or is lost through volatilization, leaching, and surface transport. Less then 1% actually comes in contact with an insect" (CEQ, 1981, p. 92).

Facility Compliance

A common way of gauging the performance of programs oriented toward facility planning, construction, and operation is to look at facility performance.

- The federal government measures the performance of (1) air pollution facilities that are regulated under State Implementation Plans, (2) air pollution facilities governed by New Source Performance Standards (NSPS), and (3) air pollution facilities that are regulated under hazardous air standards (NESHAPs). Compliance status reports in the mid-1970s indicated that usually less than 5% of the facilities in these categories were out of compliance with either the emission limits or the schedules (U.S. EPA, 1978).
- Water pollution control facilities are either municipal or industrial. The effectiveness of this program is gauged in terms of its coverage of the population in need and the compliance of the facilities themselves. By 1982, some 155 million people or two-thirds of the U.S. population were served by wastewater treatment facilities (CEQ, 14th Annual Report–1983, p. 319). A recent EPA progress report indicated noncompliance for about one fifth to one quarter of the municipal and industrial facilities (Association of State and Interstate Water Pollution Control Administrators, 1984). The

NPDES permit program is responsible for monitoring the performance of these facilities.

POINTS TO REMEMBER

The goals of environmental policy have substantially shifted from conservation to preservation and public health concerns. Goals now clearly reflect the complex interrelationships between human activity and the natural environment, have a more enlarged scope, and operate at a much finer level of detail—the level of individual chemicals. At the same time that goals were changing, technological developments have expanded the limits of detectability of environmental pollutants and the ability to reduce these pollutants in the environment so that their releases do not conflict with natural resource constraints.

The institutions that manage environmental quality have responded to changing goals and technology at all levels of government. New goals and technological change have acted as a driving force to initiate changes in the laws, administrative organization, and role of the public in shaping and implementing environmental policy. The number of environmental laws has risen dramatically and the complexity and number of requirements for compliance, environmental monitoring, and analysis has increased as a reaction to the greater number of chemicals and health risks that have emerged as environmental concerns. The administrative organization of environmental programs has also shown a dramatic increase in complexity and scope. Administrative arrangements initially went through a period of fragmentation, having been overwhelmed by the sheer complexity and magnitude of concerns of the past decade. This was followed by successive periods of centralization of environmental programs within federal government, decentralization and delegation of programs from the federal government to state and local government, and finally consolidation and coordination of intergovernmental efforts. The role of the public in environmental policy formulation and implementation became more institutionalized, more technically specialized, and more influential politically.

Within this institutional framework technical strategies and management programs arose that were aimed at integrating multiple environmental concerns simultaneously into comprehensive analytical frameworks. The techniques included multipurpose resource use, land use management, environmental planning and impact assessment, risk assessment, and dispute resolution. The management programs, such as the development of standards, areawide environmental plans, and regulatory programs, reflected environmental interrelationships by emphasizing at least a theoretical progression from sources of pollution through transport mechanisms and finally to health effects. In actual fact, data limitations often precluded this theoretical orientation from being fully implemented. The components with which these techniques and programs dealt increased considerably in number and complexity in response to new goals and technological capabilities. Faced with this potentially unmanageable situation, elaborate priority setting schemes were developed, consisting of facility size criteria, indicator chemicals, and ranking systems, all aimed at selecting out areas that would have more significant environmental impacts.

While the overall performance of these institutions is hard to measure, there are indications that the success of their accomplishments has been mixed. Goals and technology may have been an effective driving force for institutional change. At the same time, however, these changes may have overwhelmed institutional capacity to deal with them, and thus, explain performance deficiencies that exist. Legislated deadlines were often missed, compliance was lagging, and programs were not used to their capacity. While not being refined measures of performance, these give indications that government was having a hard time assembling and managing the resources to meet the ambitious requirements of new legislation. The severe budget cuts experienced by environmental agencies and the increased emphasis upon economic goals in the early to mid-1980s at a time when technical requirements were increasing has been a large contributor to the lag in institutional performance (Vig & Kraft, 1986). Environmental institutions will need a better match of resources to program needs in order to effectively achieve the new goals and take advantage of the technological changes that have occurred.

References

Ackerman, B. A., Ackerman, S. R., Sawyer, J. R., Jr., & Henderson, D. W. (1974). *The uncertain search for environmental quality*. New York: Free Press.

Advisory Commission on Intergovernmental Relations. (1972). *Multistate regionalism*. Washington, DC: Advisory Commission on Intergovernmental Relations.

Anderson, R. F. (1973). *NEPA in the courts*. Baltimore, MD: Johns Hopkins University Press.

Andrews, R. N. L. (1976). *Environmental policy and administrative change*. Lexington, MA: Lexington Books.

Ashford, N. A., Ryan, C. W., & Caldart, C. C. (1983a). A hard look at federal regulation of formaldehyde: A departure from reasoned decisionmaking. *Harvard Environmental Law Review, 7*, 297–370.

Ashford, N. A., Ryan, C. W., & Caldart, C. C. (1983b). Law and science policy in federal regulation of formaldehyde. *Science, 122*, 894–900.

Association of State and Interstate Water Pollution Control Administrators and the U.S. Environmental Protection Agency. (1984). *America's clean water. The states' evaluation of progress 1972–1982*. Washington, DC: Association of State and Interstate Water Pollution Control Administrators.

Baldwin, J. H. (1985). *Environmental planning and management*. Boulder, CO: Westview Press.

Baram, M. S. (1982). *Alternatives to regulation*. Lexington, MA: D. C. Heath.

Bardach, E., & Kagan, R. A. (1982). Introduction. In E. Bardach & R. A. Kagan (Eds.), *Social regulation: Strategies for reform*. San Francisco: Institute for Contemporary Studies.

Bick, T., & Kasperson, R. E. (1978). The CPSC experiment: Pitfalls of hazard management. *Environment, 20*, 30–42.

Bishop, A. B., Fullerton, H. H., Crawford, A. B., Chambers, M. D., & Mckee, M. (1974). *Carrying capacity in regional environmental management*. Washington, DC: U.S. Government Printing Office.

Bosselman, F., & Callies, D. (1971). *The quiet revolution in land use control*. Washington, DC: U.S. Government Printing Office.

Bosselman, F., Callies, D., & Banta, J. (1973). *The taking issue*. Washington, DC: U.S. Government Printing Office.

Bosselman, F., Feurer, D., & Siemon, C. (1976). *The permit explosion*. Washington, DC: Urban Institute.

Boulding, K. (1971). The economics of the coming spaceship earth. In H. Jarrett (Ed.), *Environmental quality in a growing economy*. Baltimore, MD: Johns Hopkins University Press.

Breyer, S. (1982). *Regulation and its reform*. Cambridge, MA: Harvard University Press.

Burton, I., Kates, R. W., & White, G. F. (1979). *The environment as hazard*. New York: Oxford.

Caldwell, L. K. (1982). *Science and the National Environmental Policy Act*. University, AL: University of Alabama Press.

Carter, S., Frost, M., Rubin, C., & Sumek, L. (1974). *Environmental management and local government*. Washington, DC: U.S. Environmental Protection Agency.

Cole, H. S. D., Freeman, C., Jahoda, M., & Pavitt, K. L. R. (Eds.). (1973). *Models of doom*. New York: Universe Books.

Conservation Foundation. (1982). *State of the environment 1982*. Washington, DC: Conservation Foundation.

Commoner, B. (1971). *The closing circle*. New York: Knopf.

Cotgrove, S., & Duff, A. (1980). Environmentalism, middle-class radicalism and politics. *The Sociological Review, 28*, 333–351.

Council on Environmental Quality. (1981). *Environmental trends*. Washington, DC: U.S. Government Printing Office.

Council on Environmental Quality. (n.d.). *Twelfth annual report. Environmental quality 1981*. Washington, DC: U.S. Government Printing Office.

Council on Environmental Quality. (n.d.). *Thirteenth annual report. Environmental quality 1982*. Washington, DC: U.S. Government Printing Office.

Council on Environmental Quality. (n.d.). *Fourteenth annual report. Environmental quality 1983*. Washington, DC: U.S. Government Printing Office.

Council on Environmental Quality. (1984). *Fifteenth annual report. Environmental quality 1984*. Washington, DC: U.S. Government Printing Office.

Dee, N., Drobny, N.L, Baker, J. K., Duke, K. M., & Fahringer, D. C. (1973). *Environmental evaluation system for water quality management planning*. Columbus, OH: Battelle Columbus Labs.

Derthick, M. (1974). *Between state and nation*. Washington, DC: The Brookings Institution.

Downs, A. (1972). Up and down with ecology: The issue-attention cycle. *Public Interest, 28*, 38–50.

Ehrlich, P. (1970). *The population bomb*. New York: Ballantine.

Forrester, J. (1969). *Urban dynamics*. Boston: MIT Press.

Gould, G. (1980). Regulation of point source pollution under the federal Water Pollution Control Act. In B. L. Lamb (Ed.), *Water Quality Administration*. Ann Arbor, MI: Ann Arbor Science.

Harris, L. (1985). *Environmental pollution causes deep concern*. New York: Louis Harris.

Haskell, E. H., & Price, V. S. (1973). *State environmental management*. New York: Praeger.

Kaiser, E. J., Elfers, K., Cohn, S., Reichert, P. A., Hufschmidt, M. M., & Stanland, R. E. (1973). *Promoting environmental quality through urban planning and controls*. Washington, DC: U.S. Environmental Protection Agency.

Keyes, D. L. (1976). *Land development and the natural environment*. Washington, DC: The Urban Institute.

Kneese, A. V., & Schultze, C. L. (1975). *Pollution, prices and public policy*. Washington, DC: The Brookings Institution.

Kundell, J. E. (1977). *Municipal environmental conservation commissions in New York State*. Springfield, VA: National Technical Information Service.

Lamb, B. L. (Ed.). (1980). *Water quality administration*. Ann Arbor, MI: Ann Arbor Science.

Lee, D. B. (1973). Requiem for large scale models. *Journal of the American Institute of Planners, 39*, 163–178.

Leontief, W. (1970). Environmental repercussions and the economic structure: An input-output approach. *Review of Economics and Statistics, 52*, 262–271.

Leopold, L. B., Clarke, F. E., Hanshaw, B. B., & Balsley, J. R. (1971). *A procedure for evaluating environmental impact*. Washington, DC: U.S. Geological Survey.

Lisk, D. J. (1974). Recent development in the analysis of toxic elements. *Science, 184*(4142), 1137–1141.

Marcus, A. (1980). Environmental Protection Agency. In J. Q. Wilson (Ed.), *The politics of regulation*. New York: Basic Books.

Marsh & McLennan Co., Inc. (1980). *Risk in a complex society*. Philadelphia, PA: Marsh & McLennan.

McAllister, D. M. (1973). *Environment: A new focus for land-use planning*. Washington, DC: National Science Foundation.

McHarg, I. L. (1971). *Design with nature*. Garden City, NY: Doubleday.

Melosi, M. V. (1980). Environmental crisis in the city: The relationship between industrialization and urban pollution. In M. Melosi (Ed.), *Pollution and reform in American cities, 1870–1930*. Austin, TX: University of Texas Press.

National Research Council. (1977–1978). *Analytical studies for the U.S. Environmental Protection Agency*. Washington, DC: National Academy Press.

National Research Council. (1980). *Regulating pesticides*. Washington, DC: National Academy Press.

National Research Council. (1983). *Risk assessment in the federal government: Managing the process*. Washington, DC: National Academy Press.

Noble, J., Banta, J., & Rosenberg, J. (1977). *Groping through the maze*. Washington, DC: Conservation Foundation.

Office of Technology Assessment. (1983). *Technologies and management strategies for hazardous waste control*. Washington, DC: Office of Technology Assessment.

O'Riordan, T., & Turner, R. K. (1983). *An annotated reader in environmental planning and management*. Oxford: Pergamon.

Pepper, D. (1984). *The roots of modern environmentalism*. Dover, NH: Croom-Helm.

Schumacher, F. (1973). *Small is beautiful*. London: Abachus.

Sorensen, J. C. (1971). *A framework for identification and control of resource degradation and conflict in the multiple use of the coastal zone*. Berkeley, CA: Department of Landscape Architecture, University of California. Unpublished monograph.

Susskind, L., Bacow, L., & Wheeler, M. (1983). *Resolving environmental regulatory disputes*. Cambridge, MA: Schenkman.

U.S. Environmental Protection Agency. (1978). *National water quality inventory. 1977 report to Congress*. Washington, DC: U.S. Environmental Protection Agency.

U.S. Environmental Protection Agency. (1984). *Risk assessment and management: Framework for decision making*. Washington, DC: U.S. Environmental Protection Agency.

U.S. General Accounting Office. (1981). *EPA slow in controlling PCB's*. Washington, DC: U.S. General Accounting Office.

U.S. General Accounting Office. (1982a). *Cleaning up the environment: Progress achieved but major unresolved issues remain*. Washington, DC: General Accounting Office.

U.S. General Accounting Office. (1982b). *Environmental protection: Agenda for the 1980's*. Washington, DC: General Accounting Office.

U.S. General Accounting Office. (1982c). *Problems in air quality monitoring system affect data reliability*. Washington, DC: General Accounting Office.

U.S. General Accounting Office. (1982d). *Implementation of selected aspects of the Toxic Substances Control Act*. Washington, DC: General Accounting Office.

U.S. General Accounting Office. (1983a). *Delays in EPA's regulation of hazardous air pollutants*. Washington, DC: General Accounting Office.

U.S. General Accounting Office. (1983b). *Interim report on inspection, enforcement, and permitting activities at hazardous waste facilities*. Washington, DC: General Accounting Office.

U.S. General Accounting Office. (1984). *EPA could benefit from comprehensive management information on Superfund enforcement actions*. Washington, DC: General Accounting Office.

U.S. General Accounting Office. (1985a). *EPA's inventory of potential hazardous waste sites is incomplete*. Washington, DC: General Accounting Office.

U.S. General Accounting Office. (1985b). *Status of the Department of Energy's implementation of the Nuclear Waste Policy Act of 1982 as of December 31, 1984*. Washington, DC: General Accounting Office.

U.S. General Accounting Office. (1986). *EPA's strategy to control emissions of benzene and gasoline vapor: Air pollution*. Washington, DC: General Accounting Office.

Vig, N. J., & Kraft, M. E. (1984). Environmental policy from the seventies to the eighties. In N. J. Vig & M. E. Kraft (Eds.), *Environmental policy in the 1980s: Reagan's new agenda*. Washington, DC: Congressional Quarterly.

White, G. (1969). *Strategies of American Water Management*. Ann Arbor, MI: University of Michigan Press.

White, L. J. (1981). *Reforming regulation*. Englewood Cliffs, NJ: Prentice-Hall.

Zimmerman, R. (1980a). The administration of regulation (PB 80-223647). Springfield, VA: National Technical Information Service.

Zimmerman, R. (1980/1982). *The management of risk*. (Report to the National Science Foundation. 2 volumes and Executive Summary). New York: Graduate School of Public Administration, New York University.

Zimmerman, R. (1983). Risk assessment and environmental health. *Environmental Planning Quarterly, 3*, 5–7.

Zimmerman, R. (1985a). The environmental impact assessment process and urban development in New York City. *New York Affairs, 8*, 132–144.

Zimmerman, R. (1985b). The relationship of emergency management to government policies on man-made technological disasters. *Public Administration Review, 45*, 29–39.

COLLABORATING TO WIN

Donald B. Straus
American Arbitration Association

DISPUTES OVER UNDERSTANDING, NOT WINNING

This chapter discusses the need to understand an issue first, before trying to win a victory. There are two reasons for this focus. In the first place, there is already a rich literature on dispute resolution, almost all of it devoted to some variation of the adversarial system. It concentrates on how to win, or how to reach accommodation among those who are fighting to win. This is an important part of our lives as individuals, family members, workers, and as citizens of a community or nation, and therefore, much attention has been paid to the problems of winning and settling. Nothing that I say in this chapter is intended to deny this fact of life.

Second, I will argue that when it comes to matters of public health and the environment, it is initially more important to understand how the system works than to win, even from the essential perspective of self-interest. I make this declaration right from the start because it runs headlong into conventional wisdom and deep-seated American cultural patterns that winning is everything. The burden of the argument is on me. All I ask of the reader is to keep an open mind for the few minutes it takes to read this chapter.

We begin with a look at that whole mixed bundle of human feistiness that we label with many names.

WHY CONFLICTS OCCUR

This section briefly reviews the different types of conflicts and their origins, and examines them as a type of pathology that is subject to treatment.

271

Types and Origins of Conflicts

Conflicts come in many shapes and forms. If we are to make any progress in considering how they affect health and the environment, we must make careful distinctions among the many varieties of conflicts and what causes them. Consider this list of words that are often used interchangeably to mean conflict: disagreement, argument, controversy, dispute, debate, quarrel, strife, strike, row, brawl, war. I have arranged these words in an ascending scale of anger and violence.

An underlying basis for conflicts can result from differences about:

- how things work,
- how we can make them work better for us, or;
- how I can make them work better for me.

There is a crucial difference between conflicts over how a system works and over how we want it to work for our benefit. It is important to realize that if the consequences of a decision may be long-lasting and of great importance—as is frequently the case when we modify the delivery of public health or alter the environment, then it is in our self-interest to understand how the system works before we take up the cudgels for a favored course of action—even if it means collaborating with our "perceived" enemy to learn something new and unexpected about the system that we couldn't understand from our own resources. But such collaboration is not part of our present conventional wisdom.

One source of conflict about how things work is disagreement about facts, scientific theories, predictions, and the impacts of different solutions. These can be approached either with a desire to learn or a determination to win. It is not unusual for the "truth" to be tailored to fit a preconceived solution because of people's perceptions about how things work best for them.

Facts can be accepted, uncertain, or disputed:

- Accepted and undisputed facts: It is 10 o'clock. The temperature is 60°F. All fish were killed.
- Uncertain facts: When did an event occur? What temperature increase will damage fish?
- Disputed facts: A 10°F. increase in water temperature will kill all fish in 2 hours. A 15°F. increase will not harm fish in 14 hours.

Another source of conflict is over values and the linkages between values and analytical judgments. Until and unless we understand the roots from which values grow, they are usually impervious to analysis or reasoned debate. Closely related to values are attitudes about risks—the judgment of whether the hoped-for benefits of a course of action are worth the feared costs when both the benefits and the costs cannot be precisely determined.

Another useful distinction is whether the conflict is about: (1) the best way to increase the size of the pie, or (2) how to divide it. If the argument is about how best to augment environmental arrangements to produce more benefits and fewer costs than existed before the proposed action, then we are facing a problem that needs innovative thinking to find a solution. But if the conflict is over how to distribute an existing amount of benefits and costs, then the question is one of justice, ethics, fairness, or rights under the law. The legal system and its courts are best at reaching distributive judgments and interpretations of existing laws but are not very proficient at inventing new solutions outside the narrow adversarial boundaries of the issues presented to them. By custom, our adversarial society relies upon the courts for the settlement of both kinds of conflicts without much apparent awareness of their differences.

The time frame from which a participant views an issue can influence the nature of the conflict. If the time frame differs for different participants, matters can become much more complicated. Today's employment and profits are often in conflict with tomorrow's health and environmental quality. Some decisions must be made long in advance, such as the future of energy sources, health standards and accompanying costs in the design of a plant, or the desired population density of an urban complex. Some decisions can be made only after an event has occured, such as the means for cleaning up an oil spill or other disaster. One of the most difficult barriers to agreement is to reconcile different time frames of concern. Many disputes require trading a current and clearly perceived benefit for a future and dimly perceived cost.

The Pathology of Conflicts

I have spent most of my working life as a professional in conflict resolution, and I now believe that to focus on disputes isolated from the context in which they arose obscures more than it reveals and deflects attention away from the real objective. The creative process, in which conflicts are an incident, is making decisions. In this context, disputes are a pathological form of decision making and can be addressed much as physicians seek a cure for obesity. Many of the processes that cause a person to be fat are also essential to growth and survival. Survival and good health, not the elimination of the processes that turn food into fat, bone, and muscle, are the goals. Competition and argumentation are creative and extremely important to progress and evolution. They become pathological when those engaged in decision making stop searching for solutions and seek only to win at all costs.

Of course, in both the animal and human worlds, "pathological" disputes, as just defined, do occur. Animals will fight for territory and food for themselves when these essentials are too scarce to supply the needs of all. Otherwise, most animals typically find "solutions" for the distribution and division of food and territory through nonlethal methods. Even more rarely do animals engage in mortal combat with others of their own species. When they do, something has gone wrong with the environmental balance—there is a pathological condition in both the physical environment and in animal behavior that needs correction. For example, primates are normally peaceable creatures. They will posture, bare their teeth, and otherwise attempt to scare each other until they have established their organizational pecking order, but they will seldom injure one another. But if there is destruction to their forest habitat, lethal combat may follow until the population is reduced and a new organizational structure emerges that permits survival in the new environment (A. Carr, personal conversation, 1984).

Humans engage in competition and confrontation to achieve personal and/or group goals. Out of this competition and confrontation can come improved solutions for managing ourselves and our environment—in other words, progress and evolution. But humans also engage in extreme forms of adversarial combat even when there are no environmental constraints making such combat essential for survival. This behavior is pathological.

There are at least two plausible explanations for why humans engage in this kind of behavior and seek to win at all costs:

1. More often than not, the winner of such fights has in fact won—ending up with more of what was desired than if he or she had not fought at all or had lost;
2. Such fights, whether individual or national, have not yet threatened the survival of the human species—on the contrary, perhaps, they have even contributed to progress.

Self-centered adversarial behavior that focuses on a single issue becomes more serious when the results of such conflicts leave both combatants worse off, and when their survival, and that of many others not directly involved, is also threatened. When these conditions become evident, it is a challenge to human intelligence to invent procedures (cures, to continue the pathological analogue) for preventing harmful conflicts while preserving the benefits that result from the competition of ideas and energies.

There is an encouraging example of such a cure from labor relations history. Before World War II, there were many strikes over the firing of an employee or other forms of disciplinary action. These disputes, often directly involving only a few individuals, could shut down a whole plant or industry and, once the war was on, they could threaten the war effort as well. The War Labor Board developed a system of arbitration that required, whenever this kind of dispute arose (to be distinguished from disputes over wages or new contract terms that affected the whole plant) that it be submitted to an arbitrator for final and binding decision. So that arbitration benefited both parties directly involved as well as the war effort, the union agreed to give up the right to strike and management agreed to yield its unilateral right to make such decisions. Both union and management also agreed to accept the award of the arbitrator.

After the war, in a national labor-management conference, both sides agreed that conduct of American labor relations should henceforth be to submit all disputes of this kind to arbitration and to give up the right to strike or to take unilateral action for the duration of any existing contract. No laws were passed other than those to make such voluntary agreements final and binding once they were made, but the incorporation of arbitration and no-strike clauses in labor agreements became almost universal practice. This example illustrates how humans can redirect pathological and needlessly destructive disputes into constructive and relatively harmless confrontations.

Single-issue activism can become pathological in environmental conflicts. Citizen groups have coalesced on both sides of the clean air, nuclear energy, birth control, pure water, and many other issues. These ''single-issue activists'' have become powerful forces in our politics and in our decision-making processes. The resulting conflicts have had both constructive and destructive consequences. On the constructive side, environmentalists have forced an awareness of potential dangers that would otherwise have gone unnoticed until they became too far advanced for effective action. On the other hand the narrow focus and single purpose of some groups have all too often frustrated efforts to find holistic and comprehensive solutions that our complex society demands.

In our increasingly complex and technological society, there is an ever-present danger that understanding what is best for our self-interest will become buried under an overload of too much conflicting information and a resulting inability to examine the consequences of different choices logically. When confronted with more information than we can absorb, there is a tendency to resort to previous prejudices and intuition about parts of the problem with which we are most familiar and which seem of paramount importance rather than to face the seemingly hopeless task of trying to comprehend the complex web of interlocking issues. Before we will give up our adversarial instinct to win a victory that is based on limited knowledge, we must first be convinced that it is more in our self-interest in such matters to reach a rationally correct solution than to seek an instinctively desired but, in practical consequences, Pyrrhic victory. We must accept the obvious—but also culturally underrecognized—truth that it is the quality of the decision, not the winning of conflict, that should be our goal.

DISPUTE RESOLUTION PROCESSES

This section considers the major types of dispute management techniques and argues for a paradigm shift that will make collaboration and resolution key elements of decision making. Most disputes are settled through one of the major adversarial fora: the courts, administrative tribunals, or arbitration. A general characteristic of such procedures is that they are entered into only after negotiations have become deadlocked, the positions of the parties have become hardened, and the objective is to devise a fair division of the goods or issues in dispute.

Mediation is an old and honored method for resolving conflicts. The essential difference between mediation and arbitration is that an arbitrator has the power to make a decision, while a mediator must use his skills to get the parties to reach their own agreement.

A newer branch of adversarial conflict management can be found under the classification of ''alternate dispute resolution'' or ADL. These systems are designed to avoid crowded court calendars with their resulting delays, to minimize the increasing costs of litigation, and in part to reduce the adversarial atmosphere of the courts. A comprehensive listing of the literature of such procedures can be found in a bibliography of alternative dispute settlement methods compiled by the American Bar Association (Sanders & Snyder, 1982).

All these processes are a form of dispute settlement and assume that the participants are adversaries. Most of the literature about these adversarial kinds of conflict settlement are part of the larger body of legal literature.

Dispute resolution, a process of special interest in this chapter, seeks a mutually acceptable and beneficial solution to a common problem confronted by the parties. We will have more to say later about the distinction between settlement and resolution. The academic home of these developments has been the graduate schools of business administration and in the institutions where systems dynamics and public policy are taught. Quite often these have been developed as aids to decision making and not consciously designed for dispute settlement or avoidance. Only recently, and only by a few researchers, have their potential use in connection with conflicts been recognized.

THE DECISION CYCLE

Most people think of disputes in very personal terms: as a barrier set up by enemies or wrong-headed people between them and their goals. Disputes are ignored or avoided as long as possible; typically they are confronted at the end of the decision process, and then only if they effectively block the action that is desired.

Most of the disputes that concern the readers of this book are embedded in or are the result of a long period of analysis and decision making—a "Decision Cycle" that begins with the awareness of a problem, moves in stages through analysis, identification of participants, negotiations, conflict resolution, and eventually to a decision which, once again, produces problems. The cycle then begins all over again. When the decision cycle is long involves many parties and complex issues, early recognition and resolution of disputes is desirable. Differences about the definition of issues or goals, disagreement over what data to select or its validity, different interpretations of scientific evidence, who should participate, or where the meetings should be held are all examples of disputes that should be resolved as soon as possible. Each is capable of human understanding and solution but, if ignored or unnoticed when they first arise, they can accumulate into a large bundle of complex and intertwined conflicts, and become imbedded in the different packages of solutions advanced by adversarial parties. By then it is almost impossible to resolve them in the aggregate.

In the context of the decision cycle, the early resolution of such disputes can result in solutions that more accurately reflect the needs of the parties and more reliably predict their impacts. It converts dispute resolution into a constructive element in the entire decision process, giving an opportunity for the exercise of human ingenuity to find creative and mutually acceptable alternatives. More often, however, if the management of disputes is postponed until the negotiations have become deadlocked, analysis is muted by the pressures of time, emotional tensions, complexity overload, and political forces. There are no presently known or available techniques that can effectively manage a dispute at the end of the cycle involving complex issues. That is why we must recognize the frailty of the available dispute resolution techniques and employ them early in the cycle, when the issues and the controversies are less complex.

The participants in a conflict almost always feel an emotional involvement. The more personal the conflict, the higher the level of emotion. It is therefore often difficult to maintain a perspective that distinguishes between winning victories and reaching rational decisions. It really doesn't matter how you define "rational decision" other than one that satisfies the goals, needs, and expectations of the parties—excluding only the goal of defeating a person or group considered hostile or evil. In other words, the end is not simply winning, but deciding wisely. What is deceptive about this statement is that it sounds so logical, and yet it often runs counter to the emotions and motives that parties bring to the forum where decisions are to be made.

In my practice as a mediator, I often opened a meeting by asking the parties to consider each other as stupid, not evil. With this attitude, I explained, they would become constructive teachers rather than militant warriors. Surprisingly, this tactic often worked.

The importance of this distinction between the *settlement* of a conflict and its *resolution* cannot be overemphasized. Settlement results in a compromise of sorts that depends as much upon physical or political power as upon a rational judgment of what solution might make the system work best, while resolution produces a decision based upon creative problem-solving efforts. In matters as important and far reaching as public health and the environment, resolution of differences should be pursued as long as possible, with resort to settlement only when all other efforts have been exhausted.

A Needed Paradigm Shift

What has preceded may seem both idealistic and unrealistic. If so, this is a perception based on a world that *was*, rather than the world that we are now capable of making. Our inherited culture is predominantly adversarial, and our feisty and combative instincts have, on the whole, served us well as a species. But as our society has grown more complex, technical, crowded, and dependent, the rewards of winning have become diminished as the costs of poor decisions have increased. Many of us are beginning to realize the truth of this statement on an intellectual level, but most of us have not yet been able to make the emotional jump—the kind of mental leap that has been called a "paradigm shift."

Thomas Kuhn (1970) introduced the notion of a paradigm shift in his landmark book, *The Structure of Scientific Revolutions*. He defined a paradigm: "to be universally recognized scientific achievements that for a time provide model problems and solutions to a community of practitioners'' (p. viii).

Most of Kuhn's concern was with paradigms in the physical sciences, but he recognized that his concept also had relevance to political and social science. He made the linkage this way:

> Political revolutions are inaugurated by a growing sense, often restricted to a statement of the political community, that existing institutions have ceased adequately to meet problems posed by an environment that they have in part created. (Kuhn, 1970, p. 92)

It is in these terms that I see both the need and the emerging reality of a paradigm shift in decision making and conflict resolution. There is widespread recognition that the way we resolve conflicts is inadequate to the dimensions of the problems we confront. I have phrased the paradigm shift that I see as follows:

> In my self-interest, it is more important first to understand how the system works, even if it means that I must collaborate with perceived enemies to reach this understanding, than to win a victory based on my present, and perhaps inadequate, understanding of the system.

Collaboration and nonadversarial behavior have become ''in'' ideas in circles of new management theories. But the paradigm shift in the management of conflict arising from public health and environmental issues will not occur until and unless it is accepted both intellectually and emotionally as promoting self-interest. It is discouraging to observe how seldom this new ''paradigm'' is actually practiced. There is great interest in reading and hearing about it, and even of ''advocating'' the collaborative approach to others. But when it comes close to home, when the issues are ours, there is still strong, and understandable, resistance to trying something that seem so counterintuitive to our culture. We have been taught to win, we have been told that good guys finish last, and our heroes are more often bloodied than benign.

Acceptance of this paradigm shift would result in the following progression from first awareness of a problem to a decision:

- The current situation will be carefully analyzed. Every temptation to jump immediately to a solution and to get ready to fight for it at all costs will be resisted.
- All concerned participants will be identified, and arrangements will be made to seek their collaboration in resolving the issue.
- Goals will be discussed and formulated by all participants. Common goals will be listed. Where goals differ, distinctions will be made between those that involve different distribution of available resources, those that might be resolved through strategies for increasing the resources, those that result from different opinions of how the system works, and those that are rooted in different values and priorities.
- Facts and information useful to finding a solution will be identified, and attempts will be made to achieve as much agreement as possible. Where agreement cannot be reached, the differences will be narrowed through

further discussion. Attempts will also be made to see if some of the differences can be discarded because they have little impact on the outcomes.

- After there has been discussion about, and as much agreement as possible has been reached on, how the system works, on the goals of the participants, and on the underlying facts and information, then and only then will the parties begin to develop strategies for achieving their respective goals.
- A final step in the collaborative process will be to attempt to select a mutually acceptable solution to the problem. Only when and if this cannot be fully achieved:
- Adversarial processes will begin, and maximum efforts to win on the remaining issues will be made. But if the previous steps have been followed, the adversarial debates and power struggles will take place on a foundation of far greater understanding of the system by all of the participants, there will be less likelihood of serious mistakes that will harm the whole society, and the intensity of conflict should be reduced.

An important difference between this idealized description of decision making and what now occurs is that in the collaborative process adversarial attitudes, behavior, and actions are minimized until as much understanding and agreement as possible has been achieved through collaboration.

COLLABORATION IN THE DECISION-MAKING PROCESS

By now it must be evident that for the purposes of this chapter, I view dispute management as part of, and subordinate to, the decision process. Without this perspective there is grave danger that our energies will be absorbed by adversarial posturing and unnecessary combat that at best will delay the achievement of objectives and at worst will increase the barriers to be overcome before our goals can be reached. But again I must stress that this does not mean that fighting the opposition is no longer necessary—only that there is far more of it being done now than is necessary, to the detriment of all. What it *does* mean is that we should try the nonadversarial methods first, and we should be clear what we are doing and with what tools.

Let is begin with an illustration. Several years ago I was asked to help manage a conference of environmentalists, industrialists, and government officials for the discussion of some amendments to the Clean Air Act. As usual in such meetings, emotions were running high as we convened, and there was an atmosphere of mutual distrust. There was, however, every expectation that some legislation would be enacted and a strong desire to reach some formula that would "satisfice," if not satisfy. There was a readiness to try a "paradigm shift" toward collaboration if only some nonthreatening method could be found for doing so without yielding basic principles or giving up perceived bargaining advantages.

After a brief discussion of the differences between collaborative and adversarial approaches, the group agreed that there were a number of factual issues in dispute, mostly about recent research findings on the impacts of acid rain on the lakes of the northeastern states. It was further agreed that it would be in everyone's interest to seek as much information and understanding about this new research without letting such investigation become part of the adversarial bargaining process. To emphasize this distinction further, we agreed that the collaborative investigation of the research findings should be conducted in a room in which all participants sat in a semicircle facing a board on which the scientists and experts could display their information. There would be no assigned seating, and all participants would interact primarily with the experts and not with each other. Then, when we had gone as far as possible with a mutual search for new or improved information on a specific topic, the group would reassemble in their teams of industrialists, environmentalists, and government officials in another room arranged in more conventional fashion to accommodate frankly adversarial negotiations.

The results were quite satisfactory. The group moved back and forth between these two rooms over the course of the 3-day conference. More progress was made, in the opinion of most of the participants, toward better understanding and some measure of agreement than could have been accomplished had we remained in an "adversarial configuration." The skills of problem-solving facilitation were employed in the collaborative room, and the skills of mediation and negotiation were dominant in the adversarial room. A simple recognition that the skills and behavioral attitudes of the parties were different under these different conditions, and that more progress could be made toward *resolution* in the collaborative mode and more toward *settlement* in the adversarial mode, seemed to be beneficial.

Managing Complexity

Complexity is a great breeding ground for conflict. It interferes with an ability to consider alternatives—there are just too many variables for human manipulation. To comprehend an issue, we must either use mechanical aids or oversimplify the problem. The danger in the use of mechanical aids, such as computers or other forms of system analysis, is that the inputs for building a model of the system are in themselves subject to different values and preconceived ideas of how the system works. If both the inputs and the resulting outputs are different and are used adversarially, this will obscure an understanding of the issues and will increase the polarity of the parties.

There is also danger in oversimplification without the use of mechanical aids. When our mind faces too much complexity, it must perform its own mechanics of aggregation, and it will use inputs that are rooted in previous experiences, prejudices, and beliefs. We often leap to conclusions without fully understanding, ourselves, just what were the components that our minds assembled subliminally.

When two parties confront each other with highly simplified, aggregated concepts of how the system does work and what the solutions should be, whether these aggregations were achieved with conscious use of complexity-managing aids or with the unconscious hunches and intuition of the mind, logical discussion is difficult. Analysis requires examination of the parts, and no matter whether the parts are embedded in the subliminal recesses of the brain or in the hidden program of a computer model, the ensuing dialogue over a controversial issue is unlikely to produce understanding or agreement.

Rivlin (1971, p. 1) has addressed the problem of decision making amid complexity by suggesting, "one has to have sufficient faith in rationality to believe that analysis of a problem generally leads to a better decision." Then she warns of the danger of oversimplification in the use of rationality:

> Single measures of social service performance should be avoided. They will always lead to distortion, stultification, cheating to "beat the system" and other undesirable results.—Health service systems cannot be judged simply and solely by the number of patients treated or by the number of patients cured or even by health problems prevented.—Multiple measures are necessary to reflect multiple objectives and to avoid distorting performance.—One can imagine health programs developing a variety of measures of health status and satisfaction of patients, also with different time lags. (Rivlin, 1971, p. 142)

To provide such measures for managing complexity, and to avoid the oversimplification of aggregated prejudices and preconceived ideas of how things work, we must employ mind-aiding tools. The most powerful of such tools now at our disposal is the computer if—and this is a critical *if*—it is used collaboratively and not as an adversarial weapon. Jointly designed and used computer models can be effective tools for helping the participants understand a complex system. If used adversarially, they can be devastatingly effective weapons for obfuscating the interactions of the system being studied, and for freezing adversarial positions. Such use can result in a "battle of the print-out."

When entered collaboratively, computer modeling provides abundant opportunity during the design stages to identify and resolve early conflicts. Disputes will of course arise over the details, and even the basic design, of the model. But these will be smaller, more human-sized, comprehensive, and presumably more easily resolved than those resulting from the use of competing models. While it is unlikely that a totally acceptable single model will be achieved, the process itself will produce a more complete understanding of the underlying differences and assumptions, and a better chance to resolve them, than would otherwise be possible.

Collaborative computer modeling adds another dimension to the management of complexity: an ability to "zoom" from a macro perspective of the problem as a whole to a detailed examination of any one of its parts. This permits the parties to look holistically at the interrelated parts and the impacts of different strategies on the whole model. If there are details that puzzle them or are in dispute, they can zoom down to that part of the model, where the problem can be discussed in a humanly manageable dimension. After gaining better understanding of that part, or resolving a dispute over how it works, the new understandings or agreements can be reinserted into the model, and then the parties can zoom back up for another holistic look to see how their new agreements impact on the whole or any of its other parts. This process helps avoid the twin dangers of oversimplification based on aggregated prejudice and intuition, and overcomplication based on analytical but serial observations of bits of the problem without a capacity to integrate them into the holistic model.

Science-Based Conflicts

When scientists disagree, the warring tribes of single-issue activists have a field day. In almost any debate over an important and complex issue it is possible to find scientists with impeccable credentials who will support a favored course of action. With few exceptions, scientists argue from convictions based on their research. There are many reasons why good scientific research can result in different conclusions. Often questions that scientists address differ in ways that are understandable to scientists but difficult for laymen, who are the decision makers, to grasp. The data chosen or available to each may also be different. There are many other possible causes for variations in the findings. Scientists differ in training, in attitudes toward some types of mathematical and other methods, and in their values. Under these conditions, it is easy for those who espouse one side or another to find a "hired gun" scientist who will champion their cause with complete integrity. For the lay decision maker in a legislature or a regulatory agency, or for the average citizen, such disputes are particularly troublesome and confusing. There is a very human tendency under such circumstances to retreat to prior convictions or even prejudices—both because there are no conclusive reasons not to do so and because it is a far easier course of action than to try to understand the mysteries of the particular science involved.

There have been a number of efforts to clarify scientific controversy for the lay decision maker. Various procedures have been written into recent legislation for this purpose. The environmental impact statement in the National Environmental Policy Act (NEPA) is one example. Another is the process used by the National Academy of Sciences (NAS) to convene top scientists of the nation to study and publish their findings on controversial issues of importance. The Office of Technology Assessment (OTA) undertakes scientific studies and interpretations for members of Congress. Others have suggested various versions of a science court composed of qualified but supposedly uncommitted experts to hear scientific adversaries argue for their different views. The science court would issue an explanation of why the views of reputable scientists differ and suggest what can be accepted with some confidence as "truth" under the present state of the scientific art, and finally suggest what are the probabilities of "truth" where there is little hard scientific evidence. These efforts produced a good deal of the information that was presented in the first part of the book. The NAS, in particular, in recent years has produced important reports on the following topics: diet and cancer, synthetic organic chemicals in public water supplies, hazardous waste management, biotechnology, acid rain, and ionizing radiation. These studies have not necessarily led to changes in government policies, but they have provided realistic assessments of what is known about many life-style, occupational, and ambient environmental risks.

Furthermore, communications between scientists and the average citizen have been notoriously bad. The task of translating science into language that the layman can comprehend is of course difficult, but the difficulty is increased many fold by the adversarial setting in which most efforts have been tried. The Council for the Advancement of Science Writing (CASW) has begun a major effort to deal with the scientist-public communication problem by offering programs to journalists on how to improve their reporting of public health and environmental stories. Part of this effort consists of having scientists and journalists discuss how reporters can isolate findings of fact, possible fact, and value. For example, the editor of this book has spoken to journalists about how to do this with environmental cancer studies. The same thing has been done with acid rain, dioxin, and many other subjects. These meetings have been videotapped and will be distributed to schools of journalism. The effectiveness of the CASW and similar efforts to inform those who inform the public cannot be judged at this time.

Closely related to scientific conflicts is the problem of risk assessment. There is almost no decision of importance that can be made without determining what the risks are and whether they are worth taking. This too is important ground for the most intransigent kinds of adversarial conflict.

Risk assessment has become a science itself. Among the techniques used to measure risks and benefits that can help in reaching a decision are:

- Cost-benefit analysis: to help judge how much the risk is worth taking.
- Comparison with national standards: to compare this risk with ambient levels, with the permissible levels in other localities, nations, or industries.
- Expressed preference techniques: to ask people what risks are acceptable to them.
- Revealed preference techniques: to ask individuals if they think projected risk levels are higher than current levels.

Related to risk assessment is "technology assessment" providing information about alternative futures. Both risk and technology forecasting have a high element of uncertainty, and when faced with uncertainty, experts can be expected to disagree as often and as violently as the rest of society. The acceptable level of risk is a value that must be made through the political process, but just who within this process does this is not always clear. The government has many bureaus charged with making such decisions: the Nuclear Regulatory Commission for atomic safety, the Federal Aviation Agency for aircraft safety, the Food and Drug Administration for supervising the safety of edibles and pharmaceuticals, the Consumer Product Safety Commission for product safety, the Occupational Safety and Health Administration for worker protection, the Environmental Protection Agency, and many others. But with increasing frequency citizen groups have been dissatisfied with the laxity of official judgments, and industrial groups often complain when the rulings seem too restrictive. This dissatisfaction has been one of the reasons for an increasing demand for direct participation in the governmental decision process by ordinary citizens and citizen groups. We will return to this theme in more detail later.

Putting It All Together

When we try to analyze a complex issue, we are forced to think about it serially, one relatively simple piece at a time. This is how our minds work—we cannot *consciously* think about more than half a dozen variables at one time. But when we make decisions, the *subconscious* mind takes over, and there are literally millions of separate "processes" that may be involved. This puts a special burden on rational conflict resolution. Our means of communication, through both conversation and the written word, is also a serial string of thoughts and ideas, and most of the tools we have developed for aiding us in analytical efforts have similar characteristics. Waldrop (1984, p. 802) touched on this dichotomy between the way we think and the way we decide:

> A neuron is very slow compared to a microchip, but the brain makes millions or billions of neuronal calculations simultaneously and in parallel; our current generation of serial, one-step-at-a-time computers are hopelessly outclassed.—Whatever is going on within our skulls when we learn something or when we figure something out, whatever is involved in recognition and memory, it is not a series of neuronal if-then statements.

Herbert A. Simon (1983) deals with this problem at some length in *Reason in Human Affairs*. He notes that our political institutions must attend to big problems one at a time. Therefore, important and controversial questions require that both the legislators and the voters must direct their attention to one issue at a time. But in complex matters like environmental protection, this can be a serious block to good analysis because the preservation of the environment cannot be reasonably considered without also taking into consideration the energy needs of the country, employment, and the economy, and other related matters. Our human propensity, based on the way we think analytically, is to concentrate on one issue while neglecting the others. As Simon puts it:

> In the context of our political institutions, it seems difficult to remember that a society may have more than one pressing problem at a time. . . . Both political faddishness and one-issue politics stem from the same underlying cause: people's inability to think about a lot of things at once. As a consequence, political institutions that are supposed to be dealing with a whole range of problems in the society sometimes have great difficulty in giving them balanced attention. (pp. 80, 82)

There is a growing recognition of the need for tools to assist us in managing, at the conscious level, many variables and interconnected issues. Fortunately, there are also a growing number of such tools being developed. In addition to computers, new techniques such as operations research, systems analysis, management sciences, mathematical game theory, and many others make possible the simultaneous manipulation of many variables. Almost all these tools rely on quantitative or mathematical expressions of the factors and variables, and this is just where they seem (at least superficially) to depart from the way we traditionally have made decisions. What goes on in the brain when the time comes to make a decision is, as we have noted, largely subconscious and therefore difficult to get at with reasoned argument or analysis. Those who advocate the use of more rational procedures are often rebuffed with the worldly put-down that values, power, and politics are the final arbiters and that any process that fails to take into account these "intangibles" is a waste of time and energy and will be ineffective.

Even if we could make more explicit and rational some of the subconscious reasons that make people differ over the way the system works, and therefore what strategies for change should be adopted, would this make the resolution of conflict and the pathway to good and reasoned decisions any easier? There are some who say that such explicit exposure of the subconscious "reasons" underlying conflict would only make the conflict more difficult to reconcile, that many settlements were more easily achieved because the underlying causes were successfully obfuscated.

Others however believe that any technique that can help us make more explicit the working of our own intuitive convictions and beliefs, and of those with whom we are involved in reaching decisions, would be more helpful than harmful. As we increase our physical ability to change the environment for better or worse, we must seek to be more conscious, analytical, and collaborative in how we go about doing it. Bad decisions, reached in the search for some compromise to avoid or terminate conflict, are also bad bargains as well.

Not to seek as much rationality as possible is irresponsible. But not to recognize that there are important emotional, political, and other "intangible" concerns of the parties is blind and stupid. We must do both, and do both better.

No matter how hard we try to achieve rationality in the decision process, there will always remain a hard core of irreconcilable values. One view, expressed well by Eric Ashby (1978), is that hunches are, in the end, the final determining factor in people's decisions:

> There is copious literature on decision theory under conditions of uncertainty, but most of it deals only with very simple problems, and I do not think it is of much use to those who have to make complex policy decisions. My impression is that at this stage of the chain reaction, in everything from environmental politics to the making of foreign policy, the politician relies on *hunch* (though he may dignify the process by calling it political judgement). (p. 73)

I agree that hunch and intuition may appear to be, or even are, dominant. What is important for our purpose is to identify as precisely as possible what are the different value judgments and beliefs that produce the hunches, so that these can be discussed and resolved with as much good information and analysis as possible. This requires the application of our best genetically evolved human endowments aided by the most powerful complexity-managing tools and systems that we can develop.

Resistance to analytical and collaborative efforts to resolve disputes stems from a belief that hunches and intuition are unrelated to rational thought and that the wrong-headed, or even evil, views of our opponents are not subject to reasoned discussion. But Ashby (1978, p. 78), who earlier in his book seemed to minimize reasoned judgment, later suggests that values (and presumably hunches as well) are not random motivations to decisions that float around inside our brain, but are the products of prior decisions and experiences:

> If you study the history of political decisions about the environment, or, for that matter, decisions about some other social issues, you find that there are no new Jerusalems at the end of the road; goals for society are redefined by the process of choice every time a choice is made. This is notably true for the politics of protecting people's health. Each political decision implants a choice into our system of social values; this imperceptibly changes the system of values, and this in turn effects the next choice.

Eric Kandel (in Lavigne, 1983) reports findings that the brain can be *physically* changed by experience. In this sense, he believes that the brain has some similarity to the computer because:

> The brain is a precisely wired device that performs a series of logical operations on the input it receives from a variety of sensory receptors. But as a biological computer, it differs from an electronic computer in at least two critical ways: The brain is remarkably plastic—it is capable of changing its performance and even its strategies as a result of experience. (p. 16)

This confirms my own hunch (based of course on experience!), that when parties in a dispute are willing to explore the underlying reasons and assumptions for their differences, rather than arguing on an aggregated level that expresses only their strong convictions and beliefs, they can often both understand the underlying causes for their dispute as well as develop some inventive and new ideas for resolving it. Their joint efforts and shared experiences change their hunches as well as their analytical reasoning.

We must, however, temper our zeal in searching for rationality and logic with the recognition that uncertainty and unknown risks will always be present. Never was this better expressed than in the report of the licensing board (in the matter of Consolidated Edison Company) that heard one phase of the Indian Point No. 2 plant dispute involving an atomic plant on the banks of the Hudson River in New York state (Public Interest Law, 1978):

> No one knows in detail what activities of life go on in the unseen depths of the Hudson River nor what the future response to changing inputs is going to be. Under these conditions the experts are free to choose those assumptions which best fit their beliefs about what may go on, and the arguments that follow produce thousands of pages of testimony and documents without providing answers that can be agreed upon, or that can give clear guidance to a Board.

Under circumstances like these, collaborative attitudes will recognize the uncertainties and will frankly admit that hunches and estimates of risks must dominate the decision making process. Adversarial attitudes will masquerade beliefs and hunches as scientific truths. The more critical the issue, the more dangerous this masquerading becomes. Ignorance masquerading as knowledge is far more dangerous than ignorance itself.

Third Party Assistance

Third party, or impartial, assistance is typically used for the resolution of disputes near the end of the decision cycle when the positions have become hardened and emotions are running high. Most of these procedures are also designed to manage conflict under adversarial conditions. This is, of course, true of the traditional legal processes of the courts and of the various tribunals found in administrative agencies. It also applies to most of the informal procedures such as mediation, conciliation, arbitration, or fact-finding.

Facilitation, one of the newer concepts of impartial intervention, is concerned with the management of the decision cycle from start to finish, including keeping a meeting on track and moving constructively, selecting and using appropriate tools for assisting in the management of complexity or other requirements of analysis, identifying potential disputes, or invoking the appropriate dispute-resolution measures.

The appropriateness of third party assistance will depend in part on where the parties are on the adversarial-collaborative spectrum. Courts, arbitration, and conciliation are typically used to resolve disputes among adversaries. Facilitation, ombudsmen, and fact-finding are most often used when the parties are ready to collaborate. Mediation, though typically used for adversarial situations, can be used at any point along this spectrum.

There are many books written about third party conflict resolution. Almost all have been written either for, or from the viewpoint of, third party professionals. Since this book is written for practitioners in quite different fields, it will be more valuable to examine the third party function from the viewpoint of participants in a dispute. We can get at this by asking five questions:

- How was third party assistance invoked?
- Who is the third party?
- Is this intervention good for our side?
- How can I use this process for our side?
- How can we use this process to help us—to collaborate?

Third parties enter conflicts in several ways. The most common way is for a third party, usually an arbitrator empowered to hand down a final and binding decision, to enter the dispute at the demand of one party under the provisions of an arbitration clause in an existing contract. Since this procedure must have been voluntarily agreed to at the time the contract was negotiated, such intervention was anticipated and is presumed by law to have been accepted by the parties in preference to either a lawsuit, a strike, or other form of adversarial behavior. Under these conditions, both federal and state laws will enforce the agreement to arbitrate, and will also enforce compliance with the decision of an arbitrator.

But this kind of intervention is rarely applicable to the kinds of issues that are the subject of this book. There is seldom a previously existing contract, there are almost always more than two parties, and there is seldom mutual acceptance of either the notion of submitting a dispute to final and binding arbitration, or exactly who that arbitrator might be.

If there is intervention, it usually comes in the form of mediation, fact-finding, or some other form of impartial assistance with a mandate only to seek agreement through persuasion leading to some mutually agreeable solution. Sometimes the impartial person is appointed by a high government official who, at the same time, seeks the cooperation of the parties in the public interest. Much less frequently one of the parties may seek impartial assistance and, in so doing, attempts to persuade the other participants to join the process. This is infrequent, because if one party seeks such assistance, the other parties might interpret the action as weakness. The less adversarial the attitude of the parties, the more likely that such spontaneous and party-initiated intervention will occur. What does occur, however, more frequently, is a less formal kind of mediatory intervention by a representative of one of the participants. Not infrequently, an individual of stature will remove himself to some extent from his own constituency and play an unofficial, and often unrecognized, role of peacemaker.

When a third party does begin to act in one of these roles, his or her identity is of paramount importance to each of the parties involved. Sometimes such a person is a professional "impartial," although again this is rare in the kinds of disputes we are discussing. More often it is a person with great knowledge and reputation in matters over which the dispute arose. In a public health conflict, it could be a prominent doctor, a former commissioner of health from some government agency, or a professor. In an environmental dispute it could be anyone with special expertise in either public administration or in one of the issues in dispute. Of course the person must always be someone considered impartial by all parties.

The greatest need for third party intervention is at the local government level because there are too few unbiased technical experts at the town, city, and county scales. The earlier chapters in this book provide a wide selection of current disputes that might be resolved with a better or at least more credible decision with intervention by impartial parties: smoking in public places, providing alcohol to minors at parties, the advantages and disadvantages of removing asbestos from schools, locating hazardous waste management facilities, and locating municipal solid waste incineration facilities.

The image of impartiality is very subjective. A participant in a conflict should be careful not to assume that the designated impartial person is biased against his side before seeing evidence of it in the specific case in which he is involved. This advice is particularly applicable if the impartial person is appointed by a high government official, and it is inevitable that the mediation process will begin with this individual playing the impartial role. In this event, it is wise to behave toward the impartial person as though indeed he or she were without bias. Individuals who are asked to assume this role usually take their responsibility seriously, subordinating previous experience or prejudice as they seek to fulfill their duties. Parties who might at first consider themselves to be at a disadvantage because of the identity of the appointed impartial could find that, in his effort to "lean over backwards," he favors them more than the other parties. This potential advantage, if indeed it does exist, could be jeopardized by an antagonistic attitude.

The question of whether or not intervention is good for your side is natural, but it is difficult to answer in advance with any assurance. The dynamics of mediation in any one of its many forms tends to increase the power of the weaker parties and diminish the power of the most powerful. On the other hand, since agreement must be voluntary and cannot be imposed, the more powerful participants have the right to refuse a solution if they think they can continue to resist and win by other means. When powerful parties accept a mediated settlement and claim they were unfairly pressured into doing so, the more accurate statement in most cases is that, through the process of mediation, they perceived the need to settle because of public relations, because they had less power than they had previously thought, or because there were other outside forces of which they were previously unaware—any or all of these reasons would have made the settlement inevitable under any conditions. The lesson is this: If you think that mediation is bad for your side and you can successfully oppose it, it may well be your duty to try. But once the process becomes inevitable, resistance is usually counterproductive.

This last statement clearly suggests an answer to the question of how mediation can be used to the best advantage for one's own side. Cooperation with the mediator, under most circumstances, is advisable. It is usually unwise to maintain an unreasonably rigid position or to advance patently specious arguments. But a cautionary note must be added: The timing of concessions is of paramount importance. If too much is given too quickly, both your own position and that of the mediator are undermined. For this reason, it is best to work with the mediator and to seek his or her guidance about when, in the light of what the opposition is saying, a concession should be made. It is often possible to link a concession to something that you wish to receive in return. Then, if the mediator does not come back with what you demanded in return for your offer, you are free to withdraw it. These maneuvers require both frankness with and confidence in the mediator. If both are not possible, mediation that can result in benefit to your side is also probably not possible. Under these conditions, it may be advisable either to withdraw from the mediation process or to seek to repudiate the impartiality of the appointed mediator. But these are dangerous tactics and should be adopted only as a last resort.

There is one other condition under which third party intervention occurs, and it requires a different kind of strategy. Sometimes there is either an agreement or just the likelihood that if mediation fails, the dispute will be submitted to some form of binding resolution. It could be that the dispute would go to arbitration, to a legislature for final determination, or to the courts. Under these conditions, it might be advisable not to give to the mediator the ultimate concession you are willing to yield, but rather to withhold something that the arbitrator or other outside final decision maker can use to "sweeten" the package. There are no easy formulae for choosing the correct tactics. Each situation must be judged separately.

All these situations assume adversarial behavior and attitudes by the parties.

Whenever there is a willingness to collaborate in a joint effort to understand the issues and to find mutually acceptable and effective solutions, then third party assistance moves from the role of mediator to that of facilitator. A mediator seeks a mutually acceptable compromise among adversarial parties, acting as a kind of umpire. A facilitator helps the parties to move toward a mutually advantageous solution as a kind of coach. Since the facilitator's role is primarily applicable to parties who are willing to collaborate, his appointment is generally a cooperative effort as well. Intervention by a facilitator, as we have previously discussed, can come at the very beginning of the decision cycle. One of his important roles is to identify at an early stage smaller disputes as the decision cycle moves along its course. No cycle will be purely collaborative throughout; there will always be a mixture of collaborative and adversarial activities. The intervention of facilitators, and the roles they play, is still uncommon. It will only become more prevalent when and if the desire to understand and to invent dominates the present preference to fight and to win.

Citizen Involvement

As a nation, we are going through an identity crisis. Are we a representative democracy that elects decision makers and then lets them make the decisions, or are we a direct democracy that gives the decision power to the individual citizen as expressed through majority vote? We are, of course, a mixture of both systems, and we obscure clear thinking about this question if we pose it in either/or terms. But it is one that needs to be addressed because we often act as if both methods are available to suit our immediate preferences.

We must improve the linkages between citizen participation and the decision process of government. Without such linkages, it will be increasingly difficult to implement changes that will reconcile the long- and short-term interests of the entire nation rather than reflect only its more powerful or vocal parts. Exclusive reliance on the traditional methods of balancing the various interests through lobbies, single-issue groups, and fragmentation of the parts have proven to be inadequate as the levels of technology and complexity increase. At the same time, a simple reliance upon the "will of the majority" as expressed in periodic votes is also inadequate. Yes/no, win/lose ballots cast by inadequately informed citizen-generalists at widely spaced intervals fail to meet the rigorous demands of decision making as we approach the twenty-first century. The tyranny of an ill-informed majority can be as devastating as the tyranny of a despot. As we survey the possible reforms for more effective citizen participation, we should seek procedures that:

- Clearly distinguish and help make choices between direct citizen participation at various stages in the decision cycle and other kinds of participation such as referenda, polls, and the election of representatives.
- Choose criteria for determining at what level citizen participation should

occur for different kinds of decisions (e.g., educational policies, zoning regulation, immigration policies, international affairs).

- Encourage citizens to remain engaged and responsible rather than becoming "drop-outs" or reverting to single-issue participation.
- Assist generalist citizens to gain an understanding of the technical aspects that should be considered in judging alternative actions for a specific issue.
- Allow citizen access to information in ways that will be understandable and will help them select pertinent information without becoming overloaded.
- Provide citizens with both intellectual and emotional simulated experience for judging the impacts of various solutions when trial and error experiments seem inappropriate or too dangerous.
- Help manage complexity in various ways including: early participation in defining issues and goals, aids in "zooming" from manageable chunks of information to a holistic and aggregated view of the whole issue.
- Help participants and facilitators identify those stages in the decision cycle most appropriate for different kinds of discussion, negotiation and ways of managing complexity, and particularly the differences between the uses of adversarial and collaborative processes.

POINTS TO REMEMBER

1. There is an important difference between understanding how things work and how to distribute the things the system can provide.

2. There is an important difference between the short-run interests of a few and the long-run interests of both that few and the community as a whole.

3. There is a need for collaboration and complexity management tools to resolve conflicts over understanding.

4. There is the likelihood that conflicts of values, beliefs, emotions, and ethics may have rational roots that are often hidden in the subconscious recesses of the mind but that, if uncovered, could be more easily resolved.

5. There is a role for the ordinary citizen as a balancing force in the decision-making process, and the complementary need for improved methods of communication and education to create of our citizenry a majority elite.

6. Lastly, the most important point to remember is the paradigm shift that states:

> In my self-interest, it is more important first to understand how the system works, even if it means that I must collaborate with perceived enemies to reach this understanding, than to win a victory based on my present, and perhaps inadequate, understanding of the system.

This chapter on conflict resolution deliberately ignored traditional methods of litigation and the many new alternate dispute resolution techniques that include arbitration and mediation. These will surely continue to be the dominant methods for resolving adversarial conflicts. But as the inevitable growth in the complexity of our society continues, their use in helping determine new directions for technology will decline.

There is an old saying that if you change anything by three orders of magnitude, it isn't the same thing any more. These are assuredly the dimensions of change in health and environmental issues through which we are passing.

For conflict resolution to remain effective, it needs to change as well. It has as yet changed very little in comparison to the technological revolution, and therefore has a lot of catching up to do. The new ideas and attitudes suggested in this chapter will surely need much testing and modification before they will be widely applicable, but if they serve only to stimulate some new thinking and experimentation among those who must make the decisions, then this chapter will have served a useful purpose.

References

Ashby, E. (1978). *Reconciling man with the environment*. Leon Sloss, Jr., Memorial Lectures. Palo Alto, CA: Stanford University Press.

Kuhn, T. (1970). *The structure of scientific revolutions* (2nd ed., Vol. 2). Chicago: University of Chicago Press.

Lavigne, M. (1983, December). The secret mind of the brain. *Columbia—The Magazine of Columbia University*, p. 16.

Public Interest Law, 1978, 187.

Rivlin, A. (1971). *Systematic thinking for social action*. Washington, DC: The Brookings Institution.

Sanders, F., & Snyder, F. (1982). *Alternative methods of dispute settlement: A selected bibliography*. Washington, DC: American Bar Association, Division of Public Service Activities.

Simon, H. A. (1983). *Reason in human affairs*. Palo Alto, CA: Stanford University Press.

Waldrop, M. (1984). Artificial intelligence. *Science, 223*, 802.

C H A P T E R   1 0

EDUCATION-FOR-HEALTH
Strategies for Change

Audrey R. Gotsch
University of Medicine and Dentistry of New Jersey
Robert Wood Johnson Medical School

Clarence E. Pearson
National Center for Health Education

At the turn of the twentieth century, communicable diseases, such as influenza, pneumonia, tuberculosis, and diarrhea and its related diseases, were the primary threats to one's health in the United States (see Chapter 1). The health education strategy was primarily didactic—telling people what to do, giving information—responding to the teachable moment when an individual was suffering from or threatened with an illness. The information tended to be very specific to the communicable disease, and the treatment plan was designed for short-range compliance. The function of the health professional tended to be providing information, since descriptions of health matters at that time were rarely available in print format for the nonprofessional.

The concept of an education-for-health program has changed from a short-range goal of assisting an individual through a relatively brief illness to a long-range goal of helping people prevent debilitating illness like heart disease, cancer, stroke, or accidents, the leading causes of death (Bowman, 1982). Education-for-health is now recognized as a national, even international, priority to improve the quality of people's lives and also to reduce the high cost of treatment (Hamburg, 1983). Perhaps the greatest support for education-for-health was the 1977 Resolution (WHA30.43) of the World Health Organization (WHO) urging that "the main social target of Governments and WHO in the coming decades should be the attainment by all the citizens of the world, by the year 2000, of a level of health that will permit them to lead a socially and economically productive life" (Mahler, 1983, p. 11). To achieve this goal, education-for-health was identified as an important strategy.

Education-for-health has become critical because the public's awareness and concern regarding the potential health impact of the presence of toxic substances in the workplace as well as the community has greatly increased during the past decade. The litany of chemicals appears endless with the toxic substance of the month frequently appearing on the front page of community newspapers. The focus in spring 1984 was on EDB (ethylene dibromide), a pesticide routinely used to fumigate citrus fruit and grain until the chemical was identified in drinking water and food products. The chemical making the headlines in 1983 was dioxin, a contaminant found in many chemical products such as Agent Orange. The list of toxic substances suspected or known to cause cancer and often other health or environmental damage stretches back over the past decade and includes such familiar items as the pesticide DDT, the artificial sweeteners cyclamate and saccharin, the synthetic hormone DES, consumer products such as hair dyes and children's night-clothes treated with Tris, and yes, even steaks cooked to perfection over the backyard grill.

In addition to the ever-present chemicals that alarm consumers, one is also faced with what appears to be conflicting advice regarding the prevention of chronic illnesses as discussed in Chapter 2. During the late 1970s and early 1980s, the consumer was informed that adults should severely restrict cheese and other dairy products from their diet only to learn in 1984 that such restrictions may be upsetting the delicate electrolyte balance in their bodies. Conflicting information also appears in the press regarding other life-style choices such as the advocated reduction in the use of sodium (particularly table salt) as one nonpharmacological approach for the treatment of hypertension (elevated blood pressure) or the daily consumption of a glass of wine to reduce the risk of a heart attack.

As a result of a heightened awareness of many potentially hazardous elements in the work and community environments as well as conflicting data concerning life-style choices, a concerned public is frequently bewildered by the differing points of views expressed by a variety of scientists as well as conflicting interest groups. The consumer at this point can either become defeated, giving in to the feeling of powerlessness over factors which appear to be beyond one's control, or seek strategies that can assist in the development of programs designed to address either individual or community needs.

Chapter 10 has been written for those unwilling to give in to factors that sometimes appear to be beyond one's control. To assist in understanding the development of education-for-health in the United States, the chapter begins with an overview of education-for-health and the agencies that have evolved to support the effort. This is followed by a discussion of the usual settings selected for education-for-health interventions with illustrations of specific strategies that are having an impact on individual behaviors.

THE CASE FOR EDUCATION-FOR-HEALTH, IMPROVED LIFE-STYLES, AND ENVIRONMENTAL PROTECTION

The 1970s produced the first strong epidemiological evidence of the relationship of life-style to health status. N. B. Belloc and Lestor Breslow (1972) published the results of their 5½-year study of the health habits of nearly 7,000 adults in Alameda County, California. For the first time life expectancy and improved health could be significantly linked to the observance of seven common health habits. The habits were:

- Drink in moderation (no more than 4 alcoholic drinks at one time)
- Sleep 7–8 hours each night
- No eating between meals
- Moderate physical exercise (such as swimming or taking long walks)
- Maintain weight at normal level
- Usually eat breakfast
- Never smoke cigarettes

The data revealed that a 45-year-old man could expect to live another 21.6 years (to age 67) if he practiced three or fewer of these habits or have an additional life expectancy of 33.1 years (to age 78) if he practiced six to seven of these health habits. It was noted that "the magnitude of this difference of more than 11 years is better understood if we consider that the increase in the life expectancy of white men in the United States between 1900 and 1960 was only 3 years" (Belloc, 1973, p. 79). In addition, "those who reported all or many of the good practices were in better physical health, even though older, than those who followed fewer such habits. These relationships were independent of economic status" (Belloc & Breslow, 1972, p. 420).

Shortly after the Belloc and Breslow study was published, the Canadian government released a landmark report, which introduced for the first time the concept that all causes of death and disease have four contributing elements (Lalonde, 1974):

- Inadequacies in the existing health care system
- Behavioral factors or unhealthy life-styles
- Environmental hazards
- Human biological factors

A methodology was developed by a group of American experts to determine the relative contribution each of the four elements would make to the ten leading causes of death in the United States in 1976. Based on their analysis, the data suggest that "perhaps as much as half of the U.S. mortality in 1976 was due to unhealthy behavior or lifestyle; 20% to environmental factors; 20% to human biological factors; and only 10% to inadequacies in health care" (U.S. Department of Health, Education and Welfare, 1979, p. 9). This analysis provided additional validation of the Belloc and Breslow study by further supporting the significant relationships of lifestyle choices to heath status.

Based on studies such as these, the first Surgeon General's Report on Health Promotion and Disease Prevention was published in 1979. The report was a cooperative effort of the Department of Health, Education and Welfare (now the Department of Health and Human Services), with the National Academy of Sciences Institute of Medicine and the 1978 Departmental Task Force on Disease Prevention and Health Promotion. Central to the theme of the report is that "the health of this

Table 10-1. Major Causes of Death and Associated Risk Factors, 1981

Cause	% all deaths	Risk factor
Diseases of heart	38.1	Smoking,[a] hypertension,[a] elevated serum, cholesterol[a] (diet), lack of exercise, diabetes, stress, family history
Malignant neoplasms	21.3	Smoking,[a] worksite carcinogens,[a] enviromental carcinogens, alcohol, diet
Cerebrovascular diseases	8.3	Hypertension,[a] smoking,[a] elevated serum cholesterol,[a] stress
Chronic obstructive pulmonary diseases and allied conditions	3.0	Smoking,[a] atmospheric pollution,[a] industrial inhalation hazards[a]
Pneumonia and influenza	2.7	Smoking, vaccination status[a]
Motor vehicle	2.6	Alcohol,[a] no seat belts,[a] speed,[a] roadway design, vehicle engineering
All other accidents and adverse effects	2.5	Alcohol,[a] drug abuse, smoking (fires), product design, handgun availability
Diabetes mellitus	1.8	Obesity[a]
Chronic liver disease and cirrhosis	1.5	Alcohol abuse[a]
Arteriosclerosis	1.4	Elevated serum cholesterol[a]
Suicide	1.4	Stress,[a] alcohol and drug abuse, and gun availability

[a]Major risk factors

Nation's citizens can be significantly improved through actions individuals can take themselves, and through actions decision makers in the public and private sectors can take to promote a safer and healthier environment for all Americans at home, at work and at play'' (U.S. Department of Health, Education and Welfare, 1979, p. 10). The experts working on the report concluded that measures that would significantly reduce the risk for many diseases are available to most Americans and include such personal actions as:

- Elimination of cigarette smoking
- Reduction of alcohol abuse
- Moderate dietary changes to reduce intake of excess calories, fat, salt, and sugar
- Moderate exercise
- Periodic screenings (at intervals determined by age and sex) for major disorders such as high blood pressure and certain cancers
- Adherence to speed laws and the use of seat belts

The relationship of personal actions to the ten major causes of death in 1981, responsible for 85% of the nation's deaths in that year, is illustrated in Table 10-1 (the table, based on work initially described in 1980 [published in 1984 by the U.S.

Department of Health and Human Services and the National Center for Health Statistics] consists of data subsequently updated by the Metropolitan Life Insurance Company). "In each instance, the association of the risk factors with the diseases here listed either has been statistically established as significant or has been suggested as relevant, as in the case of stress and lack of physical exercise" (U.S. Department of Health and Human Services, 1980a, p. 274 [original report]).

Just as in the days of Prohibition, government is attempting to alter personal actions that had been considered an individual decision. Five and a half years after the Surgeon General's Report advocating the use of seat belts, New York State has become the first state in the nation to pass a state law mandating the use of seat belts by drivers and their front-seat passengers; it went into effect January 1, 1985. How this law will be enforced remains to be seen. Reports from New York, New Jersey, and Connecticut regarding the use of safety restraints required by law for several years for children under 6 years of age indicate that compliance has been very low (Simmons, 1984). Even in states such as Tennessee, the first state to pass a child-restraint law in 1978, compliance is estimated to be less than a third of parents with young children despite strict police enforcement in Tennessee (12,000 summonses each year) and positive results (60% drop in traffic injuries and deaths of children younger than 4 years of age). Another example of recent efforts to control behaviors through legislative actions is the recently passed congressional bill to require a legal drinking age of 21 in all states in an effort to reduce alcohol-related traffic accidents. According to the *New York Times* (Molotsky, 1984), this bill is the "first significant Federal move against drinking since Prohibition ended in 1933." Twenty-seven states will be affected by the bill and will risk losing federal highway construction funds if they do not comply with the federal bill.

Life-style modification is not the sole concern of the professionally trained health educator. During the past decade, the scientific community as well as the public have become increasingly concerned about the potential health hazards of toxic substances in communities where our children play and in the settings where many of us work (Hammond & Selikoff, 1979; Rom, 1983; U.S. General Accounting Office, 1980). Although the evidence is not usually conclusive (see Chapters 3 through 6), the need to develop innovative education-for-health strategies to counter these trends is imperative. There are some very specific actions that educators can take (U.S. Department of Health and Human Services, 1980b):

- Inform the public about the hazards of exposure through the media and health education courses in elementary and secondary schools.
- Educate health professionals and directors in industry about such topics as toxicology, epidemiology and hazardous substance control.
- Expand the sensitivity of practicing physicians and other health professionals in diagnosis and reporting of environmental and occupational disease.
- Educate managers of industrial firms with a special emphasis placed on those trained in chemical and mechanical engineering, law, and business administration.

- Staff regulatory agencies with professionals well trained in their discipline as well as policy analysis.

EDUCATION-FOR-HEALTH DEFINED

A goal for education-for-health accepted throughout the world is one by the World Health Organization's Expert Committee on Planning and Evaluation of Health Education Services: "The focus of health education is on people and on action. In general, its aims are to encourage people to adopt and sustain healthful life patterns, to use judiciously and wisely the health services available to them, and to make their own decisions, both individually and collectively, to improve their health status and environment" (World Health Organizations, 1974). In an effort to delineate the scope, purpose, and methods of education-for-health more precisely, Green, Kreuter, Deeds, and Partridge (1980, p. 7) provide the following definition: "Health education is any combination of learning experiences designed to facilitate voluntary adaptions of behavior conducive to health." Green and his colleagues theorize that this definition will encourage the planner to consider all appropriate programs, methods, and activities that make up a learning experience whether or not labeled as an education-for-health program or activity.

In an effort to delineate the range of activities that are subsumed in the definition of consumer health education, the Task Force on Consumer Health Education, established by the John E. Fogarty International Center for Advanced Study in the Health Sciences of the National Institutes of Health and by the American College of Preventive Medicine, developed the following definition. "Consumer health education" includes activities that (Somers, 1976):

- Inform people about health, illness, disability, and ways in which they can improve and protect their own health, including more efficient use of the delivery system;
- Motivate people to want to change to more healthful practices;
- Help them to learn the necessary skills to adopt and maintain healthful practices and life-styles;
- Foster teaching and communications skills in all those engaged in educating consumers about health;
- Advocate changes in the environment that will facilitate healthful conditions and healthful behavior; and
- Add to knowledge through research and evaluation concerning the most effective ways of achieving these objectives.

The task force also pointed out that consumer health education (or education-for-health) and health promotion are not synonymous. Education-for-health should be viewed as one strategy of health promotion; other strategies would include research, education for the health professions, public health, environmental protection, occupational health, health care including diagnosis and treatment of illness and disability, and health economics (Somers, 1976). In an effort to distinguish between education-for-health and health promotion, Bates and Winder (1984, p. 45) define health promotion "as any combination of health education and related organizational, political and economic interventions designed to facilitate behavioral and environmental adaptions that will improve or protect health." Education-for health as a strategy focuses on voluntary changes in behavior. Health promotion relies on interventions such as media advertising, availability of products or services, and laws that affect health or the environment which are usually imposed on the individuals or groups without a personal free choice being made.

Another concept that should be differentiated from education-for-health is health protection, which relates more specifically to workplace health hazards and toxic substances in the environment. Health protection may be defined as "any combination of political and economic interventions designed to facilitate behavioral and environmental adaptions to protect health" (Bates & Winder, 1984, p. 45). Education-for-health may be one strategy to achieve the goal of health protection.

Definitions for education-for-health in the 1980s all emphasize the critical role of health behaviors. There has been a definite shift from the earlier emphasis on changing attitudes and knowledge to more aggressive attempts to change health behaviors directly. Understanding human behavior is difficult and complex. We know that progress is being make, however, because it can be systematically observed. "Such observations can be made in a reliable and reproducible way, and as knowledge progresses they [behaviors] can be increasingly quantitative and have useful predictive power" (Hamburg, Elliott, & Parron, 1982, p. 26).

An innovative planning model for designing and evaluating education-for-health programs, proposed by Green (1974), has been used successfully in the development of education-for-health strategies that range from evaluation of clinical trials (Maiman, Green, & Gibson, 1979), to development of programs for local health departments (Health Education Center, 1976) as well as special population groups such as mothers and children (Green et al., 1978). Green, Kreuter, Deeds, and Partridge (1980) identified three types of factors that should be considered before an educational plan is designed: predisposing, enabling, and reinforcing. Predisposing factors include personal attitudes, beliefs, values, and perceptions that can either facilitate or hinder one's motivation to make a change. Enabling factors, such as limited facilities, inadequate resources, or restrictive laws, may be considered as barriers to changing specific health behaviors. Reinforcing factors are related to the feedback the learner receives, which can either encourage or discourage a behavioral change. All three types of factors should be carefully assessed for each behavior that is to be changed, as they will determine the directions and nature of the education-for-health interventions.

FEDERAL SUPPORT FOR EDUCATION-FOR-HEALTH

The 1970s saw the emergence of new legislation and agencies to support the education-for-health and health promotion movement. The formation of two new agencies to reduce the fragmentation in health education grew out of the recommendations of the President's Committee on Health Education in 1973. The committee recommended that one agency be established in the public sector, the Bureau of Health Education of the Centers for Disease Control, Department of Health, Education and Welfare; and one agency in the private sector, the National Center for Health Education. Both have experienced some reorganization since their inception with the Bureau of Health Education being renamed the Center for Health Promotion and Education (CHPE), Centers for Disease Control, in the reorganized Department of Health and Human Services. The Center for Health Promotion and Education is still administratively based in Atlanta, Georgia. The National Center for Health Education has recently moved its administrative base from San Francisco to New York City and has sought to expand its constituency by inviting individuals to support the center by subscribing as associate members. The primary functions of advocacy, technical assistance, and communication have continued.

The Health Maintenance Organization Act, which became law in 1973, mandates that preventive and educational services be provided by all health maintenance organizations (HMOs) receiving federal certification (Dorsey, 1975). Metropolitan Life Insurance Company (1980) recently surveyed all HMOs in the United States to assess the current range of programs offered and has published a report summarizing the survey findings.

With the passage of the National Consumer Health Information and Health Promotion Act of 1976 (Public Law 94-317), the Office of Health Information and Health Promotion was established under the Assistant Secretary of Health in the Department of Health, Education and Welfare. This office has been renamed the Office of Health Information, Health Promotion, Physical Fitness and Sports Medicine in the reorganized Department of Health and Human Services. This agency was established to (National Consumer Health Information and Health Promotion Act, 1976):

- Coordinate all activities within the Department which relate to health information and health promotion, preventive health services, and education in the appropriate use of health care;
- Coordinate its activities with similar activities of organizations in the private sector; and
- Establish a national health information clearing house to facilitate the exchange of information concerning matters relating to health information and health promotion, preventive health services, and education in the appropriate use of health care, to facilitate access to such information and to assist in the analysis of issues and problems relating to such matters.

Helping to shape the health promotion strategies of the 1980s was the federal publication of *Healthy People: The Surgeon General's Report on Health Promotion and Disease Prevention* (U.S. Department of Health, Education and Welfare, 1979), as well as the subsequent publications, *Promoting Health/Preventing Disease: Objectives for the Nation* (U.S. Department of Health and Human Services, 1980b) and *The 1990 Health Objectives for the Nation: A Midcourse Review* (U.S. Department of Health and Human Services, 1986). These reports were the work of health experts from both the public and private sectors. *Healthy People* identified 15 priority areas where gains in the health of the U.S. citizens could be made by the year 1990 to include: high blood pressure control; family planning; pregnancy and infant health; immunization; sexually transmitted diseases; toxic agent control; occupational safety and health; accident prevention and injury control; fluoridation and dental health; surveillance and control of infectious diseases; smoking and health; misuse of alcohol and drugs; physical fitness and exercise; and control of stress and violent behavior.

Promoting Health/Preventing Disease takes the next logical step of establishing measurable objectives for each of the 15 priority areas and *The 1990 Health Objectives for the Nation* provides a midcourse status report of how well we are attaining our 1990 targets. For the 1990 objectives to be achieved will require interest and action not only by physicians and other health professionals, but also "by industry and labor, by voluntary health associations, schools, churches, and consumer groups, by health planners, and by legislators and public officials in health departments and in other agencies of local and State governments and at the Federal level" (U.S. Department of Health and Human Services, 1980b, p. 2). Setting priorities among the 15 areas has been left up to the states and local agencies, based upon regional and local needs. Strategies that are being taken by various communities will be discussed in the next section.

The thrust in the 1980s is for people to participate actively in the process of maintaining the highest possible state of individual health. As the economic cost for treating disease that can frequently be linked to poor life-style choices continues to reach new heights (see Table 10-1), the U.S. Secretary of Health and Human Services, stated, "A very significant part of the cost-control equation is the role each of us can play in preserving and maintaining our own health. In many cases, our destiny has been placed in our own hands" (Heckler, 1984, p. 6). To achieve a positive state of individual health, however, requires a substantially enhanced body of information-specific education that can apply to experiences as encountered over an entire lifespan, and at times specific help when difficult choices are faced.

SETTINGS FOR EDUCATION-FOR-HEALTH

This section briefly reviews common settings for health education, including a description of specific strategies that are being implemented in the 1980s. The settings are distinctly different, and each provides a unique focus as illustrated by the following synopses:

• Workplace. Over 100 million people are employed in the United States. While the health of workers is extremely important to both workers and employers, another concern is containing health care costs. Health education has an important

Table 10-2. Where We Work

Firm Size (Number employees)[a]	Firms		Employees	
	Number	%	Number	%
1–9	3,404,299	74.2	11,450,490	15.3
10–99	1,077,863	23.5	29,296,037	39.1
100–499	91,662	2.0	17,976,990	24.0
500–999	7,986	0.2	5,497,316	7.4
1,000 or more	4,700	0.1	10,629,569	14.2
	4,586,510	100.0	74,850,402	100.0

Note. From U.S. Bureau of the Census (1981).
[a]These census data exclude all self-employed, government, and railroad employees.

role to play in the reduction of absenteeism, retention of employees, maximization of productivity, and maintenance of high morale.

• Schools. Most leaders would agree that there will be little effect on cost containment of health services if we don't begin the educational process earlier. Out of 15,500 school districts in the United States, fewer than 1,000 have an organized, comprehensive, K-12 education-for-health curriculum.

• Health care system. There are tens of thousands of physicians and approximately 7,500 hospitals in the United States, providing an opportunity to reach patients and family members with critical information about management of illness and promotion of health. Some experts would contend that consumers of medical services, especially hospital services (either inpatient or outpatient), are the most receptive of all consumer groups to educational interventions, taking advantage of the "teachable moment."

• Community. Many consumers of health services, such as unemployed young adults, individuals who have retired, or homemakers, cannot be reached at work, in school, or in health care settings. In addition, exposure to health information in a variety of settings is desirable. Consequently, the judicious use of mass media and community programs becomes extremely important in reaching these groups.

Workplace: Health Protection/Health Promotion

Regardless of the product produced or the size of the firms (see Table 10-2), the workplace provides a unique setting for health protection/health promotion programs (Yenney, 1984). The workplace, where employees spend 30% of their waking hours, not only is convenient but also provides peer support for an individual's attempt to adopt health and safety recommendations.

Protection of the worker from health hazards in the workplace has been a critical issue to government for many years as reflected in the passage of Public

Law 91-596, the Occupational Safety and Health Act of 1970 (commonly known as OSHAct). In the general duty clause, the OSHAct requires employers to provide "employment and a place of employment which are free from recognized hazards that are causing or are likely to cause death or physical harm to employees" (Occupational Safety and Health Act, 1970) and to meet the standards established by the Occupational Safety and Health Administration (OSHA) in the Department of Labor.

The establishment of standards, however, has been very slow (Berman, 1978; Bingham, 1983). It has been estimated that "of the more than 20,000 toxic substances found in the workplace, only a very small percentage (approximately 450) have OSHA standards" (Nelson, Mazzocchi, Edelsack, & Eller, 1983, p. 886). While the Occupational Safety and Health Administration frequently has to enforce the act by issuing citations for violations and imposing fines, it relies heavily upon achieving voluntary compliance to health standards through on-site consultations, dissemination of educational materials, and provision of training programs (Bingham, 1983). The OSHAct of 1970 states that there shall be "programs for the education and training of employers and employees in the recognition, avoidance, and prevention of unsafe or unhealthful working conditions." Congress allocated funds in 1978 through OSHA's New Directions grants for educational and training programs for both workers and employers; however, the funding was discontinued in 1986.

What should the worker know? Felton (1983) states, "workers must know the nature of the work substances to which they are exposed, the disease states that may result from undue contact, the procedures involved in medical surveillance, the meaning of various test results, and the measures to be taken to avoid the ill effects from the absorption, ingestion, or inhalation of toxic substances" (p. 954). Many states have or are in the process of passing "right to know" legislation, which will also have an impact on what the worker learns (Tepper, 1980).

In addition to the training and development activities of OSHA, the National Institute of Occupational Safety and Health (NIOSH), the research agency established by the OSHAct within the Department of Health and Human Services, also has training responsibilities. Although NIOSH provides technical assistance to workers and employees, the primary target for training activities is the professional in the field of occupational safety and health. Through a network of 14 regional educational resource centers (ERCs) funded through academic institutions since 1977, health care professionals can be trained in occupational medicine, occupational health nursing, industrial hygiene, and safety. The training includes both continuing education courses and degree programs.

It is the responsibility of the occupational health professionals not only to advise workers regarding the current health risks, hazards, and protections, but also to anticipate and plan preventive approaches for the occupational hazards of the future, many of which will be due to nontoxic problems. For example, "already ergonomics issues are more common. Today millions of workers find themselves seated all day in front of video display terminals, where they experience stress and discomfort that are not related to any chemical or radiation exposure" (Robbins, 1983, p. 977). Preparing professionals to anticipate health hazards that will result from new enterprises such as biotechnology, electronics, and office work is critical if the worker's health is to be protected in the 1980s.

Usually when consideration is given to toxic substances in the workplace, the objects of concern are substances used during the manufacturing process or produced when a product is manufactured. One toxic substance in the work environment that poses a health threat for many employees is produced by employees who smoke in the workplace. Tobacco smoke can be harmful to a nonsmoking worker on the job as well as to the smoker. The hazard to the smoker may be compounded due to the synergistic effect of the chemicals in the smoke with other substances in the workplace. To address this issue, a "Model Policy for Smoking in the Workplace" has been developed by 21 national nonprofit organizations as recommended by the Work Group on Smoking Control in the Workplace during the 1981 National Conference on Smoking or Health. The rights of the smokers as well as the non-smokers are protected by the model policy. However, when conflicts arise and accommodation is not possible, the policy states, "the rights of the nonsmoker should prevail" (American Cancer Society, 1983, p. 3).

The National Center for Health Education and the American Cancer Society advocate that a written policy for smoking in the workplace should be established by every employer. Having such a policy also may increase the interest of an employee who smokes to participate in a program to quit. An educational program to encourage and assist employees to stop smoking may be considered as a health protection as well as a health promotion measure. (A copy of the model policy may be obtained through the National Center for Health Education or the American Cancer Society.)

Health protection of the worker has long been a concern to labor and management (Berman, 1978). Health promotion in the workplace, on the other hand, is a recent innovation that has generated interest since the late 1970s (Cunningham, 1982; Parkinson & Associates, 1982; Ware, 1981). At a 1983 conference entitled "Worksite Health Promotion and Human Resources: A Hard Look at the Data," Roger B. Smith, chairman of the General Motors Corporation, provided one explanation for industry's recent interest in wellness programs.

> By promoting the concept of preventive health care at the worksite, we won't be solving the problem of soaring health care costs. But we'll be contributing toward a solution—and a fiscally responsible approach to cost containment. More important, we'll be promoting good health, longer, more productive careers, and a higher quality of life in general for our employees. . . . The fact is, American industry can't afford not to expand the wellness movement in the workplace. (Smith, 1984, p. 4)

According to a report published by the National Center for Health Education (1984a), the costs of employee poor health, including payment of health services and lost work days, are tremendous. For example, consider that:

- Over $300 billion—almost 11% of the U.S. gross national product—was spent on health care in 1982. Corporations paid $77 billion. Before the year 2000, the total will hit at least $1 trillion.

- Cardiovascular disease annually costs the United States economy $80 billion.
- Drug abuse costs the economy $26 billion per year.
- The economic cost of cigarette smoking amounts to $47.5 billion.
- Diseases of the heart are the leading cause of mortality—over 750,000 deaths in 1981; 38.2% of total deaths.
- Among employed persons, there are more than ten times as many deaths from coronary heart disease, hypertensive disease, and stroke as there are deaths resulting from industrial accidents.
- About 29 million work days, representing $2 billion in earnings, are lost each year because of coronary heart diseases, hypertensive disease, and stroke.
- Cancer is the second leading cause of death in the United States and accounts for about 420,000 deaths a year. Tobacco's contribution to all cancer deaths is estimated to be 30%.
- Lung cancer accounts for about one quarter of all cancer deaths, and 85% are due to cigarette smoking.

Speaking at the 1983 worksite conference, John J. Creedon, president and chief executive officer of Metropolitan Life Insurance Company, identified three approaches that business and industry could take to reinforce the commitment of many Americans to health improvement through self-care strategies:

> (1) We should recognize the importance of this developing trend toward illness prevention through self-care and its potential for improved health and happiness of our employees, their families and society; (2) as corporate policy makers, we should consider starting and supporting health promotion programs to encourage employee health improvements; and (3) we might consider reaching out beyond our employee population and helping to encourage similar commitments to health improvement on the part of families, dependents, and indeed, entire communities where a corporation is a significant factor in the community. (Creedon, 1984, p. 10)

Host companies attending the October 1983 conference focusing on health promotion in the workplace provided an update of their health promotion and wellness programs and were summarized in issue number 1 of *Center*, the publication of the National Center for Health Education. The following descriptions of health promotion programs developed to enhance employee health provide an introduction to the innovative strategies that are being implemented in the workplace.[1]

Control Data Corporation offers three distinct programs oriented to employee health welfare. The Staywell program, developed by the Life Extension Institute, a subsidiary of Control Data, has been implemented at 17 sites. Of the 25,000 employees eligible, 68% are

---

1. From "Capsule Reports of Health Promotion Programs of 9 Corporations" by the National Center for Health Education, 1984, *Center, 1*, pp. 31–32. Reprinted by permission.

enrolled for health screening, education (offered as the traditional seminar, as self-study, or as a computer-based activity), and employee Staywell action teams.

The Employee Advisory Resource (EAR) is available to employees by telephone 24 hours a day. EAR responds not only to chemical dependency problems but also offers counselling in personal, marital, legal, or financial matters. Approximately 18% of the 50,000 U.S. employee population use EAR annually.

The Control Data occupational health service has developed an extensive hazard identification and evaluation process which monitors and manages employee exposure. Medical examinations, short-term and long-term disability programs, and an extensive correction and compliance procedure help to ensure maximum employee safety.

General Motors Corporation. As a regular course of business, General Motors Corporation has for many years devised, promoted, and maintained numerous programs that contribute to health promotion. In general, the wellness programs involve substance abuse counselling, cardiovascular risk assessment, cancer screening, antismoking campaigns, nutritional counselling (including diabetic screening), physical fitness, and stress management.

GM has extensive programs in substance abuse (54,000 clients) and hypertension (182,000 have been screened). The cancer screening and antismoking campaigns are primarily associated with GM's cancer investigations. In addition, nutritional counselling, physical fitness, and stress management programs receive considerable attention. In the medical department, well over 325,000 employees annually receive a physical exam, health consultation, and/or test procedures.

These programs have an excellent effect on employee health. GM believes in the positive health influence on employees of the 5,000,000 health and medical services given annually in GM medical plan departments.

IBM Corporation. In addition to the recreational facilities at many IBM locations throughout the country, and the athletic activities conducted by the IBM Clubs to help . . . employees in the area of physical fitness, IBM established a voluntary health education program—A Plan for Life—in 1981.

This health education program includes nine comprehensive courses lasting from two to twelve weeks and includes exercise, smoking cessation, stress management, weight management, healthy back, first aid, CPR and obstructed-airway maneuver, drivers' improvement, and water safety. Mini-courses are also offered on the subjects of health and nutrition and risk factor management. The courses are taught by qualified instructors with such community organizations as YMCA, Red Cross, American Lung Association, hospitals, and colleges. To date, there have been over 70,000 enrollments in these courses.

IBM's entire in-house health and safety program is oriented toward prevention. Services range from intensive pre-employment screening examinations to periodic job-related exams designed to ensure that the individual is suited to his or her job and will not be adversely affected by the work environment. A comprehensive voluntary health screening is also administered every five years to employees thirty-five and older. IBM was one of the first companies to institute a policy that acknowledges the rights of nonsmokers. Self-instruction manuals on smoking cessation, driver safety, and home safety have been requested by 75,000 employees.

Johnson & Johnson's Live for Life program is a comprehensive health promotion effort intended for all Johnson & Johnson employees world-wide. The Live for Life program is specifically designed to encourage employees to follow lifestyles which will result in good health, based upon the assumptions that lifestyle activities such as eating, exercise, smoking, and stress management contribute substantially to an individual's health status; and that lifestyle activities which support good health can be successfully promoted in the work setting.

Objectives include improvements in nutrition, weight control, stress management, fitness, smoking cessation, and health knowledge. Proper utilization of medical interventions such as high blood pressure control and the EAP is strongly encouraged. The expectation is that such improvements will lead to positive changes in employee morale, relations with fellow employees, company perception, job satisfaction, and productivity, as well as reductions in absenteeism, accidents, medical claims, and total illness care costs.

As of August, 1983, the corporate level Live for Life staff served about 22,000 employees in active programs at thirty-five separate Johnson & Johnson locations throughout the United States and Puerto Rico. By the end of 1986, Live for Life will be available to all 75,000 Johnson & Johnson employees worldwide.

Metropolitan Life Insurance Company's workplace health promotion programs represent a continuation of the company's 112-year history of promoting good health among its employees and the general public.

In 1979, Metropolitan founded the Center for Health Help for its own employees, through which it pilot-tested health risk intervention programs: cholesterol reduction, diabetes education, reduction of heart risks, nutrition education, weight control, fitness, smoking cessation, stress management, and breast cancer education. The Center has consistently achieved a 35% success rate at one year in smoking cessation, an average 10% reduction at six months in cholesterol levels, food changes consistent with those recommended by the U.S. Dietary Goals, and an average nine-pound weight loss sustained over one year.

Combining its long experience in implementing national health promotion programs as well as workplace health experience developed in the Center for Health Help, Metropolitan started offering consultation services to companies nationwide in 1982. The consultants, including staff of the Center, help client companies assess employees' health needs and concerns, develop risk intervention programs and education materials, and evaluate all aspects of the programs. Client companies include: General Motors, American Can, Borden, Holly Farms, Georgia-Pacific, Genuine Parts, Louisiana Pacific, the City of Dayton, and the Dade County School District.

Just as industries have taken different approaches in the development of work-site programs, so has the approach to evaluation varied by program. Windsor, Barenowski, Clark and Cutler (1984) provide a comprehensive review of the evaluation of health promotion programs and discuss how one determines the appropriate data to collect as well as specific collection techniques.

With companies, both large and small, actively becoming involved in health protection/health promotion activities, the U.S. Department of Health and Human Services (1984) projects that it should be possible to achieve the following workplace health promotion objectives by the year 1990.

Smoking and health. Thirty-five percent of all workers should be offered employer/employee sponsored or supported smoking cessation programs at the worksite or in the community.

Misuse of alcohol and drugs. The proportion of workers in major firms whose employers provide a substance abuse prevention and referral program (employee assistance) should be greater than 70%.

Nutrition. The prevalence of significant overweight (120% of "desired" weight) among the U.S. adult population should be decreased to 10% of men and 17% of women, without nutritional impairment.

Physical fitness and exercise. The proportion of employees of companies and institutions with more than 500 employees offering employer-sponsored fitness programs should be greater than 25%.

Control of stress. Of the 500 largest U.S. firms, the proportion offering work-based stress reduction programs should be greater than 30%.

Occupational safety and health. Workers should be routinely informed of life-style behaviors and health factors that interact with factors in the work environment to increase risks of occupational illness and injuries.

Based on the corporate programs described in this chapter as well as the authors' experience in other programs such as one designed for the University of Medicine and Dentistry of New Jersey, the following elements are considered critical in the development of education-for-health/health protection/health promotion programs in the workplace:

- Obtain the support and commitment for the program from top management. Encourage executives to serve as role models.
- Sell the educational program to middle management; this is the group most affected by release time granted to employees to attend programs.
- Define clear goals and objectives based on the morbidity and mortality statistics for your employees. The needs of the target group should be reflected in program's priorities.
- Establish a planning committee composed of all constituencies.
- Identify resources for the educational programs and activities. Support for programs/activities can range from full company support to total self-pay by the employee. According to data compiled by the STAYWELL program sponsored by Control Data, the cost can range from $400 to $700 per employee over a three-year period (Cunningham, 1982).
- Identify content experts who can provide the program on site or in the community. Use existing programs within the company such as the medical and food service departments as well as community agencies such as the YMCA, American Cancer Society, American Heart Association, or American Lung Association.
- Establish a policy regarding release time to participate in the program. Decide if participation will be totally on company time, employee time, or a combination.
- If the program is offered on site, decide who will be eligible to participate. For example, will the program be open to family members and/or the surrounding community?
- Motivate employees to participate in the program, but be sure to adhere to the principle of voluntary participation. One approach that appears to be very successful is the health risk assessment which provides a health risk profile based on the employee's life-style choices. This assessment not only

helps the individual to understand his current health status better, but also identifies an individual priority among the available program offerings.

- In addition to the personal health gains, build into the program incentives, such as T-shirts or recognition through the company newsletter when goals are met. Continued employee participation relies on constant feedback and reinforcement.
- Develop an action plan, including a marketing strategy.
- Highlight unique aspects of the programs.
- Design an evaluation plan. Due to the lack of experimental rigor that one can usually obtain in a work setting, the evaluation may address more of the process issues of implementation rather than behavioral outcomes such as a change in eating or exercise habits attributable to the educational program. Identify the variables that will be monitored early in the planning stage as well as the standards that will be used to determine success. In addition to the formal evaluation plan, also keep an anecdotal record of development.

Schools: Health Education/Promotion

Outside the family structure, the school system can have the greatest impact on personal decisions made on a daily basis regarding health matters (McGinnis, 1983). Unfortunately, education-for-health frequently continues to be the rainy day subject offered when inclement weather cancels the physical education class. Unlike other academic subjects, there have been no consistent benchmarks regarding the achievement of specific health content areas by grade levels. In addition,

> where health education is provided, it is often treated as an afterthought, tacked onto another subject such as biology or physical education. . . . Traditionally, school health has been limited to dry, moralistic discussions of sex, drugs, and alcohol almost guaranteed to ''turn off'' students. Exercise at school has centered on organized team sports rather than individual activities, such as tennis, swimming, and running, that children can carry on into adult life. (Lehmann, 1979, p. 432)

Education-for-health programs in schools have been plagued by a lack of continuity of subject matter and coordination within as well as between school systems (Bruess, 1978). In reviewing the status of school-based education-for-health programs, the National School Health Education Coalition identified nine major obstacles that have prevented school systems, both public and private, from providing comprehensive education-for-health (Strategic Planning Group, 1984). The obstacles include:

- Disunity and silence of health care professionals and health education professionals in their support for school health education.
- Lack of assertive community support for school health education.
- Lack of coordinated national and state leadership.

- Lack of commitment to school health education by school boards and administrators.
- Lack of concise collation of the potential educational, economic, and social benefits of comprehensive school health education to the school and the community.
- Lack of appropriate and effective inservice education for teachers, administrators, and support staff.
- Lack of incentives and rewards for administrators, teachers, and support staffs who support education.
- Lack of long-term philosophic and financial support to effect school change.
- Public perception that school health education programs are more extensively implemented than is actually the case.

The recent development of a comprehensive school-based education-for-health curriculum for grades K–12 is expected to have an impact on these constraints as national implementation takes place. The comprehensive education-for-health curriculum, known as "Growing Healthy," grew out of curriculum projects started in 1969 for two age groups: units for grades K–3 were previously identified as the Seattle Project and the Primary Grades Health Curriculum Project; units for grades 4–7 were previously known as the Berkeley Project and the School Health Curriculum Project. Major funding for the development of the units for both age groups K–7 was provided by the Bureau of Health Education, Centers for Disease Control (CDC). Through support received from CDC, the National Center for Health Education has had the responsibility for implementing the "Growing Healthy" curriculum since 1977. This support has continued from CDC and has recently expanded to include funding to the American Lung Association. In a collaborative effort, these two organizations provide information and technical assistance to those wishing to implement the curriculum within their school system.

According to a recent report in *Center* (National Center for Health Education, 1984c), the curriculum has now been implemented by 595 school districts in 41 states, though the number of school districts participating varies greatly by state (see Figure 10-1). The number of students involved in the hands-on curriculum grew dramatically from just over 300,000 children in 1980 to 528,000 children in 1983. Through this curriculum, children learn how their bodies function, the relationship between feelings and health, and how life-style choices made today can affect their health now as well as in the future. The curriculum covers such areas as alcohol and drug abuse, nutrition, cancer, heart and other chronic illnesses, eye health, safety, communicable diseases, disabilities, family and communicable health, and the importance of rest, cleanliness, and exercise. The curriculum has been designed to integrate easily with other subjects such as reading, language, science, math, physical education, music, and art.

The teenage Health Teaching Modules developed by the Educational Development Center through grants from the Center for Health and Education, Centers for Disease Control, Department of Health and Human Services (HHS); the National Heart, Lung and Blood Institute, HHS; American Heart Association; and Aetna

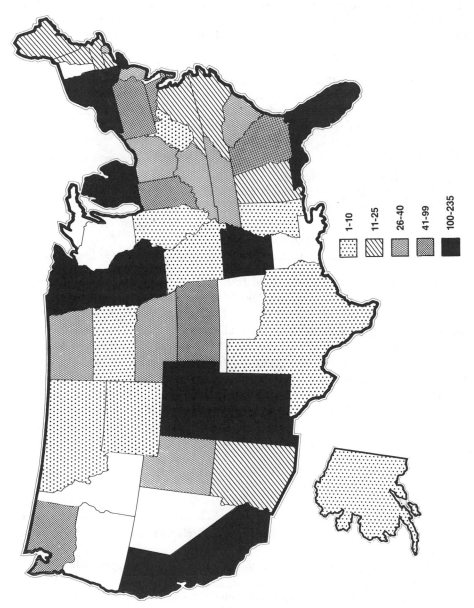

Figure 10-1. Number of school districts in 42 states that have districts participating in Growing Healthy, 1983.

1-10
11-25
26-40
41-99
100-235

Life and Casualty Company were implemented in 1983. The units in this curriculum continue to build on the base established in Growing Healthy and focus on key issues faced by developing adolescents as well as enhancing their understanding of the major health risks. The Teenage Health Teaching Modules provide ''junior and senior high school students with the knowledge and skills to act enthusiastically on behalf of their own health and the health of others, now and as they grow older'' (National Center for Health Education, 1984, p. 38). The curriculum has been designed to help students:

- Understand and feel comfortable about the physical and social changes they are experiencing as adolescents;
- Develop the confidence and skills to make informed decisions about the use of cigarettes, alcohol, and other drugs;
- Recognize and deal with stress in their lives;
- Expand their understanding of interpersonal relationships among friends and family members;
- Improve their physical fitness and eating habits;
- Improve their ability to locate and use health resources;
- Work toward improving health conditions in the community, in the physical environment, and eventually in the workplace;
- Understand the health research process and make better use of health news.

With the completion of the field testing of the Teenage Health Teaching Modules, it is now possible for a school district to implement a comprehensive education-for-health curriculum beginning with kindergarten and progressing through grade 12. As school districts continue to adopt this curriculum nationally, it will be possible for children to move from one school district to another without jeopardizing the progress of their incremental learning in education-for-health any more than the progress in math or science would be affected by a move from one school to another.

The National School Health Education Coalition has identified six priority strategies that would enhance the implementation of a comprehensive education-for-health program (Strategic Planning Group, 1984).

- Compile a statement of the potential educational, economic, and social benefits of comprehensive school health education to the schools and to the community.
- Find angel(s)-source(s) of long-term (5–15 years) philosophic and financial support for the strategies leading to comprehensive health education in the schools.
- Aid the establishment of state and local coalitions to support school health education.
- Urge National School Health Education Coalition members at the state level to assist in providing comprehensive health promotion opportunities similar to Oregon's Seaside Conference.
- Identify and encourage school superintendents who support model com-

prehensive school health education programs in their districts to help proselytize their peers, and provide support and recognition for these administrative leaders.

- Support through administrative and legislative action the continuation of comprehensive school health education leadership/coordination positions in the federal government (primarily within the Department of Health and Human Services) and in state departments of education.

In addition, the following steps should be taken before the curriculum is implemented at the local level:

- Secure the support of the district administration.
- Identify professionally qualified teachers as well as those who are interested in teaching health.
- Establish the educational team that will be responsible for the on-site implementation. This team is usually composed of at least two classroom teachers, an administrator and a resource person such as the school nurse, curriculum coordinator, or health educator.
- Review the content of the curriculum. Determine if there are teaching units that will have to be notified for your setting. For example, following a demonstration period in New York City, it was determined that the curriculum should be modified to meet the special needs of the urban population. Since refinements for some settings have already been made to the Growing Healthy curriculum, these changes should be reviewed before launching new revisions.
- Provide teacher-training workshops to increase familiarity with the program's content, teaching methods and materials, and community resources.
- Build in an evaluation process to provide feedback regarding the appropriateness of the curriculum materials and the needs and progress of the students.

Patient Education: Disease/Trauma Management and Health Promotion

Patients receive health care in a variety of settings that include hospitals, nursing homes, long-term care facilities, health maintenance organizations (HMOs), private offices, free-standing clinics, worksite clinics, and since the late 1970s, hospices. With the exception of hospices, which provide care and support to the terminally ill and their family members, the focus of care for the majority of medical care facilities has traditionally been on the treatment of disease and trauma; consequently education-for-health programs, when they exist within these settings, have traditionally been designed for people with specific diseases or health problems. As recently as 1979, the most common patient education-for-health programs found in hospitals were developed for adult inpatients and included diabetes, nutrition, prenatal, ostomy, heart attack, mastectomy, postnatal, preoperative, respiratory, postoperative, stroke, and pacemaker education (American Hospital Association, 1979). With the emphasis in the 1980s on chronic illnesses, however, medical care providers, particularly hospitals, are now expanding their area of responsibility to include health promotion. Examples of the type of programs offered include health risk appraisal programs; health risk reduction programs such as nutritional classes, smoking withdrawal clinics, and physical fitness exercise activities; cardiopulmonary resuscitation (CPR) classes; accident prevention; and assertiveness training.

The recognition that education-for-health should be a key element of all care plans for patients and that the care givers' responsibility should extend beyond the treatment of a presenting disease or disorder has received support from a number of organizations during the past decade. Taking a lead role in 1964, Metropolitan Life Insurance Company financed the First Invitational Conference sponsored by the American Hospital Association focusing on the hospital's role in patient education. This was followed 5 years later by a Second Invitational Conference to plan an action strategy to advance the cause of patient education in the coming 10 years. Growing out of recommendations and discussions at this meeting was the formulation of the *Patient's Bill of Rights* by the American Hospital Association (1972). The bill contains twelve provisions, six of which relate to patient education. The patient has the:

- Right to obtain information about one's diagnosis, treatment, and prognosis;
- Right to give informed consent before procedures and/or treatments are started;
- Right to receive complete information regarding the need for transfer to other facilities as well as alternatives;
- Right to information regarding hospital's relationship to other institutions as well as professional relationships of those providing care;
- Right to be advised of research projects that may affect the care of the patient; and
- Right to understand the process for continuity of care upon discharge from the hospital.

The importance of growing attention to patient education was formally recognized through the development and adoption of position statements by professional groups, legislative action, and other measures. The following examples from these statements not only support the rationale for including patient education with other patient services but also illustrate the change in emphasis of patient education that was occurring during this period of time.

The Health Maintenance Act of 1973 mandated that education-for-health be one of the principal responsibilities of any health maintenance organization (HMO) that was developed with federal support. The law states that an HMO should "encourage and actively provide for its members education services and education in the contribution each member can make to the maintenance of his own health." It was hypothesized that not only would the health education services be of direct benefit to the patient, but that there would be some cost savings to the health care system as well. Studies have documented the benefits to patients (Egbert, Battit, Welch, & Bartlett, 1964; Levine & Britten, 1973; Miller & Goldstein, 1972). Self-care educational interventions in an HMO have been reported in another study to have a statistically positive impact on decreasing the number of medical visits and minor illness visits (Vickery *et al.*, 1983).

The revised New Jersey Nurse Practice Act of 1974, states that the "practice of nursing as a registered professional nurse is defined as diagnosing and treating human responses to actual or potential physical and emotional health problems, through such services as case-finding, health teaching, health counseling, and provision of care supportive to a restoration of life and well-being, and executing medical regimen as prescribed by a licensed or otherwise legally authorized physician or dentist." This act makes explicit the importance of health teaching and counseling. Similar revisions of Nurse Practice Acts in other states were approved around this time.

The Blue Cross Association issued its White Paper on Patient Health Education in 1974, which concludes that "the available information regarding patient health education indicates that, where conducted by a coordinated mix of educational and clinical specialists and directed to individual needs and capabilities, it both increases the quality of health care and presents cost savings to the health care system and to the public it serves." The statement continues, "accordingly, plans should encourage health care institutions to establish and operate programs in patient education and should support them financially through the existing payment mechanism."

The American Medical Association's (AMA) Statement on Patient Education (1975) called for "planned programs of patient education developed and supervised by patient education committees whose membership would include health professionals, educators and consumers." The statement notes that "planned patient education programs are distinct from general health education programs for the public and from programs intended as education for prevention of disease or for health maintenance." The AMA statement limits the scope of the planned program to patients under treatment.

Also in 1975, the American Hospital Association (AHA) issued a Statement on Health Education: Role and Responsibility of Health Care Institutions, taking a much broader view than the AMA. "Health education is an integral part of high-quality health care. Hospitals and other health care institutions . . . have an obligation to promote, organize, implement and evaluate health education programs." The AHA statement was concerned specifically with the education-for-health of three target groups: "the patient and his family; personnel, including employees, medical staff, volunteers, and trustees; and the community at large."

A position statement on Patient and Family Education of the Society for Public Health Education (SOPHE) in 1976 emphasized that "irrespective of the location or situation in which care is offered, those responsible have an obligation to provide to the best of their ability an organized approach to patient education." The SOPHE statement states that the "patient and family should receive education as to the accessibility of care, the system of care, and the role which each can play in prevention and treatment. The latter should include both the physical and emotional aspects of the illness."

The Health Insurance Association of America (HIAA) published in 1979

HIAA's Financing In-Hospital Patient Education: Proposed Criteria. The statement stresses that "health education is the means by which illness and disability can best be prevented or its impact minimized. Basic to the health education process is its potential for encouraging more effective, efficient and economic use of health services." The statement continues, "accordingly, the Health Insurance Association of America gives strong support to organized hospital-based patient education programs."

In respect to health promotion, the American Hospital Association (AHA) issued a strong statement in 1979 regarding the leadership role that hospitals should take. The AHA's Policy and Statement on the Hospital's Responsibility for Health Promotion acknowledged that while the primary mission of the hospital was to provide health care services including education specific to the health care received, the hospital also has a responsibility to "work with others in the community to assess the health status of the community, identify target health areas and population groups for hospital-based and cooperative health promotion programs, develop programs to help upgrade the health in those target areas, ensure that persons who are apparently healthy have access to information about how to stay well and prevent disease, provide appropriate health education programs to aid those persons who choose to alter their personal health behavior or develop a more healthful life-style, and establish the hospital within the community as an institution which is concerned about good health as well as one concerned with treating illness." With this statement, the American Hospital Association was attempting to shift the focus of a hospital from that of a disease/ trauma treatment center to that of a health center where a comprehensive range of health service and support could be obtained.

The American Hospital Association in 1981 issued a new Policy and Statement on the Hospital's Responsibility for Patient Education Services. These services should be planned to "enable patients, and their families and friends . . . to make informed decisions about their health; to manage their illnesses; and to implement follow-up care at home." The statement points out that in addition to the benefits received by the patients and the hospital when patient education is planned and coordinated, inclusion of these services will also help the hospital when responding to the pressures of "accreditation standards for patient education; requirements for informed consent; need for cost efficient use of resources; increased numbers of persons needing education to help manage chronic conditions or information about new diagnostic and treatment services; and increased consumer interest in making health decisions."

With strong statements from the care providers, which included the American Hospital Association, the American Medical Association, state nursing associations, and the professional health educators, as well as from those who pay for the majority of the costs of services, which includes the Health Insurance Association of America and the Federal government, the support for patient education in the 1980s became firmly established. Of the health care settings (physicians' offices, nursing homes, public health clinics, etc.) affected by these position statements, organized patient education programs are most frequently found within the hospital setting.

Group Practice–Based

Frequently physicians form a group practice composed of several specialties, such as family practitioners, internists, obstetricians/gynecologists, and pediatricians. Using this practice arrangement, an innovative approach for integrating preventive services into the office setting is currently being implemented and evaluated in Wisconsin, Pennsylvania, and Florida. Known as the INSURE Project on Lifecycle Preventive Health Services (LPHS), sponsored by the American Council on Life Insurance and the Health Insurance Association of America, the project was "undertaken to determine the feasibility of implementing preventive services, including patient education in the primary medical care setting as a covered health insurance benefit and to evaluate the short-term effects of these services on providers and consumers" (Logsdon, Rosen, & Demak, 1983).

The protocols for the INSURE Project are based on the work of Breslow and Somers (1977), the Institute of Medicine, Ad Hoc Advisory Group on Preventive Services (Fielding, 1979) and the Canadian Task Force report on the periodic health examination (1979), which identifies the minimum recommended preventive medical services and patient education for ten age groups in place of the usual annual exam. The ten age groups include (Demak *et al.*, 1983):

1. Pregnant women/prenatal care
2. Infants (under 2 years of age)
3. Preschool children (2–5)
4. School-age children (6–11)
5. Adolescents (12–17)
6. Young adults (18–24)
7. Adults (25–39)
8. Adults (40–59)
9. Older adults (60–74)
10. Aged (75 and over)

For each of these groups, as illustrated for a 40-year-old male in Table 10-3, the protocol identifies the recommended health history and physical examinations, laboratory examinations, immunizations and the focus for the education-for-health effort with indicated referrals.

The first phase of the project, to determine the feasibility of developing age-specific protocols for preventive services and integrating them into a busy group practice, has just been completed. Findings from study sites and matched control sites for adults 18 years of age and older are promising, as indicated by the following summary (Industrywide Network for Social, Urban and Rural Efforts, 1984):

- The "quit rate" for study-site cigarette smokers was 18.7% versus 11.6% at control sites, and study patients who began regular exercise was 32.2% versus 27.2% for those at control sites. Weight loss was recorded by 41.2% at study sites compared with 35.4% at control sites, although the median weight change of 5 pounds was the same for both groups.
- 75% of females at study sites began practicing breast self-examination

Table 10-3. Lifecycle Preventive Health Services Protocol for 40-year-old Male

History and Physical Examination
Interval history and risk factors
Height and weight
Blood pressure measurement
Hearing screening
Rectal exam
Laboratory Examination
Serum cholesterol
Blood glucose
Stool for occult blood
Immunizations
Tetanus
Pneumoccocal vaccine—high risk groups only
Patient Education with Referrals as Indicated
Nutrition, especially dietary salt and cholesterol
Accident prevention
Physical activity and exercise
Alcohol and other drug use
Cigarette smoking
Weight control
Skin self-examination
Daily oral hygiene and dental referral

Note. From "Prevention in Primary Health Care: The Insure Project" by M. M. Demak, M. D. Rosen, & D. N. Logsdon, 1983, *Maryland State Medical Journal, 32,* p. 281. Reprinted by permission.

(BSE) as compared with 26% at control sites. For those women who, in the past, had practiced BSE irregularly, 54% at the study site now do so monthly, while 38% of women at the control site do so.

- At the study sites, 35% of high-risk drinkers now report consuming less than 14 drinks per week. Figures from the control sites for high-risk drinkers showed a 13.4% reduction.
- 21.5% began regular use of seat belts at study sites compared to 8.8% at control sites.

Although the number of elderly study patients, age 65 and older, was relatively small, positive changes in all of the above risk categories were reported.

The initial results from this study are very encouraging, and it will be interesting to see if these early findings will be replicated in Phase II of the project when longitudinal data are analyzed.

Hospital-Based

Education-for-health programs in hospitals, which initially began as a fringe benefit to patients, are perceived in the 1980s by the American Hospital Association (AHA) as a way for hospitals to respond to inquiries for help from consumer groups and to meet the requirements of accreditation bodies (American Hospital Association,

1981). Hospitals have been dramatically increasing the number of coordinated patient education programs, from 1,218 in 1975 to 2,009 in 1978, according to the AHA's survey (E. Lee, 1979).

During the 1970s the Office of Consumer Health Education, University of Medicine and Dentistry–Rutgers Medical School (now known as the Robert Wood Johnson Medical School), assumed a leadership role in the development of hospital-based health education programs. Through funding received primarily from the Hunterdon Health Fund, nine New Jersey hospitals were supported as 1-year demonstration sites. The primary purpose of the demonstration was to develop models of coordinated and comprehensive health education services to both the patient and the community. In addition to the demonstration sites, formal linkages were established with other institutions in an effort to develop a statewide network of hospital-based education-for-health programs. As the programs were developed by the various institutions, it became apparent that there were a variety of reasons why hospitals elected to provide comprehensive education-for-health services (Office of Consumer Health Education, 1980):

- Patients have become more knowledgeable about their conditions and their rights. So much public information exists, especially about certain chronic illnesses, that many patients who have limited understanding of their conditions know that more information exists and want to have a greater understanding.
- It is becoming increasingly difficult to exclude patient teaching as an element of hospital care. Adequate hospital care should equip patients both to understand and to be able to care for their disease or condition in order to facilitate recovery and prevent an unnecessary recurrence of hospitalization.
- It is important in determining cost-effectiveness to document patient activities to see which programs are resulting in positive outcomes and which are not.
- Evaluated programs have indicated patient satisfaction and reduction in readmissions.
- Hospitals have responsibilities in matters of informed consent, malpractice, patient's rights, and other legal matters. Patient education programs help address aspects of hospitalization that, if neglected, may lead to litigation.
- Meeting requirements of accrediting bodies, the 1975 Joint Commission on the Accreditation of Hospitals (JCAH) standards on patient care evaluation state, in part: "Criteria shall include demonstrated knowledge of the patient concerning health status, level of functioning and selfcare after discharge" (JCAH, 1976).
- Hospital inpatient education, in many cases, has not been a coordinated effort. This results in a fragmented approach to patient education as well as misuse of financial and personnel resources.
- Hospital inpatient education must meet certain criteria in order to meet third-party reimbursement requirements.

As a result of this demonstration program as well as several recent publications, "how-to" guidelines for the development of hospital-based health education programs are currently available (Breckon, 1982; Office of Consumer Health Education, 1980; Squyres, 1980).

Just as health education programs are beginning to receive some acceptance within the institutional structures, however, their viability appears to be threatened by the advent of a new reimbursement system known as Diagnostic Related Groups (DRGs). DRGs were initially implemented in New Jersey in 1980 and have now been incorporated within the fee structure used nationally by Medicare. Because the reimbursement system pays a specific amount per diagnosis, it is to the hospital's advantage to discharge the patient as early as possible, which may shorten the time period for inhouse patient education. As a result, providing patients with necessary "survival skills" and linkages to community agencies for followup becomes even more critical, particularly for patients who are being treated for mental health problems. How this new reimbursement mechanism will affect hospital-based patient education programs remains to be demonstrated.

Through the UMDNJ-Office of Consumer Health Education's demonstration program, strategies for implementing a hospital-based education-for-health program were identified to include the following components (Office of Consumer Health Education, 1980):

- Secure the commitment of the hospital administrator as well as key department heads.
- Establish a hospital-wide policy concerning patient education.
- Identify the barriers that may exist for an integrated, health education program.
- Determine the most appropriate administrative location for the program. Usual locations include the following departments: inservice, nursing, education, personnel, or public relations.
- Develop a specific written plan for the institution.
- Develop a policy statement supporting health education and identify the responsible department(s). This statement should be developed jointly by the board of trustees, the administration, and the medical staff in collaboration with the individual responsible for coordinating the health education program. (The policy statements of national organizations previously described could serve as guidelines.)
- Secure support for the education-for-health program from all levels of the institution.
- Establish a schedule for implementing the program. At least 6 months should be allowed for the planning and assessment phases of the patient education program.
- Establish an advisory board form various hospital departments, community organizations, and consumers.
- Establish short- and long-range goals for the program based on an assessment of patient and community needs.

- Identify inservice training needs and programs to meet the needs.
- Identify resources, both material and personnel, available from the hospital as well as the community.
- Design an evaluation plan that includes both process and outcome measures.
- Establish a budget for the program.
- Market the program.

Community: Preventing Premature Mortality and Disabilities

Although health goals and program funds are frequently generated on the federal and state level, the action and support for change is found at the community level (Kreuter, 1984). The primary focus for community education-for-health is to prevent premature deaths and disabilities. Consequently, "the mission of community health education is to generate a health-conscious, health-informed, and health-motivated public that is willing and able to engage as much as possible in consistently health-supportive [behaviors] and to refrain as much as possible from health-threatening behaviors" (North Carolina Chapter, SOPHE, 1980).

The key elements for a professional working with a community were identified by Mayhew Derryberry (1949), who could be considered the father of community education-for-health. In his opinion, professionals must:

- Have faith, yes, even conviction, that every citizen has a potential contribution to make for the betterment of his (her) community;
- Have faith in the democratic principle that the decisions of an informed majority are right;
- Be sufficiently patient to let a group take such time as is necessary to arrive at its conclusions; and
- Develop insight and an understanding of interpersonal and intergroup relations so that we can help individuals and groups get satisfaction from their participation, and increase their feelings of worth among their fellow men.

Basic to any community education-for-health program is to begin "where the people are." Consequently, to be successful requires that all sectors of the community be involved in the process of designing an action plan. As Raymond Carlaw points out, to "focus on a disadvantaged or problem group is an agency-oriented rather than a community-oriented response to a health condition" (Carlaw, 1982, p. 9). An excellent example of this process was the community education program conducted in North Karelia, Finland. Following an epidemiological investigation in seven countries, which included Japan, Netherlands, Italy, Greece, Yugoslavia, Finland, and the United States, the Finnish province of North Karelia (175,000 population) was found to have unusually high rates of stroke and cardiovascular disease. Through a community action plan initiated and implemented by residents, the rates of cardiovascular disease and stroke were significantly lowered within 5 years by a community-wide education program using a broad mix of methods (Salonen, Puska, Kottke, & Tuomilehto, 1981).

In the United States, the best known success story of recent years is probably the Stanford University Heart Disease Prevention Program, which was conducted in California. This experiment was designed to determine if an intensive education and mass media campaign could increase the public's awareness of recognized significant contributing factors for cardiovascular disease and convince a significant proportion of the population to change behaviors to eliminate or lower these risks. Two communities, Gilroy and Watsonville, reported significant reduction in cigarette smoking and consumption of saturated fats following the health education interventions, when compared to the control setting located in Tracy (Farquhar *et al.*, 1977). With these promising results, the National Heart, Lung and Blood Institute has funded three additional large-scale studies designed to reduce risk factors for cardiovascular disease through community education. The demonstration projects are being implemented in California, Rhode Island, and Minnesota. Initial findings from the California-based project involving five cities were recently reported (Farquhar, 1984). Following the first 30 months of the educational interventions, statistically significant changes in the expected direction were observed for knowledge, diastolic and systolic blood pressure, and cholesterol. Changes in behaviors as well as morbidity and mortality linked to cardiovascular disease will continue to be tracked during the next 42 months of the intervention phase. The role played by the community to reinforce behavioral changes, such as the flow of communication in various social networks, will also be measured.

An important tool for stimulating community participation in education-for-health programs aimed at risk factor reduction is the Health Risk Appraisal (HRA). Formulated by Dr. Lewis Robbins in the late 1940s and early 1950s, the instrument has been adapted by the Centers for Disease Control to identify, quantify, and appraise risks to one's continued wellness or health. The data base includes a personal health history; physical measurements such as height, weight, blood pressure, and serum cholesterol level; and life-style habits that include smoking and drinking patterns. After the individual completes a self-administered questionnaire, the data are processed by computer, producing a printout that provides the participant with three ages: chronological age, an appraisal age, which is the age group into which the participant is placed as a result of the risks produced by his life-style (this age can be higher or lower than the chronological age), and an achievable age, which identifies the age group the individual could join if he controlled or eliminated the risks identified on the printout (Goetz & Bernstein, 1984; Hall & Zwemer, 1979). With this instrument, it is possible to survey large groups of well individuals, identify those who are at risk of developing a chronic illness during the next 10 years, and design an educational plan to eliminate or minimize the risk. By pooling participants' data within a community, it is also possible to identify the major priority risk areas for attention in community-wide programs.

One way to reach large numbers of well individuals with the HRA has been through health fairs. Health fairs, sponsored by public and voluntary agencies, have traditionally offered a mix of exhibits, demonstrations (aerobics, judo, etc.) and screenings (blood pressure, diabetes, etc.). By adding the HRA to the health fair offerings, it is now possible to make explicit how a specific habit, such as smoking cigarettes, may be jeopardizing personal life expectancy. The HRA will relate the smoking habit to other health history information and help the individual to understand the relative importance of this risk to his own longevity. Receiving this information appears to encourage behavior change (Althafer, 1982), which can be reinforced by other community-based programs.

To focus attention on the importance of fitness and to encourage people to assume a greater responsibility for their own health, the University of Medicine and Dentistry of New Jersey (UMDNJ) through the Office of Consumer Health Education has sponsored cross-county bicycle races with health fairs taking place at the start/finish lines (Gotsch, Troxel, & Fersht, 1986). The event is held in cooperation with the Governor's Council on Physical Fitness and Sports, the New Jersey State Department of Health, Blue Cross and Blue Shield of New Jersey, the New Jersey Department of Community Affairs, and the New Jersey Department of Commerce and Economic Development. Known as the UMDNJ–Bicycle Race for Health, the 1986 race brought riders through ten counties of New Jersey as they raced from one community to the next over a 3-day period. The sporting event, a bicycle race, stimulates the citizens of the communities to consider their own physical fitness and to identify at the health fairs the factors that may be placing their health at risk. By having public and voluntary health agency participation at the fair for demonstrations, consultations, and follow-up programs, the individual's knowledge of community resources is also enhanced. Such an innovative approach, by arousing awareness and building upon other interests, is often key to the success of motivating individuals to make needed behavioral changes.

To highlight the importance of health promotion as a strategy, the U.S. Department of Health and Human Services awarded the Secretary's Award for Excellence in Community Health Promotion to 35 community programs in December 1983 (National Center for Health Education, 1984e). Four programs were selected from the group of 35 to demonstrate the variety of community approaches, range of target groups and types of health education interventions that can be employed in community programs.[2]

Chicago Uptown Coalition and Health Department Reach Needy, Underserved with WIC Service. A common saying in Chicago's racially and culturally integrated northside Uptown neighborhood is: "How ya doin'?" And the frequent answer is "Doin' without."

For nearly 3,000 Uptown mothers, infants, and children, there has been a new answer, and it is "Eatin' and feelin' better because of WIC." The change is a result of a cooperative effort of a streetwise community organization known as Heart of Uptown Coalition (HOUC), the Chicago Department of Health, and the federal Women's, Infants', and Children's (WIC) program.

A large percentage of the area's 65,000 residents depend on social welfare to survive.

2. From "Community: Health Promotion" by the National Center for Health Education, 1984, *Center*, 2, pp. 8, 11, 14, 15. Reprinted by permission.

Almost 6,000 are under five years of age. Data from the 1980 census show that of the area's 28,300 families, only 2,800 have incomes of $10,000 to $12,500; 4,700 have incomes between $2,500 and $5,000.

An HOUC survey in 1981–1982 found that most eligible mothers were not aware of WIC and also learned that the Chicago Department of Health had returned $700,000 in WIC instruments because low staffing made it difficult to locate and process eligible mothers and children. Clearly, according to Slim Coleman of HOUC, "there was a problem in communication as well as staffing." By the spring of 1982 a cooperative agreement had been worked out between HOUC and the health department.

Six goals were set: (1) to process at least 40 persons a week and to give WIC clients nutritious foods; (2) to screen for lead poisoning and sickle-cell trait, and provide follow-up; (3) to promote regular health care; (4) to recruit at least 12 volunteers, provide training, and encourage continuing education to improve employability of volunteers; (5) to provide nutrition information and education; and (6) to cut the infant mortality rate by 10 percent.

Volunteers and potential WIC clients were recruited through HOUC's own newspaper, at HOUC meetings, and by distributing flyers in grocery stores, women's and emergency shelters, and hospitals. Classes were provided for volunteers. Screening centers were set up—and the first day eight mothers and 60 children began arriving as early as 8:30 in the morning.

"Community outreach and preventive health strategies will be the prime thrusts of the Chicago Department of Health during the 1980's," says Dr. Bernard J. Turnock, acting commissioner. "We now know that it's not enough for us only to provide traditional medication services. We must reach out to overcome the attitudes, behavior patterns, and other constraints that have reduced access to and utilization of such services."

Emerging Council Stimulates Community of 3,500 to Change Health Attitudes and Behavior. In this (Arizona) community of 3,500 people, 24 percent of them Spanish speaking, there is emerging a community project designed to focus on changing personal attitudes and behavior within the individual's social and personal support systems.

The goal of the Community Health Action Model Project (CHAMP) is to build a community environment supportive of good health practices and thereby contribute to a reduction in premature deaths and disabilities. CHAMP has been developed by the Office of Health Education of the Arizona Department of Health Services and modified, approved, and implemented by a local health council.

Participating organizations in the health council include the county and city government, the Willcox Unified School District, churches, the 24-bed community hospital, the Chamber of Commerce, voluntary agencies, and social groups.

According to Christine Liberato, health educator in the Department of Health Services, "the family is the key to both changing negative health behaviors and to reinforcing positive ones. In addition, CHAMP recognizes the contribution that the community plays in providing an enabling as well as a reinforcing environment for healthy living."

At present, CHAMP is planning a preteen health fair and a community forum series on alcohol abuse. Already it has published a directory of available health and human services resources in Willcox and its surrounding communities.

Interaction, Support via TV Facilitate Community Weight Control Program. Commercial TV played a central role in a community weight control program aimed at a viewing audience of 100,000 people who were provided with a degree of interaction and support usually found only in face-to-face settings.

Fight Against Fat was a cooperative project of KATU-TV's "AM Northwest," a popular one-hour morning show, and the Kaiser-Permanente Health Services Research Center. It has "blossomed into an ongoing freedom-from-fat program" open to any adult in the community, according to Herman M. Frankel, M.D., of Kaiser-Permanente.

Six volunteers, representative of the 600 women who had applied, appeared on camera monthly to be weighed and interviewed. A team of health professionals met with them weekly, and appeared on the program at least once a month. Sometimes these were hour-long "specials" to present an integrated approach to the development of self-management and social support skills, gentle endurance training, and a gradual transition to an eating pattern consistent with U.S. dietary goals.

Some televised segments consisted of the program's hostess, Margie Boule, who proposed the project, interviewing members of the intervention team. Others were in the form of short didactic presentations; and others presented responses to questions from the studio audience or by telephone from the home audience.

There were also individual and group interviews with the six on-camera volunteers, staged scenes examining restaurant eating and food preparation, split-screen images of volunteers at various stages of weight loss, on-camera additions to each volunteer's cumulative weight-change graph, taped home visits, and interviews with family members. Over 5,000 packets of printed materials were mailed in response to viewers.

At 18 months a questionnaire was sent to a random sample of 600 viewers who had requested information. Thirty-five percent of 288 respondents said they participated in Fight Against Fat, and a telephone survey of nonrespondents showed that they were just as likely to be participants.

"Growing Younger" Reality for Those "60 and Better." A person's health age is not always the same as his or her actual age, participants in the Growing Younger program of Boise have found as they seek to improve their health and "prove" their youth.

Developed by the Healthwise Wellness Center, Growing Younger is a health promotion program for citizens "60 and better." Its aim is to help older people have a good time while making positive health changes.

In its first two years, the program, jointly sponsored by the Boise Council on the Aging under funding from the Centers for Disease Control and the state of Idaho, reached almost 10 percent of the senior population of Boise. Following the demonstration period, local sponsors have continued their support, and Growing Younger now is operating in 18 communities in 12 states.

Preliminary (six-month) evaluations of program effectiveness show statistically significant positive changes in participants' weight, body fat, flexibility, and cholesterol level, as well as improvement in fitness, nutrition, stress, and medical care behaviors.

Recruitment is accomplished by a system of neighborhood outreach, supported by television and radio messages and other media material geared to enhance participant expectation and performance.

Workshops stress "learning-by-doing" activities to build knowledge, skills, and friendships among participants. Informal sessions flow out of the regular meetings, establishing a pattern of continued neighborhood group meetings after workshops are completed. Supporting activities involve representation in monthly Neighborhood Group Network meetings, which allow groups to share ideas and coordinate multigroup activities designed to stimulate and maintain interests in health.

A national organized training approach on the community level is currently being mounted by the Centers for Disease Control. The program contains four basic steps (Mason, 1984):

- Gathering and analysis of local community opinion and health data for the purpose of identifying priority problems;
- Setting objectives and standards to denote success;
- Design and implementation of multiple strategies based on behavioral and educational diagnosis to achieve objectives; and
- Continuous monitoring of problems and intervention strategies to evaluate progress and detect the need for change.

In addition, one should also:

- Obtain community leadership commitment for the program.
- Develop an overall advisory/planning committee, representing the various community constituencies, with appropriate task forces organized for specific projects.
- Identify local resources to accomplish objectives.
- Develop a marketing plan.

POINTS TO REMEMBER

Education-for-health is a critical element of health program development and implementation and is increasingly supported by governmental and voluntary health agencies, business and industry, legislators, consumer groups, and professional organizations. There is a renewed interest in education-for-health, partly supported by the consumer movement and the realization that a magic pill for health does not exist. The message that one's state of wellness is in a large way the result of personal decisions made on a daily basis is beginning to have an impact on the attitudes and behaviors of consumers as well as the professional health worker.

Certainly, there are a variety of approaches that can be taken as well as a variety of strategies that can be employed to support individual and community actions as illustrated by the model programs in this chapter. By implementing the strategies identified in the 1970s for education-for-health, significant progress will be made during this decade toward the achievement of the 1990 objectives for the nation.

References

Althafer, C. (1982). Background and perspective on the Center for Disease Control and its Bureau of Health Education. In M. M. Faber & A. M. Reinhardt (Eds.), *Promoting health through risk reduction*. New York: Macmillan.

American Cancer Society. (1983). *Model policy for smoking in the workplace*. New York: American Cancer Society.

American Hospital Association. (1972). *A patient's bill of rights*. Chicago: American Hospital Association.

American Hospital Association. (1975). *Statement on health education: Role and responsibility of health care institutions*. Chicago: American Hospital Association.

American Hospital Association. (1979a). *Policy and statement on the hospital's responsibility for health promotion*. Chicago: American Hospital Association.

American Hospital Association. (1979b). *Survey of inpatient education*. Atlanta: U.S. Public Health Service, Bureau of Health Education.

American Hospital Association. (1981). *Policy and statement on the hospital's responsibility for patient education services*. Chicago: American Hospital Association.

American Medical Association. (1975). *Statement on patient education*. Chicago: American Medical Association.

Bates, I. J., & Winder, A. E. (1984). *Introduction to health education*. Palo Alto, CA: Mayfield.

Belloc, N. B. (1973). Relationship of health practice and mortality. *Preventive Medicine, 2*, 67–81.

Belloc, N. B., & Breslow, L. (1972). Relationship of physical health status and health practices. *Preventive Medicine, 1*, 409–421.

Berman, D. M. (1978). *Death on the job: Occupational health and safety struggles in the United States*. New York: Monthly Review Press.

Bingham, E. (1983). The Occupational Safety and Health Act. In W. N. Rom (Ed.), *Environmental and occupational medicine*. Boston: Little, Brown.

Blue Cross Association. (1974). *White paper on patient health education*. Chicago: Blue Cross Association.

Bowman, R. A. (1982). Changes in the activities, functions, and roles of public health educators. In S. K. Simonds (Ed.), *The philosophical, behavioral, and professional bases for health education. SOPHE heritage collection of health education mimeographs* (Vol. 1). Oakland, CA: Third Party.

Breckon, D. J. (1982). *Hospital health education: A guide to program development*. Rockville, MD: Aspen Systems Corporation.

Breslow, L., & Somers, A. R. (1977). The lifetime health monitoring program. *New England Journal of Medicine, 296*, 601–608.

Bruess, C. E. (1978). National scope of school health education. In *Conference proceedings of school health education: A shared responsibility*. Piscataway, NJ: College of Medicine and Dentistry of New Jersey–Office of Consumer Health Education.

Canadian Task Force for the Periodic Health Examination. (1979). Task Force Report: The periodic health examination. *Canadian Medical Association Journal, 121*, 1193–1254.

Carlaw, R. W. (Ed.). (1982). *Perspectives on community health education: A series of case studies*. Oakland, CA: Third Party.

Creedon, J. J. (1984). Remarks. In *Program summary of a conference on worksite health promotion and human resources: A hard look at the data*. Washington, DC: U.S. Government Printing Office.

Cunningham, R. M. (1982). *Wellness at work: A report on health and fitness programs for employees of business and industry*. Chicago: Blue Cross Association.

Demak, M. M., Rosen, M. A., & Logsdon, D. N. (1983). Prevention in primary medical care: The INSURE project. *Maryland State Medical Journal, 32*(4), 279–283.

Derryberry, M. (1949). Health is everybody's business. *Public Health Reports, 64*, 1293–1298.

Dorsey, J. L. (1975). The Health Maintenance Organization Act of 1973 (P.L. 93-222) and prepaid group practice plans. *Medical Care, 13*(1), 1–9.

Egbert, I. D., Battit, G. E., Welch, C. E., Bartlett, M. K. (1964). Reduction of postoperative pain by encouragement and instruction of patients: A study of doctor-patient rapport. *New England Journal of Medicine, 270*, 825–827.

Farquhar, J. W. (1984). *Risk factor reduction from community education: Preliminary results of the Stanford five city project*. Paper presented at the American Heart Association, Council on Epidemiology National Meeting, Tampa, Florida.

Farquhar, J., Maccoby, N., Wood, P. D., Alexander, J. K., Breitrose, H., Brown, B. W., Haskell, W. L., McAlister, A. L., Meyer, A. J., Nash, J. D., & Stern, M. P. (1977). Community education for cardiovascular health. *Lancet, 8023*, 1192–1195.

Felton, J. S. (1983). The industrial medical department. In W. N. Rom (Ed.), *Environmental and occupational medicine*. Boston: Little, Brown.

Fielding, J. E. (1979). Preventive services for the well population. In U.S. Department of Health, Education and Welfare, *Healthy people: The Surgeon General's report on health promotion and disease prevention* (background papers) (DHEW pub. no. 79-55071A). Washington, DC: U.S. Government Printing Office.

Goetz, A., & Bernstein, J. (1984). Computer developments in health risk management. *Corporate Commentary, 1*(1), 26–33.

Gotsch, A., Troxel, D. A., & Fersht, K. (1986). From Scotland to New Jersey: Health race held in U.S. *Hygié, 5*(3), 18–21.

Green, L. W. (1974). Toward cost-benefit evaluations of health education: Some concepts, methods and examples. *Health Education Monographs, 2*(1), 34–64.

Green, L. W., Kreuter, M. W., Deeds, S. G., & Partridge, K. B. (1980). *Health education planning: A diagnostic approach*. Palo Alto, CA: Mayfield.

Green, L. W., Wang, V. L., Deeds, S., Fisher, A., Windsor, R., Bennett, A., & Rogers, C. (1978). Guidelines for health education in maternal and child health. *International Journal of Health Education, 21*(3), 1–33.

Hall, J. H., & Zwemer, J. D. (1979). *Prospective medicine*. Indianapolis: Methodist Hospital of Indiana.

Hamburg, D. A., Elliott, G. R., & Parron, D. L. (Eds.). (1982). *Health and behavior: Frontiers of research in the biobehavioral sciences*. Washington, DC: National Academy Press.

Hamburg, M. V. (1983). Education-for-health: Perspective and prospects. In Mental Health Materials Center (Ed.), *Education-for-health: The selective guide*. Baltimore, MD: John D. Lucas Printing Company.

Hammond, E. C., & Selikoff, I. J. (Eds.). (1979). Public control of environmental health hazards. *Annals of the New York Academy of Sciences, 329*, 1–405.

Health Education Center. (1976). *Health education strategies for local health departments*. Baltimore: Maryland State Department of Health and Mental Hygiene.

Health Insurance Association of America. (1979). *Financing in-hospital patient education: Proposed criterion*. Washington, DC: Health Insurance Association of America.

Health Maintenance Act of 1973. Sec. 1301, (C-9).

Heckler, M. H. (1984). Remarks. In *Program summary of a conference on worksite health promotion and human resources: A hard look at the data*. Washington, DC: U.S. Government Printing Office.

Industrywide Network for Social, Urban and Rural Efforts (INSURE). (1984). INSURE project improves health and controls costs. In *INSURE Update*. New York: INSURE.

Joint Commission on Accreditation of Hospitals. (1976). *Manual for hospitals*. Chicago: JCAH.

Kreuter, M. C. (1984). *Orientation on the role of CDC's Center for Health Promotion and Education*. Paper presented at a seminar, Update on Health Promotion in New Jersey, Trenton, N. J.

Lalonde, M. (1974). *A new perspective on the health of Canadians*. Ottawa: Ministry of National Health and Welfare.

Lee, E. (1979). *Reimbursement forum proceedings*. Chicago: American Hospital Association.

Lehmann, P. (1979). Health education. In U.S. Department of Health, Education and Welfare, *Healthy people: The Surgeon General's report on health promotion and disease prevention* (background papers) (DHEW pub. no. 79-55071A). Washington, DC: U.S. Government Printing Office.

Levine, P. H., & Britten, A. F. (1973). Supervised patient management of hemophilia: A study of 45 patients with hemophilia A and B. *Annals of Internal Medicine, 78*, 195–201.

Logsdon, D. N., Rosen, M. A., & Demak, M. M. (1983). The INSURE project on lifecycle preventive health services: Cost containment issues. *Inquiry, 20*, 121–126.

Mahler, H. T. (1983). Education-for-health: Priorities in the real world. In Mental Health Materials Center (Ed.), *Education-for-health: The selective guide*. Baltimore: MD: John D. Lucas Printing Company.

Maiman, L., Green, L. W., & Gibson, G. (1979). Education for self-treatment by adult asthmatics. *Journal of the American Medical Association, 241*, 1919–1922.

Mason, J. O. (1984). *Focal Points, 1*, 1.

McGinnis, J. M. (1983). Remarks, Annual Meeting of the American School Health Association.

Metropolitan Life Insurance Company. (1980). *A summary of a survey of HMO health education programs in the United States.* New York: Metropolitan Life Insurance Company.

Miller, L., & Goldstein, J. (1972). More efficient care of diabetic patients in a county hospital setting. *New England Journal of Medicine, 286*, 1388–1391.

Molotsky, I. (1984). Drinking-age bill goes to President. The *New York Times*, June 29.

National Center for Health Education. (1984a). Magnitude of the problem. *Center, 1*, 32.

National Center for Health Education. (1984b). Capsule reports of health promotion programs of 9 corporations. *Center, 1*, 31–32).

National Center for Health Education. (1984c). Growing healthy now in 595 school districts; 528,000 pupils participate in 41 states. *Center, 2*, 16–17, 19.

National Center for Health Education. (1984d). Carnegie-cited education-in-health curriculum now ready for use in high schools throughout the country. *Center, 1*, 38.

National Center for Health Education. (1984e). "Wogging" teams up lung association and local firm. *Center, 2*, 11.

National Center for Health Education. (1984f). "Growing younger" reality for those "60 or better." *Center, 2*, 8.

National Center for Health Education. (1984g). Chicago uptown coalition and health department reach needy, underserved with WIC service. *Center, 2*, 11.

National Center for Health Education. (1984h). Interaction support via TV facilitates community weight control program. *Center, 2*, 14.

National Center for Health Education. (1984i). Emerging council stimulates community of 3,500 to change health attitudes and behavior. *Center, 2*, 15.

National Consumer Health Information and Health Promotion Act of 1976, Sec. 1706 (1-3).

Nelson, M., Mazzocchi, A., Edelsack, P., & Eller, S. W. (1983). The labor union's perspective on occupational health. In W. N. Rom (Ed.), *Environmental and occupational medicine.* Boston: Little, Brown.

New Jersey Nurse Practice Act of 1974, P.L. 1974, Chapter 109, Senate No. 665.

North Carolina Chapter, SOPHE. (1980). *A self-assessment tool for use in the professional practice of community health education.*

Occupational Safety and Health Act of 1970. Section 5(a)(1).

Office of Consumer Health Education. (1980). *Consumer health education: A guide to hospital-based programs.* Wakefield, MA: Nursing Resources.

Parkinson, R. S., & Associates. (1982). *Managing health promotion in the workplace: Guidelines for implementation and evaluation.* Palo Alto, CA: Mayfield.

Robbins, A. (1983). New frontiers in occupational medicine. In W. N. Rom (Ed.), *Environmental and occupational medicine.* Boston: Little, Brown.

Rom, W. N. (Ed.). (1983). *Environmental and occupational medicine.* Boston: Little, Brown.

Salonen, J. T., Puska, P., Kottke, T. G., & Tuomilehto, J. (1981). Changes in smoking, serum cholesterol and blood pressure levels during a community-based cardiovascular disease prevention program—the North Karelia Project. *American Journal of Epidemiology, 114*(1), 81–94.

Selikoff, I. J. (1983). Forward: Preventing preventable disease. In W. N. Rom (Ed.), *Environmental and occupational medicine.* Boston: Little, Brown.

Simmons, N. (1984). Compliance with seat belt laws said to be low. The *New York Times*, July 14.

Smith, R. B. (1984). Remarks. In *Program summary of a conference on worksite health promotion and human resources: A hard look at the data.* Washington, DC: U.S. Government Printing Office.

Society for Public Health Education. (1976). *SOPHE's position statement on patient and family education.* San Francisco: Society for Public Health Education.

Somers, A. R. (Ed.). (1976). *Promoting health: Consumer education and national policy.* Germantown, MD: Aspen Systems Corporation.

Squyres, W. D. (Ed.). (1980). *Patient education: An inquiry into the state of the art*. New York: Springer.

Strategic Planning Group, National School Health Education Coalition. (1984). *Obstacles and strategies* (Interim Report). New York: National School Health Education Coalition.

Tepper, L. B. (1980). The right to know, the duty to inform. *Journal of Occupational Medicine, 22*(7), 433–437.

U.S. Bureau of the Census. (1981). *County business patterns*. Washington, DC: U.S. Government Printing Office.

U.S. Department of Health, Education and Welfare. (1979). *Healthy people: The Surgeon General's report of health promotion and disease prevention* (DHEW pub. no. 79-55071). Washington, DC: U.S. Government Printing Office.

U.S. Department of Health and Human Services. (1980a). *Health United States 1980: With prevention profile* (DHHS pub. no. 81-1232). Washington, DC: U.S. Government Printing Office.

U.S. Department of Health and Human Services. (1980b). *Promoting health/preventing disease: Objectives for the nation*. Washington, DC: U.S. Government Printing Office.

U.S. Department of Health and Human Services. (1984). Workplace health promotion objectives— 1990. In National Center for Health Education, *Center, 2*, 25.

U.S. Department of Health and Human Services. (1986). *The 1990 Health Objectives for the Nation: A Midcourse Review*. Washington, DC: U.S. Government Printing Office.

U.S. General Accounting Office. (1980). *Indoor air pollution: An impeding health peril* (GAO #CED 80-111). Washington, DC: General Accounting Office.

Vickery, D. M., Kalmer, H., Lowry, D., Constantine, M., Wright, E., & Loren, W. (1983). Effect of a self care education program on medical visits, *Journal American Medical Association, 250*(21), 2952–2956.

Ware, B. (1981). A view of occupational health education: Practice, problems, prospects. In Association for the Advancement of Health Education and Society for Public Health Education, *Health Education of the public in the 80's*. New York: Metropolitan Life Insurance Company.

Windsor, R., Barenowski, T., Clark, N., & Cutter, G. (1984). *Evaluation of health promotion and education programs*. Palo Alto, CA: Mayfield.

World Health Organization. (1974). *Health education: A programme review* (offset pub. no. 7). Geneva: World Health Organization.

Yenny, S. L. (1984). *Small businesses of health promotion: The prospects look good*. New York: National Center for Health Education.

THE MEDICAL CARE SYSTEM AND THE PROTECTION OF HEALTH

Michael K. Miller
University of Florida

C. Shannon Stokes
Pennsylvania State University

Since the turn of the century the physical health status of Americans has improved dramatically (see Chapter 1). In 1900 the infant mortality rate in the United States approached 162 infant deaths per 1,000 live births (Kotelchuck, 1976). By 1940 the rate had declined to 47.0 and in the 12 months ending with June 1986, 1,000 live births were accompanied by approximately 10.5 infant deaths (National Center for Health Statistics, 1986). Other indicators have shown equally impressive declines. Tuberculosis as a cause of death has been virtually eradicated; in 1900 the rate stood at about 194 per 100,000 population. Americans are also living longer than ever before. In the early 1900s Americans could expect to live only 47 years. In 1982 the average life expectancy was 74.5 years, 70.7 for newborn males and 78.2 years for females. Thus, even though deaths from cancer have shown a steady increase over the last century, most indicators point to an improved physical health status for Americans.

Concurrently with the marked improvement in population health status have been changes in American society such as urbanization, an improved economic level of living along with altered life-styles, and substantial environmental alterations. At the same time Americans have witnessed a rapidly expanding, ever more costly and complex medical care system. In 1950 the health care enterprise cost $12 billion and accounted for roughly 4.6% of the gross national product (GNP). Fueled by costs that are increasing more rapidly than those in any other sector of the economy, the health care industry cost Americans $160.6 billion in 1977 (8.6% of the GNP) and established itself as the third largest industry in the nation, (behind agriculture and construction (Culliton, 1978; Walsh, 1978). In 1982 outlays for medical care amounted to $322.4 billion (Rice, 1983), and current estimates put the 1983 price tag for medical care at approximately $340 billion or $1,400 for every man, woman, and child, a figure that represents more than 10% of total GNP.

The medical care system has prospered for a number of reasons including the American bent toward professional autonomy and a capitalist political philosophy (Duval, 1977; Knowles, 1977; Rogers, 1977; Wildavsky, 1977). Probably the most important reason for the expansion, however, has been the public's perception of the role medicine played in the historical improvement of health, as well as estimates of the role it plays now and will play in the future production of health (McKeown, 1976; Rogers, 1977; Thomas, 1977).

The prevailing assumption is that a long, full life requires the application of more and more complex medical knowledge and technology, whatever the price. In fact, the impact that medical care has actually had or is currently having on health is, by and large, assumed but empirically unsubstantiated (Carlson, 1975; Cochrane, 1972; Dubos, 1960; Illich, 1976; McKeown, 1976; Mendelsohn, 1979; Miller, Dixon, & Fendley, 1986; Miller & Stokes, 1978). Indeed, using historical data from England and Wales, McKeown (1976) argues that the bulk of mortality decline was due to the reduction of deaths from infectious diseases. Further, the primary influences that led to the reduction, both from infectious and noninfectious causes, were nutritional, environmental (particularly improvement in water and food sources), behavioral (reduced birth rate), and intrinsic resistance resulting from interaction of organism and host. In most instances mortality rates were declining prior to the introduction of immunization or treatment procedures, and the subsequent rates of decline were not materially affected (Knowles, 1977; McKeown, 1976). In short, it can be argued that medical intervention via vaccination had very little impact on the historical overall decline in mortality.

In the nineteenth century vaccination did contribute to a measurable decline in rates of smallpox. In this century vaccines have, arguably (Collins, 1982), contributed to declines in diphtheria, poliomyelitis, tuberculosis, and measles. Nonetheless, over the course of the last century vaccinations probably accounted for less than 10% of the overall reduction in mortality (McKeown, 1976). The independent effect that can be attributed to the introduction of medical and surgical therapy, particularly antibiotics and tumor excision, is probably even smaller (Knowles, 1977).

The above discussion provides some evidence that the formal medical care system did contribute, albeit minimally, to historical mortality reduction. Some recent literature suggests that, under certain circumstances, the existing system can play a beneficial role in the further reduction of mortality and morbidity rates in the United States (Gordis, 1973; Hadley, 1982; Kessner, 1973; Lipscomb, 1978; Radtke, 1974; U.S. Department of Health, Education and Welfare, 1972). Others are less convinced by the available evidence and suggest that the contribution of the medical care system to health status has been significantly overstated and potentially misinterpreted (Callahan, 1977; Carlson, 1975; Illich, 1976; Kisch, 1974; Knowles, 1977; McKeown, 1976; Mendelsohn, 1979; Miller & Stokes, 1978; Miller, Dixon, & Fendley, 1986; Miller, Voth, & Danforth, 1982; Wildavsky, 1977).

Clearly there is disagreement surrounding the role medicine has played and will play in the improvement of health status. A central component of any explanation for the disagreement must consider the pivotal question: What is health and how should it be measured? If the measures of health differ, so should the expected role of the medical care system. The remainder of this chapter examines the issues involved in the measurement of a population's health and the structure of the American medical care system. Finally, empirical evidence on the relative role of the medical care system in the production and protection of health is examined, and some implications for health care policy are discussed.

ISSUES IN THE MEASUREMENT OF THE HEALTH STATUS
OF A POPULATION

The increasing magnitude of expenditures on health (over $340 billion annually), in combination with a growing skepticism of the system's role in the production and protection of health, has intensified the call for accountability. What gains have been derived from the public's investment in health care? The production of such evidence to guide decisions about health policies and resources is contingent upon an "appropriate" measurement of health status. To the extent that the measures differ, so too may the conclusions reached and the policy decisions made.

At present a universally valid and accepted definition of health (or illness) is nonexistent. Health means different things to different people, with those differences reflecting, at least partly, the cultural and societal context from which the definition emanates as well as the prevailing paradigm of the interested science (e.g., clinical medicine, public health, sociology, psychology). In the United States and most other industrialized countries most definitions of health relate by and large directly to interests doctors have in defining what constitutes health or illness (Schroeder, 1983). A generally acceptable definition will, necessarily, be broad. Accordingly, the World Health Organization (WHO) has offered a definition of health as a state of complete physical, mental, and social well-being. While such a definition does provide an ideal end state that easily transcends cultural and socioeconomic class boundaries as a health policy objective, operationally it is unmanageable.

Although of limited utility from a research standpoint, the WHO definition of health is useful because it recognizes the multidimensional nature of the concept. The three different "types" of health (physical, mental, and social) are clearly interrelated. An ideal measure would include appropriately weighted components of all three. Unfortunately, both data availability and the present stage of knowledge concerning measurement procedures constrain the development of such a measure (Chen & Bush, 1979; Culyer, 1983; Hennes, 1972; Sullivan, 1971). It is common practice, born of necessity, to focus investigation on one of the three dimensions. The remainder of this chapter concentrates on the physical dimension of the concept of health. The choice is guided to a large extent by the fact that health planners and legislators tend to judge the physical health dimension as relatively more important and most useful in health policy debates (Goldsmith, 1973).

Within the physical dimension of health, it is useful to examine subclassifications. Health is more than the absence of disease. Health implies a positive dimension. It is necessary to define a set of health states that correspond to the sundry conditions that an individual can experience or that are prevalent in a given population. These states position themselves along a continuum ranging from perfect health or high-level wellness at one extreme, through a neutral midpoint where disease and disability are absent, but positive health is also lacking, then through various stages of ill health or disability to the ultimate level of physical disability and dysfunction—death (Belloc, Braslow, & Hochstein, 1971). While the notion of the continuum from death to high-level wellness is straightforward, the determination of where an individual or a population's health status falls along that continuum and how that determination should be made is open to debate. At this point issues of health status measurement come into play. The key issue is what type of information should be used to measure health status. More concretely, the issue is the degree to which the information used to measure a population's health status is objective, with generally easy access, or subjective, requiring special surveys to collect the data. Again, it is possible to conceptualize this dimension as a continuum ranging from maximally objective information such as death rates at the one extreme, through such things as illness prevalence rates, medical consultation rates, to maximally subjective measures such as self-perceived and self-reported health or illness.

It is apparent from the above discussion that very different kinds of data would be required to measure health depending upon the location of the intersection of the information dimension and the nature or state of health (i.e., positive or negative). Further, with the possible exception of the extreme case of an objective measure of maximum physical disability (i.e., death), any two attempts at somehow quantifying or measuring health status may arrive at different conclusions depending on where the intersection takes place. It then comes as no surprise that attempts to measure health status formally have a long and varied history with little agreement on the superiority of the product. Rosser (1983) provides an excellent historical review of the issues of measurement of general health status. What follows is a brief introduction to some of the varied attempts.

Early attempts at guiding health policy and resource allocation by examining a population's health status were limited to using various mortality and life expectancy statistics (Mushkin & Dunlop, 1979). As the health of the nation improved, the use of conventional mortality statistics became increasingly less acceptable as empirical surrogates or proxies for health status. The arguments against mortality data were straightforward. They had become insufficiently sensitive for adequately measuring the increasingly subtle changes taking place. Increasing life expectancy did not tap such things as the changing prevalence of disabilities or the fact that acceptable "thresholds" of disability were declining. This allowed for development of a situation in which a particular statistic might be perceived as increasingly severe at the same time the aggregate statistic was actually on the decline (Culyer, 1983).

The response to these concerns was the construction of complex health status indexes or indicators that incorporate information beyond simple mortality statistics. The indexes were conceptualized as needing to include information on such things as the duration and severity of disability in order to inform policies on such matters as preventable infectious disease, degenerative diseases, and even minor malaise (Draper, 1963).

In 1963 came the Index of Activities of Daily Living (ADL) (Katz, Ford, Moskowitz, Jacobson, & Jaffee, 1963). Included in the index were restricted activity, mobility limitation, bed disability, and other degrees of handicap, which purportedly measured the health states of elderly patients. More comprehensive measures included Chiang's (1965, 1976) annual index of health (H_x), which was intended to measure the average duration of health per year for a given age group, with the state of health weighted according to a scale of severity. The P health score (Kisch, Karner, Harris, & Kline, 1969) used information about admissions to hospitals, existence of chronic and/or acute conditions, and medication histories that were collected from interviews to assess levels of health. Depending on the cumulative score, an individual was classified as being in good, medium, or poor health. A still more complex measure of health was J. E. Miller's (1970) Q index designed for purposes of planning health services for the Indian Health Service. The index uses information on days of restricted activity, days in hospital, number of outpatient days, and mortality data. The differential weights given to the various components of the index are based on decisions about degrees of loss of productivity of the individual. A day as a hospital inpatient is equivalent to a day lost by premature death while a day spent as an outpatient is equivalent to a third of a day lost as an inpatient or by death.

An attempt to develop a formal measure consistent with the theoretical conceptualization of health presented earlier was that of Fanshel and Bush (1970). They defined eleven "functional states" ranging from complete wellness to death. The functional states represented a composite or level of dysfunction (e.g., complete wellness) and the probability (prognosis) that the individual would move to every other functional state (e.g., moderate dysfunction or death). While the formulation is theoretically appealing, the practical applications have been very limited because of (among other things) data requirements and the problems of determining what the actual transition probability (prognosis) would be in any given instance.

Card and Good (1970) approached the measurement of health from a classic economic perspective. The major concern was to provide information to be used in formalizing clinical decisions. To achieve this end, Card and Good focused primarily on the utilities of different states of illness and on the more general valuation of life. The underlying logic was straightforward. The various utilities would be converted into monetary values that would then be employed in cost-benefit analysis used to inform resource allocation decisions (Card, 1975). For example, what is the potential impact on a lifetime health or disability of some specific intervention? Similar decision theory approaches to health status measurement have been advocated by Torrance, Thomas, & Sackett (1971), Card and Good (1970), and Barnoon and Wolfe (1972).

Similar to these decision theory approaches, Culyer, Lavers, and Williams (1971) and Shonfield and Shaw (1972) approached the measurement of health status from the classic utility conversion framework of economists. However, from a health policy perspective they made a significant theoretical move forward. They defined conceptually distinct types of indicators: (1) state of health indicators, which measured the prevailing level of health, and (2) system input indicators or measures of the existing health care resources. In short, Culyer, Lavers, and Williams and Shonfield and Shaw defined an input-output system that allowed explicitly for an evaluation of the effect that varying medical care resources (system inputs) has on the health status of a target population (state of health or output indicators).

While the general theoretical perspective of Culyer, Lavers, and Williams and Shonfield and Shaw represents a move forward for health policy, the data requirements (i.e., individual medical records as well as medical and social "judgments" about level and duration of pain and dysfunction) necessary for operationalization of the system make its use in policy decisions questionable. Indeed, although attempts to "improve" the measurement of health status by including data beyond mortality statistics (i.e., morbidity, feelings, "expert judgments") have been voluminous (Chen, 1976; Goldberg, Dab, Chaperon, Fuhrer, & Gremy, 1979; Moriyama, 1968; R. M. Rosser, 1974; R. M. Rosser & Benson, 1978) the utility of such complex indexes for planning and health care policy is questionable (Bickner, 1969; Damiani, 1973). Further, Bickner (1976) argued that not only were combined measures of questionable utility, but that the attempted measurement of positive health rather than ill health was folly. As R. Rosser (1983) points out, Bickner's statement is no less true in 1984 than it was in 1976. A valid, practical, and comprehensive measure of prognosis, a necessary forerunner to the legitimate combination of statistics on morbidity with those on death rates, has yet to be developed. Further, it has not been convincingly demonstrated that health policy decisions based on complex health status indices would differ materially from those based on mortality statistics alone. This is particularly true when the focus is on policies aimed at macro or community health (R. Rosser, 1983).

The Use of Mortality Statistics to Measure a Population's Health: The Concept of Community Malady

As just noted, mortality statistics, although less than ideal, are useful as measures of collective health. Further, as Goldsmith (1973) has pointed out, certain types of data are more widely accepted as policy relevant by health planners and legislators than others: infant mortality rates, rates of preventable deaths, and mortality rates by major causes. And, although there is not complete consensus, infant mortality is considered by many to be the single most sensitive index of "the level of health existing in an area" (Anderson, 1973). Further, to the extent that the etiology of life-threatening maladies is postnatal and somewhat tractable, the medical care system is, theoretically, capable of exerting some positive impact. This is true for many nongenetic causes of death and thus an appropriately adjusted death rate (all causes) can legitimately serve as an overall measure of physical health status for a population. Employing this rationale does not negate the fact that it is virtually impossible to measure health as an absolute. It does, however, lend itself to a relative definition of community health that is measurable.

Among the most basic essential functions of a community is the maintenance of a pool of individuals physically capable of filling necessary roles. At some point, the community's failure to maintain that pool of individuals becomes critical, and the collective well-being of the community is decreased. Furthermore, any inability to maximize the pool of vital individuals represents a diminished return on the community's investment in its inhabitants. Specification of the level at which failure to protect or extend an individual life represents an unacceptable return on the community's investment is not easily resolved. For example, when is a death premature? Or when is death less dysfunctional than prolongation of disablement? Nonetheless, using aggregate mortality statistics, it is still possible to provide a relative operationalization of community malady. Specifically, any community "A" has a higher malady status than any other community "B" when the mortality rate in "A" is larger than the counterpart rate in "B."

THE AMERICAN MEDICAL CARE SYSTEM:
A MACRO-STRUCTURAL PERSPECTIVE

We have suggested the existence of a deeply held belief about the functioning of the American health care system. The assumption can be succinctly stated as one that puts virtually unquestioning faith in the investigation and treatment of disease by formally trained medical personnel, particularly physicians, and to a somewhat lesser degree nurses and physician assistants (Callahan, 1977). Malady intervention is deemed critical, not only as a restorative strategy for the acutely ill, but also as the solution to long-term health prospects (Thomas, 1977). It is this presumption about the efficacy of medicine in producing and restoring health—a presumption made by both the profession of medicine and the general consuming public—that serves to justify the massive investment in medical care (Bennett, 1977). This section examines the structure of the existing medical care system as a precursor to evaluating what impact it has had on community health.

Health care arrangements in the United States have been depicted as being in a crisis (McKinlay, 1973; Somers, 1973). Glasser (1974) argues that the existing health care pattern is more a nonsystem than a system. The empirical arrangements may be ineffective, but arrangements do exist. Thus, it is possible to construct a conceptual model of the health system.

Recent literature (Field, 1973; E. Levy, 1977; Miller & Stokes, 1978) has defined the macro health care system as a societal mechanism or subsystem that has been mandated to preserve, repair, or enhance the capacity of social actors whose role performance is imperiled by ill health or premature death. As such, the system would include the aggregate of resources (to include personnel in designated roles) that society actually invests in the improvement and maintenance of the population's health. It can be argued, however, that ours is not an integrated system with collective health as the target. Rather, it is a loose assembly of medically related elements that focus on malady and mortality.

The emphasis of the system is on diagnosis and treatment of existing disease in the individual patient (Black, 1968; Reiser, 1977). Unfortunately, this focus on individual acute curative medicine comes at the expense of preventive or community health. Further, the focus of the existing system leads away from a consideration of the environmental and behavioral causes of disease, despite the increasing evidence of the importance of such public health considerations for improving collective health in postindustrial America.

So the medical care system is not comprehensively integrated with positive or community health as the focus. It is nonetheless possible to specify a general structure of the restricted medical care system. The minimum commitments that society makes to it can be organized into four major categories: knowledge, personnel, physical facilities, and economic resources. Embodied in the knowledge commitment are such things as basic biomedical research and training of personnel to fill specialized roles within the system. The personnel commitment includes all those directly involved in the health occupations such as nurses, X-ray technicians and, of course, physicians. The physical facility component embraces all objects these people need. Central among these facilities are hospitals, clinics, and technical equipment.

The economic resource component, of necessity, plays a central role in all three of these commitment areas. In addition, it includes more direct elements such as per capita expenditures for health and actual medical care payments.

Organized in this manner, the medical care system can be formally conceptualized as an input-output system depicted in Figure 11-1. The four components (knowledge, personnel, facilities, and economic resources) constitute the inputs to the system, and population health status or levels of mortality is the output.

It is useful to differentiate between internal and external components of the medical care system. The internal components are such things as medical research and education and training of physicians and other health personnel. These internal components have an indirect effect on health by affecting the level of knowledge and skill of the medical care personnel (Field, 1973). The external components of the system include the physical facilities, personnel, and economic resources devoted to health. They have a direct impact on health through the modalities or major activities of diagnosis, treatment, and rehabilitation. Additionally, medical personnel could have an impact on health through prevention and health education, but neither activity is fully integrated into the existing system (Knowles, 1977; Reiser, 1977).

As pointed out above, the medical care system is a differentiated subsystem of society. As such, it is neither unconstrained nor self-supporting, but rather operates in a given structural or community context with a target population of defined scope. Hence, the structure of the community constrains or sets limits on the operation of the system and thus influences what impact the system can theo-

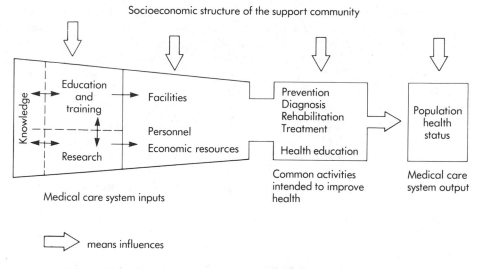

Socioeconomic structure of the support community

Medical care system inputs

Common activities intended to improve health

Medical care system output

means influences

Figure 11-1. An input-output conceptualization of the medical care system.

retically have on the physical well-being of the population (Rushing, 1971, 1975). Different settings demonstrate widely varying abilities to furnish the needed supports for the system to function optimally. At the same time, the very community or socioenvironmental structure that constrains the operation of the system also demonstrates a direct impact on the health status of the target population. In this context the concern is not only with the carcinogens in the air we breathe but also the occupations we pursue, the ethnicity and homogeneity of the area, the mobility or stability of the population, urbanization and crowding, and the overall socioeconomic conditions of the area. In short, the concern is with the general residential life-style of the community (Rosen, Goldsmith, & Redick, 1979).

Within the broad socioenvironmental milieu, it is possible to delineate conceptually two classes of interrelated factors that have been shown to have significant impacts on the health status of a population. Foremost in this category is the socioeconomic status of the area. The nature of the relationship was put most succinctly by Antonovsky and Bernstein (1977) when they stated that higher socioeconomic status was a major factor (mediated by public sanitation, preventive health, and available health treatment) in staying alive longer. Miller and Stokes (1978) and Wolinsky (1980) examined the relationship at the macro level and concluded that communities that have relatively high socioeconomic status tend to have better levels of health. The relationship persisted after controlling for medical care resources available in the area.

A second class of factors that is of increasing importance in explaining differential health status in postindustrial society is physical crowding and social disorganization. Although the results are inconclusive (Booth & Cowell, 1976), there are empirical studies that demonstrate a link between population concentration, both intradwelling unit concentration (crowding) and areal density, and increased mortality (Levy & Herzog, 1975). While there are some who argue that density per se is a cause of increased mortality (Galle, Grove, & McPherson, 1972), the stronger argument would seem to be that density forces increased contact (personal press) with others; thus, the results are increased chances to contract diseases. Density also appears empirically and theoretically to be an indicator (as well as an integral component) of a residential life-style that, in total, has adverse consequences for health (Rosen et al., 1979).

This discussion places the socioenvironmental structure of the community squarely at the center of the community health and medical care issue. The health status of a given population is a function of both the general environment of the community and the specific medical care system operating within the constraining context. Which is more important?

The Relative Role of the Medical Care System in the Production and Protection of a Population's Health: Empirical Evidence

One of the major underlying justifications for spending billions of dollars on the medical care system in the United States has been the assumed validity of what Wildavsky (1977) has termed the "Great Equation, to wit: Medical Care Equals Health." Given this equality, many presume that the real problem with the American medical care system, and thus by definition with American health status, is basic insufficiency (Thomas, 1977). There are not enough doctors (450,000), there are not enough nurses (1.7 million RNs), there are not enough medical schools, and there are not enough hospitals (about 7,000 with 1.4 million beds) (Rice, 1983). Clearly, then, if there were only enough money to expand personnel and resources, the medical care system could function to enhance good health in the population. But, as just discussed, the socioenvironmental milieu and accompanying residential life-style of an area also vie for prominence in the complex matrix of causes that help explain differential mortality in the United States. What follows is a brief look at some empirical evidence that attempts to assess the relative role played by the medical care system and the community structure in the determination of mortality levels in a community.

The literature reviewed in the introduction provided some evidence that the formal medical care system did contribute to historical mortality reduction. Some recent literature suggests that, under certain circumstances, the existing system can further reduce mortality in the United States (Gordis, 1973; Kessner, 1973; Lipscomb, 1978; Radtke, 1974; U.S. Department of Health, Education and Welfare, 1972). Studies by Minnesota Systems Research (1972) and Farmer, Miller, and Voth (1984) also reported positive impacts, but they were attributable to preventive and primary care programs rather than to typical after-the-fact curative interventions. To counterbalance claims of positive medical system impact, there is a growing literature that suggests the contribution of the medical care system to reduced mortality has been significantly overstated (Callahan, 1977; Carlson, 1975; Kisch, 1974; Mendelsohn, 1979; Miller, Dixon, & Fendley, 1986; Miller & Stokes, 1978; Wildavsky, 1977). Miller (1983) used two mathematical methods called correlation and regression analysis to assess the relative importance of community structure and the medical care system on infant mortality rates and age-sex standardized death rates for all causes for the 3,079 counties of the continental United States. Indicators of community structure employed in the analysis included: (1) percent nonwhite population, (2) median school years completed for all persons 25 years and older, (3) percent of the labor force classified as white-collar, (4) median family income, (5) percent of homes with no plumbing, and (6) percent urban population. All these indicators are structural characteristics that differentiate among communities. Communities that are relatively advantaged should theoretically have lower mortality rates than those lower in the hierarchy.

Eight indicators were used to measure medical care resources for the age-sex adjusted mortality model. Personnel resources were indexed by (1) medical specialists per 1,000 population, (2) surgical specialists per 1,000 population, (3) general physicians per 1,000 population, (4) registered nurses per 1,000 population, and (5) licensed practical nurses per 1,000 population. Physical facilities were measured by (1) number of hospital beds per 1,000 population, (2) presence or absence of at least one hospital in the county, and (3) presence of two or more hospitals in the county. Finally, items selected to represent use of existing resources include (1) inpatient days per 1,000 population, and (2) outpatient visits per 1,000 population.

The model for infant mortality employed basically the same indicators of population structure, but added one indicator of poverty: average number of Aid to Families with Dependent Children (AFDC) recipients per 1,000 population. In addition, the medical care system for the infant mortality model was more complex. The indicators of personnel were unchanged, but several additional indicators of physical resources pertaining directly to infant mortality were included: (1) presence or absence of a hospital with a neonatal intensive care unit, (2) presence or absence of a hospital with a premature nursery, (3) presence of two or more hospitals with premature nurseries, (4) presence or absence of a pediatric program in the county, and (5) presence or absence of an obstetrics and gynecology program in the county. Finally, because of known variation in mortality and resource distribution, an explicit control for region of the country was included in both models. Table 11-1 summarizes the relative importance of the top ten medical system and socioenvironmental factors in explaining mortality differences among counties.

The socioenvironmental milieu of the community had a much stronger impact on mortality than did the medical care system. For both infant mortality and mortality from all causes the percent of nonwhite population was the single most powerful negative contributor to increased death rates in a community, reflecting continuing racial disparities in American society. It accounted for approximately half of the total explained variation in both the infant mortality model and the age-sex standardized mortality model. Further, communities that have higher average incomes and higher educational levels tended to have lower overall mortality rates. In the

Table 11-1. Relative Importance of Top Ten Medical System and Environmental Factors in Explaining Mortality Differences

	Rank in importance[a]	
Factor	Infant mortality	Standardized death rate
Medical manpower and facilities		
Medical specialists/1000		3 −
RN/1000	10 +	4 −
Surgical specialists	4 −	2 +
Total physicians/1000	9 −	9 −
LPN/1000		9 +
Hospital beds/1000		5 +
Community structure		
Percent nonwhite	1 +	1 +
Percent urban	3 +	
Percent in white-collar occupations	2 −	
Median education	8 +	7 −
Percent homes without plumbing	7 +	8 +
Median family income	5 −	6 −
AFDC recipients/1000	6 +	

[a]Plus and minus signs indicate direction of association.

case of infant mortality those communities with relatively low concentrations of AFDC recipients, higher concentrations of white-collar occupations, and smaller proportions of the population living in urban areas tend to have lower rates.

Consistent with the arguments made by the proponents of the medical care system, it did have a net, albeit very small, impact on mortality. More specifically, the system accounted for only 4.02% of the variation among the more than 3,000 counties in age-sex standardized death rates, and even less (1.4%) of the variation in infant mortality. Consistent with the macro model developed earlier, the personnel and physical facilities dimensions both have variables that are statistically significant predictors of mortality. Once the impact of the socioeconomic milieu has been removed, communities that have relatively high concentrations of medical specialists and registered nurses tended to have lower levels of age-sex standardized death rates. Conversely, as concentrations of hospital beds and surgical specialists increased, the mortality rates in the communities also increased. The evidence on medical system influence on the narrower (but, arguably more sensitive) problem of infant mortality is quite different and easily summarized. The existence and concentration of traditional medical personnel, programs, and facilities at the county level have no measurable impact on infant mortality rates.

To illustrate the differences more formally, Table 11-2 contains a profile for the ten counties in the United States with the lowest and highest average death rates. For the least healthy counties the average death rate was 14.8 per 1,000 population. The counties were primarily poor rural counties with relatively large nonwhite populations (40.1%). The median family income for the group in 1970

Table 11-2. Profiles of Counties With Highest and Lowest Mortality Rates in the United States

	Average death rate	% urban population	AFDC recipients/ 1000	% white collar occupation	Median education	Median income	% nonwhite population	MD's/1000 population	RN's/ 1000	Hospital beds/ 1000
Age-Sex Adjusted Death Rate										
10 highest counties	14.8	9.7	76.7	35.8	10.1	$5864	40.1	.31	2.3	4.9
10 lowest counties	5.89	15.3	7.9	25.9	10.5	7009	4.6	.41	1.5	1.2
Infant Mortality Rate										
10 highest counties	55.9	2.0	32.9	29.7	10.1	5751	18.7	.23	.97	2.5
10 lowest counties	3.0	2.7	21.2	29.9	11.1	6582	.80	.35	2.2	5.2

was $5,864, and there were approximately 77 AFDC recipients per 1,000 population. This group of counties included such places as Nantucket, Massachusetts, with a death rate of 21.1, Buffalo and Shannon counties, South Dakota, with a rate of 15.4, and Russell County, Alabama, with a rate of 13.3.

The ten healthiest counties averaged 5.8 deaths per 1,000 population, or approximately 39% of the average for the least healthy counties. A profile describes a relatively affluent, somewhat more urban set of counties with small nonwhite populations. The median family income was $7,009, and they averaged fewer than 8 AFDC recipients per 1,000 population. Most notably this group of counties averages less than 5% nonwhite population, or approximately nine times less nonwhite population than the group of "worst" health counties. Included in this group are such places as Loving, Terrell, and Franklin counties, Texas; Sioux and Wheeler counties, Nebraska; and Brookings County, South Dakota.

Finally it should be noted that there is virtually no difference in the concentration of medical doctors for the two groups, and the less healthy group has a slightly higher concentration of registered nurses. The healthier group does, however, have higher concentrations of hospital beds.

If health is measured by infant mortality, there are equally divergent figures. The least healthy group of counties average almost 56 infant deaths per 1,000 live births, a figure that is close to some underdeveloped countries. Conversely, the healthiest group has an infant mortality rate of 3.0. And, while the profile differences are similar to those for deaths from all causes (i.e., the least healthy have lower incomes, higher concentrations of AFDC recipients, and higher levels of nonwhite populations), the counties that make up the groups are not the same. The counties with the highest rates of infant mortality include such places as Issaquena and Noxubee, Mississippi; Dickens, Irion, and Stonewall, Texas; and Glades, Florida. At the other extreme are places like Shannon and Knox counties, Missouri; Traill and Dunn, North Dakota; and Cass County, Illinois. However, once again there is little difference in medical personnel concentrations for the two groups. The least healthy have .23 doctors per 1,000 population compared to .35 for the most healthy. Clearly there are issues other than medical care that determine levels of mortality in communities.

The evidence on overall mortality and infant mortality demonstrates the notion presented earlier with regard to differing measures of health status. If the measure of health differs, so too should the expected role of the medical care system. This is true not only in comparing the system's impact on mortality versus morbidity, or some measure of positive health, but also in comparing the system's impact on different types of mortality.

If the structure and focus of the existing system are consistent with the model drawn earlier, it should be expected to influence certain causes of death differently than others. Specifically, the health system should respond to situations that lend themselves to after-the-fact curative intervention of acute conditions much more than it does to situations that are produced from chronic conditions. Mortality from accidents and from arteriosclerosis provide comparative information on how well the medical care system responds to these two very different circumstances.

In both cases the vast majority of variation in mortality is not explained either by the medical care system or the socioenvironmental milieu of the community. However, the relative explanatory ability of the models is largely consistent with the expectations developed earlier. Specifically, deaths that are related to chronic conditions as well as to residential life-style and environmental influences (i.e., deaths from arteriosclerosis) are less well explained. In the arteriosclerosis model 3% of the variance is explained, but only 18% for the accidental death model. Further, rates of death from arteriosclerosis exhibit no significant relationship to any component of the medical care system. In the case of deaths from accidents the situation is reversed. In this instance, an increase in the availability of medical personnel results in a reduction in the death rate.

Further examination showed that although availability of medical personnel was important, the level of affluence of the community was the single most important explanatory variable in the model for deaths from accidents. Affluence explained approximately 10% of the variation compared to approximately 2% for medical personnel. However, in the case of arteriosclerosis, increased affluency is found in conjunction with higher mortality rates (see Miller *et al.*, 1982, for a complete analysis). This finding is consistent with a growing literature that suggests that an affluent, overly indulgent life-style is an increasingly important determinant of differential population health status in postindustrialized society.

POINTS TO REMEMBER

Implications for Health Care Policy

The intent of this chapter was to provide some insight into the role played by the medical care system in the protection of the health status of communities. To accomplish this, a statistical analysis was made of the relationship between mortality rates on the one hand and the medical care system and environmental influences on the other. The analysis tests the hypothesis that the system improves health. The expected impact of the system would, however, vary greatly depending upon how health is measured. Mortality statistics are less than ideal indicators of health, but at the level of the community they still provide the best available evidence of aggregate health status. Thus, one function of the medical care system should be, at minimum, to prevent premature death.

Duval (1977), Wildavsky (1977), and a number of other authors have suggested that most of what the medical care system does or is capable of doing is irrelevant to collective good health even if measured by levels of mortality. The evidence presented here is equivocal. Certain components of the system do appear to play a minor role in reducing rates of mortality that have their genesis in situations such as accidents that require after-the-fact curative interventions. In the increasingly important area of mortality from chronic conditions the effectiveness pales. Indeed, the marginal value of putting one thousand or several billion additional dollars into the existing medical care system to equalize access would appear very close to zero in terms of reducing mortality rates, let alone improving the collective health status of Americans. This is a hypothesis that we are presently testing, but which appears to be true, at least in the west south central United States (Miller, Dixon, & Fendley, 1986).

If the goal is actually improved health or even simply reduced mortality and if, for whatever reason, the existing medical care system does not address many of the factors that ultimately have an impact on health, a great deal of rethinking and reallocation of funds appears to be necessary.

The data reported here are conclusive in identifying race as a major contributing factor to differential mortality in the United States. However, race is not tractable from a policy perspective. This would suggest the need to identify and examine those things that are associated with the racial factor but are more amenable to public policy solution. In this context it is increasingly evident that many health problems in the United States have their genesis in social class differences and associated personal behavior patterns generally. Hence, in some relatively low socioeconomic class communities, the major maladies result from environmental conditions and behavioral pattern (e.g., sewage disposal, water supplies, nutrition, hygiene, and reproductive practices) that are not conducive to good health. At the other extreme are the relatively affluent communities that may have equally deleterious, but very different, environmental conditions and collective behavior patterns. Overconsumption of alcohol, fatty foods, and tobacco, combined with a sedentary, generally stressful life-style, are clearly not health producing.

The conclusion is inescapable. There are priority changes that must be made if an improvement in the health status of Americans is to be realized. There are a number of alterations that loom large as needed first steps. First, it is essential that it become common, but more importantly, *accepted* knowledge by the consuming public, policymakers, and the profession of medicine that health cannot be purchased by simply pouring endless amounts of money into the traditionally structured medical care system. Life-style, social inequality, and environmental conditions are the prime determinants of health, or its antithesis, death. Second, it will be necessary to invest significant resources, part of which may need to be expropriated from the current medical care system, into the health education of Americans. It is a telling statistic that of the billions of dollars spent annually on health, only one-half of one percent is spent on health education (Knowles, 1977). This becomes particularly disheartening when it is realized that significant strides in improved health status could very probably be realized by convincing the public to observe simple and prudent behavioral guidelines relating to exercise, diet, rest, and personal habits. Three meals each day at regular times, moderate exercise, adequate sleep, maintenance of a reasonable weight, no smoking, and alcohol only in moderation (if at all) can do more for health, and at far less expense, than all the efforts of the medical care system combined.

In addition, it will be necessary for the commitment to environmental health research and primary preventive "medicine" to be substantially increased. Prevention must be fully integrated into the activities of the medical care system. It is a peculiar logic which encourages attempted medical cure of cancer when existing knowledge indicates that the vast majority of human neoplasm (about 80 to 90%) have their genesis in environmental factors such as the food we eat, the water we drink, the air we breathe, self-indulgent habits (we spend $30 billion plus for cigarettes and alcohol), and even the occupations we choose. Obviously there is a misalignment between cause and concern, on the part of both the medical establishment and the public. A health system that improves health requires a rational setting of priorities and a materially different distribution of scarce resources.

References

Anderson, J. G. (1973). Causal models and social indicators: Toward the development of social systems models. *American Sociological Review, 38,* 285–301.

Antonovsky, A., & Bernstein, J. (1977). Social class and infant mortality. *Social Science and Medicine, 11,* 453–470.

Barnoon, S., & Wolfe, H. (1972). *Measuring the effectiveness of medical decisions: An operations research approach.* Springfield, IL: Charles C Thomas.

Belloc, N. B., Braslow, L., & Hochstein, J. R. (1973). Measurement of physical health in a general population survey. *American Journal of Epidemiology, 93,* 328–336.

Bennett, L., Jr. (1977). Technology as a shaping force. In J. H. Knowles (Ed.), *Doing better and feeling worse: Health in the United States.* New York: W. W. Norton.

Bickner, R. E. (1969). *Measurements and indices of health in methodology of identifying, measuring and evaluating outcomes of health service programs, systems and subsystems.* Health, Education and Welfare Department, Public Health Series, Conference Series 1967. Washington, DC: Health Services and Mental Health Administration.

Black, D. A. K. (1968). *The logic of medicine.* London: Oliver and Boyd.

Booth, A., & Cowell, J. (1976). Crowding and health. *Journal of Health and Social Behavior, 17,* 204–220.

Callahan, D. (1977). Health and society: Some ethical imperatives. In J. H. Knowles (Ed.), *Doing better and feeling worse: Health in the United States.* New York: W. W. Norton.

Card, W. I. (1975). Development of a formal structure for clinical management decisions: A mathematical analysis in outcome of severe damage to the central nervous system. *Ciba Foundation Symposium* 34 (New Series). Amsterdam: Elsevier—Excerpta Medica.

Card, W. I., & Good, I. J. (1970). The estimation of implicit utilities of medical consultants. *Mathematical Biosciences, 6,* 45–54.

Carlson, R. J. (1975). *The end of medicine.* New York: Wiley.

Chen, M. K. (1976). A comprehensive population health index based on mortality and disability data. *Social Indicators Research, 3,* 257–271.

Chen, M. M., & Bush, J. W. (1979). Health status measures, policy and biomedical research. In S. J. Mushkin & D. W. Dunlop (Eds.), *Health: What is it worth? Measures of health benefits.* New York: Pergamon Press.

Chiang, C. L. (1965). *An index of health: Mathematical models* (PHS pub. no. 1000, Series 2, No. 5). Washington, DC: U.S. Government Printing Office.

Chiang, C. L. (1976). Making annual indexes of health. *Health Services Research, 11,* 442–451.

Cochrane, A. L. (1972). *Effectiveness and efficiency: Random reflections on health service.* London: Nuffield Provincial Hospitals Trust.

Collins, J. J. (1982). The contribution of medical measures to the decline of mortality from respiratory tuberculosis: An age-period-cohort model. *Demography, 19*(3), 409–427.

Culliton, B. J. (1978). Health care economics: The high cost of getting well. In P. H. Abelson (Ed.), *Health care: Regulation, economics, ethics, practice*. Washington, DC: American Association for the Advancement of Science.

Culyer, A. J. (1983). *Health indicators*. New York: St. Martin's Press.

Culyer, A. J., Lavers, R. J., & Williams, A. (1971). Social indicators: Health. *Social Trends, 1*, 31–42.

Damiani, P. (1973). La mesure du niveau de santé. *Journal de la société de statistique de Paris, 2*, 129–144.

Draper, J. (1963). A suggested method for constructing indices of morbidity. *Applied Statistics, 3*, 26–37.

Dubos, R. (1960). *The mirage of health*. London: George Allen and Unwin.

Duval, M. K. (1977). On the science and technology of medicine. In J. H. Knowles (Ed.), *Doing better and feeling worse: Health in the United States*. New York: W. W. Norton.

Fanshel, S., & Bush, J. W. (1970). A health status index and its application to health service outcomes. *Operations Research, 18*, 1021–1066.

Farmer, F. L., Miller, M. K., & Voth, D. E. (1984). Evaluation of rural health care programs employing unobserved variable models: Impact on infant mortality. *Rural Sociology, 49*(1), 127–142.

Field, M. G. (1973). The concept of the health system at the macrosociological level. *Social Science and Medicine, 7*, 763–785.

Galle, O., Grove, W. R., & McPherson, J. M. (1972). Population density and pathology: What are the relations for man? *Science, 176*, 23–30.

Glasser, M. A. (1974). The approaching struggle to provide adequate health care for all Americans. In H. W. Demone, Jr., & D. Harshbarger (Eds.), *A handbook of human service organizations*. New York: Behavioral Publications.

Goldberg, M., Dab, W., Chaperon, J., Fuhrer, R., & Gremy, F. (1979). Indicateurs de santé et sanométrie: Les aspects conceptuels des recherches recentessur la mesure de l'état de santé d'une. *Population Revue Epidemiologic et Santé, 27*, 51–68, 133–152.

Goldsmith, S. B. (1973). A reevaluation of health status indicators. *Health Services Reports, 88*, 937–941.

Gordis, L. (1973). Effectiveness of comprehensive care programs in preventing rheumatic fever. *New England Journal of Medicine, 289*, 331–335.

Hadley, J. (1982). *More medical care, better health? An economic analysis of mortality rates*. Washington, DC: Urban Institute Press.

Hennes, J. D. (1972). The measurement of health. *Medical Care Review, 29*, 1268–1288.

Illich, I. (1976). *Medical nemesis*. London: Calder and Boyars

Katz, S., Ford, A. B., Moskowitz, R. W., Jacobson, B. A., & Jaffee, M. W. (1963). The index of ADL: A standardized measure of biological and psycho-social function. *Journal of the American Medical Association, 185*, 914–919.

Kessner, D. M. (1973). *Infant death: An analysis of maternal risk and health care*. Washington, DC: Institute of Medicine, National Academy of Sciences.

Kisch, A. (1974). The health care system and health: Some thoughts on a famous misalliance. *Inquiry, 11*, 269–275.

Kisch, A. I., Karner, H. W., Harris, L. J., & Kline, G. (1969). A new proxy measure for health status. *Health Services Research, 4*, 223–230.

Knowles, J. H. (1977). The responsibility of the individual. In J. H. Knowles (Ed.), *Doing better and feeling worse: Health in the United States*. New York: W. W. Norton.

Kotelchuck, D. (1976). *Prognosis negative: Crisis in the health care system*. A Policy Advisory Center book. New York: Random House.

Levy, E. (1977). The search for health indicators. *International Social Science Journal, 29*, 433–463.

Levy, L., & Herzog, A. (1974). Effects of population density and crowding on health and social adaption in the Netherlands. *Journal of Health and Social Behavior, 15*, 228–240.

Lipscomb, J. (1978). Health status and health programs. *Health Services Research, 13*, 71–77.

McKeown, T. (1976). *The role of medicine: Dream, mirage or nemesis?* London: Nuffield Provincial Hospitals Trust.

McKinlay, J. B. (1973). *Politics and law in health care policy.* New York: Prodist.

Mendelsohn, R. S. (1979). *Confessions of a medical heretic.* Chicago: Contemporary Books.

Miller, J. E. (1970). An indicator to aid management in assigning program priorities. *Public Health Reports, 85,* 725.

Miller, M. K. (1983). Health systems vs. sickness systems: Implications for the physical well-being of Americans. In R. F. Morgan (Ed.), *The iatrogenics handbook.* Toronto: IPI Publishing.

Miller, M. K., Dixon, B. L., & Fendley, K. (1986). The economic costs and benefits of adding medical manpower to rural and urban communities: A human capital perspective. *The Journal of Rural Health, 2*(2), 17–36.

Miller, M. K., & Stokes, C. S. (1978). Health status, health resources and consolidated structural parameters: Implications for public health care policy. *Journal of Health and Social Behavior, 19,* 263–279.

Miller, M. K., Voth, D E., & Danforth, D. M. (1982). The medical care system and community malady: Rural, urban, and suburban variations in impact. *Rural Sociology, 47*(4), 634–654.

Minnesota Systems Research. (1972). *Children and Youth Project*, Report Series 18 and 20. Minneapolis–St. Paul: Minnesota Systems Research.

Moriyama, I. W. (1968). Problems in the measurement of health status. In E. B. Sheldon & W. E. Moore (Eds.), *Indicators of social change.* New York: Russell Sage Foundation.

Mushkin, S. J., & Dunlop, D. W. (1979). Health: What is it worth? Measures of health benefits. New York: Pergamon Press.

National Center for Health Statistics. (1986). *Monthly vital statistics report.* Hyattsville, MD: Public Health Service.

Radtke, H. D. (1974). Benefits and costs of a physician to a community. *American Journal of Agricultural Economics, 56,* 586–593.

Reiser, S. J. (1977). Therapeutic choice and moral doubt in a technological age. In J. H. Knowles (Ed.), Doing better and feeling worse: Health in the United States. New York: W. W. Norton.

Rice, D. P. (1983). The burden of illness: Past trends and future projections. In *Priorities in Health Statistics.* Proceedings of the 19th National Meeting of the Public Health Conference on Records and Statistics (DHHS pub. no. (PHS) 81-1214). Hyattsville, MD: U.S. Department of Health and Human Services.

Rogers, D. E. (1977). The challenge of primary care. In J. H. Knowles (Ed.), *Doing better and feeling worse: Health in the United States.* New York: W. W. Norton.

Rosen, B. M., Goldsmith, H. F., & Redick, R. W. (1979). Demographic and social indicators: Uses in mental health planning in small areas. *Mental Health Planning, 32,* 102.

Rosser, R. (1983). Issues of measurement in the design of health indicators: A review. In A. J. Culyer (Ed.), *Health indicators.* New York: St. Martin's Press.

Rosser, R. M. (1974). The measurement of hospital output—A case study. Paper presented to the Royal Society of Health Congress. Published in the *Proceedings.*

Rosser, R. M., & Benson, T., Jr. (1978). New tools for evaluation: Their application to computers. In J. Andersen (Ed.), Lecturer Notes on Medical Informatics, 1, Medical Informatics Europe 78. New York: Springer-Verlag.

Rushing, W. A. (1971). Public policy, community constraints, and the distribution of medical resources. *Social Problems, 19,* 21–36.

Rushing, W. A. (1975). *Community, physicians, and inequality.* Lexington, MA: Lexington Books.

Schroeder, E. (1983). Concepts of health and illness. In A. J. Culyer (Ed.), *Health indicators.* New York: St. Martin's Press.

Shonfield, A., & Shaw, S. (1972). Health indicators. In A. J. Culyer, R. J. Lavers, & A. Williams (Eds.), *Social indicators and social policy.* London: Heinemann.

Somers, A. R. (1973). Some basic determinants of medical care and health policy—An overview of trends and issues. In J. B. McKinlay (Ed.), *Politics and law in health care policy.* New York: Prodist.

350 / CHOICES AND SOLUTIONS

Sullivan, D. F. (1971). A single index of mortality and morbidity. *Health Services Mental Health Administration Health Report, 86*, 347–354.

Thomas, L. (1977). On the science and technology of medicine. In J. H. Knowles (Ed.), *Doing better and feeling worse: Health in the United States*. New York: W. W. Norton.

Torrance, G. W., Thamas, W. H., & Sackett, D. L. (1971). A utility maximisation model for evaluation of health care programs. *Health Services Research, 7*, 118–133.

U.S. Department of Health, Education and Welfare. (1972). *Infant mortality rates, socioeconomic factors* (pub. no. 72-1045). Washington, DC: U.S. Government Printing Office.

Walsh, J. (1978). Federal spending passes the $50 billion mark. In P. H. Abelson (Ed.), *Health care: Regulation, economics, ethics, practice*. Washington, DC: American Association for the Advancement of Science.

Wildavsky, A. (1977). Doing better and feeling worse: The political pathology of health policy. In J. H. Knowles (Ed.), *Doing better and feeling worse: Health in the United States*. New York: W. W. Norton.

Wolinsky, F. D. (1980). *The sociology of health: Principles, professions and issues*. Boston: Little, Brown.

ECONOMIC ISSUES IN PROTECTING PUBLIC HEALTH AND THE ENVIRONMENT

Joseph J. Seneca

Rutgers—The State University of New Jersey

This chapter discusses some economic aspects of protecting public health and the environment and the questions they raise for public policy. Economists often observe that environmental health programs require the use of some of society's scarce resources—labor, capital equipment, human capital, materials, and so on. Economists also note that these resources, once used, are no longer available for other purposes, and thus their commitment to protecting public health and the environment represents a *cost* to society. In turn, however, such environmental programs generate socially desirable *benefits*, such as various measurable improvements in public health. The relative magnitude of the costs versus the benefits of environmental protection is a major concern of economists and represents a recurring theme of this chapter.

It is sometimes distressing at first glance to think of environmental health protection in such terms of inputs and dollar costs to be weighed coldly and dispassionately against outputs, frequently expressed as reductions in morbidity and mortality rates, or lower exposure levels to hazardous substances. Nevertheless, focusing on the benefits versus the costs of social decisions which absorb limited resources leads to useful insights concerning how such decisions could be made. It also makes explicit a number of difficult economic issues that are inherent in such decisions, issues that do not disappear even if they are unrecognized or purposefully ignored in the policy decision process.

The first section of this chapter briefly presents the economic issues of resource scarcity, choice, and efficiency inherent in any commitment of scarce resources to a specific use, private or public. The second section reviews the major federal environmental laws and examines the macroeconomic (international and national) implications of environmental protection efforts in the United States and provides some estimates of their past and future effects on the U.S. economy. It also speculates on the general outlook for environmental protection in the current decade, given the overall national economic conditions that are likely to prevail. The economic issue of environmental benefit estimation is discussed in the context of health protection in the third section, and some estimates of the benefits of environmental programs are reviewed. Finally, we examine the available evidence on the incidence of pollution control benefits and costs and who benefits from, and who pays for, environmental protection programs.

ECONOMICS AND PROTECTING PUBLIC HEALTH AND THE ENVIRONMENT: AN OVERVIEW

One fundamental point of economics is the concept of *opportunity cost*—the idea that once a decision is made to use scarce resources for one purpose, the opportunity is necessarily forfeited to use those same resources for any other purpose (see Seneca & Taussig, 1984; also Baumol & Oates, 1979; Downing, 1984; Titenberg, 1984). If all of society's available resources are employed in productive activities, a decision to produce more missiles, for example, necessarily means that fewer highways, or hospitals, or social services, or other "public" outputs can be produced, including environmental protection. Alternatively, the increase in missile production can come at the expense of private goods and services as taxes, public borrowing, or inflation increase to pay for the additional military output, and resources are transferred from the private into the public sector.

Economists note that society's ability to satisfy all possible private economic desires (autos, houses, TVs, legal services, football games, and the rest) *and* public output desires (education, defense, health protection, highways, parks) is limited. This implies that we must somehow choose among all the combinations of the potential "outputs" society *could* produce. This limit on the ability to produce exists even in an affluent society such as the United States because of ultimate resource, technological, and knowledge constraints. Increases in resources and improvements in technology and know-how raise the ability of an economy to produce more of all goods and services, public and private. Choice is still required, however, since the scarcity constraint must again be confronted, at the new, higher level of potential production. Individuals in their capacity as private consumers may have different ideas on how to use any additional production potential compared to the same or other individuals in their public capacities as voters, legislators, and government decision makers. The combination in the U.S. economy today of privately motivated resource decisions in market transactions, along with public output decisions at all levels of government yields a mix of what private and public goods and services actually get produced. Our opinions may differ on the appropriateness of this mix but must acknowledge that at some point, collectively as a society, we cannot have more of everything. It is within this context of scarcity and opportunity costs, and the necessity that these conditions create to make choices, that we can view environmental protection.

Trade-offs and Margins

Consider a public decision to implement a regulatory program to reduce the ambient levels of a particular pollutant, say, sulfur dioxide, by mandating the installation of a specific pollution control technology on all emitters of this pollutant. Many complex legal, governmental, and epidemiological issues arise from such a policy decision, but from an economic perspective one obvious question is, how much should sulfur dioxide concentrations be reduced? One tempting answer to this question and one which is frequently embodied in environmental legislation is, "reduce ambient air pollution to a level which is 'safe' for human health." While alluring, this answer contains several significant problems. It assumes that a "safe" level of the air pollutant can be determined—a dubious proposition for many pollutants, given the uncertain state of knowledge concerning the relation between pollution levels and human health. Second, for what target group of the population is air to be made "safe"? Urban residents? An "average healthy person"? Asthmatics living in urban areas? Each of these groups may easily require a significantly different "safe" level of ambient air quality for the pollutant in question. Third, even given an accepted definition of the targeted population group, the implication that there is a binary choice between "safe" versus "unsafe" air quality levels may be misleading. There is evidence that in many cases the relation between pollution levels and human health is a continuous function over a considerable range of air quality. Incrementally better air quality will result in incremental improvements in public health. Economists refer to this situation as one involving *marginal* conditions, that is, some additional reduction of pollution levels leads to some additional, measurable, benefits in terms of health protection. After some point, the incremental health benefit is likely to decline as ambient air quality continues to improve. Removal of 80% of a pollutant may provide significant improvement, but a further 10% reduction may result in much smaller benefits. An additional 5% yields still less, and the elimination of the final 5% may bring only a barely detectable improvement. Similarly, as air pollution levels are reduced, the additional (marginal) costs of achieving further reductions rise. In other words, the opportunity costs of further pollution control increase. Eliminating the last 5% of the pollutant costs more (often significantly more) than the 5% between 90% and 95% removal.

These conditions imply that there is a *trade-off* between the health benefits of improved air quality versus the costs of achieving these benefits. Moreover, it is likely that as environmental conditions improve, the terms of this trade-off worsen. That is, with improving air quality, it takes an increasing amount of dollars (resources) to obtain a further, given amount of additional health benefits, or equivalently, the health benefits *per dollar spent* decline as air quality continually improves.

The Issue of Efficiency

The policy question initially posed in our sulfur dioxide program example can now be restated . Where does, or should, society stop in this trade-off process? What level of ambient air quality (health protection) should be chosen? It may still be tempting to answer: Choose that level of air quality where no further health benefits are detectable; that is, accept the trade-off between dollars (scarce resources) and health protection until the additional, *marginal*, benefits disappear.

Two fundamental problems arise with this answer, and both concern different aspects of what economists call *efficiency*. One deals with this specific pollution control program, and the other is within the broader context of all other public efforts to protect health. First, since the marginal benefits of health protection in this single program are likely to decline as air quality improves, it follows that the additional value (in dollars) of improved ambient air quality to society (the reductions in morbidity and mortality) is declining as well. (Note that the health benefits—reduced morbidity rates—have been given a dollar value.) That is, we are getting less output per additional dollar spent. On the other hand, since the marginal costs of air quality improvement are increasing, marginal benefits and marginal costs will coincide at a level of air quality less than the level where no extra health benefits can be detected (that is, where human health is "safe" from any adverse effect of this pollutant).

Improving air quality beyond the point where the additional dollars spent are matched by the additional benefits they produce would be inefficient. Controlling pollution beyond this level of air quality would cost society more in resources than the value we stand to gain. Therefore, the efficient level of air quality control is to reduce this pollutant to the level where the marginal gains equal the marginal costs of air quality control.

An understandable reply to this efficiency analysis is to argue that dollars (resources) shouldn't count when it comes to health protection, and as a wealthy, well-endowed society we should ignore this efficiency issue—air quality should still be made "safe" for all. Indeed, decision makers are rarely concerned with efficiency issues. Concerns for fairness, avoiding all public risks, or constituency interests often dominate the decision process. However, the efficiency issue does not disappear even if it does not guide decisions. Its implications remain. Accordingly, making these efficiency aspects explicit can increase the likelihood that decision makers will, in the end, take efficiency into account.

But there are many ways to protect human health, save lives, and reduce illness and suffering. These goals obviously are not the sole domain of any one program or even of environmental health programs in general. Thus, the resources used in this program have opportunity costs; they have alternative uses in other public health or broader public safety programs such as, highway safety, innoculations, fire protection, mobile cardiac units, nutrition, control of other air, water, and hazardous substances. Increases in resources devoted to these other programs will also result in reduced morbidity and/or mortality. It is also important to remember that for almost all such programs the *identity* of the individuals whose health protection is improved is unknown, either beforehand or afterwards. The benefits are anonymously distributed and generally consist of small reductions in small risk probabilities over relatively large numbers of unknown individuals. Thus, the possibility of making emotional choices among programs for additional resources based on the identity of the specific individuals protected is, fortunately, precluded.

Thus, taking health protection beyond the efficient point in this one specific air pollution control program denies society the opportunity to use those additional resources elsewhere where the health benefits per dollar spent at the margin may be higher. The general efficiency criterion for any given commitment of scarce resources is to allocate resources among all public health protection programs until the marginal benefits obtained per dollar spent are equal across programs. This will result in the largest possible *total* health benefits for any given amount of expenditure for public health purposes (broadly defined).

An even broader efficiency issue is what determines the appropriate amount of resources to devote to public health in general? Here it is necessary to weigh the opportunity costs of resources used for public health protection against other competing public uses (schools, job training, basic research, transportation) and/or private uses (consumer goods and services of all types, capital equipment).

Recognition of the fact that public health programs must compete for scarce resources with other public as well as private uses returns us to the importance of measuring the benefits of these programs and expressing them in dollars. We have already seen that within public health programs it is useful to know what an extra dollar spent on, for example, air pollution control will "buy" versus an extra dollar spent on nutrition education, or on water pollution control, or on safer toxic waste disposal. Over all, society will receive more health protection—and this would seem an objective acceptable to most—by using the dollar where its health return is the highest. This obvious point confirms the need to measure the benefits in a common denominator—dollars—so that comparisons across programs can be made. It is important to do this even if the efficiency criterion will not dictate the policy decision. That way, we can at least make rational, informed judgments concerning what we are giving up by making resource allocation decisions based on other than efficiency grounds. Okun (1975) discusses this general point of efficiency versus equity as a guide for public decisions.

From a macroeconomic dimension, it is also important to measure the benefits of environmental health protection and express these benefits in dollars. While placing dollar values on lives or human health may be morally repugnant at first thought, it is imperative if environmental and public health protection is to withstand the economic pressures that have recently been placed upon it and which are likely to increase in the rest of this decade. The reason is that the *costs* of environmental health protection as expressed in dollars are all too obvious. Direct federal, state, and local government expenditures on all forms of environmental protection, the significant costs imposed on industry by federally mandated pollution control regulations, the resulting economic effects of these regulations in terms of increases in consumer prices, reductions in output, declines in productivity, and losses in employment and income all are readily expressed in dollars. These costs appear in our national income accounts, employment figures, the balance sheets of firms, prices, individual tax bills, and government budgets. Because of the magnitude of these costs it is not surprising that they have focused attention upon, and invited criticism of, the commitment of large amounts of society's scarce resources to environmental health protection programs.

In times of national recession or slow economic growth these criticisms are likely to mount. It becomes of paramount importance, therefore, to reply to such criticisms in concrete terms and to show, if true, that expenditures for environmental protection have bought us something significant. Only with such a reply can environmental protection hope to retain a legitimate efficiency claim on society's scarce resources over time. Hence, economists argue the necessity to measure those elusive environmental health benefits in the same common denominator of dollars by which the costs of improving health protection are continually being made obvious; in other words, to demonstrate that a commitment to environmental protection is an efficient use of society's scarce resources.

NATIONAL ECONOMIC DIMENSIONS OF POLLUTION CONTROL

We turn now to a brief review of the objectives and regulatory methods of some of the major federal environmental laws. Any widespread public perception that legally mandated pollution control programs cost our country jobs, raise prices, lower incomes, and reduce our ability to compete in international markets will certainly jeopardize the long-run viability of environmental programs and create substantial economic pressures to reduce their effectiveness. Thus, the main focus of this section is to examine the magnitude of the costs that these laws impose on our society and to assess the effects of these costs on the performance of the nation's economy.

Major Federal Environmental Laws

Since 1970, the nation has passed a series of laws that attempt to improve the quality of our environment and protect public health. A general review of these laws is beyond the scope this chapter; see, however, Chapter 8, this volume.

An important point about these laws for economics is that the regulations developed to enforce them affect a wide range of the nation's industries. Obviously, each of these laws, in its pursuit of environmental objectives, imposes costs on the economy. An important economic concern is the extent of the costs of improving public health and environmental quality and their effect on the nation's economy.

Expenditures on Environmental Protection

Administering, enforcing, and complying with environmental laws costs the country a great deal of resources. What are the costs imposed on society by the pollution control requirements mandated by these federal laws and resulting state and local regulations? The estimates given here measure the expenditures that individuals, business, and the various levels of government have made, or will have to make, in order to comply with federal environmental legislation. These expenditure estimates are not identical to the concept of the *opportunity cost* of pollution control discussed earlier. Nevertheless, they are a rough minimum estimate of the value of resources currently devoted to environmental protection. (See Table 12-1.) It is immediately obvious that these expenditures are large—a total of more than $518 billion for the decade. Of this, over half (57.5%) is for air pollution control with the largest part of that, $115.8 billion, attributable to motor vehicles. Water pollution control expenditures represent almost another 33% of the total. Although toxic waste control costs are only a relatively small amount ($8.2 billion), significant amounts of these expenditures are also included in the air, water, and solid waste totals.

Economists argue that these direct costs of environmental regulation are likely to understate the true opportunity costs of pollution control. For example, federal emission regulations impose costs on auto producers, and these costs can be measured by estimating the expenditures auto manufacturers must make in order to comply with the emission regulations. However, these costs raise car prices and reduce the number of autos purchased. Consumers experience a loss in the form of fewer auto purchasers, in addition to the increased price (due to the installed pollution control equipment) of the autos that they do buy. This reduction in auto sales does not appear in the estimates of the direct costs of auto pollution control imposed on producers (Portney, 1981).

On an annual basis, pollution control expenditures represent a major portion of all federal spending on health care (nearly 75% in 1979). Moreover, expenditures on pollution control programs are estimated to increase from $36.9 billion per year in 1979 to $69 billion by 1989. This increase implies a growth rate of over 6.5% per year, or considerably above the 2% to 3% annual increase in real gross national product (GNP) expected over the same time. Thus, pollution control expenditures, as a share of GNP, are expected to increase. Nevertheless, these expenditures have been, and will remain, quite small relative to GNP (about 1.5% of GNP in 1979). Even if the growth rates projected here are realized, pollution control expenditures will only rise to approximately 2.5% of GNP by 1988.

Of the total estimated costs for the three major pollution control programs (air, water, and solid waste) almost 78% are imposed on private industries. These costs directly affect prices, employment, output, and productivity. Public sector costs, financed by tax revenues, will indirectly influence these same variables through their effect on personal income, corporate income, and other taxes. These taxes, in turn, may affect resource allocation decisions, investment choices, and the amount and direction of discretionary expenditures by individuals and businesses. A question of national importance follows from the cost estimates in Table 12-1: what is the effect of these costs on the performance of the national economy?

Economic Effects of Environmental Protection

A number of econometric studies have attempted to answer this exceedingly complex question. The studies use comprehensive models that describe the U.S. economy

Table 12-1. Estimated Incremental Pollution Abatement Expenditures,[a] 1979–88 (billions of 1979 dollars)

Program	1979			1988			Cumulative (1979–1988)		
	Operation and maintenance	Annual capital costs[b]	Total annual costs	Operation and maintenance	Annual capital costs[b]	Total annual costs[b]	Operation and maintenance	Capitol costs	Total costs
Air pollution									
Public	1.2	.3	1.5	2.0	.5	2.5	15.7	3.7	19.5
Private									
Mobile	3.2	4.9	8.1	3.7	11.0	14.7	32.1	83.7	115.8
Industrial	2.0	2.3	4.3	3.0	4.1	7.1	25.8	33.0	58.8
Electric utilities	5.5	2.9	8.4	7.6	5.7	13.3	62.3	42.7	105.0
Subtotal	11.9	10.4	22.3	16.3	21.3	37.6	136.0	163.1	299.1
Water Pollution									
Public	1.7	4.3	6.0	3.3	10.0	13.3	25.1	59.2	84.3
Private									
Industrial	3.4	2.6	6.0	5.4	4.5	9.9	42.0	34.0	76.0
Electric utilities	.3	.4	.7	.3	.9	1.2	2.9	6.5	9.4
Subtotal	5.4	7.3	12.7	9.0	15.4	24.4	70.0	99.7	169.7
Solid waste									
Public	<.05	<.05	<.05	.4	.3	.7	2.6	2.0	4.6
Private	<.05	<.05	<.05	.9	.7	1.6	6.4	4.4	10.8
Subtotal	<.05	<.05	<.05	1.3	1.0	2.3	9.0	6.4	15.4
Toxic Substances	.1	.2	.3	.5	.6	1.1	3.6	4.6	8.2
Drinking Water	<.05	<.05	<.05	.1	.3	.4	1.3	1.4	2.7
Noise	<.05	.1	.1	.6	1.0	1.6	2.6	4.3	6.9
Pesticides	.1	<.05	.1	.1	<.05	.1	1.2	<.05	1.2
Land reclamation	.3	1.1	1.4	.3	1.2	1.5	3.8	11.5	15.3
Total	17.8	19.1	36.9	28.2	40.8	69.0	227.5	291.0	518.5

Note. From Council on Environmental Quality (1980).
[a] Incremental costs are those made in response to federal legislation beyond those that would have been made in the absence of the legislation.
[b] Interest and depreciation.

358

by a large number of equations and simultaneously link all sectors of the economy. These models are capable of estimating the effects of changes in broad measures of economic activity (e.g., government spending or business investment) on economic performance—output, employment, prices, and costs. The key advantage of these models for our interests lies in the simultaneous nature of the predictions they can generate, that is, changes in one sector like federally mandated pollution control expenditures on autos, affect costs and prices in all other sectors, and hence ultimately influence the overall performance of the entire economy. These predictions can be compared to a "baseline" set of predictions generated by assuming no federal environmental regulations. The result is two projections of the performance of the national economy; one "with" and the other "without" environmental regulations. A comparison of these two paths permits an assessment of the macroeconomic effects of pollution control efforts.

A study conducted for the Council on Environmental Quality (Data Resources, 1979) provides an analysis of this issue. Table 12-2 gives estimates of the investment expenditures on air and water pollution control by sector—manufacturing, non-manufacturing, and state and local government. It is interesting to note the relative effects of environmental regulations across sectors of the economy. Of the estimated total incremental pollution control investment of $14,193 million in 1986, over 71% occurs in manufacturing industries, and mobile source emission control (essentially autos) represents 40% by itself. Expenditures by utilities (14%) and state and local government (primarily for municipal wastewater treatment) comprise almost all the rest (12%). Within the manufacturing sector (but excluding autos) the industry most affected by pollution controls is chemicals, with an estimated investment requirement of $1.36 billion in 1986. The econometric simulation takes these cost estimates for the period 1970–1986 and traces their effect on the performance of the national economy. Table 12-3 is a summary of the results of this study. There are many significant technical caveats that accompany these results, and caution must be exercised to avoid too literal an interpretation of the numbers. Nevertheless, even though many of the forecast's underlying assumptions have changed dramatically, the results are at least indicative of the direction and general magnitude of the effect of environmental regulations on the U.S. economy. Table 12-3 provides five measures of national economic performance—consumer prices (CPI), unemployment rate, real GNP, imports, and exports. The level for each measure is shown "without" and "with" the effect of environmental regulations, and then the difference between the two is given.

In terms of consumer prices, the effect of pollution control requirements has been to increase the rate of inflation. For the entire period of the study (1970–1986), federally mandated pollution controls added .25% to the inflation rate *each year*. For the most recent period, 1979–1986, the average increase in prices due to pollution control has been lower, .13%.

The overall effect on employment, somewhat surprisingly, has been positive. Pollution control expenditures have led to an estimated *net* reduction of .25% in the annual unemployment rate between 1970 and 1986. It is important to understand that this is a *net* change in unemployment. Some industries have been adversely

Table 12-2. Estimated Incremental Investment for Pollution Control, Selected Years[a]
(millions of 1977 dollars)

	1970	1975	1980	1984	1986
All industries	2,458	5,181	7,338	8,413	6,659
Manufacturing industries	1,450	3,671	4,095	4,740	4,337
Primary metals	269	892	979	572	481
Electrical machinery	14	23	44	48	37
Nonelectrical machinery	10	30	41	26	17
Transportation equipment	59	54	137	287	219
Stone, clay, and glass	76	157	154	378	170
Other durables	47	130	90	69	61
Food including beverage	117	139	554	788	806
Textiles	16	36	156	266	248
Paper	208	572	640	629	623
Chemicals	251	733	793	1,351	1,357
Petroleum	373	864	414	174	214
Rubber	2	15	40	67	39
Other nondurables	9	26	53	84	64
Nonmanufacturing	1,008	1,510	3,243	3,674	2,322
Mining	59	63	85	102	58
Public utilities	750	1,297	3,061	3,418	2,109
Commercial	200	150	97	154	155
State and local government	− 38	1,548	3,190	1,542	1,778
Mobile source emission control	505	2,123	3,633	5,667	5,756
Total	2,925	8,852	14,161	15,622	14,193

Note. From Data Resources, Inc. (1979).
[a]Only air and water pollution control expenditures.

effected by pollution regulations—costs have risen, prices have increased, sales have declined, and employment has been reduced, while activity in other industries producing, installing, and maintaining pollution control equipment has been stimulated.[1] The results in Table 12-3 potray this *net* effect on the jobless rate, and on balance employment has increased modestly due to the federal environmental regulations.

The effect on real GNP has been mixed. Real national output increased in the initial period (1970–1978) when the stimulative effects of increased spending on pollution control equipment exceeded the contractionary effects on output of higher prices and lower productivity (output per unit of labor input). However, by the mid 1980s, this net effect had turned negative, with real GNP in 1986 estimated to be over $24 billion (a change of less than 1%) less that what it would have been without environmental regulations.

---

1. This point demonstrates the advantage of the simultaneous nature of macroeconomic models: They estimate the implications of economic changes in all sectors of the economy, not only in the immediately and directly affected parts.

Table 12-3. Estimated Impact of Pollution Control Expenditures on the Economy, Selected Years

	1975	1980	1984	1986
Percentage growth rate of CPI[a]				
Without	8.7	6.8	5.8	5.7
With	9.1	6.9	5.9	5.7
Difference	0.4	0.1	0.1	0.1
Percentage unemployment rate				
Without	8.6	6.4	5.4	5.2
With	8.5	6.0	5.2	5.0
Difference	−0.2	−0.4	−0.2	−0.2
Gross national product, 1977 dollars				
Without	1698.2	2109.5	2473.7	2646.7
With	1702.6	2118.8	2457.0	2622.3
Difference	4.4	9.3	−16.7	−24.5
Imports, 1977 dollars				
Without	137.5	215.2	262.4	292.9
With	142.0	221.6	267.0	295.6
Difference	4.5	6.4	4.6	2.7
Exports, 1977 dollars				
Without	161.0	210.7	255.8	280.4
With	160.9	210.2	254.0	278.1
Difference	−0.2	−0.6	−1.8	−2.3

Note. From Data Resources, Inc. (1979).
[a]Consumer Price Index

The trade balance has also been adversely affected, with imports higher and exports lower due to the presence of pollution controls. This effect is attributable to the increase in prices and the decline in productivity, which have lead to a reduction in the competitiveness of domestic U.S. industries, thus encouraging imports and reducing exports. Recently, the nation's trade deficit has increased dramatically (to an estimated $170 billion in 1986). Opinions differ on the extent of the problem that a chronic and growing trade deficit creates for the U.S. economy. Nevertheless, the results shown in Table 12-3 indicate that some long-term deterioration in the trade balance is attributable to environmental controls. Separate studies also conclude that a small but detectable part of the decline in U.S. productivity growth is due to environmental regulations (see Haveman & Christainsen, 1981). Slower productivity growth increases international economic competition in U.S. markets and is directly related to the deterioration of the trade balance.

The overall picture conveyed by this (and similar) studies is that environmental protection has brought slower economic growth, higher prices, some net stimulation to employment, and reduced international competitiveness (Congressional Budget Office, 1985). These effects, however, are quite small, a conclusion that necessarily follows from the relative small size of total environmental control expenditures as a percent of GNP (2.0%). Nevertheless, the existence of such effects and the concerns they cause imply that environmental protection is vulnerable to erosion.

Pressures are likely to increase to relax pollution control efforts as one way of coping with inflation, slow growth, sluggish productivity, and employment uncertainties. It is useful, therefore, to reverse the analysis of the national economic effects of pollution control and now ask the obverse question: What do the economic conditions that are likely to prevail in this decade imply for the country's ability to sustain or increase its efforts in environmental protection?

The Outlook for Environmental Protection

Thus far, this decade has witnessed two national recessions. The 1981–1982 recession was particularly severe, coming as it did so close on the heels of the 1980 recession. At the recession's worst, unemployment reached 10.7%, and several major industries—steel, autos, construction—experienced especially difficult times for long periods. An economic recovery began in early 1983. Unemployment rates fell, real income and output grew, and the economic policy issue for the future is whether this growth can be sustained without a return to accelerating inflation or severe economic recession. The ability of policy to steer the economy on this narrow path of healthy economic growth, without slipping into high inflation as we did in the late 1970s or into severe recession as in the early 1980s, is highly uncertain. It is against this uncertainty that environmental protection must try to make its claim for additional amounts of society's scarce resources.

   The prevailing and expected national economic conditions will define the potential scope for environmental protection. For the foreseeable future, the issues of controlling inflation, reducing unemployment, and improving U.S. productivity and the international competitive position of our industry will probably remain the dominant national economic policy objectives (Bosworth, 1981). Unfortunately, what also seems apparent is that environmental protection is a potential casualty in attempts to cope with each of these problems. This is not because environmental regulations are the major cause of these problems or even represent a significant factor. We have seen their relatively small effect on national economic performance. It is simply because they present an inviting, visible target that can be directly controlled, in contrast to the many other complex and less manageable factors that influence economic performance. An examination of each of these major national economic issues indicates that the economic pressure upon environmental protection is likely to prove formidable.

   First, the disruption experienced because of the high inflation rates of the late 1970s and early 1980s, and the nation's trauma with the bitter cure for this inflation—the severe recessions of the early 1980s—implies that economic policy is likely to be quite wary of any possible acceleration of inflation. The Federal Reserve, in particular, will remain reluctant to return to policies that lead to any build-up of inflationary pressures, given the dearly bought gains it achieved against inflation with its restrictive, recession-inducing policy of monetary constraint of 1981–1983. The presence of significant federal deficits, extending into the foreseeable future with their expansionary effects on the economy and their pressures on credit markets, will further constrain monetary policy to essentially an anti-inflationary priority. Thus, government regulations in general, and environmental controls in particular, are likely to continue to come under pressure as one way of reducing production costs and hence lowering inflationary pressures.

Second, the concerns about unemployment and trade deficits are related in terms of their implications for environmental protection. While the econometric studies discussed above indicate that federal environmental regulations have provided a small net stimulus to employment, it is also true that they have adversely effected employment in some specific industries. In particular, the primary metals and auto industries have been required to make large investments in pollution control. Simultaneously, and for a variety of other reasons, these and other U.S. manufacturing industries have lost a considerable share of their domestic markets to foreign competition. Employment in these industries has declined significantly, and the nation's trade balance has worsened.[2] Considerable pressure has been put on Congress to restrict auto, steel, and other imports and protect U.S. industries and jobs.

In general, with the increasing importance of international trade in the U.S. economy, calls for import protection are certain to increase.[3] One obvious means of improving the competitive position of domestic industries is to reduce the costs imposed upon them by environmental requirements. Although environmental protection accounts for only a small part of production costs, it is, once again, a visible, available, and readily controllable factor. Pollution control costs are also a convenient scapegoat for both labor and management to blame as one cause of import penetration of U.S. markets, rather than addressing the more fundamental reasons behind declining competitiveness—poor management decisions, the large federal deficit, high labor costs, and low productivity growth. Our conclusion is that conditions in the nation's foreign trade sector, with their resulting implications for employment, will continue to threaten environmental protection programs.

The final major economic issue likely to be of continuing concern is how to improve U.S. productivity growth. Growth in productivity, conventionally measured as private sector output divided by labor input, has declined significantly. From 1945 to 1965, labor productivity in the U.S. grew by an average annual rate of 3.5%; between 1965 to 1975 it fell to 2.2%, and since then it has averaged significantly less than 2% per year. This slowdown has had significant and negative implications for inflation, employment, the trade balance, and economic growth. It also means that as our ability to produce more private output with additional inputs has declined, we face tighter constraints in allocating resources for public sector uses and redistributive purposes. A great deal of research has attempted to understand the causes of the decline in U.S. productivity growth, and considerable

2. Again, this does not mean that environmental regulations have caused these events. Although they have contributed, in a relatively small way, the major reasons lie elsewhere—high interest rates, a strong dollar, relatively high labor costs, lower productivity, and slow economic growth abroad.

3. Imports and exports now represent approximately 11% of our GNP compared to 6% in 1970.

public policy efforts have been directed at reversing it (Christainsen & Haveman, 1981; Denison, 1979; Northsworty, Harper, & Kunze, 1979). Since productivity growth lies at the heart of economic performance, we can expect that there will be a continuing emphasis on devising means to improve its performance.

Again, and unfortunately, environmental protection is likely to suffer from efforts to raise U.S. productivity growth. As noted previously, a small but detectible amount (10%) of the nation's recent productivity decline is attributable to environmental regulations. The basic reason is that environmental regulations add to costs (pollution control equipment must be bought, additional labor hired to install, operate, and service it, production processes changed). However, these activities do not add to the (measurable) output of industry. The result is that while inputs and costs have risen because of environmental regulation, output has not, and thus, output per unit of input is lower than it would have been without the regulatory requirements. It is important to emphasize that it is *measured output* that has not increased. Environmental regulations may reduce mortality and morbidity, and this represents the "output" society receives for the use of its scarce resources to produce and operate the pollution control equipment mandated by federal regulations. Nevertheless, this "output" does not directly appear, for example, as additional production of tons of steel, or number of autos, and hence conventional measures of productivity are lower. It seems obvious, therefore, that in a time of a national economic policy emphasis to improve productivity in order to address our chronic macroeconomic problems, any policy which adds to inputs (and costs) without raising economic output will be in jeopardy.

An additional problem for environmental protection in this productivity context is the likelihood that real interest rates (actual interest rates minus the expected rate of inflation) will remain historically high. This will mean that business investment expenditures will face relatively high borrowing costs. Accordingly, requirements for costly investments in pollution control equipment, which do nothing to increase output, revenues, and profits, are likely to be met with increasing resistance by businesses. The continuation of high real interest rates will, therefore, reinforce the pressures to reduce environmental protection efforts.

In summary, all major economic issues that are likely to prevail in the foreseeable future—concern about inflation, unemployment, the trade balance, and productivity growth—represent potential threats to public health and environmental protection programs. Given this background, two implications emerge. First, if environmental protection is to retain, or possibly increase, its claim on scarce public resources in the next decade, it is vital that our environmental objectives be achieved in least-cost manner. If we can devise new, less expensive policies that achieve the same environmental goals, pressures for reducing the nation's commitment to environmental protection will be lessened. Economists have long argued that certain changes in the basic federal regulatory approach to environmental protection could substantially reduce the costs of reaching environmental standards. These changes involve the use of economic incentives—pollution taxes, emission banks, transferable emission reduction credits—and modify the direct regulatory command approach of most of our federal environmental laws. The incentives would give industry more flexibility in deciding how to reach federal environmental standards. A discussion of these proposals is beyond the scope of this chapter, but considerable evidence exists that such changes could lead to significant savings in the nation's pollution control costs (Baumol & Blackman, 1980; Harrington & Krupnick, 1981; Liroff, 1980; O'Neill, David, Moore, & Erhard, 1980; U.S. General Accounting Office, 1982).

A second implication of our discussion is that it will be increasingly important to measure what the nation is getting for its pollution control efforts. What are the *benefits* of environmental protection? Quantifying these benefits offers the opportunity to justify environmental protection in the very terms critics use against it. We have claimed that the national economic concerns of the next decade are likely to threaten environmental protection because of the effects of environmental protection on business costs, output, and productivity. Having some estimates of the magnitude of the health, property, agricultural, amenity, and other benefits of environmental protection is ultimately the most effective means of answering these criticisms. Accordingly, we turn now to an examination of the issue of determining the benefits of environmental protection.

BENEFITS OF ENVIRONMENTAL PROTECTION

Economists have tried to estimate the benefits (costs) of environmental improvement (deterioration) by a variety of methods (Feenberg & Mills, 1980; Freeman, 1979a, 1979b; Hershaft, Freeman, Crocker, & Stevens, 1978). A first step in environmental benefit analysis is to identify the physical effects of any environmental change upon human activity. This is a formidable problem, but it has received an imposing amount of scientific investigation. The evidence of environmental effects on human and ecological activities is large and growing, but far from complete. Moreover, as pointed out in earlier chapters, considerable uncertainty remains in many areas (Lave, 1982). Nevertheless, it is obvious that if we are to attempt to measure what society gains by devoting scarce resources to environmental improvement, we must begin with some idea of what effects changes in ambient levels of environmental quality have upon human and natural activities. There are several links between environmental conditions and human activity, and each represents a potential source of benefits.

First, there are the direct effects on human health—mortality and morbidity—attributable to the biological effects of environmental conditions. Second, environmental changes affect ecological systems and through these natural processes, affect the economic productivity of these systems. Thus, there can be environmentally induced damage to agricultural, forestry, and fishing production and hence economic damage to the human use of these resources. A related aspect of environmentally induced ecological changes is the effect they may have on recreational and aesthetic uses of natural environments. Also, the stability and diversity of ecological systems may be threatened (in uncertain or unpredictable ways) by environmental deterioration, and thus lead to future potentially large losses to human welfare (e.g., the depletion of the available gene pool for scientific research as more plant and animal species become extinct, the loss of rainforests in tropical areas, climate changes, long-term acid rain damage to lakes, streams, and forests). Finally, environmental changes may adversely affect human activity through nonbiological processes. Damage to materials and structures, soiling, increases in production costs, and aesthetic disamenities are all possible additional environmentally induced effects upon human activity.[4]

There have been economic benefit studies in all these areas (Kneese, 1984). Each study confronts the difficult problem mentioned previously—identifying the actual relationship between ambient environmental changes and their effect on human activity (beneficial or detrimental). The complexity of this task cannot be overstated. However, given this imposing hurdle, a second, and almost equally formidable, problem follows. Namely, what is the *economic value* of the predicted improvements in environmental quality? For example, a benefit study of air quality and agricultural productivity would have to assemble scientific evidence on the relation between, for example, ozone concentrations and the photosynthestic processes of a particular crop, such as soybeans. Then, the study would have to estimate the gain in crop yields that would result from any given reduction in ambient ozone concentrations and *then* estimate the economic value of the increased crop yield. This is necessary in order to obtain an estimate of the dollar benefits of an ozone reduction environmental program. It is important to recall that expressing environmental benefits in dollars is required in order to make any economic efficiency assessment *across* environmental programs; an assessment that will be useful for policy decisions given the unfortunate fact that infinite resources are not available for all possible socially beneficial programs. Thus, a benefit study would indicate that the ozone reduction program results in a certain estimate of the dollar gains in soybean production. These benefits can then be compared to a benefit estimate of an alternative environmental program (such as acid rain reduction or particulate matter control), and the benefits of each can be expressed on a per dollar cost basis for an efficiency comparison across programs.

In the soybean example here, the procedure to estimate benefits is somewhat straightforward. The "output" of the improvement in environmental conditions— a measurable increase in soybean yields per acre—has a directly measurable market value—the going market price of a ton of soybeans. Thus, the increased yield can be given a price—a measure of value—and an estimate of dollar benefits of ozone reduction obtained.[5]

---

4. Significant acid rain and other air pollution damage to buildings and structures throughout the world has been detected. Airborne particulate matter causes soiling and results in more frequent cleaning costs. Degraded water quality conditions often require changes in technological processes and hence raise production costs.

5. This is only a simplified example to illustrate the basic issues. Many complications would occur in an actual study. For example, the ozone reduction will have other benefits beyond improved soybean yields, and these additional benefits would have to be estimated as well. Agricultural market prices

In general, where market prices of environmental benefits exist—house and property prices, cleaning costs, lumber products, agricultural crops, commercial fishing activities, material damages—economists use these prices, with appropriate technical adjustments, to measure the potential economic value of improved environmental conditions. Where no direct market prices exist such as the value of reductions in human mortality and morbidity, ecological system benefits, improved recreational opportunities, aesthetic gains, preservation of future scientific research options and potential, economists attempt to impute economic values by a variety of methods.

Estimates of the magnitude of environmental benefits, while subject to considerable and unavoidable uncertainty are, nevertheless, substantial. Table 12-4 lists one careful estimate of the dollar value of benefits that have resulted from the reduction in air pollutants actually achieved during the decade following the Clean Air Act of 1970. The total estimate of benefits is $21.4 billion (in 1978 dollars) and is attributable to gains in five benefit categories—health, soiling and cleaning, vegetation, materials, and property values. Each benefit category is subdivided into stationary source benefits (benefits due to reduced pollution from power plants and industry) and mobile sources (benefits due to auto emission controls). While the best estimate of the total benefits is $21.4 billion, the study notes that the possible range in total benefits could be as low as $5.4 billion or as high as $57.4 billion. Such a degree of uncertainty is inherent in this type of research. Nevertheless, estimating environmental benefits, in this case for air quality improvements, permits a dollar comparison with the costs of air quality protection. As a result, an efficiency judgment, and ultimately a defense, of environmental programs can be made.

Significantly, over 80% ($17 billion) of the total benefits of air quality improvement are health related. While the estimation of the remaining benefits listed in Table 12-4 is somewhat intuitive—from actual market prices for the benefits achieved in reduced soiling and cleaning costs, higher agricultural yields, and material and property values, it is less obvious how the *health* benefits of air quality improvement have been measured. Since this category represents the largest component of total benefits, and since it is also likely to have a similar rank in the benefits of other environmental programs such as toxic and hazardous substance control, the procedure used to estimate health benefits warrants a more detailed examination (Freeman, 1979b; Rhoads, 1978; Seneca & Taussig, 1984; Singer, 1978).

The basic idea—to estimate the dollar value of human life—is in many ways an appalling concept. The corollary is that human life is priceless, infinitely valuable. Certainly everyone feels that way about particular individuals—one's spouse, children, relatives, or public health or geography professor! However, environ-

---

might be distorted by government price supports and therefore not represent valid measures of economic benefits—what individuals willingly pay for products. A forecast of the price of soybeans in future years would have to be made, since the benefits of a permanent reduction in ozone levels would not be confined to one crop harvest. Future benefits would have to be expressed in terms of current dollars requiring a discounting procedure over time.

Table 12-4. Air Pollution Control Benefits by Category
(billions of 1978 dollars)

Category	Benefits
Health	
Stationary source	
Mortality	$13.9 billion
Morbidity	$ 2.9 billion
Total	$16.8 billion
Mobile Source	$ .2 billion
Total health	$17.0 billion
Soiling and cleaning	$ 2.0 billion
Vegetation	
Stationary source	0
Mobile source	$ .7 billion
Total vegetation	.7 billion
Materials	
Stationary source	$ .7 billion
Mobile source	$ .2 billion
Total materials	$ .9 billion
Property values	
Stationary source	$ 2.3 billion
Mobile source	$ .4 billion
Total property values	$ 2.7 billion
Total benefits	$21.4 billion
Range	$5.4 to $57.4 billion

Note. From Freeman (1979a).

mental (or other) programs do not save lives or reduce health risks for specific, identifiable people. Rather, they reduce the risk (by a small amount) of premature death for large numbers of *anonymous* individuals. Thus, the actual identity of those who benefit from an environmental program is not known, either before or after the program is put into practice. In other words, a program that reduces anonymous health risks cannot be viewed as infinitely valuable, even though any specific, known life may indeed be priceless. If such programs were viewed as infinitely valuable, then *all* society's resources should rationally, be used to save lives.[6]

As we noted earlier, there are many alternative life-saving projects—environmental protection, driver training, public nutrition, prenatal care, lower speed limits.

6. To see this point more clearly, consider the implications if society valued *anonymous* lives as infinitely valuable. Then, logically, all cigarette smoking and driving should be banned because each of these activities (and obviously many others as well) results in premature, *ex ante* anonymous deaths (an estimated 200,000 annually from smoking and 50,000 annually from driving). Society doesn't ban driving or smoking, and hence *implicitly* is deciding that reducing the risk of (anonymous) premature death is not infinitely valuable.

The economic issue is how to value the reduction in health risks that each of these programs represents.

Economists have attempted to measure the dollar benefits of life-saving programs by a variety of methods. We will discuss the two that have been most frequently used. The first is the human productivity method, which uses an individual's future income earnings as a *minimum* estimate of the value of a life. This methods assumes that an individual's income represents the value of the output that person produces for society. The argument is that a person is paid what he or she produces, and upon premature death, society (and obviously the individual) loses, *at a minimum*, the dollar value of this output.[7]

Considerable criticism has been leveled at this approach, and it is now only infrequently used in benefit studies. The basic criticisms are, first, that it has no theoretical basis as a benefit measure, that is, it is not developed from any voluntary assessment of the value of risk reduction to the affected individuals. Second, this method obviously can only capture labor market values. It omits the value of nonmarket economic activity, and even labor market values can be distorted by unions, discrimination, lack of mobility, or national economic conditions. Finally, and most objectionable, if you cannot work, this method assigns your life no value.

A second approach (and the one used for the health benefits reported in Table 12-4 estimates individuals' willingness to pay for reductions in the risk of premature death and uses this measure as the value of preventing a premature, anonymous death. This method assumes that individuals make rational employment choices among different jobs, the varying incomes that these jobs entail, and the health risks associated with each. As a result, individuals reveal by how they make these choices their valuations of small changes in health risks. In turn, these valuations can be used as the basis for identifying the amount of compensation individuals require to accept higher risks. This procedure can be described as follows:

> Suppose two occupations are identical in every respect—education and experience requirements, skill levels, and so on—except that one carries a .001 higher annual risk of job-related mortality. Suppose also that the riskier job pays $300 per year more than the other. This market information can be used to estimate the value of a human life. In the job with higher risk, there will be one additional death per 1000 workers in this occupation each year. However, each of the 1000 individuals must be paid an additional $300 per year to work in the riskier job. The total risk premium paid, therefore, for the life lost is $300,000, and this becomes the estimated value of an anonymous statistical life. In other words, the affected individuals must be compensated a total of $300,000 in order for each to accept an increase probability of premature death of .001 per year. (Seneca & Taussig, 1984, p. 264)

The validity of this method, although superior to the human productivity approach, depends upon several questionable assumptions. First, it assumes that individuals possess accurate information concerning health risks and then make

---

7. Many court cases involving liability for premature death use such calculations as part of the damage claims against the alleged liable party.

considered, informed choices. This assumption is tenuous at best, for environmental risks given the significant uncertainties of available scientific evidence. Second, the method also assumes that the choice of risky occupations is not forced upon people by lack of mobility, discrimination, or poverty (the underlying distribution of income is assumed to be acceptable). Finally, it assumes that the valuation of voluntarily assumed labor market risks can be used to value those types of risks, such as environmental risks, which are often involuntarily imposed.

Several empirical studies have used information from labor markets to estimate the wage differential across occupations attributable to risk differentials, after adjusting for other factors that affect wages. Given this differential, these studies then estimate the risk premium of premature death following the procedure discussed in the above example. A second empirical approach uses carefully designed survey techniques to elicit the willingness of individuals to pay for risk reduction. Unfortunately, these studies have yielded widely varying estimates, but a consensus estimate is approximately $1 million dollars (in 1978 dollars) as the value of avoiding the premature death of one anonymous, statistical life (Bloomquist, 1979; Jones-Lee, 1976; Thaler & Rosen, 1976). This $1 million per life estimate is used in Table 12-4 to compute the mortality reduction benefits attributable to air quality improvements.[8] Much work obviously remains to be done to improve both the theoretical foundations of health benefit estimation and to resolve the formidable empirical problems that confront such benefit studies.

EQUITY AND ENVIRONMENTAL PROTECTION

The efficiency issue that has been a theme of most of this chapter is overly simple. Given all the technical problems of estimating benefits and costs, the efficiency criterion adds these benefits and costs and produces a net gain or loss. This net gain or loss can then be used to guide policy decisions concerning the desirability of any given environmental or public health program. However, this net calculation masks the fact that the benefits and costs of environmental protection are usually bestowed on different individuals. This issue of the *equity* of environmental protection—who benefits and who pays—is necessarily and unavoidably linked with an efficiency judgment. For example, a government prohibition on the discharge of wastes by a firm into a nearby river may force the firm to close down. The beneficiaries of this program are the current users of the river; the costs of the program fall on the owners, employees, suppliers, and customers of the firm. The decision to enact the program may be efficient (total benefits exceed total costs),

---

8. In general terms, the arithmetic procedure is straightforward; based on epidemiological evidence, the improvements in air quality are estimated to reduce mortality by so many lives. This number of lives is then multiplied by $1 million to obtain an estimate of the *dollar* benefits of the health improvements (mortality reduction) attributable to air pollution control.

but the identities and economic circumstances (incomes) of the beneficiaries and those who pay the costs may differ widely.

Another version of the same environmental program would give a different equity result. Suppose the government undertakes a program to restore water quality in a now polluted river by a program of subsidies, investment tax credits, and direct public cleanup expenditures. In this case the beneficiaries remain the same—the users of the river—but now the costs are paid by the taxpayers who finance the program and/or the beneficiaries of other government programs (of all kinds) that have to be reduced or eliminated in order to pay for this environmental protection program. Thus, decisions on programs to protect public health must inevitably confront both efficiency and equity issues.

Equity Issues in Environmental Protection

This question of the distribution, or *incidence*, of the benefits and costs of environmental protection is part of several general equity issues in public finance. The distribution of the costs of environmental protection clearly depends upon how such programs are financed. In the river example above, the three alternative ways of improving the river's water quality—a prohibition that closes the local firm(s) down, a government subsidy and expenditure program financed by new taxes, or reductions in public expenditures elsewhere—all entail markedly different distributional outcomes. The choice of financing method can mean the difference between a program being, on balance, progressive or regressive in terms of its total equity effect.[9]

Consider the incidence of several basic methods of financing public health programs in general. Environmental program costs could be paid for by the sources of environmental deterioration via regulations, effluent taxes, and/or prohibitions. Such an approach is likely to cause higher production costs, higher prices, some direct and indirect employment losses, and reduced profits. All these effects would be manifested in a complicated and often delayed manner. The incidence of such costs is extremely difficult to estimate but is likely to be generally regressive, because one lasting, long-term effect is a general increase in the price level (see Table 12-3). Since expenditures on goods and services as a percentage of income decline with income, the equity effect of this method of pollution control is likely to be regressive.

If environmental programs are financed, however, by reducing or eliminating expenditures on other governmental programs, then the costs of the program fall on those whose benefits (from the other programs) are reduced. In such cases, it

9. The costs of any public program are said to be progressively distributed if costs, as a percentage of income, rise with income. Costs would be regressively distributed if the opposite were true. The benefits of a program can be similarly characterized. A progressive program would bestow larger benefits, as a percentage of income, the lower the income of the beneficiaries. A regressive program, in terms of its benefits would have benefits, as a percentage of income, rise with income. The *net* incidence of the program would be the difference between the incidence of benefits minus the incidence of costs.

would be necessary to know which programs are cut back in order to assess the incidence of the costs of the environmental program. Generalizations here are extremely risky, but at the federal level at least, the benefits of most domestic spending programs (with some notable exceptions) are thought to be distributed progressively. Thus, if general federal domestic spending is reduced in order to finance additional environmental programs, the costs of the environmental programs are again likely to be regressive.[10]

Finally, if (additional) public health programs are financed by (new) taxes, then the incidence of the costs of the new programs will be directly related to the type of taxes that pay for it. At the national level, the overall incidence of the federal tax structure—the personal income tax, the corporate income tax and payroll taxes—is generally regarded as mildly progressive.[11] A final related point is that increases in taxes may also affect work incentives, the allocation of resources between consumption and investment, and between current and future generations. Thus, increases in taxes may have both current and future efficiency effects by lowering national output, employment, investment, and real income. These effects, in turn, carry equity implications—many of them regressive—and such effects should at least conceptually be included in any full incidence analysis.

On balance, it is difficult to assess the incidence of the costs of environmental improvement. The answer depends directly upon which method of financing is chosen. Much of the federal effort in direct pollution control for air, water, and toxic substances follows the first method of financing—the polluter pays, via regulations, prohibitions, and other costs imposed by EPA restrictions. This would suggest an ultimately regressive distribution of costs via the effect on the general price level. On the other hand, more general public health programs—medical care, nutrition, innoculations—are largely financed out of general (federal) taxes pointing to a progressive distribution of costs.

The distribution of the *benefits* of environmental protection and public health programs is expected to be progressive, with proportionally larger benefits accruing to lower-income individuals. This is certainly the case for general public health programs and is likely to be true for environmental protection as well. Exposure to air pollution, water pollution, and toxic substances is often inversely related to income level, as the worst environmental conditions frequently occur in lower-income areas. Accordingly, improvements in air, water, and general environmental quality are likely to be progressively distributed.

Even this expectation of a progressive distribution of benefits, however, is complicated. First, if one major effect of environmental protection is to improve outdoor recreation opportunities[12] and aesthetic conditions conducive to outdoor

10. The *net* incidence in such a case is still an open question, since the incidence of the benefits of the new environmental programs must be weighed against the incidence of reducing benefits elsewhere.

11. Determining the incidence of various taxes is the subject of ongoing debate in public finance. This is an extremely complicated and unresolved question.

12. Water quality control programs are primarily thought to result in enhanced outdoor recreational conditions. Indeed, the stated purpose of the Clean Water Act is to make the nation's waters "fishable and swimmable."

activities, then benefits are likely to accrue proportionally more to upper-income groups because participation in outdoor recreation is directly related to income (R. Dorfman, 1977).

A second complication concerns the possible long-run economic adjustments to any improvement in environmental quality. It may be that improvements in urban air quality primarily benefit the low-income residents of central cities. However, partly as a result of improved air quality, central cities may again become attractive places to live. Over time, upper-income groups may return to urban centers in significant numbers and displace the current urban poor via higher rents and house prices. In this situation, the incidence of the long-term benefits of improved urban air quality would differ significantly from their initial effects.

Evidence on the Distribution of Benefits and Costs of Environmental Protection

Several studies have attempted to estimate the distribution of environmental protection. The preceding discussion implies that significant conceptual and empirical problems complicate these studies, and their results can only be taken as suggestive.

One comprehensive study (N. S. Dorfman & Snow, 1975) examined the incidence of three components of pollution control costs: (1) auto emission control costs, (2) price increases attributable to required pollution control expenditures by private industry, and (3) additional taxes needed to finance the public sector's environmental control efforts. The study concluded that the total distribution of the three components of costs was decidedly regressive. Pollution control costs were about 2% of income for individuals in the lowest 20% of the income distribution and only 1.25% for individuals in the highest 20%.

Using a different methodology, Gianessi, Peskin, and Wolff (1979) examined the distribution of air pollution control costs by income class. Again, a regressive pattern emerged, with costs as a percentage of income declining throughout the income distribution. Families earning below $10,000 paid about 5% of their income for air pollution control, but those with incomes above $25,000 paid less than 2%. The same study also estimated the distribution of air pollution control benefits and concluded that they were progressively distributed—benefits, as a percentage of income, were greater the lower the level of income. Interestingly, the *net* incidence of air pollution control (the incidence of benefits minus the incidence of costs) was progressive to the middle ranges of income, and then proportional at higher income levels, that is, the percentage of costs (or benefits) was the same, regardless of income level.

A different approach examined the spatial distribution of air pollution exposure levels with respect to income (Asch & Seneca, 1978). Annual particulate matter levels in 76 air pollution monitoring sites in three U.S. cities (Chicago, Cleveland, and Nashville) were matched with the incomes of individuals residing in the census tracts where the sites were located. Each tract was classified as to whether the observed level of particulate matter met or violated the national ambient air quality standard (75 micrograms per cubic meter of air). If air quality was randomly distributed with respect to income, then each income group would be represented in all census tracts (both in those where the standard was met and in those where it was violated) in the same proportion that the income group was represented in the population at large. A ratio was devised to measure whether this, in fact, was true, and the summary results for all three cities are given in Table 12-5. Values in Table 12-5 of less than 1.0 indicate that an income group is underrepresented, and values greater than 1.0 indicate the opposite. A clear pattern emerged; the poor were underrepresented in those census tracts where the standard was met (ambient particulate levels of less than 75 $\mu g/m^3$) and overrepresented in those tracts where it was violated (greater than 75 $\mu g/m^3$). The conclusion for this large urban sample, encompassing almost 100,000 families, was that exposure to particulate matter was regressively distributed, and hence improvements in air quality would result in a progressive distribution of benefits. Other studies, using earlier pollution data and different pollutants (e.g., Freeman, 1972) have found similar patterns. An analysis of water pollution (Asch & Seneca, 1980) also suggested a regressive incidence.

POINTS TO REMEMBER

This review of some of the basic economic issues inherent in protecting public health and the environment has revealed a number of complex and difficult problems. Unfortunately, these problems are inevitable, given the finite ability of our resources and the economy to satisfy all our desirable private wants and our public objectives.

Accordingly, the implications of having to make economic choices necessarily confronts environmental protection efforts. Choice brings with it the basic efficiency question of determining the extent of resources to devote to any public health and environmental quality program. Answering this question requires measurement of benefits and costs in order to make rational resource use decisions—among alternative public health programs or between private versus public uses of scarce resources. Such measurements should be made even if economic efficiency is not the main social objective, since they will at least tell society what it is giving up (opportunities foregone) by ignoring the efficiency criterion.

The national economic conditions likely to exist in the foreseeable future all tend to create pressures for reducing our commitment to environmental protection. Such pressures can be effectively withstood only if we have some idea of the dollar value of the benefits obtained from environmental programs. Tentative evidence in certain areas of environmental protection suggests that the magnitude of these benefits is large. Further, more comprehensive efforts at measuring environmental benefits are certainly warranted. Finally, the unavoidable concern for equity within these efficiency issues introduces another difficult measurement problem into environmental policy analysis.

In sum, it is tempting to be easily frustrated by the empirical difficulties that accompany the basic economic issues of environmental protection raised in this

Table 12-5. Pollution Exposure Index: Particulate Matter (National Primary Standard)

Particulates	Income ($000)						
	<3	3–5	5–7	7–10	10–15	15–25	25+
All three cities							
<75 µg/m³	0.659	0.815	0.867	0.912	1.025	1.147	1.329
>75 µg/m³	1.428	1.233	1.169	1.112	0.969	0.815	0.589

Note. From "Some Evidence on the Distribution of Air Quality" by P. Asch and J. J. Seneca, 1978, *Land Economics, 54,* p. 289. Reprinted by permission.

chapter. However, the difficulty of measuring benefits and costs does not, unfortunately, diminish their importance in decisions concerning any specific public health or environmental program. Arguing that such information cannot be meaningfully measured, or more cynically that, regardless of the available information, political policy decisions will be made anyway, creates a dual risk. First, ignoring the benefits and costs of public health protection increases the likelihood that wasteful policy choices will be made. Second, the cumulative effect of repeated inefficient policy decisions will threaten the entire effort to protect public health and the environment.

References

Asch, P., & Seneca, J. J., (1978). Some evidence on the distribution of air quality. *Land Economics, 54,* 278–297.

Asch, P., & Seneca, J. J. (1980). The incidence of water quality: A country level analysis. *Water Resources Research, 16,* 319–324.

Baumol, W. J., & Oates, W. (1979). *Economics, environmental policy and the quality of life.* Englewood Cliffs, NJ: Prentice-Hall.

Baumol, W. J., & Blackman, S. A. B. (1980). Modified fiscal incentives in environmental policy. *Land Economics, 56,* 417–431.

Bloomquist, G. (1979). Value of life saving: Implications of consumption activity. *Journal of Political Economy, 87,* 540–558.

Bosworth, B. P. (1981). The economic environment for regulation in the 1980s. In H. M. Peskin, P. R. Portney, & A. V. Kneese (Eds.), *Environmental regulation and the U.S. economy.* Baltimore, MD: Johns Hopkins University Press.

Christainsen, G., & Haveman, R. (1981). Public regulations and the showdown in productivity growth. *American Economic Review, 71,* 320–325.

Congressional Budget Office. (1985). *Environmental regulation and economic efficiency.* Washington, DC: Congress of the United States.

Council on Environmental Quality. (1980). *Eleventh annual report.* Washington, DC: U.S. Government Printing Office.

Data Resources, Inc. (1979). *The macroeconomic impact of federal pollution control programs.* Report submitted to Environmental Protection Agency and Council on Environmental Quality. Washington, DC: Council on Environmental Quality.

Denison, E. (1979). *Accounting for slower economic growth.* Washington, DC: Brookings Institution.

Dorfman, N. S., & Snow, A. (1975). Who will pay for pollution control? *National Tax Journal, 28,* 101–115.

Dorfman, R. (1977). Incidence of benefits and costs of environmental programs. *American Economic Review, 67,* 333–340.

Downing, P. (1984). *Environmental economics and policy.* Boston: Little, Brown.

Feenberg, D., & Mills, E. S. (1980). *Measuring the benefits of water pollution abatement.* New York: Academic Press.

Freeman, A. M., III. (1972). The distribution of environmental quality. In A. V. Kneese & B. T. Bower (Eds.), *Environmental quality analysis.* Baltimore, MD: Johns Hopkins University Press.

Freeman, A. M., III. (1979a). *The benefits of air and water pollution control: A review and synthesis of recent estimates.* Washington, DC: Council on Environmental Quality.

Freeman, A. M., III. (1979b). *The benefits of environmental improvement: Theory and practice.* Baltimore, MD: Johns Hopkins University Press.

Gianessi, L. P., Peskin, H. M., & Wolff, E. (1979). The distributional effects of the uniform air pollution policy in the U.S. *Quarterly Journal of Economics, 93*, 281–301.

Harrington, W., & Krupnick, A. J. (1981). Stationary source pollution policy and choices for reform. In H. M. Peskin, P. R. Portney, & A. V. Kneese (Eds.), *Environmental regulation and the U.S. economy*. Baltimore, MD: Johns Hopkins University Press.

Haveman, R. H., & Christainsen, G. B. (1981). Environmental regulations and productivity growth. In H. M. Peskin, P. R. Portney, & A. V. Kneese (Eds.), *Environmental regulation and the U.S. economy*. Baltimore, MD: Johns Hopkins University Press.

Haveman, R. H., & Smith, F. K. (1978). Investment, inflation, unemployment and the environment. In P. R. Portney, A. M. Freeman, R. H. Haveman, H. M. Peskin, E. P. Seskin, & V. K. Smith (Eds.), *Current issues in U.S. environmental policy*. Baltimore, MD: Johns Hopkins University Press.

Hershaft, A., Freeman, A. M., Crocker, T. D., & Stevens, J. B. (1978). *Critical review of estimating benefits of air and water pollution control*. Washington, DC: U.S. Environmental Protection Agency.

Jones-Lee, M. W. (1976). *The value of life: An economic analysis*. Chicago: University of Chicago Press.

Kneese, A. V. (1984). *Measuring the benefits of clean air and water*. Washington, DC: Resources for the Future.

Lave, L. B. (Ed.). (1982). *Quantitative risk assessment in regulation*. Washington, DC: Brookings Institution.

Liroff, R. A. (1980). *Air pollution offsets: Trading, selling and banking*. Washington, DC: Conservation Foundation.

Norsworthy, J., Harper, M., & Kunze, K. (1979). The slowdown in productivity growth: Analysis of some contributing factors. *Brookings Papers on Economic Activity, 2*, 387–421.

Okun, A. M. (1975). *Equality and efficiency: The big tradeoff*. Washington, DC: Brookings Institution.

O'Neill, W., David, M., Moore, C., & Erhard, J. (1983). Transferable discharge permits and economic efficiency: The Fox River. *Journal of Environmental Economics and Management, 10*, 346–355.

Portney, P. R. (1981). The macroeconomic impacts of federal environmental regulation. In H. M. Peskin, P. R. Portney, & A. V. Kneese (Eds.), *Environmental regulation and the U.S. economy*. Baltimore, MD: Johns Hopkins Press.

Rhoads, S. E. (1978). How much should we spend to save a life? *Public Interest, 51*, 74–92.

Seneca, J. J., & Taussig, M. K. (1984). *Environmental economics* (3rd ed.). Englewood Cliffs, NJ: Prentice-Hall.

Singer, M. (1978). How to reduce risks rationally. *Public Interest, 51*, 93–112.

Thaler, R. H., & Rosen, S. (1976). The value of saving a life: Evidence from the labor market. In N. E. Terleckyj (Ed.), *Household production and consumption*. New York: Columbia University Press.

Tietenberg, T. (1984). *Environmental and natural resource economics*. Glenview, IL: Scott, Foresman.

U.S. General Accounting Office. (1982). *A market approach to air pollution control could reduce compliance costs without jeopardizing clean air goals*. Washington, DC: U.S. General Accounting Office.

G L O S S A R Y

Abruptio placentae—tearing away from or the premature detachment of a normally situated placenta.

Acetaldyhyde—metabolite of alcohol which accumulates in the liver when excessive amounts of alcohol are consumed.

Acidosis—pathologic condition resulting from accumulation of acid in, or loss of base from, the body.

Addiction—compulsive habits that may be detrimental such as drug abuse.

Adrenal—ductless gland located above the kidney.

Adrenalin—*see* epinephrine.

Adsorption—adhesion by a liquid or gas to the surface of a solid.

Aerobic decay—breakdown of organic matter by microorganisms that use oxygen.

Aerosol—small particles of liquid or solid suspended in a gas.

Age-specific rate—death or incidence rate for a group calculated by dividing the number of occurrences by the population at risk. For example, there were 18 male white lung cancer deaths for age group 55–59 during 1980 in County X; there were 10,000 male whites in County X in 1980. The age-specific rate is 18/10,000 or 180/100,000.

Agent of disease—something whose presence or absence can cause a disease. Agents can be biological, chemical, and physical.

Aliphatic amines—halogenated organic compounds having an open-chain structure and consisting of paraffin, olefin, acetylene hydrocarbons, and their derivatives.

Allergy—hypersensitivity in which a person experiences symptoms (e.g., red eyes, sneezing) upon coming into contact with a substance.

Alzheimers disease—premature organic loss of intellectual function.

Ambient—the surrounding environment, usually used to mean the surrounding outdoor air, water, and land environments.

Amblyopia—dimness of vision due to lack of use of eye as well as refractive error.

Ames test—developed by Dr. Bruce Ames, this (*in vitro*) test employs bacteria to assess initially the capability of a chemical to cause mutations.

Amniotitis—inflammation of the ammion, the innermost fetal membrane which forms the bag of waters and encloses the fetus.

Anaerobic decay—breakdown of organic matter by microorganisms in the absence of oxygen.

378

Anesthetic—agent producing insensibility to pain.

Angina pectoris—syndrome characterized by short attacks of chest pain which radiates to the shoulder and arm.

Animal bioassay—testing the relative strength of a drug or substance on animal organisms at various doses in a controlled environment.

Antagonism—the combined effect of two or more factors is less than the sum of each of their effects; opposite of synergism.

Antioxidants—organic compounds used to prevent oxidation of substances like oils, rubber, and fats.

Aromatic substances—hydrocarbons that are ring-structured and related to benzene (C_6H_6) or its derivatives.

Arteriosclerosis—degenerative vascular disorder characterized by thickening and loss of elasticity of arterial walls. It assumes three types: atherosclerosis, arteriolosclerosis, and medial calcinosis.

Asthma—chronic disease characterized by periods of shortness of breath and labored breathing caused by the accumulation of mucous in the air passageways.

Athermoma—mass of plaque of degenerated, thickened arterial lining occurring in arteriosclerosis.

Atherosclerosis—the most common form of arteriosclerosis in which a plaque is produced by focal lipid deposits. In the beginning it is soft and pasty. With time the plaque may undergo fibrosis and calcification or it may ulcerate into a blood clot and eventually artery blockage.

Autonomic—self-controlling; functionally independent.

Autopsy—examination of a body after death.

Axons—nerve junctures associated with the process of conducting impulses away from the cell body.

Bacteria—usually one-celled microorganisms (rod, spiral, or spherical shaped) that can be seen only with a microscope. Some can cause diseases such as tuberculosis and anthrax. Others are essential to life.

Bile—fluid secreted by the liver, poured into the small intestine via the bile ducts, and used in fat digestion.

Bioaccumulate—process by which toxins accumulate in larger concentrations in higher order species when they consume species contaminated with low concentrations of toxins.

Birth weight—neonatal weight at time of birth; 2,500 grams (5½ lbs.) or less used as indicator of potential health problem.

Bladder—hollow, muscular, distensible organ serving as a temporary reservoir for urine.

Bronchi—two primary divisions of the trachea, resembling it structurally.

Bronchitis—inflammation of the lining of the air passages of the lungs.

Bubble policy—an air pollution policy permitting an emitter to treat all its discharge points as a single discharge point. This means that the emitter can choose to curtail emissions from some points and not from others, rather than to curtail the same proportion of emissions from every discharge point.

Cancer—a malignant growth anywhere in the body characterized by local and distant spread; *see also* malignant and carcinogen.

Carcinogen—any cancer-producing agent.

Cardiomyopathy—general diagnostic term meaning disease of the heart muscle, often of obscure or unknown cause.

Cardiovascular disease—disease pertaining to the heart and blood vessels.

Case—in epidemiology, a person with the disease (or other outcome) under investigation.

Case-control study—research that starts with the identification of persons with the disease (or other outcome) and a control (comparison) group without the disease. The rates of the disease among the cases and controls are compared; also called retrospective study.

CAT (Computerized Axial Tomography) scan—method of obtaining serial X rays of the body in predetermined planes. The resulting cross-sectional views are displayed by a cathode ray tube.

Cervix—neck of the uterus.

Chemistry—study of the atomic and molecular structure of matter.

Chlorination—process of adding the chemical chlorine to water, sewage, and other substances to kill pathogens.

Cholera—a bacterial-caused infection of the bowel marked by diarrhea and vomiting leading to dehydration, loss of electrolytes, and cramps.

Cholesterol—pearly, fatlike substance found in animal products (e.g., red meat, poultry, eggs, and dairy products); also found in bile, blood, brain tissue, outer covering of nerves, liver, kidney, and adrenal glands.

Chromosome—threadlike body of chromatin in cell nucleus that bear hereditary substances called genes.

Chronic obstructive lung disease (COLD)—group of noncancerous diseases characterized by increased resistance in the airways of the lungs or by overinflation of the lungs.

Cirrhosis of the liver—chronic disease of the liver leading to loss of liver cells and increased resistance to flow of blood through the liver.

Cluster—observation of an abnormally high number of diseases in an area.

Cohort study—epidemiological study in which subsets of the population are followed in order to determine the effect of hypothesized risk factors; also called prospective study.

Coliform—bacteria found in the colon; a high coliform count in a water body is used as an indicator of fecal contamination.

Communicable disease—a disease capable of being transmitted from one person to another.

Confounding factor—factor that makes it difficult to determine the effect of an agent (e.g., exposure to a chemical in a workplace) because it also effects the outcome (e.g., smoking).

Congenital—born with a condition.

Coronary—relating to the arteries or veins of the heart.

Correlation—in statistics, a number ranging from 1 to -1 that summarizes the extent to which two variables covary (e.g., when one increases, the other increases).

Criterion organics—eight inorganic substances defined by the Safe Drinking Water Act and

Resource Conservation and Recovery Act as toxic when found at certain levels (arsenic, barium, cadium, chronium, lead, mercury, selenium, silver).

Cytogenetics—study of chromosome behavior.

Depression—psychiatric condition consisting of dejected mood insomnia, weight loss, psychomotor retardation, sometimes associated with guilt feelings.

Diabetes—disorder characterized by excessively high levels of sugar (glucose) in the blood and a real or relative deficit of blood sugar controlling hormone, insulin.

DNA (deoxyribonucleic acid)—chromosomal material that transmits genetic information.

Dose-response curve—relationship between effect and exposure in which the effect increases or decreases as the amount of exposure, duration of exposure, and intensity of exposure changes.

Dracunculiasis—infestation caused by a parasitic crustacean; also known as Guinea-worm infection.

Duodenum—first part of the small intestine.

Dysfunction—impaired or abnormal function.

Ecology—study of relationship between living organisms and their environment.

Efficacy—extent to which a specific intervention, procedure, regimen, or service produces a beneficial result under ideal conditions.

Electromyogram—a graphic record of muscle contraction as a result of electrical stimulation.

Emission offset—air pollution policy requiring those proposing to add emissions to make compensatory reductions in emissions from other sources.

Emphysema—overinflation of aveoli and smaller bronchial tubes of the lungs with air.

Endometrium—lining the inner surface of the uterus.

Enteric fever—infectious disease caused by *salmonella typhosa*; characterized by fever, headache, abdominal pain; also known as typhoid fever.

Enteritis—inflammation of the mucous and submucous tissues of the small intestine.

Environment—biological, cultural, physical, mental, and other things that influence health; everything that is external to the person.

Epidemic—a disease that is prevalent and rapidly spreading among a population.

Epidemiology—study of the determinants and distribution of morbidity, mortality, and prevalence of disease.

Epinephrine—hormone that is a potent stimulant of the nervous system and increases blood pressure, stimulating the heart muscle, accelerating the heart rate, and increasing cardiac output.

Ergonomics—study of how to design jobs for safety and efficiency.

Ethanol—alcohol.

Etiology—study of the factors that cause disease and the methods of their introduction to the host.

Filtration—process of passing water or other liquids through a porous medium (e.g., sand, charcoal) in order to eliminate particles.

Gas chromatograph—equipment capable of detecting very low concentrations of gases.

Gastroenteritis—inflammation of the intestinal tract and stomach.

Giardiasis—waterborne disease caused by protozoa (*Giardia lamblia*) and characterized by diarrhea, loss of appetite, dehydration, cramps, and vomiting.

Hardness of water—in water quality, the amount of calcium, magnesium, and iron salts in water; opposite of soft water.

Hazard—natural or human-made danger.

Health—a state of physical, mental, and social well-being.

Hemoglobin—a chemical component of red blood cells containing two substances, globin and hematin, an iron pigment which is responsible for the transport of oxygen to cells.

Hemorrhage—excessive blood loss.

Hepatitis—inflammation of the liver of viral or toxin origin.

Hydraulic gradient—movement of water related to the slope of the land surface or subsurface contours.

Hydrocarbons—compounds containing exclusively hydrogen and carbon.

Hydrological cycle—cyclic movement of water on the earth; includes surface movements, evaporation, percipitation, and underground water movement.

Hyperkenesis—excessive, involuntary movements; in children may be due to brain dysfunction.

Hypertension—a consistent elevation of blood pressure.

Hypnosis—semiconscious state during which the patient's attention is focused on the therapist's procedure.

Hypoxia—reduction of oxygen supply to the body tissues.

Immunocompetence—ability to develop an immune response (e.g., antibody production and cell-mediated immunity) following challenge by bacteria, toxins, and other foreign bodies.

Incidence—the number of new events (e.g., new cases of a disease in a defined population) within a specified period of time.

Industrial hygiene—practice concerned with identification, evaluation, and control of workplace hazards.

Inorganic—substances which do not contain carbon, not derived from living organisms.

Inversion—in air pollution, the trapping of cooler air beneath warmer air.

In vitro—outside the body.

In vivo—inside the body.

Ion—an electrically charged atom or group of atoms produced when atoms gain (anion) or lose (cation) electrons.

Ionizing radiation—energy which causes compounds to be disassociated into their constituent ions.

Ischemic heart disease—heart disease due to functional constriction or actual obstruction of a blood vessel of the heart.

Landfarming—disposal of hazardous waste by application onto the soil surface or by mixing into soil.

LD50—lethal dose for half of an experimental animal population.

Larynx—tone-producing organ, the voice box, composed of muscle and cartilage.

Leachate—chemical mixtures resulting from the contact between water and landfill contaminants.

LEL—lower explosion level; for example a soil column containing 5% by concentration of methane gas may explode.

Linear model—a mathematical expression of the relationship between a dependent Y, and an independent variable X. $Y = a + bX + e$, where e represents random variation.

Lipid—substances including fats, waxes. phospholipids, and related compounds. The most prominent in diets are fats.

Lipoprotein—protein containing a lipid group.

Malaise—feeling of body discomfort.

Malignant—virulent, pertaining to the properties of tumors to spread locally and throughout the body.

Mass spectrometer—equipment capable of detecting very low concentrations of chemicals.

Menarche—beginning of the menstrual function.

Methemoglobinemia—a condition in which more than 1% of hemoglobin in blood is oxidized to the ferric form, which means that oxygen transport is greatly reduced; also known as blue baby disease.

Microgram—one-millionth part of a gram, abbreviated μg.

Migration study—comparative analysis of mortality and morbidity rates among native born and those not born in the local area.

Model—a qualitative or quantitative (*see* linear model) representation of reality.

Mongolism—birth defect caused by the absence of a chromosome or triplication of a chromosome; also known as Down's syndrome.

Morbidity—any departure from health.

Mortality—death.

Municipal solid waste—garbage, refuse, sludge from waste treatment plant, water supply treatment plant, or air pollution control facility, and other discarded material resulting from industrial, commercial, mining, agricultural operations, or community activities.

Mutagen—chemical or physical agent that induces genetic changes.

Mycotoxin—fungal toxin.

Myelin sheaths—a soft white material surrounding nerve fibers.

Myocardial infarction—syndrome manifested by persistent, usually intense cardiac (chest) pain, followed by sweating, pallor, difficulty breathing, faintness, nausea, and vomiting. The underlying disease is usually coronary atherosclerosis, which progresses to coronary thrombosis (blood clotting) and blockage and results in a sudden curtailment of blood supply to the heart muscle and myocardial ischemia.

Myopathy—any disease of a muscle.

Natal—pertaining to birth.

Neuroendocrine—the interaction between the nervous and endocrine systems.

Neurons—granular cells with specialized processes that are the fundamental unit of nervous tissue.

Neurosis—functional disorder of the nervous system.

Neurotoxin—a poison that attacks nerve cells.

Norepinephrine—hormone that acts as a transmitter and counteracts abnormally low blood pressure.

Obesity—increase in body weight beyond the requirement of the body due to excessive accumulation of fat in the body.

Onchocerciasis—infestation by a parasitic worm that is spread by black flies; also known as river blindness.

Organic—animal or vegetable forms of life.

Ovary—female reproductive gland producing eggs after puberty.

Ozone—form of oxygen with three atoms per molecule.

Papanicolaou (PAP) test—a screening test for premalignant and malignant changes of cells from the vagina and uterine cervix.

Parasite—organism that lives on or within another organism.

Particulate—a minute particle that may cause harm through toxic properties and interference with respiratory and other defense systems of the body.

Pathogen—agent capable of producing disease.

Pathology—study of the structure and functional nature of disease.

Pavlovian conditioning—method of modifying behavior so that an act or response previously associated with one stimulus becomes associated with another.

Pharmacology—study of the action of drugs on human organ systems.

Pharynx—fibromuscular tube extending from the nose and mouth to the esophagus and serves as a common pathway for food and air.

Phtalic anhydride—a crystalline cyclic acid used in making alkyd resins.

Placenta—spongy structure in the uterus through which the fetus derives its nourishment.

Placenta previa—displaced placenta, implanted in lower segment of uterine wall.

Plasma—clear, straw-colored liquid of blood, devoid of blood cells.

Pneumoconiosis—respiratory ailment due to inhalation of dust; in coal miners known as black lung disease.

Pneumonia—inflammation of lungs due to infection which results in the lung air spaces and passages becoming filled with fluid, cells, and celluar debris.

Poliomyelitis—inflammation of the gray matter of the spinal cord caused by a virus.

Population—entire collection of people, animals, houses, counties, or other units from which a sample may be drawn.

Prevalence studies—study of the relationship between diseases (or other health-related outcomes) and other variables of interest in existence at one particular time.

Prostate—in males, a gland surrounding the neck of the bladder and urethra. Enlargement of the prostate is common in middle age. This often results in urethral obstruction, impeding urination. Benign and malignant tumors and other problems are common in elderly men.

Psychosis—mental disorder characterized by defective or lost contact with reality.

Pulmonary—involving the lungs.

Putrescible wastes—organic wastes decomposing by bacterial and fungicidal processes and forming gaseous emissions of an explosive and malodorous nature.

Regression analysis—in statistics, a method of fitting a line in order to model the relationship between a variable that is being predicted and a predictor variable(s).

Relative risk—usually defined as the ratio of the effect (e.g., disease rate) among those exposed to an agent to the effect among the unexposed.

Renal—of or near the kidneys.

Resin—class of solid or soft organic compounds of synthetic or natural origin (polyvinyl, polyethylene, polystyrene) that are combined with chemicals such as plasticizers, pigments, and epoxides to form plasticizers.

Respiratory disease—disease of the lungs and air passageways (bronchi).

Risk factor—usually used to mean a factor that increases the chances of an effect; in this way it is a subset of etiologic factors (*see* etiology).

Sample—a subset of a population that may be selected in many different ways, for example, so that each member of the population has an equal chance of being chosen, or some age groups, racial groups, geographical areas may be more represented than others.

Sanitary landfill—a covered facility for municipal solid wastes that meets the criteria published under Resource Conservation and Recovery Act, Section 4004; may result in leaching into environment.

Schistosomiasis—illness caused by a parasite (blood flukes), which bore into humans wading in water; also known as bilharziasis.

Serum—clear liquid portion of blood devoid of fibrogen, a substance involved in blood clotting.

Shigellosis—bacterial-caused disease ranging in severity from mild diarrhea to severe and fatal dysentery.

Sister chromatid exchange—disruption of germ cells which transfer the genetic code from adults to offspring.

Solvent—liquid holding another substance in solution.

Somatic cells—cells that become part of tissues and organs of the body; as opposed to germs cells (e.g., ovum or spermatozoon).

Standard—a criterion to protect public health and the environment recognized by law, custom, or common consent, or all of these.

Standard Metropolitan Statistical Area (SMSA)—a geographical unit for which data are collected by the federal government composed of cities and contiguous suburbs which have demographic and economic interactions. The U.S. Bureau of the Census has specific criteria.

Standardization—process of calculating a single (e.g., mortality, morbidity) rate for a population by averaging age-specific rates according to a standard population or other characteristic.

Stroke—severe attack caused by a rupture or blockage of an artery of the brain and often followed by permanent brain and nervous system damage.

Sudden infant death syndrome—sudden and unexplainable death of an infant, typically occurring between the ages of 3 weeks and 5 months.

Surface impoundment—pits, ponds, or lagoons designed to hold an accumulation of liquid wastes.

Synergism—the combined effects of two or more factors is greater than the sum of each of their effects; *see* antagonism.

Synthetic liner—a plastic or engineered clay sheet separating wastes accumulated in a landfill or surface impoundment from underlying soil strata with the intention of preventing leaching.

Teratogenic—substance or event which produces malformations of the fetus.

Thyroid—gland that produces two hormones, thyroxin and triiodothyronine, which help to control metabolism.

Toxic—poisonous.

Tranquilizer—agent which acts on the emotional state, quieting or calming the patient without affecting clarity or consciousness.

Trihalomethanes—Chloroform and other halogenated derivatives (e.g., bromodichloromethane) in drinking water presumably due to the chlorination of raw water containing organic substances.

Trypanosomiasis—disease transmitted by the tsetse fly and caused by a species of trypanosoma protozoa; also known as sleeping sickness.

Uterus—a pear-shaped, thick-walled, muscular organ situated in the pelvis of a woman between the urinary bladder and the rectum.

Vagina—tube which connects the uterus with the external female genital organ.

Variance—a measure of numerical dispersion; square of the standard deviation around the mean.

Vectors—vehicles for transmitting infectious agents (e.g., flies, mosquitoes, rodents).

Vegetarianism—living upon vegetables, fruits, grains, and nuts, and sometimes eggs and dairy products.

Vertigo—a disordered state of dizziness.

Virus—microscopic or submicroscopic biological agents that can cause a variety of infections.

Vital records—records of births, deaths, marriages, and divorces collected by the government.

Volatile—substance that readily changes from a liquid to a gas.

References

Friel, J. (Ed.). (1974). *Dorland's illustrated medical dictionary* (25th ed.). Philadelphia: W. B. Saunders.

Frenay, A. (1969). *Understanding medical terminology* (4th ed.). St. Louis, MO: Catholic Hospital Association.

Last, J. (1983). *A dictionary of epidemiology*. New York: Oxford University Press.

National Research Council. (1977–1980). *Drinking water and health* (Vol. 1–3). Washington, DC: National Academy of Sciences.

Pryde, L. (1973). *Environmental chemistry*. Menlo Park, CA: Cummings.

Robbins, S., & Angell, M. (1971). *Basic pathology*. Philadelphia: W. B. Saunders.

Thomas, C. (1982). *Taber's cyclopedic medical dictionary* (14th ed.). Philadelphia: F. A. Davis.

Walter, J. (1982). An introduction to the principles of disease (2nd ed.). Philadelphia: W. B. Saunders.

Webster's New Twentieth Century Dictionary of the English Language (1961). (2nd ed.). New York: Publishers Guild.

I N D E X

Health Maintenance Organization Act, 300, 314
Health maintenance organizations, patient
    education, 313–315
Health Risk Appraisal (L. Robbins), 322–323
Healthy People (DHEW), 300–301
Heart disease
    and diet, 48, 49, 56–58
    education programs, 322
    psychosocial factors, 64, 65, 67
    smoking, 29, 30, 48, 56
    temporal trends, 6–7
Heart rate and exercise, 59–60, 63
Hepatitis, water-related, 118
Herpes simplex II and sexual behavior, 66
Hospitals, patient education, 318–321
Hydrocarbons
    indoor air pollution, 154
    sunlight and nitrogen oxides, 143, 144, 147–
        149

IBM Corp., 306
Incidence, definition, 4
Incineration, municipal waste, 181
Index of Activities of Daily Living, 335
Indian Point nuclear plant, 285
Industrial Bio-Test Laboratories, faked data,
    224–225
Industriplex Industrial Park, Woburn, Mass.,
    hazardous waste, 195–197
Infant mortality, 341–343
Inflation, 359
Information about technology, 223–226
    faked data from industry, 224–225
    proprietary data, 225
Input-output analysis, 338, 339
INSURE project, 317–318
Interagency Regulatory Liaison Group, 245
Interest rates and pollution control, 364
International trade, effects of environmental
    protection, 361, 363
Intervention/prevention
    alcohol, 44–46
    diet, 55–56
    and exercise, 62–63
    psychosocial factors, 68
    smoking, 34–36
        workplace, 36
    and water-related disease, 128–129
    see also Education-for-health
Investment, industrial, pollution control, 360
Irrigation and political power, 106

Jacobs, L., 19
James I, King of England, 27
Johnson & Johnson, 306–307

Kandel, E., 286
Kuhn, Thomas, 277–278

Labor data, pollution control and environmental
    protection, 359–360, 363, 369–370
Labor unions, occupational health and safety,
    98–99
Land use management, 247–248
Lead
    air quality regulation, 146, 148, 149
    occupational health and safety, 81–82, 102
    water-borne, 130
Legal issues, costs, 356; *see also* Policy, public
Life expectancy, 334
    temporal trends, 4–8
Life-style education, 294–298; *see also*
    Education-for-health
Lipoproteins, 49, 61
Liver
    cancer and aflatoxins, 51
    cirrhosis and alcohol, 40–41
Logic of Collective Action (Olson), 225
London
    air pollution crisis, 1952, 140–141
    cholera epidemic, 1854, 26, 108
Love Canal, 183, 190–193, 197, 198, 236
    wet vs. dry areas, 191
Lovins, Amory, 207–209, 215
Lung, smoking-related diseases
    cancer, 28–30
    chronic obstructive disease, 29–30

Malaria, 107
Market mechanisms and risk, 20–21; *see also*
    Economics *entries*
Massachusetts Department of Environmental
    Quality Engineering, 193, 195
McHarg, Ian, 248
Medical care system. *See* Health care system
    and health protection
Methane, municipal waste, 180–181
Methemoglobinemia, infant, water-related, 124–
    125
Methyl isocyanate, 207, 213, 218, 219, 234
Metropolitan Life Insurance Co., 305, 307, 314
Meuse Valley, Belgium, air pollution, 1930,
    140
Migrant studies, diet, and cancer, 50
Mormons, cancer, 50
Mortality
    alcohol abusers, 40
    counties with highest and lowest rates, 343,
        344
    environmental protection, benefits, 365
    and health status of population, 334, 336–337
    infant, 341–343
    reduction, 340–341, 343–345
Mortality rates, geographic trends, 12–16
    cancer, changing city-suburban-rural
        differences, 14–16
    changing city-rural differences, 13–14
    changing city-suburban differences, 12–14
    SMSAs, 12